2009-2010

NIV®

Standard
LESSON COMMENTARY®

LARGE PRINT

NEW
INTERNATIONAL
VERSION®

INTERNATIONAL
SUNDAY SCHOOL
LESSONS

Edited by
Ronald L. Nickelson

Published by
Standard Publishing

Jonathan Underwood,
Senior Editor

Sixteenth Annual Volume

Standard®
PUBLISHING
Bringing The Word to Life

Cincinnati, Ohio

In This Volume

Index of Printed Texts, 2009–2010

The printed texts for 2009–2010 are arranged here in the order in which they appear in the Bible. Opposite each reference is the page number on which the lesson that treats the passage begins in this volume.

Cumulative Index of Printed Texts

A cumulative index for the Scripture passages used in the
NIV Standard Lesson Commentary® for September 2004–August 2010
is presented here for your convenience.

vi

Fall Quarter 2009

Covenant Communities

Special Features

Lessons

Unit 1: Leaders in the Covenant Community

Unit 2: An Open Invitation to Covenant Living

Unit 3: The New Covenant Community

About These Lessons

Covenant is a vital concept in both Old and New Testaments. The three units in this quarter all focus on God's covenant as manifested in communities. We will consider the persons whom God chose to be covenant leaders, the invitations God offered to enter into covenant, people's responses to the invitations, and the nature of God's new covenant community.

Sep 6
Sep 13
Sep 20
Sep 27
Oct 4
Oct 11
Oct 18
Oct 25
Nov 1
Nov 8
Nov 15
Nov 22
Nov 29

Don't Go on a Reader Strike!

Each 18-month segment features six themes: Creation, Call, Covenant, Christ, Community, *and* Commitment.

As I write these words, the Writers Guild of America is on strike. This has brought to a standstill the production of the scripted Hollywood shows. This is serious, high-visibility stuff for a culture addicted to entertainment!

The writers of the Bible and of this commentary have never gone on strike. Sadly, however, some folks go on a "reader strike" when it comes to Bible study. The reason is often a drift away from God as distractions of the world take priority. We avoid drifting into a reader strike when we recall that "the world and its desires pass away, but the man who does the will of God lives forever" (1 John 2:17). We are able to *do* the will of God only when we *know* the will of God. This commentary will help you do just that.

—R. L. N.

International Sunday School Lesson Cycle
September, 2004—August, 2010

YEAR	FALL QUARTER (Sept., Oct., Nov.)	WINTER QUARTER (Dec., Jan., Feb.)	SPRING QUARTER (Mar., Apr., May)	SUMMER QUARTER (June, July, Aug.)
2004-2005	The God of Continuing Creation (Bible Survey)	Called to Be God's People (Bible Survey)	God's Project: Effective Christians (Romans, Galatians)	Jesus' Life, Ministry, and Teaching (Matthew, Mark, Luke)
2005-2006	"You Will Be My Witnesses" (Acts)	God's Commitment— Our Response (Isaiah; 1 and 2 Timothy)	Living in and as God's Creation (Psalms, Job, Ecclesiastes, Proverbs)	Called to Be a Christian Community (1 and 2 Corinthians)
2006-2007	God's Living Covenant (Old Testament Survey)	Jesus Christ: A Portrait of God (John, Philippians, Colossians, Hebrews, 1 John)	Our Community Now and in God's Future (1 John, Revelation)	Committed to Doing Right (Various Prophets, 2 Kings, 2 Chronicles)
2007-2008	God Creates (Genesis)	God's Call to the Christian Community (Luke)	God, the People, and the Covenant (1 & 2 Chronicles, Daniel, Haggai, Nehemiah)	Images of Christ (Hebrews, Gospels)
2008-2009	The New Testament Community (New Testament Survey)	Human Commitment (Character Studies)	Christ and Creation (Ezekiel, Luke, Acts, Ephesians)	Call Sealed with Promise (Exodus, Leviticus, Numbers, Deuteronomy)
2009-2010	Covenant Communities (Joshua, Judges, Ezra, Nehemiah, Mark, 1 & 2 Peter)	Christ the Fulfillment (Matthew)	Teachings on Community (Jonah, Ruth, New Testament)	Christian Commitment in Today's World (1 & 2 Thessalonians, Philippians)

Something for Everyone

by J. Michael Shannon

The lessons in this quarter are drawn from different kinds of Bible passages. That variety is expressed both in the parts of the Bible they come from (Old and New Testaments) and in the types of literature they represent (history, Gospels, and letters). But that variety comes together in a unity as we see the selected passages stress the responsibilities and privileges that come from being part of God's covenant community.

A *covenant* is an agreement. Another word for covenant is *testament.* That is why we refer to the Hebrew Scriptures as the Old Testament. It tells of God's agreement to bless his people and be their God. The New Testament tells of God's creating a new way of dealing with people. That new way comes through his Son, Jesus Christ. God's covenants are at his initiative. We cannot demand of him that he make a covenant with us. When he offers a covenant, it is our responsibility to accept it and live by its terms.

The concept of covenant goes beyond our individual relationships with God. Whether in the Old or New Testament eras, there is always a covenant community. Through the pages of the Bible we see the nature of this community progress from family to nation to church. It appears that God never intends there to be "lone ranger" believers. Believers need a community through which to both give and receive support.

Our first unit looks at the covenant community of the nation of Israel by examining some of its leaders. The second unit focuses on the incipient church, as Jesus calls people to a forming community of faith. The third unit addresses the church proper, as the new covenant community faces various challenges.

Unit 1: Leaders in the Covenant Community

SEPTEMBER

All communities need leaders. Covenant people need leaders who are in touch with God's priorities. Our first unit takes us into the world of the Old Testament to meet four such leaders. We will notice that times change, but people do not. Customs are different, but principles are eternal.

We meet Joshua in *Lesson 1,* a man who had the unenviable task of following the revered Moses. Joshua's task was to lead the people into the promised land, to complete the task first assigned to Moses. Joshua was Moses' God-picked successor, but how do you follow a legend? How do you stay courageous? How do you stay focused on God? Joshua will show us.

In *Lesson 2* we make friends with Gideon. He was "a nobody" by his own admission. We first meet him doing farm work while hiding from enemies. Yet he was able to put aside timidity to become a man of courage. A man who cowered while threshing grain in a winepress ended up taking on a mighty army with a small band of soldiers. God's help and unconventional weapons brought victory.

Gideon was among those Old Testament leaders called *judges.* While they did do some settling of disputes, they were mainly military leaders. Gideon's accomplishments in that role resulted in an invitation to make himself king, but he wisely refused (Judges 8:22, 23). Can Gideon's courage and wisdom teach us anything today?

Lesson 3 brings us face-to-face with Ezra. He is perhaps not as widely known as the others in this unit. Ezra was a Jewish exile in Babylon, but when allowed to do so he went to Jerusalem to teach the law of the Lord. We learn from him the virtues of prayer and repentance. He was called on to intercede for a people whose return from exile brought new possibilities but also old problems. He challenged returning exiles to recommit to God.

In *Lesson 4* we join up with Nehemiah, a man who rebuilt walls and morale. Like Ezra, he came back from exile to serve his homeland. He was held in such favor in a foreign king's court that he was given not only permission to return, but also material to help the capital city of his homeland. We can learn from his prayer life, his leadership ability, his single-mindedness, and his courage. But most importantly, we learn things about God.

OCTOBER

Unit 2: *An Open Invitation to Covenant Living*

Our second unit will be a change of pace in more ways than one. Here we will come to the New Testament, specifically to the Gospel of Mark. This fast-moving account of Jesus acting and ministering will allow us to imagine ourselves as observers of his ministry. We will follow Jesus as he travels and interacts with various people. Some desired to come into a covenant relationship with Jesus Christ. Some made the change and some didn't. This unit gives us insight into how Jesus ministered to individuals as he traveled and taught.

Lesson 5 allows us to see through the eyes of the crowd of people clamoring to be helped by Jesus. One such person was an outcast leper. Lepers in first-century Palestine were virtual nobodies. Thanks to Jesus, the unclean was made clean. Jesus does this yet today.

Lesson 6 takes us to Gentile territory. There we will meet a demonized man. He had been rejected by others (who are difficult to blame for doing so). But through Jesus the unacceptable became acceptable. Jesus does this yet today.

Lesson 7 casts the spotlight on two more "outsiders." One was a foreign woman, and the other was a man who is deaf and mute. Their problems were quite different, but the solution was the same: Jesus. Jesus does this yet today.

Lesson 8 will bring us face-to-face with a man whose problems were self-inflicted. He had made himself a spiritual outcast, though he could have been very useful to the kingdom of God. This man was rich, he was young, and he was a ruler. That was a lot, but it wasn't enough. Jesus loved him much, but in the end the young man walked away. In so doing he revealed his priorities. People still walk away from Jesus today.

NOVEMBER

Unit 3: *The New Covenant Community*

Our third unit changes the tone yet again: we move away from personal stories of encounters with Jesus as we open the letters of 1 and 2 Peter. These letters are often neglected since we more frequently study the letters of the apostle Paul.

Yet Peter's words are instructive and worth studying as well. Since Peter walked with Jesus personally, how could it be otherwise? Even though we will no longer be looking at the personal stories we see in the Gospels, things actually are just as personal because those two letters are intended to speak to the thoughts and actions of each and every believer.

Lesson 9 shows us how and why to become a holy people. *Holiness* is a quaint or even downright unattractive word to many folks. It smacks of "intolerance" in a culture that wants to tolerate just about everything. To be holy is to be set apart, and Peter will help us understand the implications of that. We will learn how to be holy, not "holier than thou." The world needs holy people who know the difference.

Lesson 10 convinces us that Christians are God's special people. Being chosen or special denotes both privilege and responsibility. Our special place is not a motivation for pride, but for gratitude and service. That's the nature of our royal priesthood.

Lesson 11 warns and comforts us as a suffering people. Since suffering is a universal experience, it is vital that we learn how to face it in a Christian manner. Sometimes we may act as if the Bible promises us that we will never suffer, but it actually promises the exact opposite. We can learn how to bear up as we suffer for our benefit and the benefit of the gospel. Sometimes we suffer precisely because we are Christians.

Lesson 12 admonishes us to be a faithful people. We will see how faith relates to faithfulness. Our beliefs really do determine our behavior. After more than three decades of ministry, the elderly Peter knew this for certain.

Lesson 13 highlights that we are to be a hopeful people. Hope is what enables us to live victoriously as we prepare for the day we shall meet God. The worst thing we can say about a person is that he or she is hopeless. Christians are never without hope.

Conclusion

Maybe God will use you as a leader; if so, our Old Testament lessons will encourage you to know that God is with you. Maybe you are among the extremely needy, either physically or spiritually; if so, our Gospel lessons will demonstrate that Jesus is still the answer. Maybe you have been a Christian for a while, but your commitment and sense of Christian identity seems to drift at times; if so, Peter will teach you how and why to stay the course. There is truly "something for everyone" this quarter!

Using and Not Using Lecture

by James Riley Estep, Jr.

Lecture is one of the most ancient and reliable methods of instruction. The notion that lecture methods are dead or ineffective is wrong. But that does not mean that this method is free from problems. In a lecture scenario students often do not learn to think for themselves.

Even so, lecture still can be the preferred method of instruction in certain situations. We suggest that lecture may be appropriate

WHEN TO USE THE LECTURE METHOD

. . . *when information is not readily available to the student.* This can be the case when a teacher has studied a topic that is obscure to the student.

. . . *when the teacher needs to synthesize information from a variety of sources.* Perhaps the teacher has studied several commentaries regarding the interpretation of a given Bible passage.

. . . *when the teacher needs to highlight relationships and points that may not be recognized by students.* It is easy to overlook facts from one part of the Bible when studying another part.

. . . *to deepen the student's motivation to learn additional information.* As long as the teacher is not providing "the" definitive answer, lecture can be used to raise questions in the student's mind, causing him or her to seek answers.

. . . *if there is a need to correct a misunderstanding of the Bible or doctrine.* For example, Mormon doctrine teaches that Jesus and Satan are brothers. The lecture method can be used to refute this teaching.

. . . *to remove obstacles to learning, such as wrong assumptions.* For example, students often develop assumptions unconsciously regarding the interpretation of the book of Revelation. Lecture can provide insight into these.

. . . *to resolve conflicting perspectives on a given subject or text.* Lecture can be used to explain opposing viewpoints. This may provide an opportunity to search for common ground among those viewpoints.

. . . *when the teacher's personality is best seen in lecture.* Lecture often allows the student to go beyond lesson content to learn from the teacher's life.

All this is not to suggest that lecture is the *only* valid method of instruction. At least four factors should cause the teacher to consider using a method other than straight lecture. Lecture may not be appropriate

WHEN NOT TO USE THE LECTURE METHOD

. . . *if your learning objectives require you to go beyond mastery of content.* Note that each lesson in this commentary features not only a *content* lesson aim, but also *concept* and *conduct* aims.

. . . *if your class has students who can contribute insight to the subject at hand.* Why lecture about missions if your class has three former missionaries?

. . . *if you have time to use more creative teaching methods.* Once when teaching at an adult retreat at church camp, I literally had *hours* of time to fill. That amount of time was ideal for me to use other teaching methods.

. . . *if your classroom is not designed for lecture.* If your learning area is equipped with chairs at round tables, with a projector and no lectern, etc., then why force a lecture method into a physical context not designed for it?

In short, lecture is a good method, but not always. Recognizing this fact is part of being "able to teach" (2 Timothy 2:24).

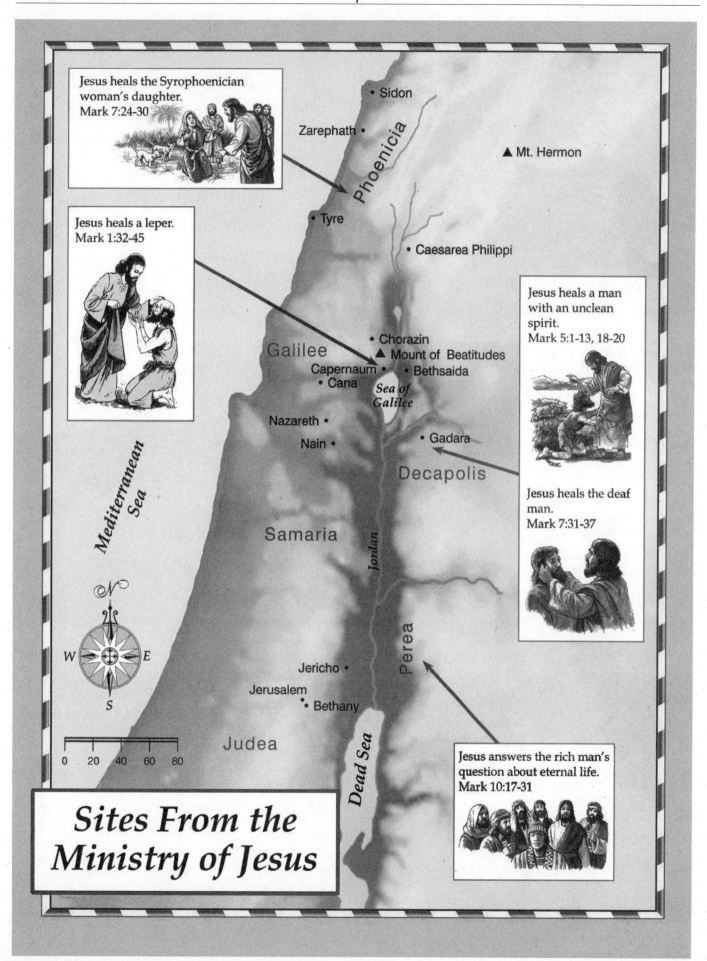

Jesus heals the Syrophoenician woman's daughter.
Mark 7:24-30

Jesus heals a leper.
Mark 1:32-45

Jesus heals a man with an unclean spirit.
Mark 5:1-13, 18-20

Jesus heals the deaf man.
Mark 7:31-37

Jesus answers the rich man's question about eternal life.
Mark 10:17-31

Sidon

Zarephath

▲ Mt. Hermon

Phoenicia

Tyre

Caesarea Philippi

Galilee

Chorazin

▲ Mount of Beatitudes

Capernaum

Bethsaida

Cana

Sea of Galilee

Nazareth

Nain

Gadara

Decapolis

Mediterranean Sea

Jordan

Samaria

Perea

N

W   E

S

Jericho

Jerusalem

Bethany

Judea

Dead Sea

0   20   40   60   80

Sites From the Ministry of Jesus

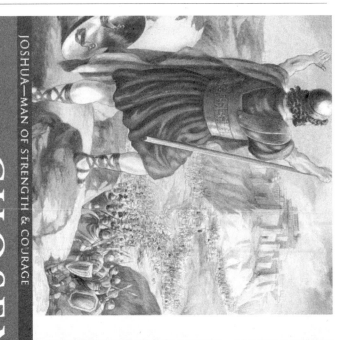

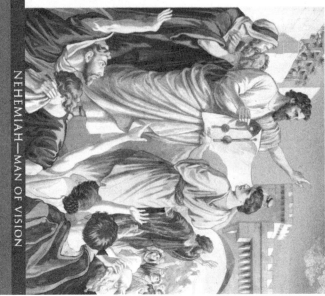

CHOSEN LEADERS OF GOD

JOSHUA—MAN OF STRENGTH & COURAGE

PETER—MAN OF ENCOURAGEMENT

NEHEMIAH—MAN OF VISION

JESUS—MAN OF HEALING

GIDEON—MAN OF VALOR

EZRA—MAN OF PRAYER

Quarter Review

Use this page to form questions for the class to answer and discuss.
Then provide the information as a handout to summarize the lessons of the past quarter.

Lesson 1: Joshua: Leader for the People

The transition from one leader to another can be difficult. When Joshua took up the position of leading God's people, the transition was seamless. He was prepared, he was gifted, and he was faithful. Does that describe our leaders?

Lesson 2: Gideon: Deliverer for the People

Sometimes leadership comes from unlikely sources. Gideon was hiding from his enemies and doubtful of God's providence when he was called. Are you thinking less of your opportuniies for service than God is?

Lesson 3: Ezra: Priest for the People

Good leaders learn the lessons of history. When the former exiles began to drift into the same kind of sin that had caused the exile in the first place, Ezra had to take action—he prayed. What is your first action in a crisis?

Lesson 4: Nehemiah: Motivator for the People

Nehemiah arrived in Jerusalem with authority granted by the king. But instead of giving orders, he made a motivational appeal. How do you use the authority you have?

Lesson 5: Looking for Jesus

The sick were looking for Jesus. Peter was looking for Jesus. A leper was looking for Jesus. Everyone wanted something from Jesus, but not everyone wanted what Jesus wanted. Are you looking for Jesus? Do you want what he wants?

Lesson 6: Recognizing Jesus

It is nice to be recognized, but only if the ones who recognize you are friends! When the demons recognized Jesus, he silenced them. It would be up to his friends to get people to recognize him as Lord. Are we helping in that effort?

Lesson 7: Begging to Get In

Having heard of God's grace "for whosoever will" for so long, it's easy to forget it was not always so. Gentiles were once excluded from the promises, like dogs hoping for table scraps. Do we appreciate the free gift of God's grace?

Lesson 8: Opting Out!

A young man with great potential approached Jesus and asked about the way to life. But when he learned of the commitment Jesus demanded, he chose to walk away. Are you aware of the Lord's expectations? Are you willing to give all?

Lesson 9: A Holy People

Like *pious,* the word *holy* has become unpopular. For some reason, no one wants to be known as "holy." But holiness is one of God's traits. To be holy is to be like him. And only the holy will be *with* him! Will you be holy?

Lesson 10: A Chosen People

"Beggars can't be choosers," we say. But we can be chosen! When it comes to righteousness, we are beggars. On our own, we cannot attain it. But God has chosen us! He has made us righteous. Are you living as one who has been "chosen"?

Lesson 11: A Suffering People

Suffering has been part of the Christian experience from the beginning. Some believers suffer much more than others, but none of us is immune from suffering. Are you suffering faithfully? Do you count it a privilege?

Lesson 12: A Faithful People

Faithful and *steady* are often paired, as if faithfulness were static. Peter makes it clear that faithfulness is dynamic; it's a growing thing. "Add to your faith goodness . . . knowledge . . . perseverance. . . ." Are you growing in faithfulness?

Lesson 13: A Hopeful People

"This world is not my home," the old song says. It's right: we look forward to a new home with the Lord. While some may scoff at our faith, this hope keeps us going; it gets us through the pain. How has your hope helped you?

Lesson Planning Page

List the aims here, either directly from the lesson or revised to suit your individual needs.

LESSON AIMS

Begin with an opening activity like the illustration from the beginning of the lesson, "Into the Lesson" from the Discovery Learning page, a discussion question, or some other appropriate opener.

GETTING STARTED

List in order the activities you will use. These include discussion questions, activities from the discovery learning page and the reproducible page—as well as key points from the commentary section.

LESSON DEVELOPMENT

I.

II.

III.

How will you bring the lesson to a climax, stressing the key point and desired action steps?

CONCLUSION & APPLICATION

Dismiss the class with an activity that reinforces the Bible lesson.

CLOSING ACTIVITY

JOSHUA: LEADER FOR THE PEOPLE

LESSON 1

INTRODUCTION

A. LEGENDARY LEADERS

Think of any sports celebrity of a generation or so ago. After you do that, try to recall the immediate successor to that person. In many cases, there was a series of people who tried to fill the void. Often a successor ends up "living in the shadow" of a famous predecessor. This has happened regarding famous kings or political leaders as well. How many people can name the immediate successors to Alexander the Great, Charlemagne, or Lincoln?

What a challenge it is to follow in the footsteps of such leaders! Think also of outstanding ministers who serve several decades in one place. They may become famous for their preaching and their people skills. But what happens after they retire, leave, or die? Often the forward momentum slows, and a downward spiral begins. This can happen even if the famous minister hand-picks the successor.

Today's lesson is about Joshua, the man who was chosen to follow a legend and then to establish his own. Moses was used of God to lead an enslaved people away from a very powerful nation. He forged this people into a new nation under God and provided it with laws. Moses is recognized as the author of the first five books of the Bible, and he wrote at least one psalm (Psalm 90). His name occurs more than 750 times in the Old Testament and more than 80 times in the New. By contrast, Joshua's name appears less than one-third as often in the Old Testament, and there are only 2 references to him in the New (Acts 7:45; Hebrews 4:8). How do you follow a legend?

B. LESSON BACKGROUND

As today's lesson opens, the Israelites were near the end of their 40-year journey from Egypt. The promised land was immediately before them, on the other side of the Jordan River. They probably had arrived in the plains of Moab during the previous summer (Numbers 22:1; 36:13).

Much happened during that encampment. The king of Moab had sent for Balaam to come from his Mesopotamian home to curse Israel. Balaam consented to come on the second appeal. Those who went to secure him thus made the 1,400-mile round-trip twice, and that took time (Numbers 22–24). Also, a second military census was conducted, revealing that the number of soldiers over age 20 had dropped slightly since the first census 39 years before at Sinai (601,730 compared with 603,550; see Numbers 1:46; 26:51). A military campaign against the Midianites is recorded in Numbers 31.

DEVOTIONAL READING:
1 TIMOTHY 2:1-6
BACKGROUND SCRIPTURE:
JOSHUA 1
PRINTED TEXT:
JOSHUA 1:1-11, 16, 17

LESSON AIMS

After participating in this lesson, each student will be able to:

1. Summarize the Lord's charge to Joshua as Joshua assumed leadership of the people of Israel.

2. Compare and contrast the task facing Joshua with the responsibility of a church leader today.

3. Make a list of ways to support church leaders.

KEY VERSE

Have I not commanded you? Be strong and courageous. Do not be terrified; do not be discouraged, for the LORD your God will be with you wherever you go.
—Joshua 1:9

LESSON 1 NOTES

Moses had been the recognized leader for over 40 years. He was challenged on occasion, for the rebels did not comprehend that to resist Moses was to go against God. Moses was God's instrument to provide governance, food, etc. But Moses is dead as today's lesson opens (Deuteronomy 34).

In every social unit, a basic question is *Who is in charge?* God did not leave the Israelites in doubt. He was the one who determined that Joshua would be Moses' successor (Numbers 27:18-23). Joshua had been Moses' adjutant or valet for 40 years. Joshua also seems to have been the leader in the battles the nation conducted during the wilderness wanderings (Exodus 17). Moses recognized early on that Joshua had leadership qualities. To make sure that Joshua knew the source of his capabilities, Moses changed his name from Hoshea ("salvation") to Joshua ("the Lord is salvation", see Numbers 13:16).

I. CONFIRMATION FOR JOSHUA (JOSHUA 1:1-9)

A. LEADER DESIGNATED (vv. 1, 2)

1. After the death of Moses the servant of the LORD, the LORD said to Joshua son of Nun, Moses' aide:

This time *Moses* is not the intermediary, since the Lord addresses *Joshua* directly. This is the first of several times in the book when Joshua has this privilege. This is a definite source of confirmation to Joshua after the death of Moses. Few people in the Old Testament are described as being a *servant of the Lord,* and it is a special title for Moses. It is used 14 times in the book of Joshua for Moses. In the last chapter of the book, Joshua himself receives this designation (24:29).

Joshua is said to be *Moses' aide* in Exodus 24:13, etc., but he is much more than that. The first reference to him is in Exodus 17:8-13, where he led in the memorable battle against the Amalekites before the people reached Sinai. Joshua was 1 of 2 spies whose minority report 39 years earlier urged the nation to have faith in God and to begin the conquest of Canaan (Numbers 13, 14). It is interesting that the names of the 2 "good" spies are still remembered, but the names of the other 10 are only a part of a listing.

2. "Moses my servant is dead. Now then, you and all these people, get ready to cross the Jordan River into the land I am about to give to them—to the Israelites.

The impact of the phrase *the Jordan River* should not be overlooked. At this time of the year, the Jordan is a wild, wide, rushing torrent. It is now the end of the rainy season, and melting snows from northern mountains add to the flow. *To cross* the Jordan successfully when it is in flood stage will validate the leadership of Joshua in the minds of the people. Comparisons are often made between the crossing of the Red Sea under *Moses* and crossing the Jordan in Joshua's day.

When Abram reached Shechem shortly after entering Canaan, God first promised to *give* his descendants that *land* (Genesis 12:7; see also 50:24). Centuries have passed, and the time for the fulfillment has come (a total of 615 years, with 430 of them in Egypt; see Exodus 12:40, 41). God's ways often require patience.

HARMONIOUS LEADERSHIP

It was a fateful day in November 1963 when U.S. President John F. Kennedy was assassinated. Kennedy and his vice president, Lyndon B. Johnson, had been bitter enemies during the primaries, yet they reached an accommodation that allowed them to run on the same ticket in the 1960 general election.

An assassin's bullet stopped JFK's life before much of his *New Frontier* program of reform could be turned into law. Yet despite their previous (and, some say, continuing) animosity, Johnson's experience in Congress enabled him to enact much of Kennedy's legislative agenda when LBJ succeeded JFK as president.

Unlike Kennedy and Johnson, Moses and Joshua had long worked in harmony. We do not see the kind of struggle for power that typifies so much of modern political and organizational leadership. This was because both Moses and Joshua were in harmony with regard to God's plan for Israel. They provide a good example for all who follow them in leadership among God's people even today. Commitment to divine principles is superior to combat over human proposals. Any congregation will be blessed when its leaders work together in harmonious obedience to God.   —C. R. B.

Visual for Lesson 1.
Keeping this visual posted throughout the quarter will stimulate thinking and dialogue about the nature of godly leadership.

B. LAND DESCRIBED (vv. 3, 4)

3. "I will give you every place where you set your foot, as I promised Moses.

The first dimension given to the land is very distinctive: it is anywhere that Joshua travels as he conquers the seven nations of Canaan (Deuteronomy 7:1). Similar language is used by *Moses* in the exhortation that he gives in Deuteronomy 11:24.

4. "Your territory will extend from the desert to Lebanon, and from the great river, the Euphrates—all the Hittite country—to the Great Sea on the west.

Geographical designations are also used to describe the scope of the land. It extends from *the desert* region (recently traversed) to the far north—to *Lebanon* and the *Euphrates* River. The northern territory, *all the Hittite country,* includes the land occupied by the descendants of a grandson of Noah through Ham (Genesis 9:18; 10:15).

In the days of David and Solomon, the area dominated by Israel did indeed reach these dimensions (about 975 BC). The combined kingdoms of Jeroboam II (king of the northern nation of Israel) and Uzziah (king of the southern nation of Judah) reached approximately the same extent again later (about 750 BC).

The men with Joshua, however, will display a weakness as they develop the "good enough" syndrome. They will not obey Joshua completely. Instead, they will conquer only "enough" land for their perceived needs. This will bring disastrous consequences.

C. GUARANTEES (v. 5)

5. "No one will be able to stand up against you all the days of your life. As I was with Moses, so I will be with you; I will never leave you nor forsake you.

It is a solid "blessed assurance" to know that the enemy is not *able to stand* in your way. Joshua had a recent experience of this type in a battle against the Midianites (Numbers 31:7). In the end, not one Israelite soldier was missing (31:49). This background, considered with the promise in the verse before us, may help explain Joshua's great shock after the first battle against Ai, when Israel loses 36 men (Joshua 7:5, 6). The loss turns out to be the result of a sin problem among the people.

The final phrases of the verse express the recurring theme of God's presence. The same thoughts are expressed in Hebrews 13:5. In that context, we are warned about the love of money and encouraged to be content

WHAT DO YOU THINK?

In what ways are we guilty of employing the "good enough" syndrome in our walk with the Lord? What would our lives look like if we were to reach our full, God-given potential instead?

with what we have. To fail to be content leads to covetousness, which ends up being the problem in Joshua 7:20, 21.

D. GUIDELINES (vv. 6-9)

6. *"Be strong and courageous, because you will lead these people to inherit the land I swore to their forefathers to give them.*

The quality of having courage or being *courageous* is mentioned several times in various admonitions to Joshua. Moses expressed this twice in his own exhortations to Joshua (Deuteronomy 31:7, 23). The Lord uses the word three times in Joshua 1:6, 7, 9. It is difficult to think that Joshua would need to be encouraged. Perhaps Moses' presence previously gave him confidence, but now Joshua, without Moses, may be hesitant about the outcomes of future conflicts. The cautiousness associated with age may also be a factor.

The final time for Joshua to receive an admonition of encouragement is given in the last verse of the chapter, and it is by members of his army. It has been said that courage consists in equality to the problem before you. It is meeting difficulties with firmness and, in some cases, by casting aside fear.

In this chapter Joshua is given two primary assignments: to conquer Canaan (which happens in Joshua 6–12) and to consign *the land* among the tribes of Israel (which happens in Joshua 14–19). Eleazar, who became the high priest when Moses' brother Aaron died, will assist Joshua in the task.

7. *"Be strong and very courageous. Be careful to obey all the law my servant Moses gave you; do not turn from it to the right or to the left, that you may be successful wherever you go.*

The elements of being *strong and very courageous* are repeated, and a new factor is mentioned: *the law* that *Moses* left behind for the people of Israel. It is a law that is written down, for the next verse states that it is a "Book of the Law." This law is not simply to be admired or put in a cabinet. It is to be obeyed with exactness.

8. *"Do not let this Book of the Law depart from your mouth; meditate on it day and night, so that you may be careful to do everything written in it. Then you will be prosperous and successful.*

The promise of success is conditioned on obeying the law. The word *meditate* in this context has a distinctive meaning that is different from our usual understanding of it. The word may also be translated "speak" or "utter a sound." In this light, it depicts the ancient way of reading, which is done orally. To read silently as our teachers instructed us is fairly new historically. Reading aloud engages more of the senses, and it can provide a greater comprehension.

This oral reading is not to be the end of the matter. The goal is to obey completely the things that are *written*. Such obedience will lead to Joshua's being able to succeed and be *prosperous* as he fulfills what he is commissioned to do. In this case the prosperity may be partly the material wealth that can come from conquest, but it is more than that. It is the spiritual rewards that are in view.

9. *"Have I not commanded you? Be strong and courageous. Do not be terrified; do not be discouraged, for the LORD your God will be with you wherever you go."*

WHAT DO YOU THINK?

What are some situations in which even the most capable leaders may lack courage? How can we encourage even those who seem to "have it all together"?

WHAT DO YOU THINK?

Is meditating on God's Word a guarantee of material prosperity? Stated in an opposite way, is a lack of material prosperity proof that a person is not meditating enough on God's Word? Why, or why not?

[Matthew 16:24 and Mark 10:29, 30 will help you frame your answer.]

The communication from *the Lord* is coming to an end. These words provide a summary of what has already been said and a final challenge. Joshua and the people are ready to begin the tasks of crossing the Jordan and conquering Canaan.

A final assurance is given that *the Lord* will be *with* Joshua. Joshua has been aware of the Lord's presence for 40 years, for the fiery pillar or cloud has accompanied the Israelites ever since they left Egypt (Exodus 13:21). The verbal reaffirmation, however, provides further support for what Joshua is about to do.

II. COMMANDS BY JOSHUA (JOSHUA 1:10, 11)
A. DELEGATED TO THE OFFICERS (v. 10)
10. *So Joshua ordered the officers of the people*:

Joshua has a system of some kind by which he can delegate to others what is necessary to accomplish the objectives. The Hebrew word translated *officers* is the same word used for the Israelite foremen in Egypt (Exodus 5:6, 10). The people Joshua has in mind are mentioned in Joshua 3:2 as following his instructions.

B. DETAILS FOR THE PEOPLE (v. 11)
11. *"Go through the camp and tell the people, 'Get your supplies ready. Three days from now you will cross the Jordan here to go in and take possession of the land the LORD your God is giving you for your own.'"*

The space of the Israelite encampment probably covers several thousand acres. But the nation is organized so that the words of Joshua can be communicated quickly. It has been 40 years since they left Egypt, but in just *three days* they will reach their destination just beyond *the Jordan*. The Jordan River is in flood stage (Joshua 3:15), and the announcement of the pending crossing undoubtedly creates excitement and wonder. In addition to the daily manna, perhaps another great miracle will occur.

First, however, there are preparations to be made. The length of the journey for those on the easternmost side of the encampment will be several miles. This means that the ones closer to the Jordan (that is, those on the westernmost side of the encampment) must travel a good distance beyond the river in order to make room for those who are behind them. Even though a 12-mile wide strip will be available (Joshua 3:16), the distance to be traveled will not allow time for the people to stop and prepare meals.

III. COMMITMENTS TO JOSHUA (JOSHUA 1:16, 17)
A. ENCOURAGEMENT (v. 16)
16. *Then they answered Joshua, "Whatever you have commanded us we will do, and wherever you send us we will go.*

Verses 12-15 (not in today's text) relate Joshua's important reminder to the two and one-half tribes that had been permitted to settle on the east side of the Jordan: they must help the other tribes in the conquest that is before them. In reply, those tribes promise that they *will do* what Joshua commands and they *will go* anywhere Joshua sends them.

The statements in verses 16, 17 are interpreted in two ways. The majority view is that they are made by the soldiers of the two and one-half tribes, for that is the immediate context. A minority opinion is that the word *they* refers

---

HOW TO SAY IT
Ai. AY-eye.
Amalekites. AM-uh-leh-kites
   or Uh-MAL-ih-kites.
Balaam. BAY-lum.
Canaan. KAY-nun.
Charlemagne. SHAR-luh-
   main.
Eleazar. El-ih-A-zar
   or E-lih-A-zar.
Hoshea. Ho-SHAY-uh.
Jeroboam. Jair-uh-BOE-um.
Mesopotamian.
   MES-uh-puh-TAY-me-un.
Midianites. MID-ee-un-ites.
Shechem. SHEE-kem
   or SHEK-em.
Sinai. SIGH-nye
   or SIGH-nay-eye.
Uzziah. Uh-ZYE-uh.

VISUALS FOR THESE LESSONS
The visual pictured in each lesson (example: page 13) is a small reproduction of a large, full-color poster included in the Adult Resources packet for the Fall Quarter. That packet also contains the very useful Presentation Helps on a CD for teacher use. The packet is available from your supplier. Order No. 192.

to representatives of all the tribes, for this gives greater assurance to Joshua. The important aspect is that Joshua has confirmation that his leadership is accepted.

B. EXAMPLE (v. 17)

17. *"Just as we fully obeyed Moses, so we will obey you. Only may the LORD your God be with you as he was with Moses."*

These words are those of a new generation. This is not the complaining, disobedient, rebellious, fearful generation that left Egypt. The people are aware that 603,548 men of the original military census of 603,550 have died along the way. Only Caleb and Joshua are still alive from that earlier group of men.

This younger group knows from experience that it is better to obey God. Their words may be only a generalization, or they may be saying that as they obeyed *Moses* during the recent months of their journey, so they will *obey* Joshua.

WHAT SHALL WE DO WITH THE PAST?

A brand-new Plymouth automobile was buried in Tulsa in 1957 as part of the state of Oklahoma's 50th anniversary celebration. The "Tulsarama" committee of 1957 apparently wanted the citizens of the year 2007 to remember what things were like in 1957, hence the car buried in a time capsule.

The concrete vault in which the car was placed was designed to withstand an atomic blast, but that was not enough to protect it from the forces of nature. When the car was dug up on June 15, 2007, its rusted hulk was sitting in four feet of water, the upholstery had disintegrated, and the engine would not start as had been hoped. This outcome did indeed teach the citizens of 2007 something about the year 1957, but not the lesson the original Tulsarama committee had hoped for!

History is a tricky thing. On the one hand, we don't want to ignore the valuable lessons that history can teach. But on the other hand, we don't want to revere history to the point of "living in the past." The Israelites were to anticipate a future that revealed the Lord's blessings. Israelite confidence was to be grounded firmly in the fact that God had been with Moses every step of the way.

But Moses was gone. And no matter how good or bad the past might have been, the Israelites had to live in the present with an eye to the future. The same principle is true for us, whether we are talking about our nation, our church, or our personal lives. Israel's history subsequent to the passing of Moses has much to teach us about the successes and failures in this regard.   —C. R. B.

CONCLUSION

The leadership transition from Moses to Joshua is notable in the way it was accomplished. The encouragement Joshua received by all the parties involved can make us wonder if Joshua was reluctant to assume the role that was thrust upon him. The encouragement prompted him to move ahead.

Churches sometimes experience difficulty with leadership changes. The older generation may be unwilling to relinquish control. The younger generation perceives that property and programs are slowly deteriorating, and they want to make changes. Spiritual maturity on the part of everyone involved is needed to bring about a productive, peaceful resolution.

WHAT DO YOU THINK?

Obedience to military leaders is essential to winning battles. Is the same true in the church? Why, or why not?

PRAYER

Dear God in Heaven, grant me the wisdom and words to accomplish the tasks that are mine for the cause of Christ and his church. May I do my part to encourage the ones who have leadership roles. In the name of Jesus. Amen.

WHAT DO YOU THINK?

What are some other ways a church can prepare for a smooth transition of leadership to the next generation? Why is it important to do so?

The work of the church is so important that emotions must be controlled. Studies of biblical principles of leadership must be undertaken. Prayers on bended knees are essential for those who desire what is really best.

THOUGHT TO REMEMBER
Encouragement can produce results.

Discovery Learning

The following is an alternative lesson plan emphasizing learning activities.
Classes desiring such student involvement will find these suggestions helpful. At the
back of this book are reproducible student pages to further enhance activity learning.

INTO THE LESSON

Give each student an index card. Say, "Without talking, write down the name of someone from history who was a great leader. Then write three or more characteristics of that person." Ask for about five volunteers to read aloud the characteristics they have written. Class members should try to guess who the leader is. As volunteers read their lists, write recurring characteristics on the board (for example, if two people say "strong personality"). When the volunteers have finished reading their characteristics, draw students' attention to the list you made on the board. Ask them if there are any other characteristics of a good leader they'd like to add.

Next, discuss the circumstances that helped cast these people into their leadership roles. Ask students whether leaders are "made" or "born" or a combination of both. From this discussion, transition into the circumstances that were present that catapulted Joshua into the leadership position of today's lesson.

INTO THE WORD

Before class, prepare the headings *God's Directions* and *God's Promises* on a poster board. Affix the poster board to the wall. Tell students that they may work independently or with a partner on the following activity. Assign, as evenly as possible, the 13 verses from today's text to individuals or pairs of students. Distribute blank strips of paper.

Have students study their assigned verse(s) and look either for a direction God gave to Joshua or for a promise God made. (Some verses may contain both.) Then have each write out the direction or promise on a sentence strip. Ask for volunteers to affix their strips under the appropriate heading on

the poster board. *Alternative to using poster board:* Prepare handouts with the above headings so students can fill them in.

When students finish, discuss the results. (*Option:* Have a map available to show students the area spoken about in verse 4.) Particularly look at the directions God gave to Joshua and see what promises may be considered to be natural consequences of following the directions (such as verse 7, which says to "obey all the law" and a natural consequence is that God will make Joshua prosper wherever he goes).

Next, discuss what characteristics Joshua already possessed that made him a good candidate to be a leader. (See Exodus 17:8-14; 24:13, 14; 32:17; Numbers 14:5-9; 14:28-31; Deuteronomy 31:1-8, 14; 34:9.) Mention that those characteristics alone would not have been enough. Say, "Joshua was a good leader because he allowed God to prepare him for the task at hand. This preparation took many years, but Joshua served God faithfully." (You can substitute the first reproducible exercise on page 116 here.)

Then look at verses 10, 11 and note Joshua's response to God. Finally, look at verses 16, 17 and discuss how the people reacted to Joshua.

INTO LIFE

Make in advance a poster (or handout) listing the following 12 dimensions of leadership: *enthusiasm; integrity; self-renewal; confidence; perceptiveness; judgment; performance; boldness; team building; collaboration; ability to inspire; aptness to serve others.* Have students identify the characteristics that pertain to Joshua and justify their answers (example: serving others in verses 16, 17). Gain a fuller picture by examining the texts from

Exodus, etc., listed above. Discuss how the characteristics involve relationships.

Next, discuss ways these 12 can manifest themselves in the church. Focus on specific ministries that need someone with these characteristics. Identify people in your congregation who possess these qualities (some of whom may be in your class). Conclude with prayer, asking God to continue to strengthen those who are currently in leadership positions in your church and to convict those he has been preparing for service to follow his guidance.

Option #1: Distribute a handout for matching the 12 dimensions with the 4 broader topics of *character, analysis, accomplishment,* and *interaction.* There will be 3 matches each: *character* to enthusiasm, integrity, and self-renewal; *analysis* to confidence, perceptiveness, and judgment; *accomplishment* to performance, boldness, and team building; *interaction* to collaboration, ability to inspire, and aptness to serve. Ask how the 4 broader topics relate to church leadership. *Option #2:* Use the reproducible exercise "Good Leaders Take Action" on page 116 to enhance this part of the lesson.

GIDEON: DELIVERER FOR THE PEOPLE

LESSON 2

INTRODUCTION

A. WHEN THE GOING GETS TOUGH

Johnny Weissmuller (1904–1984) won five gold medals in swimming in the Olympics of 1924 and 1928. He set dozens of swimming records between 1921 and 1929. When he retired from amateur swimming, he had never lost a race.

Yet his life did not begin with the promise of any such accomplishments. He came to America with his German-speaking parents when he was less than a year old. His father worked first as a coal miner in Pennsylvania, then later as a brewer in Chicago. Johnny was sickly, but the move to Chicago gave him access to Lake Michigan, where he could build his strength through swimming. With parental encouragement, he developed some swimming skills, and he began to pursue the sport with a passion. He went on to become even more famous in the role of Tarzan in 12 movies.

Haven't we all at some time benefited from the persuasion and encouragement of others? Today's lesson is about Gideon, and he also needed some extra persuasion to reach his potential. For Weissmuller it was in swimming that he needed parental persistence; for Gideon it was the Lord who moved him to commit himself to deliver the nation of Israel from her enemies.

B. LESSON BACKGROUND

Joshua (last week's lesson) had fulfilled his commission. Having led Israel in the initial conquest of Canaan, he had worked with Eleazar to consign the land among the tribes. Joshua's major military campaigns occurred between about 1406 and 1400 BC. This conclusion is based on Caleb's statements in Joshua 14:7-10. Caleb was age 40 when he was a spy, which means he was about 39 when he left Egypt, and therefore 79 when the Jordan was crossed 40 years later. The fact that he was 85 as land was assigned to him thus indicates that the initial conquest took about 6 years.

As Joshua's life was coming to a close, he assembled the people to renew their commitment to the Lord's covenant (Joshua 23, 24). He expressed skepticism that they could keep their word, but they vowed their determination to do so. The book of Judges, which covers the period about 1380 to 1050 BC, relates how they did not keep their part of the covenant. Israelite faithfulness was like the morning dew that evaporates into the air.

God had promised that if the people were faithful, they would have children, great crops, full barns, and protection from enemies (Deuteronomy 28:3-14). The people had no taxes to pay except their tithes, and the Lord

DEVOTIONAL READING:
1 CORINTHIANS 1:26-31
BACKGROUND SCRIPTURE:
JUDGES 6–8
PRINTED TEXT:
JUDGES 6:1-3, 7-16

LESSON AIMS

After participating in this lesson, each student will be able to:

1. Describe the situation facing Israel at the time Gideon was called to be judge.

2. Compare and contrast Midianite oppression of Israel with cultural oppression of the church.

3. Write a prayer that asks God to use him or her in a specific way to resist the cultural oppression of the church.

KEY VERSE

The LORD turned to him and said, "Go in the strength you have and save Israel out of Midian's hand. Am I not sending you?" —Judges 6:14

LESSON 2 NOTES

would take care of them. Moses had predicted severe punishment if the Israelites served other gods (Deuteronomy 28:15-68). The book of Judges sets forth the fulfillments of the curses that came upon them—punishments for their disobedience.

When Joshua died, Israel did not have a leader designated, and there was no procedure to select one. According to Judges 1, it seems that each tribe operated independently and was expected to help expedite the mopping up operations against the Canaanites. The mopping up began well. Then an exception appears in Judges 1:21. That is followed by a list of failures in verses 27-36.

In Judges 2, an angel of the Lord appeared and rebuked the people for their disobedience. The generation that entered Canaan did not teach the next generation to know the Lord (Judges 2:10). As a result, their descendants were attracted to the gods of Canaan. The people did not keep their word. God, however, kept his word and sent other nations to punish Israel.

A cycle thus began that is given six times in the book of Judges. It is often summarized as *sin, sorrow, supplication,* and *salvation* (the words *slavery, servitude,* and *silence* are sometimes added to the description of the cycle). The Israelites repented and prayed for help each time. Then God would send a savior in the form of a judge, who served as a military deliverer, magistrate, or both. The book of Judges has 13 such judges, and 6 of them are major delivering judges. Today's study is about Israel at the beginning of the judgeship of Gideon. He is the fifth judge, and he is the fourth major deliverer. We date his exploits between 1192 and 1152 BC. The first phase of the four-part cycle is ready to be repeated, for repentance often has a short duration.

I. DEVASTATION BY MIDIAN (JUDGES 6:1-3)

A. DURATION OF THE PUNISHMENT (v. 1)

1. Again the Israelites did evil in the eyes of the LORD, and for seven years he gave them into the hands of the Midianites.

Six rebellions by God's people are recounted in the book of Judges. Each begins the same way: affirming that the people *did evil in the eyes of the Lord* (Judges 3:7, 12; 4:1; 6:1 [here]; 10:6; 13:1). The phrase is defined more fully in Judges 2:11-13 as abandoning the worship of the Lord to serve the local deities (Baals and Ashtoreths, who are gods and goddesses of agriculture and fertility). Such worship is often associated with immoral practices.

While the Israelites were still at Sinai, God had warned them about the peoples of Canaan. The Israelites were not to make covenants with them, intermarry, or participate in their worship (Exodus 34:12-17). Yet God's prohibitions are treated like a warning about wet paint—people have to test it.

In the case before us, the evil is followed by punishment—a seven-year period of affliction from the Midianites. This group of people is also descended from Abraham, but through his second wife (Genesis 25:2). That was many centuries before the event being described here, so any sense of kinship has long since been lost. The Midianites live in the deserts east and south of Israel. Moses had found refuge for 40 years with these people after he fled from Egypt (Exodus 2:15).

WHAT DO YOU THINK?

What tools does the Christian have available to break or avoid the cycle of "sin, sorrow, supplication, and salvation" that the Israelites experienced? How will you use these tools in the week ahead?

WHAT DO YOU THINK?

Why do you think idol worship was such a strong temptation to Israel? In what ways do we succumb to the same temptation, and how do we prevent this?

The people of Israel have been given a foundational charge by the Lord: they are to be a holy people, because they have a holy God (Leviticus 19:2; compare 1 Peter 1:15, 16). The gods of their religious neighbors are grossly immoral and so are the religious practices associated with them. To follow in those ways is to bring the promised disasters.

AFFECTED BY THE PAST

The past has a way of catching up with us. Take, for example, the town of Picher, located in the northeast corner of Oklahoma. Picher was once a center for lead and zinc mining. The mines finally played out in the 1970s, and the town's population dropped from a pre–World War II high of 16,000 to about 1,600. Now, Picher is underlain with a maze of old tunnels and caverns that are subject to collapse at any time.

In 1967, nine houses fell into a single sinkhole. In 2005, a cave-in appeared beside the primary road into Picher, forcing the highway to be closed to large trucks. In 2006, the Environmental Protection Agency met with the townspeople to tell them the whole town was in danger of falling into the earth. The EPA announced its plans to buy the whole town—houses, mobile homes, church buildings, and businesses—at a cost of at least $20 million. An even greater cost is the lead poisoning that affects the children who have grown up in Picher. That which seemed at one time to promise the good life has come back to haunt the town.

Past sin has a way of coming back on us as well. Israel's "evil in the eyes of the Lord" undoubtedly seemed fun and satisfying at one time. But it proved to be the nation's downfall. The principle still applies: what we did yesterday and in years past affects our lives today. We can't change the past, but we can act on the fact that what we do today will affect our lives tomorrow. —C. R. B.

B. DESPERATE RESPONSES (v. 2)
2. Because the power of Midian was so oppressive, the Israelites prepared shelters for themselves in mountain clefts, caves and strongholds.

The oppression continues year after year. *Caves* and remote areas become places for the people to find safety for themselves and their crops.

C. DESCRIBING THE OPPRESSION (v. 3)
3. Whenever the Israelites planted their crops, the Midianites, Amalekites and other eastern peoples invaded the country.

God has withdrawn his special protection from Israel. As a result, nomadic groups are able to enjoy the fruits of Israelite labors. *The Israelites* are allowed to sow and harvest *their crops.* Then the marauders help themselves to the harvest, leaving just enough so that there will be seed for the next year. It is a time of desperation. The *Amalekites* seem to be descendants of Esau (Genesis 36:12). This is the group that attacked Israel just before it reached Sinai (Exodus 17:8-16). They are also a part of the oppression that preceded Israel's second judge, Ehud (Judges 3:13).

II. DECLARATIONS BY A PROPHET (JUDGES 6:7-10)
A. PRAYER FOR RELIEF (v. 7)
7. When the Israelites cried to the LORD because of Midian,

When you have to live in the dens of the foxes, you finally get "foxhole religion." This is usually defined as offering prayers and vows while in extreme

DAILY BIBLE READINGS

Monday, Sept. 7—The Standards of God's Choice (1 Corinthians 1:26-31)

Tuesday, Sept. 8—Crying for Help (Judges 6:4-10)

Wednesday, Sept. 9—Seeking Proof of Favor (Judges 6:14-24)

Thursday, Sept. 10—Cautious Obedience (Judges 6:25-27)

Friday, Sept. 11—Thinning the Ranks (Judges 7:2-8)

Saturday, Sept. 12—Assured for the Task (Judges 7:9-15)

Sunday, Sept. 13—Go and Deliver (Judges 6:1-3, 7-16)

WHAT DO YOU THINK?

What are some promises that you or others have made to God during extreme situations? Did those promises lead to a lasting change in your (or their) relationship with God? Why, or why not?

situations, but the commitments tend to be forgotten after the dangers pass. After seven years, however, the prayers are more sincere. For the time being at least, the people intend to keep their pledges.

B. PROPHET'S REBUKE (vv. 8-10)

8. . . . he sent them a prophet, who said, "This is what the LORD, the God of Israel, says: I brought you up out of Egypt, out of the land of slavery.

An unknown *prophet* is *sent* to remind the Israelites that they have broken the covenant. The words are very similar to the message given by the angel of the Lord in Judges 2:1, 2. They are also reminiscent of the verse that immediately precedes the first of the Ten Commandments (Exodus 20:2). Many generations have come and gone since the Mosaic covenant was given. But the passing of time does not lessen responsibility.

9. "I snatched you from the power of Egypt and from the hand of all your oppressors. I drove them from before you and gave you their land.

The deliverance from Egyptian bondage was only the beginning of God's gracious acts on behalf of Israel. He had protected the Israelites during their wilderness wanderings. The nation had met opposition as the people approached the area east of the Jordan (Numbers 21:22-35). But they easily had routed the foes. The battle of Jericho (Joshua 6) and the battle of the long day (Joshua 10) are among the blessings that God bestowed on his people in their conquest of the Canaanites. Such victories allowed God to give *their land* to Israel.

10. "I said to you, 'I am the LORD your God; do not worship the gods of the Amorites, in whose land you live.' But you have not listened to me."

The mention of *the Amorites* brings to mind Joshua's challenge in Joshua 24:15. The Amorites ordinarily live in hill country, but the term is sometimes used to refer to all the peoples of Canaan. The unknown prophet's concluding statement *but you have not listened to me* justifies the punishment that has been received by Israel. The people are not grateful for the privilege of living in the *land*. Their subsequent disobedience involves gross idolatry.

REJECTION HOTLINE

The "dating game" is nearly as old as the human race. Traditionally, the male of our species makes the first approach. Men have developed all sorts of pick-up lines to impress and interest the women they are attracted to. An important step in the process is a request for the woman's phone number.

What if the woman is totally uninterested, but doesn't want to crush the poor fellow's fragile ego in a public place? The option of giving a false phone number has been around a long time, but now a new twist has been added: she now can give him the phone number of the local "rejection hotline," smile, and walk away. The would-be suitor thinks he has hit the jackpot.

When he calls the following day, however, he hears this recording: "Hello, this is not the person you were trying to call. You've reached the rejection hotline. . . . Unfortunately, the person who gave you this rejection hotline number did not want you to have their real number." The rude voice goes on to list numerous negative characteristics that the woman may have noticed.

Israel presumed she could worship idols with impunity. Her "big time" rejection in the form of the Babylonian captivity is far in the future in Gideon's day. When the leaders of that later time tried to call on the Lord, they found themselves

HOW TO SAY IT

Abiezrite. A-by-EZ-rite.
Amalekites. AM-uh-leh-kites
   or Uh-MAL-ih-kites.
Amorites. AM-uh-rites.
Ashtoreth. ASH-toe-reth.
Baal. BAY-ul.
Boaz. BO-az.
Canaanites. KAY-nun-ites.
Ehud. EE-hud.
Eleazar. El-ih-A-zar
   or E-lih-A-zar.
Joash. JO-ash.
Manasseh. Muh-NASS-uh.
Midianites. MID-ee-un-ites.
Mosaic. Mo-ZAY-ik.
Ophrah. AHF-ruh.

reaching God's rejection hotline (Ezekiel 14:3). The unknown prophet in today's text gave Israel something of a warm-up to that heaviest of Israel's rejections. How does God rebuke disobedience yet today?

—C. R. B.

III. DIALOGUE WITH GIDEON (JUDGES 6:11-16)

A. ANGEL (v. 11)

11. The angel of the LORD came and sat down under the oak in Ophrah that belonged to Joash the Abiezrite, where his son Gideon was threshing wheat in a winepress to keep it from the Midianites.

Angel is the general word for "messenger." The phrase *angel of the Lord* thus points to a heavenly being that appears in order to deliver a message. In certain contexts, this messenger is interpreted to refer to a function of the Son of God before he comes as a babe in Bethlehem. The ground is holy when this being appears (Exodus 3:2, 5), and he receives acts of worship (Judges 6:18-23). In addition, the language in the text before us and in Exodus 3 frequently changes from *angel* to *Lord* and/or *God* as the spokesperson. The apostle John is told twice that only God is to receive worship (Revelation 19:10; 22:8, 9), so *angel of the Lord* likely refers to a divine being here.

The location for this event is given as *under* a well-known *oak* tree that is *in Ophrah;* verse 15 indicates that it is in the tribal territory of Manasseh. This serves to distinguish it from other communities that may have the same name. A *threshing* floor for grain is usually in an open area. This is so that the wind may blow away the chaff after a threshing sledge is pulled over the grain by oxen. Such places become targets for raiding parties (1 Samuel 23:1). *Gideon*, however, is doing this task in a *winepress* in order to conceal himself from *the Midianites*. A winepress is often a pit or recessed place in a rock.

B. ANNOUNCEMENT (v. 12)

12. When the angel of the LORD appeared to Gideon, he said, "The LORD is with you, mighty warrior."

The sudden appearance of the heavenly messenger is intended to arouse Gideon's attention. The greeting itself may have a certain irony or sarcasm in it, for this *mighty warrior* is hiding in a winepress to conceal what he is doing! The salutation also may be interpreted to mean that Gideon is simply a member of a family of distinction (compare Ruth 2:1, where the same words in Hebrew describe Boaz). Another possibility is that the phrase prophesies Gideon's future accomplishments.

C. ANXIETY (v. 13)

13. "But sir," Gideon replied, "if the LORD is with us, why has all this happened to us? Where are all his wonders that our fathers told us about when they said, 'Did not the LORD bring us up out of Egypt?' But now the LORD has abandoned us and put us into the hand of Midian."

Gideon responds to the first part of the angel's greeting by asking a series of questions that seem to challenge the assertion that *the Lord* is present with Israel. His first question is the *why* question that is often associated with tragedies.

Gideon is aware of the history of his people. At least in his family, it has been told by the *fathers,* and he is able to cite the acts of God associated with the deliverance from bondage. He changes from questions to the assertion

Visual for Lesson 2. *Point to this visual as you ask, "How will we make sure we recognize God's call when it comes?"*

WHAT DO YOU THINK?

Who is a "mighty warrior" you know who may not at first glance stand out as a courageous person in the eyes of the world? In what ways is this person a Christian example to emulate?

WHAT DO YOU THINK?

Why does God allow the righteous to suffer along with the guilty? What instances of this have you seen?

that *the Lord* has deserted Israel, in spite of the promises of his presence. Now Israel is being oppressed by others.

Gideon conveniently overlooks or is not aware of the denunciation by the unknown prophet (vv. 8-10, above). We may assume that the angel appears to Gideon because he is, in some sense, a righteous man. But the righteous often have to suffer along with the unrighteous.

D. COMMISSION (v. 14)

14. The LORD turned to him and said, "Go in the strength you have and save Israel out of Midian's hand. Am I not sending you?"

In response, *the Lord* does not answer Gideon's questions of verse 13. Instead, the Lord tells Gideon to *go* in order to *save Israel*. The speaker has the authority to send Gideon on the mission that is planned for him. Some see an implication in the phrase *go in the strength you have* that Gideon is being bestowed with the ability to fulfill his assignment.

E. CONCERNS (v. 15)

15. "But Lord," Gideon asked, "how can I save Israel? My clan is the weakest in Manasseh, and I am the least in my family."

The task given to Gideon is formidable. Thus he expresses what he considers to be valid and serious reservations about his abilities and self-worth. Although not stated here, the text reveals later that two of his brothers have been slain by the Midianites (Judges 8:18, 19). If the intention of such slayings is to intimidate, the purpose has been accomplished in the mind of Gideon.

F. COMFORT (v. 16)

16. The LORD answered, "I will be with you, and you will strike down all the Midianites together."

The assurance given to Gideon is the same as was given to Moses—that the Lord *will be with* him (Exodus 3:12). Like Moses, this is only partially comforting to Gideon. The narrative that follows shows that he is not fully persuaded. He receives the promise that he will be able to be victorious over *the Midianites*, but he is not totally convinced. Like Moses, Gideon needs some signs to validate what he is to do. These will be given to him according to his requests.

CONCLUSION

Gideon was reluctant at first to do what the Lord asked him to do. Yet God patiently worked with him, and he became more confident and trusting in the Lord. He is mentioned in the listing of heroes of the faith in Hebrews 11:32: "I do not have time to tell about Gideon, . . . who through faith conquered kingdoms; . . . whose weakness was turned to strength; and who became powerful in battle and routed foreign armies."

One of the challenges for every believer is simply to do what God wants to be done as revealed in his Word. Most people are fully aware of the areas in which they need to make changes. But to have the resolve and then make the changes is the real test.

Teachers of this lesson are strongly encouraged to read the entire account that relates the subsequent events in Gideon's life: the water test involving

PRAYER

Almighty God, I am grateful for the example of Gideon. May I use it to become more what you want me to be. Then may I encourage others in the same way. In Christ's name. Amen.

the wetness of the fleece left on the ground overnight, the reduction of his army from 32,000 to 10,000 to 300 (against 135,000, Judges 8:10), the attack on the Midianite camp at night, and the pursuit of those who were able to get away. The total number of verses given to Gideon and his son is more than that given to any of the other judges.

A certain preacher once used the record of Gideon in a sermon, saying that he always wondered if he would have been among the 300 who were selected to be in Gideon's final army. Afterward, one of the church leaders asked pointedly, "What makes you think you would not have been among the 22,000 that went home when they had the opportunity?" Good question!

THOUGHT TO REMEMBER
God plus one committed person equals victory.

Discovery Learning

The following is an alternative lesson plan emphasizing learning activities. Classes desiring such student involvement will find these suggestions helpful. At the back of this book are reproducible student pages to further enhance activity learning.

INTO THE LESSON

Before students arrive, write this question on the board: *What Scriptures speak to the paradoxes of God's Word (the weak shall be strong, the first shall be last, etc.)?* Have students save their answers for later.

Before class, research the stories of several people who were unlikely successes (example: Wilma Rudolph, who won three Olympic gold medals in track and field despite the fact that she had polio as a child). Distribute handouts with all the names listed on each. Read the circumstances of their lives and have students try to match the names on their handouts with the person's story. Discuss what it was in each of these people that enabled them to succeed.

Ask students to share a time when they were asked to perform a duty for which they felt unprepared or unqualified. What did they do? What was the result? Transition into the lesson by saying, "Today we have a story of another person who seemed an unlikely choice for the job God called him to do."

INTO THE WORD

Distribute handouts of the questions below. Allow time for students to provide answers from Judges 6:1-3, 7-16. (You can turn this into a crossword puzzle by using one of the free puzzle makers available on the Internet.) To make the exercise slightly harder, do not include the verse numbers,

which indicate where the answers are located.

1. The people of _____ were oppressing Israel for seven years (v. 1); 2. The Israelites hid from their enemies in _____, _____, and _____ (v. 2); 3. When the Israelites cried to the Lord, he sent them a _____ (v. 8); 4. The prophet reminded Israel that God had brought them up from _____ and had given them _____ (vv. 8, 9); 5. The angel of the Lord found Gideon threshing _____ (v. 11); 6. The angel called Gideon a mighty _____ (v. 12); 7. Gideon doubted the angel because God had already delivered Israel into the _____ of the Midianites (v. 13); 8. Gideon was an unlikely choice because his family was _____ in Manasseh (v. 15); 9. Gideon's victory was secure because the _____ would be with him (v. 16).

Go over the answers, stopping to discuss key aspects of the text.

Ask students to refer to the Scripture assignment they completed at the beginning of class. Let three or four students share the paradoxes they found. Discuss how God uses the weak or seemingly unqualified to accomplish his purposes. Discuss how God still works that way today.

Divide students into six groups. Give each group one of the following sets of Scripture references: Genesis 6:9-12, 17, 18; Genesis 12:1-5; Exodus 3:1-15 plus 4:13-20; 1 Samuel 3:9-21; Isaiah 6:1-8; Luke 1:26-38. (If your class is not large enough to form six groups, double-up some of the assignments.) Have the students work in their groups to identify the characteristics they see present in "the call" God gives in each of the passages.

When groups finish, make a list on the board of the characteristics they found. These may include the following: there is an aspect of righteousness/faith in the one called (Noah, Samuel, Mary); God revealed his plan and commissioned the one called to be part of it (Noah, Abram, Moses, Samuel, Isaiah, Mary); some who were called doubted their ability to do what God asked of them (Moses, Isaiah, Mary); God empowered those he called (Moses, Samuel, Isaiah, Mary); each person who was called obeyed God (all). Discuss the context of these calls and relate them to Gideon's call. (*Option:* Use the reproducible exercise "Others Hear God" from page 117 to extend this discussion; you can also use this as part of the Into Life segment since it is personalized.)

INTO LIFE

Ask students whether they have ever sensed God calling them to a particular task. What was the task? How did they respond? Discuss whether there are any areas of service within your church or community where God may be calling them to serve right now. Write these on the board and have students identify which needs they can fill.

Encourage each person to make this a matter of prayer and commit to at least three months of service in that area. For the remainder of the fall quarter, have students periodically report on how their service is going. Distribute copies of the reproducible exercise "Gideon Hears God" from page 117 as take-home work.

EZRA: PRIEST FOR THE PEOPLE

LESSON 3

INTRODUCTION

A. SECOND CHANCES

At the age of 17, Alan Simpson and some other teenagers were found guilty of shooting mailboxes and otherwise destroying property. It was a first offense, and he was given the proverbial second chance. The boys had to pay for the damages, and they were put on probation for two years.

As this was unfolding, Alan saw his parents look at each other in disbelief, and he saw his father cry. He just wanted another chance, and he completed probation successfully. Eventually, he became an attorney, went into politics, and was elected to be a multiterm U.S. senator from the state of Utah (1979–1997). He served in that capacity as the minority whip and then the majority whip for his party. In these positions, he did what he could to help others. But at the same time he had no use for those who used false persuasion to con their way out of deserved punishments.

God is also "a God of second chances" and much more—if the ones who have turned their backs on him are sincere in their repentance. In Jeremiah 32:33, the Lord says that he instructed his people "again and again," but they would not listen. Through the centuries his prophets preached and wrote the books that recorded the messages they had received from God. At times there were temporary responses of repentance, but the idea of the need for repentance is difficult to pass from one generation to another. Yet God continued to provide warnings because of his love. He provided opportunity after opportunity for his people to return to the path of righteousness.

B. LESSON BACKGROUND

Some seven centuries have passed from last week's lesson on Gideon to today's lesson involving Ezra. In the interim, the exceeding sinfulness of the northern kingdom of Israel had caused God to use Assyria to take it into captivity in about 722 BC (2 Kings 17). In 586 BC, the southern nation of Judah was deported by the Babylonians. Jerusalem and the temple were destroyed, and the people of Judah experienced a 70-year captivity.

Under ordinary circumstances, a nation that had been out of existence for that period of time was gone forever. But with God all things are possible. After the Persians captured Babylon in 539 BC, Cyrus the Great issued an edict that all captive peoples could return to their homelands. Then the big question became this: had the captivity cured the Israelites of idolatry, or would history repeat itself?

DEVOTIONAL READING:
PSALM 32:1-5
BACKGROUND SCRIPTURE:
EZRA 9
PRINTED TEXT:
EZRA 9:5-11, 15

LESSON AIMS

After participating in this lesson, each student will be able to:

1. Summarize Ezra's reactions when he heard of the sins of his people.

2. Identify the most important element in Ezra's prayer and tell why that element is so important.

3. Adjust the wording in Ezra's prayer to make it applicable to today.

KEY VERSE

[Ezra] prayed: "O my God, I am too ashamed and disgraced to lift up my face to you, my God, because our sins are higher than our heads and our guilt has reached to the heavens.
—*Ezra 9:6*

LESSON 3 NOTES

HOW TO SAY IT

Achan. AY-kan.
Assyria. Uh-SEAR-ee-uh.
Babylonian. Bab-ih-LOW-
   nee-un.
Cyrus. SIGH-russ.
Darius. Duh-RYE-us.
Ezra. EZ-ruh.
Midianites. MID-ee-un-ites.
Nehemiah. NEE-huh-MY-uh.
Pentecost. PENT-ih-kost.
Persia. PER-zhuh.
Pilate. PIE-lut.

Visual for Lesson 3. *Point to this visual as you ask, "When was the last time you said these words? How can a sense of shame bring us closer to God?"*

Ezra 1–6 describes the initial wave of the return from captivity of roughly 538 BC. The dedication of a new temple took place in March 515 BC. In the years immediately after the return, the Israelites maintained a separation from the peoples of the land, refusing their assistance and any corrupting influence that association with them might have brought.

Yet in the decades that followed there was a change of attitude. Marriages began to occur with those who worshiped other gods. In 458 BC, God's answer was to send Ezra and others from Babylon to Jerusalem (almost 900 miles away). Ezra 7 and 8 tell of this return, which numbered almost 1,800 men, plus women and children.

Ezra himself was both a priest and a scribe (Ezra 7:1-6). He set himself to have these purposes concerning God's law: to study it, to do it, and to teach it (Ezra 7:10). We assume that Ezra was thrilled that he actually could live in Jerusalem and be a part of the worship at the temple. There he taught God's Word, and he gained the respect of the leaders.

But any jubilation Ezra felt was short-lived. The first verses of Ezra 9 relate that the leaders came to him to report that there were intermarriages by men of Judah with the peoples of the land. God's original restrictions on intermarriage applied to the seven nations of Canaan as listed in Deuteronomy 7:1. The other nations listed in Deuteronomy 23:3-8 had only a prohibition about being a part of the assembly until several generations passed.

Even so, Ezra 9:1 indicates that a consensus had developed among the leadership that it was safer not to marry anyone who worshiped other gods. This included people belonging to groups listed in Deuteronomy 23:3-8. When Ezra was informed of the problem, his response was threefold: (1) he tore his garment, (2) he pulled hair from his head and beard, and (3) he sat down appalled until mid-afternoon and the time of the evening sacrifice (Ezra 9:3, 4). This is the point where today's lesson picks up.

I. REPENTANCE EXPRESSED (EZRA 9:5-7)

A. PERSONAL REACTIONS (vv. 5, 6a)

5, 6a. Then, at the evening sacrifice, I rose from my self-abasement, with my tunic and cloak torn, and fell on my knees with my hands spread out to the LORD my God and prayed:

Ezra demonstrates vividly that he is distraught and disappointed. After spending time sitting (vv. 3, 4), probably without uttering a word, he changes his position, falls on his *knees*, and spreads his *hands* in prayer toward *the Lord*. This sincere prayer of repentance is a first step in a dramatic reformation that must take place.

B. PRESENT SINS (v. 6b)

6b. "O my God, I am too ashamed and disgraced to lift up my face to you, my God, because our sins are higher than our heads and our guilt has reached to the heavens.

Ezra's first words describe his personal shame and embarrassment even to approach *God.* Then Ezra describes the magnitude of the transgressions. He expresses the vertical dimension that is a part of every sin: it reaches all the way to *the heavens,* where God is. Sin has its effects even in Heaven.

The fact that Ezra says *our* is not to be taken to mean that Ezra himself is personally guilty of the sin under discussion. Even so, he is identifying himself with his community (compare Nehemiah 1:6; Daniel 9:5-19). Those not guilty of a sin may still suffer the collateral effects of God's wrath when he punishes the guilty. Ezra knows this.

C. PAST REVIEWED (v. 7)

7. *"From the days of our forefathers until now, our guilt has been great. Because of our sins, we and our kings and our priests have been subjected to the sword and captivity, to pillage and humiliation at the hand of foreign kings, as it is today.*

Ezra continues his prayer by recalling that Israel tested God even before it became a special nation at Sinai (see Exodus 15:22–16:7). Ezra is surely aware of the account in Joshua 7 about Achan, who sinfully kept some of the valuables of Jericho for himself. The sin of that one man caused God to say that the nation of Israel had sinned (Joshua 7:11). Ezra knows that many of the Israelites are not personally guilty. But he understands the principle that an entire group may be considered guilty because of the sins of one or a few. Ezra also knows the consequences of national sin: *captivity*, death, poverty, and *humiliation*. The Jewish people have "been there, done that." He does not want his people to go through these things again.

THE NEED TO ACKNOWLEDGE PAST SINS

Holocaust was an NBC miniseries that first aired in April 1978. It told the story of Nazi Germany's persecution of Jews before and during World War II. It was a success in America, as was ABC's blockbuster miniseries *Roots* of the previous year. The latter series acquainted viewers with the emotional impact of America's shameful experiment with slavery.

When *Holocaust* was broadcast in West Germany in 1979, the reaction was unexpected. Fifteen million people (about half the nation's adult population) saw at least some part of the program. One commentator described it as "breaking a thirty-five-year taboo on discussing Nazi atrocities." Seventy percent of teenage viewers said they had learned more about Nazi atrocities from the miniseries than from all their years of studying German history in school. The statute of limitations on Nazi war crimes, set to expire that year, was canceled.

Critics of both TV miniseries claimed the productions took liberties with the facts. Perhaps. But the result was an increased awareness of a dark part of each nation's history. However, no one could criticize Ezra's recounting of the sins of Israel. He spoke the unvarnished truth. Every nation (as well as every person) needs to find the strength of character to acknowledge past sin. Otherwise there is no hope for redemption. —C. R. B.

II. RELIEF ENJOYED (EZRA 9:8, 9)

A. FAITHFUL REMNANT (v. 8)

8. *"But now, for a brief moment, the LORD our God has been gracious in leaving us a remnant and giving us a firm place in his sanctuary, and so our God gives light to our eyes and a little relief in our bondage.*

Ezra rejoices that *the Lord* permits *a remnant* to have a brief period of time of freedom from oppression. It now has been 80 years (538–458 BC) since Cyrus the Great gave his gracious proclamation that permitted all captives to return to their homelands (Ezra 1:2-4). The edict of Darius the Great for the resumption of work on the temple is over 60 years in the past at this point. Historically, these time spans are viewed as brief (*a little relief*).

WHAT DO YOU THINK?

What national sins (historic or present) should we confess to God right now? What may be the result when we do this?

DAILY BIBLE READINGS

Monday, Sept. 14—Confession and Forgiveness (Psalm 32:1-5)

Tuesday, Sept. 15—Skilled in the Law of Moses (Ezra 7:1-6)

Wednesday, Sept. 16—A Heart Set on Study (Ezra 7:7-10)

Thursday, Sept. 17—Guided by God's Hand (Ezra 7:25-28)

Friday, Sept. 18—Seeking God's Protection (Ezra 8:21-23)

Saturday, Sept. 19—Hearing the Law of God (Nehemiah 8:1-12)

Sunday, Sept. 20—A Fervent Prayer for the People (Ezra 9:5-11, 15)

What Do You Think?

What are some things that can hinder the church from being a strong influence to provide moral stability in modern society? How do we overcome these hindrances?

The use of the word *remnant* shows that Ezra is familiar with this important doctrinal term in God's plan and in the messages of the prophets. (This word appears dozens of times in the Old Testament.) Regardless of the sins of the nation and any subsequent punishments, there is always a faithful remnant that is recognized by God (compare 1 Kings 19:18; Romans 11:4, 5). He will bring his remnant people back from wherever they have gone (Isaiah 10:21; 11:11, 12; Jeremiah 23:3; etc.). Until now, the restored nation of Judah has had *a firm place* in God's *sanctuary*. The image is that of stability for what would otherwise be a tenuous existence.

The "Only-est" Ones

"It's the only-est one there is!" In some parts of the American South, that's a way to speak of something's uniqueness. Unique things attract us. As a parallel, many enjoy being part of a group that has relatively few members; it makes us feel special. That's part of the appeal of groups and causes such as "outlaw" motorcyclists, the Daughters of the American Revolution, and supporters of the most hopeless of political candidates.

Religious leaders throughout the centuries have tried to endow their followers with a sense of uniqueness. God certainly wanted Israel to be unique. He also wants the church to be unique. With that uniqueness should come a great deal of humility. When pride takes over, a perceived uniqueness may become a "holier than thou" exclusivity. The result can be an attitude expressed by this sarcastic bit of verse:

We are the chosen few; / All others will be damned.

There's no room in Heaven for you; / We don't want Heaven crammed!

When Ezra spoke of being part of a remnant, he spoke the truth with repentant humility. Although Israel had largely been unfaithful, there were a few who had not turned from God (or had turned back to God). Now God was going to use those faithful few to renew the nation.

The *remnant ideal* at its best says "regardless of what others may do, we will strive to be faithful!" Ezra's attitude gives those in the remnant an important reminder: humility is always more appropriate than pride. —C. R. B.

B. Favored Reactions (v. 9)

9. "Though we are slaves, our God has not deserted us in our bondage. He has shown us kindness in the sight of the kings of Persia: He has granted us new life to rebuild the house of our God and repair its ruins, and he has given us a wall of protection in Judah and Jerusalem.

The captives from Judah receive favored nation status from *God* and *the kings of Persia*. Since their return, there have been times of provocation by Judah's neighbors (see Ezra 4 for Ezra's summary of such opposition). But the people have been able to complete the temple. God has been a spiritual *wall* for *Judah and Jerusalem* in all this. The fact that the wall cited here embraces Judah as well as Jerusalem shows that this is not a physical wall. Jerusalem's literal, physical wall is still down at this point. It will not be rebuilt until the time of Nehemiah, about 14 years down the road.

Another distinctive blessing is mentioned in Ezra 7:24—that the priests, Levites, and other full-time workers at the temple are exempt from tax or tribute. By granting this exemption, the kings of Persia show their intent not to offend the God of the Jews or any other gods.

What Do You Think?

In what ways may God still be using secular authorities to accomplish his purposes for the spread of the gospel?

III. REMORSE EXPANDED (EZRA 9:10, 11)

A. SPEECHLESS RESPONSE (v. 10)

10. "But now, O our God, what can we say after this? For we have disregarded the commands

Ezra is overwhelmed by three things: (1) the goodness of God that has permitted him and others to return, (2) the favorable actions of the kings who have allowed the nation to be restored when such a task was considered to be impossible, and now (3) the ingratitude of some of those who have disobeyed so flagrantly by having wives and children who can lead the entire nation back into idolatry. Ezra is well aware that the cycle of punishment and exile can begin again. Ezra is a person who learns from history.

B. SPIRITUAL ASSESSMENT (v. 11)

11. . . . "you gave through your servants the prophets when you said: 'The land you are entering to possess is a land polluted by the corruption of its peoples. By their detestable practices they have filled it with their impurity from one end to the other.'"

The commands for Israel to avoid spiritual compromise began with Moses. The same message has been repeated through the centuries (Exodus 23:32, 33; Deuteronomy 7:1-3; 12:1-4; 23:6; Judges 2:1, 2; 2 Kings 17:15; Jeremiah 10:2). It will be repeated after Ezra passes off the scene (Malachi 2:11; 2 Corinthians 6:14-18).

It is absurd to worship a god that is not a god. Absurdity is compounded when such a practice is used to justify immoral acts that accompany such a practice. The subsequent loss of decency and respect will eventually lead to the destruction of whatever nation is involved. This is a lesson of history that has been repeated time after time. Nations that are considered to be the most powerful in their eras have crumbled and fallen because of corruption from within.

We recall that these kinds of warnings are prompted ultimately by the motive of love. The warnings may be from God or from parents, for both have concerns about their children. It would be criminal to see a child start to run into the street when a car is rapidly approaching and then not warn the child with whatever it takes to get his attention. God is a God of love, and he warns his people.

WHAT DO YOU THINK?

In what ways has the moral condition of society both improved and declined? What would revival in our land look like?

IV. RIGHTEOUSNESS CONTRASTED (EZRA 9:15)

A. GOD'S POSITION (v. 15a)

15a. "O LORD, God of Israel, you are righteous! We are left this day as a remnant.

Ezra's sermonic prayer concludes with a confession. The opening phrase affirms that *God is righteous.* This word has been defined simply as "doing what is right" or "being in conformity with a recognized standard."

God is the one who sets the standard. God's ethical standard grants forgiveness if sin is sincerely acknowledged. The consequences of sin may remain, and there may be a period of testing to determine if the repentance is genuine. But forgiveness may be expressed nonetheless.

B. PEOPLE'S STATUS (v. 15b)

15b. "Here we are before you in our guilt, though because of it not one of us can stand in your presence."

WHAT DO YOU THINK?

What are some situations (if any) where we should not offer another chance to an individual who has done something wrong? How do we forgive while still enforcing consequences?

Ezra knows that a God who is righteous also mandates that sin must be punished in some way. There are consequences for sin, and these cannot be escaped by an easy confession. The ultimate demonstration of this is the fact that Jesus' death was a punishment for sin; as such, that death satisfied God's righteous requirements. Jesus' death served as atonement for the sins of others in this once-for-all-time case (Hebrews 9:24-26).

CONCLUSION

How long has it been since you heard a sermon on repentance? A suggested guideline to apply to this lesson is that encouragement be given for the learners to look for those occasions in which they should repent and offer prayers of confession. Repentance, however, is not a popular topic, for a necessary implication is that sin and guilt precede the occasion to repent.

A starting point is to define repentance. One definition is that repentance is "a change of mind that leads to a change of heart (affections) and a change of life." The context of *repent* in the New Testament primarily indicates a change of mind. It is therefore a decision—it is a decision to quit sinning.

John the Baptist, as the forerunner for the Christ, came preaching a message of repentance. He said that the Jews should repent, for the kingdom of Heaven was at hand or near (Matthew 3:2). Jesus preached the same message as he began his ministry on earth (Matthew 4:17). On one occasion Jesus was asked to comment on Pilate's punishment of a group of people and on any crimes that may have preceded the punishment. Jesus' response seemed to say this: do not attempt to shield your own sins by citing the sins of others, for unless you repent you will perish (Luke 13:3, 5).

The church began on the Day of Pentecost (Acts 2). Peter's sermon recounted the rejection of the Lord's Christ, and that message had a dramatic effect on the hearers. They were persuaded of the truth of Peter's message, and they asked what they should do. Peter's reply included the need for repentance (Acts 2:38).

While in Athens, Paul gave his famous sermon about the "unknown" God. One of his statements was that God commanded all people everywhere to repent (Acts 17:30, 31). The reason he gave was that the day was coming when the world would be judged by the one whom God had appointed. That person is Jesus.

Peter sounded a warning in his second epistle about those who scoff at the promised return of Jesus (see Lesson 13 of this quarter). Peter stressed that the apparent delay in the return is because of the patience of God. He does not want anyone to perish, but for everyone to come to repentance (2 Peter 3:3, 9).

By its very nature, repentance is preceded by an awareness of God and the seriousness of going against what he has ordained. The person who wants to be right with God will have a godly sorrow that leads to repentance (2 Corinthians 7:9). In addition, the goodness or kindness of God in desiring to provide salvation should lead a person to repent—to decide to quit sin in order to follow Jesus permanently. Repentance is not only a crisis moment in accepting Christ, it is also a continuing process in the Christian life. "If we confess our sins, he is faithful and just and will forgive us our sins and purify us from all unrighteousness" (1 John 1:9; compare Revelation 2:5).

A prominent teacher in the early twentieth century reportedly said that if he could have any special gift, he would not ask for the gifts of speaking

PRAYER

Our God in Heaven, we are grateful that you have given us the absolute standards of right living. Without those standards, we drift on a sea of relativism. May we repent of the times we have walked in our own ways. In the strength of your Holy Spirit, we resolve to walk in the way that leads to eternal life. In Jesus' name. Amen.

in tongues, healing, etc. Rather, he said that he would ask for the ability to preach in a manner that would bring people to repentance.

Repentance—how long has it been since you heard a sermon on that subject?

Discovery Learning

The following is an alternative lesson plan emphasizing learning activities. Classes desiring such student involvement will find these suggestions helpful. At the back of this book are reproducible student pages to further enhance activity learning.

INTO THE LESSON

Write the word REPENTANCE on the board before class begins. As students enter the room but before they sit down, ask each to go to the board and write the names of public figures who have made public professions of repentance. Do Internet research in advance on this topic. Your research can yield names such as Jimmy Swaggart, Bernard Law, Marion Jones, Don Imus, and Eliot Spitzer. Make printouts of their stories for students to consider.

After everyone has had the chance to write a name on the board, discuss the various actions that accompanied these events (crying, resignations, accepting punishment, etc.). Write these on the board. Then ask, "What other actions may (or should) also accompany repentance?" List them on the board.

Alternative: If you don't want to use public or historical figures, use biblical characters (example: David's repentance over the Bathsheba incident) or just have students identify the various actions that can (or should) be associated with repentance.

INTO THE WORD

Say, "The people we listed committed sin or wrongdoing for which they realized the need to repent. Some repented in order to continue to function in a certain role. Others repented because they needed to have a clear conscience. Still others repented to receive forgiveness. In today's lesson, Ezra recognizes Israel's need to repent. His prayer can be divided into five stages of repentance."

Divide the class into five groups (or, if your class is smaller, five pairs or five individuals). Give each group some chart paper with one of the following five headings and Scripture references: *Humbly Acknowledge Sin* (vv. 5, 6); *Recognize Consequences of Sin* (v. 7); *Appreciate God's Grace* (vv. 8, 9); *Respond to God's Warnings* (vv. 10, 11); *Confess Personal Limitations* (v. 15).

Have each group read the identified verses from today's text and jot details that describe the heading at the top of the paper. (Students should write large enough on the chart paper for others to read it when it is posted on the wall.) Expected answers: (1) *Humbly Acknowledge Sin:* tore clothes, fell on knees, spread hands out to God, felt ashamed; (2) *Recognize Consequences of Sin:* country delivered into enemy hands, people killed and taken captive, land plundered; (3) *Appreciate God's Grace:* remnant return to Judah, relief from oppression, mercy from kings of Persia, restoration of Jerusalem and the temple; (4) *Respond to God's Warnings:* remember the law of God, which commanded religious purity among the people; (5) *Confess Personal Limitations:* acknowledgment that God is righteous and Israel is not.

Have groups share their findings with the class. Use the background information from the lesson text to bring clarity to the imagery in Ezra's prayer. Bring the discussion back to the actions the students listed on the board at the beginning of class. Put the groups' sheets of paper next to the board. Compare and contrast what is on the board listing with what is on the chart listings. Discuss actions identified by groups that were not listed on the board.

INTO LIFE

Ask students to discuss those aspects they find the hardest to include in their own times of repentance. Discuss what it is in human makeup that inhibits us from coming to God in complete repentance. Relate this back to the prayer of Ezra and identify certain actions that Christians would do well to emulate (kneeling, holding our hands up to God, naming the potential effects of our sin, listing the blessings God has given us in spite of our sins). Suggest students spend time in prayer this week asking God to bring them to full repentance.

Alternative: Have students work as a class to write a prayer that emulates the components of Ezra's. The result may look something like this:

Lord, I humbly acknowledge my sin to you. I recognize the effects my sin has had on me and others. Thank you for placing people and circumstances in my path to warn me of my folly. In spite of my rebellion, you have showered your grace and blessings on me in so many ways! Guide me in your righteousness and help me to submit to your will. In Jesus' name. Amen.

You may wish to use the reproducible exercise "Moving Through Repentance" on page 118 in place of this alternative. Distribute copies of Biblical Repentance from the same page as students leave.

NEHEMIAH: MOTIVATOR FOR THE PEOPLE

LESSON 4

INTRODUCTION

A. WHICH TYPE OF VOLUNTEER ARE YOU?

The military method for getting volunteers is familiar: "I want three volunteers—you, you, and you!" It is more like coercion than volunteerism. Even so, there are benefits to this method of finding volunteers: the needed quota is quickly filled, the projects that are pending are finished in a timely way, and the drafted "volunteers" sometimes discover that they actually enjoy what they have been assigned to do.

A second method is the normal procedure of announcing the nature of what needs to be done and then putting out a call for volunteers to accomplish it. The success of this approach varies greatly. Young ministers may have an idealized concept that if they announce the need for volunteers for church-related tasks then such needs will be filled easily. Reality, however, says that most people have already scheduled their time, or they do not want to be involved. The young minister soon comes to understand that this is not the best way to fill those empty slots of service.

A third approach to finding volunteers is direct and usually produces good results: capable individuals are asked personally to accept a task. One benefit of this approach is that sincere but incapable people who would volunteer under the second approach will not be hurt or offended by having their offers of help declined since they will not be asked in the first place.

Yet another type of volunteerism occurs when a talented individual perceives what needs to be done and then does it without being asked. This type of person can be a blessing. Nehemiah was such a one. He heard of a need, evaluated the circumstances, and decided that he was the best person to accomplish it. The excuses that he could have offered were many. But he sacrificed his comfortable position to do what needed to be done.

B. LESSON BACKGROUND

Six books of the Old Testament were written after the Jews returned to their homeland from Babylonian captivity. The six books include three historical books (Ezra, Nehemiah, and Esther) and the last three books of the Minor Prophets (Haggai, Zechariah, and Malachi).

Three Persian kings interacted with the Jews after the exile. Cyrus the Great captured Babylon in mid-October of 539 BC. The next year he gave his famous decree that all exiled peoples had permission to return to their native lands (see Ezra 1:2-4). Cyrus was named in a prophecy written in

DEVOTIONAL READING:
ISAIAH 62:1-7

BACKGROUND SCRIPTURE:
NEHEMIAH 2

PRINTED TEXT:
NEHEMIAH 2:5, 11-20

Sep 27

LESSON AIMS

After participating in this lesson, each student will be able to:

1. Tell how Nehemiah assessed the challenge before him, the opposition, and the resources available.

2. Explain the value of assessing a problem.

3. Assess the need in one specific ministry area in his or her church and volunteer to be a leader (or assist a leader) in that area.

KEY VERSE

I also told them about the gracious hand of my God upon me and what the king had said to me. They replied, "Let us start rebuilding." So they began this good work.

—Nehemiah 2:18

Lesson 4 Notes

How to Say It

Ahasuerus. Uh-haz-you-EE-rus.
Ammonite. AM-un-ite.
Artaxerxes. Are-tuh-ZERK-seez.
Cambyses. Kam-BYE-seez.
Geshem. GEE-shem
  (g as in get).
Horonite. HOR-oh-night.
Kidron. KID-ron.
Nehemiah. NEE-huh-MY-uh.
papyrus. puh-PIE-russ.
Salamis. SAL-uh-mis.
Samaria. Suh-MARE-ee-uh.
Sanballat. San-BAL-ut.
Tobiah. Toe-BYE-uh.
Xerxes. ZERK-seez.
Zechariah. ZEK-uh-RYE-uh.

What Do You Think?

What opportunities do people who work in secular professions have to advance God's kingdom in ways that a full-time minister does not?

Isaiah 44:28; 45:1 over 160 years before he conquered Babylon and other nations of that region. During his reign, the Jews who returned built the altar of burnt offerings, and they laid the foundation for the temple. Then opposition began by the neighbors of the Jews, and the building programs ceased.

Cambyses succeeded his father, Cyrus. Cambyses in turn was followed by Darius the Great in 522 BC. Two years later Haggai received four messages from God. That prophet exhorted the Jews to resume the work on the temple (Haggai 1:1; 2:1, 10, 20). The people again encountered opposition, but the work was allowed to continue while a search was made to see if the claim of the Jews was true—that Cyrus had authorized them to build. The decree was found, and the temple was completed in early 515 BC (Ezra 5, 6).

Xerxes (also given as Ahasuerus) followed Darius. Xerxes desperately wanted to avenge the defeat of his father by Greek forces at the battle of Marathon in 490 BC. The lengthy banquet recorded in Esther 1 may have been a planning session for the campaign that ended with a Greek victory at the sea battle of Salamis in 479 BC. Xerxes chose Esther as his queen when he returned from battle.

Artaxerxes I came to the throne in 464 BC when his father was assassinated. He permitted Ezra to return in 458 BC with other Jews (Ezra 7, 8). See last week's lesson. About 13 years later, in 445 BC, Nehemiah's brother arrived in Susa and told him of the plight of the Jews back in Jerusalem. The walls were still broken down, and a city without walls had no respect or defense. Nehemiah evaluated the matter, developed a plan of action, and waited for the right opportunity to present it to the king. The last verse of Nehemiah 1 notes that he was the king's cupbearer, a very responsible position of influence. Nehemiah could have used this opportunity to explain why he should stay in Susa in order to use his influence to help those in Judah. But this man of prayer decided that the task was his.

I. REQUEST BY NEHEMIAH (NEHEMIAH 2:5)

As our text opens, it has been four months since Nehemiah heard about the conditions in Judah (Nehemiah 1:1; 2:1). The early verses of this chapter reveal a crisis: Nehemiah has a sad countenance in the presence of the king. This can be interpreted as being unhappy with the king, and it puts a person at risk of being thought of plotting a coup.

The king evidently thinks highly of Nehemiah. After hearing the explanation, he asks what Nehemiah desires (2:4a). Nehemiah offers a "snap prayer" (2:4b) and begins his answer. It is evident that his answer is not off the top of his head. It is well developed. He is also aware that this king had given an order previously that a building program in Jerusalem had to be discontinued (Ezra 4:21). Nehemiah's words must be chosen carefully.

5. And I answered the king, "If it pleases the king and if your servant has found favor in his sight, let him send me to the city in Judah where my fathers are buried so that I can rebuild it."

Nehemiah begins with phrases that show his submission to *the king*. He avoids the word *Jerusalem* and simply requests to go to a *city* of *Judah* where his ancestors *are buried* so that he may make it a city again.

II. RESEARCH BY NEHEMIAH (NEHEMIAH 2:11-16)

Nehemiah makes his journey to Jerusalem with official papers and a military escort (Nehemiah 2:7-9). The soldiers provide protection, and their presence adds to the credentials and purposes he gives to the regional governors. His having an escort is different from Ezra's refusal to have such (Ezra 8:22). Ezra thought that having soldiers to accompany him would demonstrate a lack of faith. Nehemiah believes it is necessary for the purposes he has in mind.

A. TIME FOR REFRESHING (v. 11)

11. I went to Jerusalem, and after staying there three days

Jerusalem is almost 900 miles from Babylon. But Nehemiah has been in Susa, where kings spend a few months of the year. That is over 200 miles east of Babylon. Thus Nehemiah's journey is more than 1,000 miles. He uses *three days* after his arrival to become acclimated to the city, to become acquainted with the leaders of Jerusalem, and to refresh himself. Nehemiah 5:14 reveals that he is the governor for 12 years, starting at this time.

B. TIME FOR RECONNAISSANCE (vv. 12-15)

12. . . . I set out during the night with a few men. I had not told anyone what my God had put in my heart to do for Jerusalem. There were no mounts with me except the one I was riding on.

Nehemiah's leadership traits are exhibited again in that he has a plan for checking details and making changes from his plan. A full moon almost certainly fills the night sky for this inspection to take place. This enables him to see the difficulties his project may encounter. He can determine how difficulties may be overcome before anyone has a chance to raise an objection. His method is vastly superior to someone's saying, "Men, I think we should repair the walls. What do you think?"

Just one animal (perhaps his horse or a sure-footed donkey) is quieter than several. The *few men* with Nehemiah are probably the personal servants who have accompanied him from Susa. Nehemiah is not ready to tell the local leaders what is in his mind. Riding allows Nehemiah to survey the situation from a perspective that he would not have were he walking.

13. By night I went out through the Valley Gate toward the Jackal Well and the Dung Gate, examining the walls of Jerusalem, which had been broken down, and its gates, which had been destroyed by fire.

Nehemiah's nocturnal inspection of *the walls* gives the names of two *gates*. The next chapter refers to other gates, including the two cited here. The precise locations are unknown, but the names themselves help to indicate probable sites. The first gate mentioned probably is located on the western side of the city. The second gate is thought to be on the eastern side of the southern part. Nehemiah's tour confirms that the wooden gates, the weakest part of a city's defenses, will have to be rebuilt.

RESEARCHING FOR RESTORATION

The rectangular worship auditorium in a small church building had a platform built in the corner. Thus most of the congregation had to look somewhat sideways to see the pulpit. A new minister persuaded the church to rebuild the platform across the front of the room. One elder objected on the grounds that

---

WHAT DO YOU THINK?

Ezra refused the king's offer of a military escort while Nehemiah accepted it. How does this compare with situations today where some believers choose to proceed on "faith alone" while others take precautions and prepare for contingencies? Is one of these approaches more "spiritual" than the other? Why, or why not?

DAILY BIBLE READINGS

Monday, Sept. 21—Hope for God's Vindication (Isaiah 62:1-7)

Tuesday, Sept. 22—Mourning over Jerusalem (Nehemiah 1:1-4)

Wednesday, Sept. 23—Confession and Petition to God (Nehemiah 1:5-11)

Thursday, Sept. 24—Identifying the Problem (Nehemiah 2:1-4)

Friday, Sept. 25—Preparing for the Task (Nehemiah 2:6-10)

Saturday, Sept. 26—Dealing with Opposition (Nehemiah 4:15-23)

Sunday, Sep. 27—Rallying Support (Nehemiah 2:5, 11-20)

"It's *always* been this way," but the project went forward nevertheless. When the old platform was demolished, that elder marked a code on each piece of lumber being removed, noting where it was in the old platform. He then stored the wood in his barn.

A new minister came on the scene many years later. Using a dubious argument for "the value of historical preservation," the same elder persuaded the new minister to agree to restoring the platform to its original state. So out of the barn came the original wood! The questionable restoration could not have been accomplished without careful observation of the original platform.

Nehemiah was just as careful in his inspection, but for a much better reason. He wanted to see where the old walls were and what their condition was so they could be restored for a valid reason. In a negative sense, regard for "the way things used to be" can be whimsical at best and harmful at worst. In a positive sense, Nehemiah's concern for the walls of Jerusalem reflects the concern we should have for being faithful in rebuilding our broken lives according to Scripture.

—C. R. B.

14. Then I moved on toward the Fountain Gate and the King's Pool, but there was not enough room for my mount to get through;

The *gate* mentioned here is thought to face the Kidron Valley, on the east side of Jerusalem. The steepness of the slope into the valley is good for defensive purposes. But the accumulated debris combine with the steep slope to make it impossible for Nehemiah to continue riding.

15. . . . so I went up the valley by night, examining the wall. Finally, I turned back and reentered through the Valley Gate.

Nehemiah continues his inspection as he moves along *the wall* to the north. Most scholars think he retraces his route to the first *gate*.

C. TIME FOR REFRAINING (v. 16)

16. The officials did not know where I had gone or what I was doing, because as yet I had said nothing to the Jews or the priests or nobles or officials or any others who would be doing the work.

Five groups of people are mentioned here as being not yet informed by Nehemiah about his real goal. This is more specific than the "anyone" of verse 12. The precise distinctions among these groups are not known.

Ecclesiastes 3:7 states that there is a time to speak and a time to be silent. Nehemiah knows the difference. In his wisdom, he determines when others will be informed. Not everyone is entitled to know everything all the time, in spite of wanting to have his or her curiosity satisfied.

ON BEING SECRETIVE

Some secrets need to be kept. Consider the growing problem of identity theft. A lost wallet may provide a thief with enough information to open bank or credit card accounts with the stolen identity and run up thousands of dollars of bills. Sometimes the theft is done by "dumpster diving"—going through trash to find papers with sensitive personal financial information.

The high-tech approach to identity theft is *phishing*—usually an e-mail that throws out some "bait" in hopes of getting someone to "bite" and reveal financial information. Thus *phishing* is electronic *fishing*. An example is the e-mail purportedly from a wealthy political refugee whose accounts have been frozen by a dastardly government of a third-world country.

WHAT DO YOU THINK?

What was a time when you needed to form a plan of action before sharing with others what was on your heart? What negative consequences could there have been of sharing prematurely?

The e-mail promises a substantial reward for allowing the deposit of millions of dollars in your bank account. But, of course, you must first reveal your account numbers! Those who do not know when to be secretive about their financial information and when not to will get into trouble.

Nehemiah was secretive because a premature disclosure of his plan could have brought unthinking, knee-jerk opposition from his own people. Needed changes in the church are sometimes prevented because resistance builds as a result of partial information that gets out; when "the grapevine" takes over, watch out! There comes a time when people are to be informed, of course. As the old saying goes, "timing is everything." —C. R. B.

III. REPORTS BY NEHEMIAH (NEHEMIAH 2:17, 18)

The time has come, and Nehemiah is ready to make his announcement. His audience probably includes the groups cited in the previous verse.

A. PRESENT REVIEWED (v. 17a)

17a. Then I said to them, "You see the trouble we are in: Jerusalem lies in ruins, and its gates have been burned with fire.

Have the people of *Jerusalem* become accustomed to their unpleasant and uncomfortable existence? Things can be in a certain state for so long that people get used to it. They may be unable to envision circumstances being any other way. So Nehemiah needs to cast a vision of a better tomorrow. This starts with a frank assessment of the current situation.

The visual aids are all around. He reviews the troubles, the rubble, and the situation of the *gates*. He has been in Jerusalem only a few days, but he identifies with the people by using the word *we*. He is the governor, but they are in this together.

B. PROPOSAL TO BUILD (vv. 17b, 18a)

17b, 18a. "Come, let us rebuild the wall of Jerusalem, and we will no longer be in disgrace." I also told them about the gracious hand of my God upon me and what the king had said to me.

The residents of *Jerusalem* undoubtedly are curious about the arrival of a new governor with his servants and his military escort. So they assemble because of respect for him and his authority. Perhaps they assume that this will be a routine exhortation to be good citizens, to avoid any incidents that may be reported to the king, and to pay their taxes.

Instead, Nehemiah gives a radical proposal that seems impossible. The city has not had fortified walls for over 140 years! But Nehemiah reinforces his plan by recounting the providential acts that have brought him to them, and he reveals that he has royal approval.

C. PEOPLE'S RESPONSE (v. 18b)

18b. They replied, "Let us start rebuilding." So they began this good work.

Nehemiah is persuasive! The people combine their inner desires with their emotions, and they encourage one another for the *good work* ahead of them. Their response "Let us rise up and build," as some older translations put it, is one of the classic statements of the Bible. It has been used by many congregations that are entering into building projects.

WHAT DO YOU THINK?

How can a building campaign be a unifying experience for a congregation?

Visual for Lesson 4. *Point to this visual as you ask, "In what ways can this imperative be applied in a spiritual sense?"*

IV. RESISTANCE TO NEHEMIAH (NEHEMIAH 2:19, 20)

We all know that big projects can bring big resistance. It is unlikely that the resistance that comes next is a surprise to Nehemiah.

A. REACTIONS OF THE ENEMIES (v. 19)

19. But when Sanballat the Horonite, Tobiah the Ammonite official and Geshem the Arab heard about it, they mocked and ridiculed us. "What is this you are doing?" they asked. "Are you rebelling against the king?"

Sanballat and *Tobiah* are mentioned earlier in verse 10 as being aware that Nehemiah has arrived to promote the general welfare of the Israelites. Sanballat's name has been found on a papyrus in Egypt, dated just 37 years later; he is identified as the governor of Samaria (compare Nehemiah 4:1, 2). Samaria is the capital of this immediate area, and fortifying Jerusalem is seen as a political threat. Tobiah's area is to the east, across the Jordan River. He is, at least, an *official* of the king of Persia. A person with that name could not prove his Israelite heritage (Ezra 2:59, 60). He and his descendants (the Tobiads) are renowned far into the period between the Old and New Testaments. *Geshem* is a powerful Arabian leader to the south (Nehemiah 6:1). His name has also been found in Egypt.

Thus the people of Judah and Jerusalem have enemies on three sides: north (Sanballat), east (Tobiah), and south (Geshem). Later, Nehemiah 4:7 says that the people of Ashdod, which lies to the west, join this confederation. Thus the opposition surrounds Nehemiah and his followers.

The enemy leaders know that using force against Nehemiah can bring the wrath of Artaxerxes. So they resort to a war of words: mockery, threats, and ridicule. Perhaps they hope that Nehemiah will retaliate with force, for that will justify the accusation of rebellion *against the king.*

B. RESPONSE TO THE ENEMIES (v. 20)

20. I answered them by saying, "The God of heaven will give us success. We his servants will start rebuilding, but as for you, you have no share in Jerusalem or any claim or historic right to it."

Nehemiah's response to the three leaders also gives encouragement to the residents of *Jerusalem.* There are three parts to Nehemiah's reply. They include a strong statement of trust in *the God of heaven,* a mutual affirmation of determination, and a recounting of three ways that the opponents are excluded from any participation in a project ultimately intended to bring honor to God and his people.

This thrilling chapter comes to a close at this point. It has been exciting from its tense beginning in a capital city of Persia, to the secretive nighttime inspection of the walls, to the challenges to a lethargic people, to the forceful response of scorn from enemies who plan to stop Nehemiah.

The next few chapters tell of more opposition and of the remarkable success of organization and leadership. The gates and walls are built in 52 days in the summer of 444 BC (Nehemiah 6:15)—what previous generations could not do in 140 years.

CONCLUSION

A person may read about Nehemiah and be moved to take risks. Some make major purchases without any means of making the payments, for they

PRAYER

Lord, we are thankful for the examples of leadership and trust in the life of Nehemiah. Whether it is ours to lead or to follow, may we do so with a complete trust in you. In Jesus' name. Amen.

WHAT DO YOU THINK?

What may have been the outcome if Nehemiah had given a more conciliatory response to his opposition? How do we decide if our responses to the enemies of the church should be sharp or conciliatory?

[Titus 1:13 may be important for your answer.]

have "faith" that God will somehow provide at the right time. There are incidents in which the funds did arrive at the last minute, but there are also the failure accounts in which people had to move or surrender what they bought. The failures do not make good illustrations in lessons or sermons!

Nehemiah is an outstanding example of a person who had goals and plans, but he was also realistic. He planned and investigated in order to cause his dreams to become reality. Throughout his book he mentioned times when he prayed to God, for his was a reasoned faith. When the king of Persia granted him the unlikely request, he was on solid ground.

THOUGHT TO REMEMBER
Leadership may include sacrifice.

Discovery Learning

The following is an alternative lesson plan emphasizing learning activities.
Classes desiring such student involvement will find these suggestions helpful. At the
back of this book are reproducible student pages to further enhance activity learning.

INTO THE LESSON

Before class, recruit four students to help with the following scenarios. After you begin class, say, "I need a volunteer to help me move this table. Tom, you'll do." Then the two of you will move the table. Then say, "I forgot my Bible in the hallway. Would someone be willing to go get it for me?" Your second prearranged volunteer should immediately raise his or her hand to accept. This student should return exasperated because he or she cannot find your Bible.

Next say, "Judy, will you come to the board and be the secretary for today?" When this third prearranged volunteer comes to the board, make sure there is no chalk or marker for her to use. Your fourth volunteer will notice this need, and he or she will get up and get the chalk or marker that the secretary needs.

When the four scenarios are finished, ask the class to identify the "types of volunteers" that you used. Ask your volunteer secretary to record answers on the board. (Student #1 was coerced; #2 was a willing volunteer but was unable to help; #3 was called on and agreed but lacked the equipment to help; #4 saw a need and met it without being asked to do so.)

After the class has identified the types of volunteers, ask which of the descriptions best fits them. Allow those who are willing to share their answers to do so. Transition to the lesson by saying, "Many times one of the hardest jobs a leader has is motivating God's people to volunteer for service. Let's see how Nehemiah accomplished that in today's lesson."

INTO THE WORD

Before you begin the learning activity below, spend a few moments establishing the historical context (found in the Lesson Background) for the lesson. Prepare pieces of poster board with the following "steps" on them, one each (but do not include the italicized Scripture references): Evaluates the situation *(vv. 12-15)*; Develops a plan of action *(vv. 17, 18a)*; Recognizes potential problems *(vv. 13-15)*; Identifies the situation at hand *(v. 17)*.

Distribute the pieces of poster board to four students at random. Ask those four to stand in front of the class so everyone can read what is written on their cards (the lettering will have to be sufficiently large). Have other volunteers read verses 11-18a, one verse at a time. As the reader finishes each verse, students need to decide which of the cards that verse best characterizes. As each card is identified, put it on the board or on a wall at the front of the class.

When all the cards have been affixed to the board or wall, discuss the logic of this "plan" following a certain order. Have students identify any other steps that could be added to the plan and explain why.

Transition to the rest of the text by saying, "It's one thing to have a good plan of attack; it's quite another thing to motivate people to volunteer to implement the plan. Let's look at the rest of the text to see how the people responded to Nehemiah's leadership."

Have a volunteer read the remaining verses aloud. Identify the different reactions: the Israelites were ready to start rebuilding (v. 18b); enemies tried to bully Nehemiah into aborting the plan (v. 19); Nehemiah held firm in his resolve to build (v. 20). Discuss the significance of each reaction and relate them to the steps you identified earlier. How did Nehemiah's preparation contribute to Israelite reaction?

INTO LIFE

Say, "One of the reasons Nehemiah was such a good leader is that he was also a good volunteer. Reflecting on the four types of volunteers we identified at the beginning of the lesson, which type describes Nehemiah?" (Answer: The fourth.)

Tell the class that they are going to put the lesson into action over the next few weeks. Choose a proj-ect (in the church or the community) that your class will be willing to sponsor. Once you have agreed on the project, divide the class into two teams. One team will put together a plan of attack for the project. Make sure to encourage them to follow the steps Nehemiah used in today's lesson. The other team will focus on ways to advertise the project and motivate others within the church to volunteer to help.

When both teams are ready (this may require time outside of class to complete the assignments), have three students present the project to the leadership of your church for input and approval. Distribute copies of the reproducible exercise "How Do I Rate as a Volunteer?" from page 119 as students depart.

LOOKING FOR JESUS
LESSON 5

INTRODUCTION

A. To Whom Do We Look?

Athletic stadiums and arenas are packed with fans who want to catch a glimpse of the stars in action. The crowd roars with delight to see a winning touchdown or slam dunk in the last few seconds of the game. Even though these sports heroes cannot heal, save souls, or answer prayers, they receive so much attention and devotion that an outsider might wonder what special powers they have! If Jesus walked our streets today, what would be our expectation of him? The people of Jesus' day expected that Jesus would work miracles for those who were either physically ill or demon-possessed. What faith they had! While Jesus is not present in human flesh in our midst today, we can still take hope in John 20:29: "Blessed are those who have not seen and yet have believed."

Consider also 1 Peter 5:7. That passage encourages us to cast all our anxiety on Christ, for he cares for us. Many people of Jesus' day did just that. Jesus did the seemingly impossible for those afflicted in body, mind, and spirit. To be sure, not everyone who sought Jesus had good motives (example: John 6:26). But many did. Do we have an eager expectation today that Jesus can transform lives? Do we still revere him and gather in his presence, looking to him for blessings? Or has our faith grown complacent over time, lacking the initial flame that once burned within our souls?

B. Lesson Background

The Gospel of Mark is a fast-moving account of Jesus' actions in his ministry. While other Gospels spend a lot of time describing what Jesus *said*, Mark likes to focus on what Jesus *did*.

Today's text—a text of action—takes us into Jesus' initial preaching tour of Galilee. By the time we get to today's text, John the Baptist already had prepared the way (Mark 1:1-8). Jesus had been baptized and tempted (1:9-13). He had called his first disciples (1:14-20). He had taught; he had performed exorcisms (1:21-28). He had healed Peter's mother-in-law, who had been bedridden with a fever (1:29-31). So much action in only 31 verses!

News of Jesus had spread throughout Galilee (Mark 1:28). His fame was growing as people flocked to the one who seemed to have the solutions.

I. JESUS HEALS (MARK 1:32-34)

A. Acts of Faith (vv. 32, 33)

32. That evening after sunset the people brought to Jesus all the sick and demon-possessed.

When we take a bird's-eye view of Mark 1:21-38, we get the idea that the events described in these verses take place within a 24-hour period of time. It

---

Devotional Reading:
Ezekiel 34:11-16
Background Scripture:
Mark 1:21-45
Printed Text:
Mark 1:32-45

Oct
4

Lesson Aims

After participating in this lesson, each student will be able to:

1. Describe the extension of Jesus' ministry to the diseased and demon-possessed in Galilee.

2. Identify reasons why people seek Jesus today.

3. Commit to a greater degree of "seeking" Jesus in his or her life and to helping others who seek him to find him.

Key Verse

When they found [Jesus], they exclaimed: "Everyone is looking for you!"
—Mark 1:37

had been the Sabbath day according to verse 21. But since it is now *evening after sunset,* the Sabbath is over. Old Testament regulations forbid carrying loads on the Sabbath (example: Jeremiah 17:21, 22). Now, however, the people may freely bring their loved ones to the feet of Jesus.

What desperation the people must feel! Their desperation leads to faith, and faith leads to deliverance. We see this desperation and faith elsewhere in Mark (example: 2:1-5). This should cause us to ask ourselves if we have this same kind of outlook today. Do we bring to Jesus the cares and concerns of ourselves and of our loved ones? And when we do, is Jesus our last resort or our first priority?

The faith of the people in this verse challenges us to refocus our eyes on our Savior and behold his glory for what it truly is: life-changing. While our problems may not instantly vanish before our eyes, we can rest assured that Jesus hears our prayers. We take hope that he can deliver us out of the depths of despair.

33. *The whole town gathered at the door,*

The *town* in question is Capernaum (see Mark 1:21), located on the northwest shore of the Sea of Galilee. The population of Capernaum at this time probably is somewhere between 1,000 and 2,000 (the lower number is more likely). The phrase *whole town* need not signify exactly 100 percent of that population. But it's clear that quite a crowd is present! This gives us a sense of the desperation of the people to have Jesus answer their needs. They are eager with expectation to meet Jesus and be in his presence.

B. Acts of Deliverance (v. 34)

34. *. . . . and Jesus healed many who had various diseases. He also drove out many demons, but he would not let the demons speak because they knew who he was.*

The people do not wait in vain. The sick are *healed.* The *demons* are driven out of the afflicted.

We may find it fascinating that Jesus does not allow the demons to *speak.* They know who he is (see the parallel account in Luke 4:41). But Jesus does not want his identity revealed. He wants to keep a lid on things, at least for a while. We may find this curious. Doesn't Jesus come into the world to make himself known (compare John 7:4)? Jesus has a plan of revealing his identity according to his own timetable. Bad things happen when that timetable is violated, as we will see when we get to Mark 1:45.

II. JESUS PRAYS (MARK 1:35-37)

A. Alone (v. 35)

35. *Very early in the morning, while it was still dark, Jesus got up, left the house and went off to a solitary place, where he prayed.*

Jesus needs to break away from the crowd to seek some solitude. Consider Jesus' words for us to do the same in Matthew 6:6—when we pray, we are to go into a room and shut the door. Jesus withdraws to a lonely place in order to free himself from distractions. We are encouraged to do likewise.

There are many around Jesus who will try to co-opt him for their own purposes, as time will tell (example: John 6:15). Mark often notes that Jesus retreats from the public arena and the pressure of the crowds (Mark

What Do You Think?

What are some benefits of praying in solitude? What about praying early in the morning? Should you do more of either or both?

1:45; 3:13; 6:31, 32, 46; 7:24; 9:2, 30). Solitary prayer will help him keep his mind clear and stay focused. If Jesus has a need to do this, can we say that we do not?

I once knew a minister who was in charge of Adult Life-Changing Bible Study (also known as Sunday school) at his local church. I asked him how he spent his quiet time with the Lord. He gave me some wise advice when he said that he tithed a tenth of his time each day to God. That is, every day he specifically gave God about two and one-half hours of time. This time included studying the Word of God and communing with the Lord in prayer.

Many of us do not have such an amount of time at our disposal on a daily basis. Even so, we may be able to invest that much time on a weekly or biweekly basis. Time spent with the Lord is time well spent. While it may involve sacrifice or having to rearrange priorities, we can rest assured that our time spent seeking our Father is never wasted. It yields fruit in due season (see John 15:4).

Visual for Lesson 5. *Keep this map posted as you study this unit to give your learners a geographical perspective.*

B. NOT ALONE (vv. 36, 37)

36. *Simon and his companions went to look for him,*

This particular *Simon* is also known as Peter (Mark 3:16; 14:37). Naturally, he is not to be confused with the other Simon of Mark 3:18. Simon and his companions are looking for their leader, desperate for the company of Jesus. Despite the fact that Jesus wants to be alone, can we blame Simon and his friends for trying to stay close to him? After all, Jesus has just healed Simon's mother-in-law (Mark 1:29-31). No one seems to be content to allow Jesus to return on his own initiative.

37. . . . *and when they found him, they exclaimed: "Everyone is looking for you!"*

Simon and company are not the only ones *looking for* Jesus. Jesus has become a popular figure. Because of the miraculous acts, Jesus has achieved instant fame. Simon and the others probably urge Jesus to return to Capernaum because of the impact that he already has had on that city. That's the natural way to think, isn't it? "Keep building on the momentum you've already achieved" may be the idea. But as we soon find out, Jesus has other plans.

SUCCESSFUL AND UNSUCCESSFUL SEARCHES

Adventurer Steve Fossett set numerous world records. These involved airplanes, gliders, and balloons. The records included the first solo around-the-world balloon flight and the first solo around-the-world plane flight without refueling. On September 3, 2007, he took off from a private airstrip in Nevada to seek a site for his next big attempt: he wanted to capture the world land-speed record.

When Fossett did not return, a massive ground and air search covering 20,000 square miles was launched—what the Civil Air Patrol called "one of the largest, most intensive searches for a missing aircraft in modern history." As of this writing, Fossett's body has not been found (he was declared legally dead on February 15, 2008). Thus both the searches *by* and *for* Fossett ended in failure.

Several searches took place in our text—all of them more successful than the searches by and for Fossett. In one, Jesus sought time alone with God. He found it—at least until another search intruded. That was his disciples seeking him. They felt their need for Jesus' leadership, based on yet another search that was taking

HOW TO SAY IT

Capernaum. Kuh-PER-nay-um.
Galilee. GAL-uh-lee.
Hebrews. HEE-brews.
Jeremiah. Jair-uh-MY-uh.
Leviticus. Leh-VIT-ih-kus.
Moses. MO-zes or MO-zez.
Samaritans. SUH-mare-uh-tunz.
synagogues. SIN-uh-gogs.
Zealot. ZEL-ut.

place. As they told Jesus, "Everyone is looking for you!" According to Acts 17:27, God is easy to find. Will we make the attempt? —C. R. B.

III. JESUS PREACHES (MARK 1:38, 39)
A. DESIRE EXPRESSED (v. 38)
38. Jesus replied, "Let us go somewhere else—to the nearby villages—so I can preach there also. That is why I have come."

Jesus has a larger vision than what his followers may have for him. Jesus' goal is not to *preach* and minister only to the people at Capernaum, but to go to neighboring *villages* as well. Sometimes our vision may be clouded by the opinions of others. Others' expectations of what we are to do with our lives or our personal circumstances may not always be what the Lord has in mind for us. What are we to do?

Consider Jesus' example. Before Jesus makes this ministry decision, he spends time with his Father. His decisions are birthed in prayer, and this venture into the nearby towns can be seen as an answer to his prayer in verse 35. Are our decisions in life birthed in a context of prayer? Or are we more susceptible to the whims of others? One thing is certain: we must be able to discern God's will for ourselves. Sometimes we will need to take a stand against the desires of the crowd to pursue the will of God.

B. DESIRE FULFILLED (v. 39)
39. So he traveled throughout Galilee, preaching in their synagogues and driving out demons.

This verse summarizes Jesus' first preaching tour *throughout Galilee.* This is the first of three such tours. (Luke 8:1 notes the second preaching tour; the third tour is mentioned in Matthew 11:1 and Mark 6:6.) Jesus demonstrates the saving message of the gospel in both word and in deed.

IV. JESUS HINDERED (MARK 1:40-45)
A. REQUEST (v. 40)
40. A man with leprosy came to him and begged him on his knees, "If you are willing, you can make me clean."

Following the general description of Jesus' itinerant ministry (v. 39, above), Mark now focuses on one particular *man* who makes a request. He has *leprosy.* This is a general designation in the ancient world for some kind of skin disease (not necessarily leprosy in the modern sense of Hansen's Disease).

The priests are charged with determining the severity of such problems along with the necessary course of action (Leviticus 13:1-46; 14:1-32). The afflicted person may be excluded from social contact and forced to warn all who come near with the words "Unclean! Unclean!" (Leviticus 13:45, 46).

Thus those with leprosy are isolated and ostracized from Jewish society. The banishment is not rooted in a medical concern of spreading infection, but rather in the religious impurity and uncleanness attached to such afflictions. To associate with a leper can cause one to become ceremonially unclean. Like touching a corpse, any contact with a leper means religious contamination.

Therefore, lepers are left to take care of themselves. This particular leper wisely recognizes that Jesus is the one who has the power to cleanse him of his malady.

WHAT DO YOU THINK?

Thinking about how Jesus both proclaimed the good news and healed people, what have you discovered about the relationship between words and deeds in your Christian experience?

WHAT DO YOU THINK?

What groups today feel as ostracized as the lepers of the first century? How does the church move from being "part of the problem" to being "part of the solution" in this regard?

B. RESPONSE (vv. 41, 42)

41. Filled with compassion, Jesus reached out his hand and touched the man. "I am willing," he said. "Be clean!"

Jesus isn't appalled, and he doesn't turn his back on *the man*. Rather, Jesus breaks the barrier of "no physical contact allowed" that separates him from the leper. Jesus touches that which is impure and unclean, which potentially means becoming unclean himself according to the Law of Moses (see Leviticus 5:2, 3; 13:45, 46).

42. Immediately the leprosy left him and he was cured.

No uncleanness transfers to Jesus, however, because Jesus' touch and word result in cleansing. In contrast with some medical procedures today, Jesus does not just treat the disease. He cures it. When Jesus touches someone, there is no need to seek additional medical assistance. Today, people may need to go back to physicians over an extended period of time. Numerous visits are no guarantee of a cure, however.

Personally, I had a skin disorder that affected my foot for many years. I finally sought the help of a podiatrist, who prescribed medication that cost a pretty penny. And despite the pricey visits to this expert, my foot, he remarked, "only got worse." It reminded me of Mark 5:26—the woman who spent all she had on physicians and only grew worse. However, it gave me hope as well because it opened the door to Jesus intervening in my life. When the doors are closed in the natural, the door is still open to the spiritual.

NO LONGER "UNTOUCHABLE"

The Western world has long known about India's caste system. At the very bottom of the caste system are the *achuta*—the "untouchables." They prefer to be known as the *Dalits*—the "broken and crushed ones."

Millions of Dalits have turned to Christianity, finding in Christ their true value as human beings. This is a value they never found either in Indian society in general or in the Hindu religion in particular. The founder of the Gospel for Asia mission, K. P. Yohannan, observes that "You see a long, drawn-out, so-called awakening among the 250 million untouchables. . . . They see that unless you give up this caste system, there is no hope."

In December 2007, India's National Commission for Scheduled Castes gave an unintended compliment to the Christian gospel's power. The NCSC ruled that since Dalits who convert from Hinduism to Christianity do not suffer the same disadvantages as those who are Hindus and Buddhists, they do not need special access to federal jobs or admission rights to government-funded universities.

Lepers were literally the first-century "untouchables." The man with leprosy in today's text knew that in Jesus he would find acceptance and the means to a better life. The leper was undoubtedly focused on the physical rather than the spiritual. Our task is to take Jesus to modern untouchables, whoever they may be, in both senses. Will we do it?   —C. R. B.

C. SENT AWAY (vv. 43, 44)

43. Jesus sent him away at once with a strong warning:

Isn't it interesting that right after Jesus cleanses the man with leprosy, the man essentially is ordered to leave Jesus' presence? The man is not invited to hang around. The man has received exactly what he came for: healing. So there is no reason for him to linger. In fact, there are some things the man needs to do. See the next verse.

DAILY BIBLE READINGS

Monday, Sept. 28—*The Shepherd's Search (Ezekiel 34:11-16)*

Tuesday, Sept. 29—*Seek the Lord (1 Chronicles 16: 8-13)*

Wednesday, Sept. 30—*Set Your Mind and Heart (1 Chronicles 29:17-19)*

Thursday, Oct. 1—*Seeking God and God's Law (1 Chronicles 28:6-10)*

Friday, Oct. 2—*Seeking God's Face (2 Chronicles 7: 12-18)*

Saturday, Oct. 3—*The Search That Brings Peace (2 Chronicles 14:1-7)*

Sunday, Oct. 4—*Search for Healing (Mark 1:32-45)*

WHAT DO YOU THINK?

Jesus told the healed leper to be quiet. Are there times today when Christians need to be quiet? If so, what would be the circumstances for this?

[Make sure to look at Psalm 40:9, 10; Amos 5:13; Matthew 28:19, 20; 1 Corinthians 14:28, 40; and 2 Timothy 2:16.]

WHAT DO YOU THINK?

When Jesus acts in our lives today, how and to whom should we testify concerning what he has done?

PRAYER

Father, help us to keep our eyes fixed on your Son during the trials and tribulations in our lives. May he always occupy first place in our lives. In Jesus' name. Amen.

44. "See that you don't tell this to anyone. But go, show yourself to the priest and offer the sacrifices that Moses commanded for your cleansing, as a testimony to them."

Before getting to what the man needs to do next, Jesus tells him what he is *not* to do: he is not to go around blabbing. Jesus is concerned that his own popularity may grow to a level that will hinder his ministry.

The man's *testimony* is silenced in one regard, but not in another. Instead of running his mouth to anyone who will listen, the man's testimony is to be that of showing himself to a *priest*. Leviticus 14:2-31 speaks of this important practice. The examination is to be followed by certain cleansing procedures and sacrifices. Whether the healed man carries out Jesus' order in this regard is uncertain, for the text is silent on this.

D. SOUGHT OUT (v. 45)

45. Instead he went out and began to talk freely, spreading the news. As a result, Jesus could no longer enter a town openly but stayed outside in lonely places. Yet the people still came to him from everywhere.

Just look at what happens because of the man's disobedience: Jesus' ministry is hindered. Perhaps it is hampered to such an extent that Jesus isn't able to help all the hurting that he could otherwise. While people still come *to him from everywhere,* we are left to wonder who is not able to reach Jesus because of the disobedience. What about those who are completely paralyzed? Are they able to go and meet the healer *in lonely places*? Perhaps not.

We learn from this verse that Jesus knows best. When he gives us a task to do, we can rest assured that his way is perfect. We may ask and pray for clarification, but we dare not think that we have a better idea than God.

CONCLUSION

It is often said that you can look at people's checkbooks or day planners and determine what or who is first in their lives. If a complete stranger got hold of yours, could he or she tell that you are a Christian? In other words, are our money and time prioritized toward earthy pursuits that have no heavenly significance? Does our money go toward laying up for ourselves treasures on earth while investments in the kingdom of God go wanting? Do we give Christ only our leftover time, or do we set aside sufficient time each day in conversation with our heavenly Father?

From this lesson, it is clear that we are to look to Jesus. This not to be an occasional glance, but a soul-searching pursuit. We need to become desperate to seek his face; desperate for deliverance from the cares of this life that weigh on our souls; desperate for answers that can come only from Jesus.

I dare you to pray the "impossible," to think the "unbelievable," and to recapture the hope that once burned within your soul. Resolve today to go deeper into your pursuit of God than you did yesterday. Determine to get closer to him. Modifying your routine will be critical. In other words, it is essential to carve out time to be with the Lord. I've heard it said, "Seeking the Lord morning and night will cause everything to be all right." Before we dismiss this as simplistic, remember that the Bible speaks much the same message (see Matthew 6:33).

This goes back to the basics. Are we seeking the Lord with a fervent pursuit of his presence? The Bible tells us that "the prayer of a righteous man is powerful and effective" (James 5:16). Don't be afraid to "approach the throne of grace with confidence" (Hebrews 4:16). Tell God your concerns, your cares, and your worries. Expect him to give you answers that only he can give. Look to Jesus as your sole and soul provider.

> **THOUGHT TO REMEMBER**
> *Look to Jesus in the midst of life's storms—and at all other times.*

Discovery Learning

The following is an alternative lesson plan emphasizing learning activities. Classes desiring such student involvement will find these suggestions helpful. At the back of this book are reproducible student pages to further enhance activity learning.

INTO THE LESSON

Recruit a class member to deliver the following short monologue to introduce today's study. Give your presenter at least a week to read today's text and practice "speaking on behalf of the leper."

I had forgotten what it was like to be touched. My leprosy had set up an invisible wall of fear around me. But that did not keep the news away. Good news blasts its way into a community of lepers. We all heard it.

Some believed. Some did not. I did. So that explains why I slipped out in darkness and hid myself until the miracle worker came by. My words were carefully planned: "If you will, Lord, you can!" That was my belief. That was my expectation and hope. And that is my result: *Clean! Clean! Clean!* At the hand of him who said, "I will!"

After the monologue, ask one of your good oral readers to read today's text. At the end of the reading, ask, "Did the monologue fairly represent the Scriptures?" Let your learners note any exceptions they see.

INTO THE WORD

Divide your learners into four groups. Give them the labels POWER, PRAYER, (COM)PASSION, PREACHING. Have a good oral reader read today's text aloud. Distribute handouts to the groups that list the following questions to answer.

For the *power* group: 1. Why could Jesus keep the demon from speaking but not the man? 2. Why could Jesus not hide himself from those seeking him? 3. Which, if either, requires greater power: to heal disease or to cast out demons? Why?

For the *prayer* group: 1. What did Jesus have to pray about? 2. What is the best time and place to pray? Why do you say so? 3. When is the last time you were interrupted in a prayer time? How did you react? How did your reaction compare with that of Jesus?

For the *(com)passion* group: 1. How do you explain the passion and compassion Jesus had for those in distress? Are these natural human reactions? Why, or why not? 2. Surrounded by human woe and weakness, how could the compassionate Jesus get anything done other than healing? 3. How can we passionately demonstrate compassion for the physically distressed?

For the *preaching* group: 1. Which was Jesus' primary task: preaching or healing? Why do you say so? 2. How could Jesus be so committed to preaching and yet constantly interrupt that duty to perform miracles? 3. Which had the greater effect: Jesus' preaching in synagogues or in public spaces? Why?

Allow groups at least five minutes. Then ask them to reveal their questions and their responses to the whole class. Be certain to connect the comments to the text if the groups do not do so adequately.

Finish this section by saying, "The words we have used as group designations say much about Jesus' life and ministry: he came with divine power as the Son of God; he lived in full relationship with the Father, even in the matter of regular prayer; he showed all the righteous emotions of being both human and divine, being passionately compassionate; he came as the announcer of God's good news in preaching and teaching, in complete consistency with his daily behavior." Point out the obligations the church has in all these areas.

INTO LIFE

Say, "We use the term *seeker* for those today who appear to have an interest in the gospel. Many churches try to be 'seeker-friendly.' How do you recognize a seeker?" Let class members respond. Ask, "What is it that the seeker is actually looking for? Or can this question even be answered without first knowing the individual seeker?" Let learners respond. Ask, "How will a seeker realize that Jesus is the one to be sought?" Emphasize the important role each Christian has in encouraging the seeker attitude in non-Christians. (*Option*: Use the reproducible exercise "Everyone Is Looking for You" on page 120 to enhance this exercise.)

Give each learner a slip of paper or card with the phrase *I am the seeker's secret source*. Ask each to carry it in a pocket or purse for a week as a reminder that one's personal speech, choices, and attitudes are the best way to cause seekers to seek Christ. Distribute copies of the reproducible exercise "Jesus Prayed" from page 120 as students depart.

RECOGNIZING JESUS

LESSON 6

INTRODUCTION

A. BOUND BY CHAINS

Kathy has been in a clinical depression since her mother died in a car accident over a year ago. Kathy has not been able to forgive herself for her mother's death, even though she was not to blame. "If only I had been there," she mutters. "Or if I had prayed for her safety more often, maybe things would have been different," she says as tears cascade down her face.

Kathy has tried antidepressants, but she cannot escape the pain. Her friends have abandoned her, for she has weighed them down with her worry and tears. We would not say this is a modern case of demon possession, but Kathy definitely has "a monkey on her back." Encouraging Kathy to seek medical help is important, but would we also encourage her to seek Jesus?

Then there is Tom. Tom grew up in the slums and has never been able to break the curse of poverty in his life. He never had enough to eat as a child and struggles even now to put food on the table for his own children. Tom works countless hours from dawn to dusk just to try to make ends meet. He doesn't get to spend much time with his family. Tom is not chained due to demon possession. Yet he is figuratively chained to his job and to his circumstances, which he believes will never change. In his struggle to deal with his situation, has Tom tried turning to Jesus, the one who helps people realize their blessings despite circumstances?

B. LESSON BACKGROUND

Today's text takes us well into Jesus' three-year ministry. Just before today's text, Jesus had calmed the storm on the Sea of Galilee. While this may appear to be in no way connected to the account of the healing of the man possessed by a demon in today's lesson, it may surprise us to see a parallel. In Mark 4:35-41, a storm is raging, with crashing waves and strong winds; in Mark 5, we encounter a storm in the inward person of the man dominated by a demon. Like the surging storm on the sea that captured the attention of the disciples, the demoniac's torment was obvious and unmistakable to all. How Jesus handled that torment is the subject of today's lesson. (The parallel accounts are Matthew 8:28-34 and Luke 8:26-39.)

I. NEED FOR DELIVERANCE (MARK 5:1-5)

A. LOCATION (v. 1)

1. They went across the lake to the region of the Gerasenes.

The incident we are about to read takes place after Jesus and the disciples have crossed from the western to the eastern shore of the Sea of Galilee. The western side is populated mainly by Jews. Beyond the eastern side, *across the lake,* is the Decapolis (v. 20, below), which means "ten cities"; this is primarily a Gentile area.

DEVOTIONAL READING:
LUKE 7:18-23

BACKGROUND SCRIPTURE:
MARK 5:1-20

PRINTED TEXT:
MARK 5:1-13, 18-20

LESSON AIMS

After participating in this lesson, each student will be able to:

1. List some key elements in Jesus' encounter with the demoniac.

2. Identify some figurative demons that confront people today.

3. Make a list of three "great things" that the Lord has done for him or her and share that list with an unbeliever.

Oct
11

KEY VERSE

Jesus . . . said, "Go home to your family and tell them how much the Lord has done for you, and how he has had mercy on you." —Mark 5:19

WHAT DO YOU THINK?

Of all the places where the demoniac could have lived, why do you think he picked a graveyard? What are some figurative graveyards where people live today?

HOW TO SAY IT

Abyss. Uh-BIS.
Decapolis. Dee-CAP-uh-lis.
demoniac. duh-MOE-nee-ak.
demonization. dee-muh-nuh-ZAY-shun.
Gadarenes. GAD-uh-reens.
Galilee. GAL-uh-lee.
Gentile. JEN-tile.
Gerasa. GUR-uh-suh.
Gerasenes. GUR-uh-seenz.
Gergesenes. GUR-guh-seenz.
Messiah. Meh-SIGH-uh.
obeisance. owe-BEE-sunts.

The location given as *the region of the Gerasenes* is too broad for us to pinpoint exactly where the boat reaches shore. Some ancient manuscripts give the name as "Gergesenes," and Matthew 8:28 calls it "the region of the Gadarenes." Gerasa (or Gergesa) is located some 35 miles from the southeast shore of the Sea of Galilee, but this city apparently owns territory that joins that body of water. In this area can be seen a fairly steep slope within 40 yards of the water's edge (that feature is important, as we shall see).

B. DESCRIPTION (vv. 2-5)

2. When Jesus got out of the boat, a man with an evil spirit came from the tombs to meet him.

Now our main character, the *man with an evil spirit,* enters the scene. The fact that he dwells among *the tombs* surely illustrates the depths of his despair. This is not the first time Jesus has confronted a person dominated by a demon (see Mark 1:23).

Look at what this demoniac does: he turns to Jesus in the midst of his despair. This indicates at least two things. First, the demon is not able to prevent the man from going to Jesus. Second, the man has hope that Jesus can do something for him.

Before we move along, we can note that the man does not suffer from mental illness. Rather, this is supernatural demonization. The people of the first century know the difference. Matthew 4:24 discusses demon possession alongside "normal" illnesses, thus distinguishing between the two.

3, 4. This man lived in the tombs, and no one could bind him any more, not even with a chain. For he had often been chained hand and foot, but he tore the chains apart and broke the irons on his feet. No one was strong enough to subdue him.

We can examine these two verses from the perspectives of both the demoniac and of those who have tried to deal with him. Those who have come in contact with the demoniac have tried to handle the situation by binding him with *chains.* Was that a cruel thing to do? Perhaps not. If the man is a danger to himself and others, then those who have tried to intervene may have taken the only action they knew for everyone's safety. Since this is a Gentile area, prayer to the true God probably has not occurred.

From the demoniac's perspective, the shackles only have added to the alienation and ostracism that he has felt, despite any good intentions. In any event, the efforts so far have been in vain, since the man has been able to break the restraints. It is probably the supernatural power of Satan that has enabled the man to do this.

The chains of disapproval and exclusion can be mental as well as physical. I recently underwent a tragedy that resulted in financial and personal hardship. I found myself rejected by others as a result. Some in my own family chastised me for "not having enough faith" or "not wanting to be healed." That was their rationale for why I was in such excruciating pain. According to them, I needed to repent (which reminds me of how Job's friends responded). Others refused to pray for me. Still others would not offer me financial assistance. Some wouldn't even speak to me, turning their backs in my hour of need.

I was dumbfounded at how I had been rejected. I did not suffer from demonization. But like the man in today's text, in this furnace of affliction I sought the Lord concerning these circumstances. God in his mercy accepted me and put the pieces of my life back together. Along the way I realized that not all Christians reflect the character of the Creator. Jesus, however, always reflects the character of the Creator because he is the Creator.

5. *Night and day among the tombs and in the hills he would cry out and cut himself with stones.*

The parallel of Matthew 8:28 tells us that the man's behavior is such that "no one could pass that way." Thus if the man has not been completely forgotten, he is at least completely avoided. Even if his crying carries far enough to be heard, anyone who lives within earshot likely has "tuned him out" by now. Being unable to associate with others in society, he thus is left *among the tombs and in the hills* in the company of another man in the same condition (again, Matthew 8:28). Some students associate the man's custom of cutting *himself with stones* with demonic worship (compare 1 Kings 18:28).

HOW MUCH THEY MUST HURT

What the psychiatric profession calls "delicate self-cutting syndrome" affects a significant number of young people. The numbers are difficult to verify, but perhaps 3 million people between the ages of 12 and 30 are affected. Females are said to account for 70 percent of "cutters." Hear what one (recovering) self-cutter says:

> I used it as my outlet for anger. . . . I caused myself pain, in believing that I deserved it. . . . I even enjoyed having the marks on myself and that I had my own little secret, but I have come to hate the scars and to realize that things don't stay a secret forever. My friends are concerned about me and so is my mother, so not only am I hurting myself but I was hurting them . . . so in the end, it isn't worth it.

We wonder how much the "cutters" must hurt and why. Anxiety about relationships, poor self-image, divorce of parents, and dysfunctional family situations are all cited as causative factors of this cry for help.

One of the more poignant reasons given by a cutter is "to feel pain on the outside instead of the inside." This may get at the heart of why the demoniac acted as he did. Perhaps the hurt from his self-inflicted wounds served to distract him from the pain of the slashes to his heart inflicted by a fearful society and Satan that isolated him and bound him in chains. Who are the people whom we isolate and bind in chains—figuratively, if not literally? Why do we do it?　　—C. R. B.

II. ACTION OF DELIVERANCE (MARK 5:6-13)

A. OBEISANCE (v. 6)

6. *When he saw Jesus from a distance, he ran and fell on his knees in front of him.*

The fact that the man is said to fall *on his knees* should not be taken to mean necessarily that he honors Jesus as the Son of God. The context essentially refers to the act of bowing. This idea is used of worshiping God or idols, of bowing in obeisance before a king, or even welcoming an honored guest.

B. SHOUT (v. 7)

7. *He shouted at the top of his voice, "What do you want with me, Jesus, Son of the Most High God? Swear to God that you won't torture me!"*

WHAT DO YOU THINK?

For the demoniac, contact with the forces of Satan resulted in physical self-cutting. In what nonphysical ways does sin cause people to harm themselves today? How can that nonphysical harm result in physical self-harm?

WHAT DO YOU THINK?

How is coming to Jesus often accompanied by inner conflict today?

In reflecting on this verse, we must clarify that this is the unclean spirit who is doing the speaking here (through the man) as verses 8, 9 will show. The man himself sees in Jesus some hope. But the evil spirit has a mind of his own, crying out *at the top of his voice.* The demon knows that his judgment is coming, thus he asks not to be tormented.

We see some presumptuous posturing on the part of the demon. Claiming to know the identity of someone and then shouting the name is an attempt to gain control over an adversary. Interestingly, the question the disciples have just asked about Jesus' identity in Mark 4:41 is correctly answered here by the demon! Although it is not true worship, the demon's confession that Jesus is *Son of the Most High God* is the highest tribute.

The punishment of which this demon speaks is that of the eternal torment that stands waiting at the final judgment (compare Matthew 25:41; 2 Peter 2:4; Jude 6; Revelation 20:10). The spirit that torments the man now fears torment himself.

C. Authority (vv. 8-13)

8. For Jesus had said to him, "Come out of this man, you evil spirit!"

The phrase *for Jesus had said* indicates that Jesus' command *Come out of this man* occurs before the demon's cry in verse 7. Thus the cry of recognition and terror in verse 7 is a result of the command here in verse 8. Clearly, Jesus realizes the urgency of the situation. He doesn't allow the man to be tormented further; relief quickly comes.

9. Then Jesus asked him, "What is your name?"

"My name is Legion," he replied, "for we are many."

A *legion* is a military unit composed of about 6,000 men! It is a term familiar to both Jew and Gentile. We should not see the asking of the demon's *name* to be a critical, necessary step in the man's deliverance. Jesus easily can cast out demons without requesting their names. Perhaps Jesus asks *What is your name?* in order for the truth to be recorded—that the man has suffered with many demonic spirits, not just one.

By revealing the name of the evil power, people will know how great a deliverance this truly is. This possibility makes sense in the light of the fact that Jesus will (in v. 19, below) ask the healed man to testify to others.

10. And he begged Jesus again and again not to send them out of the area.

By begging not to be sent *out of the area,* the demons show their fear of being sent "into the Abyss," as Luke 8:31 clarifies. The word *Abyss* is also found in Revelation 9:1, 2, 11; 11:7; 17:8; 20:1, 3. When we read those passages, the reason for the demons' fear is crystal clear! By begging not to be sent away, the demons recognize that Jesus is the one who is capable of sending them anywhere he chooses.

11. A large herd of pigs was feeding on the nearby hillside.

This verse gives us a good reason to believe that we are in Gentile territory, since *pigs* are unclean animals according to Jewish dietary laws. For Jews, pigs are just as unclean as tombs and evil spirits (Leviticus 11:7, 8; Deuteronomy 14:8; Isaiah 65:4; 66:17).

12. The demons begged Jesus, "Send us among the pigs; allow us to go into them."

The *demons* do not want to be cast into "the Abyss," so to be sent into *the pigs* is their proposed alternative. The demons cannot fool Jesus, of course,

People of the first century were able to recognize the difference between demonization (demon possession) and mental illness. How do we recognize this difference today?

Daily Bible Readings

Monday, Oct. 5—The Lord's Work for Freedom (Luke 7:18-23)

Tuesday, Oct. 6—A Bondage Imposed (Exodus 1:8-14)

Wednesday, Oct. 7—I Will Free You! (Exodus 6:2-7)

Thursday, Oct. 8—The Hope for Redemption (Romans 8:18-25)

Friday, Oct. 9—Freed from the Fear of Death (Hebrews 2:14-18)

Saturday, Oct. 10—Christ Has Set Us Free (Romans 8:9-17)

Sunday, Oct. 11—A Shackled Man Set Free (Mark 5:1-13, 18-20)

but as a bit of speculation perhaps the demons hope to create some antagonism against Jesus should he grant this request—something we see happen in verse 17. In any case, they have no alternative but to do what the Son of God orders.

13. He gave them permission, and the evil spirits came out and went into the pigs. The herd, about two thousand in number, rushed down the steep bank into the lake and were drowned.

The fact that the exorcism causes 2,000 pigs to stampede over a cliff is a clue about the amount of torment the man has been suffering. The stampede in and of itself is (or should be) a testimony to those residing in the surrounding area.

Notice also the direct result of the demonic possession of the pigs: death. One may presume that this had been the demons' goal for the man himself. The demons had wanted to make the man miserable, but undoubtedly they also sought to destroy his life. He had cut himself in the process of being tormented by devilish powers. But Jesus came "to seek and to save what was lost" (Luke 19:10).

III. RESULT OF DELIVERANCE (MARK 5:18-20)

A. REQUEST DENIED (vv. 18, 19)

18. As Jesus was getting into the boat, the man who had been demon-possessed begged to go with him.

Mark 5:14-17 (not in today's text) shows us the fear that is displayed by the people of the surrounding area. They ask Jesus to leave. They apparently value pigs over people.

We see the opposite reaction in the one who has *been demon-possessed. The man* wants to stay with *Jesus.* Perhaps the man wants to ensure that his deliverance will be permanent. But the man's deliverance does not depend on being physically present with Jesus. Whomever the Son sets free is free indeed (John 8:36). Jesus has other plans for the man. See the next verse.

19. Jesus did not let him, but said, "Go home to your family and tell them how much the Lord has done for you, and how he has had mercy on you."

This verse raises a question: Why did Jesus forbid the man who was cured of leprosy in last week's lesson to testify, but now instructs the man cured of demon possession to spread the news of his deliverance to others? Perhaps the answer lies in the different locations of the two accounts. The healing of the leper took place in Jewish territory, while the deliverance of the demoniac takes place in Gentile territory. Perhaps Jesus is not concerned that Gentiles will talk freely that he may be the Messiah, since Gentiles do not share the concept.

The fact that people have asked Jesus to leave (Mark 5:17) suggests that in this area there isn't much danger of Jesus being mobbed by those who need healing (contrast Mark 1:45). After Jesus returns to Jewish territory, he will again give instructions not to talk about healing experiences (contrast Mark 5:19 with 5:43).

SAVED FROM A LIFE UNIMAGINABLE

Lakshmi Tatma was born in India in 2005. Many people in her small village thought she was the reincarnation of the Hindu deity after whom she was named. The "goddess" Lakshmi is depicted as having four arms; baby Lakshmi, by comparison, had four arms and four legs.

WHAT DO YOU THINK?

What do Jesus' instructions to the man tell us about witnessing today, if anything?

Visual for Lessons 6 & 10. *Point to this visual as you ask your learners to brainstorm ways to tell others what God has done for them.*

Her condition, which occurs in less than two percent of conjoined twins, happens when one twin's embryo stops developing and becomes a "parasitic twin" on the other. Lakshmi was joined at the pelvis with her parasitic twin. Her extra limbs grew from that juncture. She had one head and one set of vital organs but an additional set of arms and legs from her twin.

When Lakshmi was 2 years old, a team of about 30 medical personnel spent more than 24 hours removing the extra limbs, transplanting a kidney from the twin and reconstructing Lakshmi's pelvic area. Further treatment and surgeries will be needed. We cannot really imagine what Lakshmi's life would have been like had the surgery not been undertaken.

Neither can we imagine what life must have been like for the demon-possessed man. Like Lakshmi, he had no hope for a normal life on his own; neither Lakshmi nor the demoniac could do a self-repair. She needed the removal of abnormal physical growth; he needed the removal of an abnormal spiritual factor in his life. Her restoration was due to the advance of medical science; his was a miracle only God could have provided.

Humanity has made much progress in medical science in the 20 centuries since Jesus walked the earth. Yet humanity has nothing to offer to cure spiritual ailments. God is still the only one who has that power.   —C. R. B.

PRAYER

Father, may Jesus' instructions to the man released from demons be Jesus' instructions to us as well. May people know without a doubt what great things Jesus has done for us because we have modeled and spoken of those things. In Jesus' name. Amen.

B. COMMAND FOLLOWED (v. 20)

20. So the man went away and began to tell in the Decapolis how much Jesus had done for him. And all the people were amazed.

The man is completely obedient to Jesus' command. There is no record that he questions what he is to do. This should cause us to do some self-examination: Do we ask skeptical questions when the Bible tells us to follow a certain path? Do we trust and obey, or do we try to "explain away" the Lord's directives for our lives?

When we obey the Lord, we can trust that he will bring good out of our situation. The results of the man's obedience speak volumes. The *people* of the *Decapolis* who hear the testimony are *amazed*. This incident may "soften up" the area for Jesus' return in Mark 7:31.

Interestingly, Jesus will command that people keep quiet as he conducts healings on that return trip (Mark 7:36). Today we are not to keep quiet about Christ. The Great Commission (Matthew 28:19, 20) requires quite the opposite. But many will see the gospel first in the examples of what Jesus has done for us in our personal lives. Make sure they see Christ in your daily actions.

CONCLUSION

The story of the demoniac demonstrates the extent of God's mercy. It is freely available. It breaks traditional boundaries. It reaches to individuals on the fringes of society. As recipients of God's grace and mercy, our aim is to reach those whom the world has forgotten, those who have encountered the trials of this life and have been marginalized. Embracing a call to compassion is to love the unlovable, to reach the unreachable, to touch the untouchable.

Consider the problems of the poor. Proverbs 19:7 tells us, "A poor man is shunned by all his relatives—how much more do his friends avoid him! Though he pursues them with pleading, they are nowhere to be found." How many people shut their eyes to the poor? But the poor are the very people who need a touch of God's grace the most. And keep in mind that "the poor" does not refer only to those who have little money. There are also those who are "poor in spirit" (Matthew 5:3).

The Lord has done great things for you. Don't keep quiet! While those around us may not be in physical chains, they can be chained in other ways (such as by life circumstances). When we see others in chains, we can be the love of God to them in their hour of greatest need.

THOUGHT TO REMEMBER
Proclaim what Jesus has done for you.

Discovery Learning

The following is an alternative lesson plan emphasizing learning activities.
Classes desiring such student involvement will find these suggestions helpful. At the
back of this book are reproducible student pages to further enhance activity learning.

INTO THE LESSON

Display the following scrambled word for the class to decipher: *D E E O P S S S S*. Once someone sees it as *POSSESSED*, ask, "How many ways can the word *possessed* or *possession* be used?"

Expect answers such as these: "It can mean 'owned' or 'occupied,' as in 'John just took possession of his new house.'" "It can mean 'driven' or 'compulsive,' as in 'He worked like a man possessed!'" "It can relate to the spiritual phenomenon of 'demon possession,' as in 'The devil's influence over the world is seen in the New Testament in cases of demonic possession of people.'"

INTO THE WORD

Recruit in advance a class member to research and give a two-minute overview on demon possession in the New Testament. Provide a list of relevant Scriptures. Matthew 4:24; 8:16; Mark 1:23, 24, 32-34; 6:13; Luke 9:37-42; Acts 5:16; 19:13-16 can be part of the list. A short article from a Bible dictionary or handbook may be a useful resource to provide.

At the conclusion of the overview, give your class an opportunity to ask questions regarding the biblical revelation of demonic activity. Students may speculate on such activity in the modern world, as claimed to be seen in places that are spiritually dark by the absence of the gospel.

Point out the difference between genuine demonization and sinful behaviors that some label "personal demons." Remind your class that "our struggle is not against flesh and blood, but against . . . the spiritual forces of evil" (Ephesians 6:12).

This will reinforce the idea of the existence of Satan's minions.

Prepare in advance two sets of flashcards, with lettering large enough for everyone to see. One set will have words that describe the man possessed by demons in today's text; the other set will describe the demons themselves.

The first set of cards (describing the man) will feature these words and relevant verse numbers: ostracized, v. 3; superhuman strength, vv. 3, 4; beastlike, v. 4; sad, v. 5; bloody, v. 5; loud, v. 5; perceptive, v. 6; controlled, v. 7; desperate, v. 18; obedient, v. 20; evangelistic, v. 20. The second set of cards (describing the evil spirits) will feature these words and relevant verse numbers: powerful, vv. 3, 4; intelligent, v. 7; fearful, v. 7; numerous, v. 9; persistent, v. 10; desperate, v. 12; disembodied, v. 13. (*Option:* Leave the verse numbers off both sets of cards.)

Have someone read today's text aloud. Then tell the class you have two sets of adjectives: one for the man possessed by demons in today's text and one for the demons themselves. Then begin to hold up the cards (which you have shuffled into a random order) one at a time. Have class members call out *man* or *demons* as each card is seen. Pause to resolve conflicting answers. Some answers may overlap, which will contribute to a lively discussion.

If time allows, ask someone to read Mark 5:14-17, which does not appear in today's printed text. Say, "Put yourself in the position of the townspeople who came out to see for themselves what had happened. How would you describe them?" After some responses, ask, "Why would people react so negatively to an event so positive and potentially so full of joy?" Your class may suggest anxiety at the loss of livelihood (drowned livestock). Ask how the townspeople's attitudes toward Jesus still exist today.

INTO LIFE

Say, "Martin Luther King, Jr. ended his famous speech on August 28, 1963, with the words 'Free at last! Free at last! Thank God Almighty, we are free at last!' Those words are appropriate for everyone who is free indeed in Christ—freed from the spiritual emptiness and evil intention that once characterized life."

Ask your class to notice occasions this week when breaking into that expression of praise would be most appropriate (examples: seeing an advertisement to engage in a harmful, even evil, habit once "enjoyed" by the observer; recalling a spiritually harmful vocation he or she once had). Suggest that bursting into that praise in the presence of others may give them an opportunity to explain why they feel freed from sins and circumstances that once bound them, to affirm the great things the Lord has done for them.

To reinforce today's lesson, distribute copies of one or both of the reproducible exercises from page 121 as take home work.

BEGGING TO GET IN

LESSON 7

INTRODUCTION

A. WHO BELONGS AND WHO DOES NOT?

Who belongs at church? Most of us would say "everyone belongs" or maybe "sinners belong." And we would be right.

But what impression do we often give about who belongs at church? By the way we dress or speak or act, we may give some the impression that only those who have their lives in order belong there. We may communicate that the church is only for people who are disciplined, wise, and strong. Those with worries or problems or hurts may get the feeling that church is not for them.

We are not the first to leave that impression. Jesus confronted it over and over in his ministry. He challenged those who thought that only people who appear righteous could belong to God. He welcomed those who knew that they desperately needed what only he could give.

Today's text presents two people whose desperate need was obvious. One was a complete outsider, a person commonly thought to have no claim to God's blessing. The other was one whose pitiable condition was unmistakable. Jesus used both situations to remind his disciples of his ability to help those with the most desperate needs.

B. LESSON BACKGROUND

The first of today's two stories occurs in the area of Tyre and Sidon. These two cities were on the east coast of the Mediterranean Sea, to the north of Galilee. In the Old Testament, Tyre and Sidon were notorious centers for the worship of the pagan god Baal. Jezebel, who married King Ahab of Israel and attempted to establish Baal as Israel's god, was the daughter of the king of Sidon (1 Kings 16:31). Thus for the Jewish people of Jesus' time, the region and its people were associated historically with the worst kind of paganism.

The healing of the deaf and mute man takes place in a similar area. Jesus meets the man in the Decapolis (literally, "ten cities"), a region to the east and south of the Sea of Galilee. For three centuries before Jesus, that region had been populated mostly with people who adopted Greek culture, customs, and religion. Though many Jews lived there, it was pagan territory in the minds of Jesus' contemporaries. This was also the region where Jesus cast out the "legion" of unclean spirits from a man in Mark 5:1-20, the text discussed in last week's lesson.

In Mark these events follow a long discussion that Jesus has with the Jewish religious leaders about what constitutes true purity and impurity (Mark 7:1-23). Today we will see Jesus meet two people who were commonly judged to be impure. How he responded to them is a continuation of his teaching on true purity. This is a demonstration of what it really takes to belong to the people of God.

DEVOTIONAL READING:
2 CORINTHIANS 8:1-7
BACKGROUND SCRIPTURE:
MARK 7:24-37
PRINTED TEXT:
MARK 7:24-37

LESSON AIMS

After participating in this lesson, each student will be able to:

1. Retell the stories of the Syrophoenician woman and the deaf and mute man in a way that highlights their related themes.

2. Compare the Syrophoenician woman and the deaf and mute man with those considered "outsiders" by his or her own community.

3. Plan a project that will help each student and/or the class to reach out to outsiders with the message of Jesus' love.

Oct
18

KEY VERSE

The woman was a Greek, born in Syrian Phoenicia. She begged Jesus to drive the demon out of her daughter.
—Mark 7:26

Lesson 7 Notes

I. SYROPHOENICIAN WOMAN (MARK 7:24-30)

The parallel to the story at hand is in Matthew 15:21-28 (Lesson 10 for the upcoming winter quarter). Reading both the accounts of Matthew and Mark side by side allows us to capture details that one author includes but the other does not.

A. DESPERATE SITUATION (vv. 24-26)

24. Jesus left that place and went to the vicinity of Tyre. He entered a house and did not want anyone to know it; yet he could not keep his presence secret.

Beginning way back in Mark 1:32-34, 44, 45 (Lesson 5), we see that Jesus cannot escape the attention of the crowds. Even when he commands silence about himself, he cannot keep his whereabouts a secret. That fact makes the action that follows all the more noteworthy.

25. In fact, as soon as she heard about him, a woman whose little daughter was possessed by an evil spirit came and fell at his feet.

Of all the people trying to get close to Jesus, *a woman* with a demon-possessed *daughter* is one who stands out in the case at hand. She clearly comes to Jesus because she has *heard* that Jesus can cast out *evil* spirits from those oppressed by them (see Mark 1:23-28; 3:11; 5:1-20). We see that Jesus' fame has spread beyond the boundaries of the Jewish territory.

To falls at Jesus' *feet* indicates that she submits to his authority. This posture reveals the attitude that she will express in the conversation that follows. Her actions and words come from her belief that Jesus alone has the solution to her problem.

Mark often refers to demons as evil spirits, with the idea being that of uncleanness. Thus Mark draws attention to an important question: What is it that makes a person unclean before God? As Jesus explained, it is not what goes into a person, like food, that makes one unclean. Rather, it is the actions that come from sinful attitudes within (Mark 7:18-23). This *evil spirit* serves as a reminder that uncleanness is to be found with Satan. Uncleanness comes when we think and act on the evil to which he tempts us.

26. The woman was a Greek, born in Syrian Phoenicia. She begged Jesus to drive the demon out of her daughter.

The fact that *the woman* is *a Greek* means that she speaks Greek as her first language and adheres to Greek customs. Since the time of Alexander the Great (three centuries before Jesus' birth), the nations of the area have been dominated by that culture and language. This is so much the case that for a Jew in Jesus' time, all non-Jews can be loosely referred to as "Greeks" (example: Acts 19:10). She is also described more specifically as being from *Syrian Phoenicia*. Syria and Phoenicia are regions to Israel's north. The differences between the peoples of these two regions are slight. We can assume that many people identify their cultural heritage with both groups. But for Jews, both groups are seen as traditional enemies of Israel and as pagans. Though close neighbors in geography, they are worlds apart in their views of God.

So we wonder how Jesus will respond to a woman from this area. Will he turn her away because she is a foreigner who does not know the God of Israel? The stage is set for a dramatic moment.

DAILY BIBLE READINGS

Monday, Oct. 12—Excelling in Generosity (2 Corinthians 8:1-7)

Tuesday, Oct. 13—Inquiring Nations (Isaiah 11:1-10)

Wednesday, Oct. 14—A Light to the Nations (Isaiah 42:5-9)

Thursday, Oct. 15—Salvation to All the Earth (Isaiah 49:1-6)

Friday, Oct. 16—God's Glory Among Nations (Isaiah 66:18-20)

Saturday, Oct. 17—Great Among the Nations (Malachi 1:9-11)

Sunday, Oct. 18—A Gentile's Faith Rewarded (Mark 7:24-37)

B. UNEXPECTED RESPONSE (vv. 27, 28)

27. "First let the children eat all they want," he told her, "for it is not right to take the children's bread and toss it to their dogs."

Jesus' words to the woman are blunt, even shocking. We should listen to their full force, but we should not exaggerate their severity. When Jesus refers to the children, he clearly is referring to the people of Israel as the people of God under the Mosaic covenant. Jesus' statement assumes that Israel has a position of privilege. The *dogs* in Jesus' comparison are clearly those who are not part of Israel, the Gentiles. In Jesus' time, some Jewish leaders refer to Gentiles disparagingly as "dogs." However the term they used refers to wild dogs that live as scavengers. Jesus' term refers to domestic dogs, a very different kind of creature that is not viewed as loathsome. So Jesus is not employing the kind of insulting language that some others do.

Further, Jesus does not say that "the dogs" will receive none of the food from the table. The children must eat *first,* and then the dogs may be fed. He does not say that the Gentiles have no share in God's blessings, though he does say that the blessings are offered first to Israel. His words suggest that the Gentiles will also receive the food once it has been offered to the Jews first. This order in the offer of salvation is reflected elsewhere in the New Testament. In the book of Acts, the gospel is first preached to the Jewish people (Acts 1–9) before it is offered to the Gentiles (Acts 10). In Romans 1:16, Paul says that the gospel is given "first for the Jew, then for the Gentile."

Still, with all these considerations, Jesus appears to be rebuffing the woman's request. But how we understand that rebuff depends on what follows in the conversation.

28. "Yes, Lord," she replied, "but even the dogs under the table eat the children's crumbs."

The woman's response is remarkable. First, she accepts all the assumptions of Jesus' statement: that the Jews have priority and that she, as a Gentile, is in a secondary position. Thus she remains submissive to Jesus' authority. But she offers an added perspective on his comparison: while the children are eating at *the table,* the *dogs* are free to gobble up the *crumbs* that fall to the ground. So if the woman is indeed in the position of "the dogs" in Jesus' comparison, second in line behind "the children," she can still hope to receive relief right away, not just later.

What exemplary faith! The woman knows that she has a desperate need that no one but Jesus can meet. She is fully submissive to his authority and completely dependent on his answer. So she will cling to any means available to make her need known to Jesus.

WHO YOU ARE, WHERE YOU LIVE

Location, location, location is an old platitude in real estate. During the real estate bubble in the early part of this decade, home prices over much of the U.S. rose dramatically. But certain prestigious locations saw prices escalating much more rapidly than others.

To keep tabs on all this, many folks found a new friend on February 8, 2006. That's the day that www.zillow.com went online. The site offered free estimates of property values—yours or your neighbor's. So many people went to the site

WHAT DO YOU THINK?

What was a time you heard a teacher or preacher say something that seemed harsh, but actually taught a valuable lesson?

WHAT DO YOU THINK?

How can we follow the woman's example in our approach to the Lord with our requests?

[Make sure to look at Luke 22:42 and Hebrews 4:16.]

when it opened that it crashed within hours! The whole phenomenon illustrated how fascinated we are with where we live, especially as compared with where other people live.

This interest in location can become a way to feed our pride—an "us versus them" mentality. There was a certain level of tension in that regard as Jesus interacted with the Syrophoenician woman. First-century Jews looked down on her because of where she lived. But Jesus cared enough about her to test her faith with a shocking comparison. Do we value others as Jesus did? Or is their *location, location, location* more important to us?   —C. R. B.

WHAT DO YOU THINK?

Was Jesus' response to the woman the same as what we call tough love? *Why, or why not?*

C. PUBLIC AND PRIVATE RESULT (vv. 29, 30)

29. Then he told her, "For such a reply, you may go; the demon has left your daughter."

Jesus' answer affirms her faith. She expresses the kind of trust to which Jesus consistently responds. Those who believe they have all they need are not ready to receive God's blessing. Those who know that they have no means of helping themselves are the ones who can receive God's blessing.

As we hear Jesus' response, we realize that his harsh words may be something different from what we first thought. Elsewhere in Mark, Jesus shows that he knows what people are thinking before they speak (Mark 2:8). He also challenges people with difficult sayings and proposals (Mark 6:37). It is very possible that Jesus, knowing the faith that she will express, deliberately challenges the woman with his response about children and dogs. If so, then Jesus is acting for the benefit not only of the woman but also of all who overhear, especially his disciples. For any who think that by their position they have a special claim on God's blessing, this exchange offers the opposite conclusion. Jesus is saying that he comes for those who know that they are weak and lost, who recognize that they have nowhere else to turn.

That is a truth that needs to be heard by those who believe themselves to be so far from God as to be beyond his mercy. It also needs to be heard by those who have been in the church so long that they have forgotten that they are sinners who stand by God's grace, not their own goodness.

30. She went home and found her child lying on the bed, and the demon gone.

We do not know exactly how *the demon* has affected this girl. In other texts, those who are demon-possessed are characterized by violent, self-destructive behavior (example: Matthew 17:15). Whatever her previous behavior, this girl now is lying peacefully at rest in her *bed*. The end result is not witnessed by the crowd, nor need it be.

II. DEAF AND MUTE MAN (MARK 7:31-37)

Matthew 15:29-31 offers us a general parallel to Mark 7:31-37. But the specifics of the healing of the deaf and mute man we are about to consider are found only in Mark's account.

A. NEED FOR HEALING (vv. 31, 32)

31. Then Jesus left the vicinity of Tyre and went through Sidon, down to the Sea of Galilee and into the region of the Decapolis.

Although Jesus leaves the land of *Tyre* and *Sidon*, he remains in a territory dominated by non-Israelites. The man he is about to encounter is another

Visual for Lesson 7. *Point to this visual as you ask, "What are some ways we can and should intercede for others?"*

whom some of Jesus' Jewish followers might view as beyond the reach of God's blessing. That Jesus exhibits special care toward him is an important lesson for those who count themselves on the "inside" of God's favor and others as being on the "outside."

32. There some people brought to him a man who was deaf and could hardly talk, and they begged him to place his hand on the man.

The man is described as unable to hear and speaking with difficulty, if he can speak at all. The words that describe him should remind readers in the first century of God's promise in Isaiah 35:5, 6 to give hearing to the *deaf* and speech to the mute. Mark wants alert readers to recognize this story as a sign that God's promised salvation is coming to fulfillment.

Again, people recognize Jesus as a great miracle-worker even outside Jewish territory. If the deaf man is to be helped, only Jesus can help him.

B. DELIBERATE ACTIONS (vv. 33, 34)

33. After he took him aside, away from the crowd, Jesus put his fingers into the man's ears. Then he spit and touched the man's tongue.

Jesus takes specific steps in healing the man. First he takes the man *away from the crowd.* Now only the disciples will see what happens. Jesus apparently wants this action to communicate something especially to his closest followers. Second, Jesus does not simply speak an authoritative word to perform this healing, as he often does. Instead, he touches the affected parts of the man's body. In doing this, Jesus uses a sort of sign language so that the deaf man will understand that Jesus is healing him. Merely speaking to perform the miracle will not do that.

With our modern concern for germs, we may be put off by Jesus' use of saliva here. Some in Jesus' time believe that certain people's saliva has healing powers. One can imagine, however, that such cures are not effective. But what Jesus does here shows that he can do what others cannot (compare Mark 8:23).

34. He looked up to heaven and with a deep sigh said to him, "Ephphatha!" (which means, "Be opened!").

The fact that Jesus looks *to heaven* and sighs suggests that he shares with God a burden for the man's condition. Then he utters a word in Aramaic, his native language as a Jew. This gives the command of healing to the man's ears and tongue.

There are others besides Jesus in the ancient world who are regarded as powerful healers. Most of them refuse to reveal the means by which they claim to bring healing to their patients. But here and in texts such as Mark 1:40-45, what Jesus does to heal is described plainly. Jesus' power to heal is no secret. So as we read this description of Jesus touching the man's ears and tongue and using his saliva, we realize that Mark is stressing complementary ideas: (1) there is no secret to Jesus' healings, and (2) that is because there is no one other than Jesus with such an authority to heal.

The Aramaic word *Ephphatha,* meaning *be opened,* appears to be important on more than one level. In just a few paragraphs, Jesus will be alone with the 12 disciples, and he will ask them whether they have eyes to see and ears to hear (Mark 8:18). As we read about Jesus' disciples in Mark, we see them continually struggling to trust Jesus to care and provide for them. They do not yet "see" who Jesus really is or "hear" what he is really saying.

HOW TO SAY IT

Ahab. AY-hab.
Aramaic. AIR-uh-MAY-ik.
Baal. BAY-ul.
Decapolis. Dee-CAP-uh-lis.
Ephphatha (Aramaic).
   EF-uh-thuh.
Jezebel. JEZ-uh-bel.
Mediterranean.
   MED-uh-tuh-RAY-nee-un.
Mosaic. Mo-ZAY-ik.
Phoenicia. Fuh-NISH-uh.
Sidon. SIGH-dun.
Syrophoenician.
   SIGH-roe-fih-NISH-un.
Tyre. Tire.

WHAT DO YOU THINK?

How can your church do better at curing spiritual deafness? How can your church make sure it doesn't become mute in proclaiming the gospel?

[Note: The Bible has a lot to say about spiritual deafness; see Isaiah 6:9, 10 (quoted in Matthew 13:14, 15; Mark 4:12; Acts 28:26, 27); Isaiah 42:20; 29:10 (quoted in Romans 11:8); Jeremiah 5:21; 6:10; Ezekiel 12:2.]

PRAYER

Lord, when we are honest with ourselves, we realize that we are helpless, needy sinners. We can only cry out to you for your mercy and grace. Thank you for Jesus, who came to bless needy people like us. In Jesus' name. Amen.

WHAT DO YOU THINK?

How can or should the fact that Jesus "has done everything well" affect our personal commitment to excellence and the corporate commitment of our churches to excellence?

So as Jesus heals the deaf and mute man with the disciples alone as witnesses, he shows them that they need their spiritual ears opened as well. Only then will they be able to speak about Jesus as they are called to do (Mark 6:12).

C. PUBLIC AND PRIVATE RESULT (vv. 35-37)

35. At this, the man's ears were opened, his tongue was loosened and he began to speak plainly.

Once again we see that Jesus' actions are immediately and fully effective. There can be no doubt that he can do what no other can do.

36. Jesus commanded them not to tell anyone. But the more he did so, the more they kept talking about it.

This is not the first time that Jesus commands silence in connection with a healing (see Mark 1:44, 45). Jesus is concerned that news about him not spread too widely before that news is complete. Prior to his death and resurrection, Jesus commands some to keep silent. After his death and resurrection, however, he sends his followers to preach about him to everyone.

The issue is this. Jesus has authority that belongs to God alone, as the miracles demonstrate. But what does that signify? We will understand Jesus truly only when we see the one who has supreme authority willingly giving himself up to die on behalf of sinners. We have the fullness of the good news only when we have the cross and the empty tomb. Until then, people may well misunderstand what Jesus is really doing.

37. People were overwhelmed with amazement. "He has done everything well," they said. "He even makes the deaf hear and the mute speak."

News like this cannot be kept secret, however. So Jesus' fame spreads again. The words here remind us again of the promise of God in Isaiah 35:5, 6. Jesus is demonstrating that the day of salvation is arriving.

AS IF BY MAGIC

Christianity continues to lose the strong place of priority it once held in Western culture. As a result (or, perhaps, as a cause), many Westerners have turned to the incantations of Eastern mysticism that supposedly control the forces of the universe. Others have taken up occultism and witchcraft, using magic to praise deities and attempt to manipulate people and objects.

A search of Web sites for such beliefs reveals a focus on casting spells for protection and for success in romantic endeavors. For example, an Internet testimonial for one book of incantations said, "I have recently tried some spells from this book and they worked. I tried one of the love spells. I now have a boyfriend who tells me he loves me . . . but has been afraid to tell me."

Those who dabble in this stuff are making two serious errors. First, the true God of the universe is the ultimate source of power. Second, he cannot be manipulated by incantations, etc. (See also Deuteronomy 18:9-13).

Jesus did not use a magical, occult incantation. Rather, he was using his own, divine power to command the man's ears and mouth to begin functioning as they should. When Jesus used such powers, they were always 100 percent effective—always. Since the mystics and occultists come nowhere near to matching this record, isn't it obvious whom we should serve? —C. R. B.

CONCLUSION

Jesus used his encounters with the Syrophoenician woman and the man who was deaf and mute to show us the kind of person who can receive his salvation. If we imagine that we have good standing with God because of who we are or what we have done, we place ourselves beyond the reach of God's grace. But when we recognize how helpless we are and how deeply we need what only Jesus can give, he is ready to give us what we need.

The people who most needed this lesson in the first century were Jesus' closest followers. That is a caution to us! It is easy for us to become proud, self-satisfied, and self-reliant when we have known the Lord for a long time. We can become so accustomed to belonging to him that we forget how we became his in the first place. To receive his blessing, we have to get over ourselves and learn to trust him completely.

THOUGHT TO REMEMBER
"Little ones to him belong" ("Jesus Loves Me," *lyrics by Anna B. Warner, 1860).*

Discovery Learning

The following is an alternative lesson plan emphasizing learning activities.
Classes desiring such student involvement will find these suggestions helpful. At the
back of this book are reproducible student pages to further enhance activity learning.

INTO THE LESSON

Distribute copies of the word-find puzzle on the next page. Tell the class, "In this puzzle find 12 groups that are alienated from the gospel." The answers are *addicts, alcoholics, cheats, Hindus, liars, muggers, murderers, Muslims, Pharisees, prostitutes, Taoist, thieves.* You should include this list below the puzzle.

After a reasonable amount of time, say, "Now analyze the uncircled letters to discover what the 'filler word' is." When the filler word *outsiders* is noted, say, "That's what today's study is about: outsiders—those who seem most beyond the reach of the gospel."

INTO THE WORD

Have someone read today's text aloud, or have students take turns reading one or two verses each. Then say, "A difference is easy to notice and even easier to emphasize. What are the differences between the two individuals Jesus deals with in today's text?"

Write responses on the board. Expect the following: one is female, one is male; one comes at her own will, one is brought by others; one comes on behalf of another's problem (the mother), one is there for his own problem; one is concerned with a spiritual affliction, one is there for a physical affliction; one is healed at a distance, the other by a personal touch; one is sent away without knowing if the matter is resolved (except in faith), one fully knows.

After noting differences, ask, "Now, in what ways were the two needing Jesus' touch alike?" Some quick learner will no doubt respond "they both needed Jesus' touch," but persist for other similarities. Some possible responses: both live outside the Jewish nation; both probably speak a language other than Aramaic, Jesus' native tongue; and expectations of what Jesus can do surround both.

As an additional approach, recruit in advance two students or two from outside the class—one female, one male—for a bit of acting. They will stand at the front in appropriate biblical-era costuming, wearing the identifiers that say *Woman of Syrophoenicia* and *Man Formerly Deaf and Mute.* Ask them to study today's text in preparation for answering questions.

At the appropriate time, ask the two to stand quietly with eyes shut and with arms extended left and right. Give each learner two stick-on notes as you say, "Write a question for each of our biblical characters. When you get the questions written, come up and stick the question on his or her arm."

After class members read the text and stick their questions to the arms of the actors, ask your actors to rouse and answer the questions as they are removed (or you as teacher can do the plucking and reading). Allow the actors the freedom to speculate for questions asked beyond the revelation of the text. Discuss the differences between verifiable answers and those that come from a "sanctified imagination."

Alternative: Distribute copies of the reproducible exercise "Surprise!" from page 122 for students to work on in small groups or pairs. Discuss results as a class.

INTO LIFE

Write the word *OUTSIDER* vertically on the board. Ask the class to help you make an acrostic on this, using words that name groups that are "outsiders" in some way (not necessarily sinful ways). (*Alternative*: put this on a handout as a small-group activity.) The following is a complete example: *O* = Orphans; *U* = the Unchurched; *I*

= Transients; *S* = Sexual deviants; *I* = Intellectual elitists; *D* = Deaf and hearing impaired; *E* = Ethnic groups; *R* = Radicals.

Have your class discuss the groups that they think are least likely and most likely to respond to the gospel. Challenge the class to a project aimed at one of the groups identified. One example—from the acrostic suggested above—is benevolent gifts of basic personal necessities to those in a local homeless (transient) setting. Distribute copies of the reproducible exercise "Outside My House" from page 122 as students depart.

INSIDE OR OUTSIDE?

```
O  M  U  T  S  H  I  N  D  U  S
M  U  R  D  E  R  E  R  S  E  C
I  S  S  D  E  S  R  S  T  O  I
U  L  R  R  T  T  U  H  S  L
I  I  D  E  A  E  T  A  I  R  O
S  M  O  O  G  I  U  T  E  S  H
I  S  I  D  T  G  L  E  V  H  O
R  S  S  S  O  U  U  T  E  S  C
T  I  O  D  E  R  S  M  S  O  L
U  R  T  S  S  T  C  I  D  D  A
P  H  A  R  I  S  E  E  S  I  D
```

OPTING OUT!

LESSON 8

INTRODUCTION

A. ARE YOU RICH?

How much money does it take to be rich? It is hard to say, but we might think of a person who has a million dollars as rich.

According to the U.S. Census Bureau, in 2004 the median American household income was about $44,000 per year. That's not exactly a millionaire's salary. However, from that number we can estimate the amount of money that a typical American family will control over a working lifetime. The amount is about $1.75 million, not adjusting for inflation. Quite a sum!

Most of us do not think of ourselves as rich. Maybe our income is average or below average. Maybe we think of ourselves as moderately well off. But rich? That is someone else! However, when we realize how much money we control, how many decisions we make about money, how much that money influences us, and what our standard of living is in comparison with the rest of the world, then we may need to change our thinking.

B. LESSON BACKGROUND

Today's story comes in the middle of a section where Jesus was traveling with his disciples toward Jerusalem. Along the way he told them that those who receive the blessing of God's kingdom must be like children (Mark 10:14, 15) and that those who would be great in God's kingdom must be the least, the "slave of all" (Mark 10:43, 44). Only those who recognize their great need for what only Jesus can give are ready to receive his gift, which comes through his death (Mark 10:45).

Jesus' conversation with the rich man demonstrated how hard it is to accept those truths when we believe that we can rely on ourselves. Parallels to today's account are in Matthew 19:16-30 and Luke 18:18-30.

I. CONVERSATION WITH THE RICH MAN (MARK 10:17-22)

A. WHO IS GOOD? (vv. 17, 18)

17. As Jesus started on his way, a man ran up to him and fell on his knees before him. "Good teacher," he asked, "what must I do to inherit eternal life?"

A man approaches *Jesus*. As he does, he shows tremendous enthusiasm and submission, running to Jesus and kneeling before him. That attitude is also reflected as he addresses Jesus as *good teacher*. The man asks the most significant question a person can ask: *what must I do to inherit eternal life?*

The fact that this man is rich will be evident in verse 22, below. Clearly this man has enormous respect for Jesus. He believes that Jesus can answer this most significant question.

18. "Why do you call me good?" Jesus answered. "No one is good—except God alone.

DEVOTIONAL READING:
PROVERBS 11:1-7
BACKGROUND SCRIPTURE:
MARK 10:17-31
PRINTED TEXT:
MARK 10:17-31

LESSON AIMS

After participating in this lesson, each student will be able to:

1. Retell the account of the rich man.

2. Contrast the self-reliant life with the Christ-dependent life.

3. Make a plan to eliminate one material possession or attitude that most interferes with his or her relationship with Jesus.

Oct 25

KEY VERSE

Jesus looked at him and loved him. "One thing you lack," he said. "Go, sell everything you have and give to the poor, and you will have treasure in heaven. Then come, follow me."

—Mark 10:21

What Do You Think?

Does Jesus' statement about God alone being good mean that we can never refer to any human being as good? Why, or why not?

[Make sure to look at Proverbs 12:2; 13:22; 14:14; Ecclesiastes 9:2; Matthew 12:35; Luke 6:45; Acts 11:24; and Romans 5:7 as you consider your answer.]

How to Say It

Corinthians. Ko-RIN-thee-unz (th as in thin).
Deuteronomy.
   Due-ter-AHN-uh-me.
Jerusalem. Juh-ROO-suh-lem.
Moses. MO-zes or MO-zez.
synagogue. SIN-uh-gog.

Jesus challenges the man about his understanding of who is *good*. Jesus reminds the man that, in the strictest sense, only *God* can be called good.

That truth has implications that this man needs to grasp. One implication concerns Jesus himself. We may think that Jesus is objecting to being called *good*. However, that would mean that Jesus is disqualifying himself from answering the man's question. But by giving an answer, Jesus implies that the title *good* is appropriate for him. More than that, Jesus will finally say to the man, "Follow me" (v. 21, below) at the end of their conversation. If receiving eternal life means that one must follow Jesus, then Jesus has a supreme position that belongs to God alone.

The phrase *no one is good—except God alone* has an implication for the man who is asking the question. He wants to know what he can do to obtain eternal life. But because the man, like all other sinful people, is not good in an absolute sense, there is nothing good that he can do to earn or deserve eternal life. By definition, the answer to his question is, "You can do nothing to obtain eternal life because you are not good."

Jesus does not let the point rest there, however. It is hard for us to admit that we are helpless sinners who have nothing to offer God. So Jesus will give the man a chance to realize his situation.

B. Am I Good? (vv. 19, 20)

19. "You know the commandments: 'Do not murder, do not commit adultery, do not steal, do not give false testimony, do not defraud, honor your father and mother.'"

Jesus now reminds the man of certain *commandments* in the Law of Moses (see Exodus 20; Leviticus 19:13; Deuteronomy 5). Here, he says, is the standard of goodness by which you should measure yourself. Specifically, Jesus quotes several commandments that address human-to-human relationships. God is the standard of goodness, but humans are measured on that standard by how they treat each other.

In the books of the Old Testament law, the commandments are presented with two contrasting but complementary perspectives. Keeping the commandments lies within everyone's power, and the commandments are the standard by which people are to be judged. But the reality is that those who have the law never manage to keep it. So the law is good and right, but humans have never obeyed it fully. See Psalm 14:3.

So Jesus' reminder about the commandments is a reality check. Measured by the standard of God's perfect law, this person—or any person—has fallen short of the standard of goodness that would allow him to do something to obtain eternal life. Will the man realize what the commandments reveal about him?

20. "Teacher," he declared, "all these I have kept since I was a boy."

If this man thinks closely about the requirements of the law and about Jesus' reminder that no one but God is truly good, he will remember his failure to keep the law perfectly. Instead, he applies a different standard to himself: it is not the standard set by God's absolute goodness, but the standard of relative human goodness.

Compared with many people, this man probably is indeed a shining example of obedience to the commandments of God. He is probably a highly respected religious figure in his community. (Luke 18:18 tells us that he is a "ruler," probably a leader of the synagogue.) So from the perspective that compares people with other people, he can say in all honesty that he has kept the Ten Commandments ever since he was young.

Here lies the issue that this man must confront. Compared with other people, he is indeed good. By that standard, he can perhaps rely on what he can do to obtain eternal life. But compared with God, he is not good. By the standard of God's goodness, this man can do nothing to obtain eternal life. Jesus will now confront the man with his need.

C. ON WHAT DO I DEPEND? (vv. 21, 22)

21. Jesus looked at him and loved him. "One thing you lack," he said. "Go, sell everything you have and give to the poor, and you will have treasure in heaven. Then come, follow me."

What Jesus says here is among his most difficult sayings. This is perhaps why in introducing the statement Mark stresses that Jesus loves the man. Jesus' words, though seemingly harsh, are spoken in love to bring the man to salvation. Jesus tells the man first to *sell* all his possessions and *give* the proceeds to *the poor*. From one vantage, this command might sound like a challenge to go beyond the basic requirement of the law and do something of outstanding goodness. However, what Jesus will say later will make clear that the issue is really something else.

The result of the man's giving all his possessions to the poor will be that he will have *treasure in heaven*. Here we should probably understand Jesus to be talking about more than God's blessing in eternity. To say that one has treasure in Heaven is to say that the person's real support and security, what "treasure" provides, will come from God himself, the one who is enthroned in Heaven. In other words, Jesus tells the man that when he gives up all his possessions, he will still have genuine, lasting treasure that will supply everything that his money supplies—and more. But Jesus goes on, ending his statement by saying *follow me*. The final step of these instructions is the key to everything. This man cannot obtain eternal life on his own. Even with his money, he cannot manage to be good enough to merit God's salvation. But Jesus can give freely what the man cannot possibly earn on his own.

22. At this the man's face fell. He went away sad, because he had great wealth.

The gospel writers seem to imply that giving up everything is actually harder when we have more than when we have less. Combined with what Jesus will say in the next few verses, this insight helps us understand why Jesus tells the man to sell everything. This man begins with the belief that somehow he can live with enough goodness to earn the right to eternal life. He depends on himself and his own resources to establish good standing with God. But the person who depends on self and personal goodness is doomed, for no one is good except God alone.

Now we begin to realize what makes this man's sense of self-reliance so strong: he is wealthy. Jesus repeatedly warns his followers that wealth is deceptive, giving us the illusion that we can take care of ourselves. It gives us a false sense of security, which makes it hard for us to see our real weakness and need. Wealth makes it difficult for us to turn to God and rely on his mercy and grace.

That illusion is so powerful that it turns the man away from Jesus. He leaves with a sense of grief, disappointed that he does not get the answer he has sought, but not realizing that Jesus has told him something better than what he has hoped for.

Visual for Lesson 8. *Point to this visual as you ask, "What are some specific ways that we can go about laying up treasures in Heaven?"*

WHAT DO YOU THINK?

How would you explain to someone that Jesus' requirement that the man give up his wealth in order to be saved is not "works righteousness"?

WHAT DO YOU THINK?

How are the temptations inherent in the possession of wealth the same as and different from the temptations inherent in the desire for wealth? How does this knowledge help you resist both dangers?

ARE YOU RICH?

Some time ago, I read the story of a girl and her young brother who were collecting money on a Saturday morning from customers on their newspaper route. (Obviously, this story took place "some" time ago!) It was a cold, wintry day, and the children had rather threadbare clothes. When they stopped at one house, the woman, seeing how cold they were, invited them in for a cup of hot chocolate. As they drank the chocolate, the woman went about her Saturday morning duties of cleaning the house. When she came by the living room a bit later to see how they were getting along, the girl shyly asked, "Ma'am, are you rich?"

"Land sakes, no," replied the woman. "I'm not rich."

"But your cups and saucers match," said the girl.

In the neighborhood where I grew up, we did not consider ourselves rich. In our home, my parents had two sets of dinnerware—one for special occasions and one for everyday use. The cups and saucers matched in both sets. Yet I remember families in our neighborhood who did not have cups and saucers that matched.

When we compare ourselves with Bill Gates, it is easy to convince ourselves that we are not rich. But when we compare ourselves with the majority of the world, many of us are wealthy beyond comprehension. By one estimate in 2004, about half the world's population lives on less than $2 per day. Those whose cups and saucers match perhaps should pay close attention to what Jesus has to say to the rich man in today's text! —J. B. N.

II. CONVERSATION WITH THE DISCIPLES (MARK 10:23-31)
A. HOW GOD CAN SAVE (vv. 23-27)

23. Jesus looked around and said to his disciples, "How hard it is for the rich to enter the kingdom of God!"

As the man leaves, Jesus states boldly that wealth is a hindrance to entering God's *kingdom.* This surprises *his disciples* (next verse).

24. The disciples were amazed at his words. But Jesus said again, "Children, how hard it is to enter the kingdom of God!

The disciples probably are used to thinking of wealth as an advantage. They may see wealth as a sign of God's blessing. Or they may think that the wealthy can devote more of their time and resources to keeping God's law and doing good works. In response to their surprise, Jesus addresses the disciples as *children.* It seems that he is reminding them of what he taught in the previous story: that those who enter God's *kingdom* need to be like children (Mark 10:14, 15). They cannot be like the rich man who sees himself as self-sufficient. They need to know that they are utterly dependent on God the Father, just as a little child depends utterly on a parent.

25. "It is easier for a camel to go through the eye of a needle than for a rich man to enter the kingdom of God."

This is one of Jesus' most famous sayings, and one that Christians have often misunderstood. Some have claimed that *the eye of a needle* refers to a low, narrow gate in city walls, a gate just tall enough for a person to enter but too low for a *camel.* So to enter such a gate, all the baggage must be removed from the camel's back, and the camel must get down on its knees.

This popular interpretation is not supported by any real evidence in history. We have no evidence that such gates were common, let alone that anyone ever called them "the eye of a needle." It appears instead that centuries ago a clever Christian preacher invented this story to encourage the rich to give away their wealth and get down on their knees in prayer. That's good advice, but it does not capture Jesus' exact point.

We should understand Jesus to mean (1) what the disciples understand him to say and (2) what he will explain his point to be in his next statement. The camel is the largest animal that Jesus' followers saw commonly. The eye of a needle is a very small opening. It is plainly impossible for a camel to pass through the eye of a needle. So Jesus says that it is plainly impossible *for a rich man to enter God's kingdom.*

26. *The disciples were even more amazed, and said to each other, "Who then can be saved?"*

The disciples clearly understand what Jesus is saying. They believe that wealth is an advantage in salvation. But Jesus says salvation is impossible for the wealthy. If those who have the advantage are in an impossible situation, then salvation appears to be out of reach for everyone!

27. *Jesus looked at them and said, "With man this is impossible, but not with God; all things are possible with God."*

For all humans, salvation by personal effort is *impossible* because there is no one who is truly good but God alone. Even if we were to sell everything that we have and give the money to the poor, we would not be good enough to earn eternal life. But God's grace is great enough to save us if we realize how much we need it. Only when we give up the illusion of self-reliance and cast ourselves on the mercy of God can we receive the gift that we cannot earn for ourselves.

Wealth can make it hard to admit that we need to depend on God. Even after we listen to Jesus' teaching on the dangers of wealth, we can convince ourselves that our possessions do not deceive us into depending on ourselves instead of God. The moment we think that we can handle wealth without spiritual danger is probably the moment we need to ask God to help us examine our hearts and recommit ourselves to depend completely on him. But many who lack wealth have the same problem. The truth is that we all have a "rich man" inside of us, a streak of self-sufficiency and independence, a part of us that likes to run the show. If we keep that part of us alive, we will continue to live as if we do not really need God.

B. WHAT GOD CAN GIVE (vv. 28-31)

28. *Peter said to him, "We have left everything to follow you!"*

As the disciples hear what Jesus has said, they ask about their own situation. Peter may be saying something like, "Lord, we have done exactly what you told that man to do, giving up *everything to follow you.* Does that mean that God will give us eternal life because of what we have given to him?"

29. *"I tell you the truth," Jesus replied, "no one who has left home or brothers or sisters or mother or father or children or fields for me and the gospel*

Jesus gives an overview of the kinds of things the disciples have given up to follow him. The disciples' sacrifices indeed have been enormous.

30. *". . . will fail to receive a hundred times as much in this present age (homes, brothers, sisters, mothers, children and fields—and with them, persecutions) and in the age to come, eternal life.*

Jesus says that what the disciples are already receiving is far greater than what they have given up. They have left the comforts of their *homes,* the

WHAT DO YOU THINK?

Besides finances in general and money in particular, what are some things we need to give up for (or give over to) the Lord?

provisions of their livelihoods, and the fellowship of their families. But as they travel with Jesus, God gives them many times what they have left behind. This is not in literal quantity, but in the many people who now receive them as family and who provide for their needs. Those who follow Jesus do not really lose what they give up in this life. They enter into a great family in Christ. And to that bounty is added the blessing of *eternal life,* which is greater than everything. With those blessings, of course, come hardships. Those who follow Jesus are persecuted for following him. But those troubles are "light and momentary," as Paul says in 2 Corinthians 4:17.

In sum, the disciples have not "struck a deal" with God. Their sacrifices are far outweighed by everything that God gives them, now and in the future. Even with their sacrifices, they have not given something to God that makes them "good." They receive God's blessing because God in his grace does the impossible for them.

OF GAINS AND LOSSES

I have a friend who went to Africa as a missionary several decades ago. When he went, he left behind his parents, two brothers, and a sister. His wife experienced a similar separation-loss.

They had a very successful ministry in Africa, although there were serious times of crisis as well. Because of political unrest they had to leave one country, but they then went to a different country and continued their work. They started numerous local congregations and were known and loved by thousands of natives. Most of their children were born in Africa, and the children identified with their ministry equally with the parents.

They had left much behind, but they gained an enormous support team in Africa. They had left two sets of parents behind, but they ended up with hundreds of elderly Africans who treated them as adopted children. They left behind several brothers and sisters, but they gained literally thousands of Christian brothers and sisters. They had left families behind, but they indeed received a hundredfold more than what they started with.

All this was not limited to Africa. When they returned to America on furlough and traveled among their supporting churches, they were received as family by dozens of faithful supporters across the country. Those who abandon houses, lands, and families for Jesus' sake indeed receive much more in this world, plus eternal life in the world to come.

—J. B. N.

31. *"But many who are first will be last, and the last first."*

Jesus repeats a concept he uses elsewhere (Mark 9:35; etc.). He reminds the disciples that their standing with God does not depend on the size of their sacrifice, any more than the rich man's standing with God depends on the size of his bank account. Jesus comes into the world as the Lord of all but also as the servant of all (Mark 10:45). He reverses our expectations. If we count ourselves *first,* we may be in danger of being put *last.* If we know that we are last and so depend completely on him, he makes us first.

CONCLUSION

How much does it take to be rich? Any amount, large or small, can deceive us into thinking that we can depend on ourselves instead of depending on God. At the end of this chapter of Mark, another man approached Jesus—a blind man. He knew that he had nothing to offer, that he could do nothing to change his situation. He cried out, "Jesus, Son of David, have mercy on me!" (Mark 10:47). Jesus gave him his sight, and he then followed Jesus (v. 52). Will we be more like the rich man or more like the blind man?

> **THOUGHT TO REMEMBER**
> *Allow God to do what is impossible for you to do.*

Discovery Learning

*The following is an alternative lesson plan emphasizing learning activities.
Classes desiring such student involvement will find these suggestions helpful. At the
back of this book are reproducible student pages to further enhance activity learning.*

INTO THE LESSON

Give each arriving learner a handout on which you have the heading *Building a Wall Across Heaven's Gate* as well as the following references: Matthew 7:21-23; Matthew 18:3; Matthew 21:31b, 32; Mark 10:13-15; 1 Corinthians 6:9, 10; Galatians 5:19-21; Ephesians 5:5. Have the sheet designed to look like a block wall (nine blocks, in three rows of three).

Say, "Looking at the Scriptures suggested or calling on your own general Bible knowledge, write down some unrighteous behaviors or attitudes that will keep one out of the kingdom and out of Heaven, one per block. In today's study we will see one man who allowed something to be a wall across the gate of Heaven for him." Allow a few minutes to complete the task. Indicate that you will use the sheet later in the study.

Put the question *What's in a name?* on display just before you move to the Into the Word segment.

INTO THE WORD

Say, "The individual with whom Jesus deals in today's text is not named. We often refer to him only by the facts that he is rich, he is young, and he is a ruler (Luke 18:18). Look at today's text and decide what verse or verses would allow us to refer to him by each of the following designations." Put the following designations on cards so you can show them to your class; put each card in permanent view after you reveal it and a student answers your question.

Designations: A Truth Seeker (*v. 17*); A Hopeful Do-gooder (*v. 17*); A Knowledgeable Jew (*v. 19*); An Obedient Lawkeeper (*v. 20*); A Loved Lacker (*v. 21*); A Potential Follower (*v. 21*); A Saddened Miser (*v. 22*); A Tragic Example (*v. 23*).

Do not put the verse numbers on the cards. You may wish to randomize the order of the cards before working through them. Let your class suggest other designations they see as appropriate.

Note that Jesus' listeners were startled by what they heard him say, so he clarified (see the commentary). His figure regarding the camel and the eye of the needle is well known. Ask your class to fill the blanks in this statement to make a parallel thought: "It is easier for a(n) _____ to go through the _____ of a(n) _____ than for a person who _____ to enter God's kingdom!" Give this example: "It is easier for an elephant to go through a keyhole than for a person who lies like Satan to enter God's kingdom!"

If students need help to complete this exercise, have them turn to 1 Corinthians 6:9, 10 and/or Galatians 5:19-21. The entries in those passages can help your students fill in the fourth blank of the exercise. To wrap up this segment, discuss the "walls" your students filled in to begin the session.

INTO LIFE

Make five handouts of the following quotes, one quote on each handout. Distribute one to each of five class members. Ask them to stand and read them expressively in the order given:

1. "Few rich men own their property; their property owns them" (Robert Ingersoll, nineteenth-century agnostic). 2. "Many speak the truth when they say that they despise riches, but they mean the riches possessed by other men" (Charles Caleb Colton, nineteenth-century writer and Church of England minister). 3. "My riches consist not in the extent of my possessions but in the fewness of my wants" (Joseph Brotherton, nineteenth-century Christian minister and English

Parliamentary reformer). 4. "To suppose, as we all suppose, that we could be rich and not behave as the rich behave, is like supposing that we could drink all day and stay sober" (Logan Pearsall Smith, twentieth-century Anglo-American essayist). 5. "A man's life does not consist in the abundance of his possessions" (Jesus, in Luke 12:15).

Suggest that your class use Luke 12:13-34 devotionally day by day in the coming week. The section is 22 verses in length, and it can be divided this way: verses 13-15 for Monday; verses 16-20 for Tuesday; verses 21-23 for Wednesday; verses 24-26 for Thursday; verses 27-31 for Friday; and verses 32-34 for Saturday. Suggest that your students write down one important truth regarding life and riches each day as they work through these verses. Those who like to do so may bring their lists to class for sharing and review next Sunday. Distribute copies of one or both of the reproducible activities on page 123 as students depart.

A HOLY PEOPLE

LESSON 9

INTRODUCTION

A. THE AGE OF UNHOLINESS

I recently attended a baseball game with my family. After being seated, I was bothered to hear a stream of expletives from the man behind me. This was joined by a woman's voice, equally foul. Then I was truly surprised to hear a third voice, a young child who was also a potty mouth. I quickly realized that this was a family talking in their normal conversation patterns without concern for being in public. Words that are offensive or irreverent to many people were commonplace for them.

I am not without failings in this area, but I do guard my speech and strive for conversation that is pleasing to God. In other words, although my efforts may fall short, I seek to be holy in what comes from my mouth.

We seem to be living in an age of unholiness. It is a time of moral chaos and uncertainty. Many today believe that the most important value in life is personal freedom and independence. Anyone who would impose standards or rules is intolerant. Ironically, such intolerance is not to be tolerated. Yet holiness is expected of the people of God.

The biblical understanding of holiness has two important aspects. First, holiness implies a separation, a consecration. That which is holy is set apart. It is neither worldly nor commonplace (see Leviticus 10:10; 20:26; Ezekiel 22:26; 42:20; 44:23; compare Hebrews 7:26). Second, that which is holy is morally pure. It is clean and untainted by sin (see Philippians 2:15). These dual aspects are illustrated in Psalm 24:3, 4. There the one who wants to ascend the holy hill of the Lord (separation from the world) must have clean hands (moral purity).

Holiness, then, is somewhat measurable because it involves standards and invites comparisons. All standards and comparisons for holiness come back to God, for he alone is absolutely holy (1 Samuel 2:2). We must depend on the power of God to achieve holiness. We are made holy (sanctified) through the cleansing power of the Holy Spirit (see 2 Thessalonians 2:13). This is our imperative for abstaining from sin at every opportunity (1 Thessalonians 4:3). So, yes, we live in an age of growing, strident, and public unholiness. But we are still called to be holy in word and deed.

B. LESSON BACKGROUND

Many Christians today consider Paul to be the greatest of the apostles because he wrote so much of the New Testament. But many in the first century probably considered Peter to be the greatest apostle. After all, he had been an eyewitness to the momentous events of Jesus' ministry. Peter also emerged as the leader of the Jerusalem church after Jesus' ascension.

Peter's prominence in the early church may be seen in Acts 12. Here King Herod Agrippa I discovered that the execution of a church leader increased

DEVOTIONAL READING:
DEUTERONOMY 7:6-11
BACKGROUND SCRIPTURE:
1 PETER 1
PRINTED TEXT:
1 PETER 1:13-25

LESSON AIMS

After participating in this lesson, each student will be able to:

1. Tell what Peter says is the source and the evidence of holiness in the life of a Christian.

2. Illustrate the need for holy living among Christians today.

3. Express to the class one example of personal holiness that he or she has seen in another person and intends to emulate.

Nov
1

KEY VERSES

Just as he who called you is holy, so be holy in all you do; for it is written: "Be holy, because I am holy."
—1 Peter 1:15, 16

his popularity among the nonbelieving Jews. His first victim was James, the brother of John. This choice seems to have been made arbitrarily and is not explained. When Herod realized its effect, however, he sought to take the life of the biggest fish in the Christian pond: Peter. At the time he was both the public face of the church and its primary leader. To lose him would have been a crippling blow; Acts 12 tells the story of Peter's miraculous deliverance.

Although not documented in the New Testament, reliable tradition has Peter traveling extensively outside of Palestine (compare 1 Corinthians 9:5). Strong tradition claims that Peter ended up in Rome sometime during the AD 60s. There he met his death under the persecutions of Emperor Nero, about AD 67 or 68. One often-repeated tradition says that Peter was crucified upside down at his own request, claiming that he was not worthy to receive death in the same manner as Jesus (see John 21:18, 19 for a reference to Peter's death).

While in Rome, Peter wrote two short letters that have been preserved in the New Testament. At least the first one was written with the help of Silas (1 Peter 5:12). This letter mentions being in "Babylon" (5:13), a code term for the city of Rome. The Jews referred to Rome as Babylon because it was the oppressor of their nation.

Peter's first letter is addressed to people in "Pontus, Galatia, Cappadocia, Asia and Bithynia" (1 Peter 1:1). These were Roman provinces located in modern Turkey and may have been visited by Peter during his travels. Peter knew that the recipients of this letter were confronted with persecution (see 1 Peter 3:13-15). Thus he gave them instructions that called them to live holy lives even when faced with this threat. This theme—holiness in spite of persecution—makes 1 Peter a timeless resource for the church. Every generation of believers encounters persecution.

I. MOTIVATION FOR HOLINESS (1 PETER 1:13-16)
A. Sober Anticipation (v. 13)
13. Therefore, prepare your minds for action; be self-controlled; set your hope fully on the grace to be given you when Jesus Christ is revealed.

To *prepare your minds for action* is akin to our expressions "roll up your sleeves" or "put on your work gloves." Peter is advising the readers to prepare mentally for the ordeal ahead (compare Luke 12:35).

This is reinforced by several other expressions. By instructing them to *be self-controlled*, Peter is asking the readers to get serious, because what lies ahead will not be fun. He also gives them a focus point: they are to think about the time *when Jesus Christ is revealed.* This is a reference to the *grace* we gain when we remember that Christ has not abandoned his people. He has promised to return and take his faithful ones home to be with him forever (1 Thessalonians 4:17).

B. Wise Obedience (v. 14)
14. As obedient children, do not conform to the evil desires you had when you lived in ignorance.

Christian parents are faced with the challenge of raising their children to live holy, godly lives. What motivation to this end can those parents give the children that will last a lifetime?

Peter faces this same issue when writing to his *children* in the faith. For Peter, the preparation for persecution is more than mental toughness. It should manifest itself in the *obedient* lifestyle activities of the believer. Will we strive to

In what ways can you "roll up your sleeves" for the kingdom of God?

be obedient in the matters of godly behavior? Will the general passions of our flesh be the controlling factor? For Peter, such fleshly *desires* are self-destructive (1 Peter 2:11; compare Romans 12:2; Ephesians 2:3; 4:17, 18). We should no longer yield to them after escaping the *ignorance* of unbelief.

IGNORANCE

The English poet Thomas Gray observed in 1742, "Where ignorance is bliss, 'tis folly to be wise." We may reasonably wonder what happens when ignorance is not bliss!

When I was a young boy, I read a lot of Superman and Batman comic books. Flying did not seem to be that difficult, particularly if a person had a large cape such as these two comic book figures wore. I had also seen pictures of parachutists, and I figured that if the principle worked for them, it should work for me. So one day I took a blanket off my bed, climbed up about 15 feet in an oak tree in our backyard, and prepared to descend gently with my homemade parachute.

I jumped—and hit the ground very hard. The blanket-parachute did not slow me down at all. Fortunately, I didn't break any bones, but the episode did shatter my faith in my parachutist abilities. There were a few laws of physics of which I was ignorant, and it wasn't bliss.

This principle applies in other situations. People who drive at high rates of speed are often ignorant of the risks. Eating unwashed vegetables in a foreign country often produces something far less than bliss. That's why Peter counsels against living according to the standards of our former days of ignorance. Instead, we are to live in obedience to spiritual principles.   —J. B. N.

Visual for Lesson 9. Point to this visual as you introduce the question below. Also ask, "What is your own starting point for greater holiness?"

C. DIVINE IMITATION (vv. 15, 16)

15, 16. But just as he who called you is holy, so be holy in all you do; for it is written: "Be holy, because I am holy."

Peter quotes Leviticus 19:2. The history of the church records many examples of men and women who have sought to *be holy*. The church today offers many examples also of those who struggle mightily to expunge sin and live holy lives. Yet every one of these wonderful people has failed at some level. No human being (other than Jesus when he was in the flesh) can be seen as an absolute, perfect example of holiness.

We should not conclude that we cannot be part of the people of God unless our lives are sterling examples of holiness. Holiness is not an exclusionary tactic by God; it is an inclusionary one. By yielding our lives to him and obediently serving him, he invites us to participate in his holiness.

The church is holy because God is holy and he has consecrated it. It is not made up of people who have achieved personal perfection, but of sinners who have been sanctified by God's grace. This marvelous gift serves as a powerful motivation for us to work hard at the elimination of sinful, unholy behavior. While God's gracious sanctification of the believer is a free gift, personal holiness comes from radical self-sacrifice and discipline.

II. COST OF HOLINESS (1 PETER 1:17-21)

A. REVERENT LIVING (v. 17)

17. Since you call on a Father who judges each man's work impartially, live your lives as strangers here in reverent fear.

Acts 10:34, offering a statement made by Peter many years earlier, also affirms that "God does not show favoritism." This means that social

WHAT DO YOU THINK?

In what specific areas do you need to make holiness a higher priority? What hindrances will you overcome to do this?

Daily Bible Readings

Monday, Oct. 26—
Chosen by a Loving God
(Deuteronomy 7:6-11)

Tuesday, Oct. 27—
Keeping the Covenant
(Exodus 19:1-6)

Wednesday, Oct. 28—A
Reminder to Obey (Numbers
15:37-41)

Thursday, Oct. 29—
Waiting for the Holy Spirit
(Acts 1:1-11)

Friday, Oct. 30—Filled
with the Holy Spirit (Acts
2:1-4)

Saturday, Oct. 31—Born
into a Living Hope (1 Peter 1:
1-12)

Sunday, Nov. 1—Called
to Holy Living (1 Peter 1:
13-25)

How to Say It

Asia. AY-zha.
Babylon. BAB-uh-lun.
Bereans. Buh-REE-unz.
Bithynia. Bih-THIN-ee-uh.
Cappadocia. Kap-uh-DOE-
   shuh.
Galatia. Guh-LAY-shuh.
Herod Agrippa.
   HAIR-ud Uh-GRIP-puh.
Jerusalem. Juh-ROO-suh-lem.
Leviticus. Leh-VIT-ih-kus.
Pontus. PON-tuss.
Silas. SIGH-luss.

status, race, gender, or other human standards have no role in personal holiness. Being rich does not help one be holy, for holiness cannot be purchased. Likewise, being poor is of no advantage in the pursuit of holiness, for lack of material goods does not equal sanctification. We are to live *in reverent fear*, in trembling respect of God's standards and expectations.

B. Precious Redemption (vv. 18-20)

18. For you know that it was not with perishable things such as silver or gold that you were redeemed from the empty way of life handed down to you from your forefathers,

This verse touches on the familiar biblical theme of redemption, but with a different twist. Peter reminds us that there is more to Christian redemption than a rescue from the death penalty of sin. We are also redeemed from the *empty way of life* of tradition.

Peter implies that many people assume that money is the answer to life's challenges. A common perception is that *silver* and *gold* can buy happiness and provide escape from life's difficulties. Under this line of reasoning, wealth is an end unto itself.

The Christian perspective will not allow for this, however. Wealth can make us believe the lie of independence, which is that we don't need God or his holiness (see last week's lesson). Money is not evil, but it cannot save us.

19. . . . but with the precious blood of Christ, a lamb without blemish or defect.

When we adopt an eternal perspective, we realize that true redemption is possible only through the atoning sacrifice of Jesus on the cross. At this point Peter invokes the image of the Passover *lamb* to describe Jesus (see 1 Corinthians 5:7). We are reminded of the great cost of this sacrifice for God. Jesus, his Son, was his perfect lamb; as such, he served as the necessary sacrifice to take away the world's sin (John 1:29).

20. He was chosen before the creation of the world, but was revealed in these last times for your sake.

God's holy plan for our salvation is not an afterthought or improvised plan. It has been ordained *before the creation of the world.* God's love for us is so deep that he planned for human redemption even before anyone had sinned. This is one of those places where we must scratch our heads a little and admit that we don't fully comprehend. We simply rejoice that God's love has been *revealed* to us through the saving acts of Jesus Christ.

C. Faithful Hope (v. 21)

21. Through him you believe in God, who raised him from the dead and glorified him, and so your faith and hope are in God.

Peter's eternal perspective allows him to see the ultimate goal of God's plan. The sacrificial death of Jesus was followed by his resurrection and exaltation in Heaven. The focus of our *faith* is not just a bloodstained cross or an empty tomb. It is also the mighty God of the universe, who reigns from Heaven with Jesus at his right hand.

From this perspective, the need for holiness becomes clear. We place our faith in God, and all of our hopes rest in him. How, then, can we maintain this relationship if we allow unholiness to win the day in our lifestyles? We become like Isaiah, who cried "Woe to me!" when he experienced God's holiness (Isaiah 6:5). Our own experience of God's absolute purity is a powerful motivation for us to forsake our futile, sinful ways and be like him.

III. APPLICATION OF HOLINESS (1 PETER 1:22-25)
A. AS LOVE (v. 22)
22. *Now that you have purified yourselves by obeying the truth so that you have sincere love for your brothers, love one another deeply, from the heart.*

Peter seems be a bottom-line guy. Talk is good, but action is better. Therefore, he follows up his doctrinal discussion of holiness with some practical advice for our quest of personal holiness.

Peter's action plan is surprisingly simple: show holiness by loving others. He says we must love *deeply,* meaning it must become a passion. It must be *sincere,* for there is no hypocrisy in true holiness. It must come *from the heart,* for lip-service holiness is worthless.

Peter's picture of a person pursuing holiness is neither that of the austere, unsmiling killjoy nor the disconnected, head-in-the-clouds mystic. We offer our obedience with a view to holiness when we are warm, generous, and forgiving to our Christian brothers and sisters (compare John 13:34; Romans 12:10).

B. AS REBIRTH (vv. 23-25)
23. *For you have been born again, not of perishable seed, but of imperishable, through the living and enduring word of God.*

When we commit to the pursuit of holiness, we adopt a new perspective, a new set of priorities. Our focus has shifted away from ourselves and toward God and his people. Our desire is to serve him, not ourselves. We "put on the new self," the person like God in "true righteousness and holiness" (Ephesians 4:24).

We do not instinctively know how to do this, however. This is why Peter ends this section by reminding his readers of a key factor in maintaining holiness: the *word of God.* Scripture guides God's people in the ways of righteousness. It has done so for thousands of years. It is *imperishable* and eternal. It will never fail us.

CORRUPTIBLE SEED
Genetic engineering, sometimes called biotechnology, is big business these days. Essentially, it means modifying the genetic material from a certain form of life (either animal or vegetable) to produce a different end result—hopefully, a better end result.

Those in favor of the procedure claim it can mean vast improvement in our quality of life. This can apply to improved vegetables, improved meat products from engineered animals, even superior medicines. The claim is that genetically engineered food can yield larger harvests and improved nutrition. It is now estimated that 60 percent of all food in America contains genetically altered material.

Opponents of genetic engineering contend that no one knows what the ultimate results are with these changed organisms. Some experiments have already failed because the mutations did not have long-term viability. Engineered petunias lost fertility and experienced altered leaf and root structures. Engineered salmon grew too fast and turned green. There is also concern about

WHAT DO YOU THINK?
How is faith and hope in God revealed in the lives of Christians in general and in your life in particular?

WHAT DO YOU THINK?
What does unfeigned or sincere love look like?

whether these new products will cross-fertilize with the native species and upset the balance of major ecosystems.

It is interesting to observe that Peter states that when we are born again, we are born of incorruptible seed. Corruptible seed may be liable to various scientific experiments aimed at improvement, but our spiritual DNA is not subject to scientific tampering! God guarantees it.   —J. B. N.

24, 25. For,
"All men are like grass,
    and all their glory is like the flowers of the field;
the grass withers and the flowers fall,
    but the word of the Lord stands forever."
And this is the word that was preached to you.

Peter reinforces the abiding value of the Word of God by quoting Isaiah 40:6-8. Scripture is contrasted with the annual cycle of *grass* and *flowers.* These things grow for a time and then die (compare James 1:10, 11). Such a fleeting life is like the *glory* of man, for the famous of today are the forgotten of tomorrow.

The enduring nature of *the word of the Lord* stands in stark contrast with *all men.* The central aspect of Scripture for Christians is the good news about Jesus Christ. He is "the Holy One of God" (John 6:69) who atoned for our sins. He offers the cleansing power of the Holy Spirit to all who believe in him.

CONCLUSION

Christians are bound to God and to each other by the new covenant provided by the atoning blood of Christ. The first-century church was faced with the challenge of living out this covenant in the midst of hostile surroundings. This situation was well understood by Simon Peter, that great apostle of the first century, for he had experienced it firsthand. This final unit of the quarter focuses on various aspects of the church as the covenant community of God. This week's lesson begins the series by examining the issue of holiness within the covenant community as it struggled to live faithfully according to the call of Jesus.

Some Christians are perplexed when it comes to personal holiness. Whose responsibility is it? If it is strictly our job, we are inadequate and doomed to failure before we begin. If it is God's work, then why should we be concerned about it? Shouldn't we just get out of the way and let God do it? This way of thinking misses the true basis for Christian holiness. We do not seek holiness as a way of earning God's favor. To the contrary, we have the possibility of holiness because God has been gracious to us.

We don't work to eliminate sin so that we can get merit points in God's ledger. Through the work of Christ we already are in God's ledger, the Book of Life (Revelation 20:12, 15; 21:27). He helps us be pure and holy. He does so (and wants to do so) because the unholy elements of life are the things that destroy us.

Holiness, then, is not to be a duty, but a joy. We rejoice in the holy name of the Lord (see Psalm 105:3). The "prospect of the righteous is joy" (Proverbs 10:28), the great hope of being at peace with our Creator and content to serve him.

WHAT DO YOU THINK?

How do you demonstrate confidence in the Word of the Lord?

So how does one "be holy"? It does not happen by receding into a life of passivity. It happens, rather, by pursuing righteousness with all the strength Jesus gives us to do so.

THOUGHT TO REMEMBER
Holiness is a must.
Holiness is our joy.

Discovery Learning

The following is an alternative lesson plan emphasizing learning activities.
Classes desiring such student involvement will find these suggestions helpful. At the
back of this book are reproducible student pages to further enhance activity learning.

INTO THE LESSON

Place copies of the reproducible exercise "How to Be Holy" from page 124 for your early arrivers to work on. Begin class by asking, "How many of you remember singing the children's song 'Oh Be Careful Little Eyes What You See'? We're going to sing the first three stanzas of that song right now about the eyes, the ears, and the mouth." If you think some students will be unfamiliar with it, have the words printed out for them or written on the board:

Oh, be careful little eyes [ears/mouth] what you see [hear/say].
Oh, be careful little eyes [ears/mouth] what you see [hear/say].
For the Father up above is looking down in love.
Oh, be careful little eyes [ears/mouth] what you see [hear/say].

If your class is unfamiliar with the tune, then read it as a poem. After the song, divide the class into three small groups and assign one group each the topics of the eyes, the ears, and the mouth. (If your class is smaller, use pairs; if your class is larger, form extra groups and duplicate the assignments.) Ask groups to discuss the following questions as they relate to their assigned body part: 1. If we were more careful with our [eyes/ears/mouth], what are some things we should avoid? 2. What are some resources that would help us do better in this area? 3. How should an awareness of "the Father . . . looking down in love" make us more careful about what we do?

After seven minutes say, "I'm sure you all came up with some good ways to be more careful about how we live. In today's lesson Peter also gives us several excellent reasons for being careful in what we do."

Ask students to help brainstorm a list of everything they know about the apostle Peter. Ask someone to write each answer on the board. Then say, "Peter is a very familiar figure to many of us, but the two letters he wrote may not be as familiar. Over the next five weeks we'll be working through Peter's letters, which he wrote to encourage Christians experiencing persecution. Today we'll see how he taught them and us the importance of being holy, no matter what is going on in our lives."

INTO THE WORD

Write the heading *1 Peter 1:13-25* on the board. Then distribute handouts with the following list of four-word paraphrases, one for each verse. Ask students to work within their previous groups or pairs to match each paraphrase with one of the verses. (The suggested answers are in italics, but do not include them with the handout; the verse order is randomized here.)

1. Pure and perfect lamb *(v. 19)*. 2. Here today, gone tomorrow *(v. 24)*. 3. Called to be holy *(v. 15)*. 4. Time to get serious *(v. 13)*. 5. Money can't buy redemption *(v. 18)*. 6. Glory be to Jesus *(v. 21)*. 7. What not to do *(v. 14)*. 8. Holy people love people *(v. 22)*. 9. Preaching packs a punch *(v. 25)*. 10. Best reason for holiness *(v. 16)*. 11. God's plan comes together *(v. 20)*. 12. The Word goes on *(v. 23)*. 13. The Father judges fairly *(v. 17)*.

After groups finish, ask each in turn to give an answer as you read down the list. Then use the following statements and questions to lead a discussion of Peter's teaching concerning holiness: 1. How can an awareness of Christ's return help us be more serious about our walk with the Lord? 2. What can we do to change from a mind-set of "my life is mine to live as I please" to "my life belongs to God, and I live to please him"? 3. How can the truth that we have been redeemed by the precious blood of Jesus help us to want to live holier lives?

4. Which do you think is the more difficult way to be holy: to be actively involved in loving others or to live apart from the world? Or is this a false choice? Why do you say this?

INTO LIFE

Conclude the lesson by saying, "If we define holiness as 'the ability and desire to live for God, to turn our backs on sin, and to love others,' how many people do you know are doing a good job of being holy? If you had to come up with *The Holiest Christian Award* for 2009, whom would you nominate?" (If you think this activity will be too controversial, instead have students pair off to share stories of people whom they know are living holy lives.) Distribute copies of the reproducible exercise "Holiness Habits" from page 124 as students depart.

A CHOSEN PEOPLE

LESSON 10

INTRODUCTION

A. BUILDING PROJECTS

"Measure twice, cut once." "Fresh paint covers a multitude of mistakes." "A job worth doing is worth doing right." These and many other axioms form the folk wisdom of remodelers and their construction projects. One engaged in such work soon learns, however, that slogans must be backed up by the right tools, quality materials, a good plan, and practiced skills.

Unfortunately, many church buildings look as if they have been thrown together over the years by amateurs with little advance planning. To achieve quality results in building projects requires the patience, diligence, and planning abilities of a skilled builder. The true craftsman will not use cull lumber or sloppy workers. The master will not proceed with half-baked plans. The true artisan will not hurry the project to conclusion by cutting corners or compromising the design.

The New Testament sometimes pictures the church as a spiritual "house," an edifice constructed by God for his glory. Paul uses this construction metaphor to picture the church as a temple built on the foundation of the apostles with Jesus as the cornerstone (Ephesians 2:20, 21; compare 1 Corinthians 3:9-11).

God is the master craftsman with the perfect plan. We are his building material, and he has refined us and sanctified us through his Spirit to be just as he desires. We are built by God to be his chosen household, his holy habitation, or dwelling (Ephesians 2:22).

B. LESSON BACKGROUND

In the ancient world, building construction was much more difficult than it is today. There were no big-box construction supply stores in Jerusalem or Rome. There was no precut lumber or pre-hung doors.

Abandoned structures provided the most readily available construction material, particularly in terms of their stone blocks. If one was building a structure out of stone, it was much easier to take a block from an older building, clean and dress it a bit, and use it immediately. The burdensome alternative was to find a nearby source of suitable stone, set up a quarry operation, and transport blocks to the construction site.

There were cheaper alternatives to stone buildings, of course. Tents could be lavish and spacious, but these lacked a sense of permanence and grandeur. Bricks could be made on site if the right type of soil was present, but bricks might be limited in size and function. Wood was adaptable for many purposes, of course. But most of the forested areas surrounding cities had long been harvested. So large amounts of timber usually had to be imported from considerable distances (compare 1 Kings 5). Wood was susceptible to rot, and therefore it lacked the durability of stone.

DEVOTIONAL READING:
DEUTERONOMY 10:10-15
BACKGROUND SCRIPTURE:
1 PETER 2:1-17
PRINTED TEXT:
1 PETER 2:1-10

LESSON AIMS

After participating in this lesson, each student will be able to:

1. Summarize Peter's description of the life of "chosen" people.

2. Explain the metaphors in Peter's description, showing their relevance to modern society.

3. Suggest one specific way to "declare the praises of him who called you."

Nov
8

KEY VERSE

You are a chosen people, a royal priesthood, a holy nation, a people belonging to God, that you may declare the praises of him who called you out of darkness into his wonderful light.

—1 Peter 2:9

LESSON 10 NOTES

HOW TO SAY IT

Agrippa. Uh-GRIP-puh.
anticarcinogen.
*   an-tee-kar-SIN-uh-jen.*
Corinthians. Ko-RIN-thee-
*   unz (th as in thin).*
Herod. HAIR-ud.
Hosea. Ho-ZAY-uh.
Jerusalem. Juh-ROO-suh-lem.
levitical. leh-VIT-ih-kul.
Lo-Ammi. Lo-AM-my.
Lo-Ruhamah.
*   Lo-Roo-HAH-muh.*
Messiah. Meh-SIGH-uh.
Pantheon. PAN-the-ahn.
Zion. ZI-un.

WHAT DO YOU THINK?

Which of the unhealthy, toxic attitudes and actions Peter mentions gives Christians the most trouble? How do we lay these aside?

All things considered, then, there was no substitute for stone when erecting grand public buildings such as temples. An example that Peter was familiar with was the Jerusalem temple as reconstructed by Herod the Great. Herod's builders reconstructed the foundation of the temple mount using massive "ashlars" or foundation stones. The largest of these that survives has dimensions of 12' x 12' x 48' and weighs an estimated 400 tons. Even the most ambitious of the temple destroyers since Herod has been unable to budge or crack this monolith.

While Peter does not mention the Jerusalem temple specifically in today's lesson text, he does seem to have it in mind. We know that he was a frequent visitor to the temple courts when in the holy city (see Acts 3:1; 5:42). If he were in Rome at the time he penned 1 Peter, he also would have witnessed the massive stone structures of that imperial city. These included the colossal structures of the Temple of Jupiter and the original Pantheon of Agrippa.

We should remember the general context and purpose of Peter's letters: advice on how to live as Christians in the midst of hostile nonbelievers. Peter draws on his deep knowledge of the Old Testament and his rich Jewish heritage to present his case for the church as a holy, exemplary people who are dedicated to the service of God.

I. CHOOSING A SPIRITUAL DIET (1 PETER 2:1-3)

A. ELIMINATE TOXIC FOOD (v. 1)

1. Therefore, rid yourselves of all malice and all deceit, hypocrisy, envy, and slander of every kind.

Peter begins his advice on spiritual diet with a list of five attitudes and actions that should be avoided by believers. They are toxic and will poison the soul. He divides the five into three groupings.

First, he exhorts his readers to eliminate *all malice*. This has the sense of evil actions in general. Such actions can be motivated by greed, spite, jealousy, or other moral failings. But the result is an action that intends to harm another person. The word *malice* can have the connotation of "ugly," the opposite of what is beautiful or lovely (see Philippians 4:8).

The second grouping consists of *deceit, hypocrisy,* and *envy.* These are attitudes or personality traits. *Deceit* is an orientation of general dishonesty. It describes persons who may be counted on to lie if it benefits them in some way. *Hypocrisy* describes deep insincerity. The hypocritical person will play whatever role is most beneficial to him or her on a personal level. Today, we would describe this as "phoniness." The third attitude in this grouping is *envy.* This bitter, restless spirit always begrudges the success or nice possessions of others. Envy is the opposite of gratitude, of contentment with what God has given to you (see 1 Timothy 6:8).

The last of the three groupings consists of the fifth spiritual poison of *slander of every kind.* This verbal back-stabbing behavior is the manifestation of the previous three: a deceitful person who feigns innocence and friendship yet harbors deep resentment and envy. Such persons work behind the scenes to damage the reputation of those whom they dislike.

B. THRIVE ON HEALTHY FOOD (vv. 2, 3)

2, 3. Like newborn babies, crave pure spiritual milk, so that by it you may grow up in your salvation, now that you have tasted that the Lord is good.

Peter has already reminded us of the eternal Word of God as that which results in our new birth as believers. He pictures it as spiritual seed planted in our souls (1 Peter 1:23-25, last week's lesson). Now he expands this to teach us that the Word (*spiritual milk*) is also a source for ongoing growth.

Just as the *newborn* baby denied nourishment will die, so will the Christian who neglects God's Word. For Peter, this is primarily the Jewish Scriptures, our Old Testament. But Peter also realizes that the New Testament Scriptures are coming into existence in his day (2 Peter 3:16). Even in his old age, Peter loved Scripture. He testifies that he, the great apostle, continued to grow spiritually by absorbing more truths from God's Word. He acknowledges this by thanking the source of the Word, our *Lord* who *is good*.

People are more cautious these days about what ingredients are included in the foods they eat. Some avoid trans-fats, preservatives, and various additives. But how careful are we about our spiritual diet? Do we shun the unhealthy and feast on the healthy in this realm?

MILK

Milk is an essential ingredient of life, particularly for newborns. For virtually all mammals, milk is produced for the newborn by the mother. In fact milk production is tied directly to the birth of the infant; without pregnancy and birth, there is no milk production.

As a city-bred boy, I did not initially understand this. It wasn't until I was in graduate school that I realized the connection. I thought cows produced milk as automatically as sheep produce wool, not realizing the gestation of a baby is required to initiate milk production.

Those who promote the consumption of milk point out that it provides essential nutrients, vitamins and minerals. Chief among these is Vitamin D and calcium, but milk (and other dairy products) also provide healthy amounts of protein. Evidence exists that milk also provides some anticarcinogens. A key benefit for nursing infants is that mother's milk provides antibodies to get the baby off to a healthy start. These have both antibacterial and antiviral properties. In fact, mother's milk seems to have exactly the right amount of protein, calories, and antibodies to keep a baby healthy.

Peter and others of the first century certainly were not aware of all these scientific facts. Even so, Peter presumed the healthy practice of babies being fed milk. Peter knew what he was talking about. Just as a physical milk is crucial to the health and vitality of the baby, so is spiritual milk essential to the health and vitality of the infant Christian. The Bible tells us that eventually we are to move from milk to the meat of the Word of God (1 Corinthians 3:2; Hebrews 5:11-14). But milk comes first.   —J. B. N.

II. CHOOSING A BUILDING MATERIAL (1 PETER 2:4-8)
A. BLOCKS FOR THE WALLS (vv. 4, 5)
4. As you come to him, the living Stone—rejected by men but chosen by God and precious to him—

In the verses that follow, Peter displays the value of Scripture by weaving together several themes from the Old Testament. In so doing, he intends to encourage his beleaguered readers. He begins this section by drawing on Psalm 118:22. This passage is applied by Jesus to his own person in Matthew 21:42. Peter himself used it in his earliest preaching (Acts 4:11).

DAILY BIBLE READINGS

Monday, Nov. 2— *Chosen Out of All People (Deuteronomy 10:10-15)*

Tuesday, Nov. 3—A *Happy People (Psalm 33: 4-12)*

Wednesday, Nov. 4— *Hope in God and God's Love (Psalm 33:13-22)*

Thursday, Nov. 5— *Chosen as God's Witnesses (Acts 10:34-43)*

Friday, Nov. 6—A People *One in Heart and Soul (Acts 4:31-37)*

Saturday, Nov. 7—Free *Servants of God (1 Peter 2: 11-17)*

Sunday, Nov. 8—God's *Own People (1 Peter 2:1-10)*

WHAT DO YOU THINK?

In addition to Jesus himself, what are some things that people reject that God considers precious? How can we make sure we continue to have God's point of view on these things?

WHAT DO YOU THINK?

What does it mean for you to be a "stone" in God's house?

God's building project is a spiritual house made up of people. It started with the first *chosen* and *living stone,* namely Jesus. But he was *rejected* by his human evaluators. They had no insight into the fact that Jesus, the Son of God, was the most *precious* of all human beings. This lack of recognition led to Jesus' death (see 1 Corinthians 2:8). This does not negate the truth that Jesus is indeed the cornerstone for the church (see Ephesians 2:20).

5. . . . *you also, like living stones, are being built into a spiritual house to be a holy priesthood, offering spiritual sacrifices acceptable to God through Jesus Christ.*

One stone does not make a building no matter how immense it may be. God's *spiritual house* requires other *living stones.* These are the believers—us.

Peter also now reveals the nature of this spiritual house. It is a temple, a place of worship. It is where priests offer *sacrifices* to God. Yet it is a *spiritual* temple, and the sacrifices are spiritual in nature. Too often, we view the church as a place where our needs are met. Peter gives us the picture of an organization devoted to service, to self-denial, to commitment because we are a *holy priesthood.*

Peter is not saying that the priestly class of God's people has been eliminated. He is saying, rather, that it has been expanded. It now includes all believers. It is not that I don't need a priest because I am now a priest. It is, rather, that any believer can minister to me, and I can minister to any fellow believer. I can perform intercession, that most important of priestly functions, by praying for another believer at any time or place. There is no longer a need for designated intermediaries as was the case with the Old Testament levitical priesthood because we can all assume this function.

B. CUSTOM CORNERSTONE (v. 6)

6. *For in Scripture it says:*
    "See, I lay a stone in Zion,
      a chosen and precious cornerstone,
    and the one who trusts in him
      will never be put to shame."

Peter returns to the Old Testament to reinforce the divine plan for Christ to be the *cornerstone* of the church. By using a free quotation of Isaiah 28:16, Peter emphasizes that Jesus is the essential *stone* of the building, that Jesus is the *chosen* stone, and that Jesus is the *precious* stone, God's very Son. This description is followed by a promise: faith in God's essential, chosen, and precious Messiah will be rewarded.

C. WORK-SITE HAZARDS (vv. 7, 8)

7. *Now to you who believe, this stone is precious. But to those who do not believe,*
    "The stone the builders rejected
      has become the capstone,"

Not every building *stone* delivered to a construction site can be used by the stonemasons. One might have a small crack that a mason knows will grow and become a disaster in later years. Another might have an unsightly blemish that will detract from the beauty of the finished building. This kind of evaluation process is natural. Similarly, when Jesus confronts us with his claims, it is natural for us to evaluate the truthfulness of those claims. We

WHAT DO YOU THINK?

In what areas of life have you experienced the preciousness of Christ? How do you share this fact with others?

dare not reach the wrong conclusion as the Jewish leaders did! They were *the builders* who *rejected* Jesus. Peter wants believers to find Jesus as *precious* as the Father does.

Peter equates unbelief with disobedience. In this regard, he likely has the unbelieving Jewish nation in mind. To equate faith with obedience does not imply salvation through works, but draws on the fact that both believing and obeying require a surrender of the will. Israel has not surrendered; it has rejected. The marvelous cornerstone of God results in stumbling (next verse).

8. . . . and,

  "A stone that causes men to stumble
    and a rock that makes them fall."

They stumble because they disobey the message—which is also what they were destined for.

The Greek word translated *makes them fall* is the source of our English word *scandal*. Paul uses the same Greek word to describe the Jewish reaction to his preaching of the cross in 1 Corinthians 1:23. The Jewish nation of Paul and Peter's day is scandalized to think that its Messiah had to be executed as a common criminal on a Roman cross.

Peter is resigned to this state of Jewish unbelief. He understands that God in his foreknowledge is aware that the enemies of the cross will reject the gospel, thus *they were destined for* this. We can be sure, however, that Peter's heart longs for the salvation of his nation, as does Paul's (Romans 9:1-3).

Of Clouds and Linings

There's an old saying that "every cloud has a silver lining"; but sometimes a silver lining has a cloud. There are advantages and disadvantages to almost every situation, depending on what one is looking for. Whether it's a *cloud with a silver lining* or a *silver lining with a cloud* depends on one's perspective.

To a farmer, a smooth, nicely plowed field is the silver lining that can be obtained only after the cloud of rocks is removed. I read recently of one man's reminiscences along these lines. As a 14-year-old, he and his dad would drive a tractor with a large scoop bucket across the fields. They would pick up various rocks, putting them in the scoop. When the scoop was full, they would dump the rocks in a corner of the field. The whole process was necessary because a rock the size of a softball could cause serious damage to a very expensive combine. Needless to say, the rocks were a great nuisance.

Yet what may be a cloud sometimes can turn into a silver lining. In the British Isles, farmers would be dismayed at the prospect of having to remove large stones that had worked up to the surface over the centuries. This meant having to engage in the backbreaking work of carrying those stones to the edge of the field. But this cloud of rocks then became a silver lining of useful stone fences that separated the fields. Even today many farms there are bordered by these fences.

Jesus is the cornerstone of our faith. But to the disobedient, he is a rock of offense. Sometimes a person must stumble over this rock of offense to realize how much of a cornerstone Jesus can and should be.   —J. B. N.

Visual for Lessons 6 & 10. *Point to this visual as you introduce the last question on the previous page. Also ask, "What life changes will you yet make for Christ?"*

III. CHOOSING A HOLY NATION (1 PETER 2:9, 10)

A. Selected for Royalty (v. 9)

9. But you are a chosen people, a royal priesthood, a holy nation, a people belonging to God, that you may declare the praises of him who called you out of darkness into his wonderful light.

PRAYER

Holy God, king of all, to you we offer our loyalty, our obedience, and our service. May your name be praised above all others, and may you build us into a holy church for your glory. We pray this in the name of your precious cornerstone, Jesus. Amen.

Peter continues to draw parallels between the nation of Israel and the church as he moves to the language of statehood. He does this to illustrate the nature of the church as the new people of God.

Peter lists four ways in which the church of Jesus is God's new nation. First, the church is a *chosen people*. Christ's church has not been granted its status because of its accomplishments, but because God selected it (compare his selection of Israel, Deuteronomy 7:6).

Second, for Peter the church is a *royal priesthood*. Those of royal lineage were separate from the priests in ancient Israel. In the church, believers are royalty because of their relationship to King Jesus. We are also priests in that we minister to one another.

Third, the church exists as a *holy nation*. The two concepts of *holiness* and *nationhood* draw on promises given to Israel at Mount Sinai immediately before the giving of the Ten Commandments. There God told the people that he intended them to be "a kingdom of priests" and "a holy nation" (Exodus 19:6). They were to be unlike any other people on the earth in their dedication and service to God and in God's favor to them.

Fourth, the church is seen as a *people belonging to God*. They are his unique possession. God does not share the church with any other god. He is a jealous God (see Exodus 34:14).

Why was this new people of God chosen? for what purpose? Peter portrays this in dramatic terms, describing God's act of choosing his new people as bringing them from spiritual *darkness* into the *wonderful light* of God's truth. The ultimate purpose, the church's "reason for being," is to *declare* his *praises*. The church does not exist for its own pleasure, but to glorify God in all it does.

B. ELECTED FOR MERCY (v. 10)

10. Once you were not a people, but now you are the people of God; once you had not received mercy, but now you have received mercy.

Peter ends this section by alluding to the story of the prophet Hosea and his unfaithful wife, Gomer. Hosea's second child was named Lo-Ruhamah, which means "no *mercy*" (Hosea 1:6). Hosea's third child was named Lo-Ammi, which means "not my *people*" (Hosea 1:9). This was in stark contrast with God's promise to bestow mercy and claim "my people" (Hosea 2:23). For Peter, the extension to non-Jews of the possibility of joining *the people of God* is a mighty act of mercy.

CONCLUSION

How would you react if you learned that the Queen of England were coming to visit your home? Would you clean, paint, and prepare carefully? Or would you let the trash accumulate until the house smelled like a landfill? Even if we are not British, most of us would feel honored to have a visit from royalty, and we would want to be seen at our best.

Within the church, there is (or should be) a real sense that all are royals. Do we act like royalty in the best sense of the word? Do we treat fellow Christians as if they are princes and princesses? Most of all, do we honor King Jesus in all we do? Are we his obedient servants?

One of the things that distinguished the Jews from other nations in the ancient world was their awareness of being a chosen people, a holy nation set

WHAT DO YOU THINK?

As God's chosen generation, royal priesthood, holy nation, and chosen people, how can we show forth his praises?

apart by God for his purposes. This role of being the holy people of God was continued in the church by its early leaders—leaders such as Peter. May we honor this role in the year 2010 and beyond as we work toward the unity of believers as a holy, royal nation for Jesus.

THOUGHT TO REMEMBER
God continues to build his people.

Discovery Learning

The following is an alternative lesson plan emphasizing learning activities. Classes desiring such student involvement will find these suggestions helpful. At the back of this book are reproducible student pages to further enhance activity learning.

INTO THE LESSON

Before class, prepare index cards that say *You are a chosen person*. Have enough cards so that about one in five students gets one, then tape the cards to the bottoms of various chairs. Taking into account the size of your class, ask students to form themselves into groups of any number except six. Then have students look under their chairs to see who has a card. Those who do will have a special privilege in the game of *Buzz* that you will play.

Each group is to count from 1 to 100, with each person calling a number in turn. However, when they get to a number that contains either a 6 or a multiple of 6, they must say *Buzz* instead. (Example: 1-2-3-4-5-Buzz-7-8-9-10-11-Buzz-13-14-15-Buzz-17-Buzz.) Those who get their turn wrong are out of the game. The counting continues until there is only one person left or they reach 100. However, all "chosen people" get a free pass for their first mistake. Give a small piece of candy to those who weren't eliminated and to all the "chosen people," win or lose.

Discuss the game by asking some of the following questions: "How did it feel to be a chosen person? How did the rest of you feel about the chosen people's special advantages? What did the chosen people do to earn the privilege of being chosen?" (They picked the right chair to sit in.) Then say, "In God's sight, Christians are the chosen people with special privileges." Pass around the bowl of candy again and invite those who didn't get candy the first time to take some. Then say, "Let's take a look at 1 Peter 2 to see what our special privileges include."

INTO THE WORD

Form three small groups, or keep the previous ones. Distribute one of the following assignments to each group. (Smaller classes can use pairs; larger classes can form more than three groups and double-up on assignments.) Say, "You have 15 minutes to work, but at my 2-minute warning switch immediately to question e."

Assignment #1: Read 1 Peter 2:1-3. (a) What negative attitudes and actions should Christians lay aside, and how would their lives improve by doing so? (b) In what ways does God's Word nourish one's spiritual life? (c) What does Peter say that makes us want more of God's Word? How does that work? (d) How does the Bible teach us ways to replace bad attitudes and actions with good ones? (e) What are the benefits of being a Christian that relate to these verses?

Assignment #2: Read 1 Peter 2:4-8. (a) What does it mean that Christians are part of God's spiritual house? (b) As part of God's royal priesthood, how do we offer up spiritual sacrifices? (c) In what way does having Jesus as our cornerstone give us a firm foundation for life? (d) What happens to those who reject Jesus as their cornerstone? (e) What are the benefits of being a Christian that relate to these verses?

Assignment #3: Read 1 Peter 2:9, 10. (a) In what way can the label *royal* be applied to Christians? (b) How can Christians act as priests to one another? (c) In what ways is the image of coming out of darkness into light a good metaphor for becoming a Christian? (d) How does a person's life change after becoming one of God's people? (e) What are the benefits of being a Christian that relate to these verses?

Make sure to give your two-minute warning. Then ask one person from each group to summarize answers on the board for all to see.

INTO LIFE

Ask for a show of hands of those who have a gym or health-club membership. Ask who took advantage of the membership in the past week. Inquire as to what privileges are included with that membership. Then ask, "What are some of the ways that a person might convince a friend to become a member of their gym?" (Answers may include inviting them to come and try it out, talking about the privileges that go along with membership, and showing how membership has personally benefited the member.)

After allowing time for class members to make several suggestions ask, "Which of these methods can we use to bring our friends into the church? Why does it seem easier to talk about gym membership than about being or becoming a Christian? What keeps us from explaining all the benefits of life in God's family to others?" (Do not ask all three questions at once; allow time for responses between each question.) Distribute copies of one or both of the reproducible activities on page 125 as students depart.

A SUFFERING PEOPLE

INTRODUCTION

A. HATRED OF ALL THINGS CHRISTIAN

In the last few years, we have received many news reports that trumpet radical opposition to Christianity in the Islamic (Muslim) world. It is illegal for a Muslim to convert to Christianity in some countries. Such a conversion may be punishable by death. It is easy for Westerners to condemn such intolerance.

However, there seems to be a creeping intolerance of Christianity in nations that have been historically identified as majority Christian. Christian symbols are banned from public places. Not long ago, Christmas trees (a marginal Christian symbol at best) were banned for a time from the airport in Seattle. Some schoolteachers feel free to discuss any religion in the classroom except Christianity.

We all have seen the headlines about huge monetary settlements for clergy abuse class-action suits. Yet those stories as reported seem to be heralded more for the damage they inflict on the church than the justice received by victims. Publicly funded art displays often include works that are intentionally offensive to Christians. But criticisms of such presentations are themselves attacked viciously. While there are exceptions, media portrayals of people of faith are often harsh and mean-spirited.

Why all this hostility toward the church and the Christian faith? Why are we belittled for wanting to be good moral people who seek to follow Jesus? First, we should understand that this is nothing new. From its earliest days, the church in Jerusalem was opposed by the Jewish authorities (Acts 7:54-60; 12:1-3; etc.). Jesus told his disciples to expect this treatment (see Luke 6:22; 12:11, 12).

Second, we should understand that these persecutions are directed primarily at our Lord Jesus Christ (Acts 22:7, 8). Jesus knew that the world would hate him and his message (see John 7:7; 15:18, 19), for he cut away religious hypocrisy and self-righteousness. It should not surprise us, then, if this hate is now directed toward Jesus' followers, his disciples in the current day (see 1 John 3:13). As we understand how this persecution affected those in the first century, we will be better prepared to understand our own situation.

B. LESSON BACKGROUND

At the beginning, Christianity was viewed as a sect of the Jewish faith (see Acts 24:5). Almost all the earliest Christians came out of Judaism. As Paul and others began to preach the gospel to Gentiles, the church faced its first great hurdle: the circumcision controversy.

Some proposed that Gentile men had to submit to circumcision in order to be considered Christians (Acts 15:1). What this really meant was that only

DEVOTIONAL READING:
1 CORINTHIANS 12:20-26
BACKGROUND SCRIPTURE:
1 PETER 4
PRINTED TEXT:
1 PETER 4:12-19

LESSON AIMS

After participating in this lesson, each student will be able to:

1. Describe the attitude toward suffering that Peter says the believer should have.

2. Tell how the suffering that Peter's first readers faced is similar to, and different from, the suffering of believers today.

3. Explain how he or she will rejoice in Jesus despite circumstances.

NOV
15

KEY VERSE

Those who suffer according to God's will should commit themselves to their faithful Creator and continue to do good.   —1 Peter 4:19

LESSON 11 NOTES

How to Say It

Babylonians.
  Bab-ih-LOW-nee-unz.
Ecclesiastes. Ik-LEEZ-ee-AS-
  teez.
Eliphaz. EL-ih-faz.
Galatians. Guh-LAY-shunz.
Isaiah. Eye-ZAY-uh.
Judaism. JOO-duh-izz-um
  or JOO-day-izz-um.
masochist. MA-suh-kist.
Nero. NEE-row.
synagogue. SIN-uh-gog.
Tacitus. TASS-ih-tus.

WHAT DO YOU THINK?

Why do some Christians continue to think it strange when they face trials, even though Peter says not to be surprised in this regard? How do we help those Christians?

Jews could become Christians, since being circumcised indicated conversion to Judaism. In a historic move, the Jerusalem Council affirmed that circumcision would not be required of Gentiles (Acts 15). The Christian faith was open to all.

However, the fallout from this (among other things) was that Christianity ceased to be viewed as a subset of Judaism; Christianity therefore lost certain protections under Roman law. The Romans were somewhat inclusive in their religions, absorbing aspects of the religious traditions from the peoples they conquered. Judaism, although not conforming to official Roman religion, was afforded a degree of protection due to its great antiquity and moral values. Jews were allowed to become full Roman citizens. When it became apparent that the church put forth a faith different from that found in the synagogue and was heavily populated by non-Jews, this protection no longer applied to Christians.

This opened the door for official persecution of Christians in Rome during the latter days of Nero's reign, in the mid- to late-60s AD. The Roman historian Tacitus records that Nero used the Christians of Rome as a scapegoat for the great fire that consumed much of the city in AD 64. There is no direct explanation for this horrible choice, except that those Christians were largely poor, powerless, and despised. So Nero picked a group that was already unpopular and had no ability to defend itself.

These persecutions included arrest and various types of inhumane torture and execution. This is the probable backdrop for Peter's two letters. As we read this week's lesson, we should remember that the church of Rome was either in the midst of these horrors, or the horrors were recent and fresh in the community's memory.

I. TRIAL OF FIRE (1 PETER 4:12-14)

A. EXPECT IT (v. 12)

12. Dear friends, do not be surprised at the painful trial you are suffering, as though something strange were happening to you.

Peter characterizes the persecutions his readers have faced as *painful*. And there is more pain ahead.

As we noted in the Lesson Background, the Roman historian Tacitus records the cruelties of Emperor Nero. These cruelties included tying Christians on poles, dousing them with oil, and then setting them afire to serve as human torches for his parties. Whether Peter speaks of *the painful trial* with this in mind we do not know. At any rate, Peter speaks with over 30 years' experience in being a disciple of Jesus. He knows that believers will be confronted by those who hate the church and are in a position to inflict *suffering*.

The Old Testament records the suffering of the righteous (example: Ecclesiastes 7:15; 8:14). The New Testament presumes that this will continue (Matthew 5:10). As long as evil persists in our world, evil people will hate the good and either take advantage or try to eliminate it. Righteous people following Christ as Lord should *not be surprised*.

B. REJOICE IN IT (v. 13)

13. But rejoice that you participate in the sufferings of Christ, so that you may be overjoyed when his glory is revealed.

Taken only on the surface, Peter's exhortation here sounds almost crazy. Derive joy from pain? Peter is no masochist, though. It is not the suffering that he glories in, but the privilege of sharing with Christ (compare Acts 5:41). In this we see the great humility of the apostle. He is not puffed up by his legendary stature in the Christian community, but is willing to suffer alongside other believers. Peter points to a way of being more like Jesus: being a partaker in his *sufferings.*

It is the person who enjoys this deep fellowship with Jesus who will be *overjoyed* when he is *revealed,* when he returns. When Christ comes again, he will come with judgment. His followers will share in this judging (see Matthew 19:28; 1 Corinthians 6:3).

We should consider this verse alongside Peter's earlier, perhaps difficult-to-understand statement that "he who has suffered in his body is done with sin." Peter wants his readers to know beyond any shadow of doubt that living for Christ will entail suffering, for Christ himself "suffered in his body" (1 Peter 4:1).

In a life that is patterned after Jesus' life, two "becauses" converge. First, we suffer because the world hates righteous people. Second, we suffer because this makes us more like Christ. As he suffered, so shall we. Therefore, for those who truly, passionately love Jesus, joy will overshadow the pain.

C. GLORY IN IT (v. 14)

14. If you are insulted because of the name of Christ, you are blessed, for the Spirit of glory and of God rests on you.

To be *insulted* is to be deliberately maligned. No one enjoys such abuse, but Peter sees a blessing in this: our suffering from persecution is a validation of our faith.

No enemy of Christ wastes time with false believers. Such an enemy, if he is perceptive, realizes that false disciples are supporting his cause, for they destroy the church from within. If we truly display the righteous characteristics of Christ in our lives, we will be offensive to the sinful world. Suffering inevitably will follow.

Peter reminds his readers that God is not absent when they suffer. There is a glorious presence of his *Spirit* despite the pain. To suffer for Christ is to share in his glory (see Romans 8:17, 18). We gain the hardened endurance necessary to be a true, lifelong disciple (Romans 5:3).

REPROACHED FOR THE NAME

While I was still in Bible college and seminary, I had a couple of brief ministries in rural areas of central Illinois. Most of the members of the congregations were farmers; they were honest, hardworking folk. Over a period of about five years, I served three different churches, and I do not recall that a single member of any of them was a college graduate. This does not mean they were dumb; it simply means they were not sophisticated or used to thinking in logical abstractions. These were industrious, conservative people who lived close to the soil and nature.

Many of them remembered the days of the Great Depression, when agricultural experts came around to tell them how to farm better. The farmers could not see that the "book learning" of the experts was very helpful. They tended to dismiss these agricultural experts as part of "those New Dealers." The term was usually said with a sneer and a shrug, dismissing the experts' advice as unrealistic and worthless.

The phrase *New Dealers* became a synonym for "fancy-pants" scholars who had never perched on the seat of a tractor. Actually, many of the New Dealers had

WHAT DO YOU THINK?

How do you rejoice in times of trials and sufferings without appearing to be in denial about the reality of those trials and sufferings?

Visual for Lesson 11.
Start a discussion by turning this statement into a question: "What opposition to your Christian faith have you faced?"

WHAT DO YOU THINK?

How do you normally react when a fellow believer suffers justly for wrong things he or she has committed? How should you react?

good ideas that would take another generation to become accepted on American farms. Several New Deal agencies were an immense aid to impoverished farmers. But often it was just easier to dismiss the New Dealers reproachfully, even when they deserved better.

Peter notes that we as Christians often are reproached because of our name, even when we deserve better. We do well to keep in mind that this may be due just to defensiveness or lazy thinking on the part of the critic. Given time, they may come around. God is patient. —J. B. N.

II. ORDEAL OF SUFFERING (1 PETER 4:15, 16)

A. SHAMED CRIMINAL (v. 15)

15. If you suffer, it should not be as a murderer or thief or any other kind of criminal, or even as a meddler.

Even in an ungodly world, criminals deserve to suffer. If civilization is to endure, no one should be able to engage in evil without consequences.

Peter's list here is interesting. He begins with the grossest of evildoers, a *murderer*. He then moves to another despicable criminal, the *thief*. Both murder and thievery are capital offenses under certain circumstances in the first century. They are seen as evil by even the pagans of the day. Peter follows with the general term *criminal*, which sums up most law-breaking behavior.

The *meddler* is the one who sticks his or her nose into the business of others. Some people love to do this, but they run the risk of being rudely dismissed and having a friendship ruined. For Peter, this would be suffering, for no one wants to be told in angry terms to buzz off. But that would be a type of justified suffering, and therefore like the criminal who is punished.

Peter, therefore, draws a clear distinction between the just suffering of the criminal and the unjust—yet glorious—suffering of the Christian. While Peter teaches that suffering for Jesus has an important role in God's plan for the church, suffering in general is a bad thing. We should not want to suffer. If we do suffer, it should be for no other reason than our stand for righteousness.

OBJECTS OF PERSECUTION?

We live in a culture that is becoming ever more secular. In that light, it is easy for Christians to think they are objects of persecution, even though that may not be the case. It is all too easy to take comfort in the belief that we are being "persecuted because of righteousness," when actually we are being called on the carpet justly because of our own failings.

I knew a man a few years ago who thought he was being harassed by the management of his factory because he witnessed about his faith to others at work. He claimed he was being persecuted because he was a Christian. Actually, that was not true. Yes, he was a Christian; and yes, he did witness about his faith while he was at work. The problem was that he often would leave his machine and go over to other employees to talk about his faith. It was not his Christian conversation that was the problem. In fact, he was stealing production time from his employer. He also was interfering with the work of other employees so they were not giving their full time to the employer either.

Rather than being persecuted for his faith, he actually was being reprimanded for being a busybody. Other workers resented his interference, and the management disliked it as well. Rather than exemplifying the innocent persecuted Christian of verse 16 (which we will study next), he represented the negative behavior of verse 15. Are you guilty of this? —J. B. N.

B. Unashamed Christian (v. 16)

16. However, if you suffer as a Christian, do not be ashamed, but praise God that you bear that name.

My mother taught me there is no shame in not having nice clothes if you are poor, but there is shame if you do not keep the clothes you have clean. For Peter, there is no shame for us in suffering, but we must keep our lives clean and righteous no matter what the pressures may be.

If sometimes we are at a loss as to what to do, Peter gives us a course of action that never fails: *praise God.* Worship and repentance redirect our attention away from self and toward the Lord (see Revelation 14:7; 16:9).

Paul, who certainly suffered a great deal for serving Jesus, proudly announced "I am not ashamed of the gospel" (Romans 1:16). Paul's life displayed fearless confidence that he was doing the right thing by giving his all to the service of Christ, no matter what the level of suffering (see Philippians 3:8).

III. JUDGMENT OF GOD (1 PETER 4:17-19)

A. Internal Examination (vv. 17, 18)

17. For it is time for judgment to begin with the family of God; and if it begins with us, what will the outcome be for those who do not obey the gospel of God?

It is difficult to see past the pain when we are suffering. In this next section of verses, Peter asks the church not only to see beyond their sufferings, but also to use the occasion as an opportunity for self-examination.

Persecution is never fair or consistent, for some will suffer more than others. The *judgment* of God, however, is always fair, always perfect. Therefore, the church has not been granted immunity from God's judgment simply because it is being persecuted. As Peter paints the picture for us, when God begins his universal, spiritual housecleaning, he will begin with his *family.* That is a serious warning: persecution is no excuse for compromise with the world. The warnings to the seven churches in Revelation 2, 3 show us God's intent to "clean house" in certain ways.

For Peter, this threatened judgment within God's household pales in comparison with God's judging activity for those outside. Those on the outside are the stubbornly disobedient, who *do not obey the gospel of God.*

18. And,

> **"If it is hard for the righteous to be saved,**
> **what will become of the ungodly and the sinner?"**

Those who are *saved* because of their faith in Christ have no claim to boast. Their salvation is not due to their own merit, but to the work of Christ and the mercy of God. In this, Peter can say that *it is hard* for them *to be saved.* If their ultimate salvation hangs only on the mighty lifeline of God's grace, what is the fate of unbelievers?

Peter seems to have in mind both the sinners outside the church and those false disciples within the body. Judgment will come upon all the *ungodly,* whether they call themselves Christians or not, for God truly knows the hearts of all (compare Proverbs 11:31).

B. Suffering and Trusting (v. 19)

19. So then, those who suffer according to God's will should commit themselves to their faithful Creator and continue to do good.

What Do You Think?

What methods have you seen God use to judge his house, the church? How do we know this is actually God's judgment happening and not something else?

What Do You Think?

How does (or should) the eternal fate of "the ungodly and the sinner" affect your attitude toward them?

PRAYER

Holy Father, we can only imagine the pain you felt as you watched your Son suffer on the cross for the sins of the world. When we suffer for our faith, whether it be small indignities or violent hostility, may we take comfort in our sharing of the sufferings of your Son. May we always trust you and always obey you. We pray this in the name of the one who suffered for us, Jesus the Lord. Amen.

Peter's conclusion is like the old hymn "Trust and Obey." We must *commit* ourselves to him in utter, complete faith and trust. We cannot save ourselves. He will come and save us (Isaiah 35:4). We must continue to serve him in obedience, never forsaking the path of righteousness. This is because our *Creator*, God, is *faithful* and will do as he has promised. In the end, "there is no other way to be happy in Jesus, but to trust and obey."

CONCLUSION

A proper sense of right and wrong expects that people should suffer the consequences of their wrong actions. Outrage occurs when people seem to "get away with something"—when they are able to avoid unpleasant outcomes despite unethical or criminal behavior.

But what about those who suffer innocently, having done nothing to deserve the hardships they endure? History tells us that in Peter's last years the church was targeted for persecution by the Roman government. The reasons for this are somewhat murky, but the reality of the sufferings is well documented. We may not experience persecution in the way that the church of Peter's day did, but his words about suffering still have great value for us in the twenty-first century.

Many Jews of the first century believed that suffering was a sign of God's disapproval and punishment (see John 9:2). After all, the Old Testament taught that "I, the Lord your God, am a jealous God, punishing the children for the sin of the fathers to the third and fourth generation of those who hate me" (Exodus 20:5). The poor and the sick were to be pitied and cared for, but their fate was thought to be the result of some sin and wickedness. As Eliphaz, a "friend" of Job, claimed, sinners reap what they sow and "at the breath of God they are destroyed" (Job 4:9).

All this meant that the one who was suffering had a double whammy—having real pain and believing that God was angry with him or her. By implication, then, those who were well off physically and financially were thought to be in God's favor. Jesus taught, however, that material wealth is a false gauge of God's approval (see Luke 12:16-21). Conversely, poverty is a misleading measure of God's disapproval (see Luke 21:1-4). These ideas are not foreign to the Old Testament either. The psalmist observes that the wicked seem to prosper rather than suffer (Psalm 73:3-5).

What is different is that for the Christian suffering can lead to joy. No one in his or her right mind likes pain. We are not wired that way. But suffering for Christ is a confirmation of our faith. It shows us that what Jesus taught was true: the sinful world is in violent rebellion against our righteous God. "Men loved darkness instead of light because their deeds were evil. Everyone who does evil hates the light, and will not come into the light for fear that his deeds will be exposed" (John 3:19, 20). Suffering confirms that we are truly his disciples. We have denied our own road to pleasure. We have taken up the cross, and we are following our Lord to glory (Mark 8:34).

Peter's words help us understand that we do not need to suffer for Christ in silence. The church should serve as a place of encouragement and celebration in the midst of suffering. The body of Christ should be a "shelter in the time of storm," an oasis in the desert of worldly, sinful lives. We should share in these sufferings together, bearing the burdens of our fellow believers (Galatians 6:2). It is then that we become the fellowship of the unashamed, those who are confident in their obedience to Christ.

Discovery Learning

The following is an alternative lesson plan emphasizing learning activities. Classes desiring such student involvement will find these suggestions helpful. At the back of this book are reproducible student pages to further enhance activity learning.

INTO THE LESSON

Place copies of the reproducible exercise "Why Suffer for Christ?" from page 126 in chairs for your early arrivers to work on. Prepare a handout of the following matching activity with the heading *First-Century Suffering*. On the left, list the following items with a blank in front of each: 1. Stoned to death; 2. Stoned, but not to death; 3. Crucified (according to tradition); 4. Beheaded; 5. Beaten and imprisoned with Paul; 6. Witnessed crucifixion of son; 7. Put to death with the sword. On the right, list these answers: A. James; B. John the Baptist; C. Mary; D. Paul; E. Peter; F. Silas; G. Stephen.

Ask students to form into pairs to work on the activity. Each answer is to be used only once. After a few minutes, go over the answers as a class. The correct matches are 1-G, 2-D, 3-E, 4-B, 5-F, 6-C, 7-A.

Use the information from the section of the lesson Introduction titled "Hatred of All Things Christian" to discuss some of the reasons why the early Christians were persecuted. Then say, "It is obvious that suffering was a part of the Christian life for the early church. In many parts of the world, that is still true today. As we read today's text, we'll learn how we are to respond to suffering for our faith."

INTO THE WORD

Distribute copies of the Scripture text (or have students turn to the text in their student books, if you're using that resource). As students form small groups or pairs, distribute pens and highlight markers. Ask them to read through the verses of today's text. First, they are to use the pen to underline all the words and phrases that describe negative things happening to Christians.

After that, they are to use the highlighter to mark all the positive responses to suffering and the blessings that can or should result.

After groups finish, ask each to tell either a bad thing underlined or a positive response or blessing highlighted. Possible underlinings are *painful trial; insulted; suffer as a Christian.* Possible highlightings are *rejoice; be overjoyed; you are blessed; do not be ashamed; the Spirit of glory and of God rests on you; [Christ] is glorified; glorify God; commit themselves to their faithful Creator and continue to do good.*

Lead a discussion of the following two topics:

Topic: Persecution. "Do we consider it strange to have to suffer for our faith? What ways do people suffer in our own country for being Christians? What stories have you heard of Christians around the world who are being persecuted for their faith?"

Topic: Proper Response. "What is it about being mocked for our faith that could make us happy (blessed)? How can our fellowship with Jesus be deepened when we share in his suffering? In what way does God receive glory when Christians suffer?"

INTO LIFE

Have someone look up and read Paul's statement in Romans 1:16: "I am not ashamed of the gospel." Make the point that one reason Christians don't suffer for their faith is that they don't have Paul's boldness in standing up for their beliefs. Distribute handouts of the following of situations. In small groups, have learners discuss how the Christians in each case can be better witnesses.

Situation #1: Maria works in a small office where no one else is a Christian. Her boss is outspoken in his contempt for anything related to the church and Christianity. Her approach so far has been to keep her faith to herself. What are some ways that she can begin to be bolder about her faith, while remembering that she is "on company time"?

Situation #2: Brian and his fiancée, Carrie, are strong Christians. However, because Carrie's whole family are unbelievers, she has asked Brian not to say anything related to their faith when he is around them. He is very uncomfortable whenever he's with her family, as he has to watch what he says very carefully. What advice would you give this couple?

Situation #3: Devon plans to have dinner with some of his buddies later this week. Since one friend's father recently passed away, Devon thinks the discussion may turn to the issue of life after death. As a Christian, Devon has strong beliefs about eternal life through Jesus Christ, but Devon knows he's not very articulate. What do you say to encourage Devon?

Distribute copies of the reproducible exercise "A Proper Response" from page 126 as students depart.

A FAITHFUL PEOPLE

LESSON 12

INTRODUCTION

A. TO STOP GROWING

When I was in high school, I hurt my knee playing football. The X-rays showed the damage, which was eventually corrected by surgery. The X-rays also revealed something else. In technical language that I did not understand, the doctor said my knee was fully formed. This meant that I would not grow any more.

In other words, I was about as tall as I was ever going to get, even though I was only 15 years old at the time. I would never reach 6' in height. Instead, I would have to settle for 5'11". This was a difficult pill to swallow, because my older brother was 6'2", and I had always assumed I would match or exceed him. Furthermore, my favorite sport was basketball, but I knew that my success there would be limited because of my lack of height.

All of us eventually quit growing vertically (although we seem to retain a propensity for horizontal growth). This is a simple fact of life, and it is largely determined by our genetic makeup. It is tragic, though, that some Christians cease to grow in spiritual stature. An early growth spurt may give them modest spiritual height. But then, for some reason, they stagnate. They reach the point of not having new spiritual thoughts or insights for many years. The great truths of the faith become commonplace and stale for them.

Other Christians, however, seize opportunities for lifelong growth that the faith affords. They become spiritual giants, continuing to add to their growth until death takes them. Peter was one of these. He seemed to have been a giant already when he preached the first gospel message on the Day of Pentecost, shortly after Jesus' resurrection (Acts 2:14-36). We do not know how old Peter was at that time, but our best guess is that he was in his mid-30s.

By the time Peter wrote the second letter that bears his name, over three decades had passed. Peter was surely near age 70. He had no regrets, and his primary concerns were to remain faithfully obedient, to keep growing in Christ, and to pass those challenges along to others.

Whatever our physical age today, we do not have to settle for stunted spiritual growth. The spiritual life is such that it can be renewed and refreshed. Growth can begin again, even after a long period of inactivity.

B. LESSON BACKGROUND

The book of 2 Peter includes some interesting features. First, it is written in a style of Greek very different from 1 Peter (although this may not be apparent to readers of English translations). Peter notes that his first letter was written with the help of Silas (1 Peter 5:12). Silas, a companion also of Paul, seems to have been an educated Jew from a privileged background, for we know he was a Roman citizen (Acts 16:25, 38). We speculate that his help with 1 Peter provided the polish to that letter.

DEVOTIONAL READING:
LUKE 19:12-26
BACKGROUND SCRIPTURE:
2 PETER 1:3-15
PRINTED TEXT:
2 PETER 1:3-15

LESSON AIMS

After participating in this lesson, each student will be able to:

1. Tell some key points that Peter makes about growth and faithfulness.

2. Explain the connection between godly living and faith.

3. Make a plan for Christian growth in one area.

KEY VERSE

His divine power has given us everything we need for life and godliness through our knowledge of him who called us by his own glory and goodness. —2 Peter 1:3

Nov
22

LESSON 12 NOTES

HOW TO SAY IT

Alexandria. Al-iks-AN-dree-uh.
Elijah. Ee-LYE-juh.
Galatians. Guh-LAY-shunz.
Gnosticism.
   NAHSS-tih-SIZZ-um.
gnostics. NAHSS-ticks.
gnosis. NO-sis.
heresies. HAIR-uh-seez.
Judas. JOO-dus.
Pentecost. PENT-ih-kost.
Silas. SIGH-luss.

WHAT DO YOU THINK?

In what ways has God provided for your needs for life and godliness? Why, how, and when do you express thanks to God for these gifts?

Peter's second letter, however, seems to have been written quickly, under great duress, and with no help from anyone like Silas. Peter himself wrote down the words rather than passing them over to someone else to edit. The style of 2 Peter is terse and direct, with few literary niceties.

A second thing to notice is the remarkable eyewitness recollection of Jesus' transfiguration found in 2 Peter 1:16-18. Here we find the same basic elements included in the Gospel accounts, but without the part about Peter's clumsy suggestion to build three "shelters" or shrines for Moses, Elijah, and Jesus (Matthew 17:4). It is not too surprising that this embarrassing detail had faded to the background for Peter!

A third prominent feature of 2 Peter is its frank discussion of what has been called "the delay of the second coming" (see 2 Peter 3:3, 4). The earliest church apparently expected Jesus to return very shortly. Peter, writing from the perspective of more than three decades after he first met Jesus, has come to grips with the distinct possibility that the second coming may not happen during his own lifetime. This will be discussed more fully in next week's lesson.

We should treasure these words of Peter, for they are the unrivaled message of a veteran believer at the end of his ministry. He brought to the table his experiences about the Lord Jesus as few in his generation could do—and certainly no one can do today. May we listen to him carefully.

I. GIFTS OF FAITH (2 PETER 1:3-9)

A. PRECIOUS PROFUSION (vv. 3, 4)

3. His divine power has given us everything we need for life and godliness through our knowledge of him who called us by his own glory and goodness.

As the apostle Paul faced his death, he celebrated the fact that he had "kept the faith" (2 Timothy 4:7). In a similar vein, Peter begins his letter with a reminder of the importance of remaining faithful to Christ, no matter what the future may bring. There is no other option in Peter's view.

In this light, Peter wants to talk about the nature of God's gifts. Peter divides those gifts into two categories. First, there are gifts that provide *life*. For example, Jesus had taught Peter and the other disciples to give thanks for daily bread (Matthew 6:11), the necessities for living. Second, God has granted us what we need for *godliness*. The Christian does not need to guess about what constitutes the godly life. We have been provided with Scripture and teachers to guide us in this area. God gives us what is needed for physical and spiritual nourishment.

Peter also discerns two purposes for God's gifts to us. First, there is the issue of God's call in relation to his *glory*. Thus our call is not an issue of personal fame or status in this life. Also, this is a glory yet to be revealed (see 1 Peter 5:1). It is this hope of glory that makes it possible for us to endure present sufferings (1 Peter 4:13).

Peter also commends the gifts of God that contribute to *goodness* or virtue. This is closely connected with the godliness already mentioned. Peter develops this theme further in verse 5, below. Peter reminds us that these gifts come through our *knowledge* of Jesus. He is not talking about book-learning, but about knowing the Lord through a personal relationship.

4. Through these he has given us his very great and precious promises, so that through them you may participate in the divine nature and escape the corruption in the world caused by evil desires.

Although not well known, this verse identifies one of the greatest of God's gifts to believers: the Holy Spirit. Peter describes our relationship with God's Spirit as participating *in the divine nature*. As Paul put it, the Holy Spirit is God's "seal" or down payment toward our full redemption at the end of life (Ephesians 1:13, 14).

Some Christians are very cautious in this area of doctrine. While we don't want our discussion of this to become too convoluted, we should not miss the tremendous significance of what Peter is saying. As believers, we receive the promise and the experience that we are directly plugged into God at the spiritual level. He is not distant from us or foreign to us. This indeed is a *very great and precious* promise.

For Peter, the practical aspect of the gift of the Holy Spirit is that it allows us to *escape the corruption* and *evil desires* of the *world*. This describes the longing for ungodly things, preoccupation with pursuits other than God. If we have claimed the promises and gifts that come through faith, our primary focus will be on God and on doing his will. All other things pale in significance to this glorious relationship. It is this strong faith that allows Peter and his church to remain faithful through the horrible persecution by Rome.

RELIABLE PROMISES

My wife and I enjoy watching old movies. Recently we were watching *You Can't Take It with You,* one of the well-known movies directed by Frank Capra, done in 1938. At one point in the film, Anthony P. Kirby, a powerful banker, is in the midst of pulling together an amazing business merger. He decides to make his son the president of the new corporation, but one of his subordinates had promised that role to another businessman in order to get his signed proxies.

"Tell him it was a mistake," said Kirby. "We have his signed proxies; there's nothing he can do about it."

"But I promised him," protested the unfortunate subordinate.

"It's not in writing," responded Kirby. "Forget it."

Thus the promises meant nothing to Kirby. The promises were only a means to an end, the consolidation of his own power.

Promises are precious things. All parents remember those distressing times when we make a commitment to our children, and then we are unable to fulfill our commitment because of extenuating circumstances. Our child's "But you promised!" becomes an uncomfortable prick to our conscience, perhaps for years to come.

How blessed we are that God's promises are surer than all human promises! When God makes a promise, we don't have to worry about whether he will honor his word. It is impossible for him to do otherwise. In addition, he controls all extenuating circumstances, so nothing can deflect him from fulfilling his promises.

—J. B. N.

B. SEQUENCED DEVELOPMENT (vv. 5-8)

5. For this very reason, make every effort to add to your faith goodness; and to goodness, knowledge;

The New Testament writers elsewhere present the path of spiritual development as a series of steps. As such, one step builds on another (see Romans 5:3, 4; James 1:3, 4). Peter does not minimize God's role in our spiritual formation, but Peter also expects his readers to *make every effort* in these matters. Spiritual growth is not an automatic thing for the Christian.

WHAT DO YOU THINK?

How do you live life as a partaker of God's divine nature, as Peter understands that concept? How can you do better?

WHAT DO YOU THINK?

In what ways are you being diligent in adding godly qualities to your life of faith? How will you do better in developing such qualities?

DAILY BIBLE READINGS

Monday, Nov. 16—Trustworthiness (Luke 19:12-26)

Tuesday, Nov. 17—Integrity (Psalm 101:1-4)

Wednesday, Nov. 18—Truthfulness (Proverbs 14:2-5)

Thursday, Nov. 19—Courage (Daniel 6:6-10)

Friday, Nov. 20—Readiness (Matthew 24:42-47)

Saturday, Nov. 21—Willingness (Acts 8:26-39)

Sunday, Nov. 22—Godliness (2 Peter 1:3-15)

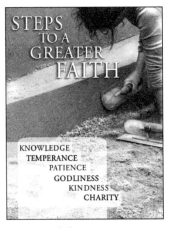

Visual for Lesson 12. *Use this visual to introduce either the previous or the following question.*

For Peter, this sequence necessarily begins with *faith*. We add to this *goodness*, which Peter has already listed as a gracious calling of God (v. 3, above). The virtuous life was sought by the ancient Greek philosophers, but it is truly realized only through faith in Jesus Christ.

The third step on this growth journey is *knowledge*. This is the ongoing expansion of one's familiarity with the ways of God and the elements of godly love. We cannot obey if we are ignorant of the expectations.

OF FAITH AND KNOWLEDGE

Clement of Alexandria was one of the key individuals in the church around AD 200. As an intellectual leader of the church in Egypt, he was concerned about fighting one of the most serious heresies facing the church at the time: the false teaching of *Gnosticism*.

The Gnostics taught that the most important thing in Christianity was knowledge (in Greek, *gnosis*, thus their name). If you had the correct intellectual understanding about spiritual things, then it did not matter what you actually did. Knowledge was salvation. The body was physical and therefore corrupt; of course it was going to do evil things. But knowledge was salvation.

Clement felt he had to fight this misconception. But at the same time, he wanted to make Christianity appealing to the intellectual classes of Alexandria, those inclined toward philosophy, even Gnosticism. Clement emphasized the importance of faith. He affirmed that even the simplest believer is saved. But the believer given to intellectual inquiry will want to go beyond simple faith to more advanced understanding. Thus Clement denied Gnosticism ("knowledge is salvation") while rehabilitating the concept of knowledge in true Christianity.

Clement did this by building on the stair steps of 2 Peter. "Add to your faith goodness; and to goodness, knowledge." We are not saved by knowledge; we are saved by faith in Christ. But knowledge becomes an important mark of spiritual maturity and development as we advance beyond the elementary basics. Your knowledge of God and his Word is either stagnant or growing. Which is it?

—J. B. N.

6, 7. . . . and to knowledge, self-control; and to self-control, perseverance; and to perseverance, godliness; and to godliness, brotherly kindness; and to brotherly kindness, love.

Christian *knowledge* should lead us to *self-control*, sometimes translated "sobriety." This is more than physical soberness resulting from avoidance of alcohol or drugs. Peter is speaking of a general attitude of moderation, of not being controlled or carried away by the things of the world (compare Galatians 5:23). Our *perseverance* in this separation moves us to *godliness*. This refers to the lifestyle that conforms to the expectations God has for his holy people. Living the godly life should imitate the great, merciful nature of God himself. The life of godliness will be evident in our *kindness* and care for our brothers and sisters within the church as well as acts of *love* for those outside the body of Christ.

8. For if you possess these qualities in increasing measure, they will keep you from being ineffective and unproductive in your knowledge of our Lord Jesus Christ.

All of these steps work together. When we begin to see loving-kindness and acts of mercy flow naturally and effortlessly in our lives, we have begun truly to live the mature, spiritual life that Peter wants for all of his readers.

This is the level of faith that Peter knows to be necessary to survive the on-slaught of persecution and testing that comes to each believer. This is just as true today as it was in the first century.

C. FAITHLESS NEGLECT (v. 9)

9. But if anyone does not have them, he is nearsighted and blind, and has forgotten that he has been cleansed from his past sins.

The gifts of God that Peter has described come to the faithful. Now Peter comments on the other side of the coin, the faithless. These are the *blind,* who lack discernment. This is an interesting illustration, for faith is the requirement for trust in that which cannot be seen (see Hebrews 11:1). Here Peter is talking about those shortsighted members of his church who fail to see the goal, the ultimate prize of faith (see Philippians 3:14). These folks have *forgotten* that their *sins* have been *cleansed* by the blood of Christ, and that salvation has been given to them, even eternal life (see Jude 21).

II. ASSURANCE OF FAITH (2 PETER 1:10-15)

A. FACT (vv. 10, 11)

10. Therefore, my brothers, be all the more eager to make your calling and election sure. For if you do these things, you will never fall,

How can we know for sure that we will be saved (that is, *never fall*)? For Christians, this is where the doctrine of assurance comes in. While we may have not yet experienced all the promised outcomes of our faith, that faith allows us to be assured of their trustworthiness.

The teachings of the New Testament say with one voice that we cannot earn salvation, because salvation is a gift. Yet we are also taught that acceptance of this gift comes with responsibilities and expectations. We have chosen to make Jesus the Lord of our lives and to live for him. It is by giving diligence to our side of the gift that we make our *calling and election sure.*

We create the assurance of salvation that our hearts crave by living out our faith; notice that vital word *if* in the phrase *if you do these things, you will never fall.* We are not caught between faith and doubt; we choose faith. Peter knows this from his own commitment and life experience. He testifies with great personal credibility that such a life will not fail.

11. . . . and you will receive a rich welcome into the eternal kingdom of our Lord and Savior Jesus Christ.

Peter reminds his readers yet again that we never need doubt God's side of the gift of salvation. For those who have true, obedient faith, a way *into the eternal kingdom* (Heaven) has been provided. This portal was forged by our spiritual trailblazer, *our Lord and Savior Jesus Christ* (compare Hebrews 2:10).

For Peter, the assurance of this salvation lies in the fact that Jesus is already there waiting for us. Peter can remember vividly that on the night Jesus was betrayed he promised his disciples that he was going to "prepare a place" for them (John 14:2, 3)—a place in Heaven.

B. REMINDER (vv. 12-15)

12. So I will always remind you of these things, even though you know them and are firmly established in the truth you now have.

WHAT DO YOU THINK?

How well are you doing in making "your calling and election sure"? What can you do better in this regard?

WHAT DO YOU THINK?

What are you doing to remind others of the things taught in the Bible? How can you do better?

PRAYER

Merciful God, we are humbled when we consider the enduring faithfulness of your servant Peter. What an example he both was and is! He loved your Son Jesus until the end. May our lives too have the evidence of Peter's dogged faithfulness, since his faithfulness never gave in, never gave up, and never gave out. We pray this in the name of the pioneer of our faith, Jesus Christ our Redeemer. Amen.

Peter knows that the great truths of the faith that he has been rehearsing are not new; his readers already *know them.* This does not make them less important, however. We are strengthened when truth is repeated. This is why we repeat pledges frequently. This is why we have favorite verses of Scripture that we quote again and again. This is why we have confessions of faith that may be repeated in unison by a congregation.

Peter has just reminded the readers that persecution becomes more tolerable when we remember that our ultimate destination is Heaven. He is careful to tell them, however, that faith must be based on the known, not speculation about the future. We have a sufficiency in the *truth* that God has provided, the truth that we already have of our salvation, which was won through the cross and empty tomb of Christ.

13, 14. I think it is right to refresh your memory as long as I live in the tent of this body, because I know that I will soon put it aside, as our Lord Jesus Christ has made clear to me.

Peter's *tent* is his earthly *body,* the current housing of his person (compare 2 Corinthians 5:1, 4). Peter writes with full awareness that his life on earth is nearly finished, for this has been revealed to him by the risen *Christ* (compare John 21:18, 19).

15. And I will make every effort to see that after my departure you will always be able to remember these things.

While Peter is at peace with this future, he is not content to ride out his last days in idleness. He is determined to use every remaining minute in ministry to encourage his flock with the great truths and promises of the faith. In so doing, he understands his influence as a great example to the believers (compare 1 Peter 5:1-4).

The New Testament does not always paint a flattering picture of Peter (example: Galatians 2:11-14). There is a sense in the Gospels that Peter's denials of Jesus after his arrest constitute a betrayal that is somewhat of a parallel to the act of Judas. The parallelism ends, however, as Judas commits suicide and Peter is restored to ministry by the Lord in the threefold question about his love (John 21:15-17). Following that, Peter never lost his faith in Christ and passion for service to him. These Peter maintained until his death, for he, as Paul, was truly "crucified with Christ" (Galatians 2:20).

CONCLUSION

Products and services to delay or mask the effects of aging are a multibillion dollar industry. One of the most amazing of these is the Botox® phenomenon. This technique involves injecting small quantities of a powerful, paralyzing poison to decrease wrinkles and other aging signs. This and other things have caused some to say that "age 60 is the new 40." Even if some of the effects of aging can be postponed or hidden, the march of the years ultimately cannot be stopped. We all grow older every day. One of the most startling things in life is the realization that other people think you are old.

We have all met people who seem to be elderly when they are still quite young, however. Their souls have fossilized long before their bodies have begun to decline. We have little control over the aging of our bodies, but we do have control over the decline of our souls. Peter promised that the Lord would provide "times of refreshing" if we put our faith in him (Acts 3:19).

Even when we are ancient in body, our relationship with God can be "new every morning" (Lamentations 3:23), for he is ever faithful. He is both the "Ancient of Days" (Daniel 7:9) and the immortal "King eternal" (1 Timothy 1:17). In him the obedient Christian's future is secure.

Discovery Learning

The following is an alternative lesson plan emphasizing learning activities.
Classes desiring such student involvement will find these suggestions helpful. At the
back of this book are reproducible student pages to further enhance activity learning.

INTO THE LESSON

Prior to the lesson, ask a student to prepare to be interviewed as Peter. Provide the student with a copy of all the sections of the lesson Introduction. Also give him a list of the questions that you will be asking. Here is a sample to adjust as you see fit:

1. The writing style of your second letter seems very different from your first. What was the reason for that? 2. How have you changed in the thirty-odd years since you preached the church's first sermon on the Day of Pentecost? 3. What final message are you trying to convey to your fellow believers? 4. What would you say to Christians who have stopped trying to grow in their faith?

To help the interview go more smoothly, do a practice interview with "Peter" before class. If you have no one willing to take on the role of Peter, ask someone else to be the interviewer while you answer the questions yourself.

Say, "We are extremely fortunate today to have a distinguished guest with us. The apostle Peter has agreed to an interview about his most recent letter—2 Peter. Peter, thank you for being with us."

At the conclusion of the interview say, "Thank you so much for your visit. To close, I wonder if you would do us the honor of reading a brief passage of your book for us." Then have "Peter" read today's text aloud.

INTO THE WORD

Say, "The verses that you just heard read are Peter's pep talk to encourage his fellow Christians not to relax and try to coast into Heaven. Even though Peter knows his life is drawing to a close, he doesn't slow down in his pursuit of godliness. Let's take a closer look at what he has to say."

Before class, prepare a handout with the following list of statements (omitting the answers in parentheses). Include these instructions: "The following statements were made by people who have a misunderstanding of the relationship between faith and godliness. In the blank write the number of the verse that contains the truth that will refute these false ideas. There is one answer per verse of 2 Peter 1:3-11, while verses 12-15 as a block take one answer."

Have your students form into groups of four or five to work on this together.

____1. I believe in taking the "tough love" approach with fellow Christians to help them shape up. (v. 7)

____2. Nobody needs to help me be good; I can do it on my own. (v. 3)

____3. The issue is *being,* not *doing.* (v. 10)

____4. Having faith is all I need; I don't need to be "good" to be saved. (v. 5)

____5. Guilt over my past sinful life haunts my thoughts, and rightly so. (v. 9)

____6. I get so tired of hearing the same truths over and over; it doesn't really help. (vv. 12-15)

____7. I'll use success principles I've learned at work to produce results for God's kingdom. (v. 8)

____8. Participating in the divine nature is grounded in my works. (v. 4)

____9. Sin means that Jesus will let me into Heaven only grudgingly. (v. 11)

___10. Sometimes the Christian life is just too hard, and I can't keep it up. If I don't seem to persevere at times, I'm sure God understands. (v. 6)

Have the groups share their answers. If their answers don't match the ones indicated above, allow for some variation as they explain. Have the person giving the answer explain how the truth of the verse would correct the person's wrong thinking.

INTO LIFE

Using construction paper make some cutouts in the shape of a flower. Hold one up alongside a package of Miracle-Gro® or some other type of plant food. Ask if anyone has used that or a similar product and if it helped. When they've related some of their ideas, make the point that there are many things that we can do in our pursuit of godliness to nourish our spiritual lives and help us grow in Jesus.

Ask for volunteers to share practices that have been helpful to them in that regard. Distribute a flower cutout to each person. Ask everyone to write on it one way he or she will nurture his or her spiritual life this week. Encourage students to put their "flowers" where they can see them all week. *Option:* Use small groups to complete and discuss the two reproducible exercises on page 127.

A HOPEFUL PEOPLE

LESSON 13

INTRODUCTION

A. KILLING TIME

Have you ever considered how much of our lives are devoted to waiting? We wait for elevators. We wait for traffic lights. We wait for the next available teller. We wait for the check to come in the mail. We wait for the rain to stop. We have special facilities devoted to waiting: they are called waiting rooms.

We also have special terminologies for waiting. We refer to being in a *holding pattern*, drawn from the language of air travel. We might refer to waiting as *time out*, originally a sports term. We push this sports analogy to say we are *playing a waiting game*, as if there is a competition when it comes to delays.

One of the most telling expressions of waiting is *killing time*. This is an odd figure of speech, for time is not ordinarily understood to be subject to death or life. Perhaps a more apt way of saying this is the sister expression *wasting time*. Unproductive waiting is truly a waste of something dear.

But is there such a thing as "productive waiting"? Something more productive than, say, reading a six-month-old news magazine in the dentist's waiting room? Today, many people fill waiting periods with chatter on cell phones. I suspect, however, that this is just a rather comfortable way to kill time, and it may have the disadvantage of wasting someone else's time.

The writers of the Bible knew a lot about waiting. Many times in the Old Testament, their advice to a suffering people was to wait on or for the Lord (Psalm 27:14). But this is not waiting in the sense of futile time-killing. Waiting for God is an expectant waiting, a waiting full of hope (Isaiah 8:17).

The two go together. We hope, therefore we wait. We wait, consequently we hope. Hopeful waiting is not wasting time, even if we are sitting on a dock beside some bay. Today's Scripture, more than any other place in the Bible, teaches us that waiting can be a joyous time if we are hoping for the glorious coming of the Lord.

B. LESSON BACKGROUND

A cardinal doctrine for the church is that of the second coming of Christ. This future event is sometimes called, in technical language, *the parousia*. This Greek word means "coming" or "presence"; it is used by the New Testament writers as shorthand for Christ's return (see 1 Corinthians 15:23; 1 John 2:28).

Some references to the second coming of Christ are very dramatic, such as these words of Jesus: "For as lightning that comes from the east is visible even in the west, so will be the coming of the Son of Man" (Matthew 24:27). Other references are more subtle as part of a larger discussion: "Each in his own turn: Christ, the firstfruits; then, when he comes, those who belong to him" (1 Corinthians 15:23, as part of Paul's discussion of resurrection). The New Testament presents the second coming of Christ in the context of hope and the need for patient waiting (see Titus 2:13; James 5:7).

DEVOTIONAL READING:
PSALM 42
BACKGROUND SCRIPTURE:
2 PETER 3
PRINTED TEXT:
2 PETER 3:1-13

LESSON AIMS

After participating in this lesson, each student will be able to:

1. Summarize what Peter said about those who scoff at the idea of the Lord's return and about the truth of the "day of the Lord."

2. Tell how the promise of the Lord's return motivates him or her to holy living.

3. Write a poem, song, or prayer expressing gratitude for God's patience.

KEY VERSE

The Lord is not slow in keeping his promise, as some understand slowness. He is patient with you, not wanting anyone to perish, but everyone to come to repentance. 2 Peter 3:9

NOV
29

Lesson 13 Notes

The first generation of Christians apparently believed that Christ would return very soon. This is why Paul taught his people to pray *Maranatha,* an Aramaic expression that means "Come, Lord!" (1 Corinthians 16:22; compare Revelation 22:20). Paul was an example of one who entertained the possibility (even the expectation) of being alive to meet the Lord when he returned (see 1 Thessalonians 4:17).

Although Jesus promised to come again, he said that he was not privy to the information regarding *when* (Mark 13:32). As time went on, the church began to understand that this return might not occur as soon as people hoped or expected. Christians came to realize that the second coming of Jesus was delayed, although this "delay" is only from a human perspective. God knows exactly when he will act in this mighty way. Even so, the earliest church needed a way to defend itself from those who would ridicule the Christian hope of the second coming. That's where Peter comes in.

I. HISTORY OF HOPE (2 PETER 3:1, 2)
A. REFRESHED MEMORIES (v. 1)
1. Dear friends, this is now my second letter to you. I have written both of them as reminders to stimulate you to wholesome thinking.

Peter understands that he can talk about the church's past like very few others in his generation. This puts him in an important position to be able to ground his readers in the timeless truths of the faith. Peter's readers are his *dear friends,* the cherished ones of his ministry. He does not say exactly what causes him to write a *second letter,* but both letters have a similar goal: calling his readers to remember.

When times are tough, we are apt to fall into a type of mental numbness. We may stumble from one day to the next like religious zombies, our spirits seeming to be more like the undead than the truly living. It is during such periods that we must remember the great blessings of the past and the powerful promises we have for the future.

B. CONTINUOUS MESSAGE (v. 2)
2. I want you to recall the words spoken in the past by the holy prophets and the command given by our Lord and Savior through your apostles.

This is an important verse for our understanding of the connection between the Old and New Testaments. For Peter, the *apostles* are carrying on some of the same functions as the *prophets* of old. Both groups communicate the authoritative Word of God. Both groups are messengers of hope, promising the comfort of God for the faithful.

Just as ancient Israel faced its various crises, so in Peter's day does the church. The message of hope is unchanged: God is in control and has not forsaken you. He hears you when you cry out (Psalm 18:6).

II. RIDICULE OF HOPE (2 PETER 3:3-7)
A. CONTEMPORARY SCOFFERS (vv. 3, 4)
3. First of all, you must understand that in the last days scoffers will come, scoffing and following their own evil desires.

Mockery is an oft used way of attacking another person. While it may be physically nonviolent, heartless ridicule can crush the spirit. The church of Peter's day is not in any position of social power or respectability. First-

---

HOW TO SAY IT
Aramaic. AIR-uh-MAY-ik.
Corinthians. Ko-RIN-thee-unz (th *as in* thin).
Maranatha. Mare-uh-NAY-thuh.
Noah. NO-uh.
parousia (Greek). par-OO-see-uh.
Shiloh. SHY-low.
Thessalonians. THESS-uh-LO-nee-unz (th *as in* thin).

WHAT DO YOU THINK?
What things stir you up in your faith as you remember them?

century Christians are able to endure their tormenters, at least in part, because of their hope that Christ will return for them. Peter understands that when the critics of the church begin to mock this core belief, they can send the believers into despair. Rather than ignore this problem, Peter confronts it head-on.

The last days for Peter is not some fuzzy future era. Those days are his own days and ours—the era of the church. Earlier, Peter had talked about "these last times" (1 Peter 1:20). John affirms that "this is the last hour" (1 John 2:18). The writer of Hebrews speaks of "these last days" (Hebrews 1:2).

A characteristic of this time is the presence of *scoffers* (compare Jude 18). There is a reason behind their mocking: they are *following their own evil desires*. In other words, they are completely irreligious, have no respect for the sacred, and ridicule the faith of others. This mean-spirited disrespect has caused them to attack the core beliefs of Peter's Christian readers.

4. They will say, "Where is this 'coming' he promised? Ever since our fathers died, everything goes on as it has since the beginning of creation."

Peter offers us two hints as to the identity of these scoffers: (1) they have a sense of the *fathers*, meaning the ancestors of past generations, and (2) they have a tradition about *creation*. We cannot be certain, but this seems to point to the Jewish background of these opponents. The Roman church of Peter's day has many Christians from a Jewish background. This common heritage makes mocking attacks by non-Christian Jews all the more painful.

The basic charge of the opponents seems very contemporary: *everything goes on as it has*. The teaching of modern atheistic materialists is similar. Those folks claim that the universe's processes can be explained by physical matter and energy interacting without reference to any outside (spiritual or supernatural) influence. These mainstream scientists seem to take pleasure in ridiculing anyone who would believe in a divine act of creation.

Yet Peter knows that belief in Christ's second coming in glory requires the expectation that everything will change radically in a cataclysmic way. To assume that things will pretty much stay the same from now on is to deny the possibility of Jesus' second coming.

B. UNINFORMED EXPERTS (vv. 5-7)

5, 6. But they deliberately forget that long ago by God's word the heavens existed and the earth was formed out of water and by water. By these waters also the world of that time was deluged and destroyed.

The Jewish identity of the mockers becomes clearer now, because Peter argues with their use of Scripture. He reminds them of two momentous events: the creation of the dry *earth* from the watery void (Genesis 1:2, 9) and the flood of Noah's day (Genesis 7:17-22). In both cases, these were acts of God, accomplished simply *by God's word*. When God acts, there need be no other explanation.

WILLINGLY IGNORANT

At the Battle of Shiloh in 1862, pickets of the Union army heard the sounds of an approaching Confederate army. They sent back the alarm, but General Sherman refused to believe it. He even told one colonel, "If your men are that nervous, they should go back to Ohio!" Within half an hour thousands of Confederate soldiers

WHAT DO YOU THINK?

What methods do modern scoffers use to ridicule Christian faith? How do Christians unwittingly give the scoffers more
ammunition to do this? How can we do better in this regard?

WHAT DO YOU THINK?

What responses can Christians offer to those who question the second coming of Christ?

were pushing their way through an unprepared federal defense. Sherman recovered, steadied his men, and fought an organized delaying action as his men retreated across the fields.

To be caught by surprise was bad enough; to ignore the warning compounded the guilt. Sherman willingly chose to ignore information that would have changed the course of that first day's fighting. It was the worst mistake Sherman made during the war. But he became a better leader because of it. He learned from his mistake.

It is one thing to be ignorant. It is something else again to be willingly ignorant. All of us are ignorant about many things. Even the most intelligent person on earth doesn't know everything about everything. Even that person has gaps in his or her knowledge. But it is a rather different situation to have the means of knowing something but then choose not to know it.

Peter chastises those who are willingly ignorant of the message that God's power can create the world as well as bring judgment on it in cataclysmic disaster. God has given us all the information we need in this regard. There is *no excuse* for being willingly ignorant of these facts.   —J. B. N.

7. By the same word the present heavens and earth are reserved for fire, being kept for the day of judgment and destruction of ungodly men.

Peter goes even further to teach that the current state of the universe (*the present heavens and earth*) is sustained by the *word* of God (compare Hebrews 1:3). There is nothing necessarily permanent or eternal about the current state of the universe. The current heavens and earth will exist only until the final *judgment*. This fate of the universe results from sin, from the need to judge the *ungodly*. Their judgment will be that of *destruction*. Although Peter does not make a direct connection, he surely has the scoffing deriders of the faith in mind here.

III. FULFILLMENT OF HOPE (2 PETER 3:8-13)
A. TIMELESS GOD (vv. 8, 9)

8. But do not forget this one thing, dear friends: With the Lord a day is like a thousand years, and a thousand years are like a day.

Having assailed the scoffers of Christ's coming, Peter now comforts his readers by reminding them of the great promises they have. He begins by discussing the nature of God himself. Point one: God is not subject to time in the sense that we are. The God of the Bible is not "immortal" like the pagan gods. The Greeks and Romans believed all their gods had a birth or point of origin, but were not subject to death (immortal). Our God, rather, is "eternal." This means that he completely transcends time in every way.

From our perspective, this makes God infinitely patient, for he is not subject to time in a way that causes him to "wait." He sits in control of time, including all the events of the future (compare Ecclesiastes 3:11).

9. The Lord is not slow in keeping his promise, as some understand slowness. He is patient with you, not wanting anyone to perish, but everyone to come to repentance.

Point two: God always keeps his promises (compare 2 Peter 1:4). *The Lord* is most specifically the risen Christ, who will return in glory for judgment (see 2 Timothy 4:8), but there is no sharp separation here between God the Father and God the Son.

Peter offers an important doctrinal reason for the seeming delay of Christ's return: it is, ironically, because of God's love for the scoffers! In the timing of

WHAT DO YOU THINK?

How should the knowledge of a coming day of judgment affect how you live your life today?

God, there is no need to rush to judgment, for this will be a judging with no appeals. It will be absolute and final. Therefore, the God who loves sinners (Romans 5:8) desires *everyone to come to repentance*.

B. UNEXPECTED RETURN (v. 10)

10a. But the day of the Lord will come like a thief.

The Lord will return with no advance alarm, no two-minute warning. He will come *like a thief* whose success depends on stealth and surprise (see 1 Thessalonians 5:2; Revelation 3:3; 16:15). For Peter, this is tied to those who need to repent. The time to repent is now, because there is no way to predict how much time remains.

A THIEF IN THE NIGHT

Night seems to be a prime occasion for crime. The chances of being "successful" in certain types of crime improve at night because the cover of darkness allows more chances for a stealthy approach and a hidden getaway. In one of the cities where my wife and I once lived, we were burglarized twice—both times at night.

A recent news report noted that robberies on Friday and Saturday nights in Washington, D.C., can average five per hour. Sometimes the crime involves no more than the unseen approach of a weaponless robber who grabs a purse and runs. Nighttime also favors the criminal because the darkness makes it harder for the victim to see clearly and identify the criminal if he is caught.

The stealth aspect of the word picture *a thief in the night* is an easily formed image. This image transfers quite readily from the first century to the twenty-first. It is an image of complete surprise. It is how the Bible describes Jesus' second coming. But the hidden-identity aspect doesn't work if we try to draw a parallel between the methods of thieves and those of Jesus. When Jesus returns, he will make no attempt to conceal his identity—quite the opposite! This calls for discernment (Matthew 24:23, 24).

Those who are watchful will welcome Jesus gladly at his return; the unrepentant, who do not expect him, will react in terror (Revelation 6:15-17). So we watch in hopeful expectation.   —J. B. N.

10b. The heavens will disappear with a roar; the elements will be destroyed by fire, and the earth and everything in it will be laid bare.

God promised Noah that he would never again destroy the earth by water (Genesis 9:11). This time *the heavens* and *earth* will be *destroyed by fire*. This is utter, complete destruction, with no recovery by simply drying out. Peter pictures this as a mighty, supernatural event as characterized by a *roar* or a great noise. The purpose of this destruction is the same as the flood, though: to destroy the ungodly. There will be no escape for them (Revelation 6:17).

C. EXPECTANT LIVING (vv. 11-13)

11. Since everything will be destroyed in this way, what kind of people ought you to be? You ought to live holy and godly lives

Peter's conclusion, then, is to advise his readers how to live. Their manner of life must be governed by a desire for godliness. Peter says, "Quit messing around. You know what kind of person you *ought* to be, so go ahead and *be* that kind of person!"

DAILY BIBLE READINGS

Monday, Nov. 23—*I Shall Again Praise God (Psalm 42)*

Tuesday, Nov. 24—*Be Strong, Take Courage (Psalm 31:21-24)*

Wednesday, Nov. 25—*God Is My Hope (Psalm 71: 1-6)*

Thursday, Nov. 26—*Hope in God's Word (Psalm 119:81-88)*

Friday, Nov. 27—*Hoping Against Hope (Romans 4: 16-24)*

Saturday, Nov. 28—*Strengthen and Encourage (Acts 14:21-28)*

Sunday, Nov. 29—*Waiting for the Day of God (2 Peter 3:1-13)*

WHAT DO YOU THINK?

What's the best way to prepare for a thief who comes in the night? What does this say about how we should expect the return of Jesus?

PRAYER

Eternal God, we are befuddled by the constraints of time. When we doubt, may you both forgive and strengthen us. May we live with joy at the prospect of the return of your Son. May our waiting for that event be an expectant, hopeful waiting. We pray this in Jesus' name. Amen.

Visual for Lesson 13. *Use this visual to introduce the questions on pages 110, 111.*

12. . . . as you look forward to the day of God and speed its coming. That day will bring about the destruction of the heavens by fire, and the elements will melt in the heat.

In addition, Peter's readers are to live expectantly. This is not to be a joyous anticipation of the judgmental destruction of the world, but for what will happen after that: the renewal of creation. God will not merely burn everything up and be done with it like some sort of cosmic firebug. See the next verse.

13. But in keeping with his promise we are looking forward to a new heaven and a new earth, the home of righteousness.

After the destruction, God will follow up by creating *a new heaven and a new earth.* These will have no place for ungodliness. It will be the *home of righteousness.* This is a snapshot version of the marvelous picture we find in Revelation 21 and 22, where the glorious city of God is presented. As Peter's friend John portrays it, "the first heaven and the first earth had passed away" (Revelation 21:1). The ungodly will be excluded (21:8; 22:15). The scoffers of the faith will be no more, and we will be with God forever. This is our final, ultimate hope.

CONCLUSION

A. CAUTION

For two millennia now, Christians have been exposed to theories about the second coming of Christ. Most theories agree that it will involve a general resurrection of all the dead and a final judgment of all men and women. It will be the final "day of the Lord," where all injustice is reversed and sin and death are conquered. As to the timing and sequence of events involved in Christ's return, there have been many competing schemes proposed.

In trying to come to grips with this important issue, we should recognize a certain tension of ideas. On the one hand, the second coming is *imminent,* meaning "could happen at any time." It has been so for nearly 2,000 years. On the other hand, Christ might not return for another 2,000 years or more.

That second idea should cause us to be careful! Think about all the wrong guesses there have been so far to predict the date of Christ's return. Some reading this will remember the booklet *88 Reasons Why the Rapture Will Be in 1988.* It was wrong. But undoubtedly there are more theories yet to come. We are reasonably certain that the crucifixion and resurrection of Christ took place in AD 30. Surely, then, there will be those who predict that his second coming will be in AD 2030, just a few years away. We can already imagine the proposals of the importance of a "double millennium"!

We must realize that Christ may come this evening or not for another 10,000 years. It should not matter to us, for our future is secured by our faith in him. Our hope in the Lord is not futile.

B. EXPECTATIONS

There is an old joke that tells of a pessimist who was in a bad accident. When the police looked in his wallet for identification, they found a card that said, "In case of accident, I'm not surprised." Many people are like this, expecting the worst.

As Christians, we should not live this way. Yes, life is hard and can be very cruel. Yes, we may have to deal with friends and relatives who ridicule us for our faith. But we have a hope that can overcome all of this pain. We look forward to our final destiny: our home in Heaven with the Lord. Christ may or may not return in our lifetimes; it doesn't matter. In the future, "so we will be with the Lord forever" (1 Thessalonians 4:17).

THOUGHT TO REMEMBER
Hope as you wait.
Wait as you hope.

Discovery Learning

The following is an alternative lesson plan emphasizing learning activities.
Classes desiring such student involvement will find these suggestions helpful. At the
back of this book are reproducible student pages to further enhance activity learning.

INTO THE LESSON

Prepare the following true-false quiz:

1. When Jesus returns, he will come so quietly that some people won't even notice (1 Thessalonians 4:16). 2. Jesus said that not even he knew what day he would return; only the Father knows (Mark 13:32). 3. Since the Bible gives us so many clues about Jesus' second coming, most Christians will know when it is about to happen (Matthew 24:44). 4. God has delayed the second coming so that as many evil people as possible can be punished (2 Peter 3:9). 5. Jesus' return will be like lightning flashing from the west to be visible even in the east (Matthew 24:27). 6. The Christians alive at Jesus' return will rise to meet him; then the dead in Christ will be raised (1 Thessalonians 4:15, 16). 7. The first time God destroyed the world he used water; next time he will use fire (2 Peter 3:6, 7). 8. Since Christians know they will go to Heaven, they don't need to be thinking about the Lord's return (2 Peter 3:11, 12). 9. Jesus will come on the clouds surrounded by glory (Matthew 24:30). 10. The events of Jesus' second coming should make us hopeful, not fearful (Titus 2:13).

As you distribute the quiz, tell students that they can work in groups of two or three. Give them seven minutes to complete it. Encourage them to answer the questions from their own knowledge, but say that they can look up two of the Scripture references if they need help. When time is up, read through the questions and ask for volunteers to give their answers. The correct answers are 1-F, 2-T, 3-F, 4-F, 5-F, 6-F, 7-T, 8-F, 9-T, 10-T.

INTO THE WORD

Before class, ask someone to be prepared to read 2 Peter 3:1-13. Before the reading, say, "Peter knew that his readers were being persecuted for being Christians. So he reminded them that Jesus was coming again and why that should give them hope. As we listen to Peter's message, see if it makes you feel more hopeful also." After the Scripture is read, ask students to work in groups to complete one of the following assignments. Each group will need poster board and colored markers.

Assignment #1: People Will Scoff. Read 2 Peter 3:1-5. What core belief of the Christians were the scoffers mocking? Why were they being so scornful? Do these scoffers remind you of people today who mock Christians? If so, give some examples. On the poster board, draw a picture of a scoffer. Surround him or her with speech balloons and write in things an antagonistic unbeliever might say today.

Assignment #2: God Is in Control. Read 2 Peter 3:5-9. Which two major events from the past show God's control over the world and everything in it? Explain. Should we be concerned that humanity will destroy the world ahead of God's schedule? Why, or why not? Name three things we learn about God's character from verses 8 and 9 that give us confidence in him. On the poster board, write the heading *God Is in Control.* Underneath list reasons from the text that provide confidence that this statement is true. Use the markers to create a border around your poster to illustrate God's power.

Assignment #3: Jesus Will Return. Read 2 Peter 3:10-13. Make a poster that features these two incomplete sentences and all the answers you can come up with: 1. When Jesus returns, we can expect . . . 2. Because we know that Jesus is returning, we should . . . Use color markers to create artwork that illustrates your answers.

Give the groups time to complete their posters. Then ask them to show their work to the rest of the class.

INTO LIFE

Create handouts for an acrostic. Have the phrase *Jesus Is Coming* printed vertically down the middle. To get your students started, have the phrase *I Have Hope* printed horizontally, with the word *I* in the horizontal phrase intersecting an *i* in the vertical phrase. Encourage your students to complete the acrostic horizontally with a list of some benefits of Jesus' coming again. Here are possible completions: ra**I**sed from death, **E**verlasting life, **C**hanged body, no more tear**S**, place prepared for **U**s, reunited with l**O**ved ones.

Distribute copies of the reproducible exercise "What a Story to Tell!" from page 128 as students depart.

Reproducible Activity Pages

Each of the following pages is designed to be used with one of the lessons of the current quarter. You'll find the activities have a variety of helpful applications. Here are a few suggestions on how to use an activity:

- Use it to supplement the discovery learning plan.

- Use it to introduce the lesson concept.

- Use it to make application near the close of your class time.

- Create an overhead transparency with the page, and use it to have the class do the activity together.

Sometimes there are two or more activities on a sheet. Sometimes there is just one. Use each activity as it best suits your own teaching style and the personality of your class.

Good Leaders Listen and Prepare

Place a D in front of the sentence below that was a direction from God to Joshua; place a P in front of a promise. There will be five of each.

_____ Get ready to cross the Jordan River (v. 2)

_____ God would give Joshua every place he set his foot (v. 3)

_____ No one would be able to stand against Joshua (v. 5)

_____ God would never leave you nor forsake Joshua (v. 5)

_____ Be strong and courageous (vv. 6, 7)

_____ Obey all the law (v. 7)

_____ Meditate on the law day and night (v. 8)

_____ Do everything that is written in the law (v. 8)

_____ Joshua would be prosperous and successful (v. 8)

_____ God will be with you wherever you go (v. 9)

Good Leaders Take Action

Circle the traits below that you possess.

Enthusiastic	Learns from mistakes	Dependable
Confident	Visionary	Anticipates needs
Organized	Problem solver	Team builder
Peacemaker	Motivates others	Servant
Good people skills	Financially astute	Self-disciplined

Which of these do you think are distinctive leadership traits? Which are traits that anyone can and should develop, whether a leader or not? Jot your ideas below.

Is there a current ministry (or needed ministry) in your church that could use someone with those traits? How could you use these abilities to help your congregation? Jot your ideas below.

Gideon Hears God

The letters that appear jumbled below this diagram need to be rearranged in the boxes to form a phrase from today's Scripture text. Any given letter may be placed ONLY in one of the boxes that is directly above it vertically. For example, the *I* and the *D* that are in the farthest column to the right may only be placed in the two boxes in the rightmost column of the puzzle box, with either the *I* above the *D* or the *D* above the *I*. The answer is one of today's verses.

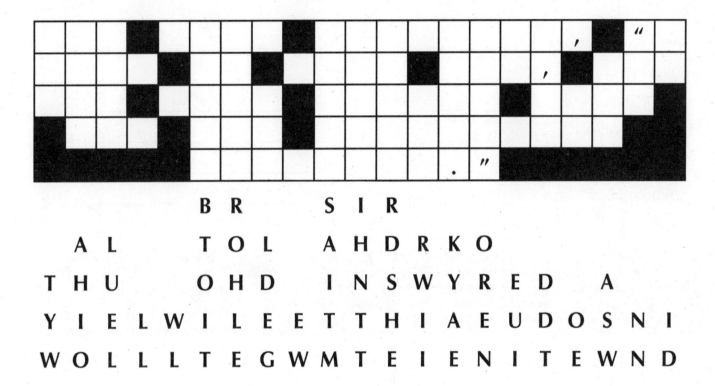

```
                B  R           S  I  R
      A  L       T  O  L       A  H  D  R  K  O
   T  H  U       O  H  D       I  N  S  W  Y  R  E  D       A
Y  I  E  L  W  I  L  E  E  T  T  H  I  A  E  U  D  O  S  N  I
W  O  L  L  L  T  E  G  W  M  T  E  I  E  N  I  T  E  W  N  D
```

Others Hear God

Joshua, Solomon, Jeremiah, Ezekiel, Jonah, and Paul are others who heard God's call. List three strengths of each. What weaknesses challenged their ability to serve God as they may have desired? Jot your ideas below.

Now make it personal. What is God calling you to do? What weakness will you have to turn over to God in order to be able to serve most effectively?

Biblical Repentance

Ezra knew the importance of repentance to Israel's future. Other Scripture writers also knew the importance of repentance to the Christian life. Take a look at each of the Scriptures below. Identify the speaker/writer in the text and the role repentance plays (or should play) in the Christian life.

SCRIPTURE TEXT	SPEAKER	RELATIONSHIP TO THE CHRISTIAN LIFE
Matthew 3:1-3	_____	_____
Luke 13:3-5	_____	_____
Acts 2:38	_____	_____
Acts 17:30, 31	_____	_____
2 Corinthians 7:9	_____	_____
2 Peter 3:8, 9	_____	_____
Revelation 2:5	_____	_____

Answers: Matthew 3:1-3: John the Baptist, prepares the way to Christ; Luke 13:3-5: Jesus, take personal responsibility for sin; Acts 2:38: Peter, leads to salvation; Acts 17:30, 31: Paul, judgment is pending; 2 Corinthians 7:9: Paul, convicts the heart; 2 Peter 3:8, 9: Peter, part of avoiding condemnation; Revelation 2:5: John, leads to changed actions

Moving Through Repentance

Using the thought-starters below, complete this prayer by identifying the specific details from your own life that could or should fit under each in order to make your repentance complete.

Lord, I humbly acknowledge my sin to you and ask you to forgive me for . . .

Some of the effects my sin has had on myself and others include . . .

I realize you have placed the following people and circumstances in my path to warn me of my folly:

In spite of my rebellion, you have showered your grace and blessings upon me in the following ways:

I confess my guilt before you, Lord, and repent of my sin. Guide me in your righteousness and help me to submit to your will. In Jesus' name. Amen.

How Do I Rate as a Volunteer?

• *Complete the survey below to assess your motivation for volunteering.* •

I volunteer to meet the needs of my church and/or my community . . . . .Agree   Disagree

I volunteer because I believe God commands me to do so . . . . .Agree   Disagree

I volunteer because it makes me feel good about myself . . . . .Agree   Disagree

I volunteer because I want to be "light" and "salt" in my community . . . . .Agree   Disagree

I volunteer when I believe in the cause or want to support an organization . . . . .Agree   Disagree

I volunteer only for projects involving my church . . . . .Agree   Disagree

I volunteer only for tasks that relate to my calling as a Christian . . . . .Agree   Disagree

I volunteer because it exposes me to people from different walks of life . . . . .Agree   Disagree

I volunteer because I want to be a blessing to someone else . . . . .Agree   Disagree

I volunteer because it is my duty as a Christian and a citizen . . . . .Agree   Disagree

I volunteer to relieve some of the guilt I have . . . . .Agree   Disagree

I volunteer whenever there is a call to do so . . . . .Agree   Disagree

I volunteer only when someone I know asks me to do so . . . . .Agree   Disagree

I volunteer for anything that comes to my attention . . . . .Agree   Disagree

I volunteer only for those tasks for which I am equipped . . . . .Agree   Disagree

I volunteer because it makes me feel less lonely . . . . .Agree   Disagree

I volunteer because it keeps me busy . . . . .Agree   Disagree

I volunteer because it helps me keep my mind off my problems . . . . .Agree   Disagree

Jesus Prayed

In today's study Jesus is found praying, early in the morning and alone (Mark 1:35). Examine each of the following texts and decide what generalization about Jesus' practice of prayer you can and should emulate. Jot your ideas to the right.

Matthew 26:36-44

Mark 6:41

Luke 5:16

Luke 6:12

Luke 23:34

John 11:41, 42

John 17:20-26

"Everyone Is Looking for You"

Peter's words to Jesus in Mark 1:37 will be no less true in the year 2009 than in Jesus' lifetime for those who understand his power and his grace. Design two lists for your own proclamation that make Jesus absolutely attractive to those in sin and need. Consider the ways and occasions you can use your lists in evangelism.

HIS POWER   HIS GRACE

Demons Out, Christ In

For each of the following 11 questions you can answer, delete (mark out) a letter from the man on the left and write it into the pigs on the right.

1. Where did the man dwell?

2. What was evidence of the man's strength?

3. What behaviors filled the man's days and nights?

4. What did the evil spirits call Jesus?

5. Where was the man assigned to witness?

6. About how many pigs were drowned?

7. What did the possessed man do when he saw Jesus?

8. What name did the evil spirit give itself?

9. As Jesus was leaving, what was the freed man's request?

10. Why did Jesus leave so soon (per v. 17)?

11. How did the people react to the freed man's testimony?

Answers: 1. the tombs; **2.** was able to break chains; **3.** crying out and cutting himself; **4.** Jesus, Son of the Most High God; **5.** home to family; **6.** about 2,000; **7.** ran to Jesus, fell on his knees; **8.** Legion; **9.** to go with Jesus; **10.** people asked him to; **11.** amazement.

Delivered!

The demoniac was blessed significantly by the coming of Christ into his life. The man was delivered from torment to peace, from alienation to rejoining society. What other elements of deliverance do you see in his circumstances?

Delivered! From _____ to _____

Delivered! From _____ to _____

And what of yourself? If you are in Christ, how do you fill in this change ? If you are not yet in Christ, what areas of deliverance you want for your life?

Delivered! From _____ to _____

Delivered! From _____ to _____

Surprise!

Decide to what extent you are surprised by Jesus' behavior and words and the other events in today's text in Mark 7:24-37. Circle 1 for "no surprise" to 5 for "very surprised."

1 2 3 4 5   Jesus was attempting to hide in non-Jewish territory.

1 2 3 4 5   A Gentile woman in the area of Tyre had heard of Jesus' abilities to heal.

1 2 3 4 5   Jesus implied that Gentiles were dogs.

1 2 3 4 5   The woman found her daughter at home to be resting in bed.

1 2 3 4 5   Jesus traveled in the Greek area of Decapolis.

1 2 3 4 5   Jesus took the deaf and mute man aside privately to deal with him.

1 2 3 4 5   Jesus put his fingers in the deaf man's ears.

1 2 3 4 5   Jesus touched the man's tongue with his own saliva.

1 2 3 4 5   Jesus spoke in Aramaic.

1 2 3 4 5   The deaf-and-mute man's afflictions disappeared instantly.

1 2 3 4 5   Jesus directed the man and his friends to tell no one of the miracle.

1 2 3 4 5   All those around the man were amazed and told everyone about it.

Discuss and compare your levels of surprise within your study group.

Outside My House

For the coming week make a list here of those "outside your house" with whom you have a regular—even if distant—relationship (such as your mail carrier). Consider if each entry on your list is also an "outsider" in relationship to opportunity to know and value the gospel. Try to enter one person, by name or description, each day of the week.

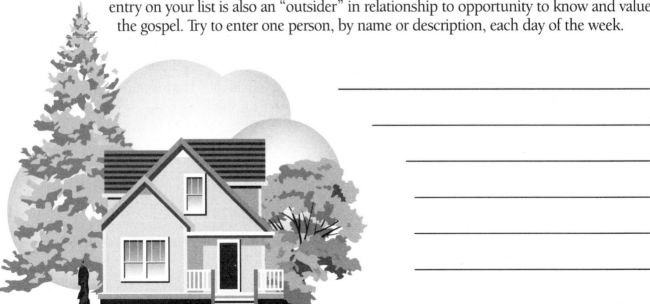

In what way can you approach one of these "outsiders" with the gospel?

It's True

The following true-false test is easy: just mark all of the statements as being true (T)! Then justify your answer with a verse number from today's text in Mark 10:17-31.

T F 1. We are incapable of saving ourselves . . . . ._____

T F 2. There are both temporal and eternal benefits of following Christ . . . . ._____

T F 3. With God anything is possible. . . . . ._____

T F 4. Jesus loves sinners . . . . ._____

T F 5. Trusting in personal wealth will keep one out of the kingdom of God . . . . ._____

T F 6. Some of Jesus' truths are so startling as to befuddle and confuse . . . . ._____

Answers: 1, v. 27; 2, v. 29; 3, v. 27; 4, v. 21; 5, v. 25; v. 24

Trusting Riches: The Kingdom of Thingdom

Living in a prosperous nation with a materialistic mind-set makes it difficult for Christians to escape the bonds of trusting riches out of proportion to their true value. Put a dollar sign ($) by each of the following sentences that "sounds like me." Establish your own scale to evaluate the level of trust one has in riches: put two, three, or four dollar signs on items you have more trouble with. What changes do you commit to making in lifestyle and attitude?

___ Shopping is one of my favorite recreational activities.

___ I flinch when my church leadership talks about money and financial needs of the church.

___ I think it is only responsible to have enough insurance to cover all possible contingencies, especially for old age.

___ My family should have all the latest electronics and comfort devices.

___ Garage sales and online auctions are the ways I dispose of items, rather than as gifts to those who need them.

___ I have replaced items—from cars to clothes— when the old were still quite serviceable.

___ My giving to benevolent causes and church causes is less than five percent of my income.

___ I would always choose a week-long cruise over a week-long service project or missions trip.

___ Extra work for extra money is more appealing to me than extra time with my family.

___ My living space is larger than I (and my family) need.

___ There are a number of items on my *need it* list that are not true needs.

___ I don't make nearly enough money to call myself "content."

___ Many who know me would call me *stingy*; I prefer the term *careful.*

How to Be Holy

Since we can't be holy on our own, we look to God as the source of our holiness. Complete the following Scriptures about God's holiness by filling in the missing words. Then unscramble the letters in the boxes/circles to spell out the two ways that Christians are to be set apart by God for holiness.

"You are to be holy to me __ ☐ __ __ __ ◯ __ I, the Lord, am holy" (Leviticus 20:26).

"There is ◯☐ ☐ __ ☐ holy like the Lord" (1 Samuel 2:2).

"Save us, O God our __ __ ☐ __ __ ◯ ; . . . that we may give thanks to your holy name, that we may glory in your praise" (1 Chronicles 16:35).

" __ ◯ __ ☐ __ ◯ __ the Lord in the splendor of his holiness" (Psalm 29:2).

"Your statues stand firm; holiness __ ☐ __ ☐ __ __ your house for endless days, O Lord" (Psalm 93:5).

"Holy, holy, holy is the Lord __ __ ◯ __ ☐ __ ☐ __ ; the whole earth is ◯ __ __ __ of his glory" (Isaiah 6:3).

Be set apart ☐☐ ☐☐☐☐☐ ☐☐☐.

Be set apart ◯◯◯◯ ◯◯◯.

Holiness Habits

One way I will draw closer to God this week is by . . .

I will find a way to serve God in the area of . . .

With God's help I will strive to overcome the sin of . . .

From Darkness to Light

A life lived apart from God is a life lived in darkness. As you think of people you know who do not know God, use the dark cloud on the left to fill in details from their lives. Some areas are suggested. In the bright cloud give a description of your life or the lives of other Christians.

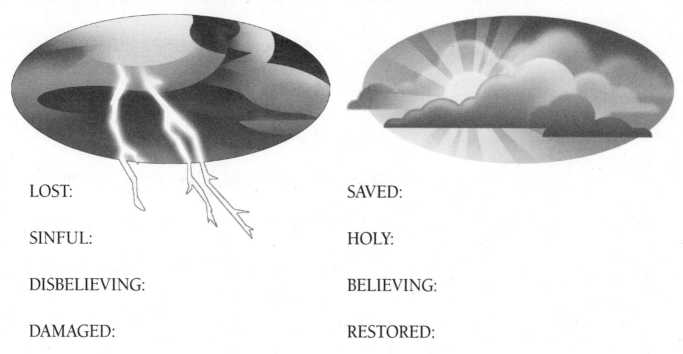

LOST:

SINFUL:

DISBELIEVING:

DAMAGED:

SAVED:

HOLY:

BELIEVING:

RESTORED:

Put It in Words

As you think about how much your life has changed since you became a Christian, use the space below to write a poem or a prayer that declares "the praises of him who called you out of darkness into his wonderful light" (1 Peter 2:9).

Why Suffer for Christ?

Today's text from 1 Peter 4 leads us to reach a conclusion regarding what Christian suffering should result in. Solve the puzzle below to find out what that is. As you answer the clues, fill in the numbers below with the corresponding letters. Several clues have verse numbers indicated if you need some help.

1. __ __ __ __ __ . . . . Something painful that Christians suffer (v. 12).
   15 21 4 10 19

2. __ __ __ __ . . . . It is ____ for the righteous to be saved (v. 18).
   16 10 21 9

3. __ __ __ __ __ __ . . . . Opposite of ugly.
   11 2 5 17 19 22

4. __ __ __ __ . . . . Suffering Christians should continue to do ___ (v. 19).
   18 8 13 9

5. __ __ __ __ __ . . . . No Christian should suffer for being this (v. 15).
   1 16 4 6 14

6. __ __ __ __ __ __ . . . . A very popular Internet search engine.
   7 2 20 3 12 17

__ __   __ __ __ __   __ __ __   __ __ __
 1 2   3 4 5 6   7 8 9   10 11 12

__ __   __ __ __   __ __ __ __ __ .
13 14   15 16 17   18 19 20 21 22

A Proper Response

Check off all of the following responses that you are likely to have when you find yourself suffering as a direct result of your Christian faith.

___ Feel sorry for myself   ___ Get discouraged   ___ Feel blessed

___ Complain   ___ Give thanks   ___ Praise God

___ Ask God, "Why me?"   ___ Rejoice   ___ Continue to do good

In the space below write one way you will try to improve your response the next time you find yourself suffering as a Christian.

Evaluate Your Virtues

How well are you doing in all the areas of Christian growth mentioned in 2 Peter 1:5-7? Look at the chart below and put an X on each line to show where you think you fall.

WORRY - FAITH
(Afraid and unable to trust God)   *(Trust in God no matter what)*

GREED - GOODNESS
(Always adding to own possessions)   *(Includes sharing generously with others)*

IGNORANCE - KNOWLEDGE
(Little knowledge of or interest in the Bible)   *(Regularly read, study, memorize the Bible)*

IMPULSIVENESS -SELF-CONTROL
(Reacting without thinking)   *(Think and pray before acting)*

DISCOURAGEMENT - PERSEVERANCE
(Give up quickly and easily)   *(Keep on praying, etc., no matter what)*

GODLESSNESS -GODLINESS
(Jesus is not the primary role model)   *(Ever striving to be more like Jesus)*

SELF-INVOLVEMENT -BROTHERLY KINDNESS
(Too busy with own life to help others)   *(Very responsive to needs of others)*

INDIFFERENCE - LOVE
(Treat people like they don't matter)   *(Respond to each person as God's creation)*

Make a Change

Look over the above evaluation, then complete the following sentences:

The one area I am especially weak in is . . .

Believing that Jesus' "divine power has given [me] everything [I] need for life and godliness through [my] knowledge of him" (2 Peter 1:3), I will try to increase my knowledge of Jesus during the coming week by . . .

I also will seek the Lord's power to help me make the following change . . .

What a Story to Tell!

Peter uses some very vivid images to teach his fellow believers about the dramatic events that will occur when Jesus returns. Match each picture below to the corresponding verse(s) from 2 Peter 3:5-13. Then on a separate piece of paper write a narrative that you could use with unsaved friends as you point to each picture and tell them why they need to turn to Jesus for salvation.

It's for everyone

Brand new!

1,000 years = 1 day

1 day = 1,000 years

Answers: water, vv. 5, 6; fire, vv. 7, 10, 12; 1,000 years, v. 8; cross, v. 9; thief, v. 10a; roar, v. 10b; person, v. 11; new Heaven and earth, v. 13.

The Lord . . . is patient with you, not wanting anyone to perish, but everyone to come to repentance" (2 Peter 3:9).

Winter Quarter 2009–2010

Christ the Fulfillment

(Matthew)

Special Features

Lessons

Unit 1: The Promised Birth Fulfilled

Unit 2: Evidences of Jesus as Messiah

Unit 3: Testimonies to Jesus as Messiah

About These Lessons

If you were to choose a favorite Gospel, which would it be? Many in the earliest church would have chosen Matthew. Being the "most Jewish" of the four Gospels, Matthew was a natural favorite for the new Christians who came from a Jewish background. Jesus came into the world in a Jewish context. Thus Matthew offers a perspective on Christ that we must not miss!

Dec 6
Dec 13
Dec 20
Dec 27
Jan 3
Jan 10
Jan 17
Jan 24
Jan 31
Feb 7
Feb 14
Feb 21
Feb 28

Quarter Review

Use this page to form questions for the class to answer and discuss.
Then provide the information as a handout to summarize the lessons of the past quarter.

LESSON 1: THE LINEAGE OF DAVID

At the end of the book of Ruth we learn that she and Boaz marry and have a son. This son brings joy, especially to Naomi. But he brings joy to the world, too, as he becomes ancestor to David, and thus ancestor to the Christ!

LESSON 2: PROPHETS FORESHADOW MESSIAH'S BIRTH

Isaiah predicted that a virgin would be with child and give birth to a son. Some 800 years later, Mary was told she would be that virgin. Luke reports she accepted her role with faith and courage.

LESSON 3: IMMANUEL IS BORN

Matthew tells of the Messiah's birth from Joseph's perspective. What great faith and courage it took for him to accept his role! He becomes an example of righteousness, mercy, and faith for us today.

LESSON 4: MESSIAH'S BIRTH CAUSES JOY AND RAGE

Christ has been the focus of opposing viewpoints from the beginning. Magi travel hundreds of miles to worship, and a jealous king plots murder. What viewpoints exist today?

LESSON 5: PROCLAIMED IN BAPTISM

John had made a name for himself, preaching and baptizing repentant sinners. How would Jesus be distinuished from them? The appearance of a dove and a voice from Heaven powerfully proclaimed Jesus as God's Son!

LESSON 6: STRENGTHENED IN TEMPTATION

Hebrews tells us that Jesus "has been tempted in every way, just as we are" (4:15). This lesson gives examples. In so doing it gives us help for facing temptations of our own. Could it be that the ministry of angels here is also relevant to us?

LESSON 7: DEMONSTRATED IN ACTS OF HEALING

Jesus' miracles were acts of temder compassion, but they were more. They were acts of power that declared him to be divine. For honest inquirers, like John, the evidence was sufficient. For scoffers, like the Pharisees, it was not.

LESSON 8: DECLARED IN PRAYER

Listening in on the prayer of one who has a deep love for the Lord is a treat. How wonderful it must have been to hear Jesus pray! His prayer, his connection with the Father, and his invitation to join him are central to this lesson.

LESSON 9: REVEALED IN REJECTION

Jesus' identity is clearly revealed his miracles, his teachings, his fulfillment of prophecy, and in other evidences. Yet there were many who rejected him. What wondrous blessings they missed! Are you missing something?

LESSON 10: RECOGNIZED IN GENTILE TERRITORY

In his hometown Jesus was rejected. How refreshing to find in Gentile territory hearts open to him! Even when her faith was challenged, the Canaanite woman did not back down. Is your faith as strong?

LESSON 11: DECLARED BY PETER

Rumors were swirling about Jesus; could the disciples sort out the truth? Peter made a bold affirmation of Jesus' identity. Would he remain as bold when the real test came? We know he didn't. Do we?

LESSON 12: WITNESSED BY DISCIPLES

Only three disciples were present when Jesus was transfigured and spoke with Moses and Elijah. By their testimony the event is well known today. By your testimony, who knows about Jesus today?

LESSON 13: ANOINTED IN BETHANY

Time was short. Jesus' life was in danger. At a dinner in Bethany, one woman alone seemed to understand the urgency of the hour. Her act of devotion was criticized by many but honored by the Lord. Can you stand up to the critics?

What Was the Reason?

by Mark S. Krause

Does everything happen for a reason? This is a deep doctrinal question. Any thoughtful person must wrestle with whether there is an all-powerful God who controls things, or if our universe is a place where things happen purely by mechanical cause-and-effect procedures.

Why did the life of Jesus play out the way it did? Was there a reason? The Bible's answer to this question is *Yes*. The reason is that the birth, ministry, death, resurrection, and ascension of Jesus were according to God's plan. This was not a make-it-up-as-we-go plan, however. It was a plan in the wisdom of God that had been foreordained long before Jesus was born.

UNIT 1: THE PROMISED BIRTH FULFILLED

The lessons for the month of December look at the birth of Jesus from the perspective of the books of Matthew and Luke. Matthew is the Gospel author most concerned with showing ways in which Jesus fulfilled Old Testament prophecy. Our four lessons also will examine Old Testament passages that give important historical context in understanding the Messiah.

Lesson 1 takes us to the book of Ruth. This book, a story of courage and faithfulness, has a larger role in the biblical story line. Ruth's marriage to Boaz is a heartwarming tale, but its lasting significance is in the great-grandson of this couple: King David. The lesson explores the ways in which the lineage of Jesus (a descendant of David) is a vital part of his identity as the promised Messiah.

In *Lesson 2* we will look at a dramatic prophecy in Isaiah and its fulfillment over 700 years later. Some may ask, "Can we still believe in the virgin birth in our world of technology and science?" At the core of this lesson is the statement from the angel, "Nothing is impossible with God." The truth of the virgin birth is a fundamental part of a Christian understanding of the Christmas story, and it will be presented using Luke's account of Mary's visit by the angel.

Lesson 3 examines the story of the birth of Jesus from the perspective of Joseph. The miraculous pregnancy of a virgin was not immediately explained to him. At first he saw her pregnancy as evidence of the defilement of his fiancée and was determined to release her from their engagement. Then he, like Mary, received an angelic message that told him to stand firm in his commitment to the woman. The lesson portrays Joseph's obedient faithfulness.

How did others respond to the birth of the Messiah? *Lesson 4* looks at two diametrically opposed reactions. On the side of faith and wonder are the Magi, mysterious scholars from the East who learn of Jesus' birth through their interpretation of a new star. On the side of jealousy and violence is bitter old King Herod, who seeks to have the baby killed. The lesson will explore why these different reactions arose and why we still see them today in people who are confronted by the message of Jesus.

UNIT 2: EVIDENCES OF JESUS AS MESSIAH

Jesus' claim to be the Jewish Messiah is not built on only a single piece of evidence. While Jesus' resurrection from the dead may be his ultimate, unquestionable stamp of approval by God, his life and ministry offer many earlier proofs of

DECEMBER

JANUARY

his true identity as the Son of God. *Lesson 5* studies the first public confirmation of his messiahship: his baptism by John. Here we consider the testimony of John himself and the heavenly voice and dove sent from the Father.

A difficult episode during the initial stages of Jesus' ministry is examined in *Lesson 6*: his experience of a period of temptation while spending time alone in the desert. Jesus was challenged by Satan in a direct, personal way that startles us. But his faithful handling of the situation is both instructive to us for our own temptation experiences and helpful in understanding the Messiah more fully.

Jesus received wide acclaim for his ministry of miraculous healing. *Lesson 7* looks at two of these healings. The lesson also looks at the various responses to Jesus and his ministry.

Lesson 8 is an analysis of one of Jesus' recorded prayers. Jesus' comments on his prayer include the gracious invitation "Come to me, all you who are weary and burdened" (Matthew 11:28). With this Scripture, we better understand the nature of Jesus' mission.

This unit of evidences for Jesus' messianic claims finishes with the account of his lack of acceptance by the residents of his home region. *Lesson 9* looks at how Jesus marveled at the lack of repentance by some despite his mighty works. Their lack of faith prevented the full power of God's mighty works from being shown in their community.

FEBRUARY

UNIT 3: TESTIMONIES TO JESUS AS MESSIAH

The lessons for February are also drawn from the book of Matthew. They are based on some of the personal testimonies that Matthew offers from people who came to faith in Jesus as the Messiah as a result of their encounters with him.

Lesson 10 begins with the testimony of a Canaanite woman who asked Jesus to save her daughter from a demon. Matthew records Jesus' delight at the great faith he found in this Gentile woman.

Lesson 11 is based on one of the key passages in the entire New Testament: Peter's confession of faith in Jesus as the Christ, the Son of the living God. All who would claim to be Christians must see their own faith mirrored in Peter's confession, for it is the very core of the gospel. This lesson will challenge students to reaffirm their personal faith in Christ.

Peter's declaration of Jesus as the Christ is followed with a confirmation from God himself: the transfiguration. *Lesson 12* will lead students through an examination of this glimpse of Jesus' glory that was given to Peter and his two companions, and it will apply this eternal reality to their own walks of faith.

The quarter ends with a lesson based on the act of a woman who anointed Jesus with costly perfumed oil. Jesus promised that her act of extravagant faith would not be forgotten. *Lesson 13* teaches us how her devotion was derided by critics, but honored by Jesus himself. From her we may learn new ways in which we too may offer acts of faithful devotion to our Lord Jesus.

PROPHECY AND FULFILLMENT

Jesus fulfilled many dramatically detailed predictions about his life, predictions given hundreds of years in advance. This is remarkable and amazing. But there is more to the fulfillment side than predictions. Jesus himself was also the fulfillment of God's plan in a larger way: he was the embodiment of God's will. He was the plan for saving sinners. This quarter's lessons drive that theme home to your students. Jesus is the fulfillment of God's plan for our salvation.

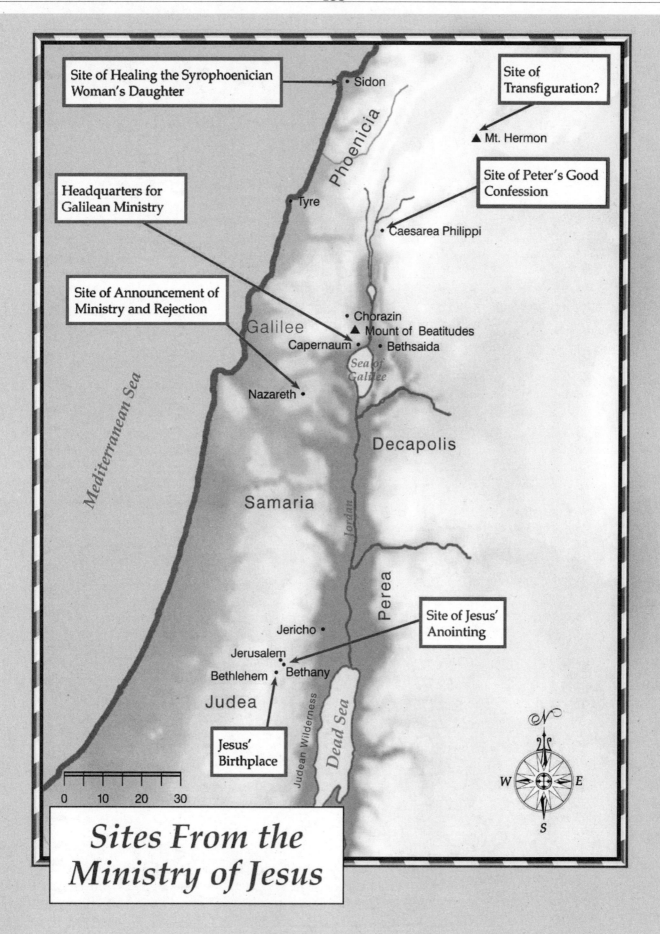

Site of Healing the Syrophoenician Woman's Daughter

Site of Transfiguration?

▲ Mt. Hermon

Site of Peter's Good Confession

Headquarters for Galilean Ministry

• Tyre

Phoenicia

• Sidon

• Caesarea Philippi

Site of Announcement of Ministry and Rejection

Galilee

• Chorazin

▲ Mount of Beatitudes

Capernaum •

• Bethsaida

Sea of Galilee

Nazareth •

Mediterranean Sea

Decapolis

Samaria

Jordan

Perea

Site of Jesus' Anointing

Jericho •

Jerusalem •

Bethlehem •

• Bethany

Judea

Jesus' Birthplace

Judean Wilderness

Dead Sea

N

W   E

S

0   10   20   30

Sites From the Ministry of Jesus

THE MARVELOUS WORKS OF GOD

ACCEPT—BLIND SEE!
REJECT—FEW MIGHTY WORKS!

ACCEPT—LEPERS CLEANSED!
REJECT—FEW MIGHTY WORKS!

ACCEPT—DEAD ARE RAISED!
REJECT—FEW MIGHTY WORKS!

ACCEPT—GOSPEL PREACHED!
REJECT—FEW MIGHTY WORKS!

ACCEPT—LAME WALK!
REJECT—FEW MIGHTY WORKS!

ACCEPT—DEAF HEAR!
REJECT—FEW MIGHTY WORKS!

Leading the Discussion

SETTING AND TIPS

by James Riley Estep

"Don't teachers just use discussion as a time-filler? I mean, some teachers come unprepared, then fill the class time with discussion!"

Unfortunately, we all have experienced discussions that fizzled. As with any teaching method, discussion sometimes is used *unintentionally*, meaning without a purpose and design. Discussions that lack purpose and design can indeed degenerate into pointless time-filling. The result may be a meandering exercise in the sharing of personal experience and perspective. When discussion is not directed toward a learning goal, you may hear one of your small groups discussing who's playing in the football game later that afternoon rather than discussing, say, the significance of Ruth in the lineage of King David (Lesson 1). This is called *discussion drift*. How do we fix this problem?

When properly used, discussion can be a most effective teaching method that values the input from your learners. Discussion sends the signal that the teacher's viewpoint is *not* the only valid one in the class, but that the insights, perspectives, and experiences of the students are also important. Discussion also can teach participants how to think biblically about life decisions and circumstances in a classroom environment before facing the issues in real life.

SETTING THE STAGE

Using discussion as an effective method of teaching requires that you set the stage in four ways. *First, make sure to use purposeful, open-ended questions.* Discussion often fizzles as a teaching method because the kind of question the teacher poses is not capable of discussion. Questions that require a simple factual answer or that can be answered *yes* or *no* fall into this category.

For example, consider this question as it might be posed for Lesson 1: "Does the Bible describe Ruth as an ancestor of King David?" Answer: "Well, yes." How can anyone legitimately *discuss* such a question? While any given discussion question can have a desired outcome—something on which the rest of the lesson can build—the question should not be so "closed" that it does not allow an open exchange of ideas.

Now think of this question: "Why is Ruth's ancestry in King David's lineage significant?" This kind of question calls for more than a one-word or yes/no response. Such a question calls for the student to analyze and synthesize biblical material. They have to *think*, not simply recall. If you are accustomed to asking the typical one-word, yes/no type of question, practice turning them into open, discussion-laden questions.

Second, you as a teacher have to want to use discussion as a teaching method and be mentally prepared to do so. Your mental preparation as teacher includes the realization that your role is somewhat different than it is under the lecture method. You as teacher must see yourself not only as the sage-on-the-stage, but also (some would say *primarily*) as a guide-at-the-side.

Many times teachers think their role is to respond quickly to questions with the "correct" answer. But when using discussion, the teacher often will turn questions back to the class to keep the discussion going. There will

When properly used, discussion can be a most effective teaching method that values the input from your learners.

Use purposeful, open-ended questions.

You as a teacher have to want to use discussion as a teaching method and be mentally prepared to do so.

be time for the teacher to provide his or her own thoughts once the class has had an opportunity to wrestle with the question. Learners will be more receptive to the teacher's thoughts once they have had a chance to discuss the matter. This requires a certain amount of patience as you assist students in working through difficult biblical or personal life questions for themselves.

Patient teachers using the discussion method also must know how to respond gently to a student whose response is way off base. Promoting discussion doesn't mean that you will allow heretical suggestions to go unchallenged. Nor does it mean that you will allow football table talk to replace the instructional discussion. Even so, a certain amount of gentleness is needed here. Too firm of a response to a student may cause others in the class to become hesitant in sharing their ideas for fear of a negative response from the teacher.

Your mental preparation also should include being thoroughly familiar with the lesson material. Such preparation often will need to be more extensive than it would be when using lecture. In a lecture format, the teacher knows exactly what is to be said and how it is to be said. Under a discussion format, the teacher's preparation includes anticipating the possible responses of students in order to be able to address them.

For example, if you are teaching a class on *How We Got the Bible,* then you should be prepared to respond to current "fad" theories that your learners are likely to mention. Of course, you can't be prepared for every possible question. In that case, don't pretend! Be honest and say, "I don't really know, but I will look into it."

Prepare your students in advance for discussion.

Third, prepare your students in advance for discussion. Discussion will fizzle if students are not ready for it. Suppose you announce, "Today we are going to discuss Ruth," but students were not asked to read Ruth prior to class or e-mailed a list of possible discussion questions to investigate. As a result, students enter class "cognitively cold," but are expected to heat up very quickly!

Effective discussions are those in which the students are equipped to engage. If students are neither informed about the subject nor provided relevant information, then their discussion is more likely to end up being a pooling of ignorance, a grasping for truth in the dark, or an occasion to talk about the big football game. The result is a discussion that does not achieve your learning goals.

This problem is avoided by providing students with relevant material in advance. This material can take the form of print media (for example, the *Adult Bible Class* student book) or digital media (for example, www.standard-lesson.com/intheworld.asp). Students also can be provided with a list of possible discussion questions in advance (perhaps by e-mail) so they can think about appropriate responses. Informed students make for an informed discussion and a genuine learning environment.

A learning environment conducive to discussion will be a great help.

Fourth, a learning environment conducive to discussion will be a great help. The physical aspects of your learning space are important. In general, someone who walks into your learning space can make an educated guess as to what method of teaching is favored by the instructor (or, at least, which method of teaching the room is designed to support) just by looking at the layout. Classrooms that feature a front-and-center podium, a projector, and rows of seats facing forward scream "lecture method!"

On the other hand, a classroom environment that favors discussion may have chairs in circles around tables. While such a classroom may have a podium, it will probably not be centered in front of the class, but located off to the side (being used to hold the teacher's notes). An environment conducive to discussion can also have a markerboard on which to write student ideas and responses.

When someone sees this kind of classroom, discussion is immediately assumed. After all, it is difficult to lecture to a class of students sitting at six round tables with some backs turned to you! When the environment is right, discussion is more readily used as a means of instruction.

CLASSROOM TIPS

Now that you know how to set the stage for discussion, we move to some practical tips. *First, make sure to provide the questions in written form.* This means writing them on the board, putting them on PowerPoint® slides, or reproducing them on handouts. (If some students have their backs to the board or screen because they are sitting at round tables, handouts may be best.) Students should not have to ask, "Now, what question are we supposed to be discussing?" or "Can you say that again?"

Second, make sure to walk around the room if you are using a small-group discussion format. Don't just stay at the front of the class or walk into the hallway. Rather, roam throughout the class, listening to the group discussions. This allows you to know what might be brought up when the groups share their conclusions. It can also allow you to correct an erroneous idea while it is still contained within one discussion group.

Third, set a time limit for discussion. When the question is provided to the class, say, for example, "Take eight minutes to discuss this question." This helps you keep the class time flowing. It also keeps the groups on task, since they know they don't have time to meander.

Fourth, don't reveal all your questions at once. Occasionally, one discussion question will build on another. For example, consider these two questions for Lesson 1 of this quarter: "How significant can one 'common person' be in the history of a nation?" and "How significant was Ruth's impact on biblical history?" Students may wrestle with the first question and conclude that common people have little significance in the grand sweep of history, but they may change their minds after seeing the second question revealed. The impact of the discussion may be diminished if you put both questions on the board at the same time.

Fifth, always bring closure. Using the discussion method does not mean allowing students to leave class with nothing more than questions. Provide directions, summations, and answers to the questions by utilizing their insights and the material you have prepared.

Finally, don't give up. The way to use discussion productively is to practice using it. Learn from the experience, correct your mistakes, and keep trying. It will be worth it!

Provide the questions in written form.

Walk around the room if you are using a small-group discussion format.

Set a time limit for the discussion

Don't reveal all your questions at once.

Always bring closure.

Don't give up.

How to Say It

Use this list to help you pronounce the names and hard-to-pronounce words in the lessons of the winter quarter.

A

Achan. AY-kan.
Agrippa. Uh-GRIP-puh.
Ahaz. AY-haz.
Ahaziah. Ay-huh-ZYE-uh.
alabaster. AL-uh-BAS-ter.
Amaziah. Am-uh-ZYE-uh.
Amminadab. Uh-MIN-uh-dab.
Antipas. AN-tih-pus.
Antipater. An-TIH-puh-ter.
Aramaic. AIR-uh-MAY-ik.
Archelaus. Are-kuh-LAY-us.
Arimathea. AIR-uh-muh-THEE-uh (TH as in THIN).
Assyria. Uh-SEAR-ee-uh.
Augustine. AW-gus-TEEN or Aw-GUS-tin.
Azariah. Az-uh-RYE-uh.

B

Baal. BAY-ul.
Bathsheba. Bath-SHE-buh.
Bethsaida. Beth-SAY-uh-duh.

C

Caesarea Philippi. Sess-uh-REE-uh Fih-LIP-pie or FIL-ih-pie.
Caiaphas. KAY-uh-fus or KYE-uh-fus.
Canaan. KAY-nun.
Capernaum. Kuh-PER-nay-um.
Che Guevara. Chay Geh-VAR-uh.
Chorazin. Ko-RAY-zin.
Cornelius. Cor-NEEL-yus.

D

Decapolis. Dee-CAP-uh-lis.
demoniac. duh-MOE-nee-ak.

E

Elimelech. Ee-LIM-eh-leck.
Ephraim. EE-fray-im.
ethnarch. ETH-nark.
eugenics. you-JEN-iks.

F

Fulgencio Batista. Fool-GEN-see-oh Buh-TEES-tuh.

G

Galilee. GAL-uh-lee.
gematria. guh-MAY-tree-uh.
Gentiles. JEN-tiles.
Gethsemane. Geth-SEM-uh-nee (G as in get).

H

Heli. HEE-lie.
Herod Antipas. HAIR-ud AN-tih-pus.
Hezekiah. Hez-ih-KYE-uh.
Hiram. HIGH-rum.
Hoshea. Ho-SHAY-uh.

I

Idumea. Id-you-ME-uh.
Immanuel. Ih-MAN-you-el.
Iscariot. Iss-CARE-ee-ut.

J

Judaism. JOO-duh-izz-um or JOO-day-izz-um.
Judas Iscariot. JOO-dus Iss-CARE-ee-ut.
Judea. Joo-DEE-uh.

K

Kidron. KID-ron.
Korazin. Ko-RAY-zin.

L

Lazarus. LAZ-uh-rus.
levirate. LEH-vuh-rut.
Louis-Sébastien Mercier. LEW-ee-Say-bass-TYUN MER-see-yeh.

M

Magi. MAY-jye or MADGE-eye.
Messiah. Meh-SIGH-uh.

messianic. mess-ee-AN-ick.
Moab. MO-ab.

N

naiveté. noh-eve-TAY.
Nazarenes. NAZ-uh-reens.
Nazareth. NAZ-uh-reth.
Nicodemus. NICK-uh-DEE-mus.

O

obelisk. OB-uh-lisk.
oxymoron. ox-see-MORE-on.

P

Pekah. PEEK-uh.
Pentecost. PENT-ih-kost.
Pharisees. FAIR-ih-seez.
Pontius Pilate. PON-shus or PON-ti-us PIE-lut.
proselyte. PRAHSS-uh-light.

R

Rezin. REE-zin.

S

Samaria. Suh-MARE-ee-uh.
Sanhedrin. SAN-huh-drun or San-HEED-run.
Sennacherib. Sen-NACK-er-ib.
Sepphoris. SEF-uh-ris.
Shavuot. SHEH-vu-oat.
Sidon. SIGH-dun.
Sodom. SOD-um.

T

Taizé. Teh-ZAY.

U

Ulrich Zwingli. HUL-drik ZWIN-glee.
Uzziah. Uh-ZYE-uh.

Y

Yahweh (Hebrew). YAH-weh.

THE LINEAGE OF DAVID
LESSON 1

INTRODUCTION

A. GENEALOGY DETECTIVES

Have you done any investigation into your genealogy? Interest in discovering facts about one's family background seems to be rising steadily. Some people hope to find a forgotten jewel in the past centuries. Maybe they are actually descended from royalty!

Others are interested because of medical reasons. Genealogical research may help them understand certain genetic conditions they may have inherited. Interest is also greater because of the enormous amount of genealogical resources that are increasingly accessible. Some Internet sites allow such research for a nominal fee. This can be fascinating work. We may discover a branch of family nearby that we didn't even know about.

In the ancient world, genealogies were remembered with great care. It was important to know who your ancestors were. For example, the great families of Rome were judged on whether or not they could trace their ancestry to the city's beginnings. Julius Caesar was from the great patrician family *Julia*, which claimed to be descended from the founder of Rome. Wealth and accomplishment in Rome did not trump family background.

For believers in Christ, all this takes on added significance. Some genealogical inquiries are worthless, even counterproductive (see 1 Timothy 1:4; Titus 3:9). But just the opposite is true with regard to Jesus Christ. One of the important aspects of our belief in Jesus as the Messiah is the way the New Testament presents him as a fulfillment of prophecy. Some prophecies are tied to ancestors of Jesus who played major roles in the history of Israel.

B. LESSON BACKGROUND

The book of Ruth is counted in Jewish tradition as one of the five "Festal Scrolls," shorter books from the Hebrew Bible that were traditionally read on festival days. Ruth was read on Shavuot, also known as the Feast of Weeks. Shavuot is better known to Christians as Pentecost. It had originally marked the period from the Passover exodus from Egypt until the giving of the law at Sinai, but it developed into a harvest festival celebrating the spring crops. This seems to be its connection with Ruth, a little book whose story is bound up in the farming customs of the ancient Near East.

The book of Ruth, a story taking place about 1100 BC, is set in the time of the judges of Israel. The book tells of an Israelite man named Elimelech (meaning "my God is king") who moved his family to the neighboring land of Moab because of famine. His family consisted of his wife (Naomi) and two sons. Over a period of a decade, they apparently made a permanent home in Moab. The sons even married Moabite women.

Tragically, Elimelech and the sons died. This left Naomi without husband or sons to support her. She also had two widowed daughters-in-law. On

DEVOTIONAL READING:
2 SAMUEL 7:8-17
BACKGROUND SCRIPTURE:
RUTH 4:13-17;
MATTHEW 1:1-17
PRINTED TEXT:
RUTH 4:13-17; MATTHEW 1:1-6

LESSON AIMS

After participating in this lesson, each student will be able to:

1. Tell how Boaz and Ruth played key roles in the ancestry of Jesus.

2. Explain how God's providence works through such "normal" events as the birth of a child.

3. Suggest two or three ministry opportunities that may have come providentially to him or her and how these opportunities will be seized.

KEY VERSE

The women living there said, "Naomi has a son." And they named him Obed. He was the father of Jesse, the father of David. —Ruth 4:17

WHAT DO YOU THINK?

What are some ways that people respond to suffering today? How is one's view of God affected when difficult times come? How should one's view of God be affected in such times?

VISUALS FOR THESE LESSONS

The visual pictured in each lesson (example: page 143) is a small reproduction of a large, full-color poster included in the Adult Resources *packet for the Winter Quarter. That packet also contains the very useful* Presentation Helps *on a CD for teacher use. The packet is available from your supplier. Order No. 292.*

hearing of the availability of food in her ancestral homeland, Naomi decided to return to Bethlehem, which was located in the tribal province of Judah. This was a risky move, since she had been gone for a decade and did not know how she would be welcomed. One daughter-in-law, Ruth, decided to go with Naomi. In the process, Ruth pledged loyalty to Naomi and to her God (Ruth 1:16, 17).

When the two arrived in Bethlehem, they were received, but the male-dominated nature of their culture presented a challenge. Naomi understood that they needed to be connected with one of the men in order to ensure survival. The likely candidate was Boaz, a wealthy farmer and a kinsman of her dead husband. This resulted in Ruth attracting the attention of Boaz. She eventually married him according to the intricate customs of the time.

Ruth was a beloved book among the Jews of Jesus' day because of its story of these two strong and resilient women. This is not why the book was written, however, or why it is included in the Old Testament. The book of Ruth is important because it tells a significant story about the ancestors of King David. The amazing detail is that one of the key ancestors of David, namely his great grandmother, was not an Israelite. This detail becomes even more important for Matthew. He includes several foreign women in his genealogy of Jesus to support the point that Jesus, the promised Messiah, was to serve all nations, not just Israel.

I. DRAMA OF DAVID'S ANCESTRY (RUTH 4:13-17)
A. BIRTH (v. 13)
13. So Boaz took Ruth and she became his wife. Then he went to her, and the LORD enabled her to conceive, and she gave birth to a son.

Although some of the maneuvers used by *Ruth* and Naomi to get *Boaz* to marry Ruth are confusing to us, this verse makes it clear that their relationship is proper and respectable. Boaz does not sleep with Ruth until after their marriage, and their marriage is blessed by God with *a son.*

The earlier chapters of this book present Boaz as a confident and capable person. We should understand that he has entered this marriage willingly, not from trickery or compulsion. He must truly care for Ruth, and their marriage is welcomed by that rich farmer.

B. BLESSING (vv. 14, 15)
14. The women said to Naomi: "Praise be to the LORD, who this day has not left you without a kinsman-redeemer. May he become famous throughout Israel!

Surprisingly, the author points to *Naomi* as the one who is most blessed by the birth of Ruth's son. Her plan to return to Bethlehem has been a complete success. Not only have she and Ruth managed to survive, they have been blessed. In some ways, the return of Naomi to Israel is seen as a return to the God of Israel. God welcomes her back and rewards her faithfulness.

The women who are friends of Naomi understand the implications of these events. God has acted to preserve Naomi. He has given her a *kinsman-redeemer,* a security for the future. Therefore, the women praise God. They ask that the child of Boaz may be *famous throughout Israel.* This repeats what the elders of the city wish for Boaz himself on hearing of his pending marriage (Ruth 4:11, 12). The word for *famous* is based on a root that involves spoken communication. Boaz's son is to be one who is talked about.

15. "He will renew your life and sustain you in your old age. For your daughter-in-law, who loves you and who is better to you than seven sons, has given him birth."

In addition to the son's fame is the security that Naomi now has for her *old age*. She is too old to marry again and must count on her *daughter-in-law* and grandson to provide for her. Boaz himself is not a young man at this time (see Ruth 3:10). While Boaz's graciousness to Naomi is welcome, it will be his son who will provide for Naomi should Boaz precede her in death.

The blessing of the women also contains a remarkable tribute to Ruth. They tell Naomi that Ruth *is better* to her *than seven sons*. In a society that values boys above girls, this is praise of the highest sort. Naomi had had a good husband and two fine sons, but they are now gone. The only person who has persevered with her is this foreign woman, her loyal daughter-in-law. No amount of sons, even the "perfect number" of seven, can replace the love and honor that Ruth has given her mother-in-law.

C. BEGINNING (vv. 16, 17)

16. Then Naomi took the child, laid him in her lap and cared for him.

Although Ruth is the mother of *the child*, *Naomi* claims him too. She is determined to take an active role in his upbringing, as is her right according to the customs of that time. Today, family displacement for education and employment strains or even severs the ties of the extended family. Raising children is a challenge, and the help of grandparents can make it much easier for a weary mother. Surely, Ruth takes comfort from Naomi's help and delights in her mother-in-law's joy.

17. The women living there said, "Naomi has a son." And they named him Obed. He was the father of Jesse, the father of David.

When *Naomi* returned from Moab, she had asked that she be called *Mara*, meaning "the bitter one" (Ruth 1:20). Life to that point had been cruel to her. Now there is no room for bitterness, and *the women* affirm her as *Naomi*, which means "my delight." This is something like a girl nicknamed *Sunshine* going through a rough period and wishing to be called *Stormy*. Now the joy is back. Naomi is Sunshine again.

Realizing the significance of this birth, the local women phrase it as *"Naomi has a son."* She shares the blessing of this boy with Ruth in full measure. The name the women give the child is *Obed*, which means "servant." This can have a religious significance, so that we can understand Obed also to mean "worshiper." There are five men by the name of Obed in the Old Testament, so we should take care not to mix them up.

This verse closes by revealing the most important aspect of this story: its connection with *David*. Obed ultimately is the grandfather of that great king. David is beloved by his people, and the stories of his ancestors are of interest to Israel. This dramatic account thus provides background for the equally providential tale of David and his rise to the throne many decades hence.

THE FAMILY VOCATION

"Once upon a time," as the saying goes, sons often followed in their fathers' footsteps in terms of vocation. In biblical times, for example, the temple priests all came from the family of Levi.

WHAT DO YOU THINK?

How are modern concerns for being able to "keep body and soul together" in old age similar to and different from those same concerns in the ancient world? What do modern attitudes tell us about people's confidence in God's provision?

WHAT DO YOU THINK?

Why is it harder to sense God's sovereignty when we're in the middle of a crisis than when we are looking back later on how God used everything (including the crisis) in our lives? How can we keep from "going off the deep end" when in the middle of a crisis?

HOW TO SAY IT

Ahaziah. Ay-huh-ZYE-uh.
Amaziah. Am-uh-ZYE-uh.
Amminadab. Uh-MIN-uh-dab.
Azariah. Az-uh-RYE-uh.
Bathsheba. Bath-SHE-buh.
Elimelech. Ee-LIM-eh-leck.
eugenics. you-JEN-iks.
gematria. guh-MAY-tree-uh.
messianic. mess-ee-AN-ick.
Moab. MO-ab.
Pentecost. PENT-ih-kost.
Shavuot. SHEH-vu-oat.
Uzziah. Uh-ZYE-uh.

This following-in-the-footsteps phenomenon is much less common today than it was in centuries past. This shift is due, at least in part, to the fact that today there are many more occupations and opportunities from which to choose than was once the case. Even so, we occasionally still see cases of families whose generations follow each other in full-time church ministry or missionary work.

The naming of Ruth's son to be Obed puts something of a prophetic spin on this ancient custom. The name *Obed* means "servant" or "worshiper," and the biblical author reminds us that Obed became the grandfather of King David. David was certainly a servant of God. But David may be best known for his worship of God, given David's authorship of a vast number of the songs of praise that fill the book of Psalms.

In this sense, David continued in his grandfather's "family business." Regardless of the earthly vocation we or our descendants choose, we will serve best when we follow spiritually in our Father's "family business" (compare Luke 2:49).

—C. R. B.

II. DETAILS OF JESUS' ANCESTRY (MATTHEW 1:1-6)

A. KEY ANCESTORS (v. 1)

1. A record of the genealogy of Jesus Christ the son of David, the son of Abraham:

Matthew begins his Gospel in dramatic fashion. His Jewish readers immediately recognize the implications of *a record of the genealogy,* with certain listings of Genesis coming to mind. Genesis 2:4 introduces the "account of the heavens and the earth," that is, the creation of the world. Genesis 5:1 introduces the genealogical list of Adam's descendents. Matthew intends his readers to understand that what he is relating presents Jesus as a new creation (2 Corinthians 5:17; Galatians 6:15), as a new Adam (compare Romans 5:14; 1 Corinthians 15:22).

In this verse, Matthew also gives the three keys to understanding his genealogy of Jesus. First, Jesus is *Christ.* That means he is the promised anointed one of the Jewish nation. (The Greek word *Christ* means the same as the Hebrew word *Messiah.*) Second, he is *the son of David.* David was the king who was promised repeatedly that his throne would be eternal, his dynasty unending (see Psalm 89:3, 4). The designation *son of David* thus is distinctly messianic. Third, Jesus is *the son of Abraham.* In this, he fulfills the promise given to the father of the Hebrews that his descendant would be a blessing to all the families of the earth (Genesis 12:3; see Galatians 3:16).

B. EARLY ANCESTORS (vv. 2-5)

2. . . . Abraham was the father of Isaac,
  Isaac the father of Jacob,
  Jacob the father of Judah and his brothers,

There is no rigid form for genealogies in the ancient world. Matthew begins his genealogy at the most distant point he wants to include, which is *Abraham.* From there Matthew works forward to Jesus. In contrast, Luke begins his genealogy with Jesus and works backward all the way to Adam and to God himself (Luke 3:23-38).

This difference in procedures is because genealogies are more than simple lists of ancestors; they are lists with a purpose. Matthew's purpose is to use the lineage data to show that Jesus is the rightful heir to the promises given to

David. Thus Jesus is the legitimate Messiah. Matthew also wants to teach his readers some other lessons by using this genealogy, as we shall see.

When we look at the whole of Matthew's genealogy (Matthew 1:1-17), we see that he is selective in what he includes. He seems to use his selectivity in order to end up with 3 sets of 14 (1:17). When we compare Matthew's list with Old Testament data, we notice that some names have been dropped intentionally. For example, Matthew goes from Jehoram to Uzziah in verse 8. Uzziah (also known as Azariah) was actually the great great grandson of Jehoram. This means that Matthew has decided not to include Ahaziah (2 Kings 8:24), Joash (2 Kings 13:1), and Amaziah (2 Kings 14:1).

There seems to be a couple of reasons why Matthew presents Jesus' genealogy as 3 sets of 14. First is the value this gives to one who seeks to memorize the list. It is always easier to recite a list if we can remember how many items it contains. For example, my brother has 4 children. I may not be able to list their names immediately because of the foggy nature of memory. But I know that I must keep going until I come up with 4 names. Eventually I can do this, and the list is therefore complete.

A second, more subtle reason for the arrangement in sets of 14 may be found in the ancient Jewish practice of *gematria*. The Jews use the letters of the Hebrew alphabet for their numbering system, so each letter has an assigned numerical value. The numerical value for the name *David* is 14. Thus, the triple 14 may be another way of reinforcing the point that Jesus is the proper heir to David's messianic throne.

The first 4 names of the list are familiar to anyone who has read the book of Genesis. *Judah and his brothers* are, of course, the 12 patriarchs of Israel, the fathers of the 12 tribes. Matthew mentions them because they represent the whole of Israel. Even so, his focus is on Judah, the royal tribe, the tribe of King David (see Genesis 49:10).

3. . . . *Judah the father of Perez and Zerah, whose mother was Tamar,*
   Perez the father of Hezron,
   Hezron the father of Ram,
   In the first half of this verse, Matthew alludes to the scandalous behavior of *Judah* in his unwitting impregnation of his widowed daughter-in-law, *Tamar* (a story told in Genesis 38). The result was a set of twins, namely *Perez and Zerah* (38:28-30). Tamar is the first woman in Matthew's list. This is an unusual move in a time when genealogies include male ancestors only.

Altogether, Matthew includes four women in his listing, and it is likely that all were Gentiles: Tamar probably was a Canaanite; *Rahab* was a resident of Jericho; *Ruth* was a Moabitess; and Uriah's wife (that is, Bathsheba) probably was a Hittite. Matthew therefore shows the contribution of Gentiles to the lineage of Jesus. He is to be the Messiah for everyone, not just the Jews.

4, 5. . . . *Ram the father of Amminadab,*
   Amminadab the father of Nahshon,
   Nahshon the father of Salmon,
   Salmon the father of Boaz, whose mother was Rahab,
   Boaz the father of Obed, whose mother was Ruth,
   Obed the father of Jesse,
   The list continues, including mention of *Boaz, Obed,* and *Ruth* from the first part of our lesson. See also Numbers 1:7.

Visual for Lesson 1. *Point to this visual as you introduce either the question below or the question on page 144. [Notice also the variant spelling* Phares *for Perez.]*

WHAT DO YOU THINK?

What can we learn about God's grace and sovereignty when we see all the "problem people" in Jesus' family tree? How should this affect our attitudes toward the "problem people" in our own families?

C. ROYAL ANCESTORS (v. 6)

6. . . . *and Jesse the father of King David.*

David was the father of Solomon, whose mother had been Uriah's wife.

Matthew comes to a climactic statement in his genealogy, for we have been led to *King David*. No one else is given this title in this listing, not even the mighty *Solomon*. In fact, no one else is given any title until the very end, where Jesus is designated as *Christ* (Matthew 1:16).

David is the beginning of the true royal lineage in Israel. God's providential care of David's line allowed it to continue for 1,000 years, to find fulfillment in Jesus, the true son of David (see Matthew 1:1; 21:9).

HEREDITY VS. DECISIONS

The "notorious Jukes family" was thought by social scientists of the late nineteenth and early twentieth centuries to prove heredity to be the primary force in determining behavior. The supposedly dysfunctional Jukes clan was thought to have had a disproportionate number of social misfits in its family tree. The list included various types of criminals, prostitutes, and people with mental and physical disabilities that apparently cost society a lot of money for imprisonment and treatment.

Thus certain researchers saw the Jukes family as proof that compulsory sterilization was appropriate to relieve society of the burden of those deemed to be likely to produce "unfit" offspring. The supposed evidence of a hereditary defect that ran throughout the clan fueled a eugenics movement that advocated a terrible kind of social engineering.

More recently, however, researchers have found records at the State University of New York at Albany that show that many of the family members were leading members of society. The original research methodology was flawed, and the whole Jukes mythology has now been discredited.

The genealogy of Jesus contains some less-than-sterling characters—Rahab the prostitute to name one. Yet there is no consistent upward or downward trend in character quality of the individuals in this genealogy that would support a "heredity determines life" outlook. Jesus, as Son of God, is a special case, of course. Yet the fact that his life did not repeat the sins of his ancestors gives us hope that we too can control the quality of our character. He strengthens us to do so.

—C. R. B.

CONCLUSION

Jesus had frequent controversies with the Pharisees, who were Jews strongly committed to keeping the Law of Moses as they interpreted it. These men often asked Jesus questions in order to catch him in an inconsistency or offensive remark. In the case at Matthew 22:42, however, Jesus was the one who initiated the conversation by asking, "What do you think about the Christ? Whose son is he?" The Pharisees respond by saying, "The son of David." Jesus then proceeded to show that even the legendary King David acknowledged that the Messiah was his Lord. Such a view stood the Jewish expectation for Messiah on its head.

Trying to come to grips with the prophetic connections of the Bible can be both fascinating and frustrating. When we don't quite understand, we still must trust that God is in control of history. His purposes cannot be thwarted by the worst of human behavior. God's plan to provide humanity with a redeeming king took many odd turns over the centuries. Tamar? A shameless

PRAYER

O Mighty Father, God of Abraham, God of David, we marvel at your wisdom and patience in preparing the world for your Son, Jesus the Christ. May we commit ourselves to his service anew, for we pray in his name. Amen.

WHAT DO YOU THINK?

How far back can you trace your spiritual heritage? Why is it important for us to be aware of our spiritual roots?

trickster. Rahab? A prostitute. Ruth? Not even an Israelite. David? Committed murder and adultery. Despite these all-too-human characters, God's divine drama of salvation triumphs in the person of Jesus. He is the fulfillment of all our hopes and needs.

THOUGHT TO REMEMBER
Jesus' human ancestry reveals God's careful and deliberate plan.

Discovery Learning

The following is an alternative lesson plan emphasizing learning activities.
Classes desiring such student involvement will find these suggestions helpful. At the
back of this book are reproducible student pages to further enhance activity learning.

INTO THE LESSON

Recruit a student to deliver the following monologue. Introduce your actor as Boaz of Bethlehem.

Monologue

"It was the strangest thing. One day she was simply there . . . in *my* fields, with all the poverty-stricken gleaners. Yes, I wanted to obey Moses' law, so I welcomed the gleaners. They could pick up the fallen grain after my servants had harvested. Usually I ignored the gleaners . . . no need to embarrass them in their poverty. God had allowed me to be prosperous; I wanted to be like him, generous and kind.

"When I asked about this woman of gracious spirit and eagerness to work, I was startled to learn she was of Moab, a traditional enemy of God's people. But she was a Moabitess once married to the son of my long lost relative Elimelech. Now she was committed to serving Naomi, Elimelech's widow.

"One night she came to rest at my feet. Would God be so good to bring joy to an old man's heart? Well, to shorten my ramblings, God *is* good. May his kingdom be blessed by our union. I believe it will.

INTO THE WORD

Recruit an actress from the class to play the role of Naomi for an "interview." Give her the following questions from Ruth 4:13-17 ahead of time so she can prepare her answers both from the Bible and from a sense of being a widow and a grandmother. Also give her a copy of the lesson commentary. To begin the interview distribute the following questions to class members. (Add other questions of your choosing.)

Q1: Naomi, after you encouraged Ruth's approaches to Boaz, how did the results match up with your hopes? *Q2:* Naomi, how do you explain the blessings the women of Bethlehem gave to you? *Q3:* Naomi, what were your feelings toward your two daughters-in-law? *Q4:* What role did you see for yourself in the rearing of Ruth's son? *Q5:* Naomi, what name did Ruth and Boaz's son end up with, and what was its significance?

For the Matthew portion of today's text, distribute copies of the following alphabetized list: Abraham, Amminadab, Boaz, David, Hezron, Isaac, Jacob, Jesse, Judah, Nahshon, Obed, Perez, Ram, Salmon, Solomon. Tell your learners that you want them to put the names of these men in chronological order. Note that the first and last are already in the correct positions. Suggest that your students work from both ends, because those are the more familiar names; then, when they need help, they can look at the text.

When you look at the final list, as shown in Matthew's arrangement, note the inclusion of the women: Tamar, Rahab, Ruth, and "Uriah's wife" (Bathsheba). Point out how Matthew's genealogy ends with the name of Mary, "of whom was born Jesus, who is called Christ." Your class may find it interesting that Matthew, supposed by scholars to have been writing for a Jewish audience, was not hesitant to present women in a valued light throughout his Gospel. Examples can be found at Matthew 8:14; 9:18-25; 15:21-28; 26:6-13; 28:1-10. (*Option:* Distribute this list as a handout as students depart.)

INTO LIFE

Ask your class to suggest a definition for the word *providential.* Introduce one or more dictionary definitions at an appropriate point. After settling on a definition that includes the element of God's intentions, ask the class to respond *yes* or *no* to the following list of life events, based on whether God's providence is involved: 1. The birth of a child with physical and/or mental limitations to a Christian couple. 2. An appealing job offer that comes "out of the blue" to a young Christian professional. 3. An opportunity for elderly parents to buy a house very reasonably next to an adult child who has of-fered to help them in their senior years. 4. A small inheritance received from a distant uncle who had no children or other close family members remaining, thus enabling the purchase of a new(er) car. Allow learners to express their views freely as to what is involved in God's providence. *Option:* Use the reproducible exercise "Kinsman-Redeemer" from page 244 instead of the above.

Distribute copies of the "Looking for Ministry" exercise from the same page as students depart.

PROPHETS FORESHADOW MESSIAH'S BIRTH

Dec 13

LESSON 2

INTRODUCTION

A. FUTURISTS VS. PROPHETS

In 1771, the French author Louis-Sébastien Mercier published his utopian novel *L'An 2440* (translation: *The Year 2440*). Many previous authors had written about imaginary utopian societies. What made Mercier's work different was his projection of this one into the future. Earlier authors had placed their utopias in the forgotten past or in remote, undiscovered corners of the world. Mercier wrote as the dynamics that led to the French Revolution were gaining steam, finally to explode in 1789. He told of a philosopher who fell asleep and awoke to Paris of nearly 700 years in Mercier's future. In so doing, Mercier used his observations of trends in society to create a vision of the future. This technique has been widely applied by other futurists, such as Jules Verne, H. G. Wells, and George Orwell.

It is amazing to see how often such authors give accurate predictions of the future. For example, the 24/7 surveillance society of Orwell's *1984* seems to be more of a reality every day! Yet when we read these works many years after their original publication, it is also startling how much they got wrong.

If we think about it, though, such errors should not surprise us. Human projections about the future are no more than guesswork. Some may be highly informed and skillful, but it is still guessing. Consider that weather predictions of even a few days in the future are often wrong despite sophisticated technology. The authors of the Bible make predictions of the future too. But these authors are not like modern-day futurists. The Bible authors have been given insights by the one who knows and controls the future: God. Such predictions are prophetic and can be understood only as something supernatural and miraculous. The prophets of the Bible were not merely good guessers; they were God's instruments to proclaim his plans.

Many prophecies in the Old Testament were fulfilled in the life and ministry of Jesus, God's prophesied Messiah. Isaiah, the greatest of the prophets, made beautiful predictions about Jesus over 700 years before his birth. This week's lesson will examine some of these prophecies and their fulfillment.

B. LESSON BACKGROUND

The seventh chapter of Isaiah is set in the reign of King Ahaz of Judah, the father of King Hezekiah. Ahaz came to power around 740 BC. His reign was overshadowed by the growing threat of invasion by the mighty Assyrian

DEVOTIONAL READING:
MICAH 5:1-5a
BACKGROUND SCRIPTURE:
ISAIAH 7:13-17; LUKE 1:
26-38
PRINTED TEXT:
ISAIAH 7:13-17; LUKE 1:
30-38

LESSON AIMS

After participating in this lesson, each student will be able to:

1. List evidences from the texts in Isaiah and Matthew that confirm Jesus' identity as the Son of God.

2. Explain Mary's role in fulfilling Isaiah's ancient prophecy.

3. Suggest a plan to tell someone else who Jesus is.

KEY VERSE

The Lord himself will give you a sign: The virgin will be with child and will give birth to a son, and will call him Immanuel. —Isaiah 7:14

LESSON 2 NOTES

empire to the north. The Assyrian armies eventually conquered the northern kingdom of Israel (also called *Ephraim;* see Isaiah 7:8, 9, 17) in 722 BC. The threat to the southern kingdom of Judah must have been terrifying.

Before this move by the Assyrians, the kings of Ephraim and Syria (also called *Aram*) formed an alliance to protect themselves. They brought military pressure on Ahaz to join them (2 Kings 16:5; Isaiah 7:1). To relieve the pressure, Ahaz pledged himself to Assyria and appeased the Assyrian king with gold looted from the temple (2 Kings 16:7-9).

This high-stakes political intrigue meant that Judah had aligned herself with the Assyrians against Israel/Ephraim and Syria/Aram. This is the backdrop for Isaiah 7–12. This section of Isaiah sometimes is called the Book of Immanuel. In this section, Isaiah confronted faithless King Ahaz because he trusted in an alliance with the Assyrians rather than trusting in God.

The term *Immanuel* (or *Emmanuel*) occurs four times in the Bible. It is a straightforward combination of words that mean "with us [is] God." The only place it occurs in the New Testament is Matthew 1:23, where the author quotes Isaiah to show how the birth of Jesus fulfilled prophecy. The other three places are all in Isaiah. One of these (Isaiah 7:14) is in today's lesson text and will be discussed below. The two other occurrences are in Isaiah 8, in obvious close proximity to 7:14.

In Isaiah 8, the prophet depicts the coming invasion of the Assyrians in terms of a catastrophic flood. The waters of this flood were to reach up to the neck of Judah (Isaiah 8:8), meaning they would be highly damaging but not fatal. In the midst of this horror, Judah would still be able to cry, "O Immanuel" (again, 8:8), in this case a plea of "May God be with us!"

Isaiah goes on to say that the plans of nations are tiny and futile against the ultimate plan of God, for truly "God is with us" (= "Immanuel," 8:10). Isaiah's point is that the people should not fear the Assyrians. They should fear the Lord and only him (8:13). At the same time, they should not trust the Assyrians (as Ahaz did), for only the Lord could provide them with safety (8:14).

HOW TO SAY IT

Ahaz. AY-haz.
Assyria. Uh-SEAR-ee-uh.
Damascus. Duh-MASS-kus.
Ephraim. EE-fray-im.
Hezekiah. Hez-ih-KYE-uh.
Hoshea. Ho-SHAY-uh.
Immanuel. Ih-MAN-you-el.
Louis-Sébastien Mercier.
   LEW-ee-Say-bass-TYUN
   MER-see-yeh.
Pekah. PEEK-uh.
Rezin. REE-zin.
Sennacherib. Sen-NACK-er-ib.
Syria. SEAR-ee-uh.
Yahweh (Hebrew). YAH-weh.

I. ANCIENT INSIGHT (ISAIAH 7:13-17)
A. SUBTLE SIGN (vv. 13, 14)
13. Then Isaiah said, "Hear now, you house of David! Is it not enough to try the patience of men? Will you try the patience of my God also?

House of David is a way of referring to the king, namely Ahaz (Isaiah 7:10, 12). Isaiah has just challenged the king to ask for a sign from the Lord. Ahaz's refusal of the request is what draws Isaiah's ire in this verse.

Isaiah's response uncovers the illogic and duplicity behind Ahaz's actions. The king's secret alliance with the Assyrians has been a perversion of truth to his nation *(try the patience of men)*. Does he think he can lie to God also *(try the patience of my God)?* To ask the question is to provide the answer. There is no such thing as duplicity with God, for we cannot deceive him. To attempt to hide the truth from God is delusional thinking.

14. "Therefore the Lord himself will give you a sign: The virgin will be with child and will give birth to a son, and will call him Immanuel.

Although King Ahaz has refused to ask for a *sign,* Isaiah announces that a sign will be provided anyway. The king's stubbornness does not thwart God's plan.

The sign to come has three parts, and each is significant. The first one is the most astounding: the pregnancy of a *virgin*. There has been discussion as to whether or not the translation of this term should be softened to "young woman" or "unmarried woman." To do so may be technically possible from the standpoint of the original Hebrew. But the Greek translation made more than two centuries before Christ uses the distinct word for *virgin*.

Also, to use "young woman" would distort the clear intention of the text. This *sign* from *the Lord* will not be an ordinary event, but something extraordinary, miraculous. Young women become pregnant all the time, sometimes when they are unmarried. Furthermore, there is no possibility in understanding this as anything less than *virgin* when we read Matthew's quotation (Matthew 1:23). The Greek word used by Matthew always means "virgin."

The two other signs are easier to understand. The child will be male, *a son*. The child will be called *Immanuel*. This does not mean that just any baby boy named Immanuel is a fulfillment of this sign. In this case the giving of a certain name is less important than what the name means. *Immanuel* means "God is with us" (see the Lesson Background). The marvelous birth of a child with no natural father can be interpreted only as a sign of the presence of God.

This leads to two very important questions we should ask. First, why a virgin birth? Isaiah does not really explain it, but Matthew, writing over 700 years later, does. The Messiah is born of a virgin so that prophecy might be fulfilled. It is a striking way of confirming the activity and presence of God in a historical event. It is worth noting that neither Matthew nor Isaiah gives any hint that a virgin birth is necessary to escape the curse of original sin, as is often proposed. It is a sign, a prophecy fulfilled.

The second question is more difficult: What does this sign mean to King Ahaz? Should he expect some young woman in Jerusalem to announce that she has become miraculously pregnant? Does it point to the birth of one of Ahaz's sons or even to the birth of Isaiah's son (Isaiah 8:3), as some have suggested? These ideas don't work, because none of those conceptions was virginal. Ultimately, we must understand this as God's way of reminding Ahaz to trust in him, for God is with his people and has not abandoned them.

SAYING GOOD-BYE AND HELLO

"You know something is wrong when you enter a room and no one says 'Hello,' but when you leave, everyone says 'Good-bye'!" This joking remark is intended to be teasingly humorous, but it could be unbearably hurtful if it actually happened to someone.

Of course, this comment is taking the term *good-bye* in the way that we commonly use it: as a simple way to say, "Oh, I see that you are leaving." Yet many of us know that the term *good-bye* is a contracted form of the old wish, "God be with you." Were we to use it consciously in that way, *good-bye* would be a blessing on someone we care about, since the term then would be a request or desire for God's presence to be with that person until we see him or her again.

As a result of Judah's sin, God eventually sent that nation into exile. This dismissal was a *good-bye* in that God promised to be with the exiles during this time of punishment (Jeremiah 30:11; 46:27, 28). But that *good-bye* is not the

---

WHAT DO YOU THINK?

How do the signs and wonders of Scripture increase your faith? Why would it be dangerous to base your faith on the expectation of modern-day miracles?

[Scriptures to consider include Matthew 12:24; Mark 8:11, 12; John 14:11; 1 Corinthians 1:22; and 2 Corinthians 12:12.]

WHAT DO YOU THINK?

Are there some prophecies (such as the ones in Revelation) that will never be understood fully until after they're fulfilled? If so, then why are they included in the Scripture?

Visual for Lesson 2. Keep this map posted throughout the quarter to give your learners a geographical perspective.

subject of today's study. Instead, Isaiah foretold a *hello*—the most marvelous *hello* in history! He spoke of the time when God himself would say "hello" to the human race in the incarnation of Jesus Christ. In that event God became "with us" (Immanuel) in a way he never had been before. May that fact of history inspire us to anticipate Jesus' second coming, when he will be with us in a marvelously permanent way.

—C. R. B.

B. COMING CATASTROPHE (vv. 15-17)

15, 16. "He will eat curds and honey when he knows enough to reject the wrong and choose the right. But before the boy knows enough to reject the wrong and choose the right, the land of the two kings you dread will be laid waste.

Curds sweetened with *honey* is baby food in a wealthy household. This is a message directly aimed at King Ahaz. In the time it takes a baby to be able to eat semisolid food and learn to behave, disaster will have fallen on the *two kings* to the north. Parents know that this sort of development varies from child to child. But by the second birthday a child normally will be weaned and begin to respond to a parent's teaching of the basics of what is *wrong* and what is *right*.

King Pekah of Israel/Ephraim reigns for 20 years (2 Kings 15:27). King Ahaz begins to reign in Judah in Pekah's seventeenth year (2 Kings 16:1). If the prophecy of Isaiah came to Ahaz in the second or third year of his reign, we can see how the prophecy of Pekah's demise is fulfilled quickly. Pekah is killed by a usurper, namely Hoshea (2 Kings 15:30). Although exact information about the king of Syria/Aram is harder to put together, we know that King Rezin of Damascus (the capital of Syria) is killed by the Assyrians at about this time (see 2 Kings 16:9).

17. "The LORD will bring on you and on your people and on the house of your father a time unlike any since Ephraim broke away from Judah—he will bring the king of Assyria."

The complete fulfillment of this part of the prophecy is a few years off, to occur in 722 BC. In that year, the ruthless armies of the Assyrians destroy the northern kingdom of Israel/Ephraim (see 2 Kings 17:5, 6). *A time unlike any since Ephraim broke away from Judah*, which happened back in about 930 BC, is Isaiah's reminder to Ahaz of the devastating division of the kingdom of Solomon. What is coming will be much worse.

The northern kingdom ceases to exist in 722 BC. Ahaz dies at about age 36, in about 728 BC (2 Kings 16:2). It falls to his son, the godly Hezekiah, to live through the terror of another Assyrian invasion in 701 BC. This time, however, God delivers Judah by killing 185,000 men in the army of the Assyrian king, Sennacherib (see 2 Kings 19:35, 36; Isaiah 37:36, 37). The saving intervention offered to Ahaz is realized in the reign of Hezekiah.

II. DYNAMIC ENACTMENT (LUKE 1:30-38)

A. NO FEARS (vv. 30-33)

30. But the angel said to her, "Do not be afraid, Mary, you have found favor with God.

The appearance of an *angel* would be an awe-inspiring event for anyone. Although details of the angel's appearance are not given, *Mary* is not left to wonder, "Is this really an angel?" In Luke, God's angels begin their visits by telling the people involved *do not be afraid* (compare Luke 1:13; 2:10). They have nothing to fear from this powerful, supernatural being, for they have been chosen to receive a message from God.

The idea of Mary being chosen is expressed as *favor with God*. The word translated *favor* is often translated as *grace* elsewhere in the Bible (example: Acts 14:3). To find grace with God in this sense means that God has determined to use a person in a dynamic way. The angel's expression echoes what was said about the one whom God chose to preserve the human race from a cataclysmic flood: "Noah found favor in the eyes of the Lord" (Genesis 6:8).

31. "You will be with child and give birth to a son, and you are to give him the name Jesus.

The news for Mary must be truly shocking. She, a young unmarried girl still living in her father's house, is to be pregnant and give birth to *a son*. This is disturbing, for it has the potential of ruining her marriage prospects and any chance for a normal life in that culture.

The *name* for the boy helps to explain this, however. His name will be *Jesus*, the New Testament version of the famous Israelite name Joshua. Joshua means "Yahweh is salvation" or "Yahweh will save."

32, 33. "He will be great and will be called the Son of the Most High. The Lord God will give him the throne of his father David, and he will reign over the house of Jacob forever; his kingdom will never end."

The significance of the boy's name is explained by the angel. He is to be a new king in the line of *David*, the fulfillment of the promise to David of an eternal *kingdom* (see 2 Samuel 7:16; compare Isaiah 9:7; Daniel 7:14; Micah 4:7). He is to be God's instrument of salvation as promised to the people of Israel. What is misunderstood by Israel is that the kingdom of this Jesus/Joshua is to be a spiritual kingdom and that his salvation is to be from sin, not from the Romans (see Matthew 1:21).

B. NO DOUBTS (vv. 34-37)

34. "How will this be," Mary asked the angel, "since I am a virgin?"

Mary is very young, perhaps only 15 or 16. Yet she understands the facts of life. Pregnancy is not self-induced. She can say without pretense that there has been no sexual contact in her life. We should not understand this to be a lack of faith on Mary's part (as if she were saying "No way!"), but a desire to understand better ("How?").

35. The angel answered, "The Holy Spirit will come upon you, and the power of the Most High will overshadow you. So the holy one to be born will be called the Son of God.

The angel makes it clear that this is not some sordid, embarrassing affair. This is a *holy* undertaking, a provision of God himself. It is also plain that there is to be no physical contact between God and Mary. God is not assuming a human guise in order to impregnate Mary, such as the fictional Greek gods might have been expected to do. Mythology abounds with such stories, which amount to little more than the rape of human women by gods in human bodies. Mary's pregnancy is to be through the *Holy Spirit*. As such, it will be a miraculous event, unexplainable by the normal laws of nature.

36. "Even Elizabeth your relative is going to have a child in her old age, and she who was said to be barren is in her sixth month.

Mary's surprises are not over. The angel reveals that her elderly *relative* named *Elizabeth* has also been blessed with a miraculous (although in a

WHAT DO YOU THINK?

What level of confidence did the angel display even before hearing Mary's response? Would the angel have this same level of confidence if announcing that God had a unique task for you? Why, or why not?

WHAT DO YOU THINK?

What is it about Mary's question that sets an example for us in how we can ask questions of God?

WHAT DO YOU THINK?

What was a time when a friend or relative was going through a life situation similar to that of your own? How were you able to strengthen each other spiritually during such a time?

PRAYER

Holy God, as you chose and used Mary, may you choose and use us according to your will. Make us sensitive to your leading so that our response will not be that of King Ahaz, but will be that of humble Mary. We pray this in the name of Jesus the Christ. Amen.

different way) pregnancy. Despite her age and history of barrenness, Elizabeth is now two-thirds through her term, *a child* growing in her womb (Luke 1:24). This serves to confirm to Mary even more strongly that God is moving in a powerful and providential way, and that she is a key player in his plan.

37. *"For nothing is impossible with God."*

This is a core statement of faith, yet one that we often neglect. If there are things that are *impossible* for *God*, then is he really God? This issue comes up later in Luke concerning salvation, for Jesus teaches that salvation is not the result of human effort. Salvation is possible for the God for whom nothing is impossible (see Luke 18:25-27; compare Genesis 18:14).

C. NO WAVERING (v. 38)

38. *"I am the Lord's servant,"* Mary answered. *"May it be to me as you have said."* Then the angel left her.

At this point, we cannot help but marvel at the faith of Mary, a mere teenager. Without a doubt, she does not understand all that is happening to her. Yet she freely submits to the will of God. She makes no demand for some kind of equal partnership with God, but offers herself as his *servant*, meaning his "handmaiden" or "slave." Her acceptance is a sign of great faith.

SIXTEEN, UNMARRIED, AND PREGNANT

Juno was one of the most highly acclaimed movies of 2007. It was the story of fictional Juno MacGuff, an unmarried 16-year-old girl who had become pregnant. Critics who were proud of their own sophistication gave the movie high praise for not being a "hand-wringing, moralizing melodrama," as one reviewer put it.

The film does deserve praise for not promoting abortion as the solution to an uncomfortable dilemma that too many young women find themselves in these days. Spurning the advice of her parents and friends, Juno decides not to have an abortion. Rather, she seeks out a married couple to adopt her child and provide the kind of home she cannot provide. The film is presented as a comedy, perhaps an acknowledgment of our culture's inability to recognize the tragedy of sin and its consequences.

Mary was different from Juno. She seriously accepted her role in God's plan rather than seeing it as an opportunity for joking. But then again, her culture was not as indifferent about such things as ours is. Mary would grow up quickly and rear her son as the Son of God, with all the gravity that that responsibility entailed.

—C. R. B.

CONCLUSION

One of the ongoing promises of the Old Testament is found when God proclaims, "I will be with you." God gave this promise to Jacob as he returned to his homeland (Genesis 31:3). A similar promise was given to Moses when he was called to lead the people of Israel out of Egypt (Exodus 3:12). Joshua and the people received the assurance as they entered the promised land (Joshua 1:5). Today this promise is reflected in one of the traditional blessings of the church: "The Lord be with you." A great part of the coming of God's Messiah was the prophecy of Isaiah that the promised one would be Immanuel. God is with us and will be with us eternally.

When we combine the prophecy of Isaiah with the story of Mary, we should realize that God is always "with" his people. This "with-ness" is more than an aspect of God's ever-presence, however. It means that God is behind his people, working with them and using them to accomplish his plans and fulfill his will. Ahaz, a king of Israel, did not understand this. Mary, a teenage peasant girl, did.

The church today, as God's people, retains this promise. God is with us. He will never abandon us. He will use us if we have the heart of submission to his will that we see in Mary. We may not be visited by angels, but we too need not be afraid. God is with us.

THOUGHT TO REMEMBER
God is still with us.

Discovery Learning

The following is an alternative lesson plan emphasizing learning activities.
Classes desiring such student involvement will find these suggestions helpful. At the
back of this book are reproducible student pages to further enhance activity learning.

INTO THE LESSON

Fill your room with signs. You will want a variety that does what signs are designed to do: provide helpful information (such as restroom gender identification), give warnings (such as a biohazard or nuclear notice), advertise things to be desired (such as a concert or circus poster), announce coming events (such as a congregation notice of an upcoming special dinner), give directions (such as a traffic arrow or route marker), and other purposes as you see fit.

You can get such signs from office supply stores, download them from the Internet, or create signs of your own design.

Ask the class, "What do signs do?" If answers are slow in coming, quiz your class regarding individual signs you have displayed. Expect a variety of responses. After you have made a list of responses on the board, say, "Today's text is about a sign. Let's see how it does all the things we have decided that signs do."

INTO THE WORD

Copy and distribute the following word-find puzzle along with the word list to your learners. Give these directions: "Look at today's two texts and find in this puzzle names and descriptions given to the child who will be born as described to Ahaz and to Mary. Be sure to find and mark out all the letters so that you'll be able to read the filler messages."

```
T  H  E  B  S  A  B  Y  W  H  O  W
T  H  E  H  O  L  Y  O  N  E  I  L
L  B  E  B  N  O  R  N  T  S  O  M
A  T  R  Y  O  F  U  L  G  O  F  I
L  H  L  S  F  T  H  E  I  N  S  A
I  E  A  S  T  H  P  R  R  O  I  P
H  H  E  O  H  C  Y  O  J  E  S  K
U  O  S  N  E  I  B  S  T  H  E  S
I  L  G  O  H  N  N  A  N  D  J  T
H  Y  E  F  I  M  M  A  N  U  E  L
S  T  U  G  G  B  S  T  A  N  S  C
E  H  R  O  H  R  O  F  G  O  U  D
S  I  G  D  E  O  E  O  D  N  S  E
V  N  S  S  S  R  E  A  J  O  I  C
E  G  R  E  T  J  O  I  T  C  E  !
```

List of words and phrases to be found: *great, Immanuel, Jesus, king, Son, Son of God, Son of the Highest, the holy one, the holy thing, virgin born.*

If your class likes a greater challenge, suggest that they do not look at the list of words and phrases to be found. Note to your class that some of the puzzle answers are more "interpretive" than they are precisely and literally biblical. (*Option:* Have students work in pairs or small groups to see who can finish first. You can give inexpensive nativity sets as prizes.)

Once all these designations for the baby are found and marked, say, "The letters used as filler are, sequentially, statements of important truths regarding today's study. Who can find them and read them?"

The letters, from left to right, top to bottom, read: "The baby who will be born to Mary fulfills the Isaiah prophecy," and "Jesus is the sign and the substance of God's goodness." The puzzle then is completed with a double challenge to "Rejoice, rejoice!" Note the exclamation mark in the final position in the puzzle. After all the terms and the statements are found, work through each one individually using the commentary. Use the question *How is Jesus the fulfillment of Isaiah's prophecy to Ahaz and to us?* as a touchstone for each one.

INTO LIFE

Recruit a musically talented class member to lead the class in singing the refrain to "Go Tell It on the Mountain." You may need to provide copies of the following lyrics (which are in the public domain):

Go, tell it on the mountain,
Over the hills and everywhere
Go, tell it on the mountain,
That Jesus Christ is born!

Note to your class the key phrase: "Jesus Christ is born!" If time allows, you may wish also to sing one or more stanzas, which are easily found in hymnals.

Encourage your class to send Christmas greeting cards that are Bible-related and Christ-centered. This means avoiding the use of cards that feature merely secular images such as snowmen, Santa Claus, wreathes of holly, etc. Distribute copies of one or both reproducible exercises on page 245 as students depart.

IMMANUEL IS BORN

LESSON 3

Dec
20

DEVOTIONAL
READING:
GALATIANS 4:1-7
BACKGROUND SCRIPTURE:
MATTHEW 1:18-25
PRINTED TEXT:
MATTHEW 1:18-25

INTRODUCTION

A. HONOR VS. SHAME

Thomas Jefferson penned these words to end the United States Declaration of Independence: "We mutually pledge to each other our Lives, our Fortunes, and our sacred Honor." It is easy to understand what he meant by *lives* and *fortunes,* but what did he intend by *sacred honor*?

Honor may be defined as "moral reputation." To act honorably is to act in accordance with the recognized moral standards of one's community. To be dishonorable is to be accused of a grave violation of public morality and to be judged guilty as such in the eyes of the community. Because morality must have a religious foundation, *true honor* is always *sacred honor.*

In our increasingly amoral and immoral society, we have lost much of this traditional sense of honor. Public figures act openly in adulterous and other immoral ways. In some communities, unwed pregnancies are the norm rather than the exception. Titans of the business world who are exposed for epic financial transgressions are quickly "rehabilitated" and allowed free rein in another company. Sports cheaters seem always able to find another team if their skills are at a high level.

How different from the days of my youth! As I grew up, there were no more devastating words said by my mother than "Shame on you!" I must admit that I heard this more than once. Many of us can still feel the heartbreak of having experienced the disapproval of a parent in this regard. When used judiciously, shame is an effective childhood motivation that continues to influence us, even as adults.

In the ancient world, shame and honor were powerful motivations and controlling influences on society. A person who acted dishonorably was seen as shameful in the public eye. This shame extended to the person's entire family and could be influential for many generations. Business dealings with a shamed person were to be avoided. Social interaction with a shamed family was unwanted. Marriage, which was as much a joining of families as of individuals, was unlikely if one of the families was seen as dishonorable. These issues weighed heavily on Joseph in our lesson today, for he sought to act honorably in a difficult situation.

B. LESSON BACKGROUND

The birth of Jesus is recorded in two of the Gospels: Matthew and Luke. Luke, which we looked at last week, tells the story primarily from the perspective of Mary, the mother of Jesus. This week we look at Matthew's account, which focuses on Joseph, the earthly (step)father of Jesus.

We can learn quite a bit about Joseph from the Bible. Matthew says that his father was named Jacob (Matthew 1:16). This is a nice parallel to the Jacob and Joseph of the Old Testament (see Genesis 35:22-24). Luke,

LESSON AIMS

After participating in this lesson, each student will be able to:

1. List the facts about the role Joseph played in the birth of Jesus the Messiah.

2. Tell how Joseph is a model for men today who face difficult choices and want to act as "righteous" men.

3. Write a commitment statement that pledges to obey even when God changes his or her plan.

KEY VERSE

She will give birth to a son, and you are to give him the name Jesus, because he will save his people from their sins. —Matthew 1:21

LESSON 3 NOTES

however, lists the father of Joseph as Heli (Luke 3:23). Since we know that Matthew and Luke were both very careful authors, this is not a matter of one being wrong and one being right. We may not know the certain solution to this problem, but it is often understood as a reflection of the levirate marriage laws of the Jews (Genesis 38:8; Deuteronomy 25:5-10).

Under this theory, Jacob and Heli were brothers, but Jacob died early. In that situation, it was the custom for the brother to take the widow as his own wife, and Heli may have done this with Joseph's mother. Thus both Jacob and Heli were Joseph's fathers—one in a legal sense and one in a biological sense. Joseph himself became Jesus' father in a legal but not biological sense.

Joseph had connections in both Bethlehem, a village outside of Jerusalem, and in Nazareth, a village in Galilee about 70 miles north of Jerusalem. Luke presents Joseph and Mary traveling from Nazareth to Bethlehem then back again. Matthew's account adds the interlude in Egypt that resulted from the threat of murderous King Herod. We can see from all this that while Joseph was not a world traveler, he did his share of moving around! This means that his perspective was not that of a single tiny village such as Nazareth.

Joseph was a carpenter by trade (Matthew 13:55). The ancient role of a carpenter was often more than a simple woodworker in a small shop, as Joseph is usually portrayed by artists. Joseph may have been a skilled construction worker who traveled to various work sites to ply his trade. If true, it is likely that the sons in his house (including Jesus) accompanied him when they were old enough.

A current theory is that Joseph and his sons may have worked in Sepphoris. This was a large city, about an hour's walk from Nazareth, that was being rebuilt at this time. There would have been plenty of work for craftsmen in this city. The nature of the sacrifice Joseph and Mary offered when Jesus was eight days old indicates a family that was far from rich (Luke 2:24; compare Leviticus 12:8). But steady work in Sepphoris may have meant that the family of Joseph later came to be relatively well off for Galilean villagers.

While Joseph plays an important role in the birth stories of Jesus, he, unlike Mary, is absent in the stories of Jesus' ministry. This has led some to conclude that Joseph was dead by that time. This is, of course, an argument from silence. But the argument seems fairly strong since Mary, Jesus' other parent, *is* mentioned in those stories. Joseph probably was 25 to 30 years old when he married. Since Jesus was about 30 when he began his preaching (Luke 3:23), Joseph likely would have been age 55 or 60 by that time. Thus the assumption that Joseph already had passed away when Jesus began his public ministry is very plausible. How long Jesus may have been without his father, we don't know. But the fact that Jesus was still identified as "the carpenter's son" in Matthew 13:55 perhaps indicates that Joseph's death was not too distant from that point in time.

I. JOSEPH PROTECTS HIS HONOR (MATTHEW 1:18, 19)

A. HEARTBREAK EXPERIENCED (v. 18)

18. This is how the birth of Jesus Christ came about: His mother Mary was pledged to be married to Joseph, but before they came together, she was found to be with child through the Holy Spirit.

We may find it difficult to understand the full impact of the statement that *Mary was pledged to be married to Joseph.* Our marriage customs today usually include a period of engagement followed by a marriage ceremony. To be engaged means that a man and woman are planning to marry. While being engaged is not a casual thing, it is understood that engagements can be broken (and frequently are).

This is not the situation for Joseph and Mary. According to the arranged marriage customs of the day, they are considered to be married legally when the pledge to be married takes place. This marriage is legally binding, even though the two have not yet begun to live together as husband and wife.

It is during this period that Joseph learns of Mary's pregnancy. For a woman in this position to be found pregnant means more than unfaithfulness to her fiancé. It means she has violated her marriage covenant; she (apparently) has committed adultery.

Matthew reassures us that this pregnancy is not the product of immorality, but of the *Holy Spirit.* But how do you prove such a claim? Mary's situation gives every indication of illicit sexual contact. This is far from what Joseph expected when the marriage was arranged. His honor is threatened. He is not likely to continue a marriage with an adulteress. Joseph is not likely to agree to take a wife from a father whose house is shamed by his daughter's (apparent) sexual sin.

B. DIVORCE CONTEMPLATED (v. 19)
19. Because Joseph her husband was a righteous man and did not want to expose her to public disgrace, he had in mind to divorce her quietly.

The Law of Moses requires the execution of one who commits adultery (Leviticus 20:10). To do so definitely would bring *public disgrace,* a strong deterrent for anyone tempted to have sex outside of marriage. By this time in history, however, this remedy is rarely exercised, if ever. The fact of Roman occupation may remove this possibility completely. But any kind of public remedy would still be highly shaming.

Matthew portrays Joseph as a man of honor. He is both *righteous* and merciful. His righteous nature makes it impossible to continue with the marriage. His merciful nature causes him to be kind to Mary despite her seeming betrayal.

To *divorce her* means literally to "release" Mary from the marriage contract (compare Matthew 5:31). If he takes this action, Joseph will protect his honor, but shame will fall on Mary and her family, for such actions cannot be kept secret in a small village. Even so, Joseph is determined to do this *quietly.* Even though the secret eventually will get out, Joseph will not be a party in making the issue public. There will be no street-corner proclamation of the divorce, as is sometimes done (compare John 8:3-5). This to be privately negotiated between Mary's father and Joseph.

HONOR-SHAME CULTURES
Americans of a bygone era had a good idea of what *shame* meant (see the lesson Introduction). But the idea of *an honor-shame culture* is foreign to many in the Western world today. However, in recent years many of us have learned (to our horror) about the extreme honor-shame parts of other cultures. An Internet search will yield many examples. For instance, in 1994 a 32-year-old Muslim

WHAT DO YOU THINK?

When we are falsely accused, how much time and energy should we expend to clear our names, if any?

[Make sure to consider 1 Peter 3:16 in your answer.]

WHAT DO YOU THINK?

How can the church do a better job of demonstrating grace to those going through an out-of-wedlock pregnancy, without seeming to condone premarital sex?

WHAT DO YOU THINK?

How can the church do a better job of ministering to those who are divorced or who are going through a divorce? Should the distinction between a scriptural and an unscriptural divorce (Matthew 5:31, 32; 1 Corinthians 7:10-15) make a difference in this regard? Explain.

in Jordan slashed the throat of his 16-year-old sister. He then ran out into the street, waving the bloody knife and yelling, "I have killed my sister to cleanse my honor."

His sister's "crime" was that she had been raped by another brother. Her uncles convinced the brother who murdered her that she was too much of a disgrace to the family honor to be allowed to live. The murderer got a 15-year prison sentence, later reduced to half that. Even that was considered to be a very severe penalty for an honor crime in Jordan.

An honor-shame culture was also in force in ancient Judea. But if we read Leviticus 20:10 carefully in its context, we realize that the foundations were different. We see a "righteous" aspect of an honor-shame culture as we examine Joseph's thinking. Mary's unwed pregnancy could have shamed Joseph. His culture demanded repercussions to make sure the shame stayed where it was presumed to belong—on her.

However, to Joseph's great credit—and as evidence of why he was chosen to be Jesus' earthly father—he demonstrated his humanity and mercy in his intent to walk the tightrope between protecting his honor and shielding Mary's privacy. We do well to remember that "Mercy triumphs over judgment!" (James 2:13).

—C. R. B.

II. JOSEPH RECEIVES A DREAM (MATTHEW 1:20-23)

A. SITUATION EXPLAINED (v. 20)

20. But after he had considered this, an angel of the Lord appeared to him in a dream and said, "Joseph son of David, do not be afraid to take Mary home as your wife, because what is conceived in her is from the Holy Spirit.

God intervenes before *Joseph* can act on his plan for divorcing *Mary*. Despite his expectation of shame, *Joseph* is told not to *be afraid to take Mary home as* his *wife*. What has happened with Mary is not a sinful mistake. Joseph is to be part of a mighty act of God. Joseph will be an intimate witness to the powerful work of the Holy Spirit. The angel communicates God's approval for Joseph to receive Mary into his home. To obey God transcends any human issue of honor.

It is significant that this unnamed angel refers to Joseph as *son of David*. Just as Matthew will show that the pregnant virgin is a fulfillment of prophecy, so too is the ancestry of Joseph. The public assumption will be that the child is a natural son of Joseph; the reality will be that Joseph will be the legal (not biological) father. Even so, the arrival of Jesus will be a fulfillment of the promise to David of a descendant who will be the legitimate one to reign on David's throne (Isaiah 9:6, 7).

B. TASK ASSIGNED (v. 21)

21. "She will give birth to a son, and you are to give him the name Jesus, because he will save his people from their sins."

Joseph is given another assignment: that of naming the boy. To do so is to recognize the child as his son (see Matthew 13:55). God knows that Jesus will need a good father and mother to prepare him for the work that lies ahead. The choosing of Joseph and Mary for these roles speaks of God's view of their characters.

As we noted in Lesson 2, the name *Jesus* is equivalent to the Old Testament name *Joshua*. This is significant. Joshua was the Old Testament hero

WHAT DO YOU THINK?

What procedure should we use when we are about to make a decision that will have a lifelong impact?

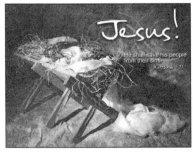

Visual for Lesson 3.
Make sure to have this visual on display as you begin your discussion of Matthew 1:21.

who led the nation of Israel into the promised land; Jesus will be God's servant to lead people to salvation (compare Romans 5:21; Hebrews 2:10). Names in the ancient world have meaning. Jesus/Joshua means "God is salvation" or "God is Savior." This meaning alludes to the angel's promise that *he will save his people from their sins.*

C. PROMISE KEPT (vv. 22, 23)
22. All this took place to fulfill what the Lord had said through the prophet:

One of the primary purposes behind Matthew's writing of his Gospel is to show Jesus as the one who fulfills the many Old Testament prophecies about the Messiah (see Matthew 5:17). Matthew often does this by relating something from the life of Jesus and then quoting Scripture. Matthew 1:22, 23 is the first instance of this; it is perhaps the most important, for here Matthew employs a marvelous text from the great *prophet* Isaiah.

23. . . . "The virgin will be with child and will give birth to a son, and they will call him Immanuel"—which means, "God with us."

It is not the birth of Jesus per se that is unusual. We can assume that he is born physically in the normal human manner. That includes labor pains, an umbilical cord, and all the rest. It is, rather, his conception that makes his arrival unique. In strictly human terms, a pregnant *virgin* is a contradiction in terms, an oxymoron. It is also a matter of faith and a cause for great wonder. God could have chosen a more spectacular sign to signal the birth of the Messiah, but it is hard to imagine a more marvelous one. Matthew's explanation of the purpose of the virgin birth is very simple: it fulfills prophecy. It is the "sign" that Isaiah anticipated (Isaiah 7:14; see last week's lesson). It is a confirmation of God's hand in the creation of this child.

There are several miraculous births recorded in the Bible (see Genesis 17:15-19; Judges 13:2, 3; 1 Samuel 1:19, 20). In none of those cases, however, was the mother a virgin. For Mary and Joseph, there can be no doubt concerning the work of God in the conception of their *son.* It is truly an instance where they can detect that God is with the two parents. By extension, it is a sign that God is with his people. He has not forgotten them.

III. JOSEPH NAMES HIS SON (MATTHEW 1:24, 25)
A. HUSBAND'S ACTION (v. 24)
24. When Joseph woke up, he did what the angel of the Lord had commanded him and took Mary home as his wife.

Matthew pictures Joseph as acting decisively. He takes Mary to be *his wife* and live in his house, being willing to bear all the implications. If there is to be shame, however unjustified, Joseph's shoulders are broad enough to bear that burden. By becoming Joseph's wife, Mary's protection and reputation have been transferred from her father to Joseph, her husband. We should neither undervalue Joseph's courage in this act nor underestimate how much this obedience has the potential of costing him.

B. FATHER'S ACTION (v. 25)
25. But he had no union with her until she gave birth to a son. And he gave him the name Jesus.

The phrase *had no union with her* means that Joseph abstains from having sexual relations with Mary. There is no record of direction from the angel to

HOW TO SAY IT
Bethlehem. BETH-lih-hem.
Galilean. Gal-uh-LEE-un.
Galilee. GAL-uh-lee.
Heli. HEE-lie.
Herod. HAIR-ud.
Jerusalem. Juh-ROO-suh-lem.
levirate. LEH-vuh-rut.
Nazareth. NAZ-uh-reth.
oxymoron. ox-see-MORE-on.
Sepphoris. SEF-uh-ris.

WHAT DO YOU THINK?
What can we learn from the immediate nature of Joseph's obedience to God?

avoid this during the pregnancy, but that is what Joseph does. He has taken to heart the holiness of what is happening.

There is no indication, however, that Mary and Joseph do not have such relations after the birth, despite the doctrine that some churches maintain of Mary's perpetual virginity. To the contrary, the Gospels record that Jesus eventually has four brothers and more than one sister (see Mark 6:3; the language of Matthew 13:56 indicates that there are three or more sisters).

Matthew does not include Luke's details about shepherds and angels at the birth of Jesus, nor does he discuss the idea of a stable serving as a delivery room. Rather, Matthew's emphasis at this point is on the prophetic and doctrinal importance of Joseph's actions. The Messiah is now among the people. God is dwelling among them in the person of Jesus (see John 1:14). Isaiah's ancient prophecy has been fulfilled.

ACTING COURAGEOUSLY

Wesley Autrey, a 50-year-old construction worker, was waiting for the subway with his two daughters in Manhattan on January 2, 2007. Nearby, Cameron Hollopeter had a seizure and fell onto the tracks just as a train was coming. Autrey later said he was thinking, "Someone has to help this guy." That's probably what most of us would have thought. But Autrey said his next thought was, "There's no one else here; you have to do it yourself."

With the train bearing down, Autrey jumped onto the tracks and pinned the thrashing man in the 21-inch-deep trough between the rails. The train brushed his cap as it rolled over him. A U.S. Senate resolution praised Autrey for acting responsibly and, as all would agree, heroically. Such courage!

Joseph is another example of courage. Awaking from his dream, he did as the angel had instructed him. He took Mary under his protection by marrying her. He named "their" son Jesus, the name that had come by divine instruction. Not many of us will be called by circumstances or divine command to risk either life or reputation as these two men did. But they stand as shining examples of what it means to act with courage.

—C. R. B.

CONCLUSION

Honor as a controlling code still exists in some places today. One of those is the military, where soldiers are still given *honorable* or *dishonorable* discharges. A foundation for a sense of honor is to realize that irresponsible and immoral actions reflect on more that just the individual who commits them. Soldiers do not (or should not) want to bring dishonor on their unit, their branch of the service, or their country.

Honor is different from pride. We can be glad for our honorable acts, but we should wince when we see people who seem to take pride in dishonorable acts. Excessive pride is toxic to our lives (see Proverbs 16:18). Honor, on the other hand, is often portrayed as the outcome of humility, the opposite of pride (see Proverbs 15:33; 29:23).

What if we are called to act in a way that is seen as dishonorable by the society in which we live? What if obedience to God's will asks us to do something that might be seen as shameful by our peers? We must remember that shame is relative to community standards. What is shameful in one community or culture may not be shameful in others. We can rest assured that God will never ask us to do something that he considers to be shameful.

It is at this point that the distinction between pride and honor must be remembered. Obeying God requires a denial of self, the opposite of pride. In today's lesson, Joseph had to swallow his pride and risk dishonor in order to obey. The verdict of history, however, is that Joseph was a man honored by God and deserving of our admiration. He sought to honor God by his obedience and was granted honor himself.

The truth is that our lack of obedience is much more likely to be a matter of pride than a matter of honor. May we take a lesson from Joseph, who sought to obey God regardless of the cost.

THOUGHT TO REMEMBER
Joseph is still an example of obedience.

Discovery Learning

The following is an alternative lesson plan emphasizing learning activities. Classes desiring such student involvement will find these suggestions helpful. At the back of this book are reproducible student pages to further enhance activity learning.

INTO THE LESSON

Place in seats copies of the reproducible activity "Who Did It?" from page 246 for students to work on as they arrive.

Recruit a male student to stand before the class while he wears a loose jacket that bears this label: *A man of God.* Give each learner a slip of paper of about 3" by 5 and a safety pin. Ask learners to write brief descriptions of "a man of God" on their slips, then come to your "model" and pin the labels onto his jacket. (The loose jacket should ensure that he will not be stuck with the sharp point of a pin.)

Once all slips of paper are affixed, have your recruit remove the jacket. Remove the labels and read them aloud to the group. At the end of this characterization of "a man of God," say, "Today's study is of a godly man who consistently demonstrated godliness in word, deed, and thought. Today we study Joseph, called to be the earthly father of Jesus."

INTO THE WORD

Establish groups of three and give each the same assignment: prepare an acrostic on the name *Joseph* that characterizes the man. Students are to use today's text and their general Bible knowledge of Joseph to complete this task. Though learners will offer a variety of words and phrases, here is a sampling of possibilities: *just, jealous, obedient, open, submissive, suspicious, excited, embarrassed, perplexed, pure, honored, husband.*

After five minutes, ask the groups to read their lists. Write responses on the board. As each entry is given, ask, "How many other groups had this word?" Put the tally with your public list. Once you have a complete list and tally, ask the class the basis for each word chosen. Some will be obvious, some not.

Prepare handouts in advance with the following clauses double-spaced down the left side: Because Joseph was a godly man; Mary's baby is not of sin, but of my Spirit; When Mary was fully committed to marrying Joseph; Your wife awaits you in purity; He did exactly as God's angel commanded; But he had no sexual relationship with her until after Jesus' birth; This is the story of Jesus' birth; He married his wife, Mary; But before they had become sexually intimate; While Joseph pondered his plans; Mary was obviously pregnant, by God's Spirit; In doing so he will complete Isaiah's written prophecy; Who did not want Mary to be shamed in the public eye; "Joseph," God said, "continue courageously with your marriage plans. David's line needs you"; Yes, a virgin will have a male child who will deserve the title "God is with us"; He decided to divorce her quietly and discreetly; Her baby is a son, who will be named for his power to save God's children; God's angel came to him as he slept; When Joseph awoke from sleep; Joseph named the baby boy Jesus.

Tell your class that the clauses are paraphrased elements from Matthew 1:18-25. Have these instructions at the top of the handout: "Rearrange and write these into a parallel, paraphrased version of the Scripture text. Use the Bible text only if you need to."

The answer, of course, is the way the thoughts are arranged in Matthew 1. This activity will provide a thorough look at this familiar text. *Option 1:* Have students work in pairs or small groups to see who can finish first. *Option 2:* Provide a pair of scissors to each student; this will allow easier visualization as students cut the phrases apart to rearrange them.

INTO LIFE

Display a container of coins. As you shake it, ask, "Got change?" Then comment, "Most of us do not like change—neither coins that we consider a nuisance nor changes in direction in life when we already have other plans." Note that Joseph had just such an interruption. He reacted nobly and rightly as he understood God's will. Give each learner an index card that is printed with this statement:

O Lord, the one who knows the future, I will submit to the changes you bring to my comfortable, well-thought-out plans. Give me the faith and courage of Joseph! Signed _____ .

Suggest that students ponder the commitment card, sign it, and keep it in a location (perhaps a Bible) until the next time God changes their plans, whether by tragedy, opportunity, or serendipity. Distribute copies of the reproducible activity "Do You Do It?" from page 246 as students depart.

MESSIAH'S BIRTH CAUSES JOY AND RAGE

LESSON 4

INTRODUCTION

A. UNNATURAL FUNERALS

Experienced ministers who have conducted many funerals will tell you that some of the most difficult are those in which the parents of the deceased are in the audience. This is particularly hard when the funeral is for a young child, but it can be almost as tough when the person being laid to rest is an adult.

A general principle of nature and of families is that the children are not "supposed" to die before the parents. This is one of the causes of the extreme grief of wartime, when parents see their young sons (and now daughters) die before their time. It is likely that some who are reading this lesson have suffered in this way.

In these cases, the grieving parents are advised to cherish the memories but move on with their lives. They are told that time heals all wounds and that the pain eases as the years go by. While this folk wisdom is oft repeated, newer studies have shown that it is not always accurate. It is true that adults may learn to cope with the death of a child in various ways, but the pain and sorrow may lie just beneath the surface for the rest of their lives.

In this week's lesson, the Bible author quotes the poignant Jeremiah 31:15: "A voice is heard in Ramah, mourning and great weeping, Rachel weeping for her children and refusing to be comforted, because her children are no more." The picture is of the grieving mother who has lost children. Nothing will relieve her grief. She cannot stop crying. Jeremiah, who certainly plumbs the depths of human sadness himself, empathizes with this ancient mother, and we can still do so 2,600 years later.

Today's lesson looks at what is sometimes called the Massacre of the Innocents, the decree from King Herod that caused the infant boys of the village of Bethlehem to be murdered. It was only through a providential act of God that baby Jesus escaped this fate.

It is futile to speculate what might have happened if Herod had been successful in killing Jesus, the target of the massacre. God did not let it happen. God would not let it happen. Even so, we can feel the combination of dread and relief experienced by Mary and Joseph.

B. LESSON BACKGROUND: HEROD

There are several men named *Herod* in the New Testament. It is difficult to keep them straight, but it is useful to do so. We start by realizing that

Dec 27

DEVOTIONAL READING:
PROVERBS 9:7-12
BACKGROUND SCRIPTURE:
MATTHEW 2
PRINTED TEXT:
MATTHEW 2:7-10, 16-23

LESSON AIMS

After participating in this lesson, each student will be able to:

1. Contrast the reactions of the Magi with that of Herod concerning the Messiah's birth.

2. Note how a similar contrast of opinions about Jesus exists today.

3. Worship the Lord in the reverent and sacrificial spirit of the Magi.

KEY VERSE

When they saw the star, they were overjoyed.
—Matthew 2:10

LESSON 4 NOTES

Herod was used as a family name, similar to how the Romans used the family name *Caesar* to designate their emperors. Today's lesson is concerned with a person sometimes called *Herod the Great.* He is probably the only Herod who ever claimed the title *king* in a meaningful way.

Herod's father, Antipater II, had been a friend of Julius Caesar (who lived 100–44 BC). Herod himself spent time in Rome growing up and was friends with Julius Caesar's eventual successor, Augustus Caesar. The Roman Senate named Herod to be the king of Judea in 40 BC, but they left it to him to win his kingdom. He raised an army and conquered Jerusalem in 37 BC. He ruled there until his death in 4 BC.

When he died, the Romans split his kingdom among his sons. Herod Archelaus, one of these sons, is mentioned in today's lesson (Matthew 2:22). Another son, Herod Antipas, was the killer of John the Baptist (Matthew 14:6-10) and presided over one of the trials of Jesus (Luke 23:7). Herod Agrippa I killed James (Acts 12:1, 2). The last of the Herods was Herod Agrippa II, who interviewed Paul in Acts 25. Herod Agrippa II died in Rome about AD 100, leaving no children. This ended the four-generation dynasty of Herod.

Herod the Great is known as a builder, and his greatest project was the rebuilding of the Jewish temple in Jerusalem. This was a massive task and was unfinished when Herod died. Work continued until about AD 62, meaning that the temple stood complete for less than a decade before its destruction by the Romans in AD 70.

C. LESSON BACKGROUND: WISE MEN

Today's lesson also features "Magi from the east" (Matthew 2:1). These wise men represent a type of scholar found in the royal courts of the rulers of Persia and other kingdoms east of Judea. (We get our word *magician* from the word *magi.*) While the academic pursuits of these men were wide-ranging, they were known for their interest in astronomy/astrology (the distinction between these two terms wasn't real clear in the ancient world) and in studying ancient texts. Both of these characteristics come into play in today's story. Those designated *Magi* were not kings in the usual sense, but they were usually from the wealthy families of their society. Some of them may have had royal blood, for not every offspring of a king could be a ruler.

The particular wise men at issue today came to Jerusalem looking for the newborn Jewish king. They apparently knew about prophecies concerning a future Messiah from their studies. They associated their observations of the appearance of a new star with this Messiah's birth.

I. WORSHIP (MATTHEW 2:7-10)

A. TREACHEROUS SEEKER (vv. 7, 8)

7. Then Herod called the Magi secretly and found out from them the exact time the star had appeared.

The *Magi* have learned from King *Herod* and his advisors that the Messiah had been prophesied to be born in the city of David, namely Bethlehem (Matthew 2:4-6). The devious Herod receives this information for his own purposes, but wants yet another piece of information. This inquiry is conducted *secretly* rather than in public. Herod wants to know when *the star had*

HOW TO SAY IT

Agrippa. Uh-GRIP-puh.
Antipas. AN-tih-pus.
Antipater. An-TIH-puh-ter.
Archelaus. Are-kuh-LAY-us.
ethnarch. ETH-nark.
Galilean. Gal-uh-LEE-un.
Herod. HAIR-ud.
Idumea. Id-you-ME-uh.
Judea. Joo-DEE-uh.
Julius Caesar.
   JOO-lee-us SEE-zer.
Magi. MAY-jye or
   MADGE-eye.
Persia. PER-zhuh.
Pontius Pilate. PON-shus or
   PON-ti-us PIE-lut.
Samaria. Suh-MARE-ee-uh.

appeared. This is because Herod, like the wise men, assumes that the appearance of the star coincides with the date of the Messiah's birth.

We wonder when the Magi first saw the star. Did they follow it for hundreds of miles across the desert? Or did they see the star "in the east" (Matthew 2:2) only after arriving in Jerusalem? The answer is not crystal clear due to the way the original text is worded. But what is clear is that the wise men are able to gain access to the court of Herod.

8. He sent them to Bethlehem and said, "Go and make a careful search for the child. As soon as you find him, report to me, so that I too may go and worship him."

The distance from Jerusalem to *Bethlehem,* to the house where Jesus is to be found, is about seven miles. The treachery of Herod is transparent to us now, but is probably not evident to the wise men. They have no reason to think that Herod is not as sincere as they are in his desire to find the newborn king. Because Bethlehem is so near to Jerusalem, Herod probably thinks this will be a quick operation, perhaps taking a day or two.

Why would any of these powerful, wealthy adults want to *worship* a baby? We should appreciate the gravity they feel, the potential impact of the birth of this *child.* For the Magi, this is a wonderful, one-time event of enormous impact. They see this as an act of God, thus a cause for worship. For Herod, this is a threat, the looming specter that his successor is now on stage. We can see that Herod's claim to desire worship is a cynical move by a person of no genuine faith.

Much of Herod's paranoia is due to the different perspectives between him and the nation of Israel. The common folk long for a Messiah to deliver them from the bondage of Roman rule. By contrast, Herod is a collaborator with the Romans. He has profited from the relationship. He has no interest in fighting them! The very idea of a Messiah is contrary to his interests.

B. TRUEHEARTED SEEKERS (vv. 9, 10)

9. After they had heard the king, they went on their way, and the star they had seen in the east went ahead of them until it stopped over the place where the child was.

The astronomical phenomenon that has prompted the inquiry of the Magi has now changed. Somehow *the star* has dropped low enough to be a precise guiding beacon for the travelers, going *ahead of them.* We should remember that these men are experts at watching stars. They are not fooled by some trickery foisted upon them by Herod or anyone else. This can be explained as nothing else but a supernatural occasion orchestrated by God himself.

The star finishes its purpose when it arrives at the dwelling *where the* young *child* is. This is not the stable of Luke 2:7, but the house of Matthew 2:11 (not in today's text). There the star stands, to move no more. We are left to wonder if this star is observed by others, or if it is seen only by the Magi. At any rate, we can assume that this is the final act of the star and that it does not reappear the next night.

10. When they saw the star, they were overjoyed.

To the wise men, the movement of *the star* confirms everything they believe. They hope that their interpretation of the astral sign and of what they

DAILY BIBLE READINGS

Monday, Dec. 21—The *Beginning of Wisdom (Proverbs 9:7-12)*

Tuesday, Dec. 22—Give *Me Wisdom (2 Chronicles 1:7-12)*

Wednesday, Dec. 23— *Gaining a Wise Heart (Psalm 90:11-17)*

Thursday, Dec. 24— *Those Who Find Wisdom (Proverbs 3:13-23)*

Friday, Dec. 25—Where *Is the Child? (Matthew 2: 1-6)*

Saturday, Dec. 26— *Overwhelmed with Joy (Matthew 2:10-15)*

Sunday, Dec. 27— *Finding and Protecting Jesus (Matthew 2:7-9, 16-23)*

WHAT DO YOU THINK?

How and with whom will you share the joy of the Magi this Christmas?

Visual for Lesson 4. *Use this visual to start a discussion regarding the ways people try to maintain a middle ground concerning Jesus today.*

know about Jewish prophecy is correct. But their faith may be tested by the experience with Herod and his advisors. Why are those Jewish leaders caught seemingly unaware of the fulfillment of their own prophecy, the birth of their own king?

The statement that *they were overjoyed* serves to express intensity of delight. This is a joy we can and should share.

FOLLOWING STARS

To mention the word *star* in an ancient culture naturally brought to mind the image of a twinkling light in the night sky. That is the normal use of the word in the Bible. But in modern culture the word *star* is more likely to bring to mind the image of a celebrity of television or movie fame. Such stars may even get "their star" on the Hollywood Walk of Fame—stretches of sidewalk along Hollywood Boulevard and Vine Street in Los Angeles.

People look up to such celebrities. The success of magazines such as *Star* and *People* offers further evidence of the existence of what may be called "a cult of celebrity." How unfortunate it is that celebrities are so often unfit role models! Foolishly, people of all ages seek to emulate "the lifestyles of the rich and famous," as one television program phrased it. It seems that about the only time many people are interested in *stars* in any other sense is when they read their horoscopes.

The ancient Magi demonstrated a wisdom that is lost on many today. To walk hundreds of miles shows how serious they were in their quest to find the one born king of the Jews. The star they followed led them to Jesus, who was to become, among other things, a role model for life as God intended it to be lived. Jesus himself is "the bright Morning Star" (Revelation 22:16). Which star means the most to you?

—C. R. B.

II. DESTRUCTION (MATTHEW 2:16-18)

A. HEROD'S MURDEROUS RAGE (v. 16)

16. When Herod realized that he had been outwitted by the Magi, he was furious, and he gave orders to kill all the boys in Bethlehem and its vicinity who were two years old and under, in accordance with the time he had learned from the Magi.

We now learn of some of the details of Herod's treachery. Previously, he had expressed his desire to know the date of the star's appearance. The reason he wants this information is so that he can estimate the age of the young king, the threat to his throne. The *two years old* part of Herod's order probably is the king's way of "making sure" by allowing for a margin of error. Jesus is perhaps several months old at this time. The fact that Joseph, Mary, and Jesus have moved from the stable of Luke 2:7 to the house of Matthew 2:11 shows us a passage of time.

Herod's character is also revealed here. He is not a potential worshiper of a new Messiah, but a jealous tyrant who will use murder to protect himself. We know from other historical accounts that Herod has ordered the deaths of sons and wives, so this fit of rage is consistent with his character.

It is likely that Herod first waits a couple of days for *the Magi* to return to him with their report. When Herod learns that the wise men have "returned to their country" without reporting back (Matthew 2:12), he interprets this as being *outwitted*. The reader knows that the wise men are not deliberately trying to get the best of Herod, however. They are following the direction God gives to them in a dream.

WHAT DO YOU THINK?

What should be the difference, if any, in our reactions to utterly evil people and "normal" sinners? Or is that distinction even valid? Explain.

B. Herod's Unwitting Fulfillment (vv. 17, 18)

17, 18. *Then what was said through the prophet Jeremiah was fulfilled: "A voice is heard in Ramah, weeping and great mourning, Rachel weeping for her children and refusing to be comforted, because they are no more."*

We are not told how many babies die in this rampage. Depending on the size of the village, it may be something like two dozen. Each household, however, feels the loss deeply. In the natural village community of young mothers, no one is unwounded. Matthew explains this by portraying it as fulfillment of prophecy in *Jeremiah* 31:15. There *the prophet* predicted this inconsolable grief as a precondition of the restoration of Israel. Jeremiah boldly proclaimed that God would gather Israel and comfort her distress because God loves Israel "with an everlasting love" (Jeremiah 31:3). *Rachel* is, of course, one of the great foremothers of Israel in the book of Genesis.

A Modern "Massacre of the Innocents"

The so-called Candelaria Massacre took place one night in 1993 in Rio de Janeiro. The tragedy involved the murder of 8 street children who were sleeping in a church doorway. In the trial 3 years later, 2 former policemen were convicted. One was sentenced to 309 years in prison, reduced to 89 years after retrial (even though Brazil has a 30-year limit on incarceration).

Some suspected the crime was part of a plot by police officers to earn extra money from shopkeepers by getting rid of street children, who commit petty crimes against the merchants. However, the defendant testified the killings happened because some children had thrown stones at a police car the previous day—as if that made the reaction excusable.

History is full of cruel ironies, and here's the one in this story: the name of the defendant given the 309-year sentence was Marcus *Emanuel*! A man whose surname means "God with us" (Matthew 1:23) repeated the crime Herod had sought to commit against the true Immanuel—the baby Jesus.

We may not know the true reason for Marcus Emanuel's crime, but Herod's motive was clear. He was so intent on eliminating threats to his kingship that he recognized no ethical or moral boundary to ensure his continued rule. Such is the power of sin that Jesus came to destroy.   —C. R. B.

III. PROTECTION (MATTHEW 2:19-23)

A. Coast Is Clear (vv. 19-21)

19, 20. *After Herod died, an angel of the Lord appeared in a dream to Joseph in Egypt and said, "Get up, take the child and his mother and go to the land of Israel, for those who were trying to take the child's life are dead."*

Matthew does not provide a time frame, but it seems that the death of *Herod* follows his Bethlehem massacre quickly, likely within the year. We know from other sources that Herod dies in 4 BC and that his death is met with great joy among the Jews of Judea. *Joseph*, Mary, and Jesus have migrated to *Egypt*, having fled Bethlehem just in time as the result of an angelic dream (Matthew 2:13-15).

Now another *dream* assures Joseph that he can return to Jewish territory, for the threat is gone. Herod probably goes to his deathbed thinking that he has killed the baby king.

21. *So he got up, took the child and his mother and went to the land of Israel.*

Joseph is a skilled craftsman. Thus he is able to find enough work to provide for his family almost anywhere he lives (compare Acts 18:3). He does not remain in Egyptian territory, however. *The land of Israel* is where his family belongs.

What Do You Think?

What do you say to someone who has experienced a tragedy that God could have prevented, but chose not to?

What Do You Think?

Why do you think God waited for Herod to die instead of just "taking him out" sooner? What does this tell us about how God may work today?

B. SAFE HAVEN IS FOUND (vv. 22, 23)

22. But when he heard that Archelaus was reigning in Judea in place of his father Herod, he was afraid to go there. Having been warned in a dream, he withdrew to the district of Galilee,

When *Herod* the Great dies, his kingdom is divided as we noted in the Lesson Background. *Archelaus* is given the provinces of Judea, Samaria, and Idumea. The Romans do not allow him to have the title *king*, instead giving him the lesser title of *ethnarch* (meaning "ruler of a people," which is also the meaning of his name Archelaus).

Archelaus is every bit as evil as Herod the Great, but not as skilled politically. He eventually is exiled to Gaul (modern France) in AD 6 by the Romans. After this, Judea is ruled by Roman governors such as Pontius Pilate, Felix, and Festus.

Although Herod is dead, *God* knows that the unstable Archelaus also poses a threat. So Joseph is directed to go farther north and settle in *Galilee*. This is the territory of Herod Antipas, the brother of Archelaus. Galilee is traditional Israelite territory, but has become heavily Gentile in this period. This provides a safer place for Joseph to raise his family, far from the mainstream of Jewish affairs.

23. . . . and he went and lived in a town called Nazareth. So was fulfilled what was said through the prophets: "He will be called a Nazarene."

The city that Joseph chooses, *Nazareth*, is insignificant as far as the ancient world is concerned. The New Testament often describes Nazareth as being within Galilee to give the readers a point of reference as to its location (Matthew 21:11; Mark 1:9; Luke 2:39).

Matthew later portrays the Galilean origin of Jesus as a fulfillment of prophecy (Matthew 4:13-16). We know from Luke's account of Jesus' birth that both Joseph and Mary have roots in Nazareth, so safety is enhanced by the presence of family (see Luke 1:26, 27; 2:4).

We do not know the exact source of the prophecy *He will be called a Nazarene*. There is probably a connection between the name of the village and the Jewish custom known as a Nazirite vow (Numbers 6:1-21). Later, the followers of Jesus sometimes are called by the designation *Nazarenes* (Acts 24:5).

CONCLUSION

Modern Nazareth is a bustling little city in northern Israel. Its focus point is a vast church built over the traditional site where Mary was thought to have received the visit from the angel Gabriel to tell her that she was to be the mother of the Messiah. Inside the church are several huge pictures of Mary and baby Jesus as portrayed by different nations. It is striking to see a Korean Mary and Jesus, a Chilean Mary and Jesus, an African Mary and Jesus, etc. This is not sacrilege, but the reflection of a natural impulse.

Each culture wants to imagine Jesus as one of its own. This is not a denial of the Jewishness of Jesus, but something much deeper. It is the result of the fact that the appeal of Jesus transcends any nationality or ethnicity. Jesus was sought by the wise men, who were pagan Gentiles from a distant country. Ironically, he was rejected by Herod, the master of the Jewish world.

WHAT DO YOU THINK?

How do we decide when we should retreat to a place of safety rather than confronting evil directly?

[Amos 5:13; Matthew 18:15-17; and 1 Corinthians 5:1-5 can be important to consider.]

PRAYER

God, you who led the wise men to Jesus, who protected Jesus from Herod, who directed Joseph to Egypt and Nazareth, to you do we offer our hearts. May they be filled with exceeding great joy when we remember the blessing you have granted us in the person of your Son, Jesus the Messiah. May the Christmas story be ever new to us. May the wisdom and persistence of the Magi be ours as well. In Jesus' name we pray. Amen.

Today, all peoples and every individual can find fulfillment in Jesus and only in Jesus. The book of Revelation pictures Heaven as a place where the people of the Lamb will be drawn from every tribe, every language, every people, and every nation (Revelation 5:9). This description crosses all possible divisions of humanity. He is the King of kings and Lord of lords.

THOUGHT TO REMEMBER

Jesus attracts both worshipers and detractors. Which are you?

Discovery Learning

The following is an alternative lesson plan emphasizing learning activities. Classes desiring such student involvement will find these suggestions helpful. At the back of this book are reproducible student pages to further enhance activity learning.

INTO THE LESSON

Prepare questions of biblical importance on small, folded slips of paper, one question per slip. Use the following questions or design your own: "Was the universe created or did it simply form on its own?" "Are miracles real or imagined?" "Is the Bible historically accurate?" "Is the doctrine of the Bible consistent throughout?" "Does the Bible have anything to say regarding contemporary life?" "If there is one true religion, what is it?" "How accurate is the Bible regarding terminal destruction of the universe?" "Is there a Heaven?" "Is Hell real?"

Hand one question to each learner as he or she arrives. Say, "Please do not open your slips of paper until I give the word." Pick learners randomly to read their questions aloud in rapid sequence. Do not allow comments. After the last question is read, say, "Wow! Important questions all. But there is one more important question." Have someone read Matthew 16:13. Ask, "Isn't that just about the most important question people need to answer personally? *Who is Jesus?* The answer to that question will help us make sense of all the other questions when we consider the full implications of the fact that he is the Christ, the Son of God."

Note that today's text pictures two vastly different approaches to this issue. Say, "One approach sees him as a threat worthy of death; the other sees him as worthy of gifts and worship."

INTO THE WORD

Give each learner a handout with the heading *The Gamut of Emotions*. List the 26 letters of the alphabet down the left side. Ask students to write one emotion, one intense feeling for each letter. Suggest they give themselves latitude in their choices for the more difficult letters; for example, suggest *exuberance* for the letter *X*.

Though you will accept a variety of choices, here is an alphabetical sampling: *anger, blue, contemptuous, depressed, elated, fearful, grief-stricken, grateful, hurt, happy, irate, joyful, kicky, love, misery, neglected, offended, paranoid, quarrelsome, rejoicing, sorrow, tenderheartedness, unashamedness, vindictive, warm-hearted, exuberant, yucky, zealous.*

After five minutes of consideration, let students share their lists aloud. Then provide handouts of today's text. Say, "Write letters where you see the emotions felt or suggested. For example, you could put a *D* for *devious* by Herod in verse 7 or an *E* for *elated* for the Magi in verse 10."

Say, "These events are full of deep emotions for real people, from Herod to the Magi to Jesus' mother and Joseph." If you do this as a whole class, ask the class members to take their marked copies of the text home for use devotionally in the coming week.

INTO LIFE

Buy a package of the typical gold or silver "reward stars" that teachers and parents use to honor good behavior and achievement. Give each learner four or five to use this week in connection with some or all of the following occasions: the congregation's worship assembly, a time of personal Bible reading or prayer, an event in the natural environment that stirs praise and awe, and/or an experience in godly service that is a response to God's goodness. Suggest the class use the stars as "markers" for their sense of true worship, sticking them in a conspicuous spot capable of reminding them of their spiritual sensitivity.

For example, if they find true worship in the congregation's assembly, they can place a star on the worship bulletin. If they visit a manger scene and it draws them close to God, they can stick the star on any handout received. Remind students that the star of the Magi was ultimately an invitation to worship, which the wise men certainly did.

Ask, "What are some potential challenges with the Christmas image of Jesus as a cute little baby, born in very humble circumstances?" Your class will no doubt note that that image in and of itself makes no demands on a person other than a warm feeling of "how nice." Ask, "How do we make certain that that incomplete picture of Jesus is not the only image the culture carries of him?" Let your class suggest specific and general steps to be taken. *Alternative:* Have your students complete the reproducible activity "Star Watch" from page 247 and discuss in small groups. Distribute copies of "Jesus: The Either/Or" from that page as students depart.

PROCLAIMED IN BAPTISM

LESSON 5

INTRODUCTION

A. ANTICIPATION

As I write this lesson, my wife and I are waiting with great anticipation for a phone call from our daughter informing us of the birth of our first grandchild. For several months we have been looking forward to this blessed event. Gifts have been purchased, a room has been prepared, and plans have been made. Now all we can do is wait.

Waiting is not something we human beings do well. We want results now! The expectation of instant gratification is a curse of our culture. But in the midst of our wanting things to happen *now,* how much do we anticipate God's ultimate fulfillment of his purpose of redemption?

B. LESSON BACKGROUND

Between the days of Malachi and those of John the Baptist, the nation of Israel had not heard the voice of a prophet of God—that's over 400 years! During those years of silence, some may have begun to feel that God had abandoned or forgotten his people. But the truth about God is that he is always at work, whether we recognize it or not. During those 400 years God had been working out his plan of the ages. That plan involved providing the ultimate answer for the problem of sin.

Our lesson today reveals the end of God's period of silence as a new prophet broke onto the scene. John the Baptist had come to announce that the one promised was close at hand. John thus served as the bridge from the anticipation of the Messiah to his actual appearance.

I. FORERUNNER COMES (MATTHEW 3:1-6)

A. IDENTITY, MESSAGE, LIFESTYLE (vv. 1-4)

1. In those days John the Baptist came, preaching in the Desert of Judea

The phrase *in those days* may sound a bit vague to us. Since Jesus begins his ministry at "about thirty years old" (Luke 3:23), we can compute this point in time to be about AD 26.

Matthew's account doesn't give us any background information on *John the Baptist.* We have to go to Luke 1 for that information. There we learn that Jesus and John the Baptist are relatives. The designation *the Baptist* identifies something about John's role as being one who baptizes. That designation also helps us distinguish him from the apostle John.

The phrase *preaching in the Desert of Judea* gives us another clue about how God likes to work. God did not choose the palace of a king for the birth of his Son, but an environment for livestock instead. Likewise, God does not choose to introduce his Son's ministry in the temple courts in Jerusalem, but rather through a spokesman in the uninhabited area of the countryside.

2. . . . and saying, "Repent, for the kingdom of heaven is near."

DEVOTIONAL READING:
ACTS 8:26-38
BACKGROUND SCRIPTURE:
MATTHEW 3
PRINTED TEXT:
MATTHEW 3:1-6, 11-17

Jan
3

LESSON AIMS

After participating in this lesson, each student will be able to:

1. Relate the account of Jesus' baptism.

2. Explain how Jesus' baptism fulfilled "all righteousness."

3. Tell how he or she can strive to fulfill "all righteousness" in his or her life situation this week.

KEY VERSE

A voice from heaven said, "This is my Son, whom I love; with him I am well pleased."
—Matthew 3:17

LESSON 5 NOTES

John's message of repentance is pointed. In a general sense, to *repent* is to change one's mind about something; in the sense of the gospel, to repent is to turn from sin. This repentance is to bring about a change in behavior based on the change of mind. It constitutes an about-face or U-turn in one's life. Repentance is based on an awareness of guilt and conviction of the conscience.

John's message of repentance is in anticipation of the imminent arrival of *the kingdom of heaven*. Mark and Luke speak of it as "the kingdom of God." Matthew, writing to a Jewish audience, is thought to use the phrase "kingdom of heaven" in deference to that audience's sensitivities. (There are 32 references to "kingdom of heaven" in Matthew, but none in the other Gospels.) A kingdom normally is thought of as the area (realm) in which a sovereign rules. However, God's kingdom is not so much a place as it is people, thus its spiritual nature.

The ancient Jews have been anticipating the inbreaking of this kingdom. What catches many by surprise, however, is that repentance is a prerequisite for entrance. Many undoubtedly think that their admission into the kingdom of Heaven is assured by birthright. After all, they are Israelites! But as verse 9 (not in today's text) makes clear, biological descent from Abraham isn't the main issue. Repentance is.

3. This is he who was spoken of through the prophet Isaiah: "A voice of one calling in the desert, 'Prepare the way for the Lord, make straight paths for him.'"

The truthfulness of the work of John is validated in fulfillment of prophecy. *Isaiah* made his prediction some 700 years prior to John's arrival. The prophecy at issue here is Isaiah 40:3.

A king in the ancient world has people who go ahead of him to herald his coming. John is in this role. His announcement of the coming of the Messiah is spoken of as one declaring and imploring through a strong *voice*. It signifies that what is being said is being said with passion.

Not only is the coming of a king heralded, but also *the way* is prepared. Rough roads are smoothed out so nothing will impede the arrival of a king. King Jesus comes to establish a spiritual kingdom and reign in the lives of people. Thus the preparation that is needed for his arrival is a spiritual preparation. It is a preparation of heart and mind. Thus the call for repentance.

4. John's clothes were made of camel's hair, and he had a leather belt around his waist. His food was locusts and wild honey.

The strange dress of this preacher of repentance is similar to that of Old Testament prophets (Zechariah 13:4). Specifically, John follows in the austere dress style of Elijah (2 Kings 1:7, 8). Clothing made of *camel's hair* is in sharp contrast with the soft robes and vestments worn by royalty. The *leather belt* about his *waist* is an article of clothing that is identifiable with the working class. Such a belt is used to fasten the clothing about the waist so the worker can labor unimpeded. It is not a linen cord, but rather a rough, strong belt.

Also startling is John's diet. The locust is a permissible food under Jewish dietary law (Leviticus 11:22). The mention of *locusts* alongside *wild honey* may not signify two things eaten separately, but perhaps refers to boiled or baked locust that is prepared in the honey. In any case, the diet is not the delectable

WHAT DO YOU THINK?

Should Christians dress in a distinctive way, or should our manner of dress "blend in" with our culture? Why? [Leviticus 19:19, 27; 1 Corinthians 9:19-23; 11:3-16; 1 Timothy 2:9, 10; and 1 Peter 3:3 can inform your discussion.]

food of the day. Rather, it is the diet of one living off the land. The lifestyle and message of John and other prophets stand in stark contrast to that of the cultured religious leaders.

COMPARING FORERUNNERS

President Nixon's visit to the communist People's Republic of China in February 1972 was truly historic. Up until the 1970s, few major nations recognized the legitimacy of that country's government. Nixon's visit had considerable political peril for the United States, since it risked straining relations with the Soviet Union, Japan, and Nationalist China.

Behind the scenes, the visit required massive preparation. In July 1971, U.S. Secretary of State Henry Kissinger held secret talks with China. Kissinger continued his secret preparations with visits in October 1971 and February 1972 to continue laying the groundwork for Nixon's visit. The details to be worked out were staggering.

The similarities and differences between the works of Kissinger and John the Baptist as forerunners are intriguing. As Secretary of State, Kissinger was one of the most powerful men in the U.S. John, for his part, had no trappings of earthly power. As "advance men," both were charged with setting the agenda of someone to follow. The agenda that Kissinger set had many topics and nuances. The one that John set was focused on one idea: people needed to repent. Kissinger worked in secret; John worked publicly. By calling attention to the sin that separates us from God, John prepared an audience to hear the gospel of the kingdom of God. Are you ready to hear it?
—C. R. B.

B. SCOPE, CONFESSION, BAPTISM (vv. 5, 6)

5, 6. People went out to him from Jerusalem and all Judea and the whole region of the Jordan. Confessing their sins, they were baptized by him in the Jordan River.

John's preaching works! Those who hear him are convicted. They repent, acknowledging *their sins*. That John teaches that baptism is to accompany repentance is seen in Matthew 3:11 (below) and Luke 3:3.

John's Jewish audience is familiar with the connection between physical water and spiritual cleansing (see Ezekiel 36:25-27; compare Hebrews 10:22). Later, Jesus will chastise the learned Nicodemus for not understanding the connection between being "born of water and the Spirit" (John 3:5, 10).

Baptism is associated with the idea of a change in state from *unclean* to *clean*. Thus baptism is appropriate for non-Jews who convert to Judaism at the time, since Gentiles are considered to be unclean by Jews. Acts 13:26 seems to refer to these converts as "God-fearing Gentiles" in contrast with those who biologically are "children of Abraham." Gentiles become spiritually clean in the Jewish proselyte baptism. This imagery carries over into the church age with Christian baptism (Acts 2:38; Colossians 2:12; 1 Peter 3:21). Baptism is a washing (1 Corinthians 6:11; Titus 3:5; Hebrews 10:22).

II. FORERUNNER PREDICTS (MATTHEW 3:11, 12)

A. WHO IS COMING (vv. 11a, b)

11a. "I baptize you with water for repentance.

The call of John is for the people to repent, or turn from their sins. Those who do so then demonstrate their repentance by submitting to *water*

DAILY BIBLE READINGS

Monday, Dec. 28—The Origin of John's Baptism (Matthew 21:23-27)

Tuesday, Dec. 29—John, More Than a Prophet (Luke 7:24-30)

Wednesday, Dec. 30—John's Testimony of Jesus (John 1:24-34)

Thursday, Dec. 31—Calling on the Name of Jesus (Romans 10:8-17)

Friday, Jan. 1—The Necessity of Repentance (Matthew 3:7-10)

Saturday, Jan. 2—Buried and Raised with Christ (Romans 6:1-11)

Sunday, Jan. 3—Jesus Baptized by John (Matthew 3:1-6, 11-17)

What Do You Think?

In what ways can John the Baptist still serve as a model for drawing attention to Jesus and away from ourselves?

[Matthew 3:13, 14; 11:2, 3; John 1:35-39; 3:22-30 will give you some ideas.]

baptism. This is no secret repentance, but rather is a full disclosure of repentance in a public act. The fact that the baptisms take place in the Jordan River is about as public as you can get!

11b. "But after me will come one who is more powerful than I, whose sandals I am not fit to carry.

John's baptism is preparatory in light of the one who is coming after John: Jesus. Think of the great prophets of the Old Testament such as Elijah, Isaiah, Jeremiah, and Jonah. John is called greater than all of these (Matthew 11:11). But when John looks at himself in relation to Jesus, he knows of his own insignificance. It is the lowest of servants whose job it is *to carry* his master's *sandals*. John does not consider himself even worthy enough to do this. He feels lower that the lowest in relation to Jesus.

So it still is that those who do great works for the Lord are, in the end, but lowly servants (Luke 17:10). This attitude of humility is what makes one a useful servant for God.

B. What He Will Do (vv. 11c, 12)

11c, 12. "He will baptize you with the Holy Spirit and with fire. His winnowing fork is in his hand, and he will clear his threshing floor, gathering his wheat into the barn and burning up the chaff with unquenchable fire."

Disagreement abounds as to what *with the Holy Spirit and with fire* means here. Some scholars say it speaks of two baptisms for two different groups. Under this theory, the water baptism is received by those who accept Christ; this constitutes a baptism unto life. The other baptism is a baptism of destruction in fire; this constitutes a baptism unto death in the final judgment. That, so the theory goes, is the idea of *burning up the chaff with unquenchable fire*. Thus what is signified by the *wheat* and chaff here are thought to be parallel to the wheat and weeds in Matthew 13:24-30, 36-43.

Another proposal is that the fiery baptism of the Holy Spirit happens when a person accepting Christ is baptized in water. This means that it is in water baptism that the Holy Spirit is received. The fire aspect symbolizes being purged from sin (chaff) at that time. Advocates of this theory point out that Ephesians 4:5 speaks of there being "one baptism," not two. Thus the singular act of baptism is thought to be like a door that naturally has two sides: the physical (water) side and the fiery (spiritual) side.

The baptism that characterizes the Christian age is different from John's baptism. Although it is still water baptism (see Acts 2:38a; 8:36; 10:47), an added element will be the receiving of the Holy Spirit (Acts 2:38b; 11:16; 1 Corinthians 12:13). John recognizes in his preaching that not only is he less than the Messiah, but also that his baptism is only preparatory to that of Christ (see Acts 19:1-6).

III. FORERUNNER SURPASSED (MATTHEW 3:13-17)

A. Baptism by John (vv. 13-15)

13a. Then Jesus came from Galilee to the Jordan

For *Jesus* to come from Nazareth in *Galilee* to the *Jordan* River means a trip of some 70 miles. To go to such an effort indicates the importance Jesus places on what is about to happen.

13b, 14. . . . to be baptized by John. But John tried to deter him, saying, "I need to be baptized by you, and do you come to me?"

How to Say It

Abraham. AY-bruh-ham.
Elijah. Ee-LYE-juh.
Galilee. GAL-uh-lee.
Isaiah. Eye-ZAY-uh.
Jeremiah. Jair-uh-MY-uh.
Jonah. JO-nuh.
Judaism. JOO-duh-izz-um or JOO-day-izz-um.
Leviticus. Leh-VIT-ih-kus.
Malachi. MAL-uh-kye.
Nazareth. NAZ-uh-reth.
Nicodemus. NICK-uh-DEE-mus.
proselyte. PRAHSS-uh-light.
Zechariah. ZEK-uh-RYE-uh.

Jesus has come to be *baptized*, but why? John's baptism is a baptism of repentance (Acts 19:4), but Jesus has nothing from which he needs to repent (Hebrews 4:15). John himself recognizes a problem, thus his question, "*I need to be baptized by you, and do you come to me?*"
15. Jesus replied, "Let it be so now; it is proper for us to do this to fulfill all righteousness." Then John consented.

If *Jesus* does not need a baptism of repentance unto forgiveness because he is sinless, then why does he insist that John baptize him? The foundational answer is that it is the right thing to do.

But we should probe further. In what way will this baptism *fulfill all righteousness*? There have been many proposals. The best approach will take into account both the repentance and end-times ("kingdom of Heaven is at hand") aspects of John's baptism. Regarding the first of these two, Jesus' baptism signifies his identification with those who are confessing their sins. Humility is expressed in this act. Part of the very reason for the incarnation is that God comes to earth in human form and faces the same issues that humans face. Jesus is the suffering servant in this regard (Isaiah 42:1).

The baptism of Jesus also marks a dividing line in God's plan for the ages. Jesus is just about to begin his public ministry, thus the kingdom of Heaven is at hand. That may be the importance of the word *now*. Jesus himself is the dividing line between those who are saved and those who are lost, between those who are in the kingdom and those who are not. Jesus thus fulfills all righteousness in coming to suffer on behalf of those who need to repent as he pushes into being the next stage of God's plan for our redemption.

THE RIGHT THING TO DO

Everett Hines was training with his crew in a bomber in 1942 before being sent to war. The plane crashed, and Hines—a white man—was knocked unconscious. Although America was segregated at that time, Abe Watson—a black man—rushed into the burning plane and rescued Hines. Both men were seriously burned. During their recovery, they met briefly and then were sent off to war separately.

Fifty years later, Hines was visiting a friend in the hospital. Nurses wheeled past him a man who had suffered a heart attack. It was Abe Watson.

Watson was dying and asked Hines to do him a favor. He had an unmarried daughter who had three small sons. Watson asked Hines to "watch out for them." Hines said, "How could I say no?" So Hines brought the family into his own home and became the grandfather Watson could not be. When interviewed in 2004 at age 85, Hines had a house full of teenagers. He said, "If it hadn't been for them, I'd be gone by now." Some people seem to know instinctively what it means to do the right thing. Hines's decision brought comfort, community, and new purpose into his life.

Jesus asked John a favor: "Would you baptize me?" John couldn't understand why, but he soon realized that the right thing to do was to honor Jesus' request. Jesus asks many things of us in the pages of the New Testament, including baptism. Have we done the right thing? —C. R. B.

B. CONFIRMATION BY GOD (vv. 16, 17)
16. As soon as Jesus was baptized, he went up out of the water. At that moment heaven was opened, and he saw the Spirit of God descending like a dove and lighting on him.

PRAYER

Father, give us a conscience to repent and a will to do so. Remind us that repentance is not a one-time thing but an all-the-time thing. As we repent, may you be able to say of each of us, "You are all sons of God through faith in Christ Jesus" (Galatians 3:26). We pray in Jesus' name. Amen.

Visual for Lesson 5.
Have this visual prominently displayed as you begin your discussion of Matthew 1: 16, 17.

WHAT DO YOU THINK?

What are some ways you have seen the Holy Spirit active in your life or the lives of others? What can we do to better understand and appreciate the work of the Spirit?

[Follow up your discussion with a consideration of John 16:7-11; Romans 8:26; 1 Corinthians 12:4-31; Galatians 5:22, 23, 25; and Ephesians 4:30.]

THOUGHT TO REMEMBER

The need to repent never goes away.

WHAT DO YOU THINK?

Is it presumptuous to think that God might say of us "This is my son (or daughter), in whom I am well pleased"? Why, or why not?

The fact that Jesus comes *up out of the water* indicates that he has been immersed in the water. As he is coming up, *heaven* is *opened* in some sense. What this looks like we can't be sure. Is the throne of God in Heaven visible to Jesus and John? Or is this more of a picturesque way of saying that God's approval is being granted? Some Christians today use terminology symbolically to speak of God's sending down a blessing. Ezekiel 1:1 and Revelation 4:1 also speak of the opening of Heaven.

The Spirit makes his arrival at this event. Isaiah 11:2 states that *the Spirit of God* is to rest on his anointed or chosen one. The image *like a dove* is clarified by Luke 3:22, which says that "the Holy Spirit descended on him in bodily form like a dove." We see the Son of God and the Spirit of God working together at other times in Scripture. One occasion is at creation itself. In Genesis 1:2 we see the Spirit of God moving on the face of the waters. We know that Jesus was part of this creation process because John 1:1-3 indicates that nothing was made except by the Word; the Word is identified as Jesus in John 1:14. See also Colossians 1:16.

God used a dove in the Old Testament as a sign of his deliverance. In Genesis 8:6-11 a dove brought an olive leaf to the ark when the earth was ready to be inhabited again after the flood. The word picture of the dove at the baptism of Jesus thus offers a certain parallel to the idea of God providing new life to a world that was filled with corruption in Noah's day.

17. And a voice from heaven said, "This is my Son, whom I love; with him I am well pleased."

In addition to the Spirit of God comes the *voice* of God. This is one of those times in Scripture when we see all three persons of the Godhead coming together at one time. In Genesis 1:26, God says, "Let *us* make man in our image." The use of the word *us* implies plurality even as God is one (Galatians 3:20).

We also see the interplay of the three divine persons in the nativity story. God speaks to Mary (by means of an angel) to tell her that she will be with child by the Holy Spirit. Of course, this child is the third member of the Godhead, Jesus. Now at the inauguration of the ministry of Jesus we see the three working together again.

God's approval and affirmation of both the person and future work of his Son is confirmed in this event. God's announcement that *this is my Son, whom I love* does not mean that it is the baptism of Jesus that somehow confers sonship on him. He was already the Son. This spoken declaration is for John's benefit and ours as well. Some students hold that God may very well be addressing the angels (and perhaps even Satan) in this declaration also.

Jesus is unique as God's Son. Yet each person who surrenders to God and is baptized into Christ is also a child of God (Galatians 3:26, 27). In that case, we can think of God saying to us, "This is my son (or daughter) in whom I am well pleased." Those who follow Jesus truly do receive the approval and recognition of God. Even so, no one is "Son" in the same sense as Jesus.

Some students link the words of God here with Psalm 2 and Isaiah 42. These passages speak of the chosen one of God and his role of service and sacrifice. This great day and this event mark the beginning of a life that is filled with this service and sacrifice. Jesus did it for us.

CONCLUSION

This is the time of year that many resolve to make changes. It may be changing an unhealthy diet, initiating an exercise routine, or correcting improper sleep habits. Some resolve to get their financial house in order or shake an addiction. The best resolution anyone can make is to heed the call of John the Baptist and repent. Perhaps there is a sin habit that is controlling your life. Determine now to turn from it. Even if you've been a Christian for a long time, you can resolve anew to honor Jesus as Messiah (1 John 1:9).

WHAT DO YOU THINK?

Why do so many of us fail to keep our New Year's resolutions? If we resolve to heed John's call to repentance, how can we carry through with that decision?

Discovery Learning

The following is an alternative lesson plan emphasizing learning activities. Classes desiring such student involvement will find these suggestions helpful. At the back of this book are reproducible student pages to further enhance activity learning.

INTO THE LESSON

Prepare a poster with the word REPENTANCE written vertically down the middle. Say, "We will build an acrostic using words and phrases that help us clarify and understand the act of repentance. Give an example by writing the words *radical change* at the letter *c*. Some other words or phrases that could be included are *forgiveness, sin, new life, faith, trust, surrender, sorrow, grief, passion, spiritual moment*, etc. As students share their words or phrases for the acrostic, also ask them to explain why their suggestion is important to the concept of repentance.

Make the transition to Bible study by saying, "Repentance was not only the key word in John the Baptist's ministry, but is a key word in our relationship with God." Stress that authentic Christians are ones who have learned repentance.

INTO THE WORD

Say, "We will share today's teaching responsibilities by doing team research and reports." Form study teams of three or four (larger classes can form more teams and double up assignments). Give Team #1 a photocopy of the lesson commentary on Matthew 3:1-6. Team #2 will need a photocopy of the lesson commentary on Matthew 3:5, 6, 11-13 plus a Bible concordance with a marker or tab on the page with the words *baptism, baptize,* and/or *baptized*. Give Team #3 a photocopy of the lesson commentary on Matthew 3:11-17. Also give each team a copy of the appropriate instructions as follows.

Team #1: Your task is to help the class understand John and his ministry. Why is John called "the Baptist"? What is the significance of *repentance* in John's messages? Why should the message "the kingdom of heaven is near" strike a chord in his listeners? Explain (1) his appearance and diet, (2) "prepare the way for the Lord, make straight paths for him," and (3) the imagery of baptism and confession in verse 6.

Team #2: Your task is to clarify the practice of baptism in the New Testament. Use the concordance to find the words *baptize, baptism,* and/or *baptized*. Read as many of those passages as possible. What procedure was used for baptism in the Bible? What clues can we use to draw reasonable conclusions for those parts of the procedure that are not precisely spelled out? How does "John's baptism" compare and contrast both with Christian baptism as inaugurated on the Day of Pentecost (hint: see Acts 2:38; 19:1-5) and with John's baptism of Jesus?

Team #3: Your task is to explain the following phrases and concepts: "baptize you with the Holy Spirit and with fire" (v. 11), "fulfill all righteousness" (v. 15), "the Spirit of God descending like a dove" (v. 16), and "This is my Son, whom I love" (v. 17).

Encourage teams to work quickly. You may wish to ask teams to assign portions of their tasks to individuals or pairs within the group to speed the process. Allow each group to report conclusions. As an alternative or additional activity, have your teams complete the reproducible activity "Appreciating Concepts and Phrases" from page 248.

INTO LIFE

Another Acrostic. Remind the students that repentance includes radical change. Say, "That change certainly includes baptism, but also much more." Write the word *CHANGE* vertically down the middle of the board. Give each person an index card. Say, "Most of us still need radical changes in our lives. Some may need to be baptized. [Write the word *baptize* on the last letter of the acrostic as you say this.] Others may identify an attitude or behavior that needs to change. Each person should identify and write down one change that needs to happen in his or her life. The word should fit in the acrostic."

Tell students not to put names on the cards because you will collect them for prayer. After collecting the cards, ask a class member to serve as a scribe to write the words on the acrostic. When the list is complete, lead a prayer that appeals for God's help.

Note: If your class is small, there is a greater danger that a confidence will be breached as it becomes easier to figure out who wrote which needed changes. In this case, have students write some general changes that all Christians should continue to make throughout their lives. Distribute copies of the reproducible activity "Understanding Repentance and Change" from page 248 as students depart.

STRENGTHENED IN TEMPTATION

LESSON 6

INTRODUCTION

A. TEMPTED JUST AS WE ARE . . .

Temptation to sin has been around since the beginning of the human race. The serpent approached Eve in the Garden of Eden and tempted her with the promise of a certain kind of wisdom. All she had to do was take a bite of some nice-looking fruit. Eve succumbed to the temptation. She then became the tempter in Adam's subsequent fall.

And so it has continued throughout history. Abraham, trying to save his own skin, gave in to the temptation to lie about Sarah's not being his wife. David was tempted by the beauty of a nearby woman who was taking a bath. He did not resist the temptation of adultery and murder.

Temptations still mark the day-to-day, hour-to-hour, even minute-to-minute lives of all people. Different things tempt different people. One person can drive past a bar or liquor store daily and never be tempted to purchase anything. Another person drives past the same bar or store and fights the steering wheel to keep from turning in. Yet another person driving past the same places stops often, giving in to temptation easily and regularly.

As we fall, we may think, "God, you just don't understand what it means to be tempted. You don't know how hard it is." But God's response to that is that he *does* understand. Scripture states: "For we do not have a high priest who is unable to sympathize with our weaknesses, but we have one who has been tempted in every way, just as we are—yet was without sin" (Hebrews 4:15). Jesus' temptations in today's text are informative in this regard.

B. LESSON BACKGROUND

The four Gospels are largely about Jesus' three and one-half year public ministry. In Matthew, that ministry does not begin until 4:12. What comes before that point are the vital preparations.

Those preparations, taking all the Gospels together, include Jesus' conception, birth, presentation in the temple, Passover visit to Jerusalem at age 12, and baptism, in addition to John the Baptist's activities as forerunner. The temptation of Jesus in the wilderness, the subject of today's lesson, is the final preparation. The parallel accounts are Mark 1:12, 13 and Luke 4:1-13.

I. SATISFYING CRAVINGS (MATTHEW 4:1-4)

A. CONTEXT (vv. 1, 2)

1. Then Jesus was led by the Spirit into the desert to be tempted by the devil.

The same *Spirit* who has just been part of the acclamation of Jesus as the beloved Son of God (last week's lesson) now leads Jesus to the place of

---

DEVOTIONAL READING:
HEBREWS 2:10-18
BACKGROUND SCRIPTURE:
MATTHEW 4:1-11
PRINTED TEXT:
MATTHEW 4:1-11

Jan 10

LESSON AIMS

After participating in this lesson, each student will be able to:

1. List the three temptations the devil offered Jesus.

2. Compare and contrast the temptations offered to Jesus with temptations he or she faces today.

3. Select and memorize a Scripture to use as a defense against temptation.

KEY VERSE

Jesus said to him, "Away from me, Satan! For it is written: 'Worship the Lord your God, and serve him only.'"   —Matthew 4:10

LESSON 6 NOTES

temptation: *the desert*. Just as God allowed Satan to test Job in the Old Testament (Job 1:6-12), he now allows Satan to tempt his Son.

The warfare between good and evil, between God and Satan, is first seen on earth in the Garden of Eden. Another pointed account is the affliction of Job. The warfare continues now with Satan *(the devil)* coming to Jesus Christ, God in the flesh. All this falls right on the heels of Jesus' baptism—with his identification with the people of God and the purpose of God. Satan is trying to thwart the work of Christ before it has a chance to begin.

2. *After fasting forty days and forty nights, he was hungry.*

This verse seems to be stating what is rather obvious: if one fasts for *forty days and forty nights,* we would expect hunger to be the result (compare Exodus 34:28). But it is important that this verse is here because it shows the way the devil works. He knows areas of weakness in the lives of people, and he strikes at those weaknesses. If someone's weakness is alcohol, he will place that temptation in his path. If the weakness if pornography, Satan knows how to attack in that area as well.

A strong desire for food naturally should be the result of a lengthy fast. Satan apparently believes that this is the best time to make his move.

B. TEMPTATION (v. 3)

3. *The tempter came to him and said, "If you are the Son of God, tell these stones to become bread."*

We see here a basic work of the devil: temptation. He is the author of temptation.

Satan is fully aware of Jesus' identity. Matthew 8:29 reveals that Satan's minions know the Son of God when they see him. Thus when Satan says *If you are the Son of God,* he is not expressing uncertainty as to who Jesus is, but rather is taunting Jesus to prove it. For Jesus to do so would be for him to bow to the command of Satan instead of acting on his own volition. Satan's view of power is that it is to be exercised for self-interest. That is the way those who sit in powerful positions in the world often use their power.

But Jesus knows that his power is to be used for the glory of God. To give in to the recommendation of Satan is to listen to the devil instead of seeking the will of God. It certainly is possible for Jesus to turn *stones* into *bread.* On more than one occasion, Jesus will feed thousands of people with a miraculous multiplication of available resources. Jesus is the very one who created the stones in the first place, so he can do anything with them he desires.

C. RESULT (v. 4)

4. *Jesus answered, "It is written: 'Man does not live on bread alone, but on every word that comes from the mouth of God.'"*

A person can live only about 50 or 60 days without food. Since Jesus now has gone 40 days without eating, he is getting close to the limit! Who could blame him if he uses his power to stave off death by starvation?

But Jesus uses Scripture to rebuke Satan. Specifically, Jesus quotes Deuteronomy 8:3. That passage was spoken some 14 centuries earlier concerning the Israelites becoming hungry in the wilderness. God allowed that wilderness wandering and the subsequent hunger to teach the Israelites to trust

WHAT DO YOU THINK?

In your experience, do Satan's temptation strategies change over time, or do they remain pretty much the same? Defend your answer.

WHAT DO YOU THINK?

What was a time you were tempted to do something that seemed good (at least on the surface), but for the wrong reason? How did you grow spiritually as a result?

him. After they became hungry, God then fed them with manna, something totally new to them. Jesus is aware of this fact of history, and he trusts God to meet his needs in his time and in his way.

Today we face temptations to put our physical needs ahead of our spiritual needs. As a result, we can end up forsaking time with God and his Word to satisfy the cravings of the flesh. It is in these times that we need to remember the priority of Scripture. Feeding ourselves the Word of God is the highest priority. Jesus knows what his priorities are.

TAKING SHORTCUTS

We've all heard of get-rich-quick schemes. A common theme is the promise of abundant returns on "too good to be true" investments.

Sometimes the hook that catches Christians is the promise that their investment will do great things for the kingdom of God. For example, in 2008 the director of a certain ministry raised funds purportedly to help foreign missions. Upon his arrest, authorities alleged that he used the money of well-meaning Christians to finance an extravagant lifestyle, which included a $1 million house and a $168,000 sports car.

The bait in such schemes essentially is the promise of a shortcut to achieving personal or ministry goals that are driven by the need for funding. Legitimate financial planners can tell you how to build financial security in sound ways. Ministries often are best funded after a lengthy season of prayer that results in sacrificial giving by many people. Taking shortcuts in either area is very dangerous.

Satan offered Jesus a shortcut. Satan will offer us shortcuts as well. Jesus knew that spiritual riches come only through the discipline of a life committed to God, not through easy shortcuts. Will we learn this lesson?   —C. R. B.

II. TESTING GOD (MATTHEW 4:5-7)
A. CONTEXT (v. 5)
5. Then the devil took him to the holy city and had him stand on the highest point of the temple.

The context of the second temptation moves from the wilderness to *the holy city* of Jerusalem. That is where *the temple* is located. The distance from *the highest point* on that structure to the lowest point in the adjacent Kidron Valley is over 400 feet. The importance of that distance is seen in verse 6, next.

B. TEMPTATION (v. 6)
6. "If you are the Son of God," he said, "throw yourself down. For it is written: 'He will command his angels concerning you, and they will lift you up in their hands, so that you will not strike your foot against a stone.'"

People spend a lot of time and effort trying to make a name for themselves. Books are written on the art of self-promotion. The goal is to make self look good in the eyes of others for personal gain and acclamation. It is this sin of pride, the pride of life, with which Satan now tempts Jesus. Satan wants Jesus to test God. Surely God will not let anything bad happen to the beloved Son in whom he is well pleased!

Since Jesus used Scripture to thwart the first temptation, Satan now decides to use some Scripture also. The passage Satan uses is Psalm 91:11, 12. This passage speaks of protection that God provides in the course of life or from harms that come in the course of living faithfully for God.

DAILY BIBLE READINGS

Monday, Jan. 4—Enduring Trials and Temptations (James 1:12-16)

Tuesday, Jan. 5—Times of Testing (Luke 8:5-8, 11-15)

Wednesday, Jan. 6—Restore Others but Take Care (Galatians 6:1-5)

Thursday, Jan. 7—Stay Awake and Pray (Matthew 26:36-46)

Friday, Jan. 8—The Way to Pray (Matthew 6:9-15)

Saturday, Jan. 9—Our Temptation and God's Faithfulness (1 Corinthians 10: 6-13)

Sunday, Jan. 10—Jesus' Victory over Temptation (Matthew 4:1-11)

But Satan is not using this passage in light of the context in which it was given originally. This promise of God is not a license for the reader to test God's faithfulness by doing foolish things. Thus Satan is doing something that false teachers still do: quoting Scripture with great disregard for context. Satan is twisting Scripture to fit an agenda.

C. RESULT (v. 7)

7. Jesus answered him, "It is also written: 'Do not put the Lord your God to the test.'"

Satan is asking *Jesus* to *test* the Father's faithfulness. But Jesus knows that it is not his task to manipulate God's power or presence in his life. To answer Satan's abuse of the intent of Scripture, Jesus draws on Deuteronomy 6:16. The context of this verse speaks to the occasion when the Israelites tested God with regard to the availability of water.

Testing God is something many still do. The person who refuses medical help and simply "trusts God" to heal him is an example. The person who "trusts God" to provide for her financial needs yet refuses to look for a job is in this same camp. Some leaders of Christian organizations launch big projects that will cost a lot of money with "trust" that God will provide. This may be genuine trust, but it also may be testing God to honor human plans instead of seeking God's plan.

The Christian is called to trust God, not demand of God. To demand of God instead of trusting his guidance and seeking his wisdom is an affront to his person.

THE "LOOK AT ME" SYNDROME

The cult of celebrity has taken a new twist in the twenty-first century: the ability to "broadcast yourself" on Internet sites such as *YouTube*. One can become instantly famous on such sites by posting an intriguing video. One's chances for fame seem to be enhanced by stupidity or even violence. For example, in 2008 eight Florida teenagers filmed themselves beating a girl, allegedly so they could post it on *YouTube*. The attackers were six girls and two boys (who acted as lookouts).

The resulting charges included battery, false imprisonment, and felony kidnapping. The victim of what the sheriff called "an animalistic attack" suffered a concussion, damage to her left eye and ear, and numerous bruises. The perpetrators are now (in)famous, not only because of their *YouTube* video, but because one of them—apparently in regret—gave the video to the police.

Satan's suggestion to Jesus was a promise of being saved from hurting himself. However, at a certain level it was similar to the temptation the eight teens succumbed to in that it invited the one being tempted to consider self only and ignore the larger consequences. It is still the "look at me" syndrome. Jesus' solution was to say, in effect, "Look at God!"   —C. R. B.

III. ACHIEVING GREATNESS (MATTHEW 4:8-11)

A. CONTEXT (v. 8)

8. Again, the devil took him to a very high mountain and showed him all the kingdoms of the world and their splendor.

One thing is certain about *the devil*: he is persistent! If he spots what he thinks is a weakness, he will continue to attack. Sometimes he will use a frontal assault (as we see here). At other times he will attack indirectly.

Visual for Lesson 6. Point to this visual as you ask, "Why should we be intentional in teaching Scripture to children?"

Jesus has demonstrated himself to be a worthy opponent of Satan in the way he has handled the first two temptations. When you remember how soundly defeated Satan was when God allowed him to put trials before Job, you would think Satan would get the message that he can't win. But on he goes, as the context changes yet again. This time the location is a *mountain* that is *high* enough to allow a panoramic view of *all the kingdoms of the world*.

B. TEMPTATION (v. 9)

9. "All this I will give you," he said, "if you will bow down and worship me."

When sin entered the world in the Garden of Eden, Satan became something of a ruler of this fallen earth. He is called "the prince of this world" in John 12:31 and "the god of this age" in 2 Corinthians 4:4. Of course, this is only an authority temporarily allowed. Though Satan may exercise some power in this world, God still remains the supreme ruler of his creation (see Daniel 4:32). What Satan is not willing to acknowledge in this temptation is that ultimately the kingdoms of the world are not his to give away.

This temptation is aimed at the lust of the eyes. In the Old Testament story of the taking of the city of Jericho, the Israelites were told not to take any of the plunder for themselves. But a man named Achan disobeyed. When he was found out his only response was, "I saw . . . I coveted . . . and took" (Joshua 7:21).

Satan is trying to short-circuit the ultimate goal of Jesus' becoming king and ruler in God's way by offering the crown without the cross. Later, Peter also will try to steer Jesus away from the cross with the declaration "Never, Lord! . . . This shall never happen to you!" (Matthew 16:22). Jesus' response indicates that Peter's thinking is in line with that of Satan (16:23; see Lesson 11 of this quarter).

Luke 24:26 says that Jesus first has to suffer before he enters into his glory. To give in to this temptation would be an attempt to force God's plan instead of allowing God's plan to play out as he has decreed. God's plan is to make Jesus ruler, but his kingdom will not be of this world (John 18:36). For Jesus to accept an earthly throne would please many in the Jewish world as they seek a military and political king (John 6:15). But Jesus knows that this is not the purpose for which he has come.

We see not only a temptation to bring about the wrong kind of kingdom, but also a wrong stipulation for receiving this kingdom in that Satan asks Jesus to worship him. Today, we hear of people who are overtly involved in the worship of Satan, but they seem to be relatively few in number. Yet Satan still tempts people to worship something on the throne of their hearts that isn't God. Satan tempts people to seek prestige and honor for themselves. He tempts people to bow down and "worship" their work, with the idea that they will have power and authority as a result. Others are tempted to pursue places of prominence by destroying others.

Many who follow these temptations may seem to have achieved the very things that Satan promises. But in the final analysis these people merely have sold their souls to the devil. They will reap only misery and destruction.

C. RESULT (vv. 10, 11)

10. Jesus said to him, "Away from me, Satan! For it is written: 'Worship the Lord your God, and serve him only.'"

HOW TO SAY IT

Abraham. AY-bruh-ham.
Achan. AY-kan.
Deuteronomy.
  Due-ter-AHN-uh-me.
Hebrews. HEE-brews.
Jericho. JAIR-ih-co.
Jerusalem. Juh-ROO-suh-lem.
Kidron. KID-ron.
Satan. SAY-tun.

WHAT DO YOU THINK?

Do the ends ever justify the means? Why, or why not?

PRAYER

Forgive us, O Lord, of those times when we willingly cooperate with the devil. Grant us awareness of his schemes. Through the power of the Holy Spirit and the example of your Son, help us resist the devil so that he flees from us. We pray in Christ's name. Amen.

WHAT DO YOU THINK?

What are some times when Satan may find people particularly vulnerable to temptation? How can our realization of these times help keep us on guard?

Jesus understands that to *worship* anyone or anything other than *the Lord your God* is to be an idolater. Again Jesus confronts the tempter with Scripture in refusing to do as *Satan* suggests. Referring to Deuteronomy 6:13, Jesus affirms that the only one worthy of worship is God.

Notice that in Jesus' response he combines two ideas to establish how one honors God: God alone is to be worshiped and served. Whatever one worships is what he or she focuses on serving. If Jesus bows to Satan, he will then be subject to Satan and be his servant.

And so it is still. Honor, prestige, wealth, and power can look very good. There are advisors who are willing to help you achieve these things. But like Satan, many of these people merely want to be exalted themselves. There is only one who always has our best interests at heart: *God.* Scripture says that we cannot serve both God and mammon (Matthew 6:24).

When we are tempted to worship the things of this world or to seek honor for ourselves, we do well to remember that these things are temporary. Such a temptation is from Satan, and he never offers anything of lasting value. Whenever we are tempted to worship and serve anything other than Christ, we must realize that Satan is behind this. Thus with Jesus we need to say to Satan *away from me* (again, compare Matthew 16:23).

11. Then the devil left him, and angels came and attended him.

The devil now leaves, but that does not mean he is finished with Jesus. Luke's account of the temptation of Jesus ends by saying that "when the devil had finished all this tempting, he left him until an opportune time" (Luke 4:13). Satan will come back when the time suits him.

It is good to have a respite from the attacks of Satan! But until this life on earth is finished, a Christian is foolish to think that he or she is ever done with Satan. Even so, it is good in the meantime to be *attended* to by those whom God sends our way as sources of comfort and encouragement.

CONCLUSION

Ultimately, the purpose of Jesus in coming to earth was to be the sacrifice for sin. But to offer a sinless sacrifice, Jesus had to be the lamb without spot or blemish (1 Peter 1:19). The episode of the three temptations was not a chance for Jesus to prove to the Father that he was worthy of this mission. Rather, the temptations that God allowed Jesus to face—not only those in today's lesson but also in places such as Matthew 27:40—demonstrated to Satan and to all humanity that victory over temptation is possible. The temptations Jesus went through mirror the temptations we face (see 1 John 2:16). In observing the response of Jesus in Satan's temptations, we learn how to deal with Satan's tactics.

We recall what we said at the beginning of this lesson: Jesus was tempted just as we are, yet he did not sin (Hebrews 4:15). The devil was beaten in the battle of the three temptations. By resisting the devil, we will be better able to overcome sin. Unlike Jesus, we will not be totally without sin because in our weakness we will continue to stumble. But as we resist by following the example of Jesus, we will develop a stronger walk with a greater capacity to deal victoriously with future temptations. A key to victory is to be aware of Satan's schemes at the outset (2 Corinthians 2:11).

When tempted, look to the one who has been where you are. Jesus endured temptation, and he will help us in our times of temptation. May the words of Hebrews 2:17, 18 encourage us all: "For this reason he had to be made like his brothers in every way, in order that he might become a merciful and faithful high priest in service to God, and that he might make atonement for the sins of the people. Because he himself suffered when he was tempted, he is able to help those who are being tempted."

THOUGHT TO REMEMBER
*We are not sinless,
but we can sin less.*

Discovery Learning

*The following is an alternative lesson plan emphasizing learning activities.
Classes desiring such student involvement will find these suggestions helpful. At the
back of this book are reproducible student pages to further enhance activity learning.*

INTO THE LESSON

Place in chairs copies of the reproducible word-find exercise "Temptation Fighters" from page 249 for students to work on as they arrive. *Brainstorming:* Ask class members to mention temptations that face Christians. Select one student to write these on the board rapidly.

Make the transition to Bible study by reminding the class that even Christians (or, perhaps, *especially* Christians) are tempted. Say, "That fact makes the temptations of Jesus an important study. Today we will discover a model for fighting temptation. We will also discover important things about God's Son."

INTO THE WORD

Dramatizations: Read today's printed text as a class. Say, "Today, you will prepare dramatizations of these temptations. However, the dramas will be drawn from contemporary life." Divide the class into three teams. Assign each a temptation of Jesus from Matthew 4:1-4, 5-7, and 8-10. Give each team a photocopy of the lesson commentary of the Scripture assigned and the following list of tasks. (Each team receives the same list.)

Task #1: Read the account of the temptation assigned. *Task #2:* Decide what is a general category for the type of temptation at issue, such as lust of the flesh, greed, pride, seeking significance, etc. *Task #3:* Prepare a dramatization of that type of temptation and a way to resist it in contemporary life. The brainstorming list may be helpful in selecting your drama theme. Make sure that your methodology for resisting the temptation incorporates Jesus' techniques.

Remind the teams they must prepare these dramas quickly (10 to 12 minutes). If you think that your learners will need more preparation time than the class session allows, distribute the list of tasks several days in advance by e-mail, etc., so students can do some preliminary thinking. Allow each team to present its dramatic sketch.

INTO LIFE

Pose the following discussion questions:

1. "What lessons do the temptations of Jesus hold for us in 2010?" List answers on the board under the heading *Lessons*. Answers may include the reality or existence of the devil (Satan) as the source of temptation, the use of Scripture as a vital tool for resisting temptation, the fact that even believers are tempted, and the types of temptations that Satan uses.

2. Read 1 John 2:16, 17 and ask, "How do you harmonize this Scripture with the concept of temptation coming from the devil?" If your students need a hint, have them look at John 12:31; 14:30; 16:11, but don't give this hint too quickly.

3. "Can temptations ever be helpful to believers?" Challenge students to defend affirmative answers, if any are offered. Ask for illustrations or experiences.

4. "How should temptation be defined?" Write suggestions on the board. Then write a dictionary definition, which you have looked up in advance. Compare and contrast.

5. "What techniques will you use to avoid or resist temptation in 2010?" List answers on the board under the heading *Temptation Fighters*. Stress the distinction between *avoid* ("staying clear of it in the first place") and *resist* ("withstand after you've been hit").

Remind your class that the lesson emphasizes the strength that Scripture offers for successfully fighting temptation. Display on a poster the following Scriptures as potential help in this regard. 1. "Man does not live on bread alone, but on every word that comes from the mouth of God" (Matthew 4:4). 2. "Do not put the Lord your God to the test" (Matthew 4:7). Explain that testing God is something we still do; examples are listed in the lesson commentary. 3. "Worship the Lord your God, and serve him only" (Matthew 4:10). 4. "The world and its desires pass away, but the man who does the will of God lives forever" (1 John 2:17).

Explain that these four Scriptures offer strength in resisting modern temptations. Give each learner an index card; ask each to list a temptation that faces him or her; then each is to select a Scripture from this list that will be helpful. Stress that students will not be asked to share this information with the class. Challenge students to use this exercise to memorize Scripture for use in facing the identified temptation. Distribute copies of the reproducible activity "Learning Our Lessons" from page 249 as students depart.

DEMONSTRATED IN ACTS OF HEALING

LESSON 7

INTRODUCTION

A. FAITH IS THE BEST MEDICINE

Medical research tends to support the old idea of laughter being good medicine. The healing power of laughter was popularized by Norman Cousins (1915–1990). He was a medical researcher who also became editor-in-chief of *Saturday Review* and author of the book *Anatomy of an Illness*.

After being diagnosed with serious heart disease and, later, a crippling form of arthritis, Cousins began to treat himself with high doses of Vitamin C and, less conventionally, a regimen of Marx Brothers' movies. He claimed that a few minutes of deep laughter could provide hours of pain-free sleep. He ended up living much longer than his doctors had predicted.

Proverbs 17:22 discusses the value of cheerfulness, although this is not a major topic in the Bible. In contrast, the Gospels clearly and frequently discuss the role of faith in healing. Again and again, people whom Jesus encountered received healing because of their belief in his divine power; on the other hand, some were unable to be blessed because they refused to believe in him. Today we explore these two responses.

B. LESSON BACKGROUND

After impressing the crowds with the authority of his teaching in the Sermon on the Mount (see Matthew 7:28, 29), Jesus performed a series of high-profile public healings that drew considerable attention to his ministry. In Matthew 8:5-13, Jesus healed the servant of a centurion. After disembarking in the region of the Decapolis, he cured demonized men who were forced to live in a graveyard (8:28-34). Crowds flocked to Jesus (8:18).

Some responded to Jesus' miracles with genuine faith; others were interested in the show, but were not truly committed to Jesus' program; some resisted him because they feared his influence; others who genuinely wanted to support Jesus wondered why he was not fitting the mold of their expectations. This is the swirl of controversy in which we find today's two lesson segments. Matthew does not always arrange his material in chronological order, and it is likely that our second segment, Matthew 11:2-6, occurs prior to our first segment of Matthew 9:27-34.

I. BELIEF AND DISBELIEF (MATTHEW 9:27-34)

Matthew 9:26 reveals Jesus' popularity as the backdrop to our first segment: "News of this spread through all that region." Mark 3:22; 10:46-52; Luke 11:14, 15; 18:35-43 offer certain parallels, although the events are different.

DEVOTIONAL READING:
LUKE 5:27-32

BACKGROUND SCRIPTURE:
MATTHEW 9:27-34; 11:2-6

PRINTED TEXT:
MATTHEW 9:27-34; 11:2-6

LESSON AIMS

After participating in this lesson, each student will be able to:

1. Tell what Jesus' healing miracles revealed about his identity and mission.

2. Explain how Jesus' miracles can be used as evidence of his identity today, even though two millennia have passed since he worked them.

3. Affirm his or her faith in the Lord and how that faith is a help in time of trial—with or without a "miracle."

Jan 17

KEY VERSE

The blind receive sight, the lame walk, those who have leprosy are cured, the deaf hear, the dead are raised, and the good news is preached to the poor.   —Matthew 11:5

How to Say It

Capernaum. Kuh-PER-nay-um.

centurion. sen-TURE-ee-un.

Che Guevara. Chay Geh-VAR-uh.

Decapolis. Dee-CAP-uh-lis.

demoniac. duh-MOE-nee-ak.

Elijah. Ee-LYE-juh.

Elisha. Ee-LYE-shuh.

Fulgencio Batista. Fool-GEN-see-oh Buh-TEES-tuh.

Galilee. GAL-uh-lee.

Herod Antipas. HAIR-ud AN-tih-pus.

Isaiah. Eye-ZAY-uh.

messianic. mess-ee-AN-ick.

Pharisees. FAIR-ih-seez.

What Do You Think?

Why do you think Jesus sometimes healed by touch but other times did not? What are some modern implications of his practice, if any?

A. Miracles of Sight (vv. 27-30a)

27. As Jesus went on from there, two blind men followed him, calling out, "Have mercy on us, Son of David!"

Matthew includes certain markers that indicate that Jesus is moving about, and *went on from there* is one of those (compare Matthew 9:1, 9). Taken together, these demonstrate that Jesus is moving around Galilee as he preaches and teaches. He may now be in the vicinity of Capernaum, where he had begun to preach (see Matthew 4:13).

The title that the *blind men* use as they approach Jesus is significant. The address *Son of David* indicates that they have concluded that Jesus is the Christ, the Messiah (see Matthew 12:23; 15:22; 20:30, 31; 21:9; 22:42). The common belief is that the Christ as Son of David will be the heir of King David. In that capacity, the Son of David will reestablish David's throne (see 2 Samuel 7). Most likely the blind men have reached their conclusion on the basis of reports of Jesus' healings in the region. Their conclusion echoes Matthew's Gospel as a whole. Matthew begins his Gospel with a lengthy genealogy that documents Jesus' ancestry. This clarifies his royal pedigree in order to establish his credentials as the Messiah.

The blind men speak to Jesus as they would to a king who has power over their lives, humbly asking him to be merciful to them. Psalm 72:12-14 describes one who will deliver the poor and needy. The blind men's request clearly reflects their belief that Jesus can and will act in this way.

28. When he had gone indoors, the blind men came to him, and he asked them, "Do you believe that I am able to do this?"

"Yes, Lord," they replied.

After sticking close to Jesus through the streets (which is not easy for blind men to do!), the two follow him into a certain house. There they press their appeal. The fact that Jesus did not heal them out in the street on their initial request perhaps reveals Jesus' intention to explore their thinking about him in more detail.

Rather than asking about the source or nature of their medical condition as a doctor would, Jesus addresses the men's spiritual situation. Jesus' question is stated in terms of their belief in his power. We may find Jesus' question to be a bit curious. Clearly, if the two men have been following Jesus through the town and even into the house begging for healing, they must *believe* that he can do something to help them!

The question, however, requires the blind men to state their faith publicly before those who are gathered. The healing to follow thus becomes evidence that their faith is valid. In other words, their public confession of faith sets a backdrop for the healing that makes Jesus' identity crystal clear.

29, 30a. Then he touched their eyes and said, "According to your faith will it be done to you"; and their sight was restored.

Jesus' reply repeats a common refrain in this section of Matthew's Gospel. While Jesus does not always heal by using touch as he does here (compare Matthew 8:13; 9:6, 7; contrast 13:58), he frequently states that a healing has come about as the result of *faith*. Sometimes this is the faith of the sick individual (see 9:22); on other occasions, Jesus honors the faith of those who make a request on behalf of someone else in need of healing (8:13; 9:2; 15:28).

We stress that Jesus does not suggest that healing will come automatically to faithful people. Neither does Jesus suggest that those who are not healed can be blamed automatically for lack of faith. If this were the case, we would have to conclude that the apostle Paul was not a man of faith since he suffered with an unhealed "thorn" in his flesh (2 Corinthians 12:7-10).

Rather, the healing of the blind men indicates that Jesus' miracles should be closely associated with a response of faith. In other words, Jesus' miracles and teaching to this point have led these men to realize that he is the Son of David. Their healing, in turn, will lead others to come to the same conclusion and place faith in him. Jesus' power proves who he is. Matthew thus closely ties Jesus' identity as the Christ to the works that he does: the miracles confirm and support the message.

"CURING" BLINDNESS

Giving (or restoring) sight to the blind is a challenge researchers are working on. The applications are still in the early stages of development, but computer technology offers hope of success.

Researchers are taking various approaches. One is called vOICe. This involves a process that sends images from a simple video camera worn on sunglasses to a laptop computer in a backpack. The computer translates the images into sound that is sent to the ears through headphones. Loudness indicates proximity, and pitch indicates the height of the object that the camera is detecting. However, this technology doesn't really result in "seeing" (www.seeingwithsound.com).

Another technology also uses a sunglasses-mounted camera, but sends the signals to electrodes implanted in the brain. In some patients this process actually has stimulated visual images. However, the images are of extremely low quality at the current state of the art, not even as good as the earliest camera/cell phone combinations.

The two blind men of whom Matthew speaks had no such technology to help them. Jesus was their only resort in their hope for sight. However, with the power Jesus possessed, there was no need for technology. He had mercy on them and healed them because they believed that he had the power and authority to do so. To what extent do you think our modern technology for restoring sight is also an extension of God's mercy?

—C. R. B.

B. EXUBERANCE OF THE HEALED (vv. 30b, 31)

30b. Jesus warned them sternly, "See that no one knows about this."

The reasons for Jesus' exhortation to *see that no one knows about this* are unclear to us. On various occasions, Jesus tells individuals who have been healed not to reveal the source of their recovery. The reason for this request is fairly easy to understand in the earliest part of Jesus' ministry, since he does not want his fame to spread too quickly (see Mark 1:43-45). Yet many of Jesus' miracles have since been performed in public places, before crowds of people. So how can (and why should) secrecy be attempted at this point?

Some commentators suggest that Jesus heals the blind men privately and asks them not to report the news specifically because they have acclaimed him to be the Son of David. In other words, under this theory Jesus wishes to avoid the political implications of that label at this point in his ministry. We note that other individuals whom Jesus heals generally do not refer to him in this way before the miracle takes place. On the other hand, Jesus had associated his power to heal with the authority to take away sins earlier in Matthew 9. That claim is no less controversial.

DAILY BIBLE READINGS

Monday, Jan. 11—A Physician Is Needed (Luke 5: 27-32)

Tuesday, Jan. 12—A Cry for Healing (Psalm 107: 17-22)

Wednesday, Jan. 13—A Prayer for Healing (2 Kings 20:1-7)

Thursday, Jan. 14—An Amazing Faith (Matthew 8:5-13)

Friday, Jan. 15—The Father's Loving Care (Hosea 11:1-4)

Saturday, Jan. 16—Sent Out to Heal (Matthew 10: 1-8)

Sunday, Jan. 17—Jesus' Healing Ministry (Matthew 9:27-34; 11:2-6)

Others students propose that Jesus is using reverse psychology, knowing that the blind men will be more likely to tell people if he asks them not to do so; under this theory, Jesus commands them to remain silent because he actually wants them to proclaim the news. This solution, however, seems inconsistent with the fact that the blind men already have been proclaiming Jesus as Son of David even before he heals them. We probably don't have enough information to draw airtight conclusions about this question. In any case, the story reaches a climax in verse 31 (next).

31. But they went out and spread the news about him all over that region.

Despite Jesus' request, the men who had been blind tell everyone what has happened. Indeed, they can scarcely avoid explaining at least to a few people how they are able to see after being blind, since family and friends cannot miss the change.

C. MIRACLES OF EXORCISM AND HEALING (vv. 32, 33)

32. While they were going out, a man who was demon-possessed and could not talk was brought to Jesus.

Jesus now meets another individual who needs help. This one has both a spiritual and a physical problem: he is *demon-possessed* and cannot speak. Evil spirits may cause various forms of disability. Some students propose that different categories of demons cause specific medical problems. In this case, it is hard to resist the conclusion that it is the demon who has rendered the victim mute.

33. And when the demon was driven out, the man who had been mute spoke. The crowd was amazed and said, "Nothing like this has ever been seen in Israel."

Just how the man is healed isn't stated. The emphasis is on the effect of Jesus' action. Witnessing this event, the astonished crowds note that Jesus' power is unique—no one has ever been able to do such things. While the Old Testament includes accounts of miraculous healings, especially in connection with the prophets Elijah and Elisha (see 1 Kings 17; 2 Kings 4–5), the scope and frequency of Jesus' healing miracles are without precedent.

D. LOGIC OF ENEMIES (v. 34)

34. But the Pharisees said, "It is by the prince of demons that he drives out demons."

Matthew clearly wishes to contrast the attitude of *the Pharisees* with that of the blind men from the previous story and of the crowds who have just witnessed the exorcism. "Seeing is believing" for the average person. But the Pharisees take a different approach to evaluate what Jesus is doing.

The fact that the mute man immediately speaks after Jesus cures him (v. 33, above) makes it impossible to deny that a genuine miracle has occurred (compare Acts 4:16). Further, almost all people in the ancient world believe in gods and also that some humans can perform works with supernatural aid. The question for people in Jesus' time, then, is not whether someone can heal miraculously (a premise that many would challenge today). The question, rather, is by what power the healing is done.

Since the Pharisees already have concluded that Jesus is a false teacher and a blasphemer (see Matthew 9:3), they interpret his miracles as proof posi-

WHAT DO YOU THINK?

In what situations today should we be silent about what Christ has done for us, if any? Explain.

[Matthew 7:6; 10:14; 21:23-27; 28:19, 20; and 1 Peter 3:15 will be helpful in framing your answer.]

WHAT DO YOU THINK?

Which brings greater criticism to a Christian leader, success or failure? Why do you say that?

tive that he is in league with Satan, *the prince of demons*. When they make a similar accusation on a later occasion, Jesus characterizes their attitude as "blasphemy against the Spirit" and warns that such a sin cannot be forgiven (Matthew 12:22-32).

People still choose to respond to Jesus in a variety of ways. Some question the source of his power. More commonly in our day, people simply deny that he was really able to do these things at all. Others, however, see the miracles as confirming Jesus' true identity as the Son of David and Son of God.

II. QUESTION AND ANSWER (MATTHEW 11:2-6)

At some point, John the Baptist is imprisoned by Herod Antipas for criticizing Herod's immoral marriage to his former sister-in-law (see Mark 6:17, 18). Our second passage picks up at a time when the imprisoned John sends his disciples to gather information about Jesus' activity. Luke 7:18-23 is parallel.

A. "ARE YOU THE ONE?" (vv. 2, 3)

2, 3. When John heard in prison what Christ was doing, he sent his disciples to ask him, "Are you the one who was to come, or should we expect someone else?"

John's question reveals his confusion. Although Jesus has become popular, he hasn't been very proactive in setting up the kingdom of God as people commonly expect that kingdom to manifest itself. If Jesus really is the *Christ*, as John originally thought back in Matthew 3, then why are the Romans still in power?

Some speculate that John's question reflects his desperation about his own situation, as he realizes that his life is in danger. The difficult circumstance may be leading John to doubt his initial confidence in Jesus' identity.

B. "JUDGE FOR YOURSELF" (vv. 4-6)

4. Jesus replied, "Go back and report to John what you hear and see:

Jesus doesn't give a straight "Yes, I am the one" kind of answer. Instead, he tells John's disciples to examine the evidence and report what they *hear and see* to *John*. Then John (and everyone else, for that matter) can draw his own conclusions. The exact evidence that Jesus suggests they examine is the subject of verse 5 (next).

5. "The blind receive sight, the lame walk, those who have leprosy are cured, the deaf hear, the dead are raised, and the good news is preached to the poor.

Jesus' response to John's inquiry clearly indicates the purpose of Jesus' ministry. The kinds of miracles and preaching that Jesus cites here appear in messianic prophecies in the book of Isaiah, such as Isaiah 29:18; 35:5, 6; 61:1, 2. In those passages we see promises of what will happen when the Christ appears.

Jesus' miracles not only reveal him to be the Christ, but also clarify the nature of the kingdom that he comes to establish. Jesus does not come to defeat the Romans, but rather to set people free from disease, demons, and sin. The last item on the list in this verse surely is the most significant: the good news of God's kingdom is being proclaimed to *the poor*, who flock to Jesus in response to his powerful works (compare Matthew 5:3). His works are, in fact, designed to generate this response.

Visual for Lessons 7 & 9.
After reviewing the entries on this visual, ask, "What works of God have you experienced in your life?"

WHAT DO YOU THINK?

If Jesus' healing miracles were evidence of the truth of his claims, what does that say regarding how we should evaluate the truth claims of modern-day healers, if anything?

WHAT DO YOU THINK?

How are Jesus' actions still "scandalous" in the eyes of some today?

PRAYER

Lord, so often we struggle in our faith and commitment. Often we feel disappointed because you don't give us the things we ask for when we want them or because you lead us to places we don't want to go. Sometimes we are tempted to doubt your love, or even your existence. Please help us remember the blessing that will come to us for accepting Christ as he revealed himself and following his word. We pray in Jesus' name. Amen.

6. *"Blessed is the man who does not fall away on account of me."*

Those who see the true meaning of Jesus' actions and recognize his identity through them will be *blessed*. Some, however, might *fall away* because of him, and thus miss the blessing. Those who have wrong expectations of who the Messiah "should" be are in danger of disappointment and, much worse, in danger of missing out on God's plan.

HOW CAN WE TELL WHO'S THE ONE?

Fidel Castro ran for parliament in Cuba in 1952. Shortly before the election, Fulgencio Batista staged a coup and became dictator. Castro—along with brother Raúl Castro and Che Guevara—began plotting a revolution that finally succeeded in 1959. Castro then nationalized privately-owned factories and plantations, eventually declaring Cuba to be a socialist state in 1962.

With the Bay of Pigs fiasco of 1961 and the Cuban missile crisis of 1962 as backdrop, Castro became something of a messianic figure to the world's political revolutionaries. But the socialist paradise he promised his people never materialized. Thousands of Cubans took political refuge in other nations as Castro tightened his grip. Even after the collapse of the Soviet Union in 1991, Castro maintained one-party Communist rule over his country. Failing in health, he finally relinquished power to his brother Raúl in February 2008. Fidel Castro never delivered his promised "paradise."

Every would-be political savior finds people asking the question, "Are you the one?" They confidently respond, "Yes!" When the question came to Jesus, he distinguished himself from every false messiah by saying, in effect, "Take a look at the evidence: what I have accomplished tells you all you need to know." The evidence of changed lives still tells us Jesus is truly who he claimed to be—the Son of God.

—C. R. B.

CONCLUSION

The concept of *truth* in the ancient world was different from what it is today. In the world of Jesus' day and for many centuries following, truth was an absolute idea. Jesus either *was* or *was not* the Messiah. The people of Jesus' day wrestled with this question (John 7:41-43). They came to different conclusions because some evaluated the evidence properly while others evaluated it improperly. But both friend and foe would agree that it's either one or the other; either Jesus *was* the Messiah or he *was not*.

This way of looking at the idea of truth does not hold sway in many quarters today. The understanding of the very nature of truth has changed. In today's world, truth is often understood in terms of personal experience: the life I have lived, what works for me, and the world as it looks through my eyes are "my truth." Many people live by this idea: "What's true for me is just that. What is true for others—which may or may not be true for me—is fine for them." This is known as the postmodern view of truth. Rather than being absolute, truth is considered to be relative to the individual. The postmodern thinker doesn't mind if I conclude that Jesus is the Messiah "for me" as long as that postmodernist can also claim that Jesus is not the Messiah for him or her.

But Jesus will have none of this kind of thinking! Jesus invites belief in him on the basis of evidence (John 14:11). Either the miracles *did* occur or they *did not* occur. In fact, Christ's powerful works reveal that he is the Son of God. This means that he is the supreme authority on all points of religious dispute. Thus his teachings are ultimate truth. As Jesus himself says, "Do not believe me unless I do what my Father does. But if I do it, even though you do not believe me, believe the miracles, that you may know and understand that the Father is in me, and I in the Father" (John 10:37, 38).

THOUGHT TO REMEMBER
Jesus' works reveal his identity.

Discovery Learning

The following is an alternative lesson plan emphasizing learning activities.
Classes desiring such student involvement will find these suggestions helpful. At the
back of this book are reproducible student pages to further enhance activity learning.

INTO THE LESSON

Give each person an index card. Tell the class that sometimes it is difficult to answer the question *Who is Jesus?* concisely and accurately. Ask each learner to write three words that describe the identity of Jesus. As they write on their cards, put this question on the board: *How do you know your descriptions are true?*

Ask class members to share their answers to the first question as someone records them on the board. Have volunteers tell how they answered the second question. Discuss.

Make the transition to Bible study by saying, "It is important for each follower of the Lord to be able to answer these questions, for two reasons: First, it is important as a foundation for our own faith; second, the ability to answer these questions must become the foundation of our testimony to unbelievers."

INTO THE WORD

Before class, recruit a volunteer to be interviewed in the class as John the Baptist (Matthew 11:2, 3). Give him a photocopy of today's lesson commentary, a copy of the questions below, and a couple basic props such as a staff and rough robe.

Read the printed text with the class. Then tell the class they're going to hear from a first-century contemporary of these marvelous events. He is mentioned as one who wondered about the identity of Jesus. He is John the Baptist. Use the following statements and questions in your interview:

1. John, welcome to our class. We have some questions about the events we've just read and how they help identify Jesus. I know that you've heard about Jesus doing quite a number of high-profile healings. What are some of these healings, and why did they draw mixed reactions? ["John" should read in advance the copy of the Lesson Background you gave him.]

2. The blind men used an important title for Jesus, calling him the *Son of David*. What is the significance that we should catch in this title for Jesus? ["John" should read 2 Samuel 7:8-16 and Matthew 9:27 in advance.]

3. How do you think the attitude or values of the blind men affected their healing? In what ways was their attitude the same as and different from yours? ["John" should read Matthew 9:29; 11:2, 3 in advance.]

4. Jesus also healed a mute man who was demonized. That healing brought a negative review from the Pharisees. How was the attitude of the Pharisees similar to and different from yours? ["John" should read Matthew 9:32-34; 11:2, 3 in advance.]

5. Now, this question is going to get personal, John. Matthew pictures you as a bit of a skeptic or questioner of Jesus' identity. Tell what kind of Messiah you expected that led you to ask your question in this regard. ["John" should read the lesson commentary on Matthew 11:2, 3 in advance.]

6. And finally, John, what is your conclusion about Jesus' identity?

Thank and dismiss "John" by inviting him to sit with the class. (*Option:* If time allows, use one or both of the reproducible exercises on page 250 as small-group activities.)

INTO LIFE

Tell the class that it is time to allow today's text to become personal. Ask the following discussion questions: 1. Why did Jesus' power to heal establish his identity? 2. Do we need (or should we expect) miracles in the twenty-first century to reaffirm Jesus' identity as Son of God? Why, or why not? 3. While genuine demon possession seems rare in the Western world, spiritual battles are a part of our lives. What are some of the great spiritual battles we still face? 4. Comparing physical blindness with spiritual blindness, what does Jesus' power over one imply about his power over the other today?

Say, "Flip over the index cards that I gave you at the beginning of the lesson." Ask students to write on their cards an answer to this question: *What new thing(s), if any, have you learned about the identity of Jesus?* Ask students to share answers with a classmate.

After a few minutes, have your learners discuss this question: *How should these discoveries equip us to face trials or doubts?* Summarize by emphasizing that the first-century miracles constitute a great body of evidence for the deity of Jesus.

DECLARED IN PRAYER

LESSON 8

INTRODUCTION

A. A LITTLE CHILD WILL LEAD THEM

Jesus uses different illustrations to describe the sort of follower he seeks. The Gospel of John, for example, refers to true disciples as those who have experienced a new birth, dying to the old way of life (John 1:13; 3:3-5). In Luke, Jesus sometimes compares believers (or those most likely to become believers) to "the poor" (Luke 4:18; 6:20; 21:2, 3). Perhaps the most striking of these comparisons, however, is the one that appears in our text for today: disciples are to be like "children."

In Jesus' view, something about children makes them a good analogy for the person who can enter the kingdom of God. Jesus warned his own disciples that "unless you change and become like little children, you will never enter the kingdom of heaven" (Matthew 18:3). On an occasion when the disciples refused to allow some parents to ask Jesus to bless their children, Jesus criticized the disciples' attitude (Matthew 19:14). Clearly, if one's citizenship in the kingdom depends on becoming like a child, it is important to understand what Jesus meant when he told his disciples to be like children.

We may wonder why it would be desirable to be like children. They are naïve and ignorant of the world; they often are self-centered; they often have no clear sense of the consequences of their actions; they often misbehave flagrantly. Surely God does not want us to act like this, does he?

The world is difficult, and children are physically weak and emotionally immature. Yet to maintain our integrity as Christians, we often are forced to make hard decisions and to face overwhelming pressures that require wisdom and maturity. Jesus himself told his disciples that they had to be "shrewd as snakes" (Matthew 10:16). This image seems to be quite different from the exhortation to be as a child. How can we, as disciples, be both "shrewd" and "like little children" at the same time? Our text for today sheds light on this question.

B. LESSON BACKGROUND

As the opening phrase "at that time" of Matthew 11:25 indicates, Jesus' remarks in today's text are closely tied to their immediate context. In 11:2 we see that John the Baptist had been imprisoned. From his prison cell, John sent his own disciples to ask Jesus whether he was really the Messiah (last week's lesson).

John's question seemed to be prompted by doubt since Jesus did not appear to be leading a revolution against Rome. Further, if Jesus really was the Christ, then why was his faithful forerunner (John the Baptist) languishing in prison? Jesus' response implied that John's expectations were wrong. While John seemed to be looking for someone who would fight Caesar, Jesus was

---

DEVOTIONAL READING:
JOHN 11:38-44
BACKGROUND SCRIPTURE:
MATTHEW 11:25-30
PRINTED TEXT:
MATTHEW 11:25-30

LESSON AIMS

After participating in this lesson, each student will be able to:

1. Tell how Jesus' unique position with the Father assures us of "rest."

2. Compare and contrast the different concepts of "rest" with "rest for your souls" that Jesus promised.

3. Identify three burdens he or she will turn over to God.

Jan 24

KEY VERSE

Come to me, all you who are weary and burdened, and I will give you rest.
—Matthew 11:28

LESSON 8 NOTES

DAILY BIBLE READINGS

Monday, Jan. 18—A Listening Father (John 11: 38-44)

Tuesday, Jan. 19— Whenever You Pray (Matthew 6:5-8)

Wednesday, Jan. 20— Praying Alone (Matthew 14:22-33)

Thursday, Jan. 21— Prayer and Blessing on Children (Matthew 19: 13-15)

Friday, Jan. 22—Pray for Your Persecutors (Matthew 5: 43-48)

Saturday, Jan. 23— Prayer and Faith (Matthew 21:18-22)

Sunday, Jan. 24—The Father's Gracious Will (Matthew 11:25-30)

bringing God's kingdom in the form of miraculous healings and the proclamation of the good news of redemption to the poor (Matthew 11:2-6).

Jesus ended his remarks on this topic by criticizing those who seemed to think that God should live up to their expectations rather than the other way around. Notably for our lesson today, he compared those who misunderstood his ministry with children (see Matthew 11:16, 17), thus criticizing the childishness of those who did not respond to Jesus and John the Baptist.

The emphasis is on the way that children often become so absorbed in what they want to do that they completely disregard what other people are saying or doing. Rather than taking the preaching of repentance seriously, many people simply complained, as children often do, that Jesus and John did not play the game that they (the children) wanted to play.

The closing verse in that section compared these "foolish children" to the wise person who heeds Jesus' words: "But wisdom is proved right by all her children" (Luke 7:35, which is the parallel to Matthew 11:19). Mature individuals will seek to conform themselves to God's outlook, rather than anticipating that God will meet their own expectations.

Building on this theme, Jesus proceeded to criticize the various towns that had rejected his message (Matthew 11:20-24). The residents of Korazin, Bethsaida, and Capernaum were guilty of failing to set aside their childish expectations and to see that Jesus' miracles both authorized his teaching and required their repentance. Their attitude was not only childish, it was worse than pagan; indeed, the Gentiles of Tyre, Sidon, and Sodom would be better off on Judgment Day than those whose "wisdom" led them to conclude that Jesus was not the one they were looking for. This is the immediate backdrop to today's text. (For more on Tyre and Sidon, see the Lesson Background of Lesson 10.)

I. REVELATION (MATTHEW 11:25-27)

A. TO CHILDREN (vv. 25, 26)

25. At that time Jesus said, "I praise you, Father, Lord of heaven and earth, because you have hidden these things from the wise and learned, and revealed them to little children.

Many people have missed the point of Jesus' ministry. As a result, they have refused to accept that God might be doing something not quite expected. Yet some realize the truth. Ironically, Jesus summarizes this situation by comparing those who reject him to *the wise and learned* while likening his disciples to *little children*. Several terms in this verse are particularly significant and require special comment.

First, Jesus does not specify what *these things* consist of. But *these things* must refer to the entirety of Jesus' proclamation. This includes his message about the kingdom of God and the things Jesus has revealed about his own identity. Matthew 11:20-24, just preceding today's text, refers to his miracles. Verse 25 shows that people respond to these in two ways: some receive this revelation of truth and accept Jesus' claims, while others refuse to listen.

They refuse because they don't accept that God's kingdom can come in the way that Jesus is introducing it. This fact sheds light on the meaning of several other key words. Essentially, the wise and learned are those who reject

Jesus' words, the little children are those who accept him, while the words *hidden* and *revealed* refer to the different effects on the two groups as a result of Jesus' preaching.

At first glance, it seems odd that Jesus refers to those who do not accept him as wise and learned. These words reflect Jesus' general suspicion toward the religious leaders of the Jews. Believing themselves to be knowledgeable about the will of God, they not only resist Jesus' works and teachings but also pressure others to reject him as well (see Matthew 9:1-3, 34; 12:24; 23:8-13; Luke 11:52). In this particular context, however, Jesus may be thinking more generally of all who doubt him because he doesn't fit their idea of what Messiah should be. All those who conclude that Jesus must not be the one he claims to be (because he doesn't do what they expect the Christ to do) have been blinded to the truth by their arrogant claim to wisdom.

By contrast, Jesus' disciples are little children. This refers to toddlers or very young children who normally have very little knowledge of anything. Because the words *little children* are specifically contrasted with *wise and learned,* the emphasis clearly lies on the ignorance of a child. But in the broader context of this remark, Jesus is not simply endorsing naiveté. His disciples are "ignorant" only in the sense that they humbly admit that God is smarter than they are. Those who accept Jesus' message are willing to set aside their preconceived ideas. They are willing to set aside what they claim to know. They are willing to consider that God may be doing something that goes beyond what they can conceive. Because the disciples are willing to humble themselves rather than depend on their own wisdom, they can see God at work in Jesus' healings and in his association with sinful people (compare 1 Corinthians 1:18–2:5).

This understanding of *the wise* and *little children* in turn sheds light on the terms *hidden* and *revealed.* In this context, these verbs should not be taken to refer to some supernatural process. Jesus is not saying that God has made it absolutely impossible for some people to understand what he is doing while giving others a special gift of faith that makes it absolutely impossible for them to misunderstand. Remember that this entire discussion takes place before the full truth of the gospel is revealed in Jesus' death and resurrection. Thus any faith possessed by anyone at this point is only preliminary to the fuller revelation of Christ yet to come. God has "hidden" these things by revealing his plan in a way that the world does not expect.

First-century Jews expect a very different kind of Messiah from what Jesus proves to be. This expectation blinds most of them to the truth. Jesus' comment here in verse 25 reflects the same kind of thinking that underlies Paul's use of the term *mystery.* On numerous occasions, Paul refers to the message of the gospel as a mystery in the sense that no one expected the Messiah to come in the way that he actually came. Before Jesus' ministry and resurrection, no one expected that the Christ would die a criminal's death on a cross. Jews did not expect that Gentile nations would be able to come to God through faith in the Messiah. We note Peter's surprise at this in Acts 10:34, 35 and others' in Acts 11:18.

At 1 Corinthians 2:7, 8, Paul admits that this mysterious plan was so unexpected that the wise and powerful people of this world missed the point entirely (see also Romans 11:25, 26; Ephesians 1:9, 10; 3:3-10; Colossians

WHAT DO YOU THINK?

What childlike qualities do you need to have that will enhance your Christian walk? How will you go about cultivating those qualities?

WHAT DO YOU THINK?

What was a time when Jesus did not meet your expectations because he did not play according to your "rules"? How did you grow spiritually through this experience?

WHAT DO YOU THINK?

Since it is difficult for "the wise" of this world to understand and accept Jesus, what should our attitude be toward secular higher education?

[Acts 18:24; 1 Corinthians 1:18-25; 8:1; and Colossians 2:8 will be important for your answer.]

1:26-28). Similarly, at Mark 4:11 Jesus himself refers to the kingdom of God as a "mystery" in the sense that it comes in a way that most people do not expect.

Jesus' declaration *Lord of heaven and earth* stresses God's authority and power. God can do things his way, regardless of whether the Pharisees or anyone else approves of what he is doing. God is smarter than all the so-called "wise and learned" people of this world who think they know better. Ultimately, no human being is in a position to criticize him or to question his judgment (compare Job 40:8). What rational person would dare to tell God that his Son shouldn't eat with tax collectors (Matthew 11:19)?

26. "Yes, Father, for this was your good pleasure.

We now see a shift in terminology as Jesus refers to God as *Father*. In connection with the earlier reference to believers as "little children," those who humble themselves and accept the truth are truly God's children. The phrase *this was your good pleasure* stresses that God's plan is no accident. God makes no apologies if our expectations don't live up to his reality.

B. BY THE SON (v. 27)

27. "All things have been committed to me by my Father. No one knows the Son except the Father, and no one knows the Father except the Son and those to whom the Son chooses to reveal him.

This verse bears a similarity to the presentation of Jesus in the Gospel of John. Matthew rarely uses *Father/Son* language to describe Jesus' relationship with God (in Matthew, Jesus is most often the "Son of Man"). But a Father/Son theme is central to John's presentation (see John 3:35; 5:19-26; 6:40; 8:36-38; 17:1). As in John's Gospel, Matthew emphasizes three special privileges that Jesus enjoys as the Son of God.

First, *all things* have been given to Christ by *the Father*. This means that Jesus bears full authority to proclaim God's truth. This claim reflects Jesus' rights as "heir of all things" (Hebrews 1:2). Under the Law of Moses, the firstborn son receives a double share of the inheritance (Deuteronomy 21:17). Obviously, an only child will inherit all the father's wealth. Since Jesus is God's "one and only Son" (John 3:16), Christ receives *all* the truth, grace, and power that God himself possesses (see John 1:14-16; Colossians 1:15). The word *committed* shows us that God allows Jesus to enjoy the benefits of the inheritance now, as is evident by his miraculous power.

Second, Christ as the Son has a special knowledge of God that no one else can grasp fully. This is only logical: obviously, a child knows his or her father better than a stranger does. Jesus alone is in a position to speak about God's nature and will since Jesus alone has seen the Father (see John 1:18). In this context, the phrase *no one knows* marks a sharp contrast between Jesus and those who claim to be "wise and learned." Ultimately, Jesus is the one who knows what he's talking about.

Third, God has given Christ the authority to *reveal* the Father in whatever way Jesus deems appropriate, as Jesus says at the end of the verse. In this context, Jesus is referring to the fact that his unexpected methods confuse those who claim to be "wise" about God while at the same time attracting "little children." Those children are the humble sinners who simply accept his miracles and teachings at face value. Again and again in Matthew's Gospel, the Pharisees are surprised by Jesus' willingness to associate with those

HOW TO SAY IT

Bethsaida. Beth-SAY-uh-duh.
Caesar. SEE-zer.
Capernaum. Kuh-PER-nay-um.
Chorazin. Ko-RAY-zin.
Gentiles. JEN-tiles.
Messiah. Meh-SIGH-uh.
naiveté. noh-eve-TAY.
Sidon. SIGH-dun.
Sodom. SOD-um.
Tyre. Tire.

on the margins of society. The Pharisees openly criticize him for keeping bad company and for violating their own standards of conduct (see Matthew 9:11; 11:19; 12:9-14; 15:1, 2). But if Jesus is God's Son and heir, how "wise" is a person who dares to question how he chooses to conduct himself?

LIKE FATHER, LIKE SON

Many years ago, a television ad campaign featured a little boy imitating his father in various everyday activities. The father sprayed the car with a water hose, then the son sprayed it with his water pistol. A voice-over then said, "Like father, like son." Similar scenes followed to cement the tone. Then the final scene showed the father reaching into his pocket and pulling out a pack of cigarettes, lighting one up, then laying the pack on the ground beside him. The son then picked up the pack of cigarettes as if to take one. The voice-over then asked ominously, "Like father, like son?"

The bond that exists between fathers and sons is a special one. It's natural for boys to "want to be like dad." Often the example the father sets is a positive one, but sometimes it is not.

When it comes to God the Father and his Son, Jesus Christ, the statement "Like Father, like Son" is always true, and the result is always positive. They share a common knowledge, purpose, and essence. As children of the heavenly Father, we should want to be like him to the greatest extent that is humanly possible. For that to happen, we need to know his Son and his Word. Only then will we be able to fulfill his purpose for us. When people see you, do they catch a glimpse of the Father?
—A. E. A.

II. INVITATION (MATTHEW 11:28-30)

A. BURDEN (v. 28)

28. "Come to me, all you who are weary and burdened, and I will give you rest.

Jesus switches to another illustration to describe his relationship with his disciples. While the previous verses referred to believers as "little children," Jesus now compares them with laborers who work hard for low pay. The words *little children* focus on the humility of those who accept Christ's message; the image of *weary and burdened* highlights the struggles we face in life.

In Jesus' culture as in ours, rich people do not bear physical burdens or dig ditches; these are the tasks of the poorer people. The large majority of Jesus' followers can relate to this reality because they literally are poor themselves. Most people whom Jesus meets can readily relate to the famous line from the Lord's Prayer, "Give us today our daily bread" (Matthew 6:11) because having something to eat just for today often is blessing enough, let alone thinking about what might come tomorrow.

But here again, the kingdom of Heaven that Jesus reveals is not what the world expects. Jesus pronounces a special blessing on the poor and says that the kingdom belongs to them (Luke 6:20). This is the case because poor people must have a childlike trust in relying on God's grace and provision. Having such a childlike trust is part of being "poor in spirit" (Matthew 5:3). Those who trust in their own wealth—either in terms of money or personal wisdom—are less likely to come to God. They see no reason to do so. They think they can carry their own burden or hire other people to do so. Thus the *rest* that Jesus offers seems laughable to them.

Visual for Lesson 8. *Start a discussion as you point to this visual and ask, "In what ways have you experienced Christ's rest?"*

WHAT DO YOU THINK?

What special challenges or burdens do the wealthy face that could make them long for the kind of rest Jesus offers?

B. Yoke (vv. 29, 30)

29. *"Take my yoke upon you and learn from me, for I am gentle and humble in heart, and you will find rest for your souls.*

The image of the *yoke* continues the "work" illustration in verse 28. Oxen wear yokes to pull plows, etc. People who think themselves "wise" often yoke themselves to the belief that they can come to God on their own terms and then try to please him by their work. Jesus' words challenge that approach. In fact, God is *not* pleased when we work on our own terms, but rather when we submit to Christ's way. That is a much easier load to bear.

In ancient Judaism, the teachings of a prominent rabbi were sometimes called his *yoke*. The phrase *taking the yoke* meant submitting to that person's doctrine and becoming his disciple. But the yoke or teaching that Jesus offers his disciples (*learn from me*) is different. In fact, one could question whether Jesus really gives his followers a "work yoke" at all, since once we accept his teaching, our work actually turns into *rest*!

30. *"For my yoke is easy and my burden is light."*

This verse contrasts the peace that Jesus offers with the impossibility of pleasing God on our own terms. It should be stressed that Jesus does not mean that he replaces one set of burdens with another, so that we swap the Law of Moses for a new set of demands. The emphasis lies, rather, on the words *easy* and *light* (compare Jeremiah 6:16; 1 John 5:3).

Of course, Jesus does have expectations for his disciples. But he also offers a supernatural peace to those who submit to him. Here again, those who are "little children"—those who put away their pride to trust his judgment and power—receive a blessing that is hidden from the wise and powerful.

THE YOKE'S ON YOU

Myths and legends of the childhood of Jesus abound in nonbiblical literature. These legends include everything from his making birds out of clay and giving them life to that of a boy who dropped dead when he ran into Jesus.

One legend involves Jesus making yokes. Following in the steps of his father Joseph, Jesus worked in his father's carpentry shop. There he made custom-fitted yokes for oxen. Those yokes were always a perfect fit, providing the ideal comfort and efficiency for work. Thus Jesus made the best oxen yokes in the area. Or so the story goes.

We do not know the validity of this legend. But we do know that Jesus is the master builder of yokes for his followers. Being in a yoke does not mean total ease, but being in a perfectly fitted yoke does lessen the burden. We know this is the way Jesus works with us, as he does not allow more to be applied to us than what we can bear (1 Corinthians 10:13). Instead of fretting over our burdens, we rely on the promise of Jesus that his "yoke is easy" and his "burden is light."

—A. E. A.

CONCLUSION

In 1910, only 13.5 percent of people in the U.S. age 25 and over had completed high school or its equivalent. By 2006 that figure had risen to nearly 86 percent. The percentage of those holding a bachelor's degree or higher rose from about 3 percent to 28 percent over the same time frame. One organization reported that more than half of young adults across the globe will enter college at some point. This increased learning clearly has not fixed our serious social problems. The most destructive wars of the twentieth century were fought between the most educated countries on earth. The World Health Organization reported in 2004 that suicide claims more lives yearly than homicide and war combined. It seems we still have a lot to learn.

Our passage today stresses that earthly wisdom ultimately cannot teach us what we most need to know: that peace comes from admitting that God is smarter than we are. Real relief comes only when our confidence in our own knowledge ends. Relief comes when we abandon our expectations about how God "should" operate. Only then can we lay down our burdens.

THOUGHT TO REMEMBER
Cast all your burdens on Christ.

Discovery Learning

The following is an alternative lesson plan emphasizing learning activities. Classes desiring such student involvement will find these suggestions helpful. At the back of this book are reproducible student pages to further enhance activity learning.

INTO THE LESSON

Before class begins, prepare a poster with the heading: *What makes you really tired? Deep-down-exhausted tired?*

Affix the poster to the wall. As students enter the classroom, pass out markers and ask each to draw a simple sketch representing what makes him or her tired. (Larger classes may require several such posters; make sure the poster board is thick enough to prevent the ink from bleeding through onto the wall.)

Begin class by allowing volunteers to explain their drawings. Then ask, "What are some of the options in correcting this sense of exhaustion?" (Sample answers to expect: take a nap, soak in a hot tub, change the circumstances that cause the exhaustion, drink coffee, pray, reexamine priorities.) Jot answers in bold letters across the poster(s).

Make the transition to Bible study by saying, "Accepting Jesus as Savior does not mean that our exhaustion and its causes magically disappear. But he does offer relief in the most important way. Let's find out what, how, and why."

INTO THE WORD

Create four study teams. (If your class is smaller, use pairs or double up the assignments.) Give each team a photocopy of the appropriate pages of the lesson commentary with copies of the assignments below. Say, "Today's study has numerous interesting concepts and teachings. The text is a prayer that provides teachings for Jesus' disciples. In it we find snapshots of the character of God, of Jesus' authority and role, and of the Lord's heart for our well-being."

Study Team #1: Read Matthew 11:25, 26 and the attached commentary. Explain to the class the significance of the titles *Lord of heaven and earth* and *Father.*

Study Team #2: Read Matthew 11:25, 26 and the attached commentary. Explain to the class the declaration of Jesus that "you have hidden these things from the wise and learned, and revealed them to little children." Be sure to explain the phrase "this was your good pleasure."

Study Team #3: Read Matthew 11:27 and the lesson commentary for it. List and explain the three special privileges of Jesus that are implied in this text.

Study Team #4: Read Matthew 11:28-30 and explain the concepts of *rest, weariness, burden,* and *yoke.* Discuss the reward and responsibility implied. Also compare and contrast the concepts of rest after physical labor with "rest for your souls."

Allow each team to report its conclusions.

INTO LIFE

Brainstorming: Remind the class of the list created at the beginning of the lesson of things that make us physically tired. Say, "There are many other burdens Christians carry in today's world. These may make us emotionally tired or feel mentally depleted or simply frustrated."

Ask the class to share some of the burdens or cares that challenge Christians. Depending on the nature of your class, you should decide in advance if the answers you request will be personal or will be "generally speaking." You may stimulate class thinking by listing examples such as "raising children to follow Jesus," "feeling guilty about not being more involved at church," or "giving proportionally and sacrificially when money is scarce." List the ideas on the board.

Identification: Give to each learner a picture of a yoke that is intended for two farm animals (easy to find on the Internet). Say, "One purpose of the yoke is to create a team. That's what we'll do right now."

Ask each learner to write his or her name in the center of one side of the yoke. Then ask each to write Jesus' name in the other side of the yoke, thus creating a team. Ask each student to identify one or more burdens that he or she is carrying and write a description of or an abbreviation of that burden underneath the yoke. Ask, "How do we cast our burdens on Jesus while not abdicating our responsibilities?"

Close with two prayers from different students. Prayer #1 is a prayer of thanksgiving for the obvious love and care Jesus demonstrates for his followers through this passage. Prayer #2 will be for God's intervention or participation in answering the burdens carried by class members. Create a class prayer list by collecting the yoke pictures from those willing to turn them in. Distribute copies of both reproducible exercises on page 251 as take-home work.

REVEALED IN REJECTION
LESSON 9

INTRODUCTION
A. SMALL TOWN, NO HERO

West of Cincinnati, travelers on U.S. Route 50 pass a remarkable monument in the small town of North Bend, Ohio. On a low hill between the highway and the Ohio River, a large American flag flies next to a massive obelisk. Those who leave the main track and make their way up Mt. Nebo Road back to this six-story tower find themselves at the burial site of William Henry Harrison, the ninth President of the United States. Harrison's grandson, Benjamin, was born in North Bend. The grandson's election to be the U.S. President in 1889 sealed North Bend's claim to "presidential pride."

The home page of the community's Web site (www.northbendohio.org) includes portraits of these illustrious former residents. The site proudly declares that only one other city in America (namely Quincy, Massachusetts) can claim to be home to two former presidents. This is no small thing for a village of 600 people!

Considering the pride that towns typically take in their famous citizens, the ancient hamlet of Nazareth should have eagerly claimed Jesus as a favorite son. But during Jesus' ministry the people of Nazareth showed no interest in promoting his name or supporting his plan. In fact, they actively opposed him despite his popularity. Our two passages today explore Jesus' reaction to the poor reception he received in his hometown of Nazareth and the surrounding region of Galilee. His rejection by the people who knew him best is troubling. This illustrates the need to avoid becoming so familiar with Christ that we take him for granted.

B. LESSON BACKGROUND

Our lesson is set during a period when Jesus' popularity was skyrocketing. But his celebrity status inevitably made him a controversial figure. He performed incredible healings and exorcisms everywhere he went. In village after village, the crowds were amazed by his power and by the authority of his teaching. The summary statement at Matthew 9:8 is typical of the crowds' reaction: "When the crowd saw this, they were filled with awe; and they praised God, who had given such authority to men."

At the same time, however, some members of the Jewish religious leadership were suspicious. In their view, Jesus' teachings were blasphemous (Matthew 9:3). Even John the Baptist, Jesus' relative and forerunner, had begun to doubt whether Jesus was really the Messiah. The preaching and healings were nice, but clearly Jesus was not organizing the expected revolutionary movement (Matthew 11:2, 3).

This mixed reception was displeasing to Jesus. We see him condemning the wishy-washy crowd in Matthew 11:16-19, just prior to today's first lesson text.

DEVOTIONAL READING:
ISAIAH 53:1-9
BACKGROUND SCRIPTURE:
MATTHEW 11:20-24;
13:54-58; LUKE 4:16-30
PRINTED TEXT:
MATTHEW 11:20-24; 13:
54-58

LESSON AIMS

After participating in this lesson, each student will be able to:

1. Tell how Jesus was rejected by some of the cities of Galilee.

2. Explain how rejection provides evidence of Jesus' identity even as cases of belief provide such evidence.

3. Articulate one of his or her own "rejection attitudes" and write a prayer to overcome it.

Jan
31

KEY VERSE

[Jesus] did not do many miracles there because of their lack of faith.
—Matthew 13:58

Lesson 9 Notes

I. CITIES WITHOUT REPENTANCE (MATTHEW 11:20-24)

Following a criticism of "this generation" in Matthew 11:16-19, Jesus proceeds to rebuke the residents of specific towns where he had performed miracles. Luke 10:12-15 offers a parallel condemnation in a different setting.

A. TWO COMPARED WITH TWO (vv. 20-22)

20. Then Jesus began to denounce the cities in which most of his miracles had been performed, because they did not repent.

The names of *the cities* in question are given in verse 21 (next). These form the string of villages across Lower Galilee where Jesus has been traveling. The larger context suggests that Jesus is concentrating on the towns clustered around the Sea of Galilee, using Capernaum as a home base (see Matthew 4:12-16).

In terms of population, Galilean villages are not really "cities" in the modern sense of the term; Capernaum, one of the largest, probably has no more than 2,000 residents in Jesus' day. However, these villages are densely populated. Their close proximity to one another may explain the quick spread of Jesus' fame throughout the region in days before modern media.

The phrase *they did not repent* may seem strange in view of the fact that the Galilean crowds have responded to Jesus in a very positive way up to this point in Jesus' ministry. Jesus' criticism directly echoes Matthew's summary of his message at 4:17. The essence of Jesus' preaching is a call to repent in preparation for the coming kingdom of Heaven. That kingdom is appearing on earth in the form of Jesus' ministry and the changed lives of his disciples.

To repent means "to change one's mind," especially with regard to one's spiritual status. Obviously, Jesus' way of doing things is not what the Jews of his day expect. This is what leads to the Jews' criticism. To see God at work in the healing of lepers, the casting out of demons, and eating with tax collectors requires a major shift in people's thinking.

The fact that they do not repent means that many people who see what Jesus is doing, even many of his closest followers, really have not changed their minds about either the reality of their sin or the nature of the kingdom of Heaven. Those who think they are "automatically in" this kingdom because of descent from Abraham see no need to repent of sin (Matthew 3:7-10; John 8:31-41). As a result, some reject Christ outright; others are enthusiastic, but profess a shallow belief as they miss the point of what he is doing.

21. "Woe to you, Korazin! Woe to you, Bethsaida! If the miracles that were performed in you had been performed in Tyre and Sidon, they would have repented long ago in sackcloth and ashes.

The village of *Korazin* is mentioned in the New Testament only here and (also negatively) in Luke 10:13. It is located in the hills above Capernaum, some two miles inland from the Sea of Galilee. Jesus doubtless visited this town more than once as he moved around the region.

Some think that *Bethsaida* is near the location of the feeding of the 5,000 (see Mark 6:44, 45). Jesus heals a blind man there (Mark 8:22-26). Those two miracles are in the future from the standpoint of today's text. Thus those miracles are not part of *the miracles* that Jesus is talking about here. But the residents of Bethsaida have seen miracles! Yet these have not

DAILY BIBLE READINGS

Monday, Jan. 25—*A Man of Suffering (Isaiah 53:1-9)*

Tuesday, Jan. 26—*No Knowledge of God (Hosea 4:1-6)*

Wednesday, Jan. 27—*Rejecting God's Command (Mark 7:5-13)*

Thursday, Jan. 28—*The Lord Disciplines Those He Loves (Proverbs 3:5-12)*

Friday, Jan. 29—*Is Not This Joseph's Son? (Luke 4:16-22)*

Saturday, Jan. 30—*Rejected at Home (Luke 4:23-30)*

Sunday, Jan. 31—*Thwarting God's Power by Unbelief (Matthew 11:20-24; 13:54-58)*

resulted in repentance. In passing, we note that the apostles Philip, Peter, and Andrew are from this town (John 1:44; 12:21).

Modern readers of the Bible may recall *Tyre* in a positive light because the Old Testament portrays Hiram, king of Tyre from 969 to 936 BC, as an ally of Israel. Hiram, apparently a close friend of King Solomon, played an important role in the construction of the temple in Jerusalem (see 1 Kings 5).

Yet the comparison Jesus draws with *Tyre and Sidon* undoubtedly is offensive to Jews. They recall that the prophet Isaiah had condemned Tyre severely, predicting its destruction (see Isaiah 23; compare Ezekiel 26:1–28:19; Amos 1:9, 10). Sidon shares this condemnation (Isaiah 23:2, 4; Jeremiah 25:22; Ezekiel 28:20-23; Joel 3:4-8; Zechariah 9:2-4; for more on Tyre and Sidon, see the Lesson Background to Lesson 10). Tyre and Sidon have come to represent the evil of pagan culture in the centuries before Jesus. Since first-century Jews pride themselves on their elect status with God and their moral superiority to Gentiles, Jesus' claim that the people of those two cities are more righteous in God's sight than Jews appears ludicrous to them.

Sackcloth is a garment of mourning (see Esther 4:1-4; Revelation 11:3). *Ashes* signify strong emotion in connection with repentance (Job 42:6; Daniel 9:3). Sackcloth and ashes together thus symbolize sincere remorse and grief over sin.

22. "But I tell you, it will be more bearable for Tyre and Sidon on the day of judgment than for you.

Jesus' remarks follow the logic that God holds people accountable for what they know. This principle is stated most clearly in the Parable of the Unfaithful Servant (Luke 12:42-48). There Jesus says that the unfaithful servant will be punished according to his level of understanding. The servant who is ignorant of the master's instructions will receive only a "few blows" from the whip, while the one who willfully disobeys will be given "many blows." Paul discusses our level of accountability in Romans 1:18-20.

Applied to the situation at hand, the citizens of Tyre and Sidon—evil as they are—can plead at least a certain level of ignorance before the *judgment* seat of God. On the other hand, the Jews who have received God's Old Testament revelation, have heard Jesus' message, and have seen his miracles have no excuse whatsoever (compare Matthew 12:41).

B. ONE COMPARED WITH ONE (vv. 23, 24)

23. "And you, Capernaum, will you be lifted up to the skies? No, you will go down to the depths. If the miracles that were performed in you had been performed in Sodom, it would have remained to this day.

If Jesus' allusion to Tyre and Sidon is ambiguous to anyone, the implications of this next comparison are crystal clear! Even today, the city of *Sodom* is infamous for its wickedness (Genesis 19). The ancient rabbis attributed all sorts of sins to the Sodomites, making the name of this city synonymous with violence and evil.

The force of verse 23 lies in the contrast between the way the citizens of *Capernaum* may see themselves and their actual situation before God. They doubtless think of themselves as good Jews who deserve God's reward; however, their unwillingness to believe makes them worthy of judgment. Jesus' words are ironic: since notable miracles have been performed in the area of Capernaum, one should expect that town to receive a special reward. But

HOW TO SAY IT

Augustine. AW-gus-teen or Aw-GUS-tin.
Bethsaida. Beth-SAY-uh-duh.
Capernaum. Kuh-PER-nay-um.
Hiram. HIGH-rum.
Korazin. Ko-RAY-zin.
Nazarenes. NAZ-uh-reens.
Nazareth. NAZ-uh-reth.
obelisk. OB-uh-lisk.
Sidon. SIGH-dun.
Sodom. SOD-um.
Solomon. SOL-o-mun.
Tyre. Tire.

WHAT DO YOU THINK?

What are some examples in our modern world of cities whose names are often associated with sin? Can you think of any ways that these cities actually might be more righteous than your hometown?

WHAT DO YOU THINK?

In what ways are we blessed today even more so than the towns in which Jesus taught and performed miracles? How might this additional blessing put us in a greater danger of receiving a "Capernaum rebuke" from Christ at the judgment? What corrective action do we take?

WHAT DO YOU THINK?

Do you find it easier to talk about your faith with family members or with strangers? Why is that? What are some of the challenges of trying to lead an unbelieving family member to Christ?

lack of faith only makes things worse. The phrase *remained to this day* implies that the Sodomites would have responded positively to Jesus' message had they heard it.

24. "But I tell you that it will be more bearable for Sodom on the day of judgment than for you."

The citizens of Capernaum no doubt are incensed that Jesus dares to compare them with *Sodom*. But Jesus is here to tell the truth.

DESIRES AND EXPECTATIONS

"Draft day" has become a major television event in professional sports. Many people watch to see what players will go to which teams. There are always the front-runners—those special players who have excelled in college. Of course, everyone wants their team to get the top prospects. Yet the top prospects who sign the biggest contracts can fail to meet expectations.

Take Heath Shuler for example. Shuler was the third overall pick in the 1994 NFL draft, receiving a multimillion-dollar contract as a result. But poor play and injury led to his being rated ESPN's seventeenth greatest "sports flop" of the last quarter of the twentieth century. You just can't see that kind of thing coming. In 2006, Shuler was elected to serve in the U.S. House of Representatives for North Carolina. No one watching the 1994 NFL draft probably expected that either!

When Jesus came to earth, he ran headlong into certain expectations that people had for the Messiah. He did not meet their expectations, so they rejected him. For his part, Jesus had desires on how people should have responded to him. They did not live up to Jesus' desires. The biblical record of both problems should keep us humble and faithful in our walk with Christ. Remember: We are here to meet Jesus' expectations and not the reverse. Eternity is at stake!   —A. E. A.

II. PROPHET WITHOUT HONOR (MATTHEW 13:54-58)

The passage above from Matthew 11 put us in Jesus' first general tour of Galilee. The next passage, from Matthew 13, puts us in Jesus' second preaching tour of Galilee and his last visit to Nazareth. In between, Jesus has to deal with opposition from Pharisees and scribes, plus an interruption by his own family members.

Intertwined are many of Jesus' famous parables. Those who seek the truth find a revelation of the kingdom in those stories; curiosity seekers, on the other hand, "don't get it" and drift away. The parables thus emphasize two ways that people can respond to Jesus: some will humble themselves and accept the truth; others will conclude that he doesn't know what he's talking about. As Jesus returns to familiar territory, which kind will he find? (The parallel is Mark 6:1-6.)

A. PEOPLES' SKEPTICISM (vv. 54-57a)

54. Coming to his hometown, he began teaching the people in their synagogue, and they were amazed. "Where did this man get this wisdom and these miraculous powers?" they asked.

The specific location of *his hometown* may seem uncertain, particularly because Matthew has portrayed three cities as Jesus' hometown in different senses: Christ is born in Bethlehem (Matthew 2:1), grows up in Nazareth (2:23), and moves to Capernaum as an adult (4:13).

The crowd's familiarity with Jesus' family members (vv. 55, 56, below) almost certainly indicates that the town is Nazareth. Jesus is now among the people who have known him longest and best. Presumably, they should be the most receptive to his message.

The crowd's remark reflects amazement at Jesus' teaching and power. Since he is now teaching in their very own synagogue, they experience his *wisdom* firsthand. They may not have seen evidence of his *miraculous powers* personally, but they undoubtedly have heard the stories. Since they know Jesus and his background, they do not understand the source of his abilities. Where is all this coming from? Their skepticism appears to reflect a belief that people draw their identities from their background; therefore people should not or will not go beyond the circumstances of their upbringing.

The word *where* thus can take one of two directions. Asking this with a sincere concern for truth will lead to the right conclusion. Asking this with a cynical skepticism will lead to a different conclusion entirely (compare Matthew 12:24).

55a. "Isn't this the carpenter's son?

The people proceed to list what they know about Jesus. They use Jesus' biographical information to confirm their suspicion that he is doing and saying things that he ought not. The phrase *the carpenter's son* associates him with Joseph. The implication is that Jesus, who apparently has been a carpenter himself (compare Mark 6:3), lacks the education necessary to speak on such important matters.

55b, 56, 57a. "Isn't his mother's name Mary, and aren't his brothers James, Joseph, Simon and Judas? Aren't all his sisters with us? Where then did this man get all these things?" And they took offense at him.

The allusion to Jesus' mother, *brothers*, and *sisters* emphasizes familiarity with the entire family. These remarks imply that Jesus had not been especially remarkable as a child, certainly not a person who would grow up to work miracles or teach in synagogues across the country at age 30!

Thus, the people close their comments by returning to a previous point: What is the source of his abilities? The fact that they *took offense at him* shows us the attitude behind their insincere questions.

SURPRISE!

Plot twists and surprise endings have always been the staple of good fiction writers. One master of this trade was O. Henry (1862–1910). In his Christmas story "The Gift of the Magi," Della cuts off her long hair and sells it to buy a watch chain for her husband. We learn at the end that Jim has sold his watch to buy ornaments to adorn her long hair! Unexpected twists and surprise endings still fascinate moviegoers to no end.

One of the greatest plot twists of all time was the death and resurrection of Jesus Christ. But in fact, Jesus' ministry was full of surprises. When he taught in his home country, the people were surprised to the point of rejecting him. They thought, "This person just cannot be who he seems to be claiming to be." But he was.

We may be certain that God has some plot twists yet in store for us. When these come, will they cause our faith to increase or to decrease?   —A. E. A.

B. JESUS' REACTION (v. 57b)

57b. But Jesus said to them, "Only in his hometown and in his own house is a prophet without honor."

Jesus notes the criticism of his former neighbors and offers a criticism of his own (see also Mark 6:4; Luke 4:24; John 4:44). Scholars are divided over

---

WHAT DO YOU THINK?

Who is someone from (or in) humble circumstances who has taught you something important about life and faith? How can your church give a wider voice to the wisdom of such people?

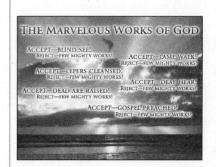

Visual for Lessons 7 & 9. *Point to this visual as you ask, "How does a periodic review of God's marvelous works help us resist the skeptics?"*

PRAYER

Lord, often we are tempted to make you in our own image and to imagine that we know you better than you know us. Please continue to surprise us by doing things that go beyond what we expect. Help us appreciate the wonders of your power. We pray in Jesus' name. Amen.

WHAT DO YOU THINK?

If you are struggling with an unanswered prayer in your life, do you think the problem is a lack of faith on your part? Why, or why not?

whether this is a familiar saying or something that Jesus makes up on the spot. Ironically, the fact that the Nazarenes reject Jesus actually proves the validity of his teaching: true prophets tend to be rejected, especially in their *hometown*, since their message of the need to repent is rarely popular. The examples of Elijah, Jeremiah, and Ezekiel confirm this. False prophets, on the other hand, tend to be welcomed, since they tell the people what they want to hear (2 Timothy 4:3).

C. SAD RESULT (v. 58)

58. And he did not do many miracles there because of their lack of faith.

The precise meaning of this verse is debated, specifically the implication of the word *because*. Does Matthew mean that Jesus simply refuses to do miracles in his hometown because he is upset with the way they treat him? In that case, Jesus' refusal to do *many miracles* is a form of judgment on those who reject him; presumably, the few works he does do (Mark 6:5) are directed to the minority who accept his teaching.

Another interpretation suggests that the hometown folks' *lack of faith* makes it impossible for Jesus to work effectively. On several occasions in Matthew, Jesus directly associates miracles of healing with the faith of those in need (Matthew 8:10-13; 9:2-7, 22, 29; 15:28). In this instance, the Nazarenes' resistance may have the opposite effect by limiting what Jesus can do for them. We point out, however, that Jesus sometimes performs a miracle when no faith is evident (8:23-27).

In any case, the tragedy of the situation is that the claim to know Jesus causes the people of Nazareth to miss out on the blessings he can bring them. There is a certain sad irony here: it is the familiarity with Jesus' background that interferes with being able to discern his true identity.

CONCLUSION

The great theologian and church father Augustine (AD 354–430) stated that the expression "familiarity breeds contempt" was already common in his time. This old Latin proverb could well be a paraphrase of Jesus' comment about "a prophet without honor." It remains a simple fact that we are less impressed with things and people the longer we are exposed to them.

This came home to me recently when my wife and I were thinking about possible Christmas gifts for my father. A number of things associated with the history of space flight immediately came to mind, a topic that has interested my dad for quite some time. Growing up in the '50s and '60s, he was fascinated by the space race. But to me, having grown up in the '70s and '80s, space travel has always seemed less impressive. Similarly, my own children take computers and DVD players completely for granted.

We run a great danger when familiarity makes us take the power and love of Jesus for granted. Those who have been Christians for some time may recall that they felt more "on fire" in the earlier days of their faith, when each page of Scripture seemed to open a whole world of insight. As we become more acquainted with Christ and his teachings over the years, some of the luster can wear off. Maybe that was the problem the ancient Israelites had during Moses' day. Seeing the miraculous "pillar of cloud" and "pillar of fire" all the time should have increased their devotion to God (Exodus 13:21, 22). But familiarity bred contempt (Numbers 14:11).

Today's passages stress that we can never let Jesus become so familiar that we doubt his ability or challenge his right to go beyond our expectations. If we do, we become worse than those who never knew him in the first place.

Discovery Learning

The following is an alternative lesson plan emphasizing learning activities.
Classes desiring such student involvement will find these suggestions helpful. At the
back of this book are reproducible student pages to further enhance activity learning.

INTO THE LESSON

As students enter the classroom, give each a handout with the following printed on it:

Welcome to _____ (*your childhood hometown*), home of _____ (*something noteworthy about your hometown*).

Ask students to fill in the blanks as indicated. Those who grew up in rural settings should list the town nearest to their childhood residence.

Ask students to tell what they wrote. Then ask for the name of Jesus' childhood hometown (*Nazareth*). Say, "Various towns today have signs at the city limits proudly proclaiming *Childhood home of . . .* , with the name of a famous athlete, politician, etc., filled in. But ancient Nazareth didn't treat Jesus like a favorite son. Jesus was rejected by his hometown. His experience there teaches us a few things about how complete our acceptance of him should be."

INTO THE WORD

In advance, write the questions below on two pieces of poster board. Tape a cover over each question. Uncover the question when ready to use it for the discussion. At the top of one poster write *Matthew 11:20-24*. At the top of the other write *Matthew 13:54-58*. Say, "Today we have some questions for Jesus about these passages. You are going to help provide the answers that you think Jesus would give."

You may wish to work on both posters together as a class, or you may divide the class into two groups to complete the two posters separately. Make copies of the lesson commentary available for reference as you think appropriate. (It is not necessary to have someone play the part of Jesus

personally; rather, anyone can answer as he or she thinks is consistent with the way Jesus would answer.)

Questions regarding Matthew 11:20-24

1. Jesus, why did you scold or denounce the three cities mentioned in this text? Why were you so hard on them? 2. What were some of the miracles to which you referred? What did you do in Bethsaida and Capernaum? 3. Comparing Capernaum to Sodom is startling. Why did you do this? 4. Jesus, it is apparent you wanted these cities to repent. Repent of what? And what would be clues that would indicate that they changed or repented?

Questions regarding Matthew 13:54-58

1. Jesus, when you arrived in your hometown, you spoke in the synagogue. What gave you the right or privilege of using the synagogue as your platform? 2. This account is fascinating with regard to how people "back home" responded to you. If you felt it necessary to clarify this passage for the twenty-first century, how would you paraphrase or restate verses 54-56? [*Option*: give students an opportunity to work in small teams to paraphrase these verses. Provide each team with a piece of paper and a pencil, if needed.] 3. What thoughts or emotions sparked the statement about a prophet's honor? 4. One more question: Can you expand a bit on Matthew's conclusion regarding the role of the lack of faith (unbelief) of verse 56? Specifically, what role does faith have to play in your interaction with people?

Option: Have small groups complete the reproducible activity "A Disappointed Lord, Part 1" from page 252.

INTO LIFE

Say, "It is easy to talk about unbelievers rejecting Jesus. But we want to do a self-examination of ways believers may reject him also, even in small ways."

Brainstorm ways that Christians may deny Jesus full access to their minds, hearts, or behaviors. If your students need an example, mention a person's denial of Jesus as creator when he or she accepts a popular theory of evolutionary origins. Another example is the practical rejection of Jesus' role as king when we deny him control over various segments of life such as stewardship of resources or our participation in questionable activities. Mention that it is entirely possible for a person to voice a belief in Jesus while living in a way that contradicts that profession of faith.

Ask students to identify one of these areas just listed that they know they have not completely surrendered to Jesus. Ask each person to write a personal prayer of confession and repentance for this act on an index card that you have provided. They are to keep the card as a prayer reminder. *Option*: the reproducible activity "Use A Disappointed Lord, Part 2" from page 252 here.

RECOGNIZED IN GENTILE TERRITORY

LESSON 10

INTRODUCTION

A. PLENTY OF FOOD FOR ALL

Many have lived through it. It is an embarrassing situation. You are a guest for a meal in an unfamiliar place. You are very hungry. Your host brings out the food. To you it looks like far too little to satisfy you and the others at the meal. So as you are served, you take only a little, insisting politely that you are not very hungry but actually intending to leave enough for others.

As the meal proceeds, however, you realize that there is much more food than you thought. Bowls are refilled; new dishes are brought out. There's plenty for everyone, but you already have said that you have little appetite. Your misunderstanding will leave you either hungry (as you decline to take more food) or humiliated (as your taking of more food proves that you are indeed hungry).

Today's text addresses a similar misunderstanding. We know that God is rich in mercy. The good news of Jesus teaches us that no sinner is too far from God to be forgiven. But we easily fall into another way of thinking. We behave as if God's love and grace are in short supply and should be hoarded. Yet today's story about Jesus and the Canaanite woman and the healings that follow is a vivid demonstration of the opposite. God has more than enough for all who have need, no matter how far from him they seem to be.

B. LESSON BACKGROUND

In Matthew's Gospel, today's episode belongs to a section stretching from 15:1 to 16:12. In this section the writer frequently mentions *bread* and other terms related to eating. Before our story, Jesus was in a controversy with the religious leaders about questions of purity in eating. Afterward, he fed a great crowd with only a few loaves of bread and some fish. Then he warned the disciples about the leaven (yeast) of the religious leaders. The disciples mistakenly take that as a comment on their own lack of food. So we will want to pay close attention to the way that *bread* plays a role in this story and connects it to the others in its context.

The first part of our lesson takes place in the region of Tyre and Sidon. This area was to the north of Galilee, which was the region where most of Jesus' ministry takes place as recorded in Matthew. Historically, Tyre and Sidon were bitter enemies of the people of Israel. The wicked queen Jezebel, who sought to replace the worship of Israel's God with the worship of the idol Baal, came from Sidon (1 Kings 16:31). The prophets had identified Tyre

DEVOTIONAL READING:
ISAIAH 42:1-9
BACKGROUND SCRIPTURE:
MATTHEW 15:21-31;
MARK 7:24-37
PRINTED TEXT:
MATTHEW 15:21-31

LESSON AIMS

After participating in this lesson, each student will be able to:

1. Retell the story of Jesus and the Canaanite woman with insights from the context and culture.

2. Explain why the woman's persistence in seeking Jesus' help displayed her faith in his ability to heal.

3. Name one area of life where he or she will seek Jesus' help with a difficult problem.

Feb
7

KEY VERSE

Jesus answered, "Woman, you have great faith! Your request is granted." And her daughter was healed from that very hour.
—Matthew 15:28

LESSON 10 NOTES

and Sidon as doomed to destruction because of their overweening pride that excluded worship of the true God (Isaiah 23; Ezekiel 26–28).

Yet God had made a promise that embraced Tyre and Sidon. In Psalm 87 God pledged that one day those who belong to him would include even people from nations that have seemed most opposed to him through history. Among these is Tyre (87:4). If God's plan is to bless all nations as he promised to Abraham (Genesis 22:18), then even these pagan, hostile cities will be included.

Still, that promise was difficult for Jesus' contemporaries to remember. For them, the people of Tyre and Sidon seemed like rich, oppressive tyrants. Those cities had made peace with the Roman government, and many of their people became wealthy with trade and seafaring. To the poorer, more isolated Jews of Galilee, the Gentiles of Tyre and Sidon posed a threat both culturally and economically. It was not easy to think warm thoughts about Tyre and Sidon one day being saved!

I. RELIEF FOR A FOREIGNER (MATTHEW 15:21-28)

The story of Jesus' encounter with a woman from the region of Tyre and Sidon highlights the tension between these cities and the Jewish people. As we read the story, we may be uncomfortable with the way Jesus seems to dismiss a very obvious need. But we need the passage's sharp language to appreciate the radical statement that Jesus makes about the woman at the end. The parallel account is Mark 7:24-30.

A. SETTING (v. 21)

21. Leaving that place, Jesus withdrew to the region of Tyre and Sidon.

As *Jesus* and his disciples leave Galilee, he has just asserted that real purity is a matter of the heart, not what or how a person eats or drinks. By implication, this means that the practices of the Law of Moses that established barriers between Israel and her pagan neighbors should be barriers no longer.

Now Jesus leads his disciples to a place where they will encounter a woman who stands on the other side of those barriers. His exchange with her will demonstrate what is in her heart, which is far more important than any external barriers.

B. FIRST REQUEST (v. 22)

22a. A Canaanite woman from that vicinity came to him,

This term *Canaanite* is quite antiquated in Jesus' time, as the people of this particular region have not been called Canaanites for hundreds of years. However, its use emphasizes the hostility between this woman's ethnic group and the Jews to whom Jesus and his disciples belong.

Canaan is depicted in Scripture as the great enemy of God's people. Canaan was the nation that was to be driven out as Israel entered the promised land (Genesis 9:24-27; Joshua 7:9; Judges 1:1, 31-33). The word *Canaan* thus is a bitter reminder of all the hostility of the past. The term conveys the full weight of ethnic and cultural antagonism.

22b. . . . crying out, "Lord, Son of David, have mercy on me! My daughter is suffering terribly from demon-possession."

In the light of that antagonism, the woman's words are most remarkable. She addresses Jesus with two terms that underline his power and her submission to it. In calling him *Lord,* she probably does not use that title to signify everything that it means when it refers to God. But one who is Lord is at the least a person of power and authority.

Then the woman calls Jesus *Son of David.* That terminology is very much part of Jewish vocabulary, so it is remarkable coming from the lips of a Gentile. The phrase is based on the promise of God to David that his descendant or son would one day rule an everlasting, righteous kingdom (1 Chronicles 17:11-14; Isaiah 11:1-5). The pagan woman is using a term that acknowledges Jesus as the promised king sent by God.

In submission to Jesus, she seeks his *mercy.* Such a request can come only from a person who realizes her profound need. At the same time, the request acknowledges the superior power of the person she is addressing. She desperately needs help, and she recognizes that Jesus can supply it.

The reason for the request is that the woman's *daughter* is afflicted by a demonic spirit. From the description of the demonized in other passages, we can imagine that the demon causes the girl to be disabled in some way (Matthew 9:32; 12:22) or to be violent and destructive (Matthew 8:28; 17:15). Such cases are hopeless unless someone with greater power than the demon intervenes.

C. SECOND REQUEST (vv. 23, 24)

23. Jesus did not answer a word. So his disciples came to him and urged him, "Send her away, for she keeps crying out after us."

Jesus' response to the woman's plea is stony silence. We may be surprised by this. After all, Jesus is noted for his compassion toward the needy (Matthew 4:24; 8:16, 28-32; 9:32, 33; 12:22). However, we need to keep reading to understand what his silence actually means.

The *disciples* seem surprised (or at least frustrated) as well. The woman continues with her plea, so they ask Jesus to do something to *send her away.* That might appear to mean that they ask Jesus to order her to leave with nothing.

However, what Jesus will say in the next verse seems to suggest that the disciples propose something more. They want Jesus to give her what she asks so that she will stop her begging and leave them alone. For the disciples, her pleas are an annoyance. They want Jesus to cast the demon out of her daughter, but not because they care about her need. They simply want her irritating requests to end.

24. He answered, "I was sent only to the lost sheep of Israel."

The bitter implication appears to be that Jesus' power to bless is for *Israel* only. Those outside Israel are not worthy of it. It exists only for the chosen. There is not enough for others.

What are we to make of this stunning refusal? Is Jesus subject to the ethnic prejudices of his day? Does he not yet realize that he is *sent* to grant salvation to all nations? We will need to keep reading to understand the significance of his statement.

D. THIRD REQUEST (vv. 25, 26)

25. The woman came and knelt before him. "Lord, help me!" she said.

The woman's deep submission to Jesus' power and her desperation now become all the more apparent. Again she addresses Jesus as *Lord,* asserting

HOW TO SAY IT

Baal. BAY-ul.
Canaan. KAY-nun.
Canaanites. KAY-nun-ites.
Cornelius. Cor-NEEL-yus.
demoniac. duh-MOE-nee-ak.
Ezekiel. Ee-ZEEK-ee-ul or
    Ee-ZEEK-yul.
Galilee. GAL-uh-lee.
Gentiles. JEN-tiles.
Jezebel. JEZ-uh-bel.
Sidon. SIGH-dun.
Tyre. Tire.

WHAT DO YOU THINK?

What response is the Lord looking for in those times when we are challenged with ministry opportunities that seem inconvenient or even irritating?

his supreme authority and submitting to it. Her submission is all the clearer as she worships him, probably lying prostrate before his feet in a gesture of complete subservience and honor. Again she pleads from a position of dire need, asking only for *help*. Will Jesus honor such a plea?

26. He replied, "It is not right to take the children's bread and toss it to their dogs."

It appears that even the woman's posture of worship does not break through Jesus' refusal to help a Gentile. More than that, his statement is even harsher than the last one! Jesus uses a figure of speech that identifies the Israelites as children at the table, who receive bread from their parents. The woman and other Gentiles like her Jesus compares with *dogs*. What kind of parent would take the *children's bread* and give it to the dogs? Surely no one can imagine such a thing.

Certainly we are taken aback by Jesus' statement! Elsewhere in Matthew Jesus is known for his compassion (9:36; 14:14; 15:32; 20:34). On other occasions he heals large numbers of people (4:23; 8:16). Does he refuse here simply because the woman is not from his own people? Elsewhere Jesus seems to take the side of those who are in need (5:3-6). Why does he not do so here?

There is another aspect to Jesus' statement, however, that we need to keep in mind. The story about giving the children's bread to dogs assumes that there is only enough bread for the children alone. It would be irresponsible for a parent to feed dogs and let the children go hungry. But is the bread really as limited as that? This is the very point that the woman will challenge.

E. FOURTH REQUEST (vv. 27, 28)

27. "Yes, Lord," she said, "but even the dogs eat the crumbs that fall from their masters' table."

Jesus has just implied that there is enough food only for the children, with none for the *dogs*. But the woman believes that Jesus' bread is abundant. She replies that there is at least some bread that the children do not eat: the *crumbs that fall* to the floor. Those crumbs the dogs can *eat* without depriving the children. The woman gladly takes the position of the dog in the story because for her, a crumb from Jesus is enough. Jesus' power is so great that just a crumb from his *table* will deliver her daughter from demonic oppression.

28. Then Jesus answered, "Woman, you have great faith! Your request is granted." And her daughter was healed from that very hour.

As *Jesus* speaks of her great faith, we notice a very important contrast in Matthew's narrative. Previously Jesus has warned his own disciples that they have little faith (Matthew 8:26; 14:31). Not long after this story, he will tell them again that they have little faith, specifically because they are worried over having too little bread (Matthew 16:8)! As he says that the woman has *great faith*, we see the contrast.

Faced with danger or need, the disciples doubt that Jesus can protect them and provide for them. But this woman has confidence in Jesus to the point of brashness—and she is a pagan who lives in a culture that does not teach her about the God of Israel! She is like the Roman officer whose faith leads him to believe that Jesus can heal his servant even from a great distance (Matthew 8:5-13; see especially verse 11).

WHAT DO YOU THINK?

While Jesus was not guilty of ethnic or racial bias, it still remains a problem. How do we overcome prejudice so that the gospel is unimpeded?

Visual for Lesson 10.
Point to this visual as you ask, "In what ways is the faith of the Canaanite woman both a model and a challenge to us?"

This contrast between the Gentile woman and Jesus' disciples probably explains the shocking harshness of Jesus' earlier responses to her. In the stories surrounding this one, the disciples repeatedly fail to exercise faith in Jesus. As they stand with him on this occasion, they see the woman as someone to despise and dismiss. In other episodes, Matthew makes clear that Jesus knows what others are thinking even when they do not speak (Matthew 9:4; 12:14, 15, 25). By the end of this story, we are led to conclude that before he speaks he understands what is in both the woman's heart and the disciples' hearts. She has a faith that provides a lesson for the disciples. That the lesson comes from someone whom the disciples are accustomed to despise makes it all the more powerful.

Throughout his ministry, Jesus consistently welcomes those who know that they have great need, no matter their social status. Conversely, he consistently warns those who believe that they have a privileged position. In this exchange, he brings that contrast to a climax. In God's mercy there are no boundaries, no limits, unless we believe that we have no need for his mercy.

OF LITTLE AND MUCH

A woman once brought two small coins to the temple and placed them in the offering. Jesus commended her. The seemingly small contribution was really a great gift (Mark 12:41-44). Hattie May Wiatt (died 1886) followed in these footsteps. She was a little girl who lived in Philadelphia near a church that had an overcrowded Sunday school, and she had trouble getting in. The preacher spoke of the day when there would be a building large enough to accommodate all who wanted to attend. But little Hattie May became sick and died before that became a reality.

After Hattie May's death, a small change-purse was found in which she had saved 57 cents toward this dreamed-of building. Through a series of events, the 57 cents became much more. This eventually became seed money for the purchase of a nearby house that would accommodate the primary department of the Sunday school.

God can indeed do much with little! Sometimes he may decrease our visible resources intentionally in order to demonstrate his power in this regard (example: Judges 7). But whether he grants us many resources or few, he expects faith. Jesus' own disciples were amazingly deficient in this regard (example: Matthew 17:19, 20). On the other hand, a Canaanite woman—of all people—was the complete opposite: "Woman, you have great faith!" Which example are you following?
—A. E. A.

II. ABUNDANCE FOR THE NEEDY (MATTHEW 15:29-31)

The next verses summarize in a few words many other miracles of Jesus. But in the way that Matthew summarizes them, he continues to emphasize the themes of the story just ended.

A. RETURN TO JEWISH TERRITORY (v. 29)
29. Jesus left there and went along the Sea of Galilee. Then he went up on a mountainside and sat down.

By giving us this short geographical note, Matthew signals to us that *Jesus has returned to Jewish territory.* Although the previous episode shows Jesus' mercy on a Gentile, the focus of his ministry is among the Jewish people. It is after his death and resurrection that he tells his disciples to go into all the

WHAT DO YOU THINK?

What modern parallels can you draw with the levels of faith of the Gentile woman and Jesus' disciples?

PRAYER

Lord, we confess that we sometimes act as if we are the only people whom you love. Help us to see others as you see them and to see ourselves as you see us. Remind us that your grace is available to all. We pray in Jesus' name. Amen.

world to make disciples of all nations (Matthew 28:19). Until that full message of salvation is ready, his focus is primarily within Israel.

Elsewhere in Matthew when Jesus goes up on a mountain, something important is revealed (see 5:1; 17:1; and 28:16). This story seems to belong among those others, since it happens in a similar place. The setting tells us to note carefully what happens and to appreciate its meaning.

B. Healing a Great Crowd (v. 30)

30. Great crowds came to him, bringing the lame, the blind, the crippled, the mute and many others, and laid them at his feet; and he healed them.

As on other occasions, Jesus is surrounded by people who have brought their sick to him for healing. The whole range of physical suffering seems to be on display. Jesus' response is to heal all of *them*. Clearly the Canaanite woman is right: there is plenty of bread at the Lord's table, so that no one needs to be turned away.

C. Response (v. 31)

31. The people were amazed when they saw the mute speaking, the crippled made well, the lame walking and the blind seeing. And they praised the God of Israel.

The Gospels often describe the response to Jesus as wonder, especially the response to his miracles. In such settings, wonder suggests the sense of awe, amazement, and joy that comes from witnessing a mighty act of God to bring blessing. The people realize that these great miracles are signs that God is bringing his promised salvation to his people.

LOST IN WONDER

Between Montrose and Silverton, Colorado, lies 195 miles of U.S. Highway 550. A portion of this stretch is known as the Million Dollar Highway. No one knows for sure the source of this name. One theory proposes that the name originates from the value of the ore in the material that was part of the road's construction. Another theory proposes that the name refers to the high cost of building the road over a mountain pass and a gorge. No matter what theory is correct, the view itself is worth a million dollars!

A few years ago my wife, younger daughter, and I were traveling this stretch of highway. It took all Sunday afternoon to make this drive because of the awe-inspiring beauty of the majestic mountains, steep cliffs, and little villages in the valleys. We stopped to take picture after picture, captivated by what we saw. On returning home, my daughter created a memory book of the trip. When she created the section about this highway, she inserted a picture and around it wrote the words to the great old hymn "How Great Thou Art."

Those who witnessed the miracles of Jesus saw the mighty wonders of God. Some may say today that if they could see these miracles firsthand, then they would be convinced of the existence of God. But how about observing the beauty of his creation? The most marvelous part of creation is people themselves. Remember: before Jesus cured the diseased and healed the afflicted, he created those people in the first place.   —A. E. A.

CONCLUSION

Clearly, the Canaanite woman was right to have the confidence that she had in Jesus. Despite her discouraging reception, she believed that Jesus had enough to give her the blessing she so desperately sought. The love of God is stronger than any social boundary; the grace of God is greater than any sin.

Sometimes we may think or act as if Jesus died only for a particular kind of people—people of our own ethnic group, nationality, or social status. Or we may think that some people are simply too far lost ever to be saved. Today's text tells us otherwise. It also reminds us that to receive Christ's mercy we need to realize how desperately we need it.

THOUGHT TO REMEMBER
Jesus didn't limit his mercy, and neither should we.

Discovery Learning

The following is an alternative lesson plan emphasizing learning activities.
Classes desiring such student involvement will find these suggestions helpful. At the
back of this book are reproducible student pages to further enhance activity learning.

INTO THE LESSON

Before class prepare the following activity titled *Asking for Help* as handouts for your class. Distribute copies as learners arrive, asking them to work individually.

On a scale from 1 ("very unlikely") to 5 ("very likely"), how likely are people, generally speaking, to ask for help in the following situations? 1. Getting directions when lost. 2. Reaching something on a high shelf at a store. 3. Asking for a few cents from a stranger to have enough money to make a purchase. 4. Seeking child-rearing advice. 5. Pursuing financial counseling to get out of debt. 6. Seeking help from a fellow Christian to overcome a sin. 7. Getting professional advice on overcoming depression. 8. Requesting prayer for wisdom in a life decision.

Ask, "In which situation are people most likely to ask for help? in which are they least likely? Why? Is it easier to ask a stranger for help or someone who is known well? What difference does it make if the stranger is someone whose reputation is known?" Conclude this section saying, "Our lesson today is about a woman who desperately needed help, and she was willing to ask for it from a stranger with a great reputation. Let's look at her story."

INTO THE WORD

Before class make five copies of the lesson text from Matthew 15:21-31 to be used for a dramatic reading. On the individual pages highlight the parts to be read by the following characters: narrator, woman, Jesus, and two disciples. If possible, pass these out before class begins and ask participants to be ready to stand up and read their parts aloud. The two disciples are to read their line in unison. Afterward thank the readers for their help.

Prepare handouts with three columns. The columns will have the following headings, one each: *Question, Obstacle Explained, Woman's Response.* Enter the following questions and Scripture references in the leftmost column and leave the other columns blank: 1. How were the woman's nationality and religion obstacles? (vv. 21, 22); 2. How was Jesus' initial response an obstacle? (v. 23); 3. How was the disciples' response an obstacle, if at all? (v. 23); 4. How was Jesus' first answer to the woman an obstacle? (v. 24); 5. How was being compared with a dog an obstacle? (v. 26).

Have your students complete the chart within small groups. After a reasonable amount of time, ask learners to share their answers. The following may be mentioned: 1. Although she knew that Jewish men usually had nothing to do with Gentile women, this worried mother followed Jesus and called out to him about her problem. 2. When Jesus did not answer her, she did not let this discourage her, but continued to follow him and cry out. 3. She probably could hear the disciples' implication that she was a nuisance, but she still continued to plead for help. 4. Jesus' first words indicated he was not there to help Gentiles; yet she knelt before him and asked for his help. 5. She might have felt hurt pride by being considered one of the "dogs," but she humbled herself and asked for any crumbs of healing Jesus might give.

Use the following questions to cement the lesson content: "How persistent was this woman in overcoming obstacles?" *(very)*; "Why was she so persistent?" *(she had faith that Jesus could relieve her daughter's suffering)*; "Would she have been this persistent if she had had doubts about Jesus' ability to heal her daughter?" *(probably not)*; "What was the result of her persistence?" *(Jesus healed her daughter and praised her for her great faith)*.

INTO LIFE

Distribute index cards. Say, "What if you knew that Jesus was going to be in church today 'in the flesh'? If you could ask him for help with one prob-

lem in your life, what would it be? Write it on the card." (Stress that the cards will not be collected.)

After a few minutes say, "Now turn the card over. Write down a prayer asking for Jesus' help with your problem." Close the class with prayer for God's help for each student to have the faith to believe that Jesus can help. Encourage students to take the cards with them and pray their prayers each day during the week ahead. Distribute copies of the reproducible activities "Obstacle Course to Faith" and "Energizing Scriptures" from page 253 as take-home work.

DECLARED BY PETER

LESSON 11

INTRODUCTION

A. WHAT IT TAKES TO KNOW A PERSON

What does it take to know another person truly? We may be introduced to someone and right away learn something about that person's work, home, or family. We might then draw conclusions about that person's character, based on what we associate with a particular profession, place, or family situation. But with time, we learn more about that person and are driven to other conclusions. People can defy our "first impression" expectations.

Today's lesson concerns what Peter knew about Jesus. By declaring Jesus to be the Christ, the Son of the living God, Peter declared what Christians ever since have affirmed as the central tenet of their faith. But by itself, Peter's confession is not sufficient to tell us who Jesus is. He is indeed the Christ, but we also must know the kind of Christ he is. We need to know that he willingly went to the cross for the sake of sinners. Jesus defied Peter's expectations. Perhaps we will need to revise our expectations of Jesus too.

B. LESSON BACKGROUND

Today's story is at the center of the plot of Matthew's Gospel. Prior to this story, Matthew presents Jesus performing miracles, teaching, meeting the challenges of his opponents, and issuing calls to repent of sins and follow him. Notably Jesus has spoken and acted with authority that some recognize can belong only to God. Yet to this point in time, Jesus has not spoken clearly and directly about his identity. He has left provocative hints but has made no explicit statements. Most prominent among those who follow Jesus is Simon, also called Peter. He is the first of Jesus' followers to be named in Matthew's Gospel (4:18) and the one most often named thereafter (8:14; 10:2; 14:28, 29; 15:15). He is usually bold, sometimes in a foolhardy way.

Today's story is set in Caesarea Philippi, a town on the northern edge of Israel's territory in Galilee. The town was famous in Jesus' time for a shrine to the Greek god Pan. It was as pagan a place as one could find within Israel's borders, a symbol of the conflict between the God of Israel and a hostile, sinful world. Our text divides naturally into two parts. The first is focused on Peter's statement about Jesus and Jesus' response to it. The second centers around Jesus' statement about his future, Peter's response to it, and Jesus' rejoinder. We must couple the two parts together to grasp who Jesus really is.

I. WHO JESUS IS: PETER'S CONCLUSION (MATTHEW 16:13-20)

A. OTHERS' EVALUATIONS (vv. 13, 14)

13. When Jesus came to the region of Caesarea Philippi, he asked his disciples, "Who do people say the Son of Man is?"

In the infamous area of *the region of Caesarea Philippi* (see the Lesson Background), Jesus asks about others' opinions of him. Jesus refers to himself as

DEVOTIONAL READING:
JOHN 10:22-30
BACKGROUND SCRIPTURE:
MATTHEW 16:13-27
PRINTED TEXT:
MATTHEW 16:13-27

LESSON AIMS

After participating in this lesson, each student will be able to:

1. Recite Peter's confession from memory and explain the context in which it was uttered.

2. Harmonize Peter's confession with Jesus' rebuke of Peter.

3. Tell how his or her life will demonstrate self-denial to exalt Jesus as Lord in the coming week.

Feb
14

KEY VERSE

Simon Peter answered, "You are the Christ, the Son of the living God.
"
—Matthew 16:16

Son of Man, as he often does. While this phrase in Jesus' time is used to mean something like "human being," it is very clear that Jesus does not use it to stress his humanity. That does not need stressing: everyone can see that Jesus is human. Rather, it is likely that Jesus uses *Son of Man* to connect himself to "one like a son of man" in Daniel 7:13, 14. In Daniel's vision, this figure defeats the evil kingdoms dominating the world, and establishes God's everlasting rule. By calling himself *Son of Man,* Jesus invites people to think about whether he might be the one who is fulfilling this promise.

But what do people think of that? How do they evaluate Jesus the teacher and miracle worker?

QUESTION AND ANSWER

In May of 2007 I went to Taizé, France, and took part in a week of activities at an ecumenical gathering. Each morning a teacher would lead the adults in a Bible study, then assign questions for small-group discussion that afternoon. One day the teacher posed Jesus' question, "Whom do people say that I am?" When we gathered in small groups that afternoon, we were to discuss that question and give our answers.

One lady said that she did not focus on Jesus because she needed a feminine figure in her life, so she talked about Mary. Another said that what really mattered was the Holy Spirit, so again Jesus was left behind for a discussion on "experiencing" the Spirit. These discussions sidestepped the vital importance of Jesus' question in today's passage.

As the people in Jesus' day should have learned—and as we should learn as well—it is imperative to understand and accept what the Bible reveals about Jesus and why. Other issues are important too, of course. But if we misunderstand Jesus' identity, we are very likely to arrive at wrong answers in other areas as well.

—A. E. A.

14. They replied, "Some say John the Baptist; others say Elijah; and still others, Jeremiah or one of the prophets."

We can imagine the disciples (*they*) one after the other making various replies to this question. Jesus is identified by *some* as *John the Baptist,* probably because both are famous for their message about the nearness of God's kingdom (Matthew 3:1, 2; 4:17); by this point in time John the Baptist is dead (14:1-12). *Elijah* is another easy comparison: Jesus' miracles resemble Elijah's miracles. *Jeremiah* was known for preaching about God's imminent judgment on his people, a theme that Jesus sounds as well.

So taken together, these opinions boil down to the last one: that Jesus is a prophet sent by God. That evaluation has a strong basis in fact since Jesus' preaching and teaching clearly resembles that *of the prophets.* Jesus is indeed a prophet. But is he merely a prophet? Or is he something more?

B. PETER'S EVALUATION (vv. 15, 16)

15. "But what about you?" he asked. "Who do you say I am?"

Jesus now focuses on the disciples' own viewpoint. They are witnesses of nearly everything that he has said and done. Are they content to see Jesus just as a prophet?

16. Simon Peter answered, "You are the Christ, the Son of the living God."

Peter's answer is forthright and clear. He first calls Jesus *the Christ,* a term that means "the anointed one." In times past, the king of Israel was desig-

WHAT DO YOU THINK?

How would you respond to someone who agreed that Jesus was "a great prophet" or "a great teacher," but no more than that?

nated by anointing his head with oil (example: 1 Samuel 16:13). So the term "anointed one" has come to mean the great, future king whom God has promised. That king will defeat God's enemies utterly and rule eternally and righteously. Old Testament texts like 2 Samuel 7:12-16; Isaiah 9:1-7; 11:1-9; Jeremiah 23:5, 6; and Zechariah 6:12, 13 announced this promise. Peter is taking the bold step of identifying Jesus as this promised king.

Peter goes on to call Jesus *Son of the living God.* By calling God "the living God," Peter is contrasting the true God of Israel with false, non-living gods such as the god Pan that is worshiped at the shrine in the town where this conversation takes place. Like *Christ,* the phrase *Son of God* is used in Jesus' time mostly to refer to the great king whom God has promised. For example, in 1 Chronicles 17:13 and Psalm 2:7 God calls the one who sits on the throne of Israel his *Son.* Again, Peter declares Jesus to be that promised king.

After Jesus' death and resurrection, his followers will use *Christ* and *Son of God* with an even more exalted meaning. They will realize that one who speaks and acts as Jesus does can be only God himself, entering the world as a human being. As Peter says these words on this occasion, however, he will need to see more. He especially will need to witness Jesus' death and resurrection in order to understand fully the sense in which Jesus is the Christ and God's Son. Still, Peter's insight here is tremendous. Jesus is much more than a prophet alone. He is God's king, the one who will defeat evil and establish God's rule.

C. JESUS' COMMENDATION (vv. 17-20)

17. Jesus replied, "Blessed are you, Simon son of Jonah, for this was not revealed to you by man, but by my Father in heaven.

In effect, Jesus says, "Congratulations, *Simon,* Jonah's *son*! You say what God says!" Peter has God's favor because he gives no mere human opinion, but the view of God himself (Matthew 3:17).

18. And I tell you that you are Peter, and on this rock I will build my church, and the gates of Hades will not overcome it.

The proper interpretation of Jesus' reply to *Peter* is one of the most disputed in the New Testament. For centuries interpreters have argued about whether this statement commissions Peter as the head of the church on earth. We start by noting that everyone recognizes that Jesus is using a play on words, since the name Peter means *rock.* But does that automatically mean that Jesus is referring to Peter personally as the rock on which Jesus will *build* his *church*? Is it more likely that Jesus is referring to something besides Peter (such as Peter's confession) since Jesus says "this rock" while speaking directly to Peter? And since the rock at issue is the foundation of Jesus' own church, is it more likely that the proper interpretation has more to do with Jesus himself than with Peter? Further, what about the differences in the sizes in rocks that the Greek text may indicate?

That dispute is important, but if we pay attention to it and nothing else we will miss much of Jesus' message. Clearly, Jesus is making a powerful, dramatic claim. We are used to the term *church* as referring to the assembly of believers in Jesus. But that usage is not yet established at the point in time when Jesus utters this statement. His disciples are familiar with the Greek and/or Aramaic word (since they likely spoke both languages)

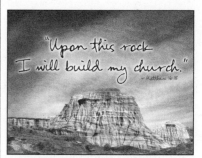

Visual for Lesson 11.
Point to this visual as you ask, "What is one way you can be a rock for Jesus in your congregation today?"

translated *church* to refer to the assembly of Israel as the people of God. Considering that, we can better hear what Jesus is saying: the assembly of God's people is now Jesus' assembly. The people of God belong to Jesus alone!

Beyond that, Jesus pronounces certain victory for his people. He implies that the church battles and defeats Satan, evil, and death. That is a tremendous statement of assurance!

19. "I will give you the keys of the kingdom of heaven; whatever you bind on earth will be bound in heaven, and whatever you loose on earth will be loosed in heaven."

The proper interpretation of this statement is also disputed. The *keys of the kingdom* have nothing to do with Peter standing at the gates of Heaven as depicted in jokes and folklore. Rather, the expression implies that Peter will provide access for people to enter the promised rule of God. Unlike the religious leaders who reject Jesus and so shut the door of God's kingdom (Matthew 23:13), Peter will open entry to God's kingdom by preaching the good news of Jesus. It is therefore no accident that later Peter delivers the first gospel message on the Day of Pentecost (Acts 2) and opens the door of salvation to the Gentiles by preaching to Cornelius (Acts 10).

The second part of this verse makes a related point. What Jesus says clearly does not give Peter or the other disciples the authority to do whatever they want. In the original language, the statement is more literally, "what you *bind on earth* will have been *bound in heaven,* and what you *loose on earth* will have been *loosed in heaven.*" We can compare this statement with this famous line from the Lord's Prayer: "Your will be done on earth as it is in heaven" (Matthew 6:10). God's promise is that his will should be done everywhere, just as much on earth as in his very presence. Jesus now promises that the church, which is made up of those who confess him as king, will achieve this. They will accomplish on earth what God has decreed in Heaven.

In sum, Jesus responds to Peter by telling him some amazing things. The message that Jesus is God's promised king is the very message of God himself. It is the means by which Jesus will establish a people who belong to him as the people of God. This will be a people who will certainly overcome death and Satan, bringing others into fellowship with and submission to God and fulfilling God's purpose for the ages. We can hardly imagine a more stirring, spectacular statement!

20. Then he warned his disciples not to tell anyone that he was the Christ.

After such an impressive declaration, we hardly expect *Jesus* to tell *his disciples* to keep quiet about his identity! But this is exactly what he does. Until the disciples understand more about what it means for Jesus to be God's promised king, they will only spread misunderstanding if they speak about it. What the disciples need to learn Jesus explains next.

SHUTTING UP OR SPEAKING UP?

The news report is all too familiar. A high-school student is standing among a crowd of people on a city street late at night. He becomes angry. He draws a gun and pulls the trigger. The fortunate thing this time is that the gun jams.

The assailant runs away. Then the police begin an investigation. But the details are sketchy because witnesses do not offer much information. They could say more, but they don't.

WHAT DO YOU THINK?

Do you think it is wise for new believers to begin sharing their faith immediately, or should they keep quiet about it until they understand it more fully? What are the advantages and disadvantages under either idea?

There is indeed a time to speak up. But there also is a time to shut up. Think of plans for a surprise birthday party. The surprise depends on information being kept silent until that special moment. Yet some people just can't seem to keep a secret!

Does it seem like there is something about human nature that causes us to speak when we should remain silent and to stay silent when we should speak? Christians are not immune to this problem. Sadly, many today seem to have taken the admonition to the disciples from this text and applied it to themselves. Thus they do not share the message of Christ. Yet Jesus has told us it's time to speak (Matthew 28:18-20).   —A. E. A.

II. WHO JESUS IS: JESUS' DESTINATION (MATTHEW 16:21-27)

A. PREDICTION AND OBJECTION (vv. 21-23)

21. From that time on Jesus began to explain to his disciples that he must go to Jerusalem and suffer many things at the hands of the elders, chief priests and teachers of the law, and that he must be killed and on the third day be raised to life.

Previously, Jesus has spoken only rarely and indirectly about his death. But now that Peter has declared him as God's Son, Jesus begins to speak frequently and directly about his coming death and resurrection (see also 17:12, 22, 23; 20:18, 19, 28; 26:2). From this point his words are straightforward in this regard.

22. Peter took him aside and began to rebuke him. "Never, Lord!" he said. "This shall never happen to you!"

This may be the most surprising verse of the whole passage. Why does *Peter*, who has just declared Jesus to be God's Son, now contradict what Jesus says? For Peter and the other disciples, the idea that God's anointed one will be killed is unthinkable. Jesus himself has just declared that his church will prevail against all opponents. The prophets had promised that God's king would establish an everlasting kingdom. So how can Jesus be killed, and by the very religious leaders who should submit to his authority?

This exchange brings us to the heart of one of the most challenging aspects of the gospel. Jesus is king, but he is the king who gives his life for the sake of his unworthy subjects. He is different from every kind of king we have ever known. To submit to him, we need to set aside our ordinary concepts of power.

23. Jesus turned and said to Peter, "Get behind me, Satan! You are a stumbling block to me; you do not have in mind the things of God, but the things of men."

Just six verses before, Jesus had told *Peter* that Peter says what *God* says. Now Jesus tells him that he speaks the opposite of what God says. Peter speaks from a purely human standpoint—or worse, he speaks from the standpoint of the devil himself! Jesus' designation of Peter as *a stumbling block* helps us understand why Peter's statement is so starkly condemned. If Jesus accepts Peter's idea, then Jesus will stumble and turn aside from the very purpose of his coming to earth, which is to die for sinners. In that case, the entire mission will fail and so will the purpose of God. What Peter and the other disciples need is a reorientation away from conventional thinking and toward God's real plan. That is what Jesus supplies next.

DAILY BIBLE READINGS

Monday, Feb. 8—My Sheep Hear My Voice (John 10:22-30)

Tuesday, Feb. 9—Believe in the Good News (Mark 1: 9-15)

Wednesday, Feb. 10— Only Believe (Mark 6:34-44)

Thursday, Feb. 11—Help My Unbelief (Mark 9:14-27)

Friday, Feb. 12—Ask and Believe (Mark 11:20-25)

Saturday, Feb. 13—Both Lord and Messiah (Acts 2: 29-36)

Sunday, Feb. 14—You Are the Messiah (Matthew 16:13-27)

WHAT DO YOU THINK?

What are some of the ways the Lord corrects us today?

[Make sure to consider Proverbs 27:6; Matthew 18:15, 16; Hebrews 4:12; and James 1:22-25 in your answer.]

B. EXPLANATION AND CHALLENGE (vv. 24-27)

24. *Then Jesus said to his disciples, "If anyone would come after me, he must deny himself and take up his cross and follow me.*

The *disciples*, as Jesus' followers, need Jesus' outlook. Jesus states this challenge in three parts. The first is the need to *deny* oneself. In Jesus' teaching, this does not mean giving up comforts or ambitions, as if such things are evil in and of themselves. Rather, Jesus tells his followers that they should deny themselves in order to serve others (Matthew 20:25-28).

The second part is the need to *take up* one's *cross*. This is not just a call to bear difficult burdens. The cross is an instrument of death. The person who bears a cross is going to his or her own execution. Jesus challenges his followers to deny themselves to the point of surrendering their lives.

The third part of the statement is to *follow* Jesus. The first two commands make sense in light of the third. Why should anyone be so seemingly foolish as to go to his or her own death willingly? Only because that person follows Jesus, the very Son of God. And Jesus shows the way by his own life.

25. *"For whoever wants to save his life will lose it, but whoever loses his life for me will find it.*

Jesus now adds a layer to the previous challenge. The way to true *life* is not in trying to keep our lives for ourselves. Ironically, that plan leads to death. Rather, the way of life is the way that Jesus is taking. He does not seek to protect himself. In fact, he will give himself willingly in death for the sake of others. Through that death he will find life, for God will raise him from the dead, as Jesus has just told the disciples.

So it is for us. If we try to live our lives just to fulfill our own desires, our lives will be empty and lost. But the person who by faith in Jesus serves others is always rediscovering real life. And that life does not end in death, for God will raise us from the dead just as he raised Jesus.

26. *"What good will it be for a man if he gains the whole world, yet forfeits his soul? Or what can a man give in exchange for his soul?*

Again, Jesus reinforces his point. A person may acquire all the selfish pleasure that this *world* has to offer. But what really has been gained if that person's *soul* is lost in the process? Jesus declares with his words and deeds that the way to eternal life is in giving of oneself to serve him. By giving our lives, we receive them back again. (The word *life* in verse 25 and the word *soul* here are translations of the same Greek word.)

27. *"For the Son of Man is going to come in his Father's glory with his angels, and then he will reward each person according to what he has done."*

Jesus closes the discussion with the note of triumph that he sounded before. Though he goes to his death, he will return as the king he truly is. As the triumphant king, he will distribute his *reward* to his loyal subjects. Those who have done what he has commanded, those who have followed him in giving their lives for the sake of others, will share in his triumph.

CONCLUSION

In many ways, today's passage is the tipping point in the story of Jesus. It confronts us with the central question: *Who is this Jesus?* Like Peter, we must take a stand on that question. It challenges us to trust Jesus enough to believe what he says about his death and resurrection and even to follow him on the same path. Believing in Jesus as the Christ, the Son of the living God, is the

PRAYER

O Lord, challenge us, as you did Peter, to consider who you really are. Give us the vision to see that as we give ourselves, we receive our lives back from you in greater measure than ever before. We pray in Jesus' name. Amen.

WHAT DO YOU THINK?

How have you found the phrase "the selfish person experiences death all the time" to be true in your life? How have you used this experience to put selfishness aside?

essence of the Christian life. Such belief is more than mere intellectual assent. It means that we are ready to give up seeking our own pleasure and prosperity. It means that we give our time, energy, and resources—our very lives—to serving others. The Jesus we confess as Christ is the Jesus of the cross. When we follow him, we go where he goes: to give ourselves and thereby to receive our lives back again.

THOUGHT TO REMEMBER

"He is no fool who gives what he cannot keep to gain what he cannot lose" (Jim Elliot).

Discovery Learning

The following is an alternative lesson plan emphasizing learning activities. Classes desiring such student involvement will find these suggestions helpful. At the back of this book are reproducible student pages to further enhance activity learning.

INTO THE LESSON

Place copies of the reproducible activity "Who He Is!" from page 254 in chairs for your students to work on as they arrive.

Prepare the following unscrambling activity in advance. Cut index cards in half and write one of the following words on each part: "You are the Christ, the Son of the living God." Mix up the 10 puzzle pieces and put them in an envelope. Prepare enough envelopes so that each group of four or five students will have one set of puzzle pieces. Say, "Each envelope contains a very important truth that we are going to study today. Let's see who can unscramble the message the fastest."

Acknowledge the team that is able to give you the answer first. Then read the phrase together as a class. Write *Matthew 16:16* on the board. Then have half of the class say the first part, the rest of the class say the second part, and everyone say the reference. Repeat this several times to help fix the verse in your students' minds.

INTO THE WORD

Ask for a volunteer to read Matthew 16:13-27 to the class. After the reading say, "When Peter made this confession, Jesus praised him for speaking the words of God. But then Peter said something so wrong that Jesus accused him of talking like Satan. Let's take a look at those two events and find out how they happened."

Prepare enough assignment sheets so that half of your groups (or pairs, if your class is smaller) can work on Assignment #1 and the other half on Assignment #2. *Option:* Distribute copies of the commentary for the verses to be studied.

Assignment #1: Peter, the Rock (Matthew 16:13-20): 1. Which prophets sent by God were named by the disciples? How many others can you name? 2. According to Jesus, where did Peter get his information about Jesus being "the Christ"? 3. What did Peter mean when he referred to Jesus as "Son of the living God"? 4. Is the rock on which Jesus builds his church to be identified as Jesus himself, Peter, or Peter's words? Support your answer. *(Caution: this one may be time-consuming and controversial.)* 5. While many cartoonists show Peter at the pearly gates, what do Jesus' words most likely mean with regard to "the keys of the kingdom of heaven"? (See Acts 2 and 10.) 6. Why was what Peter said so praiseworthy?

Assignment #2: Peter, the Stumbling Block (Matthew 16:21-27): 1. What information did Jesus discuss with his disciples that must have been hard for them to hear? 2. How did Peter respond to this information? 3. In what way was Peter acting like Satan by tempting Jesus? 4. From verse 24, what three steps must a disciple of Jesus take? 5. What are some ways in which a follower of Jesus might be asked to "lose his life"? 6. What was wrong about what Peter said?

Allow groups to share their answers. Make sure to leave enough time for groups to give their answers to question 6 in both assignments.

Next, reconcile the two assignments with the following summary: "While Peter got it right that Jesus was the Christ, the Son of the living God, he had an incomplete idea about what that really meant. How was Peter's thinking deficient?" Expected response: Peter probably thought that God's Son would set up an earthly kingdom and reign in power in that context. What he didn't understand was that Jesus would save sinners by dying on a cross. When he rebuked Jesus for talking about his death, he was showing his ignorance of God's way of doing things.

INTO LIFE

Make handouts of the activity in the next column. Give one to each student. Say, "We need to be careful that we don't fall into the trap of getting wrong ideas about what it means to be Jesus' follower. Look at the following chart and put an *X*

where you fall along each continuum. Then state one way you will improve your discipleship this week."

Indulge myself......................................*Deny myself*
Live for me..*Live for Jesus*
Live for the world...........................*Die to the world*
Reward myself.......................*Look for Jesus' reward*

Conclude the class with prayer that your students will find ways to deny themselves and follow Jesus this week.

WITNESSED BY DISCIPLES
LESSON 12

INTRODUCTION

A. THINGS ARE NOT ALWAYS AS THEY SEEM

Have you ever seen a celebrity look-alike? Some bear an uncanny resemblance to well-known people. And it seems that this is not a new phenomenon. The American author Mark Twain (1835–1910) was so annoyed by the many people who sent him photographs claiming to look like him that he offered this reply to one: "In my opinion you are more like me than any other of my numerous doubles. I may even say that you resemble me more closely than I do myself. In fact, I intend to use your picture to shave by."

Although a celebrity double looks like someone famous, the double is not really the famous person. Many things appear to be what they are not. Margarine can look like butter. An actor in a white coat can look like a doctor. Today's text is about a situation like that, only in the opposite direction. Outwardly, Jesus of Nazareth appeared very ordinary (Isaiah 53:2). But the unseen reality was that he was much more than an ordinary man of his time. The Gospels reveal Jesus as fully human but—amazingly and paradoxically—fully divine as well. He was God incarnate, the Word made flesh who lived for a while among us.

Jesus' transfiguration manifested that reality visibly to his disciples. To understand him rightly, we need to understand that event as described in today's text from Matthew.

B. LESSON BACKGROUND

The account of the transfiguration in Matthew follows immediately after Peter's confession of Jesus as the Christ and Jesus' startling prediction of his death and resurrection (last week's lesson). At the end of that episode, Jesus said to his disciples, "I tell you the truth, some who are standing here will not taste death before they see the Son of Man coming in his kingdom" (Matthew 16:28). Those words seem to point forward to Jesus' return, when he will extend the fullness of God's rule over his redeemed creation and overcome death for all time.

But Jesus' statement suggests his resurrection as well, a vital part of God's plan for redemption. And it appears that the transfiguration (today's lesson) also is part of this design, as it provides a glimpse of the glory that belongs to Jesus and will be further revealed in his resurrection and return in glory.

The account of the transfiguration provides yet another example of the disciples' struggle to understand Jesus. In the preceding story, Peter first declared Jesus to be the Christ, the Son of the living God. But then Peter rebuked Jesus when Jesus said that he was to be crucified and resurrected. Though Peter and the others recognized Jesus as God's promised king, they did not yet realize the kind of king he really was. They needed to

DEVOTIONAL READING:
2 PETER 1:16-21
BACKGROUND SCRIPTURE:
MATTHEW 17:1-13
PRINTED TEXT:
MATTHEW 17:1-13

LESSON AIMS

After participating in this lesson, each student will be able to:

1. Recall the story of Jesus' transfiguration, noting how details of the story point to Jesus' supremacy.

2. Suggest some icons of contemporary culture that might be seen by some as equal to—or even superior to—Christ.

3. Assist church leaders in planning a "mountaintop" retreat that focuses on the singular place of Jesus in the life of believers—a retreat to be open to all church members.

KEY VERSE

[Jesus] was transfigured before them. His face shone like the sun, and his clothes became as white as the light.
—Matthew 17:2

Feb 21

reckon with the fullness of his glory, and they needed to couple that with his warning that he was to suffer and die.

I. JESUS, MOSES, ELIJAH (MATTHEW 17:1-4)

A. CONTEXT (v. 1)

1. After six days Jesus took with him Peter, James and John the brother of James, and led them up a high mountain by themselves.

Specific notes about time are fairly rare in the Gospels. Matthew notes that this event takes place less than a week after Peter's confession and Jesus' prediction of his death and resurrection. That means we need to think carefully about how this event helps us understand that one as well.

Here Jesus separates from most of his disciples, taking only *Peter, James, and John* with him. Matthew tells us one other instance where Jesus does this: when he prays in the Garden of Gethsemane (26:37). By linking the stories in this way, Matthew invites us to understand each in light of the other.

We cannot determine exactly which *mountain* is the place of this scene. However, in biblical history mountains are often the sites of great acts of revelation, like the burning bush (Exodus 3:1, 2), the giving of the law to Moses (Exodus 19:20), the "gentle whisper" by which God spoke to Elijah (1 Kings 19:11-13), and Jesus' Sermon on the Mount (Matthew 5:1). By drawing our attention to the mountain setting, Matthew invites us to expect an event like those.

B. TRANSFORMATION (v. 2)

2. There he was transfigured before them. His face shone like the sun, and his clothes became as white as the light.

The description suggests that Jesus' appearance becomes one of brilliant *light*. This reminds us of the way that Moses' face shone after he spoke with God (Exodus 34:29). But this description goes far beyond that. The light that radiates from Jesus is not just exceptional, it is overwhelming—both from his *face* and the rest of his person. The effect is clear: Jesus exudes a light that suggests God himself, the very source of light (Genesis 1:3).

C. COMPANY (v. 3)

3. Just then there appeared before them Moses and Elijah, talking with Jesus.

The appearance of the two ancient prophets underlines what an extraordinary event this is. We can imagine many reasons why these two appear with Jesus. As noted above, they also had been part of great acts of revelation on mountains. Among the Old Testament prophets, *Moses and Elijah* are most notable for miracles like those of Jesus.

But likely the most important reason for their appearance is that both are connected with great promises that God made about the future. God had promised Israel a prophet like Moses, whose words they were to heed absolutely (Deuteronomy 18:18, 19). Similarly, God had promised the appearance of one like Elijah as the prelude to his final act of salvation (Malachi 4:5, 6).

Modern readers often ask how the disciples recognize these two prophets. About that we can say only two things: (1) the Gospels do not offer any explanation in that regard, and (2) whatever the means, they do indeed know that these are Moses and Elijah. See the next verse.

WHAT DO YOU THINK?

In what ways can we expect our own "mountaintop experiences" to be similar to and different from the "mountaintop experiences" of people in the Bible?

HOW TO SAY IT

Augustine. AW-gus-TEEN or Aw-GUS-tin.

Deuteronomy. Due-ter-AHN-uh-me.

Elijah. Ee-LYE-juh.

Ezekiel. Ee-ZEEK-ee-ul or Ee-ZEEK-yul.

Gethsemane. Geth-SEM-uh-nee (G as in get).

Herod Antipas. HAIR-ud AN-tih-pus.

Isaiah. Eye-ZAY-uh.

Malachi. MAL-uh-kye.

medieval. me-DEE-vul.

Moses. MO-zes or MO-zez.

Ulrich Zwingli. HUL-drik ZWIN-glee.

D. Reaction (v. 4)

4. Peter said to Jesus, "Lord, it is good for us to be here. If you wish, I will put up three shelters—one for you, one for Moses and one for Elijah."

As he does in the previous story, Peter leads with his mouth. Again, his words appear sincere, devoted, passionate, but confused. He wants to build *three shelters* or tents, like those that are built every year at the Feast of Tabernacles to celebrate Israel's deliverance from Egypt (Leviticus 23:42). Obviously, Peter understands that he is witnessing an extraordinary event, which he wants to commemorate in some way.

Not long before this, *Jesus* had asked who people were saying that he is. The disciples' response was that people thought of Jesus as a prophet. But when Jesus asked them about their own viewpoint, Peter had responded with something greater: the Christ, the Son of the living God. But now Peter seems to equate Jesus' significance with that of *Moses* and *Elijah,* given that Peter wants to build three shelters, one for each. Moses and Elijah indeed are great figures in God's plan, but is Jesus simply another like them?

We also cannot miss the contrast between what Peter says here and what Jesus recently had said in response to Peter's confession in Matthew 16:15-19. In the text before us, Peter wants to make three temporary shelters. Jesus, however, has promised to build his church on a solid "rock." The word *build* that Jesus used implies in that context something solid and permanent, so much so that the gates of Hell themselves will not prevail over it (Matthew 16:18).

Peter indeed understands that in Jesus God is doing something amazing. But he does not yet understand just how amazing.

II. JESUS, GOD, DISCIPLES (MATTHEW 17:5-8)

A. Voice of Approval (v. 5)

5. While he was still speaking, a bright cloud enveloped them, and a voice from the cloud said, "This is my Son, whom I love; with him I am well pleased. Listen to him!"

When Peter confessed Jesus as God's *Son* just a few days before, Jesus commended him by saying that he had spoken what God had revealed to him (Matthew 16:17). Now a *voice* from a *cloud,* clearly representing the presence of God (compare Exodus 13:21), speaks to remind the disciples of that very truth.

As at Jesus' baptism (Matthew 3:17), God declares that he is *well pleased* with Jesus, his Son. The statement reminds us of two Old Testament passages. One is Psalm 2:7, where God declares his support for his king, calling him "Son." The other is Isaiah 42:1 (quoted in Matthew 12:18), where God declares that he is pleased or delighted with his great servant. The way the statement before us brings together those two passages is important. As God's promised king, Jesus will rule. But as the servant of God of whom Isaiah had spoken, Jesus will suffer (Isaiah 52:13–53:12).

That astonishing contrast is clear in this text as the voice of God continues, saying to the disciples *listen to him.* Peter had confessed Jesus as king just a few days before, but Peter had refused to listen when Jesus spoke of his suffering. Peter and the others need to listen carefully to the one they now confess as the anointed one. As they listen, they are to set aside what they believe the Christ "must" do. If they listen, they will allow Jesus to revise their understanding.

What Do You Think?

Should we consistently expect "mountaintop experiences" when we want to seek the presence of God? Why, or why not?

What Do You Think?

What can we do in our Christian walk that will move us to a daily awareness of God's presence?

B. REACTION OF FEAR (v. 6)

6. When the disciples heard this, they fell facedown to the ground, terrified.

The disciples' reaction to the voice from the cloud is what we see elsewhere in Scripture when God appears to humans (Ezekiel 1:28; Revelation 1:17). It is always a fearful thing to encounter the living God.

C. RESPONSE OF COMFORT (vv. 7, 8)

7. But Jesus came and touched them. "Get up," he said. "Don't be afraid."

Jesus' response of comfort to the disciples reminds us of his actions as the disciples faced a dangerous storm (Matthew 14:27). Both cases involve physical contact (14:31).

8. When they looked up, they saw no one except Jesus.

As the experience comes to a close, the central truth is clear: now Jesus stands alone. At a certain level, he can be compared with Moses and Elijah. But only through Jesus comes the fulfillment of the promise that Moses, Elijah, and the other prophets had delivered. Jesus alone is the Son of God. He is the only one who can give the disciples what they so desperately need.

TO SEE NO ONE EXCEPT JESUS

There have been many great leaders in the history of the church. They often have led great movements for improvement. History continues to honor them because of their contributions. Martin Luther saw the corruptions of late medieval Catholicism and desired reform. He risked his life in order to achieve meaningful change, and many followers exalted him and followed his footsteps. The same is true of other Reformation leaders—Ulrich Zwingli, John Calvin, John Knox, Thomas Cranmer, Menno Simons.

The list goes on. Francis of Assisi and Dominic revolted against the corruptions of medieval monasticism. Augustine of Canterbury, the great missionary to England, and Boniface, "the Apostle to Germany," successfully planted and expanded Christianity in these two countries. They are greatly appreciated by modern students of the history of evangelism.

Moses and Elijah were great leaders too. But when the disciples came down from the mountain, they saw no one except Jesus. Even the great Moses and Elijah had faded from sight. Luther, Francis, Augustine, and all the others would have desired the same thing. We appreciate what these leaders accomplished, but their followers often have made the all too common human error of honoring the leader instead of the one to whom the leader pointed. Ultimately, all great leaders of the church should fade away so that all we can see is Jesus.   —J. B. N.

III. INSTRUCTION, QUESTION, ANSWER (MATTHEW 17:9-13)

A. JESUS' DIRECTIVE (v. 9)

9. As they were coming down the mountain, Jesus instructed them, "Don't tell anyone what you have seen, until the Son of Man has been raised from the dead."

Jesus' command to silence is puzzling to us. We assume that everyone should know about this amazing event that has just taken place. However, it is impossible to see the real significance of this event apart from the cross. To know Jesus only as the glorious Lord is insufficient. That may lead people to assume that he will rule like a super-powerful political monarch, one who destroys his enemies instantly. Such ideas are not far from the way that many in Jesus' day expect God's promised Messiah to be.

WHAT DO YOU THINK?

How can we go about developing a personal retreat program where we seek the singular presence of Jesus? How can our lives be different as a result?

WHAT DO YOU THINK?

Which parts of our encounters with God should we share with others? Which parts should we keep to ourselves? Why?

Likewise, it would be a mistake to understand Jesus only in terms of his death. Crucifixion victims are surely life's most awful losers, suffering unimaginable torture and shame.

So the disciples are to continue to think about what they have seen, while telling no one about it until Jesus has died and risen. Each of the three events will then give context to the other two. His transfiguration tells us that Jesus is the glorious, divine Lord. His death tells us that he gives his life for the sake of sinners. His resurrection tells us that he triumphs over death and evil despite his seeming defeat in death.

Will the disciples begin to understand this? When Jesus spoke of his death and resurrection in the previous chapter, Peter, speaking for all the disciples, showed a complete failure to understand (Matthew 16:21-23).

B. DISCIPLES' QUERY (v. 10)

10. The disciples asked him, "Why then do the teachers of the law say that Elijah must come first?"

Having just seen the ancient prophet *Elijah* appear before them, the disciples are reminded of the familiar teaching, based on Malachi 4:5, 6, that Elijah must come before the great day of the Lord. We can imagine that they wonder whether the appearance of Elijah that they have just witnessed is the fulfillment of that promise. If so, then the day of the Lord must be very near.

C. JESUS' RESPONSE (vv. 11-13)

11. Jesus replied, "To be sure, Elijah comes and will restore all things.

Jesus affirms the disciples' expectation. The promise of the prophet is valid. *Elijah* must come to *restore all things*. That is, he serves as God's agent to begin God's reclaiming of the sinful world. Yet the disciples' understanding of the nature of that promise may be flawed, as Jesus goes on to explain.

12. "But I tell you, Elijah has already come, and they did not recognize him, but have done to him everything they wished. In the same way the Son of Man is going to suffer at their hands."

Now it becomes clear that Jesus is speaking of John the Baptist as *Elijah*, just as he did in Matthew 11:11-14. However, Jesus warns that this promised Elijah has not been universally recognized. Many have believed, but many also opposed John, including Herod Antipas. Just two chapters before, Matthew tells us of John's execution in Herod's prison, a sordid affair that seems to show evil very much in power in the world (Matthew 14:1-12). It appears that the wicked can do whatever they please, without consequence.

But then Jesus brings the disciples up short. He states that he will *suffer* in the same way that John the Baptist did. Linked with Elijah in the transfiguration, Jesus now links himself with John the Baptist, the successor to Elijah, in death.

John, with his preaching and baptizing, inaugurated God's program of reclaiming lost humanity. Jesus will bring that program to reality with the very death of which he speaks here. His triumph as the glorious Lord will come after suffering torture and death at the hands of a ruthless human empire.

Will the disciples understand the significance of Jesus' words? Matthew gives us their reaction in the next verse.

Visual for Lesson 12.
Point to this visual as you ask your students to list distractions they have learned to resist as they focus on Jesus.

DAILY BIBLE READINGS

Monday, Feb. 15—Eyewitnesses of Jesus' Majesty (2 Peter 1:16-21)

Tuesday, Feb. 16—Witness of the True Light (John 1:6-13)

Wednesday, Feb. 17—The Kingdom Has Come (Matthew 12:22-28)

Thursday, Feb. 18—Beseeched the Lord, David's Son (Matthew 20:29-34)

Friday, Feb. 19—Hailed as the Son of David (Matthew 21:1-11)

Saturday, Feb. 20—To This We Are Witnesses (Acts 3:11-16)

Sunday, Feb. 21—Listen to Him (Matthew 17:1-13)

13. Then the disciples understood that he was talking to them about John the Baptist.

The disciples clearly understand what Jesus is saying. That is, they understand at least the first part of his statement in verse 12: that Jesus speaks *of John the Baptist* as Elijah, that John fulfills the promise of the coming Elijah (compare Luke 1:17).

But Matthew does not tell us that the disciples understand anything else. Previously they did not accept what Jesus said when he spoke of his death. Although they understand that he speaks of John here, the disciples still show an insufficient grasp of what Jesus says about himself.

For the disciples, it is unthinkable that the one who has been transfigured before them will suffer the way that John the Baptist did. But without that suffering, Jesus cannot fulfill the purpose for which he has come. Without that suffering, he cannot rule in the way that he has come to rule.

ELIJAH HAS ALREADY COME

In the 1938 movie *The Adventures of Robin Hood,* Errol Flynn and Olivia de Havilland star as the romantic couple Robin Hood and Maid Marian. Robin is leading a band of "Merry Men" against the unscrupulous Prince John. That scoundrel has taken over the throne of England in the absence of his brother, Richard I, who is off in Palestine fighting in the Third Crusade. Robin and his group are fighting to fix the situation in England where John is taxing the people outrageously—in the name of raising a ransom for his brother, but actually amassing a fortune for himself.

Toward the end of the movie, Robin Hood meets a small group of knights and laments the absence of Richard. He chastises Richard for leaving England at the mercy of the cruel John. He criticizes Richard for going off on his crusading jaunt while abandoning his English subjects to his greedy brother. How he wishes Richard were back in England! Little does Robin Hood know that indeed Richard is back in England. In fact, Richard is one of the knights right there in Robin's presence. Richard had already come!

Sometimes the very thing we are looking forward to has already come, but we are not aware of it. The disciples believed that the Messiah would not come until Elijah had reappeared. They did not realize that Elijah had already come—in the form of John the Baptist. Even then they found it hard to realize that the Messiah had come. Be honest: Do you truly believe that the Messiah has come and is in our midst today?

—J. B. N.

CONCLUSION

The center of the gospel of Jesus Christ is a paradox. On the one hand, Jesus is the Lord of glory, the almighty king, God himself who entered the world as a human being. On the other hand, Jesus gives himself willingly to suffer and die on behalf of the unworthy. We understand who Jesus is and what he has done only when we understand both sides of this paradox.

That understanding is more than a matter of theoretical doctrine. It transforms the way that we live. Christians claim to serve the risen Lord, who rules over everything. Yet we continue to suffer in the same way as other people. In fact, sometimes we suffer precisely because we are Christians, experiencing rejection and persecution from the unbelieving world.

We can understand why we experience trouble in such great measure when we realize that the Christ who saved us and who rules over us is the

Lord Jesus, we want to know you as the Lord who shines in the darkness, who brings light and love and power into our lives. But we know that you accomplished that at the cost of your own blood. Help us to remember everything that you are and everything that you did for us. We pray in your name by your sovereign authority. Amen.

Christ who suffered for us. We can be confident that beyond the present difficulties lies a glorious future, assured to us not because of our worthiness but because of his grace, the same grace that took him to the cross.

THOUGHT TO REMEMBER
"Listen to him" still applies!

Discovery Learning

The following is an alternative lesson plan emphasizing learning activities.
Classes desiring such student involvement will find these suggestions helpful. At the
back of this book are reproducible student pages to further enhance activity learning.

INTO THE LESSON

Put a copy of the following word-search puzzle in each chair for students to begin working on as they arrive. Include these instructions: "Find words of 4 letters or more from today's text that contain the letter *t* (there will be 15 such words in all)."

Make a separate handout of the following word list as puzzle answers: *Baptist, bright, brother, first, light, mountain, Peter, restore, talking, three, touched, transfigured, understood, until, white.* Offer to give this additional handout to those who need help. (*Option:* Instead of this word-search puzzle, distribute copies of the reproducible "False to True" activity from page 255 for students to work on as they arrive.)

```
T R O B T H G I R B F A P
A L O A R M T K W H I T E
K A D U A O A T B U R K E
T G M O N A T W R N S T R
S H O T S D P H I T T W H
R T N U F I E A E P F T T
B A P T I S T R T R I H N
S L T A G N E G S O G B E
T K N M U K R E S T O R E
F I S O R N T W L M O I F
A N M O E U T H G I L O S
S G U N D T F I R N T S D
L T O U C H E D L G S T E
```

Say, "When Peter saw Jesus transfigured on the mountaintop, he thought he had a suggestion that fit the situation to a *T*. But there was a fundamental flaw in his idea. Let's find out what it was."

INTO THE WORD

Ask students to listen carefully as you read aloud Matthew 17:1-13. Say, "As I read, please make

notes on the following two things: first, list details from this event that illustrate Jesus' supremacy; then decide why Peter's response shows that he missed that point." (Distribute paper and pencils as needed.)

After you have read, ask for volunteers to share evidence of Jesus' supremacy. Expect responses to include the following: Jesus' appearance changed; he appeared with Moses and Elijah, who some think represented the Law and the Prophets, respectively; they heard God speaking; God stated that Jesus was his beloved Son; they were told by God to listen to Jesus; the disciples were terrified by this experience; in the end Jesus stood alone; Jesus was the fulfillment of Old Testament prophecy, as he was preceded by John the Baptist, who "was" Elijah.

Student responses regarding Peter's reaction may include the idea that his suggestion of three shelters made Jesus equal to, but not superior to, Moses and Elijah. Caution that answers here may be more speculative than biblical. Use the lesson commentary to expand on all answers as appropriate.

INTO LIFE

Option #1. Ask students to share times when they have had "mountaintop" spiritual experiences. Have them reveal what brought them about and what they learned. Discuss the idea of planning a spiritual retreat for your class. Perhaps you could make arrangements at a nearby Christian camp, at a hotel, or in a church member's home to stay overnight. Or the retreat could be held as a day trip on a weekend. Ask for volunteers to help plan such aspects as the location, the activities, the music, and the food.

Option #2: Have your students break into groups of three or four. Give handouts of the following instructions and statements to each group: Many people have wrong ideas about who Jesus is. Select one of the following statements and have someone in your group present the arguments for it. The rest of your group is to give reasons from the transfiguration and other evidence to refute the idea: 1. "Jesus was a great prophet, just like prophets such as Muhammad, Buddha, and Gandhi"; 2. "Jesus never really claimed to be the Son of God while he was alive—His disciples just made that up after he was gone"; 3. "I accept Jesus as a wise teacher. But I can't believe he was anything more than a very smart human being."

Encourage students to look for opportunities this week to share their beliefs about Jesus' true identity as Son of God. End with a prayer that asks for the Holy Spirit's strength to do so. Distribute copies of the reproducible activity "Transformed by the Transfiguration" from page 255 as students depart.

ANOINTED IN BETHANY

LESSON 13

INTRODUCTION

A. MODERATION OR EXTREMISM?

Moderation is generally wise. Most people think it is good not to be too heavy or too thin, too rich or too poor, too trusting or too skeptical. We generally seek some kind of balance.

But moderation is not best in everything. Running for President of the United States in 1964, Barry Goldwater proposed that certain values were too important to be treated moderately when he famously claimed that "moderation in the pursuit of justice is no virtue." While we may agree or disagree with that particular statement, we have to agree that certain things in life demand extremes of devotion and effort.

For the Christian, what constitutes the right level of devotion to Jesus? Is there such a thing as too much service in his name? When we realize who Jesus is and what he has done for us, it is impossible for us to remain moderate in our response to him. While some may want to be moderate in their relationship with Jesus, he calls for something more. Today's text demonstrates that.

B. LESSON BACKGROUND

The story of Jesus' anointing at Bethany occurs in Matthew after a series of events in Jerusalem. A few chapters before today's text, Jesus had arrived to great acclaim in the city. His actions in the temple and his popularity provoked the religious leaders to challenge him publicly. They failed to overcome him in debate, and he responded with a harsh announcement of their coming judgment.

Matthew frames the story of Jesus' anointing with a description of the religious leaders' plot against Jesus. This plot led to Jesus' arrest and death, which is subsequently narrated. We might think that Jesus was overtaken by events or overcome by opponents who proved stronger than he. However, the story of Jesus' anointing shows that Jesus was well aware of everything that was taking place. He was not surprised by the plot against him, and he was not overcome by his enemies. Rather, he deliberately and willingly surrendered himself to death. In the verses just preceding our text, Jesus announced once again to his disciples that he was about to be crucified.

The events of which we are about to read took place shortly before a Passover celebration. That was the great annual feast set forth in the Mosaic law to celebrate God's liberating Israel from slavery in Egypt. During Passover, Jerusalem was filled to overflowing with Jewish pilgrims from the land of Israel and beyond. The scene of this particular Passover was one of excitement and expectation (John 11:56). Jesus' opponents had decided to put a stop to him prior to the point in time when today's text begins (see Matthew 12:14; 21:46). The parallels are in Mark 14 and Luke 22.

DEVOTIONAL READING:
DEUTERONOMY 15:7-11
BACKGROUND SCRIPTURE:
MATTHEW 26:3-16;
JOHN 12:1-8
PRINTED TEXT:
MATTHEW 26:3-16

LESSON AIMS

After participating in this lesson, each student will be able to:

1. Summarize Jesus' anointing at Bethany.

2. Note the various attitudes toward Jesus represented in the people in today's text and compare them with the attitudes commonly held toward Jesus today.

3. Make a plan to "break the perfume jar" once for Jesus in the year ahead.

KEY VERSE

I tell you the truth, wherever this gospel is preached throughout the world, what she has done will also be told, in memory of her.
—Matthew 26:13

Feb
28

LESSON 13 NOTES

I. PLOT AGAINST JESUS (MATTHEW 26:3-5)

A. PLOTTERS' PURPOSE (vv. 3, 4)

3. Then the chief priests and the elders of the people assembled in the palace of the high priest, whose name was Caiaphas,

Fomented by the priestly leadership, the plot against Jesus is hatched in Jerusalem. The exact location is the grand home of *the high priest*. This residence stands in stark contrast to the simple village house in Bethany that we will consider later. All the action in these verses is confined to a small geographical area as events accelerate toward the cross.

The *chief priests* are the leading male members of the extended family of the high priest. That man is *Caiaphas*, who presides over the temple of God. Since about 150 years before Jesus' birth, the high priest has come from a single family that acquired tremendous political power in Israel. Since the time that Israel came under Roman control, about 60 years before Jesus' birth, that family has cooperated with the Roman occupiers to maintain their power. However, cooperation with the Romans makes this group enormously unpopular with many of the Jewish people.

Elders of the people is a general term referring to men in significant leadership. They are members of the Sanhedrin. This is an assembly of 70 powerful leaders of the Jewish people. They assist the high priest in leading the nation of Israel. This group comprises Jesus' primary opposition in the days leading up to his death. They see Jesus as a challenge to their authority, so they seek to eliminate him as a rival. However, even among this group some have come to faith in Jesus. Joseph of Arimathea is one example (Matthew 27:57-60; Mark 15:43).

4. . . . and they plotted to arrest Jesus in some sly way and kill him.

The religious leaders' plot is to have Jesus arrested at a time and place away from the public eye. When their plan comes to action, Jesus will point out the contrast: he has preached openly in the temple, yet they come by night with weapons to arrest him as if he were a dangerous rebel (Matthew 26:55). In the end, it will not be the religious leaders' stealth that takes Jesus to his death. It will be his deliberate surrender.

B. PLOTTERS' PROBLEM (v. 5)

5. "But not during the Feast," they said, "or there may be a riot among the people."

The plotters' dilemma is Jesus' popularity. They fear provoking *a riot* if they arrest him publicly. A large segment of the pilgrims in Jerusalem for Passover hold Jesus in high regard. To take action against Jesus risks a violent reaction to which the Roman occupying forces will respond, first by putting down the insurrection and then by removing the religious leaders whose actions provoke it. If the religious leaders want to protect their own power, they must find a way to arrest Jesus away from the crowds. So they plan to arrest him after the Passover, when the crowds of pilgrims have left.

II. ANOINTING OF JESUS (MATTHEW 26:6-13)

A. WOMAN'S EXTRAVAGANT ACTION (vv. 6, 7)

6. While Jesus was in Bethany in the home of a man known as Simon the Leper,

This verse marks the transition to the anointing story, being placed deliberately in the middle of the plot against Jesus. The story of Jesus' anointing is set in the village of *Bethany,* which is on the east side of the Mount of Olives, just a short distance from Jerusalem. Matthew tells us that Jesus spends the nights in Bethany during his final week in Jerusalem (Matthew 21:17).

We assume that this *Simon* is a former *leper,* perhaps cleansed by Jesus. That logical assumption means that he is restored from his state of uncleanness, allowing full fellowship with others.

7. . . . *a woman came to him with an alabaster jar of very expensive perfume, which she poured on his head as he was reclining at the table.*

From John's Gospel, we learn that Mary, the sister of Martha and Lazarus, is the *woman* who anoints Jesus (John 12:1-8). Matthew omits these details, keeping the focus constantly on Jesus and his response.

The *perfume* is extravagantly *expensive.* (John 12:5 says it is worth "a year's wages.") It is stored in a vessel made of *alabaster,* which is a soft stone that is carved to be various receptacles. The vessel in view here is perhaps a narrow-necked flask, sealed at the top with wax. The bottle is opened by breaking off the top, requiring that all the contents be used at once.

The term Matthew selects for the perfume implies a substance with a powerful, pleasing aroma. The word is sometimes used to refer to perfumed oils applied to the skin. It is also used for the aromatic substances used in burials.

Mary anoints Jesus' *head* during the meal. This is a most unusual action: a woman is interrupting the men's meal to do this! Her action is unexpected, unconventional, and extravagant. How will those at the table respond?

B. DISCIPLES' INCENSED REACTION (vv. 8, 9)

8. When the disciples saw this, they were indignant. "Why this waste?" they asked.

The *disciples* react in a way that we can understand easily. The expensive anointing oil is used up in an instant and in a most unconventional way. It appears to be wasted. Of course, the disciples are about to witness another action that will seem to be a much greater *waste:* the death of Jesus. If they can understand how Jesus' anointing is not in fact a waste, then they may be ready to understand why his death will not be a waste either.

9. "This perfume could have been sold at a high price and the money given to the poor."

Passages of the Mosaic law, such as Deuteronomy 15:1-18, make it clear that everyone in Israel who has a means of livelihood is responsible to care for those who do not. So the disciples believe that selling the oil and giving the money for the care of *the poor* would have been a better use, a more godly use, than the seemingly wasteful anointing of Jesus. But is that Jesus' viewpoint?

C. JESUS' PROFOUND RESPONSE (vv. 10-13)

10. Aware of this, Jesus said to them, "Why are you bothering this woman? She has done a beautiful thing to me.

Jesus insists that the disciples' reaction is causing needless grief for *this woman* who honors him. He stresses that the work she does is *a beautiful thing,* not something to be criticized.

WHAT DO YOU THINK?

What do your choices regarding what you offer Christ and what you withhold from him say about your Christian commitment?

WHAT DO YOU THINK?

In what areas of your relationship with Jesus have you chosen moderation because of fear of how others might respond? How will you correct this problem?

11. *"The poor you will always have with you, but you will not always have me.*

The first part of this verse is often mistaken as a statement of despair, as if Jesus is saying, "Because you can never eliminate poverty with charity, there is no point in helping *the poor.*" However, nothing could be further from the case.

Jesus is quoting from Deuteronomy 15:11 in the first part of this verse. That reminds the Israelites that caring for the poor is their duty in all generations. Jesus does not respond to the disciples' suggestion by denying that responsibility. The disciples are right in their concern for the poor.

However, as great as the responsibility to care for the poor is, Jesus points out something greater: the disciples can care for the poor at any time, but Jesus is with them only for a brief time. That time is briefer than anyone but Jesus realizes. If they are to honor him, they must do it now. Jesus is beginning a startling comparison: as important as it is to give to the needy, honoring him is even more important.

12. *"When she poured this perfume on my body, she did it to prepare me for burial.*

Jewish religious teachers in Jesus' time affirm the importance of giving to the poor. But they teach that faced with the choice of giving to the poor or burying the dead, one must first bury the dead. Jesus now says something like that, affirming the importance of a *burial.* But what he says is shocking: he speaks of his own burial, and he is still very much alive!

This statement brings home the fact that Jesus stands in full control of his destiny. He knows very well that his death is drawing near. Yet he does nothing to prevent or avoid it. Speaking of it here, he shows that he will not die because he is conquered, but because he surrenders willingly.

Furthermore, we see just how clearly Jesus understands what will happen. At his death, his burial will be hasty and incomplete (Matthew 27:57-61). So he interprets this anointing as advance preparation for the burial to come. When the women return to the tomb to complete the preparation of Jesus' body, he already will have risen from the dead (Matthew 28:1-10).

13. *"I tell you the truth, wherever this gospel is preached throughout the world, what she has done will also be told, in memory of her."*

This statement is the climax of the anointing story, as signaled by its solemn introduction *I tell you the truth.* For Christians who know well the story of Jesus' death and resurrection, it may seem unremarkable. But from the perspective of Jesus' disciples, it is most extraordinary and challenging.

We are used to associating the idea of the preaching of the *gospel* ("good news") with the entire story of Jesus' life, death, and resurrection. But for the disciples before Jesus' resurrection, the good news is simply that God is about to bring his promised salvation to his people. How he will do that remains unclear at this point, but the faithful believe his promise that he will deliver them.

We also are accustomed to the idea that the preaching of the good news of Jesus is to be done *throughout the world.* This idea also does not take shape for the disciples until after Jesus' resurrection. They know that God has promised to bless all nations (Genesis 22:18), but how this will happen they do not yet grasp.

But now Jesus announces that the good news is about to be *preached* to the whole world, and it has to do with his own death and burial. His death

WHAT DO YOU THINK?

How good are you at recognizing and responding to "one-time only" opportunities for service to Christ? How can you do better?

HOW TO SAY IT

alabaster. AL-uh-BAS-ter.
Arimathea. AIR-uh-muh-THEE-uh (TH as in THIN).
Bethany. BETH-uh-nee.
Caiaphas. KAY-uh-fus or KYE-uh-fus.
Jerusalem. Juh-ROO-suh-lem.
Judas Iscariot. JOO-dus Iss-CARE-ee-ut.
Lazarus. LAZ-uh-rus.
Mosaic. Mo-ZAY-ik.
Sanhedrin. SAN-huh-drun or San-HEED-run.
Zechariah. ZEK-uh-RYE-uh.

is so central to the plan of God to save the world that even this story about a woman anointing Jesus will be told as a part of that good news.

Now we can appreciate why the woman's extravagance is so fitting. She has captured a glimpse of something that we can see clearly from the other side of the cross. In the entire world there is none like Jesus. He is the one through whom God will save a people from every nation. He is the one who brings to reality God's purpose for the ages. And because he does that with his death, resurrection, and ascension, he will be with the disciples for only a brief time. To honor him rightly, his followers need to recognize who he is and what he is doing, even as he reclines at the table with them.

OF SHORT AND LONG VIEWS

Waste is in the eye of the beholder. What one person may regard as a waste, another may regard as a good idea. Often the difference comes about because one person is taking a short view while the other is taking a long view.

When the Union Pacific Railroad was begun in the 1860s, the U.S. government gave the railroad one-mile square pieces of land alternating on different sides of the rail line. A waste? No, because the opposite square miles of land brought higher revenues to the government. Or consider the case of James J. Hill. When he developed the Great Northern Railroad in the 1890s, he gave blooded English bulls to ranchers along his rail line. A waste? No, because the ranchers raised healthy cattle and paid the railroad to ship them to market, and Hill made a significant fortune from his investment. Such is the value of the long view!

A woman poured perfume on Jesus' head. The disciples, taking a short view, said it was a waste. Jesus, taking a long view, accepted it as proper worship and honor to him. As a result, the world continues to tell the woman's story. Some of your family and friends may view as wasted the time and money you give to God. Will you react to their skepticism with a short view or with a long view?

—J. B. N.

III. BETRAYAL BY JUDAS (MATTHEW 26:14-16)
A. MEETING OF THE MINDS (vv. 14, 15a)
14, 15a. Then one of the Twelve—the one called Judas Iscariot—went to the chief priests and asked, "What are you willing to give me if I hand him over to you?"

Matthew now returns our attention to the plot against Jesus' life. One of the disciples who has objected to Jesus' anointing now joins the conspirators. For centuries, readers of the Bible have speculated about Judas's motives. The Gospel writers make no direct statement to satisfy our curiosity. However, Matthew does draw a sharp contrast between the woman's extravagant honor for Jesus and Judas's willingness to sell out his master for a relatively small sum (next verse). We ought to be impressed with the sharply different value each places on Jesus' life.

B. PRICE OF TREASON (v. 15b)
15b. So they counted out for him thirty silver coins.

What Judas offers is a solution to the leaders' problem of arresting Jesus away from the crowds. Their plan as it stands is to wait until the Passover is finished and the crowds have dispersed. But Judas can deliver Jesus to them sooner than that. That is, Judas can lead them to Jesus when Jesus is in a private, vulnerable place, away from the crowds.

WHAT DO YOU THINK?
What one act of worship do you find connects you with Jesus more closely than other acts of worship? How has this changed for you over time, if at all?

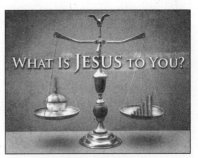

Visual for Lesson 13.
Point to this visual as you ask, "How would you adjust this image, if at all, to reflect reactions to Christ today?"

WHAT DO YOU THINK?

How do people still "sell out" Jesus for the hope of short-term gain? How do we guard ourselves in this regard?

[Make sure to consider Matthew 6:1-4, 21 as you answer.]

PRAYER

Lord, we stand amazed at what you have done for us. We want to pour ourselves out for you. Give us pure hearts to honor you with our thoughts and actions. May your name be praised in our lives. We pray in Jesus' name. Amen.

So the religious leaders agree to pay Judas 30 *silver coins*. This sum equals about a month's wage. However, it is significant as the common price for a slave (Exodus 21:32). Further, the prophet Zechariah had spoken of the same sum as the amount given to a shepherd who was rejected by his flock (Zechariah 11:12, 13). The amount underlines the inconsequential value that Judas places on Jesus.

C. PLAN IN MOTION (v. 16)

16. From then on Judas watched for an opportunity to hand him over.

Judas now looks for the chance to lead Jesus' enemies to him when he is away from the crowds. As the story develops, however, Judas's conspiracy does not produce Jesus' immediate arrest. In the next verses in Matthew, Jesus prevents Judas from arranging the arrest during the Passover meal by not revealing the place of the meal until they arrive for that meal (Matthew 26:17-20). At the meal, Jesus announces that he knows of the plot (26:21). But he does nothing to stop it. When Judas finally gathers the soldiers to arrest Jesus in the garden, Jesus tells his disciples what is happening (26:46). But Jesus refuses to take action to protect himself (26:52, 53). In the end, Jesus surrenders willingly the life on which Judas places such little value.

AN INFAMOUS NAME

The American presidential election of 1824 was tumultuous. There were no political parties as such, but there were 4 candidates. Andrew Jackson won 43 percent of the popular vote and 40 percent of the electoral vote. John Quincy Adams won 31 percent of the popular vote and 32 percent of the electoral vote. Henry Clay won only 13 percent of the popular vote and 14 percent of the electoral vote. William Crawford's numbers were similar to those of Clay. So the decision had to be made by the U.S. House of Representatives.

Jackson of Tennessee was the obvious leader, but Clay of Kentucky did not like him. Just before the voting in the House, Clay met with Adams and gave his support. Adams was elected. Soon after, he declared that Clay would be Secretary of State. Outraged Jackson supporters claimed a "corrupt bargain" and betrayal. Three of the previous four Secretaries of State had become president, and it looked like Clay had accepted a bribe—"support me now and you can become the next president."

Jackson called Clay "the Judas of the West." Clay appeared to have betrayed his fellow western politician for personal gain. Just as the action of Mary's anointing lives on, so does the infamy of Judas. Mary is still a popular name. But when was the last time you heard of a parent naming a child Judas? (By the way, Jackson later became president but Clay never did.)

—J. B. N.

CONCLUSION

Like the woman who anointed Jesus, we need to realize that Jesus is the pinnacle of all that God has done in the world. God has given us the same responsibility that he gave to Israel: to care for those who have need (James 1:27; etc.). But the greatest need is to know the one who was God made flesh, who rose to conquer death. Today we can honor him with extravagance like that of the woman who anointed him. We do it not with expensive anointing oil, but with the extravagant devotion of our lives.

It is sobering to realize how close we can come to Judas's action in selling out Jesus for a meager sum. We can spend all our time and energy trying to get ahead in life. In so doing, we end up taking the life that God gave us to pour out in Christ's service and trading it for a few pieces of silver.

Remember: "Whoever wants to save his life will lose it, but whoever loses his life for me will find it" (Matthew 16:25). There is no foolishness in the extravagant gift of our lives to the Christ who gave his life for us.

THOUGHT TO REMEMBER

"Whatever was to my profit I now consider loss for the sake of Christ" (Philippians 3:7).

Discovery Learning

The following is an alternative lesson plan emphasizing learning activities. Classes desiring such student involvement will find these suggestions helpful. At the back of this book are reproducible student pages to further enhance activity learning.

INTO THE LESSON

Place in chairs copies of the reproducible activity "What Is Jesus Worth?" from page 256 for students to work on as they arrive.

Make handouts of the following activity that you distribute to small groups of four or five: "A Web site claiming to have 'the perfect gift' offers a selection of items for various tastes. For women, there is a $20 cake server in the shape of a high-heel shoe; for men, there's a teardrop-shaped glass paperweight at $32; for a child going to camp, there's a $16 autograph pillowcase; and for a mere $265 there's a Walker Wagon set complete with an array of tantalizing toys for a toddler. Do you know someone for whom any of these would be the perfect gift? Have you ever given or received what you thought was the perfect gift? What was it, and why was it perfect?"

Allow a few minutes for discussion. Then say, "The woman in today's story gave Jesus what he thought was the perfect gift for the occasion, even though others in the room thought it was a terrible gift. Let's find out what happened."

INTO THE WORD

Prepare enough copies of the following chart so that each student will have one. Across the top label three columns *Actors, Actions,* and *Attitudes.* In the far left column, put each of these items on a separate line: Jewish leaders (vv. 3-5, 14, 15); Simon the Leper (v. 6); The Woman (vv. 7, 10, 12); The Disciples (vv. 8, 9); Jesus (vv. 10-13); Judas (vv. 14-16).

Leave space in each row so that there is room to write answers in the other two columns. At the top have these instructions: "In Luke 6:45 Jesus tells us, 'The good man brings good things out of the good stored up in his heart, and the evil man brings evil things out of the evil stored up in his heart.' In the chart below write down all the actions of the people indicated. Then examine the actions of each to determine the attitudes of their hearts."

Encourage your students to work together in small groups or pairs to complete the chart. To speed things up, suggest that they divide the characters among themselves and then share their answers within their groups.

Ask groups to name the attitudes noted for each character and defend their answers. The variety of responses might include the following: Jewish leaders (jealous and hateful); Simon the Leper (hospitable and undoubtedly grateful for Jesus' healing); the woman (generous, loving, spiritually intuitive); the disciples (sincere but clueless); Jesus (appreciative, loving); Judas (wicked, greedy, conniving).

Lead a concluding discussion on why the woman's gift was so appropriate for Jesus before his death. Be sure to mention the fact that Jesus' burial was hasty and incomplete (Matthew 27:57-61). So as the lesson writer states, "[Jesus] interprets this anointing as advance preparation for the burial to come."

INTO LIFE

Option #1: Agree/Disagree. Either in groups or as a class, discuss whether your students agree or disagree with these statements: 1. "Taking care of the poor is the government's responsibility. That's why I pay taxes." 2. "My responsibility is to be a good steward of the money God has given me. That's why I give my money to the church and leave charity to the non-Christians." 3. "Jesus said we'll always have the poor with us. To me that sounds like it's a hopeless situation, so why bother?" 4. "I'm happy to give money to responsible charities that help the poor. I prefer that to being involved personally with poor people." 5. "Whenever I'm aware of a nearby family that's struggling, I do what I can to help."

Option #2: "Break the Jar." Find an ad for an expensive perfume or cologne in a magazine or on the Internet. Distribute copies to your students.

Say, "In Jesus' day the money to pay for the expensive perfume the woman used to pour on Jesus' head would take almost a year to earn. Her decision to break the jar and use it all up showed her overwhelming love for Jesus. Is there anything in your life that you view as extremely precious and valuable? Would you consider surrendering it in some way for Jesus? Take this picture with you and think about it this week. If you are willing to make such a sacrifice, write it on the picture and place it where you can see it." Close by thanking God for his perfect gift to a lost world: the life of his only begotten Son.

Reproducible Activity Pages

Each of the following pages is designed to be used with one of the lessons of the current quarter. You'll find the activities have a variety of helpful applications. Here are a few suggestions on how to use an activity:

- Use it to supplement the discovery learning plan.

- Use it to introduce the lesson concept.

- Use it to make application near the close of your class time.

- Create an overhead transparency with the page, and use it to have the class do the activity together.

Sometimes there are two or more activities on a sheet. Sometimes there is just one. Use each activity as it best suits your own teaching style and the personality of your class.

Kinsman-Redeemer

The idea of *kinsman-redeemer* appears repeatedly in the book of Ruth (see 2:20; 3:9, 12; 4:1, 3, 6, 8, 14). Today, Jesus is our ultimate kinsman-redeemer. Even so, the Old Testament concept of kinsman-redeemer may have a continued application in the way that God expects his people to "redeem" one another in a figurative sense of providing physical and spiritual care. In that light, what is your responsibility in the following circumstances? Jot your ideas in the spaces provided.

1. A family member who "rubs you the wrong way" needs a ride to a family reunion, but has not asked you for help in this regard.

2. A family member who is a Christian is marrying a non-Christian and has invited you to the wedding.

3. A fellow Christian invites you to go to an R-rated movie with him or her.

4. A fellow Christian is about to go deeply into debt in planning to buy an expensive new car.

Looking for Ministry

The women in Naomi's circle saw an opportunity for a ministry of praise, and they exercised it! Do you have eyes to see what needs to be done in various ministry areas? What is happening (or not happening) in your congregation's life that looks as though God is providing an opportunity for someone with your spiritual gifts? Jot your ideas below each of these possible ministry areas.

Education   Fellowship   Worship   Evangelism   Benevolence

Reacting to God's News

Ahaz of Isaiah 7 and Mary of Luke 1 react differently to news from God. For the one, the news was carried by God's prophet. For the other, the news was delivered by God's angel. But the messenger was secondary in both cases; it was the message that was primary. Look at these occasions of God sending news to a person. Fill in the messenger, the basic message, and the reaction.

	MESSENGER	MESSAGE	REACTION
Genesis 18			
Joshua 5:13–6:5			
Judges 13:2-21			
Nehemiah 8			
Jeremiah 36:1-26			
Acts 10:1-8			
Acts 10:9-21			
You, in the past month			

How you answer the last one will be revealing! If a certain messenger (preacher, friend, etc.) pointed out something in the Bible that you didn't want to hear, did you react by questioning the motives or character of the messenger?

Rejoice! Our King Has Come!

We have reason to rejoice:
Our King has come!
Raise a loud, persistent voice:
Our King has come!

Sin no longer has its power;
Our King has come!
There in Bethlehem's birthing hour:
Our King has come!

There's no reason for despair;
There's rejoicing in the air:
Our King has come!
Jesus the Son!

Copy and use this simple poem, with the title above, to accompany your Christmas greetings this season. It can emphasize who Jesus is and how Christmas celebrates that fact.

Who Did It?

Matthew 1:24 says that Joseph "did what the angel of the Lord had commanded him." The Bible offers many examples of individuals who did exactly as the Lord commanded. Check the following list of texts and identify *Who Did It*.

Genesis 7:5 _____

Genesis 12:4 _____

Exodus 19:7 _____

Judges 6:27 _____

Jonah 3:3 _____

Matthew 3:13-15 _____

Luke 5:27, 28 _____

Acts 1:4 _____

Acts 9:10-17 _____

Acts 18:9-11 _____

Do You Do It?

Are you in the company of Joseph in obeying God? For each of the following, put a check mark in the appropriate box regarding what the passage says about you.

The New Testament

ME!	NOT ME!	
❏	❏	Matthew 28:19, 20
❏	❏	Acts 2:38
❏	❏	Romans 12:1
❏	❏	Romans 12:13
❏	❏	1 Corinthians 10:31
❏	❏	2 Corinthians 9:7
❏	❏	Galatians 6:2
❏	❏	Ephesians 4:32
❏	❏	Philippians 2:3
❏	❏	1 Thessalonians 5:15
❏	❏	1 Thessalonians 5:17
❏	❏	Titus 3:1
❏	❏	James 1:19

Star Watch

In modern culture, "star watch" brings mental images of red-carpet premieres with rows of adoring fans excitedly awaiting the arrival of some pop-culture icon. For the Magi, "star watch" was their way of finding the long-awaited Messiah. What about your own "star watch"? Who or what did God use to draw your attention to his Son, the "bright Morning Star" (Revelation 22:16)? By each star below, identify a person or occasion that helped point you on the way to that Star.

✳ _____

✳ _____

✳ _____

✳ _____

✳ _____

Is there someone on your list that deserves a Christmas "thank you"?

Jesus: The Either/Or

The choices about Jesus are *either/or*. He is either who he claimed to be and who the Scriptures declare him to be, or he is . . . something else. For each of the following claims, what is the skeptic's "or"? (Challenge: Put a unique answer for each description; do not use the word *not*.)

EITHER HE IS . . .	OR HE IS . . .
The Way	
The Good Shepherd	
The Light of the World	
The Truth	
The Christ, Messiah	
The Bread of Life	
Resurrected Lord	
I Am	

Appreciating Concepts and Phrases

When we read today's text from Matthew 3:1-6, 11-17, we encounter interesting concepts and phrases. Jot a note about your appreciation of each concept or phrase listed:

"Repent, for the kingdom of heaven is near" (v. 2):

"I baptize you with water for repentance" (v. 11):

"It is proper for us to do this to fulfill all righteousness" (v. 15):

"The Spirit of God descending like a dove and lighting on Him" (v. 16):

"This is my Son" (v. 17):

Understanding Repentance and Change

Repentance involves radical change. The repentant person is called to change attitudes, values, and behaviors. On to the acrostic to the right below, list one change that needs to happen in your life. Then use the remaining letters to build a prayer about the change that you desire for God's glory. On the left is an example for someone who wishes to be baptized:

Sample	My Need and Prayer
I **C** annot	**C**
c **H** ange	**H**
A nything on my	**A**
ow **N**, Lord. I seek	**N**
coura **G** e and guidance as I am	**G**
baptiz **E** d.	**E**

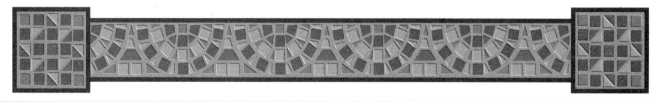

Temptation Fighters

Each of the words listed below are key words in today's account of Jesus' temptations, as found in Matthew 4:1-11. Try to find all 19 without looking at the word list at the bottom.

```
I W P B F F V T Y Y C U S D S
Y K I K R T A O I R L U F W L
T E M P T E D S O R S O R D E
G O D S T V A D T E I I H R G
D M E N K B N D J I T P R O N
C T G B H E N H D T N Z S L A
C U F K L F R H E D L G D R V
B K M P S S R N S W J T J A K
Q M S D E V I L M C V E J H T
Z C W R A O M S O V H M O G J
H W V Q L N A A D U E P W K O
Q E P I N Q J T G Z D T E P Y
P I H S R O W A N N R E I I Z
V V G A K Z G N I V D R O W Q
M G O O Q M G R K C Y S B C X
```

Words to be found: angels; bread; devil; fasting; God; holy; Jesus; king-doms; Lord; Satan; serve; spirit; splendor; tempted; tempter; test; word; worship; written.

Learning Our Lessons

After studying Matthew 4:1-11, what are the lessons you have learned

. . . about the devil?

. . . about the source of temptation (see also 1 John 2:16)?

. . . about believers and temptation?

. . . about fighting temptation?

Their Reaction and My Surprise

What a marvel as Jesus healed! Perhaps equally amazing is the various reactions of people. Look at the statements below and put them in the order from "most surprising" (with a 1) to "least surprising" (with a 4). Compare and contrast your answers with others in your group.

____ Matthew 9:27 "Have mercy on us, Son of David!"

____ Matthew 9:33 "Nothing like this has ever been seen in Israel."

____ Matthew 9:34: "It is by the prince of demons that he drives out demons."

____ Matthew 11:3: "Are you the one who was to come, or should we expect someone else?"

John's Question and My Answer

After word reached John about all that Jesus was doing, he questioned the identity of Jesus. Well, give him *your* answer . . . set to music! What are some phrases and lines from Christian music that summarize the identity of Jesus?

Reactions

Our reactions to scriptural teachings may consist of a series of phases. These phases include interpreting the passage, experiencing an emotion, and even resisting the implications of the passage. Those steps do not always occur in a straight line, and sometimes there's a back-and-forth interaction among the phases. Jot your reactions to the following words from Jesus in Matthew 11:25-27. Then set this exercise aside for a week or a month. When you pick it up again, note how your reactions have changed.

I praise you, Father

Lord of heaven and earth

Because you have hidden these things from the wise and learned

And revealed them to little children

Yes, Father, for this was your good pleasure

All things have been committed to me by my Father

No one knows the Son except the Father

And no one knows the Father except the Son and those to whom the Son chooses to reveal him

Actions

Consider also Matthew 11:28-30, below. What action steps will you take in order to accept the yoke of Christ? What burdens do you hope to have lifted as a result?

Come to me, all you who are weary and burdened, and I will give you rest

Take my yoke upon you and learn from me

For I am gentle and humble in heart

And you will find rest for your souls

For my yoke is easy and my burden is light

A Disappointed Lord, Part 1

Today's texts of Matthew 11:20-24 and Matthew 13:54-58 reveal disappointing times of Jesus' life on earth. Let the following question boxes help you understand and wrestle with the implications of these disappointments.

What was the primary purpose of Jesus performing miracles? What do his miracles tell you about him?	Nazareth's rejection of Jesus prompted the classic pronouncement, "Only in his hometown and in his own house is a prophet without honor." Why is this true?
Jesus pronounced harsh judgments on the cities that rejected him. What implications from Jesus' judgments do you find for our culture and times?	What does Matthew 13:58 tell you about the role of faith in Jesus' work?

A Disappointed Lord, Part 2

How will you complete the following?

I know that the ungodly and unbelievers are not the only ones who may reject Jesus. Christians may also reject his participation in or control of portions of their lives. I have found that I need to yield to his control in the following way:

_____. *My Lord Jesus, I do repent of this portion of my life that I've withheld from you. Please help and guide me as I try to honor you as my God.*

Signed: _____

Obstacle Course to Faith

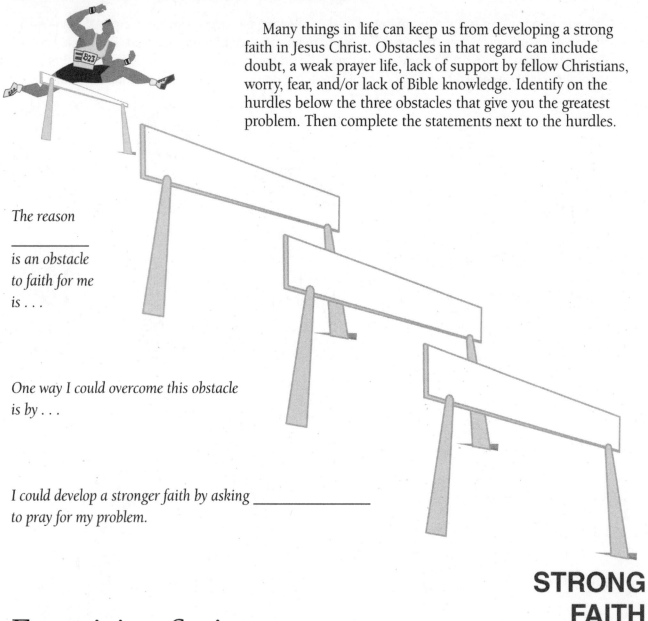

Many things in life can keep us from developing a strong faith in Jesus Christ. Obstacles in that regard can include doubt, a weak prayer life, lack of support by fellow Christians, worry, fear, and/or lack of Bible knowledge. Identify on the hurdles below the three obstacles that give you the greatest problem. Then complete the statements next to the hurdles.

The reason

_____

is an obstacle to faith for me is . . .

One way I could overcome this obstacle is by . . .

I could develop a stronger faith by asking _____ *to pray for my problem.*

STRONG FAITH

Energizing Scriptures

Select one of the Scriptures below to memorize. Recall it several times each day in the week ahead to energize and strengthen your faith.

"I can do everything through him who gives me strength" (Philippians 4:13).

"Be joyful always; pray continually; give thanks in all circumstances" (1 Thessalonians 5:16-18).

"What is impossible with men is possible with God" (Luke 18:27).

"Ask and it will be given to you; seek and you will find" (Matthew 7:7).

Who He Is!

Fill in the descriptions for Jesus that are found in the following passages. The letters you put in the 15 boxes will reveal, in the order given, the first part of the main message of today's lesson. Put those letters on the lines of Matthew 16:16 at the bottom. *Option:* Do it all backwards! Fill in Matthew 16:16 first, then transfer the letters to the 15 boxes to help you guess the descriptions before you look them up.

John 14:6 _ _ ☐

Matthew 8:2 _ ☐ _ _

Acts 10:42 _ ☐ _ _ _

John 8:58 _ ☐ _

John 1:1 _ _ ☐ _

1 Timothy 2:5 _ ☐ _ _ _ _ _

John 10:9 _ _ ☐ _

John 10:11 _ _ _ _ ☐ _ _ _

Matthew 12:18 _ ☐ _ _ _ _

Hebrews 6:19 _ _ ☐ _ _ _

Hebrews 6:20 _ _ _ ☐ _ _ _ _ _

Job 19:25 ☐ _ _ _ _ _ _

Matthew 9:15 _ _ ☐ _ _ _ _ _

John 4:42 ☐ _ _ _ _ _

John 8:12 _ _ _ _ ☐

" _ _ _ _   _ _ _   _ _ _ _   _ _ _ _ _ _ _,'

the Son of the living God" (Matthew 16:16).

False to True

All of the following statements about Jesus' transfiguration are false. Cross out the words that make the statements false; then write the words needed to make the statements true. Answers are found in the verses indicated from Matthew 17.

1. Jesus took the twelve disciples up on a high mountain. *(v. 1)*

2. When Jesus was transfigured, his face shone like the moon. *(v. 2)*

3. Moses and Isaiah appeared and talked with Jesus. *(v. 3)*

4. Peter offered to put up three altars. *(v. 4)*

5. A dark cloud enveloped them. *(v. 5)*

6. A voice from the cloud said, "This is my Son, whom I love. . . . Baptize him!" *(v. 5)*

7. When the disciples heard the voice, they fell facedown on the ground, overjoyed. *(v. 6)*

8. An angel touched them and said, "Get up. Don't be afraid." *(v. 7)*

9. When the disciples woke up, they saw no one except Jesus. *(v. 8)*

10. As they came down the mountain, Jesus told them, "Don't tell anyone what you have seen, until the Son of Life has been raised from the dead." *(v. 9)*

11. The disciples asked why the teachers of the law said that Elijah had to come second. *(v. 10)*

12. Jesus said that Elijah comes to restore some things. *(v. 11)*

13. Jesus said that the Son of Man was going to prophesy in the same way Elijah did. *(v. 12)*

14. In reference to Elijah, the disciples understood that Jesus was talking to them about John the Apostle. *(v. 13)*

Transformed by the Transfiguration

Seeing Jesus in all his glory must have changed Peter, James, and John! Imagine that you had been there too and complete the following sentences.

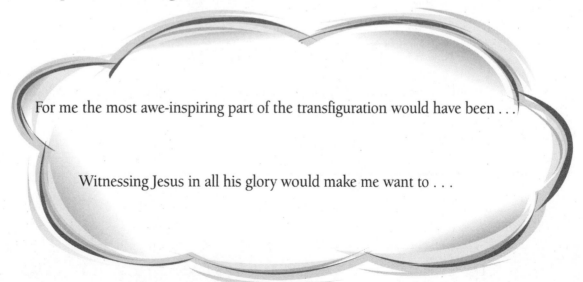

For me the most awe-inspiring part of the transfiguration would have been . . .

Witnessing Jesus in all his glory would make me want to . . .

What Is Jesus Worth?

There was such a contrast in how the people in today's lesson valued Jesus. From Judas's willingness to sell out Jesus for a mere 30 pieces of silver to the woman's spontaneous sacrifice of her most valuable possession to honor Jesus, the difference was very great. Use the numbered clues to solve the puzzle below for a hymn title that might best express how valuable Jesus was to the woman of Bethany. Answers are in Matthew 26 according to the verse numbers given.

A. __ __ __ __
   3 20 9 18

Some people thought that instead of anointing Jesus with the perfume the woman should have _____ it. (v. 9)

B. __ __ __ __
  16 6 15 11

The Jewish leaders planned carefully so they wouldn't start one. (v. 5)

C. __ __ __ __
  14 6 17 10

"The poor you _____ always have with you." (v. 11)

D. __ __ __ __ __
  1 4 18 8 5

The disciple who struck a deal with Jesus' enemies. (v. 14)

E. __ __ __ __
  12 22 8 18

The body part upon which the woman poured the expensive perfume. (v. 7)

F. __ __
  21 2

Jesus said, "You will not always have _____." (v. 11)

G. __ __ __ __ __
  14 8 7 19 13

When the disciples saw what the woman had done, they asked, "Why this _____?" (v. 8)

__ __ __ __ __   __ __   __ __ __   __ __ __
1 2 3 4 5   6 7   8 9 10   11 12 13

__ __ __ __ __   __ __   __ __
14 15 16 17 18   19 20   21 22

So, how valuable is Jesus to you? What act of sacrificial love will you do this week to show him?

_____

_____

_____

_____

Spring Quarter 2010

Teachings on Community

(Jonah, Ruth, New Testament)

Special Features

Lessons

Unit 1: Community with a Mission

Unit 2: Teachings of Jesus

Unit 3: Teachings of the Church

About These Lessons

One of the worst things that can happen to a prisoner is to be put in solitary confinement. One former prisoner described his experience in that regard as a form of torture. God designed us to interact with one another! These lessons will show us why and how.

Mar 7
Mar 14
Mar 21
Mar 28
Apr 4
Apr 11
Apr 18
Apr 25
May 2
May 9
May 16
May 23
May 30

Quarter Review

Use this page to form questions for the class to answer and discuss.
Then provide the information as a handout to summarize the lessons of the past quarter.

LESSON 1: MISSION TO THE COMMUNITY

How do you define your "community"? Your answer to that question will to a large measure determine your mission. God challenged Jonah to redefine his community. Is he likewise calling you to change yours?

LESSON 2: A COMMUNITY TO REDEEM

If Jeremiah is the "weeping prophet," then Jonah must be the "pouting prophet"! Jonah could not accept that God wanted to redeem people different from him. Are you eager to see "different" people find God's redemption?

LESSON 3: FAMILY AS COMMUNITY

The account of Naomi and Ruth is as touching a story as can be found anywhere. Ruth's pledge of devotion reveals what is unstated: Naomi had reached out to her new family member with God's love. Are you reaching out to your family?

LESSON 4: ACCEPTANCE IN THE COMMUNITY

Ruth was a Moabitesss and, thus, not entitled to a place of belonging in Israel. But Boaz saw virtue in her, and he was willing to take on both the privileges and challenges that went with accepting her. Can you be as accepting of an outsider?

LESSON 5: THE COMMUNITY FACES PAIN AND JOY

The group of disciples had seen their share of sorrow and joy—but nothing like what they were about to experience! Jesus was preparing them for that. For what is he preparing you?

LESSON 6: LOVE WITHIN THE COMMUNITY

It's old, but it's new. The idea has been around for centuries, but its practice is as challenging as learning to write with the wrong hand! To love one another seems easy, until "one another" turns out to be less than loveable! How are you doing?

LESSON 7: CONNECTING IN COMMUNITY

When Jesus said one's righteousness must surpass that of the Pharisees and the teachers of the law it must have seemed impossible. Who knows the law as well as they? But knowing and doing are not the same. And doing starts with love. Are you doing?

LESSON 8: INCLUSION IN COMMUNITY

"Blessed is the man who will eat at the feast in the kingdom of God." But just who is "the man"? Jesus' story indicates that it won't be the ones that many expect. Many unlikely guests will be at that table. Will you be included?

LESSON 9: A FAITHFUL COMMUNITY

The Colossian church was a good church. Paul praised their apparent faith, love, and hope. He commended their faithful minister Epaphras. And he prayed for their continued faithfulness. Is your church like theirs?

LESSON 10: AN ESTABLISHED COMMUNITY

Paul warned the Colossians against "hollow and deceptive philosophy" and other ungodly teachings. He reminded them of their baptism. Are you living up to what you began when you were "buried with him" and then "raised with him"?

LESSON 11: A CHOSEN COMMUNITY

God's choice makes demands on us. Paul encouraged the Colossians to live in a manner that reflected their status. The chosen treat one another with love. The chosen let the Word of God dwell in them. Are you living as the chosen people do?

LESSON 12: AT HOME IN THE COMMUNITY

Paul wrote to Philemon to ask him to forgive someone. This person had been a slave, but he had run away. In God's providence, he met Paul and became a believer. Could Philemon now welcome him home—as a brother? Could you?

LESSON 13: AT RISK IN THE COMMUNITY

Paul was not the only New Testament writer to warn about false teachings. Jude was another. His short letter encourages us to contend for "the faith . . . once for all." Believers are still at risk; for their sake, can you contend for the faith?

When The Prodigals Sang

by Lloyd M. Pelfrey

It was touching when The Prodigals sang their theme song. This group was a male prison choir under the direction of the prison chaplain. They occasionally had opportunities to travel outside the prison to present concerts at different functions in the state.

The men themselves chose the choir's name, and it is obvious that they used the popular definition of the word *prodigal*—someone who sins but repents and returns. The word actually means a person who uses money wastefully or foolishly (see Luke 15:11-32), but everyone knew what was intended by the name.

Their theme song was "No Man Is an Island." The title of this popular folk song is based on a meditation written by John Donne (1572–1631). The essential portion of the original essay expresses these thoughts: "No man is an island, entire of itself; every man is a piece of the continent, a part of the main; if a clod be washed away by the sea, Europe is the less . . . any man's death diminishes me, because I am involved in mankind."

These thoughts are in harmony with the principles in the next three months' lessons. They develop the concept of *community,* that no person is an island.

The quarter begins with four lessons from the Old Testament, followed by lessons from the Gospels and the Epistles. Differing situations demonstrate that each person must recognize that he or she is part of a community. Everyone belongs to a variety of social units. These units differ in size and function. These may include family, workplace, online "virtual communities," and a body of believers that worships God as a unit—even a prison choir. No one is an island.

UNIT 1: COMMUNITY WITH A MISSION

MARCH

The four lessons for March 2010 are from two Old Testament books: two lessons from Jonah and two from Ruth. The first two focus on Jonah's mission to save the city of Nineveh. The final two lessons also focus on survival, but in circumstances that are in vivid contrast with what is depicted in the book of Jonah.

In *Lesson 1* we will see Jonah attempt to flee from the mission that God gave him. The reluctance of a prophet of God in this case contrasts vividly with the response of the Gentile community of Nineveh.

Jonah eventually delivered the pronouncement of pending doom. The people of Nineveh demonstrated a genuine repentance. Jonah learned that God can find you wherever you are. Jonah also began to acknowledge reluctantly that God's compassion extends to people of different cultures and communities.

Lesson 2 features *the runaway prophet* becoming *the pouting prophet* as Jonah continued to learn lessons from a vine, a worm, and a scorching wind. (Previously a big fish taught him that he could not hide from God.) Jonah's self-centeredness differed sharply from God's love for others.

The country of Moab provides the setting for *Lesson 3*. It is also a different time—several hundred years before Jonah. The book of Ruth relates the struggles of a community much smaller than Nineveh—of a man, his wife, and their two sons. Major decisions were made to preserve life and faith. The climax of the lesson has Ruth making her declarations of loyalty to Naomi (her mother-in-law) and to the God of Israel.

In *Lesson 4* Ruth finds acceptance among her dead husband's people in Bethlehem in Judah. Ruth's care for Naomi and her work ethic combine to bring special favors in the harvest fields, a proposal of marriage, the marriage itself, and the birth of a son. That son becomes the grandfather of David, king of Israel.

APRIL

UNIT 2: TEACHINGS OF JESUS

Jesus' resurrection is celebrated the first Sunday of April. In this light another type of community is featured: Jesus and the apostles. The first part of *Lesson 5* takes us to the Gospel of John to give Jesus' words of comfort to the apostles on the evening before he was crucified. The final part of the lesson focuses on Jesus' concern for Mary Magdalene as she discovered that Jesus was again alive!

The first epistle of John provides the framework for *Lesson 6*. John is often called "the apostle of love," and he affirmed that people of all ages and levels of maturity who claim to be a part of the fellowship of believers must love others.

Two well-known passages have been chosen for *Lesson 7*. The first is a text from Jesus' teaching on the mount in Matthew 5.

Lesson 8 uses the setting of Jesus eating with a prominent Pharisee. In response to a statement at the banquet, Jesus told a parable about the petty excuses some offered when invited to attend a banquet. It is not enough to be invited; those who feast in the kingdom of God must accept God's invitations.

MAY

UNIT 3: TEACHINGS OF THE CHURCH

Lesson 9 uses the opening verses of the book of Colossians to express gratitude for the faith, love, and hope of the Colossian Christians. The passage continues with sound counsel on how to be a faithful member of the community.

In *Lesson 10* "the Colossian heresy" is addressed with the forceful words of the apostle Paul. He described the hollow and deceptive teaching of people who wanted to add the traditions of the world to faith in Christ. There is no need to add anything to what has been received.

The practical portion of Colossians begins in chapter 3, the focus of *Lesson 11*. It is essential that negative actions and attitudes be removed. There are also positive attributes that must become dominant in the Christian's walk. Whatever is done is to be in the name of the Lord Jesus.

Lesson 12 offers the delightful experience of reading the little epistle of Philemon. Here we will see how Paul challenged Philemon to do the right thing when his runaway slave Onesimus returned.

Lesson 13 is a reminder that Christian fellowship is not just warm and fuzzy. The epistle of Jude is a denunciation of error and a warning that there will always be those who can lead to division and scoffing about the message of redemption.

NO ONE IS AN ISLAND!

On one occasion when The Prodigals sang, the chaplain was told that a choir member was talking of trying to escape by going through a bathroom window. The chaplain then received this assurance: "Don't worry! We won't let him do it!" And there was no escape, for the other members of The Prodigals were not going to allow one person to cause all of them to forfeit their privileges.

There are serious consequences when the integrity and oneness of a community is violated. There must be a firm resolve to remain steadfast and to help the weak to be true to the Christian faith. Each believer is part of the larger family of God. We must remember: no one is an island.

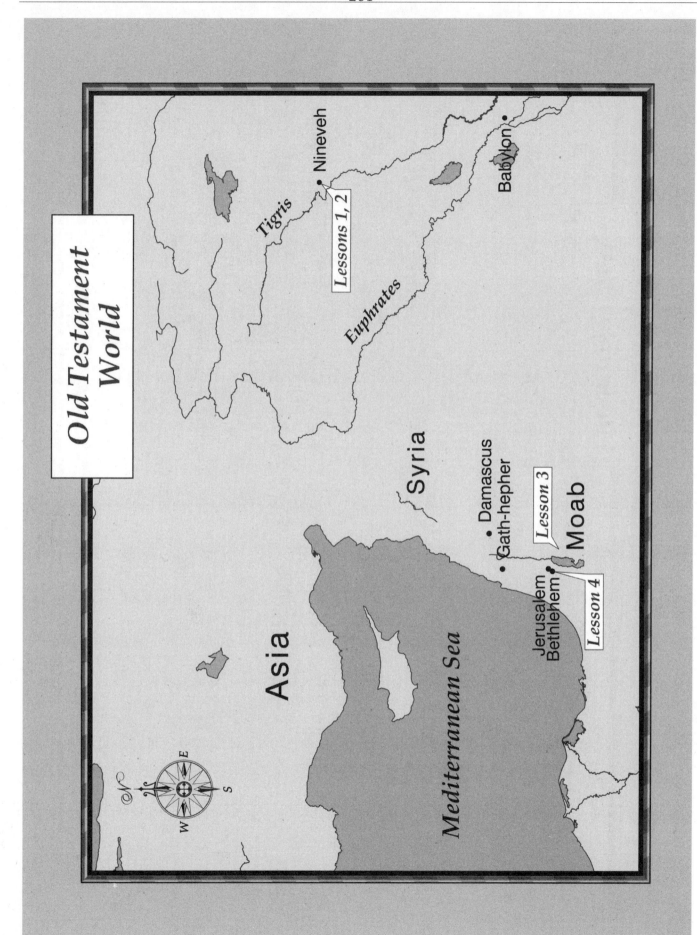

Old Testament World

Asia

Syria

Mediterranean Sea

Tigris

Euphrates

Nineveh

Babylon

Damascus

Gath-hepher

Jerusalem

Bethlehem

Moab

Lessons 1, 2

Lesson 3

Lesson 4

N E S W

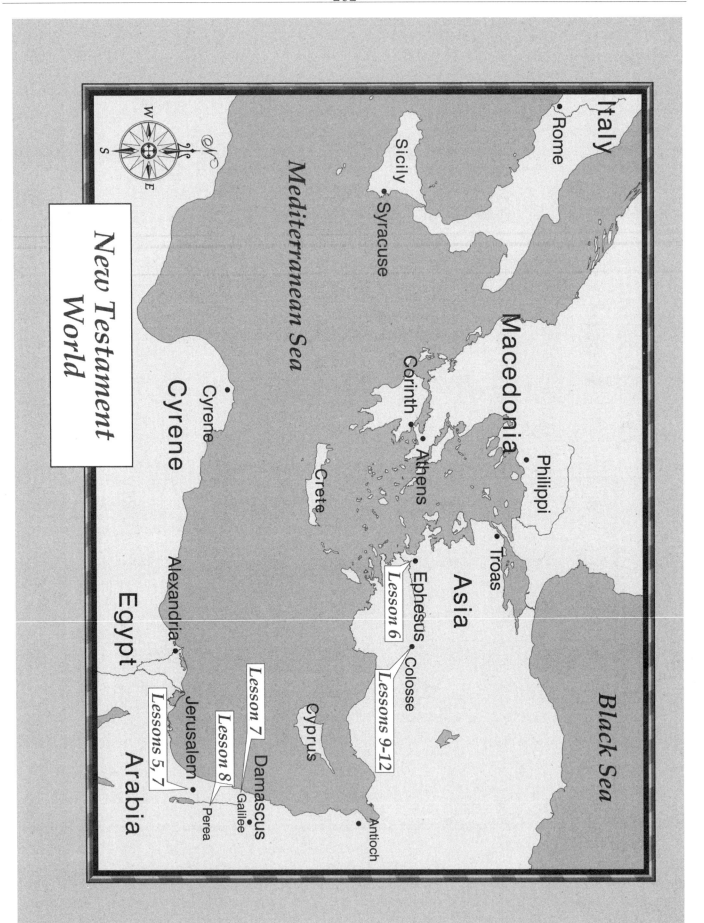

Dealing with Difficult Students

PROBLEM BEHAVIOR IN THE ADULT CLASSROOM

by James Riley Estep, Jr.

"I thought this was an adult teacher book! What do you mean difficult students? Adults aren't text-messaging, trash-talking, disrespectful teens and tweens!" Reality check: difficult students exist in learning environments at all age levels. While adults may not be running around the room or overtly and intentionally misbehaving, nevertheless they can be a distraction in the classroom.

Generally speaking, there are five types of difficult students you may encounter in adult classrooms. Deciding what approach to take in dealing with a difficult student first involves a diagnosis of which problem-type is presenting itself.

There are five types of difficult students you may encounter in adult classrooms

THE KNOW-IT-ALL

The Know-It-All uses the class setting of the Sunday school hour to demonstrate his or her "superior" knowledge and understanding of the subject. The Know-It-All often appears to be in competition with the teacher. Know-It-Alls may feel the need to comment on every statement made by the teacher, add "deeper" insights to the lesson, or (at worst) directly oppose the teacher's ideas. A Know-It-All may try to set himself or herself up as *the* definitive voice of truth for the class. This becomes a distraction to other adult learners as it tends to change the class discussion or lecture into a debate.

There are several options for handling this type of difficult student. One method is to design your class with a time designated intentionally for discussion, particularly in small groups. This may limit the Know-It-All's opportunities to interrupt.

THE KNOW-IT-ALL

Another tactic is to recruit this kind of student to be a teacher. However, some Know-It-Alls will not accept the call to teach. They may prefer to snipe at the teacher rather than assume the teaching role itself—a role that would put the Know-It-All in a vulnerable position of being on the receiving end of the sniping!

A third tactic is to get the Know-It-Alls out of your classroom by having them "promoted" to administrative positions that require them to be elsewhere during the Sunday school hour. Some may view this tactic as "chickening out," since it works around a problem without dealing with the real issue of the Know-It-All's character flaw.

That character flaw is addressed by a fourth tactic: gentle, one-on-one confrontation. This involves a spiritually mature person taking the Know-It-All aside outside of class and asking, "Do you realize what you're doing in the classroom?" The resulting discussion can be very productive if the confronter is skilled at dealing with defensive reactions that may pop up.

Caution: it is usually not wise for you, the teacher, to try to neutralize the Know-It-All by countering his or her "deeper" insights with "even deeper yet" insights of your own. This tactic can deteriorate quickly into a tawdry game of one-upmanship.

THE GRUMBLER

The Grumbler uses the classroom as a platform for expressing complaints. Regardless of the topic being discussed, the Grumbler is able to turn it into an occasion for a negative remark about the congregation, minister, or Christianity in general.

You the teacher must realize that this is a spiritual matter that originates beyond the walls of your Sunday school classroom. The Grumbler is obviously feeling some kind of pain, has unresolved issues, or has been hurt by someone. Dealing with a Grumbler requires a pastoral approach.

Hence, the best way to deal with a Grumbler is outside the class, one-on-one. That meeting does not necessarily have to include you, the teacher, but it should involve a respected leader of your congregation. Such a meeting will try to pinpoint the specific issues with which the Grumbler has concerns.

Taking an open, non-defensive posture toward Grumblers is often helpful in getting them to open up and share concerns. Many times they simply want to be heard. The fact that someone is taking time to listen to the Grumbler affirms that his or her concerns are being heard. The Grumbler needs to be made aware, however, that he or she should take the concerns directly to the church leadership rather than to your class.

THE LIGHT-SHINER

Light-Shiners use the classroom to show how they exemplify the points of the lesson. They set themselves up as a paradigm for the Christian life and tend to interpret the Scriptures in terms of their personal lifestyle. For example, when hearing a lesson on giving to the poor, Light-Shiners feel compelled to share with the class all their involvement with the homeless, everything they've given to the Salvation Army, etc. As a result, Light-Shiners can alienate others by making them feel spiritually inferior. Class members become annoyed by the self-promoting personal testimonial that occurs in every class session.

One method of dealing with the Light-Shiner is to ensure that all your learners have opportunity to share how they demonstrate the topic of the day in their lives. You can do this by asking each student, one by one, to identify how he or she practices the biblical principle at hand. In this way you end up making the Light-Shiner one candle among many rather than the solitary light.

Light-Shiners need to balance Matthew 5:14-16 with Matthew 6:1-4; thus a lesson in that regard may be in order. If they can understand that the focus is not to be on themselves, Light-Shiners can become wonderful mentors.

THE CAFÉ-GOER

I have an affinity for coffee and fellowship! But I also realize that Sunday school is more than coffee and coffee talk. I enjoy my time at the local coffeehouse and the opportunity it brings for discussion and even spiritual support. But I also know that Sunday school classrooms are not coffeehouses.

However, Café-Goers don't share this awareness. They spend an inordinate time around the class coffeepot conversing with friends, and they may have to be reminded more than once "It's time to start class." Even then they may continue chatting throughout the lesson (typically about anything but the lesson topic).

One tactic to deal with the Café-Goer is to voice a gentle hint such as, "I see some discussions going on—am I way off course on this? Questions, comments, concerns?" This should draw everyone's attention back to the topic.

Café-Goers often are simply unaware of the distractions they are causing. They may view Sunday school primarily as an opportunity for fellowship rather than as a teaching venue. A gentle hint as suggested may be all that is needed.

The High-Maintenance Individual

Do you have folks in your class who are always expressing personal issues for prayer requests, identifying themselves as examples of misfortune, or even openly crying in class? If so, you may have High-Maintenance Individuals on your hands. These are people who always seem to be in a state of spiritual or personal crisis.

Such folks need intentional pastoral support. A primary function of the church is to provide such support, of course. But an adult Bible fellowship (Sunday school) classroom usually is not the best place to provide it. Yes, the church exists to help troubled souls. But to allow your classroom to become a crisis counseling center is to change the design of the Sunday school hour into something other than a Bible-teaching venue.

None of this is meant to be insensitive to the genuine needs of people in crisis. Members of your Sunday school class can indeed serve as crisis counselors and crisis responders in times of death, spiritual doubt, financial problems, etc. These are normal and expected ministries of class members with one another. But that is not to say that the Sunday school hour is the best time for such ministries to occur.

The key response in such cases is *referral*. A person going through crisis often needs more and different help than is available during the Sunday school hour. Make arrangements for your troubled individuals to get counseling from an appropriate source, such as your minister, an elder, or Christian counselor. Referral addresses the issues of the troubled individual in the best way possible while helping minimize the chance that your Sunday school hour will become something it is not designed to be.

Why This Is Important

As you read the five descriptions above, images of certain individuals probably entered your mind. (Maybe you even saw yourself!) Teachers cannot avoid difficult students; it is part of the call to the teaching ministry.

Remember: your goal as teacher is to keep your lesson aims at the center as you teach the Word and help your students apply it. The behavior of difficult students takes you away from this goal. In effect, such behavior, if left unchecked, will change the purpose of the class. The more mature members of the class realize their responsibility to the class as a whole. Difficult students, by contrast, use the classroom as a means of fulfilling a personal agenda, either intentionally or unintentionally.

Many teachers simply tolerate the behavior of difficult students. *This is not really an option,* since such behaviors are counterproductive to a learning environment and actually may do harm to other students. Newcomers to the class may end up with a poor experience and may choose not to return as a result. In short, the teacher *must* deal with difficult students. The problem will rarely correct itself if ignored. Recognizing the problem is the first step toward fixing it.

The High-Maintenance Individual

Your goal as teacher is to keep your lesson aims at the center as you teach the Word and help your students apply it. The behavior of difficult students takes you away from this goal.

Recognizing the problem is the first step toward fixing it.

How to Say It

Use this list to help you pronounce the names and hard-to-pronounce words in the lessons of the spring quarter.

A

Abyss. Uh-BIS.
Alexandria. Al-iks-AN-dree-uh.
Amittai. Uh-MIT-eye.
Apphia. AF-ee-uh or AP-fee-uh.
Archippus. Ar-KIP-us.
Areopagus. Air-ee-OP-uh-gus.
Arimathea. AIR-uh-muh-THEE-uh
(TH as in THIN).
Assyrians. Uh-SEAR-e-unz.
Azariah. Az-uh-RYE-uh.

B

Babylon. BAB-uh-lun.
Beatitudes. Bee-A-tuh-toods
(A as in MAT).
Boaz. BO-az.
Bucharest. BU-kuh-rest.

C

Caesar. SEE-zer.
Cannes. Kan or Kanz.
Chemosh. KEE-mosh.
Colosse. Ko-LAHSS-ee.
Corinth. KOR-inth.
coxswain. COCK-sun.

E

Elimelech. Ee-LIM-eh-leck.
Emmaus. Em-MAY-us.
Epaphras. EP-uh-frass.
Ephesus. EF-uh-sus.
Ephrathites. EF-ruh-thites.
epistle. ee-PIS-ul.
Essenes. EH-seenz.

G

Galilean. Gal-uh-LEE-un.
Gath Hepher. Gath HE-fer.
Gentiles. JEN-tiles.
Gethsemane. Geth-SEM-uh-nee (G
as in GET).
Gnosticism.
NAHSS-tih-SIZZ-um.

gnostics. NAHSS-ticks.
Gomorrah. Guh-MORE-uh.

H

Hazael. HAZ-zay-el.
heresy. HAIR-uh-see.
Hierapolis. Hi-er-AP-o-lis.

J

Jeroboam. Jair-uh-BOE-um.
Joses. JO-sez.
Josiah. Jo-SIGH-uh.
Judaism. JOO-duh-izz-um or JOO-
day-izz-um.
Judas Iscariot.
JOO-dus Iss-CARE-ee-ut.
Judea. Joo-DEE-uh.

K

Kilion. KIL-ee-on.

L

Laodicea. Lay-ODD-uh-SEE-uh.
Laodiceans.
Lay-ODD-uh-SEE-unz.
levirate. LEH-vuh-rut.

M

Macedonia.
Mass-eh-DOE-nee-uh.
Magdalene. MAG-duh-leen or Mag-
duh-LEE-nee.
Mahlon. MAH-lon.
Marcion. MAHR-shun.
Mardi Gras. MAR-dee Grah.
Mesha. ME-shuh.
Messianic. Mess-ee-AN-ick.
milquetoast. MILK-toast.
Moab. MO-ab.
Moabite. MO-ub-ite.

N

Naomi. Nay-OH-me.
Naphtali. NAF-tuh-lye.

Nazareth. NAZ-uh-reth.
Nicolae Ceausescu. NIH-ko-lie
Chow-SHES-ku.
Nineveh. NIN-uh-vuh.
Ninevites. NIN-uh-vites.

O

Obed. O-bed.
Onesimus. O-NESS-ih-muss.

P

Pharisees. FAIR-ih-seez.
Phoenicia. Fuh-NISH-uh.

Q

Qumran. Koom-RAHN.

R

Rabboni. Rab-O-nye.
Rehoboam. Ree-huh-BOE-um.
Reichstag. RIKE-stagh.

S

Sadducees. SAD-you-seez.
Samaria. Suh-MARE-ee-uh.
Samaritans. Suh-MARE-uh-tunz.
Scythian. SITH-ee-un.
shalom (Hebrew). shah-LOME.
Shema. SHE-muh.
Sodom. SOD-um.

T

Tigris. TIE-griss.

U

Uzziah. Uh-ZYE-uh.

W

Waodani. Whoa-DON-ee.
Worms. Vorms.

Z

Zarephath. ZAIR-uh-fath.
Zebulun. ZEB-you-lun.

MISSION TO THE COMMUNITY

LESSON 1

INTRODUCTION

A. RED AND YELLOW

Jesus loves the little children, All the children of the world; Red and yellow, black and white, They are precious in his sight; Jesus loves the little children of the world" (attributed to C. H. Woolston). These words of a children's chorus are easy to remember, and many fondly recall singing them. To hear a new generation sing the same chorus is often accompanied by nostalgic feelings. The purpose of the chorus is to remove racial prejudice, even among the people of God. Some have criticized the chorus for having the opposite effect: that the words themselves call attention to the differences.

Differences do tend to divide, and dissimilarities may present themselves in terms of age, income, education, race, religion, cultural customs, and athletic abilities—in other words, just anything that is different. Sociologists affirm that it is normal for people to cluster with others who are similar in some way.

It is wrong to allow differences to grow into petty attitudes of jealousy, pride, or hostility. It is wrong to look down on those who are different. It is wrong to be envious of those who have "more" or to feel superior because others have "less." Wars have been and are being fought because of such dissimilarities. The fact that people are made in the image of God is conveniently ignored. Even when this is acknowledged, various reasons still are used to justify hostilities.

The great tragedy is when some express disdain about taking God's Word to others because they are "not one of us." Jonah is often cited as an example of this kind of a reluctance. The Lord commissioned him to preach a message of repentance to a foreign nation, and Jonah became "the runaway prophet." We see a certain similarity in the apostle Peter, who had to be convinced by visions and a rebuke that the message of Christ was also for Gentiles (Acts 10:34, 35; Galatians 2:11, 12).

B. LESSON BACKGROUND

Solomon, the wise king of Israel, died about 930 BC. He was succeeded by his son Rehoboam, who immediately demonstrated that his wisdom was inferior to that of his father. The result was that Israel divided into two nations: Judah as the southern nation and Israel as the northern one.

The two nations had times of mutual hostility and friendship as well as oppression from other nations. Oppression changed to prosperity when

---

DEVOTIONAL READING:
MATTHEW 21:28-32
BACKGROUND SCRIPTURE:
JONAH 1:1-3; 3:1-9
PRINTED TEXT:
JONAH 1:1-3; 3:1-9

LESSON AIMS

After participating in this lesson, each student will be able to:

1. Summarize the account of Jonah's call to preach at Nineveh and what happened as a result.

2. Compare and contrast the Ninevites' reaction to Jonah's preaching with the reaction of people today when the gospel is preached in secular contexts.

3. Pray for the success of a particular missionary who is preaching the gospel in a foreign city.

KEY VERSE

The Ninevites believed God. They declared a fast, and all of them, from the greatest to the least, put on sackcloth.   —Jonah 3:5

HOW TO SAY IT

Amittai. Uh-MIT-eye.
Areopagus. Air-ee-OP-uh-gus.
Assyrians. Uh-SEAR-e-unz.
Azariah. Az-uh-RYE-uh.
Gath Hepher. Gath HE-fer.
Jeroboam. Jair-uh-BOE-um.
Nazareth. NAZ-uh-reth.
Nineveh. NIN-uh-vuh.
Rehoboam. Ree-huh-
    BOE-um.
Samaria. Suh-MARE-ee-uh.
Tigris. TIE-griss.
Uzziah. Uh-ZYE-uh.
Zebulun. ZEB-you-lun.

WHAT DO YOU THINK?

How does the wickedness rampant in our big cities affect you?

Uzziah (also called Azariah) became king over Judah. At the same time Jeroboam II was king in Israel. Both nations expanded their territories so that the combined dominion was about the same as in the days of Solomon. The outward wealth of Israel in the days of Jeroboam II (793–753 BC) fulfilled a prophecy that was made by Jonah in 2 Kings 14:25. This helps to date the approximate time of Jonah's ministry. The educated guesses for his trip to Nineveh range between 790 and 760 BC.

The traditional view is that Jonah himself wrote the book that bears his name. The book tells of the journeys of Jonah, and it also serves as a self-indictment of his attitudes and actions. By writing the book he demonstrated a repentance similar to what his preaching prompted for the entire city of Nineveh. It is interesting that the book of Jonah is still read each fall on Yom Kippur, the Jewish Day of Atonement. It is read in the afternoon service to emphasize the theme of repentance.

The book of Jonah provides a journal of jealousy, jeopardy, joy, and judging. The book is the fifth book in the Minor Prophets, which are the last 12 books of the Old Testament. It is different from the others in that it is primarily a narrative. (A more typical approach is to blend prophetic utterances with sections of history or personal experiences.) Jonah is the only prophet among the Minor Prophets who rebelled against God and then recorded a factual account of his actions.

I. COMMISSION AVOIDED (JONAH 1:1-3)

A. DESIGNATING THE MESSENGER (v. 1)

1. The word of the LORD came to Jonah son of Amittai:

The opening phrase of the book, *the word of the Lord,* offers the standard formula that prophets often use when they proclaim or write their messages from the Lord. Jonah's identification as the *son of Amittai* reflects the custom of providing the name of the father as a means of more precise identification. The extra identification is not as essential in this case, for Jonah is the only person in the Bible with that name. The word *Jonah* means "dove."

The reference to Jonah in 2 Kings 14:25 reveals that Gath Hepher is his hometown. This is one of the cities of the tribe of Zebulun (Joshua 19:13). It is located just a few miles north of Nazareth in northern Israel. It is not known if Jonah is in his hometown when he receives the word of the Lord.

B. DELIVERING THE MESSAGE (v. 2)

2. "Go to the great city of Nineveh and preach against it, because its wickedness has come up before me."

Nineveh is both a *great city* and an ancient city, having been built shortly after the great flood (Genesis 10:11, 12). The book of Jonah describes the greatness or importance of this city three times (Jonah 1:2; 3:2, 3). It is located in what is now Iraq, across from modern Mosul on the eastern side of the Tigris River. The journey to Nineveh from Israel's capital of Samaria is about 600 miles. Nineveh is well fortified with inner and outer walls, and it is one of the major cities of the Assyrians. It became the capital of the empire in approximately 700 BC.

The *wickedness* of Nineveh is not hidden from God; thus Jonah's task is to proclaim *against* the city. Under ordinary circumstances, a prophet who represents the God of Israel will have no effect on the residents of a foreign city. The people of Nineveh, however, experience some events in the eighth century BC that may make them more receptive to Jonah's message. Two severe plagues (765 and 759 BC), military defeats, several weak kings, and a total solar eclipse on June 15, 763 BC (the darkness is considered negatively by these superstitious people)—any or all of these may prepare the way for the arrival of the prophet of God.

C. DISOBEDIENCE OF THE MESSENGER (v. 3)

3. But Jonah ran away from the LORD and headed for Tarshish. He went down to Joppa, where he found a ship bound for that port. After paying the fare, he went aboard and sailed for Tarshish to flee from the LORD.

The first two words of this verse reveal that Jonah is about to become a reluctant, rebellious, runaway prophet. The Lord has said, "Go east," *but Jonah* deliberately selects *Tarshish,* a destination that is as much as 2,000 miles the other way.

Ships of Tarshish are mentioned several times in the Old Testament (example: Ezekiel 27:25). It is therefore a city of commerce, a good place to try to hide. The location of Tarshish has not been identified precisely. Conjectures include an area of southern Turkey near Tarsus, a place on the island of Sardinia (west of Italy), and a town named Tartessus on the eastern coast of Spain. The last may be the best choice, for it is the farthest away.

Jonah's attempt to escape *from the Lord* is futile. It is assumed that he is aware of the thought given in Psalm 139:7-10—that wherever one goes, to the heavens or the depths, God is there. In his rebellion against God, however, Jonah overlooks what he knows. He is like some people whose conduct away from home is inconsistent with a professed faith in God. Selective obedience to God is not the way that leads to eternal life.

Jonah pays the normal *fare* for such a trip. Most interpret this to mean that he is purchasing a trip to Tarshish. Another view is that he rents a boat and its crew in order to leave as quickly as possible.

HEARING AND ACTING ON THE LORD'S WORD

In early 1988, Edgar C. Whisenant (1932–2001) published a booklet titled *88 Reasons Why the Rapture Will Be in 1988.* It predicted the Lord's return to occur between September 11 and 13 of that year. The booklet sold in the millions of copies. When his prophecy failed, Whisenant wrote new books that adjusted the predictions to the years 1989, 1993, and 1994.

The fact that Whisenant had been a NASA engineer meant that he was not an unintelligent person. But he definitely was a false prophet. Many false prophets try to add credibility to their predictions by claiming that "the Lord has given me a word" or "the Lord said to me." When their prophecies don't come true, they prove that God has not been speaking through them.

Self-styled prophets are all too eager to hear "words from the Lord" when it is merely their own imaginations working overtime. Ironically, Jonah's case was the opposite: he was *un*willing to hear the word of the Lord even though God *was* speaking to him! God will attempt to speak to you today through creation (Psalm 19; Romans 1:20) and through his written Word (2 Timothy 3:16, 17). When he does, will you embrace him and his will, or will you run?

—C. R. B.

Visual for Lesson 1. *Post this map throughout the first four lessons to give your learners a geographical perspective.*

WHAT DO YOU THINK?

What are some ways that people today seek to "run away from the Lord"? How have you tried to do so? How did you grow spiritually as a result?

WHAT DO YOU THINK?

God often gives second chances. What does that say about him? What does that say about us?

[John 21:15-19 and 2 Peter 3:9 may be useful in your answer.]

VISUALS FOR THESE LESSONS

The visual pictured in each lesson (example: page 269) is a small reproduction of a large, full-color poster included in the Adult Resources packet for the Winter Quarter. That packet also contains the very useful Presentation Helps on a CD for teacher use. The packet is available from your supplier. Order No. 392.

WHAT DO YOU THINK?

What is there about big cities that present both barriers and opportunities to the church?

II. COMMISSION EMBRACED (JONAH 3:1-3)

A. SECOND CHANCE FOR JONAH (v. 1)

1. Then the word of the LORD came to Jonah a second time:

The intervening verses (not in today's text) give the familiar account of Jonah's being swallowed by the great fish that *the Lord* prepares for that purpose. It is likely that the interior is dark, smelly, and dismal. One thing is certain: when *Jonah* is given a second chance to take his life in the correct direction, there is no hesitation.

It is significant that the factor of Jonah's being in the sea creature three days and nights is cited by Jesus as a sign of his own resurrection (Matthew 12:40). This tends to stamp the account as an actual, historical event.

Jonah now understands that he cannot flee from God, and that it is up to him to be God's messenger to Nineveh. The fact that God approaches Jonah a *second time* says something about God's character as well. Others, such as Peter and John Mark in the New Testament, are determined to redeem themselves from their previous failures, and God allows them to do so (see John 18:15-18; 25-27; 21:15-19; Acts 13:13; 15:37-39; 2 Timothy 4:11).

B. SERIOUSNESS OF THE MESSAGE (v. 2)

2. "Go to the great city of Nineveh and proclaim to it the message I give you."

The second summons for Jonah has a new element. Previously Jonah was told that he is to preach against *Nineveh*. This time he is informed that he is to speak only what God tells him. The implications are that he must wait until God is ready and that he is neither to add to nor subtract from God's message.

C. SUBMISSION TO GOD'S WAY (v. 3a)

3a. Jonah obeyed the word of the LORD and went to Nineveh.

Jonah has learned that obedience to God is better than disobedience. In the centuries ahead, Jesus will contrast those two responses by comparing them to building houses on sand and rock (Matthew 7:24-29). Many are intrigued by the contrast of the two foundations in that story, but the main point that Jesus makes is that of disobedience versus obedience.

D. SIZE OF NINEVEH (v. 3b)

3b. Now Nineveh was a very important city—a visit required three days.

The three-day factor is subject to different interpretations. It may refer to the fact that preaching through the city in all its neighborhoods takes *three days*. Some consider it to mean that anyone who wishes to tour the city will find that it takes three days; the inner wall has a circumference of eight miles, and that is huge by ancient standards (compare Jonah 4:11). It may be that the general area of Nineveh and its suburbs requires a three-day trip to get there from a certain point.

III. CONDEMNATION RESULT (JONAH 3:4-9)

A. PROPHET'S SERMON (v. 4)

4. On the first day, Jonah started into the city. He proclaimed: "Forty more days and Nineveh will be overturned."

Jonah is a representative of the God of Israel, and this somehow prompts the people of *Nineveh* to give him an audience. The message of the prophet is very brief: just five words in the Hebrew language in which it was first written and eight words in the English here. It is not a message that offers any hope. Yet the 40-day factor suggests a window of time in which the people might be able to do something that will please God in order to avoid another catastrophe (see the comments on Jonah 1:2).

B. PEOPLE'S RESPONSE (vv. 5, 6)

5. The Ninevites believed God. They declared a fast, and all of them, from the greatest to the least, put on sackcloth.

Those who hear Jonah are convinced! This is indicated by three responses: belief, *a fast,* and the wearing of *sackcloth.* This verse does not state how the decision to mandate a fast is reached and announced. But the next verse suggests that the king and his nobles may be the ones behind these extraordinary actions that involve every level of society. No one is above or beneath the need to repent. These outward expressions are dramatic, and they are typical for the people of the time who wish to show repentance or extreme agony.

The word *repent* is not used in the account as it is given by Jonah. But Jesus uses that term when he commends the people for repenting at the preaching of Jonah. Jesus then condemns the people of his day for a lack of repentance (Matthew 12:41, 42).

Jonah's preaching triggers one of the greatest citywide revivals of all time. Yet Jonah does not want this revival to happen, as we shall see in Lesson 2.

6. When the news reached the king of Nineveh, he rose from his throne, took off his royal robes, covered himself with sackcloth and sat down in the dust.

The precise identity of which *king of Nineveh* is involved cannot be determined. A good guess is Ashurdan III (reigns 772–755 BC). It is during his reign that most of the catastrophes cited in the commentary for Jonah 1:2 occur.

The question is often asked as to why the king is referred to as *king of Nineveh* instead of *king of Assyria* (the nation). Ancient kings like to accumulate titles that indicate their superiority. They often add the names of any region or nation conquered. A king who travels to one of his cities is king over that city. To be the king of Nineveh is a great honor, for it is a great city!

On this occasion, however, the king lays aside his kingly apparel, and he leads others in acts of humility. Regarding the combination of sackcloth and ashes, see Esther 4:1, 3; Isaiah 58:5; Jeremiah 6:26; Daniel 9:3; Matthew 11:21; Luke 10:13.

C. PROCLAMATIONS OF THE KING (vv. 7-9)

7. Then he issued a proclamation in Nineveh:
    "By the decree of the king and his nobles:
    Do not let any man or beast, herd or flock, taste anything; do not let them eat or drink.

New factors are given in this verse: the fasting includes the animals, and refraining from both food and water is the nature of the fast. Domesticated animals often demand to be fed at the times to which they have become accustomed, and they do this by the assorted noises they make. The resulting din of hungry animals and children creates a stressful reminder of the repentance.

The unknown factor in the fast is its duration. About 300 years later, Queen Esther will ask for a three-day fast when she prepares to enter the presence of the king without having been invited (Esther 4:16). A similar time period may be involved here, or there may be repeated days of fasting.

8. "But let man and beast be covered with sackcloth. Let everyone call urgently on God. Let them give up their evil ways and their violence.

The covering of animals is not unusual, but in this case the garments are *sackcloth*. This repentance is not just an outward adornment; it involves a decision to abandon *evil* of any type. The final part of the repentance is sincere and genuine prayer to *God*. This may be vocal and loud, as is customary in that region, or it may be the quiet prayers of contrite hearts.

9. "Who knows? God may yet relent and with compassion turn from his fierce anger so that we will not perish."

At this point the people of Nineveh have no assurance of respite from the promised destruction. The mercy of the God of Israel may be known to them, but it is very rare for people to think that any god cares about the people of other nations. The fact that God cares enough to send a messenger to warn them may be the element that gives them a glimmer of hope.

AN EYE IN THE SKY

Environmental scofflaws have a new enforcement technique to contend with these days. The Massachusetts Department of Environmental Protection is now comparing old aerial photos of the state's wetlands with newer images to find differences that reveal violations of environmental laws. Two examples of violations: a concrete plant illegally filled in wetlands, and a junkyard logged a wooded swamp and filled it in to expand the junkyard's operations. Monetary fines were hefty.

Similar techniques are being used elsewhere. Breaches in hog farm waste lagoons in North Carolina that pollute streams do not go unnoticed. Satellite surveillance has detected illegal loggers clear-cutting Brazil's Amazon River basin. The list goes on. But even with heavy fines, it's not known whether the violators were repentant!

God's "eye in the sky" observation of Nineveh's sin resulted in genuine repentance; this was not the "I'm sorry I got caught" attitude we so often see today. It's a common human trait to think we can escape the consequences of sin. But God watches and collects evidence from on high.

—C. R. B.

CONCLUSION

The apostle Paul gave his famous sermon at the meeting of the Areopagus when he was in Athens. He noted in that sermon that God commands everyone to repent (Acts 17:30). Several conclusions may be derived from that sermon and the story of Jonah.

1. Repentance is something that can be commanded. It may involve the emotions, but repentance is primarily an act of the will. It is a deliberate choice.

2. Repentance is a decision that is made after the individual examines his or her own life, the goodness of God, and the consequences of not repenting.

3. Sincere repentance involves both present and future obedience. Repentance is not a one-time event, but is a continuing process (1 John 1:9). The actual need for repentance may diminish as growth in Christ continues, but sensitivity about sin will increase.

WHAT DO YOU THINK?

Why is the concept of the ungodly perishing at the hand of a God of fierce anger not a greater motivation for evangelism and missions? How can it be?

PRAYER

Lord, thank you for this lesson, which compels us to examine our lives. May we find areas in which we need to repent and change. We pray in Jesus' name. Amen.

4. Repentance is a personal matter. The people of the city of Nineveh repented, but it is fundamental to understand the importance of the individual as part of the whole.

5. Repentance is to be followed by a changed life—the fruits of repentance.

If repentance is a command for everyone, then there should be sermons and lessons about it. Do we hear these as much as we should?

THOUGHT TO REMEMBER

"[The Lord] is patient with you, not wanting anyone to perish, but everyone to come to repentance" (2 Peter 3:9).

Discovery Learning

The following is an alternative lesson plan emphasizing learning activities.
Classes desiring such student involvement will find these suggestions helpful. At the
back of this book are reproducible student pages to further enhance activity learning.

INTO THE LESSON

Brainstorming. Display these words of a children's song: Jesus loves the little children, / All the children of the world; / Red and yellow, black and white, / they are precious in his sight; / Jesus loves the little children of the world. Ask, "What seems to be the intended message or purpose of this chorus?" (Answer: To remove racial prejudice among the people of God.) Next ask, "What are common obstacles or reasons that may cause Christians to be reluctant to share the gospel with those of other cultures?" Write answers on the board. Also, "What additional problems might you face as a Christian if that culture is hostile to your culture?"

Make the transition to Bible study by saying, "Sharing the gospel cross-culturally is often very challenging. In Acts 10, Peter had to have a direct vision from God before he would break ground in cross-cultural evangelism. Today's study turns back to the Old Testament to unveil another reluctant missionary. But through him we learn an important lesson in walking through doors that God opens for us.

Option: Do a brief skit about the difficulties of sharing the gospel cross-culturally. The setting: A barbershop. The characters: "Barber Bob" and "Jim," who's getting his hair cut. Barber Bob asks what's happening in the other man's family. Jim expresses concern that his daughter and son-in-law are moving to Florida to try to plant a church among Cuban refugees (or another cultural group of your choosing). Jim will respond to Barber Bob's questions about safety, learning cultural traditions, language, etc.

After the skit say, "Reaching across cultural lines is often intimidating. It is for us in our community as well as for missionaries. But that's not new as we will see today in our lesson about a reluctant prophet."

INTO THE WORD

Lecture Teams. Make the following written assignments to three small groups. Each group is to appoint a lecture team of two or more to deliver a brief lecture. Give Group #1 a photocopy of the Lesson Background and a Bible dictionary article on Jonah. Group #2 will need a photocopy of the lesson commentary on Jonah 1:2, 3; 3:3. Group #3 will need a photocopy of the lesson commentary on Jonah 3:4-9 and a Bible dictionary article on Nineveh. Each group will also need a marker pen, a poster board, and the following instructions.

Group #1: Prepare a brief lecture giving the lesson background for today's study. You may find it useful to work from an outline. One possible outline is *A. Two Nations; B. Jonah Himself; C. Yom Kippur; D. The Book of Jonah.* Group #2: Prepare a brief lecture describing Nineveh. See Jonah 1:2, 3; 3:3. You may find it useful to work from an outline. One possible outline is *A. Ancient City; B. Beautiful City; C. Great Walled City; D. Jonah's Journey to the City.* Group #3: Prepare a brief lecture describing Nineveh's response to Jonah's preaching. Read Jonah 3:4-9. You may find it useful to work from an outline. One possible outline is *A. Jonah's Second Chance; B. The Message; C. Nineveh's Response; D. Nineveh's Hope.*

Remind the groups that two or more people are needed to do the team lectures and that they have only about eight minutes to prepare.

INTO LIFE

Write the word *Preparations* on the board. Say: "In Jonah's life we get a glimpse of reaching other cultures for God's glory. To succeed, however, we may need to make preparations and develop strategies. What are some ways we can do this?" Note responses. Then write the word *Challenges* on the board. Ask the class to list some difficulties or challenges one may face in taking the gospel to another culture. Again, note answers on the board.

Next, write the word *Methods* on the board. Ask what strategies or methods may be successful in reaching others. Remind students that Jonah did "street corner" preaching, which may be successful in some cultures but not in others.

Finally, remind the class that God has people taking his message to other cultures every day. Ask the class to share examples; jot on the board the names and locations mentioned. Close the class by asking teams of two to four people to pray in small groups for the missionaries or persons cited. You can distribute copies of the reproducible activity "The Reluctant Prophet" on page 372 either to begin the class or as take-home work.

A COMMUNITY TO REDEEM

LESSON 2

Mar
14

INTRODUCTION

A. COURAGE FOR GOD

Laszlo Tokes was more than just your run-of-the-mill conscientious objector. His Bible and his conscience sparked a revolt that eventually toppled the Communist regime of Nicolae Ceausescu in Romania in 1989.

Tokes was a Protestant minister. His opposition to the Ceausescu government began several years earlier with an essay on human rights abuses. The first effort to quiet him was to relocate him to a small village. He refused to go. He then accepted a transfer to be an assistant minister in a certain congregation. The death of the senior minister six months later elevated Tokes to that position. The congregation began to grow, and his opposition to governmental procedures drew attention even from other nations.

In October 1988 he organized a cultural festival. That caused the bishop, in cooperation with the government, to issue a ban on all youth activities in the area. Tokes's response was to take the lead in sponsoring a spring festival the following year. He was ordered to move to a more remote area, and he refused to leave. With the help of his congregation, Tokes was able to withstand having his ration books taken away and having his house disconnected from the power supply. A court issued an eviction order on October 20, 1989. Armed men broke into his residence on November 2. Tokes lost his housing appeal, and forcible eviction was to take place on December 15.

When the day came, Tokes's supporters formed a barricade. The crowds grew, and by evening a revolt ensued against the governmental authorities. It spread to the Romanian capital of Bucharest. A full-scale insurrection was in progress by December 20. The army was summoned to fire on the defenseless citizens, and some were killed. Finally, the army would no longer obey such orders. Five days later Romania was freed from the oppressive regime of Ceausescu upon the execution of that leader.

The credit for toppling the government is usually given to the thousands who took part in the insurrection. But behind it all was the moral strength of one person who remained firm in his personal convictions about right and wrong—Laszlo Tokes, a minister. After a rough start, Jonah became a man who also confronted an unrighteous situation. The influence of one person can affect thousands, whether in modern Romania or ancient Nineveh.

B. LESSON BACKGROUND

This lesson continues immediately from the final verse of last week's lesson. The background is therefore the same and need not be repeated

---

DEVOTIONAL READING:
MATTHEW 9:9-13
BACKGROUND SCRIPTURE:
JONAH 3:10–4:11
PRINTED TEXT:
JONAH 3:10–4:11

LESSON AIMS

After participating in this lesson, each student will be able to:

1. Tell how Jonah reacted both to the Ninevites' repentance and to God's gracious response.

2. Draw parallels between Jonah's attitude and the attitude of some modern Christians.

3. Select and organize a group project that will cross cultural lines with the gospel.

KEY VERSE

[Jonah] prayed, . . . "O LORD, is this not what I said when I was still at home? That is why I was so quick to flee to Tarshish. I knew that you are a gracious and compassionate God, slow to anger and abounding in love, a God who relents from sending calamity." —Jonah 4:2

here. Instead, we offer some distinctive and interesting features about the prophet's life.

1. Jonah is the only prophet of the Old Testament known to attempt a sea-going excursion.

2. Jonah is the only prophet in the books of the Minor Prophets known to have delivered a prophecy outside of Israel. There are several instances of prophets in the books of the Major Prophets being away from Israel or Judah: Elijah went to Zarephath in Phoenicia (1 Kings 17:7-10); Elisha traveled to Damascus of Syria to anoint Hazael as Syria's next king (2 Kings 8:7); Jeremiah was taken by force to Egypt, where he delivered some of his last prophecies (Jeremiah 43:7-13); and both Daniel and Ezekiel carried out their prophetic careers in Babylon.

3. None of the other prophets in the books of the Minor Prophets rebelled against God and attempted to flee.

4. The book of Jonah is primarily a narrative. It is not a collection of prophecies.

5. The other books of the Minor Prophets do not record any miracles that directly involved the prophets.

6. The fact that Jonah was a prophet from *northern* Israel was conveniently overlooked in the response to Nicodemus's procedural question in John 7:50-52.

7. Jonah is the only minor prophet who was mentioned by Jesus, as a sign for a wicked and adulterous generation (Matthew 12:39, 40). Zechariah was also cited by Jesus (Luke 11:51), but not everyone agrees that that man was one of the minor prophets, for there are about 30 people in the Old Testament with that name.

I. REPRIEVE FOR NINEVEH (JONAH 3:10)

A. GOD SEES (v. 10a)

10a. When God saw what they did and how they turned from their evil ways,

Righteousness exalts a nation" (Proverbs 14:34), as long as that righteousness is genuine. Nothing escapes God's awareness, and he can see that the repentance of the Ninevites is real in that they turn *from their evil ways.*

This does not mean that the Ninevites are converted so as to serve only the God of Israel. They still worship Assur, their god of war. But these people are responding to what they know, and right living by any nation is pleasing to God.

There are questions about this event that have no answers. Why does God send Jonah to Nineveh and not to other cities? Is it because he knows there will be a repentance, or that Nineveh has the greater need, or both? We don't know. Neither is given the duration of the penitent attitude in Nineveh. National repentance in the nation of Judah lasts only as long as the king provides leadership for it. A primary example is the spiritual reformation of Josiah, beginning about 632 BC (see 2 Chronicles 34, 35).

What about personal repentance? How long does it last? One observer said that personal repentance lasts about two months. Then Satan employs the old temptations again, and it takes real effort to continue in the righteousness that God desires.

B. GOD SPARES (v. 10b)

10b. . . . he had compassion and did not bring upon them the destruction he had threatened.

The Ninevite repentance has a heavenly effect, and the *destruction* God *had threatened* is averted. Approximately a century later, in roughly 650 BC, the prophet Nahum will prophesy doom for Nineveh. That city will be destroyed totally by the Medes and the forces of Babylon (which happens in 612 BC). In the meantime, God has plans for Assyria and its capital of Nineveh to destroy the nation of Israel (which happens in 722 BC, perhaps 40 years or so after Jonah prophesies). So the time for Nineveh's overthrow is deferred.

II. REPROOFS FOR JONAH (JONAH 4:1-11)
A. PETTINESS (vv. 1-4)
1. But Jonah was greatly displeased and became angry.

Jonah's response to the repentance of the people of Nineveh is not how a preacher should react! He is *angry*, extremely angry. The last phrase literally is "it burned to him." James 1:20 says that human anger does not produce the righteous life that God desires. Jonah's reaction illustrates that principle.

Perhaps *Jonah* realizes that his own nation also needs to repent. He would rather preach there, but in his heart he may suspect that he will not have success among his own people. Several years after Jonah's time, Amos will come from Judah to Israel (where Jonah is from) to preach a message of repentance. His preaching will indeed have results: he will be told to go home (Amos 7:12)!

2. He prayed to the LORD, "O LORD, is this not what I said when I was still at home? That is why I was so quick to flee to Tarshish. I knew that you are a gracious and compassionate God, slow to anger and abounding in love, a God who relents from sending calamity.

Jonah's reaction is to channel his anger into a prayer that is more demanding than submissive. His prayer is not to overcome his anger, but to scold *God* for having sent him to Nineveh. Jonah gives an eloquent description of some of God's attributes—he is *gracious* and *slow to anger*. He recalls that while he was still in Israel, even prior to his frustrated flight to *Tarshish*, he had predicted that God would not fulfill the promised destruction.

It is important to understand that repentance is the conditional element that causes the prophecy of destruction to be averted. When the people repent, they are spared. This repentance is used by Jesus to challenge people many centuries later (Luke 11:32). Jonah, however, does have one prophecy fulfilled in addition to his prophecy of success for Jeroboam II back in Israel (2 Kings 14:23-27). In Jonah 1:12 he had said that if the sailors would throw him into the sea, it would become calm. They did, and it did.

3. "Now, O LORD, take away my life, for it is better for me to die than to live."

Jonah is exasperated. He is aware of God's kindness, but in his heart he wants to see this foreign city brought to an end. He is despondent and disappointed to the point that he says *it is better . . . to die than to live.* Not long before this, his own *life* had been in jeopardy. From inside the fish he had prayed to live and to see again God's holy temple (Jonah 2:4). He had been spared, but now he does not want the same blessing for others. His strange inconsistencies are hard to understand—as are the lives and thoughts of many others.

4. But the LORD replied, "Have you any right to be angry?"

The Lord responds with just three words in the Hebrew. The purpose is to begin an attitude adjustment for Jonah. The question we see here demands a

---

WHAT DO YOU THINK?

What do Jonah's strong emotional responses in Jonah 4:1, 3, 6, 8, 9 say about his level of spiritual maturity? How do we learn from Jonah in this regard?

WHAT DO YOU THINK?

How does Jonah's mind-set reflect the outlook of modern thinking? What do we learn from this parallel?

WHAT DO YOU THINK?

Two times (vv. 6, 9) God questions Jonah about the appropriateness of his anger. What are some justifiable, righteous occasions for anger?

[Make sure to consider Matthew 21:12, 13 and James 1:20 in your answer.]

genuine introspection, a self-examination of the heart. Jonah knows that he has no real justification for his attitude, but his anger becomes his defense mechanism. People who know that they are in the wrong frequently resort to anger or a temper tantrum. Pride keeps them from the blessing of acknowledging guilt so as to be forgiven.

The question about being *angry* is good for all of us to consider. Is anger ever justifiable? Anger can be a very toxic emotion, and the Bible has a lot to say about it (Proverbs 29:22; Colossians 3:8; etc.). Since Jesus became angry (Mark 3:5), we cannot say that anger is a sin in and of itself. The reason for and result of the anger are important to consider.

BLOWING YOUR TOP

Do you ever find yourself lashing out when others provoke or insult you? Do you ever commit a case of road rage that you later regret? Those kinds of reactions are easy to recognize as anger.

But anger may take a subtler form, such as doing a "slow burn" when things don't go our way. Anger creates problems with other people (as above), but it can also be self-destructive when it gets turned inward. When that happens, anger becomes a churning cauldron lying just beneath the surface of our seemingly cool exterior. Ancient Christian thinkers were so concerned with the problem of anger (or "wrath" in the traditional terminology) that they included it in the classic list of seven deadly sins.

Jonah "blew his top" because God didn't meet Jonah's expectations. In that light we may fairly say that Jonah's anger was more about him than it was about God. Human nature hasn't changed much, has it? —C. R. B.

B. PROTECTION (vv. 5-8)

5. Jonah went out and sat down at a place east of the city. There he made himself a shelter, sat in its shade and waited to see what would happen to the city.

The previous verses treat Jonah's emotional responses to the repentance of the population of Nineveh. In our next section, God uses objects to provide further instruction for Jonah. They center on things that Jonah values highly in his situation. He is about to learn that things do have value, but to have anger about them is indefensible.

A few years ago, news items from Iraq sometimes mentioned the town of Mosul, which is located on the western side of the Tigris River. The city of Nineveh in Jonah's day is located across that river on a large plain. It is likely that *Jonah* makes his exit through the Shamash Gate in the southeastern sector, the most important gate of the city. It is conjectured that he finds a mound at a reasonable distance from *the city* where he can wait to *see what* will transpire at the end of the 40-day period (Jonah 3:4).

So Jonah makes some kind of a hut, and this provides protection from the sun. He may use a combination of branches and stones, depending on what is available. Perhaps he has been offered accommodations within the city, but he chooses to be by himself. It is more difficult to sulk and reinforce anger when others are present. Food and drink may be provided by Nineveh's citizens or by purchases that Jonah has made.

6. Then the LORD God provided a vine and made it grow up over Jonah to give shade for his head to ease his discomfort, and Jonah was very happy about the vine.

HOW TO SAY IT

Babylon. BAB-uh-lun.
Bucharest. BU-kuh-rest.
Hazael. HAZ-zay-el.
Jeroboam. Jair-uh-BOE-um.
Jonah. JO-nuh.
Josiah. Jo-SIGH-uh.
Nicolae Ceausescu. NIH-ko-lie Chow-SHES-ku.
Nineveh. NIN-uh-vuh.
Ninevites. NIN-uh-vites.
Phoenicia. Fuh-NISH-uh.
Syria. SEAR-ee-uh.
Zarephath. ZAIR-uh-fath.

The Lord is in the business of providing. The Hebrew word given as *provided* in Jonah 1:17 is used four times in the book. The four items that God prepares or provides are a fish, a plant, a worm, and a wind. This time it is the plant. This is usually thought to be a castor-oil plant, for it grows rapidly to a height of eight feet or more. It has large leaves, each about one foot in diameter. In verse 10 God states that the plant comes up in one night, so the plant's growth appears to be providential.

The plant serves as a *shade*, probably in addition to what *Jonah* has made. Although Jonah is *very happy* with his blessings from God, Jonah has problems when others receive blessings. Love for enemies is not in Jonah's mind (compare Matthew 5:44). God's teaching about love for enemies predates Jonah (see Exodus 23:4, 5; Proverbs 25:21), so Jonah is without excuse.

7. But at dawn the next day God provided a worm, which chewed the vine so that it withered.

One preacher has a sermon entitled "Jonah and the Worm." The title catches your attention, for mentally it is contrasted with the popular expression of "Jonah and the whale." (The word *whale* comes from Matthew 12:40 in the *King James Version*.) God first used a sea creature to correct Jonah's attitude about making the journey to preach in Nineveh. Now God uses a *worm* to correct Jonah's attitude about something else.

The worm does what it is designed to do: it chews the *vine*, which withers. Castor-oil plants (if that is what this is) wilt very quickly if a stalk is injured. Jonah's extra protection from the heat of the sun comes to an end.

8. When the sun rose, God provided a scorching east wind, and the sun blazed on Jonah's head so that he grew faint. He wanted to die, and said, "It would be better for me to die than to live."

The morning *sun* is accompanied by an *east wind* that brings heat from the desert. The absence of adequate shade and the presence of wind and sun combine to cause Jonah to become dizzy or light-headed. In his physical discomfort he temporarily forgets his anger, and he expresses a desire *to die*. He is convinced that death is better than living. He is miserable, far from home, and totally frustrated.

C. PRONOUNCEMENTS (vv. 9-11)

9a. But God said to Jonah, "Do you have a right to be angry about the vine?"

God is not through with lessons for *Jonah* to learn. God begins his statements to Jonah with a question that is designed to help Jonah think correctly. To be so upset about a plant shows an immaturity no one should have, least of all a prophet of God.

9b. "I do," he said. "I am angry enough to die."

Jonah continues his petty, defensive attitude and comments. He makes the bold assertion that his anger is justified. He tries to strengthen his statement by affirming that it would be better for his life to end. God can use people who have deep emotion, but emotion must be balanced with reason and self-control.

10. But the LORD said, "You have been concerned about this vine, though you did not tend it or make it grow. It sprang up overnight and died overnight.

The Lord's previous question is designed to cause Jonah to begin to soften and change his mind (which is the heart of repentance) and to have correct thoughts about others who are created in the image of God. God now makes

WHAT DO YOU THINK?

How can a focus on personal comfort interfere with the church's evangelistic efforts? What corrective action can we implement?

[Paul's situation in 2 Corinthians 11:25-27 should be part of your answer.]

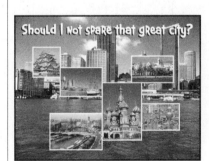

Visual for Lesson 2. *Use this visual to introduce a time of prayer. Point to it as you ask, "What great city does God want us to pray for today?*

PRAYER

Lord, as we tell our community about the righteousness that you can provide, may our attitudes attract others to the message. We pray in Jesus' name. Amen.

WHAT DO YOU THINK?

In what ways does God's affirmation about "many cattle" agree and disagree with the passions given (or not given) to human rights and animal rights today?

statements that continue in this same vein. The statements are designed to make Jonah see how petty and small his actions, attitudes, and pronouncements really are. Jonah is reminded about his extreme, inexcusable reactions over the loss of a plant. The plant is not the result of any labor or effort on his part. He has no valid entitlement to it.

11. "But Nineveh has more than a hundred and twenty thousand people who cannot tell their right hand from their left, and many cattle as well. Should I not be concerned about that great city?"

The Lord asks a final question as a challenge to Jonah. The emphasis changes from a plant to people. The answer to the Lord's question is unstated but obvious nonetheless: people are more important than plants.

The number 120,000 has two interpretations. One proposal is that this refers to children who have not yet learned the difference between *right* and *left*. Under this idea, the total population of the city is more than 500,000, counting adults. An alternative view is that the number has a spiritual dimension—that the entire population of the city is 120,000 and that spiritually they do not know right from left. This idea accords well with an event that took place a century before Jonah when another king of Assyria invited the entire population of a city to a feast—all 69,000 of them. That city was about half the size of Nineveh.

The reference to *cattle* in the final verse of the lesson is often overlooked. Here God demonstrates a concern for the domesticated animals that are part of the city of Nineveh. Throughout history, such animals have been part of communities of agrarian cultures. They are counted as more valuable than plants, and Jonah's concern for the plant is a contrast to the norm. Jonah has had prophetic experiences with two types of animal life (the fish and the worm), and now he is reminded of the value of domestic animals.

The fact that God gives this as another reason for not destroying Nineveh shows that a slaughter of animals without purpose is not in God's plan. Remember that animals were covered with sackcloth in Jonah 3:8. God's original dominion mandate makes clear that plants and animals are for the benefit of humanity, not the opposite (Genesis 1:28-30; compare Genesis 9:3, 4). It is our responsibility to apply principles of good stewardship in our use of the resources of God's creation. That responsibility especially includes our concern for taking the gospel to the lost. After all, people are the highest order of creation!

PRIORITIES

The creation narratives in Genesis place humans at the pinnacle of God's creative work. However, the slow and subtle rise of secularism in modern times has eroded humanity's sense of its uniqueness. We can see this in the silly response of a spokesperson for a famous "animal rights" organization to this question in an interview: "If a baby and a dog were in a boat and the boat capsized, which would you save first?" Her answer: "I don't know . . . it might depend if it's my baby or my dog, or my baby and someone else's dog."

Jonah's concern for the plant that had sheltered him and his lack of concern for the Ninevites indicated priorities that were out of whack. God tried to straighten out Jonah's priorities. He will try to straighten out our priorities as well.

And just to keep *our* perspective straight, we need to hear God's statement of concern for the animals of the city. God cares about *all* of his creation. We should too. But we need to prioritize our concerns to match the respective value God places on each part of it.

—C. R. B.

CONCLUSION

The Bible can be an uncomfortable book to read! This is especially true in those places where we see problems of human nature and realize that we are looking in a mirror at our own reflection. When we look at Jonah, do we see ourselves? If we do, what will we do about it?

THOUGHT TO REMEMBER
Learn from Jonah's mistakes.

Discovery Learning

The following is an alternative lesson plan emphasizing learning activities.
Classes desiring such student involvement will find these suggestions helpful. At the
back of this book are reproducible student pages to further enhance activity learning.

INTO THE LESSON

Before class, mount on the wall a large poster bearing the title *People of Significant Influence*. In larger classes, have two or more identical posters available. As learners enter the classroom, ask them to write the name of someone who has influenced thousands of people. (Make sure the posters are thick enough so that ink doesn't bleed through onto the wall.)

Begin the class with a quick review of the names on the poster(s). Mention the diversity of influence that could be on the list, including heroes, researchers, inventors, criminals, politicians, etc.

Next, ask for the names of individuals who have influenced large numbers of people for the Lord. Write these names on the board. You may need to "seed" the list by mentioning one or two famous evangelists, such as Billy Graham.

Make the transition to Bible study by saying, "Every one of these godly leaders was probably very excited when people responded to the gospel message of repentance and forgiveness. However, there was one preacher in history who was very displeased when his audience repented. In fact, he even scolded God for the outcome. We're going to discover he was in for an attitude adjustment! This adjustment should influence our own thinking and values."

INTO THE WORD

Distribute handouts entitled *Excavating Facts and Searching for Values*. Include the following instructions on the handout: "Dig out the facts of today's lesson from Jonah's preaching and experience by reading Jonah 3:10; 4:1-11. Then list your answers to the following questions about the events and lessons to be learned from Jonah's experience." (*Options*: This can be a whole-class exercise as you work through each question, or you can use study teams or study pairs.)

1. The Ninevites repented and turned from their evil ways at Jonah's preaching. What does this tell you about effective and ineffective methods in reaching another culture with the gospel? 2. God relented and did not destroy the city of Nineveh. Is that something you would expect of God? Why, or why not? 3. How does God's response to Nineveh encourage you personally? 4. Jonah and the Lord had different reactions to Nineveh's repentance. What is your reaction to the displeasure that Jonah expressed in his prayer? 5. Why do you think Jonah said he would rather die than live after his experience? What does this tell you about Jonah's view of Nineveh's people? 6. When Jonah was waiting to see what would happen to the city of Nineveh, God prepared three items. What did he provide, and what was the lesson God taught through each? 7. What was the attitude adjustment God sought for Jonah? 8. If the traditional view that Jonah himself wrote this book is true, what does this tell you about his character in being willing to write all this down? Would you be willing to write a book about your own embarrassing and sinful shortcomings?

Allow a few class members to share responses to each question.

INTO LIFE

Use the following discussion questions to help make the lesson personal: 1. Jonah's response to Nineveh's repentance was not the expected response of a prophet. However, his response and God's reactions may give us lessons that are sometimes hard to learn. What do you think is the overall principle God is teaching through this event? *(valuing all people in spite of their backgrounds, etc.)* 2. What other lessons do you discover for life in this passage? *(being obedient even when we question God's way; the power of preaching and teaching to bring about repentance; etc.)* 3. What does this event teach us about the challenges of cross-cultural witnessing? *(the need to overcome biases, etc.)* 4. What are some things we can do as a class to reach across cultural lines with the gospel? *(Create a leadership team for the project. Guide the class into organizing one of the projects discussed.)*

Option 1: Ask your students to identify personal attitude corrections they need to make. They will do this by creating an acrostic with words that may be helpful in making their attitude adjustments. Display the word *CULTURE* vertically on a poster with one letter completed such as Understand or tRy. Allow a time of sharing. *Option 2:* Ask volunteers to present the skit on page 373.

FAMILY AS COMMUNITY
LESSON 3

INTRODUCTION

A. FAMINE AND FAITH

It was the early part of the twentieth century. A family in one U.S. county heard that a family in an adjacent county had the same last name. Those who had seen both groups said that members of the two families resembled one another. Curiosity grew, and the time came when a trip was made to see if the families were related.

As the two families engaged in conversations and compared information, they discovered that they were rather closely related. Shortly after America's Civil War, a young married man living in the hills of an eastern state decided to move to a place with more opportunity, for there was no available land where he lived. The couple bade farewell to their respective families and started west. They never expected to return to their place of origin. The emotions of such a transition in that era are described by one author this way: "A departure to a distant land, with its last farewells to beloved friends and familiar scenes, has in it much of the bitterness of death."

A few months later, a young brother who had recently married made the same decision. It was a coincidence, but the two brothers settled in neighboring counties in the same state. Many years passed before their descendants found each other and experienced the joy of discovering relatives they did not know existed.

History shows that families move for three primary reasons: fortune, faith, and famine (or food). The faith factor may be seen when a couple or an individual decides to take the gospel to a foreign land. Today the trauma of separation is not as great as in the past. The communication and transportation methods that now exist tend to nullify some of the stresses of separation.

The lesson for today is about a family that moved because of famine. But it becomes evident that faith in God was a vital part of the family's orientation; thus there was an issue of faith as well. The lesson begins in Bethlehem, and the Lord will bring people together who will become ancestors of David and ultimately of Jesus.

B. LESSON BACKGROUND

Today's text from Ruth comes from one of the two books of the Bible named for women. (The other is the book of Esther.) The date for the events in the book of Ruth is uncertain. David was the great-grandson of Ruth, and he became king over Judah about 1010 BC, then over the entire nation of Israel in 1003 BC. The primary account in Ruth can therefore be no later than 1100 BC, and it may be earlier.

The author of the book is not given. Jewish tradition ascribes it to Samuel, who had anointed David as the king to follow Saul on the throne (1 Samuel 16:1-13). Samuel died before David became the king, so it is sometimes

DEVOTIONAL READING:
JOHN 20:24-29
BACKGROUND SCRIPTURE:
RUTH 1:1-16
PRINTED TEXT:
RUTH 1:1-9, 14b-16

Mar 21

LESSON AIMS

After participating in this lesson, each student will be able to:

1. Describe the circumstances of the move of Naomi and her family to Moab and the return to Bethlehem.

2. Suggest several factors that can influence someone to make a dramatic break with the past, as Ruth did.

3. Write a plan for evangelism in the community utilizing the factors identified in aim #2 as contact points.

KEY VERSE

Ruth replied, "Don't urge me to leave you or to turn back from you. Where you go I will go, and where you stay I will stay. Your people will be my people and your God my God." —Ruth 1:16

LESSON 3 NOTES

HOW TO SAY IT

Bethlehem. BETH-lih-hem.
Chemosh. KEE-mosh.
Elimelech. Ee-LIM-eh-leck.
Ephrath. EF-rath.
Ephrathites. EF-ruh-thites.
Kilion. KIL-ee-on.
Mahlon. MAH-lon.
Mesha. ME-shuh.
Micah. MY-kuh.
Moabite. MO-ub-ite.
Naphtali. NAF-tuh-lye.

WHAT DO YOU THINK?

What do individuals and families lose when they move? What is the church's ministry in these situations?

thought that a person such as Nathan, a prophet who was prominent in David's life, may have written the book. Solomon is not mentioned, and that is significant in this regard (allowing for cautions of using an argument from silence).

The book of Ruth is considered one of the finest literary works in all of ancient literature. There is drama in each chapter, and the lesson for today is from chapter one.

I. CHALLENGES FOR A FAMILY (RUTH 1:1-5)
A. DECISION TO MOVE (vv. 1, 2)
1a. In the days when the judges ruled, there was a famine in the land,

The first phrases of the book give the historical background. An entire book of the Old Testament is dedicated to the period of *the days* of *the judges,* meaning about 1375–1050 BC. In this time frame, God raises up people called *judges,* who are military deliverers or magistrates. God allows times of suffering or oppression to come on the Israelites when they sin. When repentance takes place, God rescues his people by using one of the judges as a military deliverer. A period of peace follows, and the cycle starts again.

The time frame in view here is narrowed to an occasion when there is *a famine.* Famines are usually caused by lack of rain, the presence of insects (such as a locust invasion), or the fact that oppressing nations rob the people after the harvest is complete. Famine is one of the judgments that God promises if the people of Israel do not comply with the terms of the covenant (Deuteronomy 28, especially verse 24). It seems likely that this time the cause of the famine is drought-related.

1b. . . . and a man from Bethlehem in Judah, together with his wife and two sons, went to live for a while in the country of Moab.

Geographic locations are given, and in the centuries ahead *Bethlehem* will become prominent as the hometown of David. This village is first mentioned in the Bible as being near the site where Rachel died when she gave birth to Benjamin, the twelfth son of Jacob (Genesis 35:19). The town will be cited later in Micah 5:2 as the place where the Messiah will be born.

This account is more than just a time, a tragedy, and a town. It is about people who live in that time, in that town, and who experience the tragedy of a famine. It is about a *man, his wife, and* their *two sons.* In the midst of these circumstances the father makes a major decision: they will move to *the country of Moab.* The word *Bethlehem* means "house of bread," and it is ironic that the family feels compelled to move to Moab to have bread.

On a clear day the hills of Moab are visible from Bethlehem when a person looks to the east across the Dead Sea. The journey to reach Moab involves going toward Jericho and crossing the Jordan River just before it empties into the Dead Sea. That is the lowest point on the planet that is not covered by the ocean. It is about 1,380 feet below sea level at the north end (as of 2007, with the water level dropping about 3 feet per year). The climb to Moab then begins.

2. The man's name was Elimelech, his wife's name Naomi, and the names of his two sons were Mahlon and Kilion. They were Ephrathites from Bethlehem, Judah. And they went to Moab and lived there.

Personal names in biblical times are often significant in their meaning. The name *Elimelech* means "my God is king." *Naomi* means "pleasant." The son who will marry Ruth (Ruth 4:10) is *Mahlon,* meaning "weak." His brother is *Kilion,* or "pining." The latter two names suggest physical weaknesses. The decision to move and the health of the brothers may be related factors. To move from a place that had been assigned to an ancestor is difficult, but parents will make such sacrifices for their children.

The entire family is designated as *Ephrathites.* Ephrath seems to have been a former name for *Bethlehem* (again, Genesis 35:19). The word *Judah* is added to the designation to distinguish it from another Bethlehem that is in the northern tribe of Naphtali (Joshua 19:15, 16).

B. DEATH OF A FATHER (v. 3)

3. Now Elimelech, Naomi's husband, died, and she was left with her two sons.

Naomi has already experienced the emotions prompted by moving to another land. Now she has the grief that is associated with the loss of her *husband.* She and *her two sons* have to bury their loved one in a foreign country instead of the familiar environs of Bethlehem.

C. DECISIONS TO MARRY (v. 4)

4. They married Moabite women, one named Orpah and the other Ruth. After they had lived there about ten years,

The choice of a spouse is very important. One of the deciding factors for the Israelite brothers should be the god or gods whom the young *women* worship. The brothers may know that it was *Moabite women* who had seduced some Israelite men into false worship when the Israelites were waiting to cross the Jordan River (Numbers 25:1-5), but it is possible that they feel they have converted their prospective brides. Several hundred years later (about 450 BC), Ezra will demonstrate very strong reactions when he learns that Israelite men have married women of Moab and other nations (Ezra 9:1-3). The attendant circumstances at that time may be different from what is described here.

The fact that the family remains in Moab *about ten years* indicates that they have become relatively comfortable there. Apparently there is no serious thought about returning to Bethlehem.

D. DEATHS OF THE SONS (v. 5)

5. . . . both Mahlon and Kilion also died, and Naomi was left without her two sons and her husband.

In the culture of the time, it is usually essential for a woman to have a *husband* to provide for physical necessities. Naomi has become dependent on her *sons* after her husband's death, but the deaths of the sons place all three women in difficulty. They are without husbands to provide support and protection.

Ancient Jewish interpretations of these events suggest that the deaths of the father and his sons are a divine punishment for their leaving Bethlehem and for their lack of trust that God would provide. These thoughts are not mentioned in the biblical text, so to suggest such is speculation.

II. CHOICES IN A FAMILY (RUTH 1:6-9, 14b-16)

A. NAOMI'S DECISIONS (vv. 6-9)

6. When she heard in Moab that the LORD had come to the aid of his people by providing food for them, Naomi and her daughters-in-law prepared to return home from there.

DAILY BIBLE READINGS

Monday, Mar. 15—A Shared Experience (John 20:24-29)

Tuesday, Mar. 16—A Shared Reward (1 Samuel 30:21-31)

Wednesday, Mar. 17—A Shared Advantage (Luke 3: 10-14)

Thursday, Mar. 18—A Shared Oath (1 Samuel 20: 30-42)

Friday, Mar. 19—A Shared Responsibility (Romans 14:13-21)

Saturday, Mar. 20—A Shared Love (John 15:9-17)

Sunday, Mar. 21—A Shared Faith (Ruth 1:1-9, 14b-16)

What Do You Think?

What are some godly things to do when circumstances go from bad to worse?

Naomi becomes aware (perhaps from traveling merchants) that there is *food* back in her homeland. Bethlehem, the "house of *bread*," has been blessed by *the Lord*. She decides that she can now *return* to the familiar surroundings she had left a decade earlier. When things are not going well, there is no place like *home* to find comfort.

It is interesting that the three women have remained together thus far. Their mutual losses and sorrows perhaps have helped them work through their situations. But now Naomi is suggesting a change that jars the comfort level of the young women. Naomi wants to go home—back to Bethlehem.

It has been suggested that this book of the Bible could be called *The Book of Naomi,* for it is at this point that she becomes the leader who makes plans for herself and others. She has the lead in the recorded conversations. Every social unit needs someone to rise to the top to give purpose and direction for those involved.

7. With her two daughters-in-law she left the place where she had been living and set out on the road that would take them back to the land of Judah.

The initial indication is that the three women want to stay together. The common bond they have forged in their shared grief is very strong. But to leave Moab will take them away from the place where they experienced grief, and sometimes that is good therapy. The process of packing their few possessions will provide an opportunity to think about what they are doing. Do they really want to leave Moab, or is this decision made in haste?

When There's No Choice but to Move

Statistics from www.moving.com indicate that among the U.S. population people move about 12 times in their lifetimes. About 1 in 4 adults in the U.S. will move each year. Moving is one of the most stressful events in life.

People move both voluntarily and involuntarily. Voluntary moves result from getting married, finding a new job, or simply desiring to live in a different neighborhood. Involuntary moves may result from mortgage foreclosure, health problems, and natural disasters. Naomi's move was involuntary. She found herself in a foreign country without sufficient means of support. At that time and in that culture, the only recourse she could see was to move back to Judah to be with her extended family. Survival was at stake.

How would Naomi be received when she showed up? That's a question that's relevant yet today. Perhaps you will have a relative who needs to move in with you. Perhaps your church has members who are facing the stress of an involuntary move (either arriving or departing). What will be your attitude when this ministry opportunity presents itself?   —C. R. B.

8. Then Naomi said to her two daughters-in-law, "Go back, each of you, to your mother's home. May the Lord show kindness to you, as you have shown to your dead and to me.

Naomi is genuinely grateful for the loyalty that her *two daughters-in-law* have for her. But she concludes that it will be best for them to remain in their native Moab. She therefore directs them to stay. This is the first of four such statements by Naomi. She can add that being a childless widow in Judah may be a stigma in being able to marry again, since barrenness is associated with women, not men.

Naomi's request that *each* daughter-in-law *go* to her respective *mother's home* may seem strange, especially in view of the fact that Ruth's father is later said to be alive (Ruth 2:11). It is sometimes said that widows are to go to the house of the father (Genesis 38:11; Leviticus 22:13). But when Rebekah first met Abraham's servant, she went to her mother's house (Genesis 24:28). Naomi knows the background of each daughter-in-law, and she makes the appropriate recommendation.

9. "May the LORD grant that each of you will find rest in the home of another husband."

Then she kissed them and they wept aloud.

This is often said to be the key verse of the book—Naomi's desire that Ruth and Orpah *find rest* through remarriages that will relieve them from the anxieties and stresses of being widowed. The three women have been through much together, but Naomi is persuaded that what she is recommending is best. The kisses of separation are routine, but the weeping *aloud* shows the closeness that has developed.

B. RUTH'S DEVOTION (v. 14b)

14b. Then Orpah kissed her mother-in-law good-by, but Ruth clung to her.

Orpah accepts the suggestion of Naomi, but *Ruth* demonstrates that she is at a different level. It may be that she feels an obligation to her deceased husband and that she chooses to show loyalty to him by caring for his mother. We may conjecture that Mahlon was the second son to die, and that in his final days his concern for his mother was recognized by Ruth. Thus she may have pledged to him that she will care for Naomi.

So Ruth clings to Naomi. Her concern for the older widow is in keeping with what is described as the pure religion that God recognizes (James 1:27). Ruth, however, has additional motivation, and that is given in the final words of today's printed text.

C. NAOMI'S DISSENT (v. 15)

15. "Look," said Naomi, "your sister-in-law is going back to her people and her gods. Go back with her."

Naomi urges Ruth to imitate the example of Orpah, and two very strong appeals are used: family (*her people*) and faith (*her gods*). The primary god of the Moabites is Chemosh (see Numbers 21:29; 1 Kings 11:7). But it is customary for people to worship the gods of neighboring nations also—just to be sure that they do not offend any of the gods. The famous Moabite Stone of about 850 BC tells of the revolt of Mesha, king of Moab, against Israel (see 2 Kings 3:4, 5). It refers to Chemosh several times, and it states that Moab had become subservient to Israel because Chemosh was offended.

It is somewhat strange that Naomi is willing to make the trip to Bethlehem by herself, but she is doing what she thinks is best. It may be that she is not aware of Ruth's inner feelings or commitments. Naomi's decision undoubtedly is colored by her grief and perhaps even depression. A return to Bethlehem offers the promise not only of physical sustenance but also emotional support.

D. RUTH'S DECLARATION (v. 16)

16. But Ruth replied, "Don't urge me to leave you or to turn back from you. Where you go I will go, and where you stay I will stay. Your people will be my people and your God my God."

WHAT DO YOU THINK?

Was Naomi's counsel to "go back" good advice or bad advice? Why? How do we go about rejecting bad advice when it comes from someone who is sincere and well-meaning?

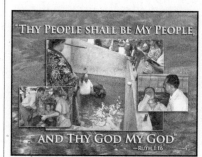

Visual for Lesson 3. *You can use this visual to introduce either question on page 288.*

WHAT DO YOU THINK?

What does Ruth's affirmation to Naomi say about the right reasons for being committed to another person?

WHAT DO YOU THINK?

In what ways does Ruth's break with her past life parallel the decision we make when we accept Christ as Savior and Lord?

PRAYER

Heavenly Father, thank you for the example of faith in the choices of Ruth. May her example help us in the choices that we make today as we walk in the way that leads to eternal life. We pray in the name of Jesus. Amen.

Ruth's statement is one of the most beautiful expressions of devotion in all literature. It begins with a response to the fact that Naomi has given four separate exhortations to her daughters-in-law to return to their own people and their gods (1:8, 11, 12, 15).

Ruth affirms her commitment to be with Naomi, and it is evident that she esteems her mother-in-law very highly. Negative jokes are sometimes made about mothers-in-law, but this has no place in Ruth's mind. Ruth and Naomi shared a mutual grief when Mahlon died. The strength, beauty, and power of Ruth's declaration have their foundations in both family and faith.

The determination of Ruth is especially revealed in verse 17, which is not part of today's lesson text. There Ruth makes a pledge that only death will separate her from Naomi. Ruth binds the statement with an oath that a judgment from God on her should result if she goes back on what she has just said. This is what proves beyond all doubt that Ruth really means what she says. Naomi no longer protests the decision of this devoted young woman. They will make their sojourn to Bethlehem together. They do not know the future, but they will have each other and God to strengthen them.

TREASURED WORDS

Some of the most poignant, enduring words ever spoken in American history are found in Abraham Lincoln's Gettysburg Address. The address was given on November 19, 1863, at the dedication of a cemetery on the site of one of the bloodiest battles of the American Civil War. Fought in July of that year, the Battle of Gettysburg resulted in upwards of 51,000 soldiers from both sides being dead, wounded, or missing.

Edward Everett, widely known as an eloquent orator, was the main speaker. He spoke for two hours, but few today know what he said. Lincoln spoke for two minutes, but his words became timeless. The speech reshaped the thinking of the nation regarding the nature and purpose of that violent conflict. (Some propose that Lincoln, in effect, rewrote the U.S. Constitution with his speech.) Lincoln gave meaning to the carnage as he spoke of the cause in which the dead "gave the last full measure of devotion."

Ruth's words of commitment to Naomi have also become treasured, at least among those who are biblically literate. There is a sense in which Ruth was "dying"—she was abandoning her culture and homeland for Naomi's. If there ever was a "full measure of devotion," that was it! Should our devotion to Christ be any less?

—C. R. B.

CONCLUSION

A college student said that when he was young, his grandmother often influenced him to do what was right. After she died, he had the idea that she was in Heaven watching him from that vantage point. He did not want to disappoint his grandmother, so he tried to do the right thing.

It is a certainty that the lives of Christians are under scrutiny. In some cases this is a good thing, for others want to know if a person's faith is genuine. They want to know if the Christian's example will show how to handle the tough situations or special trials that are a part of life.

Sometimes, however, there are those who actually want the believer to do what is wrong. This provides an opportunity to throw the *hypocrite* label at Christians, or it is interpreted that the claims of Christ are of no significance in the person's life. In this lesson, Ruth is one who makes a right decision for the right reasons after observing her mother-in-law for a length of time.

How then shall we live? The answer is obvious: in a way that pleases God and sets good examples for others! Both he and they are watching.

Discovery Learning

The following is an alternative lesson plan emphasizing learning activities. Classes desiring such student involvement will find these suggestions helpful. At the back of this book are reproducible student pages to further enhance activity learning.

INTO THE LESSON

Brainstorming. Ask students to raise hands if they have moved to your community within the last 10 years. Ask why. Jot answers on the board. Also ask, "What were some of the difficulties or challenges in making the decision to move and in settling in to the new community?" Again, list responses on the board.

Say, "The writer of the lesson commentary thinks that history shows families move for three primary reasons: fortune, faith, or famine (food)." Explore agreements and disagreements for a few minutes. Then say, "Our study today is sensitive to one or more of these issues in a famous move."

Option: Have groups of four or five list "communities" they belong to and why they are loyal to them. These loyalties may be to a civic group, family, a veterans organization, etc. After a few minutes ask, "What would it take for you to break allegiance with a community you mentioned?" Invite responses within groups. Make the transition to Bible study saying, "We are going to look at people who made that tough decision to split a family and leave a country. Of particular importance will be the issue of faith."

INTO THE WORD

You will need three "reporters" that you have recruited during the week. Each will need a photocopy of the lesson commentary to prepare five-minute mini-lectures that examine the facts in the lesson's events. The second part of the Bible study will explore the implications for faith and life that surface through this story.

Reporter #1 will report on Elimelech's decision to move and the challenges his family faced (Ruth 1:1, 2). The outline for this topic will be A. *Lesson*

Background; B. The Decision to Move; C. The Family. Reporter #2 will outline the changes in the family after the relocation (Ruth 1:3-5). Points of the lecture should include A. *Elimelech's Death; B. Marriages; C. More Death.* Reporter #3 will look at the choices facing the three women who constituted the remaining family. The suggested outline is A. *Naomi's Choice; B. Choices of the Daughters-in-Law; C. Ruth's Devotion.*

After these reports, ask the following discussion questions or allow groups of four or five learners to discuss them: 1. Some have said that this book could be called *The Book of Naomi.* What does the suggestion imply or why might this be an appropriate title for the book? 2. What does verse 9 imply about the relationship of the three women? 3. What hints do you find in this story of Naomi's faith and God's provision for her? 4. Ruth's expression of devotion in verse 16 is one of the most beautiful sayings in literature. Why does it touch us so deeply? What are its lessons? 5. What lesson(s) do(es) the events in this story teach you about cross-cultural faith or sharing your faith across cultural lines?

Alternative: Use small groups to complete the reproducible activity "Tragedy, Faith, and Love" from page 374.

INTO LIFE

Activity #1: Opportunity Awareness. Form groups of four or five. Give each group a marker and poster board. Ask them to identify groups or "communities" to which they belong and put a symbol for each on the poster board (examples: include a school building, a logo for a civic club, three stick figures for a family). Then ask groups to identify at least one way to insert their faith in God into each setting. Do not have them report their findings to the class. Instead, make the transition to the next activity by saying, "We honor God when we are using opportunities to influence groups or communities for his will. Now I'm going to challenge each of us to do so."

Activity #2: Planning. Give each learner an index card. Say, "Pick one of the communities you identified and write a plan and prayer for evangelism in that group. Consider factors that might influence someone to make a dramatic break with the past, as Ruth did." Encourage students to commit to using godly principles of influence for groups with which he or she is affiliated. Have them identify a group by drawing a symbol for that group on the card. Suggest that learners put the card on a bathroom mirror for at least a month as a continual reminder.

Activity #3: Report. If the class initiated a cross-cultural project last Sunday, ask for an update or progress report from the leadership team.

Option: Use the reproducible activity "My New Bumper Sticker!" from page 374 as a substitute for one of the above.

ACCEPTANCE IN COMMUNITY

LESSON 4

INTRODUCTION

A. TAKE THE FIFTH!

The caption above is usually associated with criminal trials and investigations in which a defendant pleads the Fifth Amendment of the Constitution of the United States: "No person . . . shall be compelled to be a witness against himself." In certain legal settings, the use of the phrase "I plead the Fifth" makes us suspicious that the one being questioned has something to hide. The phrase was used often in the legal proceedings ensuing from the Enron scandal of a few years ago.

Most believers know that the first-named fruit of the Spirit in Galatians 5:22 is *love.* The fifth fruit in the list is *kindness,* which carries the connotation of being gentle. Each community and home would be a better place if more people would "take the fifth" fruit and resolve to conduct themselves with gentleness and kindness in their interactions.

Illustrations about the effects of such an attitude abound. They include accounts showing that people of esteem have demonstrated that they really do care. For example, presidents have visited military hospitals and have used their position to help others. I heard a story of a person who was ready to attack and probably kill someone who had just insulted him. Another person heard the verbal abuse, and he responded by kindly offering to help the insulted person in some way. This action brought a sudden stop to the anger that was building, and there was no physical attack.

I also heard a story of an Arab in Israel who saw an Israeli with car trouble, so he stopped to help. The Arab took the other man to an auto parts store where items for repair could be obtained. Later someone commented that he did not know that Arabs would help Jews. The Arab replied, "Oh, I'm a Christian, and I am compelled to help those in need." Christianity is about redemption in Christ, and it is also about the fruit of the Spirit.

B. LESSON BACKGROUND

Last week's lesson was from the first chapter of the book of Ruth. It focused on the family of Elimelech as it experienced famine, a move to a foreign land, marriages, and deaths. The emphasis shifted to the three women who survived, and the famous statement of devotion by Ruth was the concluding verse: that Ruth would be loyal to Naomi and to her God.

The two women successfully made the journey to Bethlehem. As today's lesson opens, they have arrived in early spring, just as the barley harvest was ready to begin (Ruth 1:22). This fact allowed Ruth to obtain food.

DEVOTIONAL READING:
ROMANS 12:9-18

BACKGROUND SCRIPTURE:
RUTH 2, 3

PRINTED TEXT:
RUTH 2:5-12; 3:9-11

Mar 28

LESSON AIMS

After participating in this lesson, each student will be able to:

1. Describe how Ruth and Boaz met and eventually married.

2. Tell how a person's character can sometimes break down the walls that otherwise prevent an "outsider" from finding acceptance.

3. State a commitment to living a life of virtue and noble character.

KEY VERSE

"And now, my daughter, don't be afraid. I will do for you all you ask. All my fellow townsmen know that you are a woman of noble character.
"   *—Ruth 3:11*

LESSON 4 NOTES

WHAT DO YOU THINK?

How does God's Old Testament plan for feeding the poor compare and contrast with modern efforts to care for the needy, in terms of governmental, church, and personal programs?

[Scriptures to consider include Leviticus 19:9, 10; 23:22; Deuteronomy 24:19-21; Proverbs 10:4; 12:27; 26:15; Ecclesiastes 10:18; Acts 6:1; 2 Thessalonians 3:11, 12; and 1 Timothy 5:3-16.]

WHAT DO YOU THINK?

In what circumstances today is it helpful and harmful to identify and characterize people by ethnic background and/or country of origin? Why?

WHAT DO YOU THINK?

Do your work habits commend you to your supervisors? How can you use Colossians 3:23 to improve in this area?

I. BOAZ NOTICES RUTH (RUTH 2:5-12)

The Lord's economic plan for the poor in ancient Israel is not welfare, but what has been termed "workfare." The Law of Moses states that the corners of the fields are not to be harvested, and any stalks of grain that are dropped are not to be retrieved; in this way the poor and the sojourner will have food to eat (Leviticus 19:9, 10; 23:22; Deuteronomy 24:19-21).

Fitting this category, Ruth takes the initiative in asking Naomi if she can go to the fields to glean (Ruth 2:2). Ruth ends up in the fields of "Boaz, who was from the clan of Elimelech" (2:3). Most students interpret this to be an act of God's providence in leading her to the right place to bring about a phase of God's redemptive plan.

A. DISCOVERING RUTH (v. 5)

5. Boaz asked the foreman of his harvesters, "Whose young woman is that?"

A second "happening" is that *Boaz* comes to the barley fields at the time that Ruth is present. This may be his regular custom if he is involved in all aspects of the harvesting process. He evidently wants to be acquainted personally with the workers in his fields. He immediately notices someone unfamiliar to him. Boaz is listed in three genealogical lists in the Bible: at the end of the book of Ruth, in 1 Chronicles 2:12, and in Matthew 1:5 as a part of Christ's genealogy.

B. DESCRIBING RUTH (vv. 6, 7)

6. The foreman replied, "She is the Moabitess who came back from Moab with Naomi.

The *foreman* of the harvesters has several responsibilities: to employ the workers, to pay them at the end of the day, and to ensure the availability of the basic supplies they need during the day. Some have suggested that these supervisors monitor the carefulness of the workers to make sure they are not leaving an excess amount behind—just in case a worker's family members are among the poor who are gleaning for themselves.

It is sometimes thought that a generous landowner will instruct his harvesters to be deliberately careless so that the poor may have enough to eat. Whatever the situation, the work supervisor determines Ruth's identity and why she is in the barley field.

7. "She said, 'Please let me glean and gather among the sheaves behind the harvesters.' She went into the field and has worked steadily from morning till now, except for a short rest in the shelter."

The foreman reports Ruth's request to Boaz. This enables Boaz to know why she is present. The arrival of Naomi and Ruth from Moab is common knowledge in Bethlehem. Boaz is now able to have personal contact with the young woman who has come with Naomi. There is a natural curiosity to know what type of person Ruth really is, so this prompts the foreman to observe her at work. Work habits are a good gauge of character for a society in which everyone is expected take part in making a living for the family.

The supervisor is able to give a good report about Ruth in this regard. The work involves a repetitive leaning over to pick up stalks of grain that the workers ahead of her fail to gather or accidentally drop. The work supervisor is aware that Ruth has taken one break from her work to rest in the small hut or tent that is provided. Such a mid-morning break is understandable.

C. PROVISIONS FOR RUTH (vv. 8, 9)

8. So Boaz said to Ruth, "My daughter, listen to me. Don't go and glean in another field and don't go away from here. Stay here with my servant girls.

The question and imperative by *Boaz* show his compassion. This time he has a special interest and concern for *Ruth* and Naomi, who are related to him through their marriages. The expression *my daughter* is usually thought to show that he is considerably older. Some Jewish traditions suggest that he is about age 80, but that idea cannot be verified by Scripture.

In the harvest procedure of the day, it is the men who go through the fields with their sickles. The technique probably is to hold the stalks with one hand while cutting with the other hand. The worker then drops that handful on the ground and advances for the next swath.

The *servant girls* may be the women who follow to collect the small clusters of stalks. One suggestion regarding ancient harvest methods is that the women take their accumulations to a central location to make stacks. The stacks are then transported to a threshing floor. There the stalks, husks, and chaff are separated from the grain. It is understandable that handling the stalks so many times results in some falling to the ground. They are not to be picked up or retrieved, for this is God's provision for the poor.

9. "Watch the field where the men are harvesting, and follow along after the girls. I have told the men not to touch you. And whenever you are thirsty, go and get a drink from the water jars the men have filled."

Boaz continues his special considerations to Ruth. If she needs a *drink* of water, she is given permission to help herself to what has been brought to the harvest field for his workers. The *water jars* are probably the usual water skins. Boaz's statement also indicates that he has *told* his *men* not to bother Ruth in any way. He advises her to work only in the fields where his workers are. Ruth 2:14 adds that Boaz invites Ruth to eat bread with him and the others. Bread is the normal staple of that society. It will not spoil or mold quickly, so it can be safely taken to the fields. It is often dipped in a vinegar wine, perhaps mixed with some olive oil. This softens the bread and gives it an extra flavor.

CARING FOR OTHERS

Fred "Hargy" Hargesheimer's plane was shot down over the Pacific Ocean on June 5, 1943. He parachuted into enemy territory in Papua New Guinea. Finding shelter in an abandoned native hut, he lived for weeks on snails he found in a riverbed. Daily he recited Psalm 23 and reflected on the hope his faith gave him.

Natives in the area found Hargesheimer after a month. They showed him a note written by an Australian soldier that said to trust them because they had saved other pilots. They were Christians, and at great risk they protected the American from capture by the enemy.

Eventually, Hargesheimer made his way off the island by submarine. Years later, while corresponding with a missionary, he discovered his native rescuers needed a school. He raised $15,000 for a school building and brought in volunteer teachers. A few years later he built a library and clinic. Then, 27 years after his rescue, he and his wife moved to the island "to say thank you in a meaningful way."

Fred Hargesheimer knew he had lived a blessed life, so he decided to return the blessing to those in greater need than he. Boaz lived a blessed life as a wealthy farmer. He decided to share his blessing with a poor, struggling widow and her mother-in-law. Details of such stories may vary, but the spirit is always the same: godly, blessed people genuinely care for others.   —C. R. B.

D. PERPLEXITY OF RUTH (v. 10)

10. At this, she bowed down with her face to the ground. She exclaimed, "Why have I found such favor in your eyes that you notice me—a foreigner?"

Ruth's responses to these kindnesses include bowing so that *her face is to the ground*. In this manner, she begins to express her gratitude to Boaz. Ruth does not understand why she, *a foreigner* who has come to Bethlehem only recently, should even be noticed.

Ruth's comments are normal for anyone who is in a new environment or situation, for she is concerned about acceptance or about what others are thinking. She probably has been introduced to the women who are old friends of Naomi. But to be in the grain fields with these men and women can cause some unease.

E. PERSPECTIVES ABOUT RUTH (vv. 11, 12)

11. Boaz replied, "I've been told all about what you have done for your mother-in-law since the death of your husband—how you left your father and mother and your homeland and came to live with a people you did not know before.

The statement by *Boaz* is a positive commentary on both Ruth and her *mother-in-law*, Naomi. A smaller, tight-knit community often takes a long time to evaluate a newcomer. Sometimes it may take almost a generation before acceptance finally occurs.

Naomi has risen above her personal losses. One result is her positive endorsement of daughter-in-law Ruth, who recently accompanied her from Moab. It is very likely that Naomi has told of Ruth's commitments (see Ruth 1:16-18). Ruth's willingness to leave Moab, her family, and her gods commends her highly in the eyes of the residents of Bethlehem.

12. "May the LORD repay you for what you have done. May you be richly rewarded by the LORD, the God of Israel, under whose wings you have come to take refuge."

Boaz continues his affirmation of Ruth by giving what is considered a prayer of blessing or a strong wish. He is confident that *the Lord* will reward Ruth for the personal sacrifices that she has made because of her love for her mother-in-law and for God. Boaz is pleased about Ruth's commitment to serve the *God of Israel*.

Boaz uses a very striking word picture in this regard—that of a young bird taking refuge *under* the *wings* of its mother. As a mother hen provides protection for her young, so Boaz desires God to bless and protect Ruth. This vivid figure of speech is a frequent way to show God's care. It is found in both the Old Testament (Psalm 17:8; 36:7; 57:1; 63:7) and the New Testament (Matthew 23:37; Luke 13:34).

II. BOAZ RESPECTS RUTH (RUTH 3:9-11)

When Ruth goes to the harvest that first morning, she likely has feelings of uncertainty about what will happen with the people in a place where she has never been. As she returns to Naomi that evening, she carries about two-thirds of a bushel of grain (Ruth 2:17). That is the equivalent of

How to Say It

Bethlehem. BETH-lih-hem.
Boaz. BO-az.
Deuteronomy.
     Due-ter-AHN-uh-me.
Elimelech. Ee-LIM-eh-leck.
levirate. LEH-vuh-rut.
Leviticus. Leh-VIT-ih-kus.
Moab. MO-ab.
Mosaic. Mo-ZAY-ik.
Naomi. Nay-OH-me.
Obed. O-bed.

several days' wages, and it is an amazing amount for gleaning in just one day. Ruth has much to say to Naomi about the kindnesses shown to her by Boaz.

In the intervening verses not in today's text, Naomi assumes the role of matchmaker. She knows that Boaz is more than just a relative of her deceased husband. According to the Mosaic law, Boaz can be a "redeemer." Such relatives assume the responsibilities of redeeming a family's land that has been sold, purchasing the freedom of a relative who has sold himself into servitude, being the avenger for a near relative who is murdered, and/or marrying a childless widow (Deuteronomy 25:5-10). The marriage under the latter concept is known as a *levirate marriage;* that is from the Latin word *levir,* meaning "husband's brother." The barley and wheat harvests are almost complete, and the marriage proposal is about to take place.

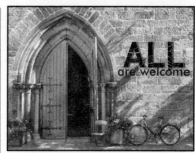

Visual for Lessons 4 & 8. *Point to this visual as you ask, "In what ways are we a welcoming church? How can we do better in this regard?"*

A. REMINDERS BY RUTH (v. 9)
9. *"Who are you?" he asked.*

"I am your servant Ruth," she said. "Spread the corner of your garment over me, since you are a kinsman-redeemer."

Ruth carefully follows the instructions of Naomi (Ruth 3:1-4, not in today's text). In that regard, Ruth goes to the threshing floor at night without being detected. She observes where Boaz lies down for the night, and at the proper time she lies down near him. During the night Boaz stirs, detects that someone has invaded his area of privacy, and quietly asks a question to determine the person's identity.

Ruth's answer reflects a boldness that she has already demonstrated in earlier choices to follow Naomi and the God of Israel. Her response has three parts to it: to provide her name, to state that she is subservient to Boaz, and to suggest that Boaz *spread* his covering over her to acknowledge the special obligations that exist because of his being a relative of Naomi's deceased husband.

Ruth's statement is fascinating because she uses one of the same Hebrew words that Boaz has used in pronouncing a blessing on her. Ruth 2:12 translates this word as "wings." The plural form is the most frequent use of this word, and that is understandable. The word may also be given as the fold or the hem of a *garment,* and that is the meaning here. In one sense Ruth is challenging Boaz to recognize that he should be the one who is used of God to provide the covering that he has mentioned previously in his oral blessing.

B. RESPONSES BY BOAZ (vv. 10, 11)
10. *"The LORD bless you, my daughter," he replied. "This kindness is greater than that which you showed earlier: You have not run after the younger men, whether rich or poor.*

Boaz has the ability to comprehend the big picture immediately and to think about it clearly. His first words are another spiritual blessing that he pronounces on Ruth. This takes away any improper motives that are sometimes assigned to this event.

The phrase *my daughter* shows that Boaz is fully aware of the generational difference between himself and Ruth. He knows that Ruth's actions are a proposal for marriage. But he understands that her real motivation is

WHAT DO YOU THINK?

How does Boaz's favor mirror the grace of God? How does all this speak to how we should treat others?

WHAT DO YOU THINK?

How can we demonstrate to others the virtue, kindness, and noble character that Boaz observes were true of Ruth? How do we balance Matthew 5:14-16 with Matthew 6:1-18 in this regard?

PRAYER

Almighty God, thank you for the blessing of being able to study this lesson and to see that all things really do work together for good to those who love you. We pray in Jesus' name. Amen.

to provide care for Naomi, and that this is the best way to do it. He sees that her goal is not just marriage, or she would have chosen a man who is younger.

11. *"And now, my daughter, don't be afraid. I will do for you all you ask. All my fellow townsmen know that you are a woman of noble character."*

The intention of Boaz may be to provide an assurance that Ruth needs to hear. A different reaction by Boaz can produce great embarrassment. He therefore speaks to relieve any fears that she has. While she is bold to do the right thing, she may have doubts about the way her proposal will be received.

Boaz continues by saying that he *will do* for her *all* she requests. He is confident that others will be receptive to this arrangement. The Hebrew word that Boaz uses to describe Ruth (translated as *noble character*) is exactly the same word that is used to describe Boaz in Ruth 2:1, there given as *wealth*.

Boaz keeps his word. He and Ruth marry, and they have a son who is named Obed (Ruth 4:17). But the story does not end there. Many believe that the reason for this book's being in the Bible is not to have a story of love and marriage, but to present more of the background of David, Israel's greatest king: Obed ends up being David's grandfather. Ruth's acceptance into a community and into a family results in blessings that lead to events that give access for anyone to have acceptance to God through Jesus, the Son of God.

A PLAN FOR SURVIVAL

Biosphere was the brainchild of Texas oil millionaire Ed Bass. It was built in the desert near Tucson, Arizona, at a cost of about $150 million. The project was designed to mimic the earth's ability to provide all the needs of its inhabitants and thus anticipate how humans might live in colonies in space. Thus Biosphere was designed to be self-contained in terms of water, food, and air.

Eight people lived in Biosphere 2 from 1991 to 1993. But the experiment was called off due to crop failure and a deteriorating oxygen supply. Jane Poynter, one of the colonists, later said, "Basically, we suffocated, starved, and went mad."

Compared with Biosphere 2, Naomi's plan for survival was much simpler. It consisted of personal relationships based on hard work, integrity, and a benevolent spirit. Our lesson suggests that Ruth's behavior was a well-orchestrated proposal for marriage. Naomi had devised the plan, Ruth carried it out, Boaz responded with appropriate integrity, and all three were blessed. In any area of life, well-conceived plans can bring blessings to everyone involved when those plans are implemented with skill, care, and godly motivation.   —C. R. B.

CONCLUSION

The opening words of Charles Dickens's *A Tale of Two Cities* are "It was the best of times, it was the worst of times." These two phrases are among the most famous in English literature. The sharp contrast between the phrases is also a commentary on the closing chapters of the book of Judges and the four chapters of the book of Ruth.

The last three chapters of the book of Judges depict such things as the low estate of women, rape, death, war, and deception. Anyone who reads these chapters is reading about "the worst of times." Then to begin reading the book of Ruth is to find an oasis of family, devotion, and faith. It is "the best of times" when common people display love, loyalty, and blessed living.

The people in the town of Bethlehem in Ruth's day did not realize the importance of their village in God's plan. The book of Ruth shows that ordinary people are very important in the eyes of God. While they live out their lives they may never know about the far-reaching consequences of their decisions for God. That is why it is important for each believer to let his or her light shine (Matthew 5:14-16). To reflect the love of God in kind acts may have results far beyond what is ever imagined.

THOUGHT TO REMEMBER
Continued faith in the worst of times brings blessings in the best of times.

Discovery Learning

The following is an alternative lesson plan emphasizing learning activities. Classes desiring such student involvement will find these suggestions helpful. At the back of this book are reproducible student pages to further enhance activity learning.

INTO THE LESSON

Art Activity. Before students arrive, place a piece of white paper and two darker colored crayons or drawing pencils at each seat. Begin the lesson by asking the students to sketch "gentleness and kindness." Most probably will draw some person performing an act that fits that phrase. Allow students to explain their drawings. (Larger classes may do the sharing in small groups.)

Next, ask the following two discussion questions: 1. If you had to name one person as "gentle and kind," whom would you name? Why? 2. What are some of the positive outcomes from acts of gentle kindness? (List answers on the board.)

Make the transition to Bible study by saying, "The personal quality we have been talking about may influence others. Today, we'll discover how this quality became an important ingredient in creating a marriage that was a part of the lineage of Jesus. We'll also discover ways that we can express this characteristic to influence others for Jesus."

INTO THE WORD

Study Teams. Form study teams or pairs to explore and report on the text through the following assignments. Give each team a copy of its task. Give Teams #1, #2, and #5 a photocopy of the lesson commentary on the verses assigned. Teams #3 and #4 will not need copies of the lesson commentary, but they will need poster board and markers.

Team #1: Read Ruth 2:8, 9 and the commentary to discover and report on the traditions of benevolent gleaning during Ruth's lifetime. *Team #2:* Discover and report on the question, "Who was Boaz?" You will find clues in Ruth 2:5-7 and the commentary. *Team #3:* Read Ruth 2:5-12; 3:9-11. List personal character traits and values demonstrated by Boaz. What would draw Ruth to this man as a potential husband? *Team #4:* Read Ruth 2:5-12; 3:9-11. List personal character traits and values demonstrated by Ruth. What would draw Boaz to this woman as a potential wife? *Team #5:* Discover and report on traditions in marriage and benevolence during the time of Ruth. Clues will be found in Ruth 3:9-11 and in the commentary.

After each group reports, remind the class that the story of Ruth, Boaz, and Naomi is an illustration about the effects of compassion, kindness, and personal virtue. Say, "In this story we find lessons for our own values and behaviors. The setting for the story of Ruth, Boaz, and Naomi is the ordinary village of Bethlehem. The marriage between Boaz and Ruth results in a lineage that takes us to King David and eventually to Jesus himself. God uses everyday people in common places to accomplish his work."

INTO LIFE

Discussion Questions. 1. Why are we drawn to people who demonstrate gentleness, kindness, and compassion? Why are these characteristics considered good virtues in life? 2. What motivates acts and expressions of gentleness, kindness, and compassion? How do these expressions contradict Darwin's philosophy of "survival of the fittest"? 3. What discourages people from practicing gentleness, kindness, and compassion? What values or parts of our nature must we conquer in order to be known for our gentleness, kindness, and compassion? 4. Who are some extraordinary everyday people through whom you see God working and influencing people? How do you see God working through them?

Wristbands. Purchase light-colored ribbon that is three-quarters of an inch wide. Cut it into wrist-sized lengths. Also purchase hook-and-loop dots to use as fasteners for the wristbands. Ask, "What does it mean when a person on trial in the U.S. says, 'I take the Fifth'?" (Answer: It means the person invokes the protection of the Fifth Amendment of the Constitution, which says that a person cannot be compelled to testify against himself or herself.) Ask, "What would it mean if we said, 'I take the fifth fruit of the Spirit?'" (Discussion should involve the *kindness* virtue per Galatians 5:22.) Have class members make wristbands from the materials supplied. Students are to write on their wristbands *I take the fifth . . . fruit of the Spirit* and assemble them. Encourage your learners to wear the bands for one week as a reminder to practice the godly virtue of gentle kindness.

Option: Use one or both of the reproducible exercises from page 375 in place of these activities.

THE COMMUNITY FACES PAIN AND JOY

LESSON 5

INTRODUCTION

A. A JOURNEY INTO THE GREAT UNKNOWN

A family of Italian traders followed the ancient Silk Road in the thirteenth century all the way to what we now know as Beijing, China. After many years in China, they returned to Italy, where the son wrote a book about their journey. This book, *The Travels of Marco Polo*, soon made him famous throughout Europe. Many people were skeptical about his claims, however. The fabulous riches of the Mongol emperor seemed too much to believe. The pictures of daily life in ancient Cathay were just too strange. Who could accept such things?

Other people did believe the stories of Marco Polo. They were excited by the idea of such a journey into the unknown. If someone had actually been there, why not listen to him? Among these believers was Christopher Columbus, who was inspired to seek an ocean route to the riches of the Far East. Among the personal possessions of Columbus was a heavily annotated copy of Marco Polo's book.

When someone can actually tell about a journey into the unknown, we should listen. This is especially true if that journey is one that we all must take. Therefore, when Jesus speaks to his disciples about his upcoming journey into death and beyond, we will do well to listen in.

B. LESSON BACKGROUND

The apostles gathered with Jesus in the upper room in Jerusalem. Together they celebrated the Passover, the ancient feast commemorating how God brought his people out of bondage in Egypt (see Exodus 12). In at least two ways the events of that night emphasized a sense of community.

First, they gathered as faithful Jews, members of a nation that was forged out of the trials of slavery and deliverance. Their ancestors had gone to Egypt few in number, but came out 400 years later as a great multitude. They would always look back to their deliverance from Egypt as the time when they became a nation. Second, Jesus and the apostles came to this point in their lives with a strong bond of sharing in a smaller, special community. They had spent three years together. They had come to recognize Jesus as the long-awaited Messiah, and they had pledged their lives to him.

It is in this tender setting, however, that Jesus uttered alarming words. He was leaving, and they could not come with him. He was, in fact, going to die. They would mourn his loss and be overcome with sorrow. Jesus promised that there would yet be cause for rejoicing in the future, but how could this be?

DEVOTIONAL READING:
PSALM 5

BACKGROUND SCRIPTURE:
JOHN 13:21-30; 16: 16-24; 20:11-16

PRINTED TEXT:
JOHN 16:16-24; 20: 11-16

Apr
4

LESSON AIMS

After participating in this lesson, each student will be able to:

1. Summarize Jesus' predictions regarding grief and joy in relation to his death and resurrection.

2. List some ways that the modern Christian's pain and joy is different from that of first-century believers.

3. Explain to one unbeliever why the joy of the Christian life far outweighs the pain.

KEY VERSE

"In a little while you will see me no more, and then after a little while you will see me." —John 16:16

LESSON 5 NOTES

I. DISCIPLES' CONFUSION (JOHN 16:16-18)

A. INITIAL SHOCK (v. 16)

16. "In a little while you will see me no more, and then after a little while you will see me."

Jesus has already warned his disciples that in Jerusalem his enemies will kill him (see Mark 8:31; 9:31; 10:33). But no matter how many times he says it, the disciples do not seem to be able to accept it (see Mark 9:32). Now Jesus tells them again, in words that are somewhat mysterious.

In a little while, in less than 24 hours, the disciples *will see him no more*. While they will later understand how these words point to his death, for the moment they are unable or unwilling to grasp the meaning. And then *a little while* later, they *will see* him. Although they do not understand it now, Jesus will conquer the tomb, rise from the dead, and appear to them.

B. ONGOING BEWILDERMENT (vv. 17, 18)

17. Some of his disciples said to one another, "What does he mean by saying, 'In a little while you will see me no more, and then after a little while you will see me,' and 'Because I am going to the Father'?"

Afraid or ashamed to let Jesus hear them, the *disciples* have a nervous discussion among themselves. *What does he mean?* they ask *one another*. Since they are unable or unwilling to accept the literal intent of Jesus' words, they can only grope for some other meaning. The disciples seem to have special difficulty with one part of what Jesus says, as they single out the words *because I am going to the Father* (see also John 16:5).

Since we live on this side of the cross, we can understand at least part of Jesus' words without difficulty: he will be taken from the disciples in death, and then he will be restored to them via resurrection. The words about *going to the Father,* however, still cause some disagreement yet today. Does Jesus mean that he will spend time with the Father during the time his body is buried? Does he mean that he will be in Heaven after his ascension and then return as the Holy Spirit at Pentecost, since that is the same as Jesus dwelling in our hearts according to (as some believe) Ephesians 3:17? Or does he mean that he will be with the Father until the second coming, even though in that case *a little while* turns out to be many centuries? Like other words of Jesus, these have more depth than first meets the eye.

18. They kept asking, "What does he mean by 'a little while'? We don't understand what he is saying."

The disciples continue to press the point with one another. *What does* Jesus *mean?* If this unwelcome separation is going to happen in just *a little while*, will Jesus leave them tonight? tomorrow? When will this unwelcome departure take place? Ultimately they concede that none of them knows what the words mean. This is not the first time they have failed to *understand* what Jesus intends nor will it be the last.

II. JESUS' PROMISE (JOHN 16:19-24)

A. SORROW LEADS TO JOY (vv. 19, 20)

19. Jesus saw that they wanted to ask him about this, so he said to them, "Are you asking one another what I meant when I said, 'In a little while you will see me no more, and then after a little while you will see me'?

Jesus is aware of the uneasy argument that is going on among the disciples. He knows they want *to ask him about* what he said, so he brings their reluctance out into the open. When he repeats his own words from verse 16, he is also repeating back to them their own questions from verse 17.

Jesus subtly identifies the heart of their ignorance and frustration when he asks *Are you asking one another what I meant?* Rather than turning to the one who has the answers, they are asking only each other. This, however, is one of those times when human answers simply are not enough. They will never know the ultimate truth as long as they are merely quizzing one another.

20. *"I tell you the truth, you will weep and mourn while the world rejoices. You will grieve, but your grief will turn to joy.*

Here Jesus states an emphatic truth. The disciples will soon face a tragic, traumatic time. They will *weep* in deep sorrow (as does Mary Magdalene in John 20:11) and will *mourn* (as do the women who watch Jesus go to the cross in Luke 23:27). But *the world,* which means all those who embrace living in their sinful and fallen state, will rejoice. Such people will think they have finally put the troublesome Galilean out of the way.

At that dark hour the disciples will be sorrowful with a deep, crushing *grief.* But then, just when the situation seems hopeless, their *grief* will *turn to joy.* This promise of Jesus echoes the promise of David in Psalm 30:5b.

B. BIRTH PAIN LEADS TO DELIGHT (v. 21)

21. *"A woman giving birth to a child has pain because her time has come; but when her baby is born she forgets the anguish because of her joy that a child is born into the world.*

To illustrate his point, Jesus compares the coming crisis with *a woman giving birth* (see also Isaiah 13:8; 21:3; 26:17; Micah 4:9; 1 Thessalonians 5:3). *When her time has come,* in the final hours of labor that lead to the moment of delivery, she has *pain* and sorrow. But finally the *baby* comes, and the tears of *anguish* turn into tears of *joy.* The mother's birth pains are swept away by the delight of welcoming her *child* into *the world.*

In the next few hours, the disciples will experience a flood of emotions: confusion, fear, panic, and utter despair. Within moments, Judas will leave to betray Jesus. The others will forsake him in the Garden of Gethsemane. In a courtyard near Jesus' trial, Peter will deny him and then rush out to weep bitterly. The next day they will watch as Jesus is crucified; he will be dead by late afternoon. Can there possibly be joy after all this?

C. JOY LEADS TO CONFIDENCE (vv. 22-24)

22. *"So with you: Now is your time of grief, but I will see you again and you will rejoice, and no one will take away your joy.*

The disciples have sorrow at the prospect of losing Jesus. All their hopes of a Messiah and the coming kingdom of God seem about to be destroyed. Other "saviors" have appeared on the scene and have gathered a following, only to have their efforts come to nothing (see Acts 5:36, 37). Will Jesus turn out to be merely another one of these?

But their *grief* will turn into *joy,* a confident joy that *no one* will be able to *take away* from them. This will happen when Jesus' words *I will see you again* come true. The disciples will be beaten and persecuted for their testimony of the risen Lord, but their joy and confidence will not be taken from them (see

WHAT DO YOU THINK?

In what cases, if any, should we take our questions and concerns only to Jesus in prayer and Bible study as opposed to trying to work out a solution with the help of other people?

WHAT DO YOU THINK?

How did your faith help you endure a time of deep grief?

Visual for Lesson 5. *Point to this visual as you ask,* "What sorrow does the empty tomb help you overcome today?"

Acts 5:40-42). After Jesus rises from the dead, the community of believers will all share this unquenchable joy. They will proclaim his resurrection with unshakable faith. They will stand against all opposition in victory.

LOOKING FOR THE RISEN SON

The word *funeral* sounds morose. Funeral services themselves often reflect (or create) that impression. There was a time within the memory of many older Christians when James H. Filmore's mournful hymn "We Are Going Down the Valley" was sometimes sung at funerals:

> We are going down the valley one by one,
> With our faces tow'rd the setting of the sun;
> Down the valley where the mournful cypress grows,
> Where the stream of death in silence onward flows.

But a shift has taken place in recent years in the way Christian funerals are conducted. Today we are likely to conduct a *memorial service* in which the emphasis is on the hope of God's promise for a great resurrection day as the life of the deceased is remembered. There are certainly moist eyes at such services. But there are also joyful testimonies of what the deceased meant to those who remain, those still awaiting their own heavenly reward.

Jesus used the facts of childbirth to illustrate the mixed feelings that are to be experienced. Temporary pain is forgotten with the joy new life brings. Those who love Jesus keep looking for the risen Son even as their own deaths approach.

—C. R. B.

WHAT DO YOU THINK?

Do Jesus' instructions mean that each and every prayer must end with the words in Jesus' name *in order to be valid? Why, or why not?*

23. "In that day you will no longer ask me anything. I tell you the truth, my Father will give you whatever you ask in my name.

In that day probably refers to the time after Jesus' resurrection and ascension. Therefore, they will not be able to ask him anything in person. But in the *name* of Jesus they will have the right to *ask* the *Father* directly. At their request he *will give* them the power to work miracles (compare Acts 3:1-10) and even raise the dead (see Acts 9:36-41).

Decades later, the apostle John will confirm that Christians have the right to go directly to the throne of God in prayer. In 1 John 5:14, 15 he assures us of two wonderful truths: (1) God hears us, and (2) he will grant the requests that are according to his will.

24. "Until now you have not asked for anything in my name. Ask and you will receive, and your joy will be complete."

The disciples have *not asked for anything* in Jesus' *name* up to this point. But henceforth they and all other Christians are given the right to approach God using the authority of God's own Son. *Ask and you will receive* is the blessed promise that attends every prayer (see Matthew 7:7-11). This is the promise that brings *joy* to God's people.

III. MARY'S DISCOVERY (JOHN 20:11-16)
A. TRAGIC SORROW (v. 11)
11. But Mary stood outside the tomb crying. As she wept, she bent over to look into the tomb

Early on Sunday morning, the third day after Jesus' death and burial, *Mary* Magdalene is at the tomb (compare Mark 16:1, 2; John 20:1). With eyes brimming with tears, she stoops down to look inside the place where Jesus had been laid. Tombs of the wealthy, such as this one belonging to Joseph of Arimathea, are small rooms carved out of rock (see Luke 23:50-53). Along the walls are low shelves, where dead bodies can be placed. Typically, the entrance to such a *tomb* is small and low, plugged with a large rock to keep out animal scavengers. With this large stone rolled back (Mark 16:4), Mary is able to peer inside.

B. PUZZLING ENCOUNTER (vv. 12, 13)

12. . . . and saw two angels in white, seated where Jesus' body had been, one at the head and the other at the foot.

Mark 16:5 and Luke 24:4 describe the *angels* as having human appearance, like young men. The angels are sitting on the low stone shelf where the *Jesus' body* had previously been placed. An angel sits at either end, *one at the head and the other at the foot*, but there is no corpse between them.

13a. They asked her, "Woman, why are you crying?"

When the angels ask Mary *why* she is weeping, they are implying that there is no need for sorrow. They know that Jesus is risen. But Mary does not yet know this. Neither does she know the angels are more than just young men who are unexpectedly present in the tomb.

13b. "They have taken my Lord away," she said, "and I don't know where they have put him."

She answers the angels' question with what she supposes to be the truth: persons unknown *have taken* away the body of her *Lord*, and she has no idea *where they have put* it. That apparent fact gives her one more reason to weep.

C. JOYFUL RECOGNITION (vv. 14-16)

14. At this, she turned around and saw Jesus standing there, but she did not realize that it was Jesus.

After Mary answers the question, she assumes there is no further need to converse with the young men. Perhaps withdrawing from the entrance to the tomb, she turns around and sees *Jesus standing there*. She does not recognize Jesus at first, for one or more reasons: her eyes are full of tears; the dawn is not yet full light; she does not turn completely around to face the man she encounters (see v. 16, below). On top of all that, she has no reason to expect that this person is Jesus. It is even possible that she is divinely prevented from recognizing Jesus, as are the two men on the road to Emmaus in Luke 24:16.

15. "Woman," he said, "why are you crying? Who is it you are looking for?"

Thinking he was the gardener, she said, "Sir, if you have carried him away, tell me where you have put him, and I will get him."

Jesus addresses Mary with the words of the angels: *Why are you crying?* It seems that everyone here knows good news that Mary does not! The second question is even more to the point: *Who is it you are looking for?*

In her grief and confusion, Mary supposes this man to be *the gardener.* (Who else would be in this area so early?) Moreover, she supposes that he has removed the body and put it elsewhere. (After all, this tomb didn't really belong to Jesus.) If he will just *tell* her *where* he has *put* the body, she will find a more appropriate place for its burial.

16. Jesus said to her, "Mary."

HOW TO SAY IT

Arimathea. AIR-uh-muh-THEE-uh (TH as in THIN).

Emmaus. Em-MAY-us.

Galilean. Gal-uh-LEE-un.

Gethsemane. Geth-SEM-uh-nee (G as in GET).

Judas. JOO-dus.

Magdalene. MAG-duh-leen or Mag-duh-LEE-nee.

Messiah. Meh-SIGH-uh.

rabbi. RAB-eye.

Rabboni. Rab-O-nye.

Waodani. Whoa-DON-ee.

WHAT DO YOU THINK?

What are some of the things that may cloud our vision so that we are not fully aware of Christ in our lives? How do we overcome these?

PRAYER

Heavenly Father, we praise you for raising Jesus from the dead. We ask you for greater confidence in the victory that belongs to your people. Please help turn all our pains and sorrows into eternal joy. We pray in Jesus' name. Amen.

WHAT DO YOU THINK?

In addition to hope for an eternal future in Heaven, what power does Jesus' resurrection give us today for our work on earth?

She turned toward him and cried out in Aramaic, "Rabboni!" (which means Teacher).

A single word jolts *Mary* to reality. When Jesus addresses her by name, she suddenly recognizes the familiar sound of that voice. Now she turns around completely to face Jesus, exclaiming *Rabboni*. This is a variant form of *rabbi*, a Hebrew title of honor that means "great teacher" or "one who is distinguished by great knowledge." Mary now shows both that she recognizes who Jesus is and that she honors him as her teacher.

Mary's joyful discovery is the discovery of all Christians. She meets the risen Jesus in person; we meet the risen Jesus in our spirits, and we recognize him for who he really is. We worship him as the Savior who has conquered sin and death. We acknowledge him as our Lord. All the pain and defeat of this life are swallowed up by the joy of his resurrection.

RECOGNIZING JESUS

A man whom we'll call *David* was walking through the exhibit area of a national Christian convention. Coming toward him was a man with white hair, a salt-and-pepper beard, and a smile on his face. The man said, "Hello, old friend; it's good to see you after all these years."

David couldn't come up with a name, so he glanced at the man's convention badge—that wonderful invention designed for just such moments. Unfortunately, the name on the badge was printed too small. Thus David was forced to say, "I'm sorry, I can't remember your name." The stranger said, "I'm John. We went to college together 30 years ago!"

When Mary failed to recognize Jesus, the problem was not the length of time since she had seen him last. It was not advancing age that had dimmed either her memory or her sight. It was because she was not anticipating Jesus to be alive when she went to his tomb. The world today has a similar problem: many do not believe Jesus has risen from the dead, and they do not expect to see him alive. Our glorious privilege as Christians is to explain not only that Jesus rose from the dead, but also to demonstrate that Jesus is alive within us! A convention badge that says *Christian* on it simply won't do. —C. R. B.

CONCLUSION

A. WE'RE IN THIS TOGETHER!

The saddest moments of Jesus' final day of life involved episodes of solitude and isolation. Judas went off alone from the upper room to betray him. Jesus prayed alone in the garden while his disciples slept. The disciples forsook Jesus, leaving him to face the trials alone. But "aloneness" can be emotional and spiritual as well as physical. Peter was surrounded by people outside a trial of Jesus, but Peter's denials isolated him. Jesus' followers shared a common grief at his death, but grief may be intensely isolating as each experiences loss in a personal way. Mary did not remain in this state. Just as Jesus promised, sorrow turned to joy! Once Mary knew the good news, she could not allow others to remain isolated in their personal grief. So she rushed back to the other believers so they could rejoice together.

B. THE VICTORY OF THE EMPTY TOMB

The disciples in the upper room could not imagine how anything good could come from the absence of Jesus. During and after the crucifixion, they could not imagine how any sorrow that deep could ever turn to joy. Their joy came when Jesus proved that death is not the end. He proved that sin is not a fatal blot, but a stain that is washed away by his blood. He proved that the promises he made would be kept. In the light of the great victory of the empty tomb, God's people can learn to face pain together. We can learn to put confidence in the promises God gives to us, expectantly ready to share joy together. The hope of resurrection is the promise of shared life in eternity.

THOUGHT TO REMEMBER
Experience the joy of the empty tomb again for the first time.

Discovery Learning

The following is an alternative lesson plan emphasizing learning activities. Classes desiring such student involvement will find these suggestions helpful. At the back of this book are reproducible student pages to further enhance activity learning.

INTO THE LESSON

During the week, locate articles on the Internet about Jim Elliot and the other four missionaries who were martyred as they tried to take the gospel to the Waodani tribe of Ecuador in 1956. (This is the same story that was retold in the 2005 motion picture *End of the Spear.*) Print off the articles and pictures; have them on display as students arrive. Present a summary of the incident and what led up to it.

Make sure to include in your summary the fact that a sister of one of those martyred and a widow of another later went to live among the Waodani. Say, "Their presence in the village afforded an opportunity for them to explain to the warriors why the missionaries had not tried to defend themselves—the men had wanted to make contact with the Waodani to tell them of a man named Jesus who willingly allowed himself to be killed in order to help all people. The missionaries' martyrdom was an illustration of the sacrifice of Christ for this savage people. One by one, the Waodani submitted their lives to Jesus. This story sets the tone for our lesson today: even in the midst of great sorrow, God can bring joy."

INTO THE WORD

Use the Lesson Background to set the context for today's study. Then write SORROW, JOY on the board. Have four students read the following verse combinations aloud, one each: John 16:16-18; John 16:19, 20; John 16:21, 22; John 16:23, 24. After each group of verses is read, put the elements of that text under the correct headings of Sorrow and Joy. Discuss reasons for your conclusions. Use the lesson commentary to add to the discussion and clear up any confusion.

Next, survey rapidly what happens between the two printed texts for today's lesson (that is, between John 16:16-24 and 20:11-16). You can do this by having students skim through the section headings in their Bibles (if their Bibles have such headings). Jot these events on the board under the correct headings.

Finally, have one or two students read aloud the final Scripture text for today, which is John 20:11-16. Discuss elements of sorrow and joy as before. There may be some disagreement, as events, reactions, etc. are intertwined. Use the lesson commentary to help students sort these out. Discuss how the empty tomb can be at first sorrowful (for those who found it empty), but then joyful. The entries you have written on the board can resemble this partial example:

SORROW...*JOY*
Will see me no more .... *Will see me*
Disciples will weep .... *World will rejoice*
Pain of childbirth ....*Joy of new life*
Trials of Jesus ....*Jesus says, "Mary"*
Crucified and buried................................*Empty tomb*

INTO LIFE

Say, "Jim Elliot wrote in his journal, 'He is no fool who gives what he cannot keep to gain that which he cannot lose.'" (Write that sentence on the board.) Then lead a discussion using the following questions: 1. How does this quotation apply to our Scripture text for today? 2. How does (or should) this quotation apply to your life? 3. How did this quotation apply to Jim Elliot and his fellow missionaries?

Wrap up the discussion by saying, "The story I read at the beginning of class is an example of God working for the good of those who love him by turning an event filled with sorrow into a story of joy and hope. But the story does not end there. Years later, Steve Saint, the son of one of the martyred missionaries met a man who had lived a faithful life for God in spite of many sorrows and trials that resulted from that faith. That man explained that his inspiration had been a story he had read years ago about the five missionaries who had died for their faith. Imagine the joy that the son of the martyred missionary felt in contrast with the sorrow he had experienced so many years earlier." Allow students to react and reflect.

Conclude: "God's providence is often beyond our comprehension, yet one thing we can understand: God will turn our sorrow to joy. As the psalmist recorded in Psalm 30:5b, 'Weeping may remain for a night, but joy comes in the morning.'" Ask for volunteers to give examples of how joy resulted from sorrowful situations in their lives. You can use the reproducible activity on page 376 for this.

LOVE WITHIN THE COMMUNITY

LESSON 6

INTRODUCTION

A. FAMOUS LANDMARKS

What is the quickest way to identify a great city? Almost everyone knows that Paris is the home of the Eiffel Tower. Rome has its Coliseum; London has Big Ben and the Tower Bridge; Moscow has the Kremlin. Around the world, many cities have landmarks by which they are recognized. Even small towns and villages often have unique features that give them a special identity.

Other cities are famous for what happens there. Los Angeles makes movies; Cannes has its annual film festival; New Orleans has Mardi Gras. Even if it is only Apple-Butter Makin' Days or the Mid-Winter Ice Fishing Festival, communities identify themselves in distinctive ways.

So what is it that identifies the Christian community (the church) as such? What is the landmark that makes us recognizable to the world? It is our loyalty to Christ, of course, but that is not all. Jesus himself said, "By this all men will know that you are my disciples, if you love one another" (John 13:35). Therefore, an identifying landmark in the church is love.

B. LESSON BACKGROUND

When the apostle John (the author of today's Scripture text) and his brother James left their nets to follow Jesus, they were not yet at the point of embracing the kind of love that Jesus was teaching. For instance, on one occasion they voiced hostility toward certain Samaritans, even offering to call down fire from Heaven to destroy them (Luke 9:54). On another occasion, those two tried to get ahead of their fellow apostles by asking for the choicest seats in the coming kingdom (Mark 10:35-41). John was not learning his lesson of love very well when he showed such hostility and selfishness!

Yet we have come to know John as "the apostle of love." Once he finally accepted what Jesus was trying to teach him, he wrote expressive letters to teach these lessons to others. His first letter, known to us as 1 John, sharply contrasts the life of love with the life of hatred or indifference. It is the contrast of light versus darkness, the contrast of living as children of God versus living as children of the world.

I. COMMUNITY'S STANDARD (1 JOHN 2:7, 8)

A. OLD COMMAND (v. 7)

7. *Dear friends, I am not writing you a new command but an old one, which you have had since the beginning. This old command is the message you have heard.*

DEVOTIONAL READING:
JOHN 13:31-35
BACKGROUND SCRIPTURE:
1 JOHN 2:7-17
PRINTED TEXT:
1 JOHN 2:7-17

Apr
11

LESSON AIMS

After participating in this lesson, each student will be able to:

1. Tell what John says about loving one another and not loving the world.

2. Explain the distinction between love and hate as John uses those terms.

3. Describe one specific way he or she will put love into action in the week ahead.

KEY VERSE

Whoever loves his brother lives in the light, and there is nothing in him to make him stumble. —1 John 2:10

LESSON 6 NOTES

God's community is not a democracy. We do not make our own rules or elect our own prime minister. God rules this community through his Son and gives the commands by which the community is to live. While we may react negatively against the idea of anyone giving us a *command*, we should recognize that God has the absolute right to do so.

The commandment of which John writes is not something *new* or novel. His readers have heard it before. It is the same commandment that Jesus taught his disciples from *the beginning* (see John 13:34, 35). Jesus demonstrated it by his own life (see John 15:13). It is the command to love one another.

In fact, this command goes back many centuries earlier than Jesus and his disciples. Moses gave the Israelites this same command from God, saying, "Do not seek revenge or bear a grudge against one of your people, but love your neighbor as yourself. I am the Lord" (Leviticus 19:18). Even though this imperative was originally given in a list of miscellaneous commands, Jesus singled it out as second only to the command to love God himself (see Matthew 22:34-40, next week's lesson).

B. NEW COMMAND (v. 8)

8. Yet I am writing you a new command; its truth is seen in him and you, because the darkness is passing and the true light is already shining.

Even though it is many centuries old, the *command* of love is ever *new*. It does not grow old and outdated with the passage of centuries; it is never covered with the dust of time. Genuine love in the community of God's people is always fresh and alive.

Love keeps its fresh vibrancy because *its truth is seen in him*; that is, it is at the essence of who and what God really is. As John will say later in this same epistle, "Dear friends, let us love one another, for love comes from God. Everyone who loves has been born of God and knows God. Whoever does not love does not know God, because God is love" (1 John 4:7, 8). John's readers must make sure that this kind of love is a reality in their lives.

The day of pagan *darkness* and ignorance *is passing*. Jesus, the light that enlightens everyone, has come into the world (see John 1:9). Through him the *true light* of God's love shines into everyone's heart. By watching love in action in the church, the world can see the love that is in the Father's heart.

II. COMMUNITY'S DISTINCTIVE (1 JOHN 2:9-11)

A. LOVE FALSELY CLAIMED (v. 9)

9. Anyone who claims to be in the light but hates his brother is still in the darkness.

There is always the danger that God's people will pay only lip service to his commands. When people truly love God, however, they will necessarily demonstrate it in their lives. Warmed by the *light* of God's love and directed by the light of God's Word, they will reflect God's love to those around them. But if someone *hates his brother*, he exposes the fact that he *still* lives *in the darkness*.

The one who claims to walk in God's light and at the same time hates a brother or sister in the Lord should hear the warning of Jesus: "Why do you call me, 'Lord, Lord,' and do not do what I say?" (Luke 6:46). Jesus gave the command to love. To obey him as Lord is to walk in his pattern of love. As it has often been said, one must "walk the walk, and not just talk the talk."

B. LOVE TRULY SHOWN (v. 10)

10. Whoever loves his brother lives in the light, and there is nothing in him to make him stumble.

There are three wonderful traits shown in the kind of person John wants us to be. First, such a person *loves his brother.* Because we have experienced God's love in our own lives, we are able to share it with everyone else in the church.

Second, such a person abides *in the light.* When we remain in God's light, which is symbolic of God's truth, we keep the command of God to love our neighbor. Third, there is *nothing* in us to *make* someone else *stumble.* This means that the one who abides in love does not become the cause of a fellow Christian tripping up spiritually.

C. LOVELESSNESS SADLY MANIFESTED (v. 11)

11. But whoever hates his brother is in the darkness and walks around in the darkness; he does not know where he is going, because the darkness has blinded him.

To show the truth about love and light more clearly, John holds them up against the opposite. If a professing Christian (see v. 9) *hates* a *brother,* it produces an ugly situation. Such a person may claim to be—even believe himself or herself to be—in the light. But that person actually is living *in the darkness.* The failure to love exposes the fact that he or she does not truly know God and God's will.

Consequently, such a person does not know *where he is going.* Groping blindly in the darkness of ignorance, such a person is unaware of being completely off the path of the journey that God intends.

The darkness that blinds may come in various forms. Perhaps the person will be arrogant because of his or her social standing. Perhaps the person will be racist or hostile toward foreigners. However expressed, the inner darkness will cause him or her to withdraw or withhold love from certain ones of God's children. A failure to love all God's people proves that any claim of love for God himself is false.

III. COMMUNITY'S VICTORY (1 JOHN 2:12-14)

A. LOVE BRINGS FORGIVENESS (v. 12)

12. I write to you, dear children, because your sins have been forgiven on account of his name.

Turning to a more positive note, John begins to single out specific groups within the church to rejoice in the victories they have been granted thus far. First, he addresses his *dear children.* While this is a favorite term that John uses for all his readers (see 1 John 2:1, 18), the contrast of the groups in the verses before us shows that John has in mind those who are either young in years or new to the faith.

The victory that belongs even to those who are spiritually "young" in the church is that their *sins have been forgiven.* They have been given this victory not because of their own merit, but *on account of his name.* The God who delivered the Jewish nation from captivity in Babylon is the God who delivers people from sin and its effects. In regard to that earlier deliverance God said, "For my own sake, for my own sake, I do this. How can I let myself be defamed? I will not yield my glory to another" (Isaiah 48:11).

"He that loveth his brother abideth in the light, and there is none occasion of stumbling in him." —1 John 2:10

Visual for Lesson 6. *Point to this visual as you ask, "What actions that might cause others to "stumble" have you learned to reject?"*

HOW TO SAY IT

Babylon. BAB-uh-lun.
Cannes. Kan or Kanz.
Corinthians. Ko-RIN-thee-unz (TH as in THIN).
Ephesians. Ee-FEE-zhunz.
epistle. ee-PIS-ul.
Isaiah. Eye-ZAY-uh.
Leviticus. Leh-VIT-ih-kus.
Mardi Gras. MAR-dee Grah.
Samaritans. Suh-MARE-uh-tunz.

B. Forgiveness Brings Triumph (vv. 13, 14)

13a. I write to you, fathers, because you have known him who is from the beginning.

The next group with whom John celebrates is the *fathers*. These are the older men among his readers who have *known him who is from the beginning*. Being more spiritually mature, they are the ones who know God, the ancient of days, best; they know the Lord Jesus, who in the beginning was with God and was God (see John 1:1). They have lived out their lives trusting God, and they can testify to his faithfulness.

13b. I write to you, young men, because you have overcome the evil one.

The third group John addresses constitutes the *young men*. Like the young warriors in a tribal village, these are the ones who have stood strong (and are yet standing strong) against the enemy. They have learned that when they resist the devil he flees from them (see James 4:7). So when *the evil one* (Satan) launches his attacks, they *overcome* him.

13c. I write to you, dear children, because you have known the Father.

John begins addressing each of the groups a second time here at the end of verse 13. To know God *the Father* and to know Jesus the Son is the essence of eternal life (see John 17:3).

14a. I write to you, fathers, because you have known him who is from the beginning.

To the *fathers* John repeats the same truth: they have *known him who is from the beginning*. In a pattern of expression that is common among Jewish writers, this kind of restatement adds emphasis to what John says.

14b. I write to you, young men, because you are strong, and the word of God lives in you, and you have overcome the evil one.

Finally, John gives a triple commendation to the *young men*. They are *strong* in the Lord (see Ephesians 6:10). They have this strength because they have Scripture—the *word of God*—as a living, permanent part of their lives. And with this strength they have *overcome the evil one*.

Little ones, young men, fathers—together they have turned to God through Jesus their Lord. With their sins forgiven they are able to stand strong against the devil, "the accuser of our brothers" (Revelation 12:10). Standing together, young and old, the church declares her victory.

Rites of Passage? Stages of Growth?

In times gone by, it was almost a rite of passage in rural communities for teenagers to tip over outhouses or put farm wagons on the tops of sheds on Halloween night. The deeds were often excused with the adage, "Boys will be boys." That saying has been used through the years to excuse everything from harmless pranks to serious misdemeanors.

"Sowing wild oats" is another phrase sometimes used to describe youthful escapades. In a beach community in California a couple of years ago, a group of young men who boasted of "partying and getting wasted" got into a fight with a professional surfer. The fight left the surfer dead, and the five perpetrators faced charges ranging from misdemeanor battery to murder. It wasn't wild oats sown in that case, but noxious, deadly weeds since that was the harvest. We assume, hope, and/or pray that children eventually will grow up to become responsible adults, both physically and spiritually, even though that journey seems to be a real struggle for many.

What Do You Think?

Would you describe your own spiritual maturity as that of a child, a teenager, or a parent? What will you do to progress to the next level?

John speaks in terms of spiritual growth in today's text as he addresses Christians of varying levels of maturity. Everyone knows that there are stages of physical growth. But there also are stages of spiritual growth. Parents get concerned and take action when their child's physical growth is not what it should be. Are we as concerned when a person's spiritual growth does not progress as God expects?

—C. R. B.

IV. COMMUNITY'S IMPERATIVE (1 JOHN 2:15-17)
A. LOVING THE WORLD (vv. 15, 16)
15. Do not love the world or anything in the world. If anyone loves the world, the love of the Father is not in him.

Love is a beautiful thing. But it becomes ugly when it is turned toward evil. That is why John now warns his readers that they must *not* love either *the world* or *anything in the world*. In this context, *the world* is not merely the physical planet Earth, but all that characterizes the people of the fallen world in their sinful state. Just as we cannot serve two masters (see Matthew 6:24), we cannot *love the world* and love *the Father* at the same time.

This verse raises an important distinction in two different ways of loving the world. God loves the world (as in John 3:16) with the intention of saving and changing it from its fallen state. This is right and good. On the other hand, it is wrong to love the world as it is in its sinfulness. To love sinful things is to set oneself in opposition to God and all he represents.

16. For everything in the world—the cravings of sinful man, the lust of his eyes and the boasting of what he has and does—comes not from the Father but from the world.

This verse makes it clear that it is not the created, physical world that is the issue. What is at issue, rather, is what *the world* stands for. John breaks this down into three broad concerns. First, John refers to the world in terms of *the cravings of sinful man*. God is the one who created our bodies to have physical appetites. There are proper ways to satisfy these appetites. But the world will tempt us to satisfy those appetites in sinful ways.

It is clear that both *lust* and pride will distance a person from God. Like the rich fool who took pride in using his possessions on his appetites (see Luke 12:14-21), such a person thinks he or she has no need of the creator. In short, a person either can be in love with God or in love with the world, but not both.

UNLIMITED APPETITES
Most of us know someone who has a voracious appetite that is accompanied by the proverbial "hollow leg." We may be envious about that person's seeming ability to eat anything desired without gaining weight.

Sonya Thomas seems to be one such person. The International Federation of Competitive Eating (www.ifoce.com) certifies and celebrates her as holding world records for eating 46 dozen oysters in 10 minutes, 11 pounds of cheesecake in 9 minutes, 11 pounds of lobster meat (44 Maine lobsters) in 12 minutes, and 8.4 pounds of pork and beans in 2 minutes 47 seconds. As of this writing, Thomas is #6 on the IFOCE's "rankings of the top eaters on the circuit worldwide." But get this: Thomas weighs only about 100 pounds! So—is she guilty of gluttony, or not?

Of course, so-called "competitive eating" has much more to do with satisfying a desire for fame than satisfying a desire for food. Yet either desire has the potential

PRAYER

Loving Father, forgive us for being too much concerned with this world. Show us how to love you with all our hearts and then to reflect your love to the rest of the world. We pray in the name of Jesus, who showed us utmost love. Amen.

What Do You Think?

What can we do when our fleshly desires threaten to overcome our better judgment?

[Make sure to consider 1 Corinthians 10:13 in your answer.]

to destroy us; thus John's warning applies to both—and to many others as well. Is there an insatiable appetite that has you in its grip today?   —C. R. B.

B. Serving the Father (v. 17)

17. The world and its desires pass away, but the man who does the will of God lives forever.

The one who loves the world should be aware of this fact: *the world* passes *away*. There is no lasting satisfaction in fulfilling *the desires* of the flesh. There is no permanent gain in securing the lust of the eyes. There is no real benefit that comes from pride in a life that will soon come to an end. The fallen world and all its desires are doomed.

The only lasting reward comes from doing *the will of God*. Only the person who serves the Father has assurance that what he or she is doing will have lasting, eternal significance. Those who devote themselves to doing the will of God will abide forever in the community of Heaven.

CONCLUSION

A. Famous for No Reason?

Andy Warhol (1928–1987) is credited with a comment about people having their "fifteen minutes of fame." There seems to be no shortage of people who want to have their brief moment of recognition, even if for no good reason. They wave their hands in the background for TV cameras. They run onto baseball fields in the middle of games. They have an urge to be noticed, but have accomplished nothing to earn it.

Similarly, there are sometimes celebrities who are really just "famous for being famous." Some of these folks stage "photo ops" merely for the publicity they bring. Then there are the demagogues who rush to every controversy, hoping to be interviewed. This kind of meaningless fame calls to mind the old adage, "Fools' names and fools' faces always appear in public places." By contrast, God's people have something substantial. They do not need to advertise their mark of distinction; their recognition comes from simply being who they are. They are the community of God—the church—and they are known by their love.

B. Famous for Love

From the earliest days of the church, God's people have been notable for their love. They sold property, shared belongings, and did whatever was necessary to be sure that everyone had what was needed (see Acts 2:44-46; 4:34-37). When widows needed food, they organized to feed them (see Acts 6:1-3). When the saints in Jerusalem faced severe famine years later, the Gentile believers were eager to help them in their need (see Acts 11:28-30). They did this even though they lived in poverty themselves (a later occasion in 2 Corinthians 8:1-4). Through the centuries, the church repeatedly has taken the lead to care for the sick, provide for orphans and widows, and offer opportunities for education. Who else will care for the lepers? Who else will leave home and safety to carry good news to distant tribes? Who else will do such things but those who have felt the love of God?

Therefore it is incumbent on every local church to have the distinguishing mark of love. It is not the sign out front by which a church is known; rather, it is the demonstration of love. Since this is true, it is vital that every individ-

What Do You Think?

What will it take for your church to mobilize to meet community needs? What will be your part in this?

What Do You Think?

If an outsider observed your life for one week, what might he or she say are the identifying "landmarks" of your life in terms of your highest priorities? What adjustments do you need to make?

ual Christian ask himself or herself what specific act of love he or she should do. Where is the specific need that love can address? Where is the specific hurt that love can heal? Christian love will seek out those needs and move vigorously to meet them.

Discovery Learning

The following is an alternative lesson plan emphasizing learning activities.
Classes desiring such student involvement will find these suggestions helpful. At the
back of this book are reproducible student pages to further enhance activity learning.

INTO THE LESSON

Before class, download pictures of famous cities from the Internet. Place a number beside each picture and affix them to the wall for students to see as they arrive. (*Option:* Instead of affixing pictures to the wall, put the pictures on sheets of paper to circulate among the students.) Give each student a sheet of paper with those same numbers listed vertically down the left side; ask students to write the names of the cities next to the appropriate numbers.

When everyone is finished, discuss the results. Ask, "What landmark or physical feature helped you identify each city?" Then say, "In today's lesson we will discuss the 'landmark' that should identify the Christian community—the church."

Alternative: Before class, prepare two sets of index cards. On one set write the names of at least five famous yearly events, one per card (examples: Mardi Gras; dropping of the giant ball on New Year's Eve). On the other set, write the names of the cities in which those events occur, one per card (examples: New Orleans and New York City for the two events above, respectively). Depending on class size, prepare enough cards for each group of three or four students to have one set of event cards and one set of city-name cards.

Distribute the cards to your small groups. Say, "Match event cards with city cards." Discuss the results. Then say, "Some cities are famous for the activities that take place there. In today's lesson we will discuss certain actions that should identify the Christian community—the church."

INTO THE WORD

Before class, make an index card for each verse of the printed text, writing the verse reference at the top of the card. In the middle of the cards, write a second reference according to the following list: 1 John 2:7 and Matthew 22:39 / 1 John 2:8 and John 13:34, 35 / 1 John 2:9 and John 3:19, 20 / 1 John 2:10 and John 3:21 / 1 John 2:11 and 1 John 4:20 / 1 John 2:12 and 1 John 2:1, 2 / 1 John 2:13 and 1 John 1:5, 6 / 1 John 2:14 and 1 John 5:3, 4 / 1 John 2:15 and John 3:16 / 1 John 2:16 and James 4:7-9 / 1 John 2:17 and 1 John 3:1-3.

Give each student or pair of students at least one of the cards. Create duplicate cards if you are using pairs and your class is larger than 22 in size; give some students more than one card if your class is smaller than 11 in size and students work alone; etc.

Say, "Look up the text at the top of the card and write a brief phrase that expresses its message. Then look up the verse in the middle of the card and do the same thing. At the bottom of the card write one sentence that summarizes the message of the two Scripture references combined." (Example: the first card, which has 1 John 2:7 and Matthew 22:39, will have something like *the old command* and *love your neighbor as yourself* as the two brief expressions; the summary of the two Scriptures could be *The command to love your neighbor is an old command.*)

Discuss the results card by card. Tape the cards to the board as you go, grouping together cards that have similar messages. Once you have discussed the last card and have completed your groupings, ask the class to suggest one sentence that summarizes each grouping. Use the lesson commentary to add any important aspects that did not emerge in the group verse studies or in the discussion. Although there will be a wide variety of ways to summarize the groupings, some possibilities are *God loved us and made us his own; We should love others as God loved us;* and *When we love others, they see God in us.*

Ask students what common theme they see emerging from all of the statements. The natural response will be *love.* Stress that this is the "landmark" (or "action," if you used the alternative activity in the Into the Lesson segment) that should identify our Christian community (church).

INTO LIFE

Ask, "What does love look like?" Have students brainstorm specific examples of the actions they, as Christians, need to exhibit in order for others to see God's love in them. Write the examples on the board. Then have each student select an action that he or she will commit to implementing this week. Close by singing the song "They'll Know We Are Christians by Our Love." Distribute the two the reproducible puzzles on page 377 as students depart.

CONNECTING IN COMMUNITY

LESSON 7

INTRODUCTION

A. BROKEN CONNECTIONS

We live in a world of broken connections. Some of it is caused by failures of technology. Cell phones drop our calls; work stops when "the network" is down; a power outage interrupts our access to entertainment. These kinds of broken connections are relatively new in the timeline of history.

Other kinds of broken connections are very old. Think of the inequities in society. Sometimes these are holdovers of racism; such may continue long after prejudicial laws have been revoked. Sometimes there is misguided nationalism, with hostility directed indiscriminately toward foreigners. Sometimes there is a great divide between the rich and the poor. The worst of the broken connections are very personal. Broken marriages set the partners adrift and put children in limbo. Old animosities fester against the boss, against the neighbor, against the in-laws. Many people just feel alienated from their own world, longing to connect with someone . . . anyone!

Jesus taught about two great laws that fix broken connections. The first law is to love God. Making peace with our Creator is the most important reconnection of all. The second law is to love our neighbor, whoever he or she may be. When people live out this kind of love, one by one the old breaks in life's connections can begin to disappear.

B. LESSON BACKGROUND

During the second century BC, the influence of Greek culture began to infiltrate the lives of God's people in Judea. Many of them began to compromise their convictions, no longer keeping distinctive Jewish laws regarding food, circumcision, the Sabbath, etc. In order to call their nation back to God's ways, a group arose that called themselves *the pious ones.*

This group tried to set a high standard of obeying every detail of the law as an example for the rest to follow. When they prayed, they prayed very publicly. When they tithed, they called attention to the fact that they even gave a tenth of what their herb plants produced. When they fasted, they made sure that people noticed. We know these *pious ones* better by their biblical designation *Pharisees.* They no doubt meant well in the beginning, but by the time of Jesus they had become self-righteous and hypocritical.

Five times in Matthew 5 Jesus drew attention to the inadequacy of keeping the Law of Moses in a merely formal way, as the Pharisees did. Jesus

DEVOTIONAL READING:
ROMANS 5:1-11
BACKGROUND SCRIPTURE:
MATTHEW 5:17-20; 22:34-40
PRINTED TEXT:
MATTHEW 5:17-20; 22:34-40

Apr
18

LESSON AIMS

After participating in this lesson, each student will be able to:

1. Quote the two greatest commandments from memory.

2. Explain how the two greatest commandments may be said to summarize the entirety of the law.

3. Make a plan to demonstrate his or her love for God in one concrete way in the week ahead.

KEY VERSE

Jesus replied: "Love the Lord your God with all your heart and with all your soul and with all your mind."
—Matthew 22:37

gave an example of how true righteousness was more than mere legalism each time he said "You have heard . . . but I tell you." God was calling his community to something higher than mere outward compliance to a list of rules.

I. DECLARATION AND IMPLICATION (MATTHEW 5:17-20)

The first section of today's lesson text is part of the Sermon on the Mount (see also Luke 16:16, 17). By this time in Jesus' ministry, he has gained great popularity with the common people. But there is still no clear idea as to exactly who Jesus is and what he intends to do. Will Jesus replace or revise the Law of Moses? Will he do away with what the ancient prophets said?

A. NOT TO DESTROY, BUT TO FULFILL (vv. 17, 18)

17. "Do not think that I have come to abolish the Law or the Prophets; I have not come to abolish them but to fulfill them.

Right here, early in the Sermon on the Mount, Jesus explains his purpose. He starts with a negative—he has not *come to abolish the Law.* Neither has he come to reverse the teaching of *the Prophets.* Instead, he has come *to fulfill them.* He will fulfill the Law of Moses by accomplishing everything it requires. Although not explained at this point, this will involve giving his life to satisfy the law's demands against sinners. Jesus also will teach about internal submission to God's will, not just external compliance. Jesus will fulfill the prophets by being and doing all that they have predicted about the Messiah. From his incarnation in the womb of a lowly virgin to his death, burial, and resurrection, Jesus accomplishes everything the prophets have foreseen.

18. "I tell you the truth, until heaven and earth disappear, not the smallest letter, not the least stroke of a pen, will by any means disappear from the Law until everything is accomplished.

Many ancient kingdoms have passed into oblivion by the time of Jesus. In so doing, they have taken their authority and their laws with them to the dustbin of history. But Jesus firmly states as a truth that God's *Law* will not *disappear* as long as *heaven and earth* exist.

To emphasize this further, Jesus declares that *the smallest letter* or *the least stroke of a pen* will not *disappear from the Law.* The Hebrew letter *yodh* is the smallest letter in that alphabet. Likewise, certain Hebrew letters have a tiny "horn" that juts out on them and requires only a slight movement of the pen. (For instance, this tiny addition distinguishes the Hebrew letter *r* from the letter *d.*) Thus neither the tiniest letter nor the tiniest corner of a letter will be stricken from what God has said.

But then Jesus adds more: *until everything is accomplished.* These words show that at a certain point in time—when all is fulfilled—God's law will somehow be revised or replaced. While this could point to the end of the world at Judgment Day, it is more likely that Jesus is pointing to the end of his earthly ministry. His death on the cross, his resurrection from the empty tomb, and his ascension to Heaven preceding the birth of the church will bring the old covenant to a close. A new covenant, ratified in his blood, will replace it (see Luke 22:20; Colossians 2:14; Hebrews 8:8-10).

B. NOT TO BREAK, BUT TO TEACH (v. 19)

19. "Anyone who breaks one of the least of these commandments and teaches others to do the same will be called least in the kingdom of heaven, but whoever practices and teaches these commands will be called great in the kingdom of heaven.

No one has the right to break even *one of the least of these commandments* of God. Until God himself changes the requirements of his covenant, anyone who violates what he has said will be considered *least in the kingdom of heaven.* Likewise, no one has the right to teach *others* to violate God's will. As long as people are still living under the old covenant, they are obligated to obey its provisions. When Jesus ushers in the era of the new covenant, people will be just as obligated to obey its stipulations. Anyone who *practices and teaches* the will of God who will be called *great in the kingdom of heaven,* the everlasting community of God.

It is important to understand at this point that even when the new covenant replaces the old covenant, the same standards of ethics and right behavior remain. In fact, as the rest of the Sermon on the Mount makes plain, when a person has the precepts of the new covenant written on the heart, his or her behavior will go beyond the letter of the law and will fulfill its intention (compare Galatians 5:14).

C. NOT TO FAIL, BUT TO EXCEED (v. 20)

20. "For I tell you that unless your righteousness surpasses that of the Pharisees and the teachers of the law, you will certainly not enter the kingdom of heaven."

Righteousness means having a track record of doing what is right. When Jesus calls for the people to have righteousness that exceeds that of *the Pharisees and the teachers of the law,* they must surely look at the task as impossible! Are not the scribes experts in the law? Do they not make their living by carefully producing exact copies of Scripture by hand? If anyone knows exactly what God requires, is it not the scribes? And are not the Pharisees virtually flawless in observing the most minute detail of the law? No one can match the Pharisees in the way they give, pray, or fast!

How then can Jesus require that people live up to an even higher standard or else *not enter the kingdom of heaven*? The answer is twofold. First, the kind of righteousness God seeks is an internal allegiance, not merely an external compliance. Real religion begins in the heart, not in external rituals. What Jesus proceeds to teach in Matthew 5:21–6:18 clearly shows this.

Second, and even more importantly, being counted as perfectly righteous is something that comes only from Jesus himself. The apostle Paul explains this in Philippians 3:5, 6 and Romans 3:21, 22.

ON LEGISLATING MORALITY

When a conversation develops about what laws ought to be passed and enforced, someone may object, "You can't legislate morality!" All too often it seems that the one expressing that sentiment is in favor of a behavior or lifestyle that he or she doesn't want to be declared illegal.

But of course, we *can* and *do* legislate morality. We have laws against murder, theft, extortion, rape, and many other behaviors that are considered immoral. It is true that such laws often are broken, but would anyone seriously argue that society would be better off without such laws? It can also be argued that many

WHAT DO YOU THINK?

What are some ways we may be teaching others by our actions to break God's commandments? How can we do better in this regard?

WHAT DO YOU THINK?

Would you be comfortable saying that your righteousness exceeds that of the scribes and Pharisees? Why, or why not?

Visual for Lesson 7.
*Post this map as you study
the New Testament lessons
for this quarter to give your
learners a geographical perspective.*

who do not break such laws are not really moral in the Judeo-Christian sense (if we may use a double negative without getting confused). Jesus' confrontations with the Pharisees are proof enough of that!

Christians have an obligation to understand God's law and its relationship to the concept of righteousness. The law makes us aware of sin (Romans 3:20). We have an obligation to obey God's law in order to avoid sin, but we dare not think that we can gain a righteousness of our own by so doing (Galatians 2:21; 3:21; Philippians 3:9). Our righteousness comes from Christ.   —C. R. B.

II. SCHEME AND OUTCOME (MATTHEW 22:34-40)

In the final week before his crucifixion, Jesus successfully answers a number of challenges to his teaching. One of those challenges comes from the Sadducees, a sect of the Jews that does not believe in resurrection. They create for Jesus a question that shows their contempt for that concept: If a woman has been married seven times, they ask, which man will be her husband in Heaven? Jesus easily handles their challenge, explaining that in Heaven people will not be paired off in marriage (see Matthew 22:23-33). That is the immediate backdrop to our next passage. Mark 12:28-34 is parallel.

A. CHALLENGING QUESTION (vv. 34-36)

34. Hearing that Jesus had silenced the Sadducees, the Pharisees got together.

The Pharisees, in contrast with *the Sadducees,* do believe in resurrection. The two groups frequently argue about it, as we see them doing in Acts 23:6-10. When the Pharisees hear that Jesus has *silenced* their opponents, they are favorably impressed according to Mark 12:28. But they are not finished challenging him.

35. One of them, an expert in the law, tested him with this question:

To be *an expert in the law* in a religious sense is to be knowledgeable in interpreting the fine details of God's law. As a legal expert, this man is clever enough to come up with yet another challenge for Jesus.

On the surface the lawyer seems to be an earnest seeker of truth. But it is clear that when he asks Jesus *a question* he is also testing him. This means that the lawyer is daring Jesus to come up with a good answer to a very difficult question. The implication is that the man wants Jesus to fail the test. The lawyer wants the crowd to see Jesus as a fraud.

36. "Teacher, which is the greatest commandment in the Law?"

The rabbis frequently argue among themselves about the relative importance of God's laws. This is an issue with practical implications, because some situations force a person to choose among laws when they apparently conflict with one another. When performing one religious duty means that another religious duty has to be ignored, which one should take precedence?

There are more than 600 laws in the Old Testament. Ideally, if the law at the top can be identified, then it will be easier to place the other laws in their proper positions below it; this procedure is called *rank ordering.* In actual practice, however, no consensus on the rank ordering is ever reached by the rabbis. What will Jesus say about this complex problem?

IT DEPENDS ON WHAT IS IS

Back when the Clinton-Lewinsky sex scandal was at its height, the president appeared before a federal grand jury on August 17, 1998 to testify. His lawyer,

HOW TO SAY IT

Deuteronomy.
    Due-ter-AHN-uh-me.
*Ecclesiastes. Ik-LEEZ-ee-AS-
    teez.*
Judea. Joo-DEE-uh.
Leviticus. Leh-VIT-ih-kus.
Messiah. Meh-SIGH-uh.
Moses. MO-zes or MO-zez.
Pharisees. FAIR-ih-seez.
rabbi. RAB-eye.
Sadducees. SAD-you-seez.
Shema. SHE-muh.

Robert Bennett, had testified previously regarding the president's behavior that, "There is absolutely no sex of any manner, shape, or form." When the president was questioned about whether his attorney's statement was true, he said, "It depends on what the meaning of the word *is* is."

President Clinton went on to "explain" what amount of time the present tense *is* covered and did not cover regarding the situation at issue. His tortured, evasive response immediately became fodder for comedians and talk shows. In the careful parsing of the verb *is,* the president technically was telling the truth while attempting to hide the fact that previously there *had been* an illicit affair.

Modern politicians of all stripes have shown themselves to be the equal of the Pharisees in their skills at verbal jousting. Quibbling about minutiae hides larger issues. The larger issue the Pharisees tried to hide was the fact that they weren't interested in the truth! Their intent was to trap Jesus. Sadly, most of us are guilty of occasionally "shading the truth" to achieve a certain goal or to avoid an unpleasant outcome. There's blame enough to go around!   —C. R. B.

B. CONCLUSIVE ANSWERS (vv. 37-39)

37. Jesus replied: "'Love the Lord your God with all your heart and with all your soul and with all your mind.'

Just as with the other challenging questions, Jesus has an immediate answer. He draws his answer from what is called *the Shema,* a Hebrew word that means "hear." That is the first word of Deuteronomy 6:4, 5: "Hear, O Israel: The Lord our God, the Lord is one. Love the Lord your God with all your heart and with all your soul and with all your strength."

In the Old Testament the *heart* and the *soul* are overlapping concepts, referring to the inner person. The original command of Deuteronomy does not so much address three separate areas of a person's life as to address the entirety of one's life. The command is to love God in every way, with everything we have.

At the same time, it is interesting that Jesus sees fit to adjust the quotation of this well-known text: "with all your mind" becomes "with all your strength." This doesn't change the meaning so much as it serves to stress the idea that our devotion to God is both internal and external.

38. "This is the first and greatest commandment.

The first duty of anyone is to honor the Creator. Appropriately, the first of the Ten Commandments says, "You shall have no other gods before me" (Exodus 20:3). Wise Solomon decreed, "Fear God and keep his commandments, for this is the whole duty of man" (Ecclesiastes 12:13).

But God desires more than just fear and obedience. Most of all God desires our love. That is why the most fundamental of all laws is the commandment to love God. It is in this light that Jesus presents Deuteronomy 6:5 as *the first and greatest commandment* in answering the question of the lawyer.

39. "And the second is like it: 'Love your neighbor as yourself.'

Even though the lawyer has not asked for it, Jesus gives him *the second* greatest commandment as well. It is *like* the first command, for it is also about *love.* Not only must people love God, they must also love other people.

When Jesus says *love your neighbor as yourself,* he is not commanding self-love as a priority, as some have proposed. What he means is that just as truly as all well-balanced, sane people take care to attend to their own needs, to that same extent we should be careful to attend to the needs of others.

WHAT DO YOU THINK?

How would your life be different if you truly loved God with all your heart, soul, and mind? How can you make progress in this regard, and why should you?

WHAT DO YOU THINK?

Should we first focus on learning to love ourselves so that we may better love our neighbors? Can we love others if we do not love ourselves first? Explain.

WHAT DO YOU THINK?

Which do you think is harder: to love God or to love your neighbor? Why do you say that?

Given the importance of this command, it is somewhat surprising to note that it is drawn from a relatively obscure list of miscellaneous laws in Leviticus 19. The law quoted by Jesus actually is just the second half of Leviticus 19:18. The entire verse says "Do not seek revenge or bear a grudge against one of your people, but love your neighbor as yourself. I am the Lord."

While the rule originally applied to fellow Israelites, Jesus elsewhere shows that this imperative has broader application. Jesus' Parable of the Good Samaritan in Luke 10:29-36 leaves no doubt that "neighbor" is defined by action, not by social status or biological descent. Interestingly, that parable is preceded by a lawyer's affirmation that the way to eternal life is to "'Love the Lord your God with all your heart and with all your soul and with all your strength and with all your mind'; and, 'Love your neighbor as yourself'" (Luke 10:27).

C. COMPREHENSIVE COMMANDS (v. 40)

40. "All the Law and the Prophets hang on these two commandments."

When *these two commandments* are correctly understood and followed, they sum up *all* the requirements of *the Law and the Prophets*. When a person truly loves God, there will be no question about profaning his name or turning to idols. When a person truly loves a neighbor, he or she does not need to be told not to harm that neighbor in terms of stealing, lying, or having an adulterous affair with the neighbor's spouse.

Every law that is necessary for the good of society is an outgrowth of these two laws. The more that people live by these two laws, the less any other law is needed. Conversely, the more that people ignore the laws of love and try to regulate society with an ever-increasing number of legal statutes, the more frustrating the situation becomes. God's people are to live out these two laws from the heart.

CONCLUSION

A. THE LETTER OF THE LAW

There are several reasons why laws are often inadequate. Some laws are written badly, such as those that prohibit a certain act but provide no means of enforcement. Some laws are unrealistic and are sooner or later repealed.

Other laws are just bad to start with. Rosa Parks saw a bad law, a law that perpetuated racial barriers. So in 1955 in Montgomery, Alabama, she defied the order to move to the back of the bus. Her action sparked the Montgomery bus boycott and helped to propel Martin Luther King, Jr., to leadership in the American civil rights movement. Bad laws and broken connections between people just seem to go together.

Even good laws do not seem to be enough to achieve the ideals that society wants. That may be why some claim that "You can't legislate morality" (see our previous illustration). The more we depend on the letter of the law, with all its fine print and clever definitions, the less we seem to be able to achieve our goals. There is something inherently wrong with living a life that is made up only of the letter of *you shall* and *you shall not* in contrast with the spirit of those laws.

B. THE SPIRIT OF THE COMMANDS

God's people have been called to live together in love. Broken relationships with God and with other people can be repaired. Jesus came not only to enable us to have peace with God (see Romans 5:1), but also to make it possible for us to live in peace with others (see Hebrews 12:14).

Living for God is not primarily about following laws written with ink or chiseled onto tablets of stone, but of honoring the laws of love written on our hearts. We do not walk by the old letter of the law, for the letter kills but the spirit gives life (see 2 Corinthians 3:3-6). As we connect with God and with one another, we demonstrate that the greatest thing of all is love.

THOUGHT TO REMEMBER
Love God. Love one another.

Discovery Learning

The following is an alternative lesson plan emphasizing learning activities.
Classes desiring such student involvement will find these suggestions helpful. At the
back of this book are reproducible student pages to further enhance activity learning.

INTO THE LESSON

As students arrive, give each two large index cards. Say, "Please give your summary of the message of the New Testament in two sentences, writing one sentence on each card." As students finish, have them affix the cards to the board (with masking tape).

Next, ask students to help you group similar statements together as you rearrange them. Then write a sentence that sums up the essence of each grouping. Say, "In our lesson today, Jesus sums up the entire teaching of the Old Testament law and prophets in two sentences." Quote Matthew 22:37, 39. Continue: "Do you see any similarities between the two commands Jesus gave and the ones we put on the wall today?" After discussion, say, "Perhaps today's lesson will give us even more insight in this area."

INTO THE WORD

Say, "Many in Jesus' day saw him as a loose cannon, as someone who simply tossed out the old rules and made up his own. But the section of the Sermon on the Mount we will study today shows that Jesus came to complete the law, not to do away with it." Have someone read Matthew 5:17-20 aloud. Ask a student to pick out the phrases that identify Jesus' purpose in coming to earth (vv. 17, 18) and what he expected his listeners to do (vv. 19, 20).

Prepare in advance the following Scripture references on large index cards, one reference on each: Exodus 20:3, 4, 7, 12, 13, 14, 15, 16, 17; 22:21, 22, 25-27, 28-30; Leviticus 19:5-8; 19:9, 10; Deuteronomy 15:12-15. Distribute them. (If your class is smaller than the number of cards you create, give some students two cards.)

Ask each student to look up his or her Scripture(s) and write a summary on the card(s). As students finish, they are to put their cards on the board (with masking tape). Then say, "Let's fast forward to the last week of Jesus' earthly ministry. Matthew 22:34-40 tells us how a teacher of the law tried to test him." Read verse 34 to the class and use the commentary for that verse to provide the context for the remaining verses. Have another student read Matthew 22:35-40 aloud. Lead the class in a discussion of the two greatest commands.

After a few minutes, say, "Verse 40 says 'All the Law and the Prophets hang on these two commandments.' Let's see if we can determine why Jesus said that." Write on the board in big letters *Love the Lord your God* and a little farther down write *Love your neighbor.* Have the class work together or in groups to put underneath the appropriate heading the "laws" they previously affixed to the board. (Under *Love the Lord* will be Exodus 20:3, 4, 7; 22:28-30; Leviticus 19:5-8. Under *Love your neighbor* will be Exodus 20:12, 13, 14, 15, 16, 17; 22:21, 22, 25-27; Leviticus 19:9, 10; Deuteronomy 15:12-15.) Lead students in a brief discussion about how those two commands do, in fact, sum up the Law and the Prophets. (*Option #1:* In place of this last section, use the reproducible matching exercise "The Law and the Prophets" from the page 378. *Option #2:* Distribute that same exercise as a take-home activity instead.)

INTO LIFE

Say, "We've seen how the two greatest commands that Jesus cited sum up the Law and the Prophets. But our next concern is how we can apply these same commands to our lives. Or do these two greatest commands even apply anymore since we're now under the new covenant?" Allow students a few minutes to express their conclusions.

Next say, "Ultimately, our Christian life focuses on two types of relationship: relationship with God and relationship with others. To make sure we understand how these commands relate to our lives today, let's spend the rest of our time identifying specific ways we can (1) love God with all our heart, soul, and mind, and (2) love our neighbors as ourselves."

Give two index cards to each group of two or three. Ask each group to come up with one specific action to demonstrate love for God and one specific action to demonstrate love for neighbor. Tell students to place cards on the board under the appropriate heading as they finish. Discuss conclusions as time allows. End by praying for God's help to put at least one action under each heading into practice this week. Distribute copies of the reproducible activity "Planning to Put Love into Action" from page 378 as students depart.

INCLUSION IN COMMUNITY

LESSON 8

INTRODUCTION

A. INVITATIONS

We all get invitations: weddings, showers, birthdays, cookouts—the list goes on. But most of these are rather routine and common. "Important" people get "important" invitations: black-tie affairs, country-club banquets, dinners at the White House, etc. Some folks even measure their success and status by the quality of their invitations. Invitations make us feel included. When we are asked to join a group, we are flattered. We feel good about ourselves when people think enough of us to want our company. Part of a person's sense of well-being comes from being included.

In the eternal scheme of things, however, most of the connections that we value are rather insignificant. Long after we have finished our lives on earth, who will care if we belonged to a certain lodge, fraternity, or chamber of commerce? The only thing that will matter is whether or not we belong to the community of God. That is why the most important invitation of all is the invitation we have from God.

B. LESSON BACKGROUND

During the final months of Jesus' ministry, he stayed away from Jerusalem because the authorities were intent on arresting him (John 10:39; 11:8). At one point even some of the Pharisees warned him of the danger that awaited (Luke 13:22, 31). But as his appointed time drew near, Jesus began the circuitous journey that would end in Jerusalem and the cross.

One Pharisee invited Jesus into his home on the Sabbath day. Some of the guests were skeptical of Jesus, so they watched him very carefully (Luke 14:1-4). Others were more intent on getting places of honor at the table. At a banquet in the first century, guests would recline around a low table. Therefore, they were not just grabbing a chair, but were trying to be the first to lie down on the couch next to the host. Jesus watched them scramble for their spots, and then had a word of rebuke: "For everyone who exalts himself will be humbled, and he who humbles himself will be exalted" (Luke 14:11).

Jesus had a further word for the host. Instead of just inviting his family, friends, and/or rich neighbors, the man should have invited the poor, the blind, and the crippled. Such people would not be able to repay the favor. God himself would repay the man's generosity at the final resurrection (Luke 14:12-14). It was the prospect of sharing in God's great banquet at the final resurrection that one guest exclaimed the words that begin our lesson.

DEVOTIONAL READING:
PSALM 65:1-8

BACKGROUND SCRIPTURE:
LUKE 14:1-24

PRINTED TEXT:
LUKE 14:15-24

LESSON AIMS

After participating in this lesson, each student will be able to:

1. Summarize the Parable of the Great Banquet.

2. Compare and contrast the excuses in the Parable of the Great Banquet with excuses heard today.

3. Adapt the Parable of the Great Banquet for the twenty-first century.

Apr
25

KEY VERSE

"Go out quickly into the streets and alleys of the town and bring in the poor, the crippled, the blind and the lame."   —Luke 14:21

I. Blessed Inclusion (Luke 14:15-17)

A. One Man's Exclamation (v. 15)

15. When one of those at the table with him heard this, he said to Jesus, "Blessed is the man who will eat at the feast in the kingdom of God."

One of the guests responds enthusiastically to what Jesus has just said about being repaid by God at the resurrection of the righteous (see Luke 14:14). The man probably assumes that he himself and the other pious Pharisees certainly will be in that number. Thus he exclaims how *blessed* is the person who will participate in the endless *feast* of Heaven.

The word *blessed* is the same word Jesus uses in the Beatitudes (see Matthew 5:3-11). It is used in ancient times in the context of congratulating people who have been successful, fortunate, or seem to have been treated favorably by the gods. For people who know the one true God, to be blessed means to receive the favor and approval of Heaven.

The guest at this Pharisee's table is correct to perceive that eating at God's table will be a wonderful thing. He is wrong, however, if he assumes that he has an automatic right to be there because of his Jewish ancestry or his pious good deeds as a Pharisee.

B. The Lord's Explanation (vv. 16, 17)

16. Jesus replied: "A certain man was preparing a great banquet and invited many guests.

Jesus puts many of his teachings in the form of a parable. A parable often is called "an earthly story with a heavenly meaning." Teaching this way has several advantages. For common people, the stories are interesting and make sense. For hostile critics, the stories give them nothing solid by which they can condemn Jesus. For all people, the stories are a way of getting past the initial resistance, slipping important truths in by a side door. Many of Jesus' parables also have a note of wry humor, as the tables are turned.

So Jesus describes *a great banquet* hosted by *a certain man.* (When Jesus tells the parable again after he arrives in Jerusalem, he makes the host of the banquet "a king"; see Matthew 22:2-14.) This is a feast much like the one these *guests* themselves currently enjoy. Only great people are *invited* to a great banquet. The people hearing this parable immediately understand how fortunate it is to be invited.

17. "At the time of the banquet he sent his servant to tell those who had been invited, 'Come, for everything is now ready.'

The host has sent word in advance that a great *banquet* is going to be held. The invitation undoubtedly includes the day and place. Thus everyone *invited* has plenty of opportunity to get ready for the important event. The host also is able to find out how many are planning to come so that he will know how much food to prepare. Then, when the banquet hall is ready and all the food has been cooked, he sends *his servant* with the great announcement: *Come, for everything is now ready.*

Jesus' audience knows that it is fashionable among upper-class people to have the two-part invitation. The second part prevents them from coming too early and then having to wait; thus they avoid embarrassing themselves and their host. Besides being true to life, though, the two-part invitation also enhances the point of Jesus' parable since God himself also offers repeated invitations.

What Do You Think?

On what basis can we affirm that we will be at the great feast in Heaven? Or is it presumptuous of us to think that we will? Explain.

What Do You Think?

As you read your Bible, what preparations do you see God making for his marriage supper (Revelation 19:9)? What is your part, if any, in those preparations?

II. RUDE EXCUSES (LUKE 14:18-20)

A. LAND TO BE INSPECTED (v. 18)

18. "But they all alike began to make excuses. The first said, 'I have just bought a field, and I must go and see it. Please excuse me.'

Astonishingly, *all* those who are invited to the great feast begin *to make excuses*. This is a shocking breach of etiquette, as Jesus' hearers know very well. (After all, they have not failed to honor the invitation to the feast they are currently attending!) At the very least, the people in the parable could have let their host know at the first invitation that they would not be able to attend. Instead, they wait until the feast is already prepared and then insult their host with feeble excuses.

The first excuse comes from a man who has just purchased some property. Now that he has made the purchase, he wants to go and take a look at it. This excuse, like the others that follow, is intended to look ridiculous. As Jesus' hearers think about the situation, they probably chuckle to themselves at how silly the excuse actually is. The implication of *I have just bought a field, and I must go and see it* is that this person has made his purchase sight unseen. But who does such a thing? While it may happen in rare circumstances, it certainly is not the normal thing to do. And why at banquet time does this man suddenly need to inspect it? This potential guest simply has decided that he has something he would rather do than honor the invitation.

B. OXEN TO BE TESTED (v. 19)

19. "Another said, 'I have just bought five yoke of oxen, and I'm on my way to try them out. Please excuse me.'

As the master's servant continues to make the rounds in giving the follow-up invitation, he comes to another potential guest who offers an excuse as well. The fact that he has bought *five* pairs *of oxen* shows that he is wealthy and successful, since most farmers can afford only one or two. Now the man wants to go *to try them out*—to put them to the test and find out if they can plow. Again, there undoubtedly is a chuckle from Jesus' audience as they consider the folly of buying oxen without first knowing if they can do the work. Like the first excuse, this one also is unworthy.

The Greek word for *please excuse me* in verses 18 and 19 is also used in Hebrews 12:19. There the children of Israel are described as standing at the foot of Mount Sinai and begging to be excluded from hearing the voice of God. The same word occurs in Hebrews 12:25 in a caution not to refuse him who speaks. Seeing the word in this context shows that making excuses to God is the sinful equivalent of stubbornly *refusing* to listen and respond.

C. WIFE TO BE CONCERNED WITH (v. 20)

20. "Still another said, 'I just got married, so I can't come.'

Finally, a third guest declines the invitation because he has just gotten *married*. This man says *therefore* he *can't come*, as if the logical connection is obvious. To Jesus' audience, it is a ridiculous excuse. Did not the man know at the initial invitation that he was planning to get married? If the supper is for men only, could he not be apart from his wife for even a few hours? And if she is also invited, what wife would not want to go to a banquet? (In the

---

DAILY BIBLE READINGS

Monday, Apr. 19—God Is the Hope for All (Psalm 65:1-8)

Tuesday, Apr. 20—All Nations Shall Come (Psalm 86:8-13)

Wednesday, Apr. 21— Come and Learn God's Ways (Isaiah 2:1-4)

Thursday, Apr. 22—King of the Nations (Revelation 15:2b-4)

Friday, Apr. 23— Ministry to All (Matthew 25:31-40)

Saturday, Apr. 24— Humility and Hospitality (Luke 14:7-14)

Sunday, Apr. 25—Invite All to Come (Luke 14:15-24)

HOW TO SAY IT

Abraham. AY-bruh-ham.

Beatitudes. Bee-A-tuh-toods (A as in MAT).

etiquette. EH-tih-kit.

Isaac. EYE-zuk.

Isaiah. Eye-ZAY-uh.

Jacob. JAY-kub.

Jerusalem. Juh-ROO-suh-lem.

Messianic. Mess-ee-AN-ick.

Pharisees. FAIR-ih-seez.

Sinai. SIGH-nye or SIGH-nay-eye.

What Do You Think?

What are some excuses non-Christians give to avoid making a decision for Christ? What are some excuses Christians use to avoid Christian service? Are there common elements across these two? Explain.

first century, Jewish women often are invited to banquets, but the women are seated separately from the men.) Would she rather stay at home and cook? If there are women in this audience, they undoubtedly exchange amused looks, knowing how quickly they would accept such an invitation.

Thus the invited guests in Jesus' parable have come up with three lame excuses for not wanting to come to the feast. Fitting an old definition, each excuse is "the skin of a reason stuffed with a lie." Ridiculous circumstances take precedence over the invitation of the host. If the guests attend the feast, will not the unseen field, the untested oxen, and the stay-at-home wife still be there later? Like other excuses listed in Luke 9:57-62, there is no sufficient reason to allow anything to come ahead of loyalty to the Lord.

Recognizing Excuses for What They Are

As a college professor, I hear a lot of excuses. Many are genuine, and I make allowances for them. One student told me of working on a paper when a friend called; the friend had been involved in an auto accident and needed someone to come to the hospital. Ultimately the student spent several hours at the hospital and was unable to finish his paper on time. Another student called me to say she was seriously ill and could not get her work done. Her normally pleasant voice was gravelly and scratchy. In both instances, I gave the students time to make up the work without penalty.

But while some excuses are convincing, others are not. I remember the time a student told me she couldn't finish her paper because her cat had died and she needed a week to recover from the loss. Now, I am not a cat hater, and I realize some people get very close to their pets, but I thought, "It's only a cat!" I suppose that marks me as insensitive. Some students oversleep and miss class on the day an assignment is due. Normally I'm not very sympathetic, unless there is some extenuating circumstance.

I realize that sometimes "real life" gets in the way of schoolwork. But some people use excuses as a crutch to hobble their way through life. Jesus calls us to something higher than that. Much of this comes down to an issue of priorities.
—J. B. N.

III. SURPRISING RESULT (LUKE 14:21-24)
A. Alternative Invitation (v. 21)
21. *"The servant came back and reported this to his master. Then the owner of the house became angry and ordered his servant, 'Go out quickly into the streets and alleys of the town and bring in the poor, the crippled, the blind and the lame.'*

As the story continues, the *servant* returns to *his master* with a complete report: the invited guests refuse to come. The *owner of the house* is understandably *angry*. His gracious invitation has been thrown back in his face.

In his anger he comes up with a plan: he will send his servant out to the *streets and alleys of the town* where homeless beggars live. He will bring in *poor* people to replace his wealthy "friends." He will invite people who are *crippled* to take their places on his upholstered couches. He will bid people who are *blind* to replace those who just could not see their way clear to come to his feast. (It should not be forgotten that these are exactly the people whom Jesus had earlier said that his host should have invited to the supper currently in progress; see Luke 14:13.)

Visual for Lessons 4 & 8. *Point to this visual as you ask, "How do we move from merely saying 'all are welcome' to actually being a welcoming church?"*

B. COMPELLING SUMMONS (vv. 22, 23)

22. "'Sir,' the servant said, 'what you ordered has been done, but there is still room.'

The servant quickly obeys his master, summoning the beggars of the city to come to the feast. These people, desperate in their poverty, gladly respond to the invitation. As soon as they enter the banquet hall, they know that they are about to enjoy a feast beyond anything they have ever known. And still, there is such abundance that there is room for more! Throughout his ministry Jesus shows a special love for such people. Wherever there are people whom society had cast aside, Jesus reaches out in love. By contrast, he often clashes with the powerful pious. As Jesus will soon tell the chief priests and elders at the temple in Jerusalem, "The tax collectors and the prostitutes are entering the kingdom of God ahead you" (Matthew 21:31).

YET THERE IS ROOM

When I was in junior high many decades ago, our church held a revival. One night the evangelist preached a sermon on Heaven. He referred to the argument of some that Heaven would not be big enough to contain all the souls that had gone there. After all, aren't there going to be only 144,000 that make it, according to Revelation 7:4? To this the evangelist pointed out 7:9, which mentions a "great multitude . . . from every nation, tribe, people and language," which no one can number. That certainly exceeds the 144,000 "from all the tribes of the children of Israel."

The evangelist then went on to read Revelation 21:16, which describes the massive dimensions of the new Jerusalem. If taken literally, that verse depicts the heavenly city as being 12,000 furlongs (about 1,500 miles) long, wide, and high. Think of a city that is 1,500 miles square and is then stacked up 1,500 miles high as well! That's room for a multitude that no one can number.

Some argue that the book of Revelation is not meant to be taken literally in these kinds of references, but that is somewhat beside the point. The point is that Heaven has enough room for everyone! The words of Jesus that the banquet hall still has room applies to the glorious banquet feast that God is preparing for all of us.

—J. B. N.

23. "Then the master told his servant, 'Go out to the roads and country lanes and make them come in, so that my house will be full.

There are still empty places at the tables, even as the great hall fills with people who are poor, lame, and blind. Determined that his hospitality will not be wasted, *the master* of the house sends *his servant* out to find even more replacements for those who were invited originally. The servant is sent beyond the boundaries of the town, to find even travelers. He is sent into the rough areas fenced by brush, where vagrants may be found.

When the servant finds such people, he is to *make them come in* to the feast. *Make them* does not mean to force them against their will, but to urge them strongly and show them convincingly the necessity. The host is determined that his banquet shall not go to waste, but that his house should *be full.*

In this parable Jesus can be seen to prophesy a future time when God will replace the "expected" guests with outsiders. God previously had established a covenant with the people of Israel, preparing them for the coming of the

WHAT DO YOU THINK?

What are some ways we can "compel" unsaved people to come to the Lord while avoiding the criticism that we are "imposing" our religion on others?

PRAYER

Heavenly Father, thank you for preparing the heavenly feast and inviting us to share your bounty. Help us never to assume that we have somehow earned the right to be there. Help us also to be passionate about carrying the invitation to others, to compel them to come in. We pray in Jesus' name. Amen.

messianic age. When that time arrives with the advent of Jesus, however, many reject him. Therefore God will find replacements!

C. COMPLETE REJECTION (v. 24)

24. "'I tell you, not one of those men who were invited will get a taste of my banquet.'"

The host is clearly angry with those who reject his invitation. Thus he vows that *not one* of them will even get a *taste* of his *banquet*. They have put matters of lesser consequence ahead of the great feast. The repercussions of their refusal will be long-lasting. They may think that there will always be more invitations in the future, but those invitations will not come.

This parable teaches us that God, the host of Heaven, is angry with those who reject his invitation. And he has every right to be (compare Proverbs 1:24-31). Whether it is the people of first-century Israel who will not accept the Messiah of the new covenant or the people of any nationality today who do not respond to the gospel invitation, it is no small matter to snub the Creator and spurn his salvation. According to John 3:18, anyone who rejects God's Son and the forgiveness of the cross is "condemned already."

CONCLUSION
A. GOD'S R.S.V.P.

The letters *R.S.V.P.* often are included at the bottom of written invitations. These four letters abbreviate a French phrase that is translated "please respond." To ignore the request to respond is a social blunder. The more important the invitation, the greater the blunder if it is ignored.

God's invitation to come to him is the greatest invitation any person can ever receive. (See Isaiah 1:18; 55:1; Matthew 11:28.) Therefore nothing in all of life should be allowed to displace it. It is God's greatest gift that "whosoever will" can come (see Revelation 22:17). Older Christians will perhaps remember a hymn written by Charles H. Gabriel (1856–1932) that reflects that idea:

> *"All things are ready," come to the feast! / Come, for the table now is spread;*
> *Ye famishing, ye weary, come, / And thou shalt be richly fed.*
> *Hear the invitation, / Come, "whosoever will";*
> *Praise God for full salvation / For "whosoever will."*

WHAT DO YOU THINK?

What is the greatest sacrifice you had to make when you accepted the invitation to receive Christ? How has God begun to repay you for what you gave up?

B. THE MARRIAGE SUPPER OF THE LAMB

The invitation to join God's community is not without cost. God's invitation demands the right to override all other claims on our time and resources. While it certainly does not demand that we abandon our families, quit our jobs, or throw away our financial assets, it does demand to come ahead of them in priority. At times we may experience conflicts that are far more pressing than the foolish excuses of Jesus' parable, but God's call must always come first. In a verse that follows the parable, Jesus even says, "Any of you who does not give up everything he has cannot be my disciple" (Luke 14:33).

But the wonderful truth is that giving up everything to accept God's invitation will be worth it! Jesus assured his disciples that even if they had to give up houses, lands, or family ties for his sake, they would be repaid many times over, and they would inherit eternal life (Matthew 19:29).

The invitation to become part of the community of God is also an invitation to the marriage supper of the Lamb (Revelation 19:7). When God's people take their place at the feast with Abraham, Isaac, and Jacob in the kingdom of Heaven, there will be great rejoicing. But for those who are not included, there will be "weeping and gnashing of teeth" at the lost opportunity (see Matthew 8:11, 12).

Any sacrifices made to attend this feast will be soon forgotten. All who are included on that day will understand the words of the angel recorded by John: "Blessed are those who are invited to the wedding supper of the Lamb!" (Revelation 19:9).

THOUGHT TO REMEMBER
*"All things are ready,'
come to the feast!"*

Discovery Learning

*The following is an alternative lesson plan emphasizing learning activities.
Classes desiring such student involvement will find these suggestions helpful. At the
back of this book are reproducible student pages to further enhance activity learning.*

INTO THE LESSON

Collect or construct invitations of various kinds (examples: birthday party, wedding, fiftieth anniversary, graduation, awards banquet, Presidential Inaugural Ball). Before class begins, spread the invitations on the tables or chairs. (You may have more than one of each type of invitation.)

Ask each student to select an invitation and devise an acceptable excuse for refusing it. Then have students describe the types of invitation they received. Ask the class to help you rank them in order of importance (example: a birthday party might rank lower than a fiftieth wedding anniversary). When you have ranked the invitations, have students share their refusals. As a class, determine whether each refusal is acceptable based on the importance of the invitation.

Say, "It seems rather crazy to us to think someone would refuse an invitation to the President's Inaugural Ball. But in our lesson today we will see people who refused an even greater invitation."

INTO THE WORD

Divide the class into three groups. Group #1 will analyze the invitations in Luke 14:7-14 (not in today's lesson text). Group #2 will analyze the invitations in Luke 14:15-24. Group #3 will analyze the excuses given in Luke 14:18-20.

Prepare the following questions on a handout for Groups #1 and #2: 1. To whom were the invitations given? 2. Why was the invitation is-

sued? 3. How did those who were invited respond? 4. What was the host's reaction to the guests?

Prepare a handout for Group #3 with these questions: 1. What was the excuse each person gave? 2. Were these excuses reasonable? Why, or why not?

After groups prepare, begin with Group #1 to set the background. Have the group summarize their passage, making sure they answer the four questions (*1. prominent people, friends, relatives, rich neighbors [v. 12]; 2. to be repaid by a return invitation [v. 12]; 3. picked places of honor [v. 7]; 4. give someone else your seat [v. 9]*). Supplement with information from the Lesson Background. Then say, "This scenario sounds somewhat familiar, doesn't it? Most of us invite those we know to parties. When we go to a party, we tend to seat ourselves (if there are no printed seating assignments) rather than wait for the host to seat us. Now let's see how another scenario compares."

Group #2 then presents its conclusions. This group should summarize the events of the passage. Make sure they answer the four questions (*1. first to specific individuals [v. 17], then to everyone—poor, crippled, lame, blind [v. 21]; 2. to fill the house [v. 23]; 3. they offered excuses [v. 18; make sure this group does not go into detail about the excuses, since that is what Group #3 will discuss]; 4. invites others to take their places [vv. 21, 23]*). Supplement this group's report with information from the lesson commentary. Give students the opportunity to compare and contrast the two banquets in other ways.

Next, have Group #3 present its report. Make sure they include the information that answers their questions (*1. just bought a field [v. 18], just bought oxen [v. 19], just got married [v. 20]; 2. answers may vary; supplement with the lesson commentary for vv. 18-20*).

Wrap up the discussion by using the lesson commentary for verses 21-24 to impress on the students the fact that God extends his invitation to all. Time allowing, have students complete the reproducible activity "Come to the Feast" on page 379.

INTO LIFE

Say, "God's invitation is not only for those who have not yet accepted his gift of salvation. He also offers certain invitations to those of us who already are part of his body." Have students work individually or in pairs to look up Proverbs 3:5, 6; Matthew 6:19, 20, 33; 7:7, 8; 11:28-30; Mark 8:34; Galatians 5:13; Ephesians 5:1, 2; 5:15, 16; Philippians 4:6-8; Colossians 3:15-17; and 1 Peter 5:7.

As students identify the invitation God gives in each passage, have them write the invitation on an index card. Then have students identify excuses that they or others have given for not accepting those invitations, writing them on the cards as well. Discuss the validity of the excuses. Have students identify invitations God has been extending to them, but that they have been reluctant to accept. *Option:* Use the reproducible activity "Excuses! Excuses!" page 379 instead.

A FAITHFUL COMMUNITY

LESSON 9

INTRODUCTION

A. TEAMWORK IN REAL LIFE

Sports seems to affect every nation on earth, especially team sports. Many children and young adults participate in such sports. They then retain their interest as fans when they can no longer play. Major events such as the World Cup in soccer, the NCAA tournament in college basketball, and the Super Bowl in football draw interest even from casual fans.

Team sports have the potential of teaching young men and women many positive lessons about life. In football, we learn that running backs don't score touchdowns unless they have teammates blocking for them. In basketball, we learn that even the deadeye shooting guard cannot score all the baskets needed to win a game by herself. In baseball, even the best pitcher needs teammates who will score some runs. Team sports by definition are not one-person shows. Team sports teach lessons about learning to work together. A team has a variety of roles that need to be filled successfully.

Churches are like teams in many ways, although the analogy can be overdrawn. (Obviously, churches are not in competitive leagues and do not function on a seasonal basis!) Paul, who seemed to be a sports fan himself (see 1 Corinthians 9:24), taught that every church was more than a gathering of individuals. Paul saw the church as a body (Romans 12:5), a unified entity working as one. Today's lesson, drawn from the first chapter of Paul's letter to the Colossians, is an excellent example of how this worked.

B. LESSON BACKGROUND

When we read the book of Acts, we may get the impression of Paul being constantly on the move, traveling from city to city to preach the gospel and plant churches. A careful reading, however, shows that Paul had two locations where he had extended stays. During his second missionary journey, Paul was able to remain in Corinth for about 18 months (Acts 18:11). On his third missionary journey, Paul was located in Ephesus for more than 2 years (Acts 19:8, 10).

Ephesus was one of the larger cities in the Roman Empire. It served as a commercial and administrative hub for the Roman province of Asia (now part of Turkey). A hundred miles to the east were the tri-cities of Colosse (also spelled *Colossae*), Laodicea, and Hierapolis (compare Colossians 2:1; 4:13). Laodicea was the leading city of this triad, and it is known to Bible readers for one of the seven churches of the book of Revelation (Revelation 1:11; 3:14-22).

While we have no record of Paul visiting these cities, it is likely that their churches were founded during his time in Ephesus. Thus they formed a network of churches associated with that apostle. Some speculate that the Colossian church was founded by Epaphras, a trusted coworker of Paul and

DEVOTIONAL READING:
JEREMIAH 29:10-14

BACKGROUND SCRIPTURE:
COLOSSIANS 1

PRINTED TEXT:
COLOSSIANS 1:1-14

LESSON AIMS

After participating in this lesson, each student will be able to:

1. List some of the things that Paul thanked God for and prayed about concerning the Colossians.

2. Compare and contrast the strengths and weaknesses of the church at Colosse with those of his or her own church.

3. Suggest a plan or program that can be implemented at his or her church that will help members grow in knowledge, wisdom, and spiritual understanding.

May
2

KEY VERSE

Since the day we heard about you, we have not stopped praying for you and asking God to fill you with the knowledge of his will through all spiritual wisdom and understanding.
—Colossians 1:9

Lesson 9 Notes

What Do You Think?

What are some non-Christian philosophies that affect churches today? How can you help protect your church from these?

Daily Bible Readings

Monday, Apr. 26—A Future with Hope (Jeremiah 29:10-14)

Tuesday, Apr. 27—A Faithful Servant (Matthew 25:14-21)

Wednesday, Apr. 28—Faithful in a Very Little (Luke 16:10-12)

Thursday, Apr. 29—Trustworthy Stewards (1 Corinthians 4:1-5)

Friday, Apr. 30—Steadfast in the Faith (Colossians 1:15-23)

Saturday, May 1—Paul's Faithful Service (Colossians 1:24-29)

Sunday, May 2—The Gospel Bearing Fruit (Colossians 1:1-14)

a native of Colosse (see Colossians 1:7; 4:12). Colosse, a moderately prosperous market city, was known for producing a type of fine, dyed wool that was prized in the ancient world.

Colossians is one of the Prison Epistles, letters Paul wrote while he was imprisoned in Rome about AD 62 or 63. A reference to this is found in the final verse of the book, (Colossians 4:18; this is a reference to his house-arrest status in Acts 28:16, 20). This letter was sent to the Colossian church primarily to combat a growing threat of heresy within that body. While the heresy is not named, it seems to have included elements of pagan philosophy and Judaism. Paul wrote to correct the problem and call the church to a return to the simple faith in Christ (Colossians 2:6, 7). He gave a strong warning to reject outside philosophies and religious teachings that were incompatible with the teachings of Christianity (2:8).

I. CAUSE FOR GRATITUDE (COLOSSIANS 1:1-8)

A. Appreciation of Faithfulness (vv. 1, 2)

1. *Paul, an apostle of Christ Jesus by the will of God, and Timothy our brother,*

We should remember that *Paul* is under a type of house arrest when he writes this letter. He has been charged with crimes by the Jewish leaders from Jerusalem (see Acts 24:5, 6). As a Roman citizen, Paul has exercised his right to appeal his case to Caesar (Acts 25:11).

He has been taken from Judea to Rome in order that his appeal to the emperor might be heard. Thus he is in a house in Rome where he can receive visitors but where there is a guard present at all times. (They didn't have electronic monitoring bracelets back then!) *Timothy*, Paul's trusted helper, is there with him. While Timothy may have a hand in writing the letter, we should understand it ultimately as the thoughts of Paul.

2. . . . *To the holy and faithful brothers in Christ at Colosse:*
    Grace and peace to you from God our Father.

The reference to the *brothers* means that Paul's greeting is for the entirety of the Colossian church. This is not a letter intended just for one or two of the church leaders (contrast 1 Timothy 1:2; 2 Timothy 1:2; Titus 1:4).

One of Paul's points of emphasis in Colossians is the appreciation he has for such faithful people (see Colossians 2:5, 7). A faithful church is made up of faithful men and women acting both individually and collectively in ways that are consistent with their trust in Christ and his commandments. Christ is the source and foundation of this faith.

As is common in his letters, Paul gives a two-fold blessing to his readers. *Grace* reflects a traditional Greek style for greeting beloved friends. *Peace* (or *shalom*) is a Jewish blessing.

B. Appreciation of Devotion (vv. 3-5)

3. *We always thank God, the Father of our Lord Jesus Christ, when we pray for you,*

Paul is unable to do much for the Colossians personally because of his situation. This does not hinder him from praying for them, however. Despite his imprisonment, Paul's prayers are not those of frustration or lament. Rather, they are prayers of thanksgiving, for this church has been an encouragement to Paul.

4. . . . *because we have heard of your faith in Christ Jesus and of the love you have for all the saints—*

Paul emphasizes two characteristics of the Colossians that make him thankful. First, they are renowned for their *faith in Christ Jesus*. Paul knows that there are some specific doctrinal concerns in this area, and these will be addressed later. These problems, however, do not overshadow the strong faith that the congregation exhibits. What a glorious compliment! How great it would be today to have the reputation of being "the church with a deep faith in Christ"!

Paul's second point of thanksgiving is the *love* that the Colossians have for *all the saints*. This is a loving congregation, so much so that its reputation for love has spread all the way to Paul in Rome. Here, Paul uses the term *saints* to refer to all the believers in the church, those who have been sanctified by their faith in Christ and the presence of the Holy Spirit in their lives. This term is applied to all Christians in the New Testament era (compare Ephesians 1:1; Philippians 1:1).

Again, what a beautiful reputation! We should realize that it is no coincidence that deep faith in Christ and a loving church go hand in hand.

5. . . . the faith and love that spring from the hope that is stored up for you in heaven and that you have already heard about in the word of truth, the gospel

Another factor in the success of the Colossian church is its high level of expectation based on the promises of *the gospel*. They have *hope* for the future, for they know that *Heaven* is their eternal home. The central element of this hope is the resurrection of Christ (compare 1 Peter 1:3, 4). Without the resurrection, the gospel is not true (see 1 Corinthians 15:14). Hopeful people tend to be happy people (see Psalm 146:5).

Notice that we now have the three core elements of the famous triad of *faith*, hope, and *love* (compare 1 Corinthians 13:13; 1 Thessalonians 1:3). Where all three of these are strong, one will find a healthy congregation made up of blessed, purposeful believers.

C. APPRECIATION OF PRODUCTIVITY (v. 6)

6. . . . that has come to you. All over the world this gospel is bearing fruit and growing, just as it has been doing among you since the day you heard it and understood God's grace in all its truth.

Paul teaches that sincere, faithful reception of the *gospel* will result in *fruit* from the believers. A well-known principle taught by Jesus is that a tree is known by its fruit (Matthew 12:33). This might be lifestyle characteristics and attitudes that Paul considers to be spiritual fruit (Galatians 5:22, 23; compare Colossians 1:10, below). Also included may be the evangelistic efforts of the Colossians that result in new disciples (compare John 15:8). *God's grace*, as seen in the sacrifice of his Son for our sins, should cause us to share the gospel and thereby grow the church.

D. APPRECIATION OF PARTNERSHIP (vv. 7, 8)

7a. You learned it from Epaphras, our dear fellow servant,

Epaphras is originally from Colosse (Colossians 4:12). At some point, he is jailed with Paul (Philemon 23). Paul views this man in two ways. First, Epaphras is a *dear fellow servant*. This is a remarkable designation, for with it Paul puts Epaphras on the same level as himself. The man from Colosse is more than Paul's assistant. They are serving together equally in some ways. The fact that they end up in prison together signifies that the Romans themselves realize this.

WHAT DO YOU THINK?

Can a doctrinally compromised church still be pleasing to God? Why, or why not?

[Titus 1:9; 2:1 and Revelation 2:13-16 can be talking points in your discussion.]

HOW TO SAY IT

Caesar. SEE-zer.
Colosse. Ko-LAHSS-ee.
coxswain. COCK-sun.
Epaphras. EP-uh-frass.
Ephesus. EF-uh-sus.
Gentiles. JEN-tiles.
heresy. HAIR-uh-see.
Hierapolis. Hi-er-AP-o-lis.
Judaism. JOO-duh-izz-um or JOO-day-izz-um.
Laodicea. Lay-ODD-uh-SEE-uh.
medieval. me-DEE-vul.
shalom (Hebrew). shah-LOME.

7b, 8. . . . who is a faithful minister of Christ on our behalf, and who also told us of your love in the Spirit.

The second way Paul views this man is as *a faithful minister* to the Colossians. Epaphras has been one of the designated leaders of the Colossian church. He is now in Rome with Paul, although we are not told why. Epaphras has brought the heartening news of the love and faith of the Colossians to the imprisoned apostle. It is "the Epaphras connection" that can cause Paul to have a strong attachment to a church that he may never have visited.

II. CAUSE FOR ENCOURAGEMENT (COLOSSIANS 1:9-14)
A. ENRICHED LIVES (vv. 9, 10)

9. For this reason, since the day we heard about you, we have not stopped praying for you and asking God to fill you with the knowledge of his will through all spiritual wisdom and understanding.

Paul has no cause to question the Colossians' faith and commitment. His concern is in the general area of *knowledge, wisdom,* and *understanding.* A genuine faith must be an informed faith. There may be areas of disagreement in Christian doctrine that do not really matter that much, but there are essentials that must not be compromised.

Paul is treading lightly here, gently preparing the Colossians to hear his plea for purity in their understanding of Jesus. Paul knows that this letter may be his only shot at correcting the heresy that is beginning to form in Colosse. Therefore, he must approach this prayerfully, trusting in the power of God to fill them with the truth.

10. And we pray this in order that you may live a life worthy of the Lord and may please him in every way: bearing fruit in every good work, growing in the knowledge of God,

Paul wants the Colossians to have the whole package: a worthy *life* (righteous living), fruitful production *in every good work* (active compassion in their community), and ever-growing *knowledge of God.* The first two seem to be in reasonably good condition according to the report of Epaphras, but the third needs help.

Before we criticize the Colossians, we should remember that they are in a smaller town far from the mainstream of Christianity in their day. There are few (if any) of the writings that constitute our New Testament available to them. They have not had the benefit of the long-term teaching ministry of someone like Paul. Their region abounds with religious teachers, both Jewish and pagan. Paul wants to give the Colossians every chance to be assured and correct in their doctrine and faith. This is why he is writing.

TO WALK WORTHY

One of the greatest knights in medieval England was William Marshall. He served faithfully under King Henry II from 1170 until the king's death in 1189, including 2 years fighting with the crusaders in the Holy Land. Marshall then served under Richard the Lion-Hearted during the 10 years of his reign. When Richard died unexpectedly, Marshall supported John as the next king, even though many barons supported a rival.

In spite of Marshall's support, however, John called him a traitor, took most of his land, held his two sons hostage, and tried to get him killed in a tournament. Yet Marshall supported the king as his rightful lord in spite of this treatment. Marshall

WHAT DO YOU THINK?

How do you go about "growing in the knowledge of God"?

WHAT DO YOU THINK?

Based on Paul's example, how should we go about trying to correct the perceived doctrinal errors in others?

[You may find Luke 6:42 to be important to your discussion.]

supported John against Pope Innocent III and even supported his king against the barons' rebellion that resulted in the Magna Carta. Why? Because Marshall had taken an oath of fealty.

In the Middle Ages, treason against one's lord was the worst crime. Marshall's oath of loyalty and his innate code of honor would not allow him to join the rebellion against his king. For Marshall to live a worthy life was to live up to his word—and that meant support for the king even if the king were wrong. We follow a king who is never wrong. But sometimes it seems as if our loyalty wavers. Why is that?

—J. B. N.

B. EMPOWERED LIVES (v. 11)

11. . . . *being strengthened with all power according to his glorious might so that you may have great endurance and patience, and joyfully*

Paul uses several terms to describe the life that is fueled by God's *power,* the *glorious* power that we receive from the Holy Spirit's ministry (compare Ephesians 3:16). It is a life that is strong, mighty, and powerful because of the Lord's presence (compare Ephesians 1:19). In this case, Paul is not talking about empowerment that manifests itself in miraculous deeds, but of inner strength, strength of character.

The person of godly empowerment will show *patience* and *great endurance.* God's power gives us the ability to endure times of stress and pain. This is much more than dogged stubbornness. We can recognize the presence of God in our lives when we patiently endure hardship *joyfully.* It is through this powerful patience that the Christian is able eventually to bear fruit for the Lord (see Luke 8:15).

C. ENLIGHTENED LIVES (v. 12)

12. . . . *giving thanks to the Father, who has qualified you to share in the inheritance of the saints in the kingdom of light.*

Paul returns to his theme of thanksgiving to praise God for the bond of fellowship between believers. The word translated *qualified* indicates that we are "suitably made" (see Genesis 2:20). Paul is thus including the Colossian believers in his larger community of Christians. These are the *saints in the kingdom of light*—those who walk in the light of God's truth (see Ephesians 1:18; 5:8, 9) and share in his promises. Through their faith, the Colossians have become "co-heirs" (Romans 8:17) with all believers and with Christ.

If we compare this passage with other places where Paul talks about an *inheritance,* we see that he is particularly addressing the Gentile believers of Colosse. The nation of Israel has long seen itself as the heirs of Abraham. Through Christ, Gentiles are able to share in the blessings associated with being citizens of the kingdom of God (Ephesians 3:6). To be an heir is to be a true child of the king (see Galatians 4:7). Gentiles may therefore be partakers of the greatest inheritance of all: salvation and thus eternal life (Titus 3:7).

D. ENABLED LIVES (vv. 13, 14)

13a. *For he has rescued us from the dominion of darkness*

What is *the dominion of darkness* from which people may be *rescued?* For Paul, this is a combination of ignorance and sinfulness. Those who have

WHAT DO YOU THINK?

Where in your life is God calling you to exercise patience today? How do you do that with joyfulness?

Visual for Lesson 9. *Use this visual to start a discussion on how bearing and harvesting spiritual fruit interrelate.*

PRAYER

Loving God, may we seek to honor Christ in our church by our faith and our faithfulness, by our love for you and our love for each other. We pray in the name of the one whose blood has rescued us from the power of sin and darkness. Amen.

not been enlightened by the truth stumble around in moral darkness without understanding God's will for their lives (see Psalm 82:5). Paul teaches that such ignorance is common (particularly among Gentiles). But this does not make it excusable, since everyone can know some things about God (Romans 1:20).

Paul also uses *darkness* as a metaphor for sin, particularly those sins that are done in private (compare Ephesians 5:12). Paul sees the combined influences of ignorance and sin as a way that unbelievers are spiritually controlled by Satan and the "powers of this dark world" (Ephesians 6:12).

RECOGNIZING DARKNESS

A staple of Hollywood productions is to pit "the good guys" against "the bad guys." Often, part of the depiction is in the color schemes of the characters' clothing. *The Wizard of Oz* features the Good Witch of the North dressed in lightly colored clothing while the Wicked Witch of the West is dressed in black. In *Star Wars*, the villain Darth Vader wears a black outfit. In the *Lord of the Rings* series, the Dark Lord Sauron is in dark clothing.

But Hollywood is not always consistent in this regard. Those of us who are familiar with the old "grade B" Western movies probably are used to thinking of the heroes wearing white hats while the bad guys wear the dark hats. But recently I picked up some DVDs of John Wayne movies from the 1930s and was surprised to discover that there was little consistency about the heroes and the color of hats. More recently, the chief villain in the 2005 movie *The Lion, the Witch, and the Wardrobe* was dressed in lightly colored clothing while in her ice fortress. The "good guy" Batman wears black. Clothing color is not always the key to being able to tell good from bad in movies.

To avoid the darkness of sin involves first being able to recognize that darkness. This requires discernment given that "Satan himself masquerades as an angel of light" (2 Corinthians 11:14). Our challenge is to look beyond mere outward appearances in our quest to recognize darkness for what it truly is.   —J. B. N.

13b, 14. . . . and brought us into the kingdom of the Son he loves, in whom we have redemption, the forgiveness of sins.

The *redemption* Christ's blood purchases has reversed our hopeless situation. We are delivered from a situation over which we have lost all control. In our distress and weakness, God has come to save us (Isaiah 35:4).

CONCLUSION

Perhaps more than any other sporting event, crew rowing requires a coordinated team effort from all involved. The rowers must pull together in complete harmony and unison if they are to be successful. If the oars on one side are pulled too hard, the boat (or "shell") will go slightly off course and waste some of its focused energy. If one rower begins the stroke too early or releases too late, again the shell will be pulled off target. All the rowers must listen carefully to the cadence of the coxswain and stay in rhythm. The rower cannot be listening to a cadence in his head of his own making or the cadence of the coxswain from the boat in the next lane.

One of the things that endeared the Colossian church to Paul was that they were "pulling together." They were united by their faith in Christ and their love for one another. Many churches are sadly lacking in this area. The members have different agendas and different goals. Some members may pull on the oar that preserves tradition and resists change. Other members may be pulling hard on an oar for radical change and dropping of tradition. The "boat" of a church like this will go in circles! May we learn from the Colossians the power of unity in purpose and faith for any church.

Discovery Learning

The following is an alternative lesson plan emphasizing learning activities. Classes desiring such student involvement will find these suggestions helpful. At the back of this book are reproducible student pages to further enhance activity learning.

INTO THE LESSON

As class assembles, have on display a large line drawing of a traditional church building (for example, one with a steeple or bell tower). Have it labeled *The Good Church*. As each learner arrives, hand him or her a marker. Say, "Go up to *The Good Church* and write something that goes into a good church." You may wish to have an example visible, such as "faithful people" or "apostolic approval."

Once all have had a chance to write something, discuss the entries. Some questions you may wish to ask are "Which of the entries do you see as being most essential?" and "Have we left out anything absolutely critical?" Preserve the drawing for possible use under *Option #3* in the Into the Word segment.

If available, display a map of the part of the Roman Empire that is now Turkey. This will help learners see the geographical relationship of Colosse to Ephesus, where Paul had a lengthy ministry. This map will be useful also for the lessons from Colossians to follow.

INTO THE WORD

Say, "As Paul writes to the church at Colosse, we get a picture of the kind of church the Christians in that city were (or ideally should have been). Consider each of the following as church mottoes or signboard sayings. Where in today's text do you see each one as a possibility?"

Reveal the following list, one item at a time, for responses. (These are listed here in random order; do not give the italicized verse references, as those are the answers the learners are to discover.) 1. Strengthened, Patient, and Joyful (*v. 11*); 2. Redeemed and Forgiven (*v. 14*); 3. Jesus Christ Is Lord (*v. 3*); 4. Love Is Our Watchword (*v. 4*); 5. We Seek Knowledge of His Will (*v. 9*); 6. The Word, the Truth, the Gospel (*v. 5*); 7. Loving the Son as God Does (*v. 13*); 8. Fellow Servants in Ministry (*v. 7*); 9. Desiring to Be Filled (*v. 9*); 10. Hoping for Heaven (*v. 5*); 11. To Live a Life Worthy (*v. 10*); 12. We Have Mail! (*v. 1*); 13. Letting His Light Shine (*v. 12*); 14. Rescued from Darkness (*v. 13*); 15. Trying to be Tried and True Saints (*v. 2*); 16. Fruit Bearers (*v. 6*).

Finish with an emphasis that these are the traits and behaviors God expects in *The Good Church*.

Option #1: Turn this into a competition between study teams to see who can finish first; in that case, put the 16 mottoes (without verse references) on handouts. *Option #2:* Make this into a matching exercise by using handouts with mottoes in the left column and verse references in the right column. *Option #3:* Return to your line drawing of the church building and ask, "Based on today's text, what do you see in the Colossian church that qualifies it as *a good church*?" Accept a variety of answers. You may wish to use one example: "Verse 4 reveals that the Colossian church has the attribute Christ said would characterize his followers: love for all the saints."

Ask your class to propose which of the 16 mottoes would be the most accurate to appear on a sign in front of your own congregation's building. This can lead to a spirited, good-natured discussion. If your learners reach something approaching consensus on one, pass the idea along to the church leaders who are responsible for publicity, whether for billboard, Web page, or literature of the church.

INTO LIFE

Form small groups of four or five to brainstorm answers to this question: "What does our congregation need to do to help members grow in knowledge, wisdom, and spiritual understanding according to Colossians 1:9?" Remind learners that brainstorming makes no initial evaluation of ideas suggested, even if they seem inappropriate. *Option:* Use the reproducible activity "The Growing Church" from page 380 here.

If you need to spur thinking, offer these secondary questions: "How can we encourage more generous financial giving?" "What changes do we need to make in our Bible-study efforts?" "How can we connect the spiritually wise and mature with new Christians and the spiritually less mature?" "How can we do a better job presenting Christ to the ungodly?"

Whatever list is developed, state you will pass it along to your congregation's leadership. (It will be better to do this in a face-to-face meeting with those who are primarily responsible for church planning, rather than simply giving a written report.) Distribute copies of the reproducible activity "Living as a Saint" from page 380 as students depart.

AN ESTABLISHED COMMUNITY

LESSON 10

INTRODUCTION

A. THE HISTORY OF HERESY

Have you ever had to deal with heresy? In matters of faith, a distinction is made between that which is "orthodox" and that which is "heterodox" or heretical. The word *orthodox* means "straight/correct praise or glory." If we are orthodox, then we understand and worship God correctly, and our beliefs are what God intends.

On the other hand, *heterodox* means "a different praise or glory." It signifies that we have strayed into false religion, away from the correct way of understanding God. Probably we are all at least slightly heterodox, because our understandings are imperfect. But to move away from what the Bible clearly teaches is to engage in heresy and to make oneself a heretic.

Heretics are nothing new to Christianity. Paul and the other apostles were already confronting them as the New Testament was being written (example: 2 Peter 2:1). Heretics in medieval Europe were punished harshly, even to the point of being burned at the stake. To be accused of heresy today will not result in prison time or a fine by a court, much less by being burned at the stake. Heresy now flourishes with few constraints. It is aided by a modern fascination for novelty and charismatic, self-promoting personalities.

Our task of guarding against heresy is to avoid the extremes of paranoid fear and relaxed indifference. Some popular television preachers teach amazingly heretical (and stupid) doctrine. It is not necessarily our job to oppose them publicly. It definitely *is* our job to turn them off and make sure their heresies do not creep into our fellowship of believers. Paul occasionally saw the need to debate doctrine in a public setting (see Acts 18:28; 28:23, 24). But he always felt an urgency to correct budding heresy within the churches.

Many of Paul's letters were written with this urgency in mind. For example, a crucial issue in Corinth was a heretical teaching concerning the resurrection. The Thessalonians were paralyzed by a heretical view concerning the second coming of Christ. False teachers taught the Galatians that they had to become Jews before they could be Christians (the Judaizing heresy).

B. LESSON BACKGROUND

The exact nature of the heresy is not as clear in the church at Colosse, but it seems to be connected with a false view of the nature of Christ. The city of Colosse was in a region with a rich heritage of Greek philosophy. This seems to have infiltrated the church in subtle ways and influenced the

DEVOTIONAL READING:
EPHESIANS 3:14-21
BACKGROUND SCRIPTURE:
COLOSSIANS 2:1-19
PRINTED TEXT:
COLOSSIANS 2:1-12

LESSON AIMS

After participating in this lesson, each student will be able to:

1. Cite some of the issues about which Paul was concerned in the Colossian church.

2. Give examples of how human traditions of the first and twenty-first centuries have been used to contradict the Word of God.

3. Confess an area where human tradition has held sway in his or her life and make a plan to change it.

May 9

KEY VERSE

See to it that no one takes you captive through hollow and deceptive philosophy, which depends on human tradition and the basic principles of this world rather than on Christ. —Colossians 2:8

Lesson 10 Notes

doctrine. Paul called the church back to a pure faith in Christ, a faith not mixed with paganism or philosophy.

The ancient world was a tossed salad of religion. We must guard against the mistake of overly simplified divisions in this area. For example, it is convenient to divide the ancient people into the sharp categories of *Jew* and *Gentile*. Yet there were many kinds of each. Regarding the Jews, think about the Sadducees, who did not believe in resurrection. Then there were the Jews of the Qumran community, known as the Essenes, who wrote the Dead Sea Scrolls; they believed that the Jerusalem temple and priesthood were utterly corrupt. Further still were the Jews of Alexandria, who translated the Hebrew Bible into Greek and adopted many Greek doctrinal terms.

The Gentile world was even more diverse. The Romans in particular had a tendency to incorporate foreign religions into their system rather than quashing them. Just as a person today may have several favorite authors, a Roman of the first century might have multiple religious allegiances.

In the Roman provinces, cities like Colosse might also have traditional gods and temples unique to their region. Each of these deities had its own priesthood and beliefs, and sometimes they were conflicting. Yet there was no pressure to make exclusive choices in religion. Perhaps the most sophisticated and mysterious of these ancient faiths was *Gnosticism*. This system emphasized the importance of esoteric knowledge.

There were several things that made Gnosticism incompatible with Christianity. Gnostics believed in many gods at many levels. Even if they eventually came to a supreme deity, this understanding of the spiritual world was at odds with the Jewish and Christian belief in a singular God.

Gnostics also made a radical division between the material world (which they believed was corrupt and evil) and the spiritual world (which they believed was the realm of truth and light). This made it inconceivable to gnostics that the Son of God could assume a human body. The fundamentals of Gnosticism required that Jesus either be a god or a man, but not both.

Gnosticism became more organized in the second century AD. In Paul's day, the elements of Gnosticism were just coming together, but their presence can be seen in his letter to the Colossians. Paul realized that faith in Christ and the way of Christianity was exclusive, meaning that it could not be combined with other faiths without losing its essence. There was no room for compromise.

DAILY BIBLE READINGS

Monday, May 3—The Power and Wisdom of God (1 Corinthians 1:20-25)

Tuesday, May 4—The Glory of God in Christ (2 Corinthians 4:1-6)

Wednesday, May 5—The Full Stature of Christ (Ephesians 4:11-16)

Thursday, May 6—One Body in Christ (Romans 12:3-8)

Friday, May 7—Grow in Grace and Knowledge (2 Peter 3:14-18)

Saturday, May 8—Hold Fast to Christ (Colossians 2:11-19)

Sunday, May 9—Fullness in Christ (Colossians 2:1-10)

I. KNIT TOGETHER IN LOVE (COLOSSIANS 2:1-5)
A. AGONIZING SEPARATION (v. 1)
1. I want you to know how much I am struggling for you and for those at Laodicea, and for all who have not met me personally.

Laodicea is a few miles from Colosse and is a growing city in this period in terms of both numbers and prosperity. Paul probably has not visited either city, for he mentions some *who have not met* him *personally*. His connection with Laodicea and Colosse comes from his extended stay in Ephesus, approximately AD 54–57 (Acts 19).

Paul understands that the churches of the two cities are in close contact and fellowship. Thus the Colossians are instructed to pass this letter along to the Laodiceans (see Colossians 4:13-16). The apostle John will later have some very sharp words for the Laodiceans in Revelation 3:14-22.

One of the most agonizing dilemmas of life is to be aware of a crisis in which one has a personal stake but be prevented from helping because of distance, infirmity, or other circumstances. This is the struggle that Paul is experiencing. He wishes he could be in Colosse to help them work through the doctrinal issues that have arisen. He must instead trust in the words of this letter (Colossians 4:7-9). This personal agony is compounded by the slow communications of the ancient world. Paul is not going to receive a cell phone call or an e-mail after the Colossians receive the letter! It may be many months before he learns of its reception and impact.

B. ASSURING TREASURES (vv. 2, 3)

2. My purpose is that they may be encouraged in heart and united in love, so that they may have the full riches of complete understanding, in order that they may know the mystery of God, namely, Christ,

Gnosticism is built on a claim to have secret knowledge that is shared only with the elite adherents. Paul counters any such nonsense by claiming that he is glad to reveal the deepest secrets of the *mystery of God*. So, yes, Christianity also has its mysteries, but these are revealed mysteries, open secrets (Ephesians 3:4-6; Colossians 1:26; 4:3).

Paul wants each and every believer to have full *understanding* of Christian doctrine. These beliefs are the *riches* of the church, for they are the truths that give us assurance of salvation through Christ.

3. . . . in whom are hidden all the treasures of wisdom and knowledge.

The truths of Christianity are universal and exhaustive. In the Christian system, we have *all the treasures of wisdom and knowledge,* not a mere taste. Jesus promised that the Holy Spirit would guide the apostles into all truth (John 16:13). Christians need never fear competing truth claims or attacks that question the truth of the Christian faith. Humans will never be able to destroy truth, no matter how fierce the attack (see 2 Corinthians 13:8).

This is not to say that other religions have no truth whatsoever. There are some parallel truths (mixed with error) that may be found in Islam, in Buddhism, even in Scientology. This is particularly true of religions that have been influenced heavily by Christianity. For example, the *Book of Mormon* quotes extensively from the *King James Version* of the Bible. But the power of the consistent truth of the gospel will eventually break down every false teaching that challenges it (see 2 Corinthians 10:4, 5). Pure doctrine, the goal for which Paul works, is truth with no mixture of error (see 1 John 4:6).

C. ATTENTIVE FAITH (vv. 4, 5)

4. I tell you this so that no one may deceive you by fine-sounding arguments.

Paul now gets to the main purpose of the letter: countering false teachers who have gained an audience among the Colossians. He fears that someone will *deceive* them. This means he is afraid they will be hoodwinked. This will be done by someone using *find-sounding arguments*. This comes from the terminology of rhetoric and refers to persuasive speech. Paul is foreseeing intentional deception by outside teachers, perhaps for the purpose of self-enrichment (compare Romans 16:18; Ephesians 5:6; 2 Timothy 4:3).

WHAT DO YOU THINK?

What difference, if any, do you think modern technology would have made to Paul in his efforts to combat doctrinal problems in the churches? How can we use technology more effectively in helping the global church grow in knowledge and faith?

WHAT DO YOU THINK?

Since all the treasures of wisdom and knowledge are found in Christ, is it useful to read literature from other religious traditions? Why, or why not?

ENTICING WORDS

Someone talked me into signing up for a life insurance policy when I was in college and about to get married. It was the 20-year, paid-up-for-life kind. He used convincing words about providing for my wife if something happened to me. He also stated that this policy could be used as a retirement nest egg (a common line of thought back then). I signed up for the policy, then realized that the monthly premium was 20 percent of my earnings, an impossible situation for me. I canceled the policy before I paid anything.

Some years ago, my wife and I sat through a presentation on purchasing a "time share." The sales rep talked about the advantages of never having to use a motel room as we traveled, since that company had vacation resorts scattered all over the country. She described luxurious surroundings. We signed up, but as soon as we left we had second thoughts. We called the company a few days later and canceled. And that was even before we learned about the maintenance fees, which the sales rep did not mention.

We dodged the proverbial bullet in both cases. Even so, both of those instances involved dollars and cents, not issues of eternal importance. Enticing words could have been financially crippling had we fallen for them. Enticing words can cost us our eternity with Christ when the issue involves Christian belief.   —J. B. N.

5. For though I am absent from you in body, I am present with you in spirit and delight to see how orderly you are and how firm your faith in Christ is.

Paul's initial reports indicate that the Colossians have resisted the false teachers. This causes him great joy and hearty approval for their stand. Paul knows that his imprisonment has resulted in his lack of personal support. Oh, how he longs to be with them in this time of danger (compare 1 Corinthians 5:3)! Paul defines himself by his faith and steadfastness, and this is an example to others (see 2 Timothy 3:10). Now he must trust in the *faith* that the Colossians have *in Christ.*

II. WALKING TOGETHER IN CHRIST (COLOSSIANS 2:6-12)

A. STEADY PACE FORWARD (vv. 6, 7)

6, 7. So then, just as you received Christ Jesus as Lord, continue to live in him, rooted and built up in him, strengthened in the faith as you were taught, and overflowing with thankfulness.

To *continue to live* is to picture life as a journey, a walk. In this journey we make choices as to which roads we take (Proverbs 12:28). From its earliest days, Christianity is pictured as the "way" (Acts 9:2) or road that leads to life. When we walk *in him,* we are trusting in Jesus' teachings and directions as the guide for our life decisions.

Even more, we are trusting Jesus for our salvation. This is the essence of a strong, established *faith.* The use of the full designation *Christ Jesus as Lord* may be a preliminary salvo at the gnostic teachers, for Paul is affirming both the humanity of Christ (v. 6: Jesus, the man) and the divinity of the Christ (v. 6: Jesus as Lord, a term reserved for God in this context).

B. WATCHFUL EYE AROUND (v. 8)

8. See to it that no one takes you captive through hollow and deceptive philosophy, which depends on human tradition and the basic principles of this world rather than on Christ.

WHAT DO YOU THINK?

What are some ways you can improve your Christian walk?

Paul now moves to four specific items of potential heresy. First is *philosophy,* the only place this Greek term is used in the Bible (although Acts 17:18 and 1 Corinthians 1:20 has *philosopher(s)* in reference to people). We still use this word today and may use it in a neutral sense. For us, philosophy is either good or bad depending on what it teaches. For Paul's context, though, philosophy has a negative sense of human wisdom that is concocted apart from God.

This is combined with the adjectives *hollow and deceptive,* which convey the idea of empty lies that are intended to mislead. Such fabulous whoppers may not even be believed by those who teach them, but they serve the teachers' purposes in devious ways (Romans 16:18; Ephesians 5:6).

Both of these components are tied to *human tradition*—wisdom from previous generations. We sometimes believe that the older the tradition, the more valuable. This obvious fallacy ignores the fact that if the teaching was false when first proposed, then the passage of time does not make it true. It is true that the passage of time does have a tendency to sift and eliminate error from human thought, but this is not a foolproof process. Think of how long people have been captive to the false idea that "might makes right."

Paul's fourth characteristic is that all of these things are fashioned *after the basic principles of this world.* We recall that "the ways of this world" is tied to "the ruler of the kingdom of the air," the devil (Ephesians 2:2). Thus the *world* includes a reference to powers from the dark spiritual forces. Paul thus recognizes that false teaching is more than the product of human musing. It may be prompted and encouraged by the evil spirits of the world, who love nothing more than to confuse and mislead Christian believers.

C. GLORIOUS LEADER AHEAD (v. 9)

9. For in Christ all the fullness of the Deity lives in bodily form,

This is one of the most wonderful and absolute statements of Christian doctrine in all of Scripture. In Christ, there is a complete presence of *the Deity,* or Godhead. When Christ walked the earth, he was God dwelling *bodily.* Paul affirms the full humanity and the full divinity of Christ in one sentence in a clear challenge to Gnostic doctrine (compare Philippians 2:6, 7). In the context of this chapter, this is important to Paul because it clinches his argument that the teaching of Christ is superior to anything proposed by human teachers, even those influenced by the spiritual world.

D. SINFUL BURDEN BEHIND (vv. 10-12)

10. . . . and you have been given fullness in Christ, who is the head over every power and authority.

Paul exhorts the readers to be satisfied, for they have *fullness in Christ,* lacking for nothing. The *power and authority* that Paul has in mind here refers to evil spiritual powers that still have vast influence in the human sphere (see Ephesians 1:21; 6:12); Christ is *head of* these in the sense that he is the one with ultimate authority, not them.

To have fullness in him is equivalent to donning the "full armor of God" as portrayed by Paul in Ephesians 6:11-17. This spiritual armor will serve to protect the believer from any attack that might come from Satan or his demons.

11. In him you were also circumcised, in the putting off of the sinful nature, not with a circumcision done by the hands of men but with the circumcision done by Christ,

Visual for Lesson 10. *Point to this visual as you ask, "What are some examples of deceptive philosophy? How do we guard against these?"*

WHAT DO YOU THINK?

How does affirming Christ as both fully human and fully divine help you mature in your own Christian walk?

WHAT DO YOU THINK?

How can Paul say that the Colossians have experienced "fullness" or completeness in Christ when they obviously are deficient in one or more areas of doctrine? How does the Colossians' completeness encourage you?

Paul now leaves the realm of philosophy to employ terms from the Jewish world of thought. It is likely that the false teaching that has challenged the faith of the Colossians also has an element of Jewish opposition to Paul's teachings.

Someone may try to claim that the Gentiles in the Colossian church need to be *circumcised* according to the tradition of the Jews. Paul counters with a better idea: they already are circumcised (compare Romans 2:29). This kind of circumcision is not done with a knife, but with the spiritual cleansing that comes from faith in Christ. As a rabbi might cut off a foreskin, Christ has sliced the guilt of sin from their souls. Our faith has allowed the atoning blood of Jesus to perform a "sin-ectomy" on our *sinful nature.*

12. . . . *having been buried with him in baptism and raised with him through your faith in the power of God, who raised him from the dead.*

Paul ties this spiritual circumcision to *baptism.* The Jews circumcise their baby boys to affirm that they are part of Israel, sons of the covenant. By contrast, the Christian believer publicly identifies with Christ in baptism, even to a reenactment of Jesus' death, burial, and resurrection (Romans 6:3, 4). Our faith in the core elements of the gospel recognizes that "Christ died for our sins . . . was buried, [and] raised on the third day" (1 Corinthians 15:3, 4).

Buried with Him

Burial customs are interesting because they indicate what is valued by various cultures. Often, what is buried with the deceased are things thought to be needed on the journey to the afterlife. Some ancient cultures placed food in the burial chamber. Graves of royalty often contained gold, silver, and precious jewels. Warriors might be buried with their swords. Musicians may have musical instruments alongside them. Hunting societies often placed bows, arrows, and spears in the grave.

Today, we sometimes put items in a casket that had special meaning to the deceased. Parents who have to bury a child may place a special stuffed animal alongside the body of their loved one. I have heard of people being buried with their lodge pins attached to their lapels. I am still debating about my wedding ring. Should I leave instructions to have it buried with me as a testimony to my eternal love for my wife? Or should I have it removed as a keepsake for my children? I haven't decided yet.

Paul says that our baptism is a burial with Christ. His presence is assurance that our journey to the next life will have the right outcome. There should be no debate about that.

—J. B. N.

CONCLUSION

Like many people my age, I walk several times a week for exercise and enjoyment. My body can no longer tolerate the rigors of basketball. Running or jogging seems to result in constant injuries. So I walk.

I like to walk outdoors and in different places. These may include a beach, along a river, or around a lake. If one is committed to outdoor walking, it must be done in good weather and bad. I like to walk early in the morning, when the sun is just rising. I especially enjoy walking after a good rain, when everything seems clean and fresh. If I can't walk for an extended period due to illness or my schedule, I miss it.

PRAYER

God of truth, may we never waver in our commitment to the essentials of the gospel: that Christ died for our sins and through him we are freed from this bondage. May we resist enticing words from false teachers and walk in Christ all of our days. We pray in his name. Amen.

Life, in many ways, is like purposeful walking. We should know where we are going. If lost, we should ask for directions. Life should be lived deliberately, not as if floating aimlessly down a river. Just as we should know why we are walking, we should know why we are living.

The most important part, however, is to know what road we are on. The Bible promises that if we choose to walk on the road that leads to life, we have the companionship of Jesus. In fact, it is a road pioneered by Jesus, for he is the trailblazer (Hebrews 12:2). How is your spiritual journey progressing these days?

THOUGHT TO REMEMBER
Walk determinedly with Christ.

Discovery Learning

The following is an alternative lesson plan emphasizing learning activities. Classes desiring such student involvement will find these suggestions helpful. At the back of this book are reproducible student pages to further enhance activity learning.

INTO THE LESSON

Recruit class members in advance to research heretical doctrines of selected groups that arose within Christianity but have departed from the truth. You may choose which groups you wish your students to research or allow them to do the choosing. Allow learners to give their reports after the following introductory activity.

Display these three scrambled words as learners arrive: *DHOOORTX, ENIRTCOD,* and *EEHRSY* (for the third, have the letters distorted in various ways but still recognizable). Say, "These are three letter-scrambled words that are key to today's study. I want you to 'decode' them in the sequence given." (Someone will see *orthodox* in the first; the second is *doctrine,* with the word simply written backward; the third, with the distorted letters, is *heresy.*)

As the word *doctrine* is deciphered, say, "Doctrine, of course, can go in the right direction or the wrong direction. The right direction draws a straight line to Christ." (If your class can handle the play on words, add, "In the wrong direction, it is always a dead fish ['inert cod'] that is ready to decay and stink!")

As the word *heresy* is identified, point out that in heresies some elements of doctrine are made almost unrecognizable. Sometimes this involves additions (as if the gospel were incomplete and inadequate) or deletions (as if some parts of the gospel are no longer relevant). In discussion, use the lesson writer's comments on these terms in the Introduction.

INTO THE WORD

Say, "Paul makes it clear as he writes to the Colossians that the gospel, pure and complete as it was initially presented to them, is fully capable of bringing forth fruit (see Colossians 1:5b-7). Any impurity—any change involving either addition or subtraction—does nothing but impede the gospel's power and progress."

Ask your class to help you make a list you will label *Basic Christian Doctrine 101.* Though the text for today is from Colossians 2, do not limit the class's search to that chapter only. Perhaps assigning each of the five chapters in the epistle to a different segment of the class will facilitate a thorough search.

Allow time for searching, then call for statements of basic doctrine. If the class needs an example, use "The Father and the Son share divine glory and power" from 1:2, 3 (and others). Allow time to develop this list before you come back specifically to today's printed text.

Ask, "What does Paul identify as the practical values of correct doctrine?" Allowing freedom of expression, the following should be noted. Pure doctrine (1) encourages us by its promises as it removes the fear prevalent in the modern culture, (2) eliminates doubt and anxiety, thus enabling mental health for dealing with the problems the world generates, (3) allows us to resist the captivity of lies, thus giving us a way to measure the validity of pop psychology, philosophy, etc., (4) gives an assurance of forgiveness, redemption, and resurrection, thus allowing freedom from the guilt of the past, (5) allows stability and steadfastness in daily living, thus giving us an anchor in a deteriorating world, and (6) creates mutual acceptance by giving us the reason to eliminate prejudice. (*Option:* List these six on a handout and have students form small groups to determine which verses in today's text support which values.)

To wrap up this segment, ask, "What do you see as the most important verse in this text relative to orthodox doctrine?" Allow the class to discuss their choices. This can be either a small-group or whole-class activity. (*Option:* Use the reproducible activity "Three Ways to Go Wrong" from page 381 as an additional activity.)

INTO LIFE

Give each learner a double-spaced copy of Ephesians 4:14, 15 with the heading *Tossed or Anchored.* Ask the class to suggest other contrasts (called *either/ors*) by which those verses may be headed (examples: *Infants or Grown Ups; Deceit or Truth*).

Next, ask learners to pick the verse from today's text that they consider to be "hardest hitting" in support of one of these either/ors. They can write out that verse next to the contrast they like best. Learners then can post this handout in a conspicuous place in the week ahead as a watchword against false doctrine. Distribute copies of the reproducible activity "In Control of My Sailboat" from page 381 as students depart.

A CHOSEN COMMUNITY

LESSON 11

INTRODUCTION

A. "SOMEBODY MIGHT BE LYIN'"

When I was a youngster trying to understand politics, one of my best teachers was an uncle from Kansas. He was a small-town newspaper editor and very active in that state's political scene. When I was a teenager, I became very confused concerning the claims of the candidates in a particular election. It seemed to me that they were in direct conflict, and I knew that they could not both be right. I had the occasion to ask my uncle about this. His wise, insightful comment was, "Don't suppose somebody might be lyin', do you?"

Somebody might be lyin'? Unfortunately, this does not surprise us all that much in the political arena. It is not too shocking in the business world either, although we loathe it. Have you ever been promised something by a salesperson that proved to be a gross exaggeration?

What about in the church? Should we be stunned to discover a church member has been spreading lies about another church member? I hope we can answer *Yes!* because this is not the way the church should be. The ideal church should be an island of respect and honesty in the worldly ocean of deceit and pretense. To lie about someone is to diminish that person purposely, a person redeemed by Jesus and precious to him. We may not have the ideal church, but we should not be satisfied with a church that shows no marked difference from the corruptions of the world.

As noted in last week's lesson, Paul probably never visited the church in Colosse, but he knew quite a bit about it. His letter to them shows that he had a high view of these people. He commended them in several areas. But he did not hesitate to remind them that they needed to leave behind the "old man" of lying and other malicious behavior, for they had put on the "new man" of peace and thankfulness for their fellowship with God and with one another. He urged them to build a community where no one ever had to wonder if "somebody might be lyin'."

B. LESSON BACKGROUND

In Colossians 2, Paul deals with doctrinal dangers to the Colossians, specifically their understanding of the nature of Christ. This may be combating an early form of Gnosticism (see last week's lesson). Paul moves to the ethical demands of Christianity in Colossians 3.

The ancient world had many competing ethical systems, just as our world does today. For example, deceit and trickery could be seen as cleverness in certain circumstances and thus counted as a virtue rather than a vice. Today, some idealize the efficiency and effectiveness of the Roman Empire's governing. But in reality the Romans could be violent and corrupt with little regard for ethical standards. They built their empire on slave labor. Julius Caesar was

DEVOTIONAL READING:
ISAIAH 41:4-10
BACKGROUND SCRIPTURE:
COLOSSIANS 3
PRINTED TEXT:
COLOSSIANS 3:1, 2, 8-17

LESSON AIMS

After participating in this lesson, each student will be able to:

1. List some of the attitudes and behaviors that Paul says should and should not characterize the church.

2. Explain how a mind that is set on Christ rises above the pettiness of the world.

3. Volunteer for a ministry in his or her church that is focused on expressing a Christlike attitude toward people in the community who do not fit the demographic makeup of the congregation as a whole.

May
16

KEY VERSE

Therefore, as God's chosen people, holy and dearly loved, clothe yourselves with compassion, kindness, humility, gentleness and patience.
—Colossians 3:12

LESSON 11 NOTES

WHAT DO YOU THINK?

What are some qualities or behaviors that are promoted in our culture but are judged as vices in Scripture? How do we keep the church pure in this regard?

murdered by the same senators who had elected him Dictator for Life. This confusing ethical stew was the environment of the Colossians as they sought to live Christian lives as a tiny group within their city.

I. EVERLASTING PERSPECTIVE (COLOSSIANS 3:1, 2)

A. NEW FOCUS (v. 1)

1. Since, then, you have been raised with Christ, set your hearts on things above, where Christ is seated at the right hand of God.

For Paul, all who have been baptized have *been raised with Christ* (Colossians 2:12, last week's lesson). This logically includes all the professing members of the Colossian church, so he is talking to everyone. Their focus in life is to be redirected to the higher things, moving past the day-to-day temptations that come from living as if they belonged to the world (Colossians 2:20). Paul's picture of Jesus seated at *the right hand of God* is an image of judgment. This prepares his readers for the strong ethical injunctions of this section of the letter. Their standard in life is determined by the demands of Christ himself, for he will be their judge (Acts 17:30, 31).

B. NEW PATTERN (v. 2)

2. Set your minds on things above, not on earthly things.

To *set* one's *mind on* something is another way of saying "think about." Paul is not necessarily appealing to the Colossians' spiritual or emotional natures at this point. He wants them to think through what he is saying as a logical appeal. Paul is convinced that the pattern of lifestyle and behavior that he advocates is that which God has ordained, that which comes from *above*. It is therefore superior to any *earthly* human concoction. The behaviors that Paul condemns as sinful are also destructive in relationships (next verse). Actions based on selfishness and self-preservation must be abandoned.

II. PREVIOUS PERSPECTIVE (COLOSSIANS 3:8, 9)

A. RELATIONSHIP WRECKERS (vv. 8, 9a)

8, 9a. But now you must rid yourselves of all such things as these: anger, rage, malice, slander, and filthy language from your lips. Do not lie to each other,

Paul's list may be seen as primarily sins of the tongue, words that destroy relationships. The first three present a progression. Something happens to make us angry. We allow this *anger* to progress to the point that we want to vent it, to express our *rage*. This may be a physical act, but most expressions of anger and rage are verbal. Even so, such expressions still can be highly injurious to the recipient. Such rage can become malicious, seeking to do serious harm to the one at which it is directed. It grows to the point that we do more than express our anger. We want to damage our offender.

The next two speech behaviors, *slander* and *filthy language,* are often present in angry talk. We use irreverent and offensive words to heighten the emotional effect of our tirade. We let our anger get out of control. The hole we dig just gets deeper and deeper, piling sin on sin.

Paul completes his concerns about speech by including a warning about lying. This seems to be a problem for the Colossians, based on what verse 9b (below) says. This problem may be tied to the false teaching and teach-

FOCUS ON THINGS ABOVE

Visual for Lesson 11. *As you discuss verse 2, point to this visual and ask, "What is one way you have been successful in focusing on things above?"*

ers that threaten the Colossian church doctrinally. There is truth-twisting and misrepresentation present. Unity and harmony in a church's life are built on trust. This trust will evaporate if there is deception and flat-out lying. The result is a fractured congregation that will not endure. See also Ephesians 4:25-31; 5:4.

DO NOT LIE

Modern culture honors telling the truth—or at least it says words to that effect. Over the past decade or so, numerous political candidates have been embarrassed by various statements they made that were later determined to be not quite true. One of these, to offer a single example, involved a military situation where the candidate claimed to have been under enemy fire, but was not.

Other leading figures have been accused of plagiarism. They copy someone else's material and claim it as their own. This is a form of lying and counts as a serious offense in the academic world. One presidential candidate had to drop out of contention because some of his academic work was plagiarized. A few years ago, the reputation of a very popular historian suffered because someone discovered that much of one of his books was simply lifted from another published source.

I remember as a child playing a game where your team scored points if you could tell a lie and get the other team to believe it. But lying is not a game. Lies sow distrust, destroy communication, and disrupt the harmony of the Christian body. The fellowship of Christians is severely hurt by falsehood. *Do not lie!*

—J. B. N.

B. BAD OLD DAYS (v. 9b)

9b. . . . since you have taken off your old self with its practices

Paul returns to the significance of baptism, although it may not appear to be that at first glance. In Romans, Paul pictures baptism as reenacting the death, burial, and resurrection of Christ. This is a symbolic crucifixion of the *old self* (Romans 6:3-6). If there is a true change in the baptized believer, it will be shown in the new convert's actions. Paul knows that good works are not a way of earning salvation. But he also knows that a lack of good works is a sign that something is amiss.

There should be no nostalgia for the "good old days" of sin. Before faith, we lived for ourselves, and our criteria for behavior was different. Now we do not live for self. We live for Christ (Galatians 2:20)!

III. PERFECT PERSPECTIVE (COLOSSIANS 3:10-17)

A. GOOD NEW DAYS (vv. 10, 11)

10. . . . and have put on the new self, which is being renewed in knowledge in the image of its Creator.

When we become obedient believers in Christ, the best days are always ahead of us. We have *put on the new self*, have made a radical change in our identity (Ephesians 4:24). Imagine the person who is dressed in a filthy, sweat-soaked gorilla suit. He sheds the suit. Then he bathes himself and dons new, perfectly tailored clothing. The transformation would be remarkable, beyond recognition. Who would be able to guess that the gorilla-suit guy had become the striking fashion plate?

The change in a new Christian can be just as remarkable. The life that is disturbing and ugly can be bright and beautiful. For Paul, this is not the

WHAT DO YOU THINK?

What are some practical ways to "put off" sins of speech? What will happen when we do?

[James 1:19 will provide talking points for your discussion.]

WHAT DO YOU THINK?

What spiritual qualities would you like to have five years from now? How will you begin cultivating those qualities today to make that goal a reality?

WHAT DO YOU THINK?

How can your church do better at demonstrating in its demographics a commitment to Christian unity?

WHAT DO YOU THINK?

Who in your family or church is good at modeling one of the qualities of compassion, kindness, humility, gentleness, or patience? How has this person influenced you in this regard?

product of a self-improvement program. A divine transformation occurs through the *renewed* power of God in a person's life. Sin has defaced the image of God in all of us (Genesis 1:26, 27). Through faith in Christ and the power of the Holy Spirit, we are remade into the *image* of our *Creator* (see 2 Corinthians 3:18). To restore the image of God is equivalent of becoming Christlike (Romans 8:29). We want to be like our Savior, and we do so more and more (see Philippians 3:10).

11. Here there is no Greek or Jew, circumcised or uncircumcised, barbarian, Scythian, slave or free, but Christ is all, and is in all.

In Lincoln's Gettysburg Address, he referred to the "proposition that all men are created equal." For Lincoln, the American experiment in government is founded on this core belief. But Lincoln's "proposition" points to an unstated presupposition: that humans are created in the image of one God, that we are all children of a common Father (see Acts 17:29). Eighteen hundred years earlier, Paul taught Lincoln's proposition in a different light. Paul writes that we are *all* equal because we are all brothers and sisters in Christ.

While we cannot seem to escape ethnic and cultural distinctions in society, they no longer matter in the church. There is no more division between Gentile and *Jew*. It does not matter whether someone has been *circumcised* or not. One can be a Roman, a *barbarian*, or even a *Scythian* (the ultimate barbarian for the Romans). Such designations are irrelevant to *Christ*. He is the one who unites us as one body (see Romans 12:5; Colossians 3:15).

B. RELATIONSHIP BUILDERS (vv. 12-14)

12. Therefore, as God's chosen people, holy and dearly loved, clothe yourselves with compassion, kindness, humility, gentleness and patience.

A chief characteristic of this new existence should be the presence of personal traits that build relationships rather than wreck them. So now Paul contrasts his vice list of verses 8, 9 with a multi-item catalog of godly virtues that must be present for a harmonious church. These are for *God's chosen people*, the *holy and dearly loved* members of the Colossian congregation.

Paul's first virtue, tender *compassion*, is closely related to his second one, *kindness*. The third virtue in Paul's list is *humility*. This is paired with the fourth, *gentleness*. These related qualities are characterized by a meekness of spirit. This does not mean that a humble, meek person is a milquetoast, allowing himself or herself to be run over by everyone else. It is not a person with a poor self-image, for such a person may actually be very proud and selfish. More than anything, the gentle and humble person understands his or her place in the universal order of things, with God as Lord and all of us as his loving servants.

We do not need to understand the next virtue, *patience*, as always involving suffering. We can be joyful in our waiting, in leaving matters in God's hands.

IDENTIFYING THE CHOSEN OF GOD

How do you identify or distinguish the chosen people of God? Through the centuries of church history, various groups have done this in different ways. In recent years, some have used outward adornment as a distinguishing factor. The women wear long dresses with high necklines in something of a nineteenth-century style;

men wear similarly modest clothing, perhaps with distinctive headwear. Others have defined themselves as "of God" by their pacifist positions on use of force.

In the fourth and fifth centuries AD, many Christian men chose to become monks as the distinguishing mark. They adopted a special regimen that marked them as holy ones of God. They wore simple robes and lived alone, often in deserted areas. They restricted themselves from the pleasures of the flesh, including sleep. Some allowed themselves to sleep only by standing in the middle of a room, with nothing to lean on. Some lived on very meager diets. Some built cages for themselves that were too small to stretch out their legs or even to sit up straight. They believed that by punishing the flesh they were purifying the spirit.

Paul describes a different distinctive. We are to demonstrate compassion, kindness, humility, gentleness, and patience. Do we? —J. B. N.

13. Bear with each other and forgive whatever grievances you may have against one another. Forgive as the Lord forgave you.

The attitude of patience is actualized in the sixth virtue: bearing *with each other*. This is the willingness to be patient with others who may do stupid or inconsiderate things. Since this includes all of us from time to time, forbearance is a crucial attitude to foster within any church.

Forbearance is promoted by the seventh virtue: forgiveness. Paul reminds the readers that they have a supreme model of forgiveness in Christ, who in his worst moment of agony and injustice said, "Father, forgive them" (Luke 23:34). Likewise, Christ has forgiven each of us and paid the penalty for our sins with his own blood. When church members can humble themselves in both seeking and granting forgiveness freely, the church will be blessed. Perhaps we will have *grievances* against each other, but we must forgive.

14. And over all these virtues put on love, which binds them all together in perfect unity.

The last virtue is Paul's most important. That virtue is *love*. Older translations render this as "charity," but this involves more than performing charitable acts for, say, the homeless. It is an overwhelming mind-set to care for the church and all of its members with selflessness and devotion. This is how the state of *perfect unity* is achieved. Without the presence of this ultimate attitude, there will be no peace in a church.

The Colossians may already be aware of Paul's teaching that Christ "loved the church and gave himself up for her" (Ephesians 5:25). As Christ taught forgiveness on the cross, he demonstrated love through the cross. The harmonious church is where the members serve one another "in love" (Galatians 5:13).

C. PEACEFUL LIFE (vv. 15-17)

15. Let the peace of Christ rule in your hearts, since as members of one body you were called to peace. And be thankful.

When the church consists of members who embrace and practice the Christlike virtues Paul has listed, it is a congregation of *peace*. Peace reigns, beginning with the *hearts* of the believers. For Paul, this ideal is what the church should be, indeed what it is *called* to be.

Paul certainly has had his share of fractious churches. Think of the church in Corinth. There he has to deal with the strife caused by selfish and prideful church members. By this time he has written them two long letters to deal with their problems. Perhaps Paul even continues to hear about those problems during his imprisonment in Rome. We should fall on our knees and *be thankful* to God if we are in a church that is peaceful and united in purpose. All too often this is not the case.

16. Let the word of Christ dwell in you richly as you teach and admonish one another with all wisdom, and as you sing psalms, hymns and spiritual songs with gratitude in your hearts to God.

Another characteristic of the peaceful church is the presence of *the word* in the church's teaching and worship. The earliest church in Jerusalem was focused on its obligation to be "teaching and proclaiming the good news that Jesus is the *Christ*" (Acts 5:42). Now, three decades later, Paul reaffirms that learning the ways of the Lord is a lifelong duty, and the teachings of Christ are an inexhaustible source of material. This ministry includes both the words of Jesus and the teachings of the Old Testament that are the foundations of his teachings. Today we have the added benefit of the writings of the apostles and their associates—our New Testament; this is a resource largely unavailable to the Colossian church at the time.

A peaceful church is more likely to be a worshiping church. It will find togetherness in singing praise in unity. Paul mentions three sources for worship songs here. *Psalms* are selections from the book of Psalms, written by David and others who expressed their deep sense of worship in poetic fashion. *Hymns* are probably Christian compositions based on the doctrine of the church. Thus the Christian faith is expressed via the medium of music. An example of this may be found in 1 Timothy 3:16, where Paul seems to be quoting a hymn that is known to him and to Timothy. Such hymns are already being shared among churches in different cities. *Spiritual songs* may be simple songs of praise composed by various musicians/teachers. Perhaps they are musical presentations of prayers and thanksgivings.

Paul's outline in Ephesians 5:19 is similar. It is important that such singing is not by rote or mere habit. Rather, it is to be a true expression of the melody of praise that the believer naturally has in his or her heart.

17. And whatever you do, whether in word or deed, do it all in the name of the Lord Jesus, giving thanks to God the Father through him.

Paul ends this section with a wise reminder: it is not about us. It is about God. Church activities and fellowship must always have this perspective, that we are doing everything for the glory of the *name of the Lord Jesus* (compare 1 Corinthians 10:31). We can measure how well we are doing this by asking whether what we say and do is in harmony with an attitude of *giving thanks to God*. Do we give thanks when we bad-mouth other believers? No. Do we give thanks when we refuse to forgive? No. We must give thanks to God with our whole hearts, leaving no room for bitterness or pettiness (Psalm 9:1). This is the essence of praise.

CONCLUSION

In the society of the street gangs that plague our cities, the most volatile offense is to "disrespect" someone. On occasion gangs can live in peace with rival gangs if no disrespect is shown. Even in this culture of lawlessness, respect may lead to a type of warped peace. Why, then, is the church sometimes a hotbed of disrespect? Why can some churches never seem to achieve the peace and harmony that Paul sees in (or at least desires for) the Colossian

PRAYER

Lord, fill our hearts with your love. Give us patience with our brothers and sisters, and help us forgive one another. May your peace rule in our hearts. We pray in the name of Jesus. Amen.

church? Can't we, the chosen people of God, learn to respect one another? Can't we muster up a powerful love that will bind us together?

We can. We should. We must. A fighting, divided church will not survive. Are there things you can do to bring more harmony to your congregation? Have you been one of the agitators, or are you one of the peacemakers?

THOUGHT TO REMEMBER
Live out your calling.

Discovery Learning

The following is an alternative lesson plan emphasizing learning activities. Classes desiring such student involvement will find these suggestions helpful. At the back of this book are reproducible student pages to further enhance activity learning.

INTO THE LESSON

As learners assemble, write on the board this sentence from the lesson Introduction: *The ideal church should be an island of _____ and _____ in the worldly ocean of _____ and _____.* Ask your class to suggest words that can complete the idea. Jot responses on the board. If you feel the learners need an example to get them going, try *mercy, grace, violence, self-centeredness.*

After an appropriate amount of time, reveal the writer's choices of *respect, honesty, deceit, pretense.* Say, "Today's study is a foundational examination of the ways a Christian must differ from the typical person of the world. It is a study of the *if/thens* of Christian living." (*Option:* This can be a small-group exercise using handouts, depending on class size.)

INTO THE WORD

Prepare handouts of a three-column worksheet based on today's text. The worksheet divides each of the 12 verses into three parts and randomizes them. The columns will have 12 entries each, as follows:

Column 1: a. Here there is no Greek or Jew, circumcised or uncircumcised; b. Set your minds; c. Do not lie to each other; d. And have put on the new self; e. Since, then, you have been raised with Christ; f. Therefore, as God's chosen people; g. And over all these virtues; h. Let the peace of Christ rule in your hearts; i. Let the Word of Christ dwell in you richly as you teach and admonish one another; j. But now you must rid yourselves of all such things as these; k. And whatever you do, whether in word or deed; l. Bear with each other.

Column 2: a. on things above; b. set your hearts on things above; c. since you have taken off; d. anger, rage, malice, slander, and filthy language; e. barbarian, Scythian, slave or free; f. which is being renewed in knowledge; g. and forgive whatever grievances you may have against one another; h. holy and dearly loved; i. put on love; j. with all wisdom, and as you sing psalms, hymns and spiritual songs; k. since as members of one body you were called to peace; l. do it all in the name of the Lord Jesus.

Column 3: a. but Christ is all, and is in all; b. in the image of its Creator; c. clothe yourselves with compassion, kindness, humility, gentleness and patience; d. Forgive as the Lord forgave you; e. which binds them altogether in perfect unity; f. your old self with its practices; g. And be thankful; h. with gratitude in your hearts to God; i. from your lips; j. giving thanks to God the Father through Him; k. where Christ is seated at the right hand of God; l. not on earthly things.

Put these directions at the top of the handout: "Each of the 12 verses of Colossians 3:1, 2, 8-17 is divided into 3 segments. See if you can connect the segments. Use your Bible only if you are stumped."

INTO LIFE

Distribute handouts that list the attributes of compassion, kindness, humility, gentleness, patience, forgiveness, love, peace, and thankfulness, per Colossians 3:12-17. Head the list *Seven Days of Christian Grace.*

Give each learner seven small peel-and-stick blank labels as you offer this direction: "The Spirit challenges us to demonstrate behavior expected of the person who is risen with Christ. Each day this coming week, select one of these nine Christian graces to make a special effort to demonstrate. Write your choice each day on one of the labels and 'put on' the sticker (where you will see it) as you 'put on' the characteristic to emphasize that day. Feel free to select the same one for more than one day if that's a particularly troublesome area for you." Wrap up with a discussion about how the attributes "put on" can make a difference in one of the congregation's ministries to those who are "not like us."

Alternative activity #1. Say, "Paul's admonitions to the Colossians might be prefaced with the common question, 'What difference does it make?'

Paul makes it clear that if we have been raised with Christ (as he affirms in 2:12), it must make a difference." Pair off your students and give them this instruction: "Say to your partner, 'Since you are raised with Christ, what difference does it make?' Responses should include phrases and concepts from today's lesson text."

Alternative activities #2 and #3: Use either or both of the reproducible activities on page 382 in addition to (or instead of) the above.

AT HOME IN THE COMMUNITY

LESSON 12

INTRODUCTION

A. FELLOW OUTSIDERS

I recently met a man who had a background that intersects with my own. We both live in Los Angeles and now work across the street from each other. As we talked about our families a little, we realized that he had been a professor at the college in my hometown while I was in high school. He had known my father a little bit. He knew some other people I had known while growing up. Although we were 1,000 miles from that town and it was 30 years later, there was an eerie, yet comforting feeling about reminiscing together. It is likely that we had even seen each other in that little town decades earlier, but we did not know each other.

In our mobile society, such stories are repeated many times. We encounter people whom we do not know, only to find we have common friends and experiences. This creates an unusual camaraderie. Being in a new city can be scary and lonely. When we are far from home, it is comforting to find someone, anyone, who shares our past. It is as if we accidentally become fellow outsiders, displaced people with common memories.

Something a little like this happened with the apostle Paul. In the early AD 60s, he found himself in the biggest city of his world: imperial Rome. He was confined under house arrest and had no freedom to explore the city (Acts 28:16, 30). He must have felt scared and lonely at times. Then he encountered a person from his past, but a person he probably did not know before. It was a person who reminded him of happier days, but a person with a terrible secret. This is the setting for today's lesson, Paul's short letter to Philemon.

B. LESSON BACKGROUND

The letters of Paul are not arranged in our New Testament chronologically, but by order of length. Romans is the longest and comes first. Philemon is the shortest and comes last. This order is somewhat misleading, for Philemon belongs chronologically with three of the other letters that we call the Prison Epistles. Two of these three are Ephesians and Colossians; these two and Philemon have overlapping recipients and themes. The fourth Prison Epistle, Philippians, was written about the same time but to a church in Macedonia; it addresses different people and issues.

Paul's missionary journeys resulted in extensive travels in Asia Minor. Ephesus was the leading city of this region, and we know that Paul spent

DEVOTIONAL READING:
COLOSSIANS 4:2-9
BACKGROUND SCRIPTURE:
PHILEMON
PRINTED TEXT:
PHILEMON 4, 5, 8-21

LESSON AIMS

After participating in this lesson, each student will be able to:

1. Summarize Paul's argument for Philemon to receive his runaway slave Onesimus.

2. Compare the social structure and class distinctions of Paul's day with those of contemporary society.

3. Resolve (repent of) any unholy class distinctions that he or she holds.

KEY VERSE

Confident of your obedience, I write to you, knowing that you will do even more than I ask.
—*Philemon 21*

May 23

more than two years in and around this city. During this period "all the Jews and Greeks who lived in the province of Asia heard the word of the Lord" (Acts 19:10). This means that Paul and his associates were busy preaching the gospel and planting churches throughout the area.

It is during this period that churches were started in Colosse, Laodicea, and Hierapolis, a cluster of cities about 100 miles east of Ephesus. We have no record that Paul ever visited these cities, but he had contact with some of the leaders of these churches. Combining Colossians 1:7; 4:9, 12; Philemon 1, 2, 23; and today's lesson text, we realize that one of these was a wealthy man named Philemon. Apphia and Archippus, believed to be Philemon's wife and son, respectively, also were known personally to Paul (Philemon 2). When Paul wrote these letters, Archippus apparently was a grown man and a leader in the Colossian church (Colossians 4:17).

While in Rome, Paul was contacted by a fourth member of the Philemon household: a slave named Onesimus. Onesimus was not in Rome legally, though, for he had run away from his master, Philemon. Somehow Onesimus found Paul, his master's old friend, in that teeming megalopolis. We do not know how old Onesimus was, maybe just a teenager. He was a resourceful young man, though, for he was able to hide his identity as a fugitive slave. Perhaps he tired of this life of running and sought out Paul's help. Paul's letter is a personal appeal to Philemon to allow Onesimus to come home.

Many of Rome's residents were slaves. Scholars estimate that slaves made up one-third to one-half of the city's population. It would have been easy for Onesimus to blend into this environment, but his life was in danger if his status as a runaway slave were discovered. The institution of slavery was maintained by an atmosphere of fear among the slaves; they knew their punishment for running away could be severe.

I. PRAISE OF PHILEMON (PHILEMON 4, 5)

A. IN PAUL'S PRAYERS (v. 4)

4. I always thank my God as I remember you in my prayers,

WHAT DO YOU THINK?

How can we make intercessory prayer a higher priority?

Paul often prays for his readers (compare 2 Thessalonians 1:11). He must have an enormous prayer list! We can imagine that his house arrest situation allows him many hours each day for systematic praying. We cannot always be physically present with the ones we love, but we can always pray.

B. IN PAUL'S REPORTS (v. 5)

5. . . . because I hear about your faith in the Lord Jesus and your love for all the saints.

While in Rome, Paul receives a visit from Epaphras (Philemon 23). That man is one of the Colossian church's leaders (Colossians 1:7; 4:12). Epaphras doubtlessly comes with news about the church, possibly including a glowing report about Philemon. Epaphras's close relationship with Paul apparently causes him to be detained also, for he is described as the apostle's "fellow prisoner" in Philemon 23.

Paul's comment gives us a key insight about relationships within the Colossian church. If we have a strong, loving relationship toward the *Lord Jesus,* it will overflow easily to our fellow believers in the church, *the saints.*

ARE YOU A SAINT?

Unfortunately, there is confusion and disagreement today about the meaning of the word *saint*. I found the following definition in a Roman Catholic encyclopedia: "A person whose heroic virtues have been confirmed by attested miracles and whose name has been inscribed in the catalog of saints." Many people have been influenced by this understanding. If this is the correct definition, it means that only a very small percentage of Christians who have ever lived qualify for the designation *saint*.

I do not mean to criticize the Roman Catholics, but their understanding is not compatible with the New Testament use of the term. The same encyclopedia article begins by stating that *saint* is derived from the Latin *sanctus*, which means "holy." In more common English, a saint is anyone who has been made holy. We are made holy by the blood of Christ (Hebrews 10:10, 14). Thus all Christians are saints.

When we sing the words of the festal song "Rise Up, Ye Saints of God," we are not calling on the ghosts of the deceased. Rather, we are urging all still-living Christians to take up the work of the church. This is our calling. Will we live up to it?

—J. B. N.

II. PLEA FOR ONESIMUS (PHILEMON 8-21)

A. FROM AN OLD MAN IN JAIL (vv. 8, 9)

8, 9. Therefore, although in Christ I could be bold and order you to do what you ought to do, yet I appeal to you on the basis of love. I then, as Paul—an old man and now also a prisoner of Christ Jesus—

Acts 7:58 describes Paul (when he was known as Saul) when he was "young." Now, some three decades later, Paul describes himself as *an old man*. We can only guess Paul's age, but he is likely in his mid to late fifties. This may seem middle-age to us, but it is considered "old" in Paul's day.

We can detect some of the effects of the pressure that Paul is feeling, for his ministry has been filled with hardship (see 2 Corinthians 11:23-28). He easily can feel sorry for himself, an old man, imprisoned unjustly in a city far from his home and friends.

Paul is not one to wallow in self-pity, however. He knows that God can still use him, even when he is unable to travel. So Paul now comes to his primary reason for writing to Philemon, a reason that causes him to *be bold*, risking damage to a friendship for what he believes he must do.

To do *what you ought* in this context means to do what is one's duty, to do what one should do. Paul is going to ask Philemon to do something very difficult, but it is what he ought to do.

USEFUL IMPRISONMENTS

We usually think of a prisoner as someone confined against his or her will, pining away the months and years in idleness. The circumstances of the imprisonment may be dire. Yet sometimes an imprisonment accomplishes good, and may even be designed to do so.

In April of 1521, Martin Luther was invited by Charles V, the Holy Roman Emperor, to defend his views before the Reichstag in Worms, Germany. Charles demanded that Luther retract all that he had written or be made an outlaw throughout Germany, with a price on his head. Luther refused. Charles would have had him arrested right then and there, but he had given Luther a promise

---

WHAT DO YOU THINK?

When, if ever, should a person retire from active ministry?

[Numbers 8:25, 26 can give you a talking point.]

HOW TO SAY IT

Apphia. AF-ee-uh or AP-fee-uh.
Archippus. Ar-KIP-us.
Colosse. Ko-LAHSS-ee.
Epaphras. EP-uh-frass.
Ephesus. EF-uh-sus.
Hierapolis. Hi-er-AP-o-lis.
Laodicea. Lay-ODD-uh-SEE-uh.
Macedonia. Mass-eh-DOE-nee-uh.
Onesimus. O-NESS-ih-muss.
Philemon. Fih-LEE-mun or Fye-LEE-mun.
Reichstag. RIKE-stagh.
Worms. Vorms.

of safe-conduct. However, Luther was captured on his return home and taken to a castle in western Germany. He had become a prisoner.

But Luther's captor was his own prince, Elector Frederick of Saxony. Frederick took Luther "out of circulation" to protect him. Luther stayed there for 11 months, where he translated the New Testament into German. He also wrote numerous tracts to advance his doctrinal views. These tracts and the translated New Testament soon circulated all over Germany, further spreading the evangelical message as Luther understood it. This imprisonment was a great benefit to the advancement of Luther's views.

Paul was a prisoner in Rome—a prisoner of the Roman Empire but also a prisoner of Christ. That imprisonment allowed him time to write four of the letters that make up our New Testament. Imprisonment also allowed him time to witness to many people, including the palace guard (Acts 28:17-31; Philippians 1:13). The next time you find yourself somewhat "imprisoned" and unable to move about as freely as you would like—such as when recovering at home from an injury or enduring a three-hour layover at an airport—will you view it as wasted time?

—J. B. N.

B. FOR A NEW HELPER IN MINISTRY (vv. 10-14)

10. . . . . I appeal to you for my son Onesimus, who became my son while I was in chains.

Paul begins his plea by naming the person at the center of his request: *Onesimus.* This name means "profitable one" or "useful one." This is an ironic moniker given what Onesimus has done! Paul uses this name to help make the point that Onesimus has undergone a radical change. He is now Paul's *son,* for Onesimus has become Paul's spiritual son during this period of Roman imprisonment (compare 1 Corinthians 4:15). Onesimus is now a fellow believer, one who has been born again in Christ.

11. Formerly he was useless to you, but now he has become useful both to you and to me.

Paul indicates the change in Onesimus's status by a play on words. The slave who bears the name *useful* has proven to be the opposite for his master, Philemon. We may assume from the name *Onesimus* that he is a purchased slave rather than one born in the household. His running away has deprived Philemon of his purchased labor, making the investment worthless. Now, Paul says, Onesimus is living up to his name. He is profitable or useful to both Paul and Philemon.

12, 13. I am sending him—who is my very heart—back to you. I would have liked to keep him with me so that he could take your place in helping me while I am in chains for the gospel.

Paul is *sending* Onesimus *back to* Philemon. But it gives Paul deep distress in his *heart* to do so. Paul's preference is to retain Onesimus as a personal assistant, much as he did with Timothy previously (see Acts 16:3).

Paul is sending Onesimus home to face the consequences of being a runaway. This is a period of transition for the status of slaves in the Roman Empire. Slaves are gaining a few rights, but masters still have near absolute power over their slaves. It is possible that Philemon can even impose a death penalty on the returned slave as an example to his other slaves. The Romans know that the institution of slavery will collapse if running away is not punished harshly. Slavery survives through fear. A slave is little more than property, and the gap between slave and slave owner is enormous.

14. But I did not want to do anything without your consent, so that any favor you do will be spontaneous and not forced.

Paul is concerned not to play the bully with Philemon. In his discretion, Paul decides that this is not the place to invoke apostolic authority. Nor does Paul seem to wish that his request regarding Onesimus be tinged by his friendship with Philemon. Paul's appeal is to Philemon's heart, for Paul wants the right treatment of the returned slave to be *spontaneous,* not *forced.*

C. FOR A NEW BROTHER IN CHRIST (vv. 15, 16)

15, 16. Perhaps the reason he was separated from you for a little while was that you might have him back for good—no longer as a slave, but better than a slave, as a dear brother. He is very dear to me but even dearer to you, both as a man and as a brother in the Lord.

The term *slave* should be understood in the strongest possible way here. This is not a paid servant or hired hand, but a slave. How can the practice of slavery survive in the church? Paul teaches the Colossians that there is no longer a category distinction of slave and free for those who are in Christ (Colossians 3:11). If both a slave and a master have become Christians, does not their relationship change to that of "brothers"?

Paul should not be thought of as a crusader against slavery, although he seems to condemn slave trading in 1 Timothy 1:10. Elsewhere, he advises slaves to be content with their situation (1 Corinthians 7:21). He asks that slaves be honest and hardworking and that masters treat their slaves well (Ephesians 6:5-9; Colossians 3:22; 4:1; 1 Timothy 6:1, 2; Titus 2:9, 10). Yet it is unlikely that Paul himself ever owned slaves. He clearly sees slaves as human souls needing the salvation offered by Christ.

Some Roman slaves are highly educated and accomplished. What if a slave were to become a leader, an elder in the church, while his master is a new believer? Could slavery survive this role reversal? Historically, we can see that within the principles of Christianity are seeds that eventually grow and cause the rejection of slavery. But it takes another 1,800 years and brave men such as William Wilberforce and Abraham Lincoln to end slavery in those parts of the world most under the influence of Christianity. In the case at hand, Paul wants Philemon and Onesimus to have more than a master/slave relationship. He wants the two to be brothers in Christ, and therefore have a relationship that lasts forever. Philemon certainly will not be Onesimus's master in Heaven. Why wait until then to begin their new relationship?

D. FROM THE SPIRITUAL FATHER (vv. 17-21)

17. So if you consider me a partner, welcome him as you would welcome me.

If Philemon has any doubts about how to react to Onesimus's return, Paul has an idea: *welcome him as you would welcome me.* What could be clearer? But Paul has even more to say.

18. If he has done you any wrong or owes you anything, charge it to me.

It is possible that Onesimus has stolen money or property from Philemon to finance his runaway *(if he has done you any wrong).* Paul promises to make this right, to stand good for any debt the slave may have incurred to his master. He does not want this to be a reason for Philemon to punish Onesimus.

19. I, Paul, am writing this with my own hand. I will pay it back—not to mention that you owe me your very self.

WHAT DO YOU THINK?

Why do you think Paul didn't condemn slavery outright and work for its abolition? Does Paul's position mean we can tolerate slavery in places where it still exists, such as Sudan? Explain.

Visual for Lesson 12. *Point to this visual as you ask, "What 'right thing' have you been putting off that you need to do today?"*

WHAT DO YOU THINK?

What areas are there, if any, where we should try to do "more" than what the Bible writers have instructed us? Will attempting to do "more" cause us to fall into the error of the Pharisees? Why, or why not?

PRAYER

Lord God, we join our voices to you in prayer along with millions of other believers. We glorify your name in every part of the earth. May our voices become one voice, as your great love for us is translated into a great love for all our brothers and sisters in Christ. We pray this in Jesus' holy name. Amen.

THOUGHT TO REMEMBER
We are all one in Christ.

At this point, *Paul* pushes his friend Philemon a little. Paul, in verse 18, steps out to take responsibility for any debt that Onesimus owes Philemon. But if Philemon contemplates sending a bill to Paul, Philemon should recall that it is through Paul's efforts that Philemon has received the gospel. Paul is saying, in effect, "*You owe me* more than you can ever repay, so do not get stingy with the matter of Onesimus. Just do the right thing."

20, 21. I do wish, brother, that I may have some benefit from you in the Lord; refresh my heart in Christ. Confident of your obedience, I write to you, knowing that you will do even more than I ask.

These verses help us understand Paul's motives a little better. He is not making any threats by reminding Philemon of his debt to the apostle for salvation itself. Salvation is a gift of God, and no one knows this better than Paul (Ephesians 2:8). Neither is Paul simply asking that Philemon have pity on this slave and act as if he had never run away.

Paul's expectations are much higher than this. He believes that Philemon, the Christian gentleman, will see Onesimus in a new light as a precious brother in Christ. Whether or not this means freedom for Onesimus is not the issue. Paul is *confident* in the godly, righteous nature of Philemon to *do even more than* he asks. This may be a step beyond brotherly love to the point that Philemon accepts Onesimus back as a wayward son and, like Paul, loves him like a father does (Philemon 10).

The great, godly optimism of Paul can be seen more fully at the end of the letter. There he asks that Philemon prepare a guest room for him in anticipation of a future visit (Philemon 22). He does not expect that this issue with Onesimus will cause any strain in their friendship and that it all will have been settled satisfactorily by the time that Paul expects to visit.

CONCLUSION

The history of the church tells us that at the beginning of the second century AD there was a prominent leader named Onesimus in the Ephesian church. We do not know if this is the same runaway slave who forms the subject of the letter to Philemon, but several things make this plausible. If Onesimus had been a teenager when Paul encountered him in Rome, he would have been in his 60s at that later time—not an unusual age for a position of leadership. Further, *Onesimus* was common as a slave name, so it is very possible that this leader was a freed slave. This might also help explain why this small, very personal letter to Philemon survived to be included in the New Testament. It tells the encouraging story of an apostle and a believer, and how their love for Jesus transcended the harsh reality of slavery in their world.

We like to think that all are equal in the church, but in certain ways this is not true. In most churches there are great income differences among families. There are those whose families have been associated with the church for many generations, making them very influential, in contrast with new believers, who have little influence. Some may have extensive educations and advanced degrees, while others can barely read and write. There are those with a deep, thorough knowledge of Scripture, and those who are novices. There are the very old and the very young. There are those who are sick and physically weak and those who are healthy and fit.

Yet in every way that matters eternally, we *are* equal. We are all saved in exactly the same way in Christ. We worship the same God. We share the gift of the same Holy Spirit. We are equally, limitlessly loved by God our Father. We are all one in Jesus Christ (Galatians 3:28).

This equality under God can be difficult and elusive to maintain in a society that has created many ways of dividing and categorizing people. It is important, however, for church leaders to recognize barriers to full, open fellowship and seek to eliminate them. The church of Paul's day seemed to be content to have slaves and masters in the same congregation, but the church today has rightly rejected slavery, the so-called "peculiar institution." What is the "peculiar institution" in your church that strains Christian equality?

WHAT DO YOU THINK?

What practices or institutions in your church challenge the idea of Christian equality? How can your church modify or eliminate those things?

Discovery Learning

The following is an alternative lesson plan emphasizing learning activities. Classes desiring such student involvement will find these suggestions helpful. At the back of this book are reproducible student pages to further enhance activity learning.

INTO THE LESSON

Prepare in advance eight miniature pyramids by trimming and taping together some large index cards; the pyramids will have four faces each, counting the bottom face (which is the base of the pyramid). On the faces of the pyramids that show (which excludes the base) put the three eight-letter words PHILEMON, ONESIMUS, and BELIEVER, one letter per face, in this manner: for PHILEMON put the P on one face of the first pyramid, the H on one face of the second pyramid, etc.; for ONESIMUS, put the O on one of the two unused faces of the first pyramid, the N on an unused face of the second pyramid, etc.; do the same thing for the word BELIEVER on the remaining eight unused pyramid faces. Put a small numeral 1 (just big enough for you to see it) somewhere on the first pyramid, which is the one that contains the letters P, O, and B. Number the remaining pyramids in sequence.

Put the pyramids on display toward your class so students can see one face of each, in numerical order from their left to right. Adjust the facings so that it is not apparent what any of the three words are. For example, you may have O, E, I, L, I, V, O, S showing. Say, "Someone call out a number from *one* to *eight* to reveal a different letter." When a number is called, turn that pyramid one face clockwise. This will proceed very rapidly once the students catch on to the idea that you're trying to spell a word.

Eventually, one of your three words will be showing. When that happens, say, "Keep going!

We have two more words to discover." When all three words have been revealed, say, "That's the core of today's study. Onesimus, a slave, is to meet his master, Philemon, as an equal believer in Christ."

INTO THE WORD

Divide your class into three groups. Give each one of the labels *Paul, Onesimus,* and *Philemon.* Try to ensure that at least one person having greater biblical knowledge is in each group. (If your class is small, use pairs; if your class is large, form extra groups and double up on the labels.)

Say, "Today's study is a picture of relationships among three Christians who were in various stages of spiritual maturity. Complicating matters is the issue of slavery in the first century. Use today's text and your general knowledge of Paul's life and ministry to answer the questions I give your group. On this handout, please fill in the two other names as you answer 'for' the person whose name your group carries." Give each group a handout with these questions: 1. "What is my relationship to ___ and ___?" 2. "What do I have in common with ___ and ___?" 3. "What is my attitude toward ___ and ___?"

Discuss conclusions as a class. Highlight the groups' conclusions that are both biblically established and "possible" regarding the relationships among Paul, Onesimus, and Philemon. Use the lesson commentary to fill in gaps, correct misconceptions, and resolve disagreements.

INTO LIFE

Create a handout with the following true/false self-evaluation statements. As you distribute them, stress that you will neither collect the answers nor ask anyone to reveal their answers.

1. I am better in some way(s) than most people I meet. 2. Most people I meet are better than I am in some way(s). 3. There are some people who are not worthy of the gospel. 4. I would be displeased to see certain people become members of my congregation. 5. I believe my country is too lenient in allowing people from other countries to become citizens. 6. People with higher levels of formal education are more likely to demonstrate moral behavior. 7. The church and the gospel seem to have the most appeal to those who are middle class. 8. Worship services should be planned in ways that satisfy and edify me. 9. I have family members I wish were not family members. 10. I am unhappy about the "kind" of people moving into my neighborhood.

Wrap up by saying, "This is not a graded test. It is simply a 'think about it' exercise, as we have considered the Christian social dynamics represented in Paul's letter to Philemon. So just think about it!"

Option: Time allowing, also do the reproducible activity "Christianity and Slavery" from page 383. Distribute copies of the reproducible activity "A Noted Prayer List" as students depart.

AT RISK IN THE COMMUNITY

LESSON 13

INTRODUCTION

A. THE CHURCH AS BATTLEFIELD

Although we like to think of the church as a place of peace and harmony, it is also a battlefield. Satan is the primary enemy on this battlefield. He will do everything he can to shred the church's harmony. He will use various tactics to accomplish this goal.

Temptation to commit sin is, of course, the main driver behind all his tactics. When uncorrected and unconfronted sin gets into the church, the result can be a cancer that spreads until the witness of the church is completely ruined. This seems to be Paul's concern in 1 Corinthians 5.

Satan especially likes to attack the church's leaders. Satan uses various approaches, and we all know of cases where church leaders exploited the sheep of the flock for devious purposes. Too many churches and Christians have been damaged by dynamic but unscrupulous and unfaithful leaders! This unfortunate pattern was already in play in the first century. It is a problem frequently addressed in the books of the New Testament. The church of any century needs strong leaders who are grounded in the Scripture, secure in their faith, and empowered by the Holy Spirit. One of the greatest voices for this need is a book often overlooked or misunderstood by Christians today. This is the 25-verse book of Jude, the source for our lesson today.

B. LESSON BACKGROUND

The Gospels record that Jesus had brothers and sisters (see Matthew 13:55; Mark 6:3). These names are rendered into English in various ways. His brothers were named James (Jacob), Joses (Joseph), Judas (Judah, Jude, or Juda), and Simon.

The third brother in the list is the one we are concerned with for this lesson. His Hebrew name was Judah, and in Christian tradition this brother of Jesus has been identified by the variant name Jude. Mark 6:3 says Judas, but we tend to shy away from that name so we don't get him confused with Judas Iscariot, the disciple who betrayed Jesus. This distinction is important, but we should remember that these two men had the same name.

When Jesus was engaged in his ministry, his brothers did not accept him as the Messiah and even scoffed at him (see Mark 3:21; John 7:2-5). After his resurrection, however, they were among the believers (Acts 1:14). The oldest of these brothers, James, became the leader of the Jerusalem church. He served as the moderator for a famous meeting in Jerusalem

DEVOTIONAL READING:
1 TIMOTHY 6:3-10
BACKGROUND SCRIPTURE:
JUDE
PRINTED TEXT:
JUDE 3-8, 19-25

LESSON AIMS

After participating in this lesson, each student will be able to:

1. List key features of the dangers that Jude discusses.

2. Distinguish between faith as an attitude and the faith as a body of doctrine to be believed.

3. Explain how he or she will avoid the extremes of license and legalism in the Christian life.

KEY VERSE

Be merciful to those who doubt; snatch others from the fire and save them; to others show mercy, mixed with fear. —Jude 22, 23

May
30

LESSON 13 NOTES

that is recorded in Acts 15. It is likely that the other brothers of Jesus, including Jude, were at this meeting.

In the greeting of the book for this lesson, the author identifies himself as "a servant of Jesus Christ and a brother of James." This is similar to the beginning of the book of James, where James claims no family relationship with Jesus, seeing himself as simply "a servant of God and of the Lord Jesus Christ" (James 1:1). This is probably because James was widely known as Jesus' brother and the leader of the Jerusalem church. Naturally, to be the brother of a brother of Jesus is to say that Jude was also a sibling of Jesus.

Jude wrote his book for believers facing the threat of false teachers within their body. The book assumes some knowledge of Jewish traditions, and it may have been written for churches that were made up largely of Christian Jews. The book was perhaps written about AD 75, which was shortly after the destruction of the Jerusalem temple in AD 70. There are many parallels between the books of Jude and 2 Peter.

I. FIGHT FOR THE FAITH (JUDE 3-8, 19)
A. BE CONTENDERS (v. 3)

3. Dear friends, although I was very eager to write to you about the salvation we share, I felt I had to write and urge you to contend for the faith that was once for all entrusted to the saints.

Jude uses some beloved and invaluable phrases in his opening statements, expressions that we cherish. He speaks of *the salvation we share,* the promise of eternal life that all Christians in all eras share. He also exhorts his readers to *contend for the faith.* The word *contend* comes from the world of athletic contests, the idea of striving for victory. It is a recognition that the church is in a fight for its life concerning some doctrinal matters. The church needs champions, warriors for the cause of Christ.

When we read that this contending is to be *for the faith,* we realize that this is not the usual way of using the word *faith.* Usually this word is understood in the New Testament to be an attitude of belief plus trust. Jude, however, uses *the faith* to mean "a body of doctrine to be believed," referring to the central truths of the church (see also Galatians 1:23). The church today still needs those who will contend for the faith, who will fight "the good fight" in that regard (2 Timothy 4:7).

A third memorable phrase, which overlaps the second, is *the faith that was once for all entrusted to the saints.* Christianity is based on solid, fixed truths. It is not an evolving religion with continuing, new revelations. The simple facts of the gospel are timeless and need no updating. This is extremely important in Jude's campaign to fight for the faith, because the false teachers are introducing ideas that are at odds with the doctrine the apostles have taught.

B. DETECT INFILTRATORS (v. 4)

4. For certain men whose condemnation was written about long ago have secretly slipped in among you. They are godless men, who change the grace of our God into a license for immorality and deny Jesus Christ our only Sovereign and Lord.

Jude now sets forth some things for his readers to keep in mind regarding the false teachers. First, they are sneaky, *secretly* slipping into positions of

---

WHAT DO YOU THINK?

What was a time, if ever, that you found it necessary to "contend for the faith"? How did things turn out? (This question should be used with caution if the situation involved a doctrinal issue or false teacher in the church you presently attend.)

WHAT DO YOU THINK?

How do you explain the sad irony that some Christian leaders have shown unscrupulous characteristics while many non-Christians display a high level of morality, kindness, love, etc.?

influence. They are not forthright concerning their true motives and teachings. Second, this type of trickster doesn't catch God by surprise, since their *condemnation was written about long ago*. God in his foreknowledge has foreseen their arrival. God's judgment on them is sure and indeed has already been issued. Another issue is their sexual *immorality*. It is a sad fact that many who are identified as false teachers yet today are also exposed as living hidden (or not so hidden) lives of sexual sin.

The final item in Jude's list is the most important: these false teachers deny *Jesus Christ our only Sovereign and Lord*. This seems to be Jude's primary point of contention, the very crux of his letter. This problem includes more than a tacit denial by devious and self-serving actions. It is, rather, the false teachers' explicit opposition to the central teaching of the church, the lordship of Christ. This problem includes any who may teach, "No, you really don't need to believe that Jesus is Lord." Such teaching can be an issue for those with a Jewish background, who might affirm *God* but refuse to confess the Jesus as Lord. Jude's point is that for a Christian to deny Christ as Lord is a denial of *Sovereign* God himself.

CREEPING IN

One of the most serious enemies the early Christians faced was *Gnosticism* (see the Lesson Background of Lesson 10 for this quarter). This belief system maintained that all things fleshly were evil by their very nature. To the gnostics, this meant that Christ could not have been human. The gnostics came up with a variety of ways to deny the Incarnation, but they all came down to the same basic thing: Christ was divine but not human.

A leading gnostic in the second century AD was Marcion. His father was the bishop of a church in northern Asia Minor, yet Marcion was thrown out of his home church because of "gross immorality." He then moved to Rome, where he became involved with the church there. Because he was a wealthy merchant and gave considerable money to the church, he was welcomed. But when his Gnosticism was discovered, that church also threw him out—and even returned all his money!

Marcion is typical of the false teachers that Jude warns about. He was guilty of immorality, he tried to sneak into the church, and he even circulated an edited version of holy writings to support his doctrines. Does history repeat itself in this regard today?

—J. B. N.

C. REJECT REBELS (vv. 5-7)
5. Though you already know all this, I want to remind you that the Lord delivered his people out of Egypt, but later destroyed those who did not believe.

The unfortunate facts of history tell us that the people of Israel participated in numerous incidents of unfaithfulness even though they were rescued from Egyptian slavery in spectacular fashion (see 1 Corinthians 10:5-11). Some incidents resulted in mass deaths at the hand of God (example: Numbers 21:4-9). God even delayed entry into Canaan so that an entire generation of unfaithful people would be *destroyed* (Numbers 14: 29, 30).

6. And the angels who did not keep their positions of authority but abandoned their own home—these he has kept in darkness, bound with everlasting chains for judgment on the great Day.

This is a mysterious reference, speaking not of rebellious people, but of rebellious *angels*. We are not privy to the rules and laws of the domain of angels, but their fate for rebellion is the same as ours: punishment by God. In this case, they are bound with *everlasting chains* as they are thrown into some kind of spiritual prison. There they await the *Day* of *judgment*. This prison seems to be similar to (or perhaps is the same as) "the Abyss," where demons are confined (see Luke 8:31; Revelation 9:1, 2; 20:3).

7. *In a similar way, Sodom and Gomorrah and the surrounding towns gave themselves up to sexual immorality and perversion. They serve as an example of those who suffer the punishment of eternal fire.*

Jude's third example of rebels against God is the shameful story of *Sodom and Gomorrah* and the other *towns* of that area (Genesis 19:24, 25). Their rebellion included unbridled sexual perversion (19:5). These towns had a lawlessness that God could not ignore (18:20, 21). Thus they were destroyed with *eternal fire*, meaning supernatural fire from Heaven. Their destruction was complete (19:28, 29).

D. RECOGNIZE DEFILERS (vv. 8, 19)

8. *In the very same way, these dreamers pollute their own bodies, reject authority and slander celestial beings.*

Jude returns to the false teachers who have infiltrated the churches. In so doing, he speaks of them in the same breath as the rebels of Israel, the rebellious angels, and the sinful cities. Described as *dreamers,* these teachers ignore the clear realities of God's intention for the church. They are charged with three specific areas of sinful rebellion.

First, they *pollute their own bodies*. This is another reference to sexual immorality. Their bodies are not pure in this regard (see 1 Corinthians 6:15, 16). Second, they *reject authority,* meaning that they consider themselves answerable to no one but themselves. They have a spirit of lawlessness like the residents of Sodom. Third, they *slander celestial beings*. This is not slander in the human sphere, but to the angels of God, who deserve our respect. Jude illustrates this in verse 9 (not in today's text) with a story from Jewish tradition.

19. *These are the men who divide you, who follow mere natural instincts and do not have the Spirit.*

After an interlude not included in our lesson text, Jude returns to the false teachers and adds charges. Their teachings cause fragmentation in the church (compare Romans 16:17, 18; Titus 3:10, 11). They are fixed on gratifying the desires of the flesh. This usually refers to sexual gratification, a charge Jude makes repeatedly. This is emphasized when Jude says they *do not have the Spirit*. They are complete charlatans no matter what their claims might be, for to be without the presence of the Holy Spirit is to be something less than Christian (see Romans 8:9, 14).

II. RESCUE FROM THE FIRE (JUDE 20-25)

A. TRAINING REGIMEN (v. 20)

20. *But you, dear friends, build yourselves up in your most holy faith and pray in the Holy Spirit.*

Jude's agenda goes beyond the identification of false teachers. He is also concerned to repair the damage they have caused. Those who will be contenders for the faith must *build* themselves *up*, fortifying their spiritual strength with their *most holy faith.* They must be well versed in the doctrines of the faith, not confused or unsure.

All this should be accompanied by an expanded and powerful prayer life, deep prayer through the ministry of the Holy Spirit (Romans 8:26). Doctrinal depth and spiritual communion form the training regimen of the spiritual warrior.

B. ATTITUDE ALIGNMENT (v. 21)

21. Keep yourselves in God's love as you wait for the mercy of our Lord Jesus Christ to bring you to eternal life.

This spiritual warrior must also be aware of the boundaries of his or her battlefield. This warrior must stay within *God's love,* not allowing self to be drawn into the deceits and immorality of the false teachers. This is best accomplished by maintaining an eternal focus, which involves looking ahead for the glorious coming of *our Lord Jesus Christ.* It is he who inaugurates the era of *eternal life* for the saved.

C. CRITICAL ASSIGNMENT (vv. 22, 23)

22. Be merciful to those who doubt;

Spiritual warfare is not a brutal, take-no-prisoners endeavor. It must be motivated by mercy for those who have been led astray from the faith once delivered. We should not hate them. Instead, we love them as the lost sheep of the good shepherd, our Lord Jesus. In this way, we can deliver them from this peril to their faith and future.

The phrase *those who doubt* probably is not referring to the hard-core unbeliever, but to one who has fallen away and is no longer sure whom to trust and what to believe. These sincere doubters deserve our love. There is no triumphalism in spiritual warfare, no joy for the crushing of our adversaries, but only the joy for those saved.

23. . . . snatch others from the fire and save them; to others show mercy, mixed with fear—hating even the clothing stained by corrupted flesh.

The second group (called *others*) that needs a rescue is in much deeper trouble. Jude pictures their deliverance as the work of a firefighter, one who puts his or her own life at risk to save those who are perishing (compare Amos 4:11; Zechariah 3:2).

The rescuer must guard his or her own life in this operation, *hating even the clothing stained by corrupted flesh.* This seems to be another reference to the sexual sin of the false teachers, a temptation that can lure the spiritual warrior away from the mission. This task of rescue is for those who are spiritually strong and secure, who have achieved a level of spiritual maturity (see Galatians 6:1). If they fall prey to the seductive teachings of the charlatans, the battle is a disaster and the losses are compounded.

D. HONOR PRESENTATION (vv. 24, 25)

24. To him who is able to keep you from falling and to present you before his glorious presence without fault and with great joy—

We have the spiritual resources of the Lord God to empower us in our rescue operations. Jude acknowledges this with his closing prayer, one of the favorite benedictions of the church. Jude's final word-picture is of the spiritual soldiers being presented for recognition after the battle has been won. They

"OTHERS SAVE WITH FEAR, PULLING THEM OUT OF THE FIRE." —JUDE 23

Visual for Lesson 13. *Point to this visual as you introduce the next question below.*

WHAT DO YOU THINK?

What are some methods we can use to rescue others from false doctrine or immorality? How do we ensure that we don't fall into their errors while attempting to rescue them?

WHAT DO YOU THINK?

What are some ways God has kept you from falling? What was a time when God worked through you to keep someone else from falling?

[Caution your students to withhold information that should be kept in confidence as they answer the second question.]

have been protected from *falling* (becoming casualties) and are presented as *without fault,* not having succumbed to the alluring lies of the false teachers. This is a time of *great joy.*

KEPT FROM FALLING

The home where I grew up benefited from the green thumb of a previous owner. We grew lots of fruit. We had an apple tree, two peach trees, two grape arbors (about 50 feet of lush grapevines), a gooseberry bush, a rhubarb patch, a strawberry patch, and three cherry trees.

The cherries were my favorite. When the cherries were ripe, my sister and I would pick them under my dad's watchful eye. We ate quite a few in the process, but he didn't mind. I remember when I was about nine years old being up on a ladder picking cherries, some of which were located on branches that curved around behind me. At one point I leaned back to get some cherries, and the ladder began to fall backward. I was about to end up on the ground with the ladder on top of me. But my dad was watching, for at the critical time he placed his hand on my back and pushed me upright.

Jude says that our God is able to keep us from falling. If watchful earthly fathers can keep us from falling, how much more can our heavenly Father!   —J. B. N.

25. . . . *to the only God our Savior be glory, majesty, power and authority, through Jesus Christ our Lord, before all ages, now and forevermore! Amen.*

The final sentence describes our heavenly leader in marvelous terms. He is *the only God.* He alone possesses absolute wisdom and understanding. His purposes may not always be clear to us, but they are perfect. Although we battle for him, we remember that he is *our Savior,* the one who has rescued us so that we might help rescue others.

We may be presented for recognition, but all the honor must go to God. We bow to him in his *glory* and *majesty,* the trappings of the King of kings. We cede to him all *power and authority,* the dominion of the Lord of lords. This is both a present and a future reality, *now and forevermore!*

Jude closes with the traditional *amen,* a Jewish way of saying, "Let this all be true!" It is a way of releasing the prayer to God, allowing him to rule utterly in our lives.

CONCLUSION

Two extremes to avoid in our Christian walk are *license* and *legalism. License* is the idea that "anything goes." It is what Jude fights against. The danger we face in fighting *license* is that we will go the other extreme and become *legalists.*

But what is a legalist? This is not a title that people usually apply to themselves. It is always "someone else" whom we think of as a legalist. No one wants to be known as the Supreme Legalist or the Legalist Par Excellence. We think of legalists as uncompromising, joyless nitpickers who are always correcting our speech and behavior in the tiniest of details.

The Pharisees are examples of legalists in that they crossed the line from contending for the faith to engaging in doctrinal minutiae. No human understanding of God can be perfect, so those who demand complete uniformity are chasing the wind. This does not mean, however, that just any teaching should be tolerated or even allowed to receive a hearing.

PRAYER

O Lord our God, may we never take the teachings of your Word for granted. Even as we make allowance for the doctrinal differences among believers, may we never develop a spirit of accommodation when it comes to false teaching. Keep us pure and spotless. Keep us from the fire. Guard us from error. We pray this in the name of our Savior, Jesus Christ the Lord. Amen.

The history of the church has shown that doctrine must be defended and protected or it will become corrupt, losing its original power. Who are the guardians of the truths of the church? Fortunately, we have the Bible as a fixed depository of doctrine. We can always go back to the source, the Scriptures, and check our teachings against the words of the inspired authors who wrote these books. Because we are not engaged in adding or subtracting from Scripture, we have a resource that transcends time and culture and can be applied to any human situation.

The church will always need faithful, experienced teachers who have immersed themselves in the Word. The church will always require defenders who will rescue the prey of self-serving teachers who would lead them astray. Jude knew this well, and we should not hesitate to heed his example.

THOUGHT TO REMEMBER
The Christian faith is worthy of our passionate defense.

Discovery Learning

The following is an alternative lesson plan emphasizing learning activities.
Classes desiring such student involvement will find these suggestions helpful. At the
back of this book are reproducible student pages to further enhance activity learning.

INTO THE LESSON

As your learners arrive, tie a bow of yarn on an index finger of each. This will represent the old memory device, once used with the assumption that such a bow cannot be ignored and that it will remind the wearer of something important. Delay your explanation of the bow until later in the lesson.

Have the following sentence on display, arranged and highlighted as shown, as your learners gather:

The early church needed *strong leaders*
who were *grounded* in the Scriptures,
secure in their faith, and
empowered by the Holy Spirit.
(see the book of Jude)

Introduce today's study by saying "Here is the reason for today's study," then delete the word *early,* change *needed* to *needs,* and change *were* to *are.*

INTO THE WORD

Refer to the yarn bows and ask, "Using one-word terms, what are some areas of major Christian doctrine to remember?" Jot ideas on the board as students call them out. Possible responses include *sin, grace, Heaven, Hell, Son, angels, Father.* Say, "Now let's see what Jude wants us to remember." Assign a verse from today's text to each learner,

repeating verses as necessary to account for class size. Say, "Write a reminder of a foundational biblical doctrine or concept from the verse assigned to you, beginning your statement with the imperative *Remember,* for Jude says in verse 5 that he writes to "remind" us.

Allow no more than one minute, then ask for reports. Here are some possible "remembers" as examples: foundational doctrines are in our possession (v. 3); deceivers can and do infiltrate leadership roles (v. 4); sin elicits God's vengeance (v. 7); there is such a thing as wrong behavior and attitude (v. 8); knowledge and mastery of foundational doctrine is expected of every believer (v. 20); sin corrupts (v. 23); God is eternal (v. 25). Your learners' decisions should promote substantial discussion.

Option #1. If time allows, distribute handouts of the following matching exercise, which will take your class outside today's printed text to other parts of Jude. Ask, "How important is Old Testament history to Jude? Let's find out." Challenge your students to make their matches without looking up the passages. *Events:* 1. The exodus from Egypt (Jude 5); 2. The destruction of Sodom and Gomorrah (Jude 7); 3. The death of Moses (Jude 9); 4. The sin of Cain (Jude 11); 5. Balaam's rebellion (Jude 11); 6. The rebellion of Korah (Jude 11); 7. The long life and success of Enoch (Jude

14). *Texts to match:* A. Genesis 4:1-8; B. Genesis 5:18-24; C. Genesis 19:24, 25; D. Exodus 13:17, 18; E. Numbers 16:1-35; F. Numbers 22–24; G. Deuteronomy 34:1-8.

Option #2: If time allows, have students complete the reproducible matching exercise "Jude the Describer" from page 384.

Have a learner read Jude's benediction (verses 24, 25). Then return to the quote with which you began the session. Note again the words *grounded, secure, empowered.* Say, "These are keys to Christian living—not just for leaders, but for everyone."

INTO LIFE

Ask, "Did you know that there is a 'spiritual tug-of-war' going on right now?" Ask a class member to help you illustrate this. Take two lengths of cord and tie one each to that person's left and right wrists. Hand the free end of one of the cords to a second volunteer as you put a sign reading *LICENSE* around his or her neck. Hand the free end of the other cord to a third volunteer as you put a sign reading *LEGALISM* around his or her neck.

Have your second and third volunteers pull gently in opposite directions as you say, "On the one hand, our freedom in Christ can have the pull of *license,* which is the idea that we are 'free' to do whatever we please. On the other hand, our love of righteousness may tempt us with the pull of *legalism,* where we deny Christian freedom to ourselves and to others."

Next ask, "How can we avoid the pull from either direction, the pull away from being centered on Christ, his holiness, and his grace?" Allow responses. (*Option:* You can illustrate this with stick-figure drawings on the board instead of using cords and signs.)

Distribute copies of the reproducible activity "Benediction" from page 384 as students depart.

Reproducible Activity Pages

Each of the following pages is designed to be used with one of the lessons of the current quarter. You'll find the activities have a variety of helpful applications. Here are a few suggestions on how to use an activity:

- Use it to supplement the discovery learning plan.

- Use it to introduce the lesson concept.

- Use it to make application near the close of your class time.

- Create an overhead transparency with the page, and use it to have the class do the activity together.

Sometimes there are two or more activities on a sheet. Sometimes there is just one. Use each activity as it best suits your own teaching style and the personality of your class.

The Reluctant Prophet

The story of Jonah and Nineveh is the story of a reluctant, yet successful prophet. Read the story in Jonah 1:1-3 and 3:1-9. Then use the following clues to discover the words that are also hidden in the grid. The answers are available below.

1. Who issued the command to preach in Nineveh? _____. (1:1)
2. Who was God's choice to be that missionary? _____. (1:1)
3. This great city became the capital of Assyria. _____. (1:2)
4. The missionary's responsibility was to _____. (1:2)
5. The reason God needed a missionary was the city's _____. (1:2)
6. Rather than go to the target city, Jonah headed to _____. (1:3)
7. Jonah found transportation at the city of _____. (1:3)
8. The transportation? _____. (1:3)
9. The reason Jonah headed to Tarshish was to _____. (1:3)
10. The Lord had to speak to Jonah a _____ time. (3:1)
11. Jonah simply was told to _____ God's Word. (3:2)
12. What was Jonah to proclaim? _____ (3:2)
13. Nineveh was not only great, but was also an _____ city. (3:3)
14. The message gave Nineveh _____ days. (3:4)
15. The threat was that Nineveh would be _____ (3:4)
16. The Ninevites declared a _____ and put on _____. (3:5)
17. Even the _____ wore sackcloth and sat in the _____. (3:6)
18. The king decreed people should _____ call on God and give up their _____ ways and their _____. (3:8)
19. The king was hoping God would _____ and have _____ from his fierce _____. (3:9)

```
U M J S H J H Y E T C S E C O N D L
R P I E H V O C W O F L O R D L G R
G E O A N I N N M I A V H J I I F L
E F L H L E P P A A C K K V P P F F
N H I W L C A W T H O K E W K U A V
T R R O E S O N H E I R E U J U S M
L W I X S K A R Z D E H A D I Q T V
Y V B I P T E P P G K R K C N F M K
T L O R R O H U N X K I N G V E S D
R N R O W E V A E E L F B P H A S U
I Y P E V T B E A P M T R H C X I S
G M S E L W I U R W Z E T K S L M T
I X N C X E Y I W T A I C C E R K W
X I P W N T N Z D C U L K E Y F T M
N Y T R O F Q T H T O R J O P P A F
F M E S S A G E R T T K N X N K B T
T J Y Y I J G S H K L C H E N B U E
L Z A Y T A R S H I S H W K D D E M
```

Stretching Ourselves in Reaching Out

Present the following skit to illustrate how challenging it may be to reach people who are in circumstances that are foreign to the Christian's worldview. The skit is written for two men and two women, but this can be changed depending on class make-up. The setting is in a living room with chairs in a semicircle. The group has just finished a Bible study from the life of Jonah.

Mark: I've got to confess, I really have a hard time understanding why Jonah was upset about the city of Nineveh repenting of their wickedness. Why wouldn't he be happy about that?

Beth: I have the same question. It doesn't sound like he really believed in his own preaching.

Mark: Yeah! Why did he even go there if he didn't really want them to repent?

Michelle: Well, I guess he *didn't* want to go. After all, he tried to go the other direction until that big fish caught up with him. But somehow that turned him around, and he decided he'd better do what God told him to do.

Jim (*who has been in deep thought*): Well, I've been thinking about this issue too. While you've been talking, I tried putting myself in Jonah's shoes in today's world. For instance, I was just notified by the city that a man who has been labeled a sexual predator has moved into my neighborhood . . . just two houses down from me. So, I wondered how I would feel if I were told to go witness to him. I've got to confess, I don't think I'd be very happy about having to do that. Now, isn't that a little like Jonah? Maybe he was just doing what God told him to do, yet not really expecting the response that he got.

Mark: I'm sorry, I still don't get it. I would expect any man of God to be happy that someone has repented.

Michelle: Well, remember that Nineveh was an enemy of God's chosen people. We know that some time later the Assyrians (of which Nineveh was the capital) would conquer God's people. Maybe this prophet suspected that might happen. Maybe he was thinking it would be better for God to wipe them out rather than let them live.

Beth: I don't know. That sexual predator is my neighbor too, and I don't want anything to do with him. I had a 13-year-old niece who was abused by a sexual predator, and frankly, I'd just as soon see him burn in Hell as be forgiven. Now, I know that's not a nice thing to say, but he did a terrible thing to that sweet girl. I just can't seem to get past the damage he did to her.

Michelle: I understand your feelings. But maybe that's God's point. Even though we don't like someone—we may even hate them—God wants us to get past that. After all, didn't God reveal through Peter that the Lord doesn't want anyone to perish, but wants everyone to repent according to 2 Peter 3:9? I suppose that even includes your predator-neighbor, strange as that seems to us.

Jim: Yeah. Wouldn't you like to see him repent and change? I agree with Michelle: It would be a good thing for the neighborhood.

Beth: It's really hard for me to try to look at it from God's eyes and see that man as someone God loves. I'm sure God wants him to change. But I'd rather not have anything to do with him myself!

Mark: Maybe I'm starting to see the point. I guess I can understand Jonah's disappointment in Nineveh's repentance. After all, they were enemies of his people. Maybe that's why God had to work so hard to change his heart. Kinda funny, huh? The preacher had to repent . . . after preaching repentance to others. This neighborhood dilemma, however, shows me that sometimes it's really tough to practice what I preach. Tougher than I like.

Jim: Well, once again, God's Word "meddles" in everyday life! That is, if we'll let it. I liked it better when we were just giving Jonah a hard time and not trying to apply the lesson he learned to our own lives! Oh well, coffee and cake anyone?

Tragedy, Faith, and Love

The story of Naomi and Ruth is laced with the dramas of tragedy, faith, and love. From this moving moment in history, we learn lessons about commitment, faith in foreign cultures, and more. Read Ruth 1:1-9, 14b-16. Then review the tragedies listed and note the cultural, economic, or other complications that could arise from the experience. Also, note the incidents of love and faith in this text. Reflect on the lessons you learn from each expression of love and faith.

RUTH 1	TRAGEDY	COMPLICATIONS FROM THE TRAGEDY
verse 1		
verse 3		
verse 5		

	FAITH AND LOVE	LESSONS FROM THIS EVENT
verses 6, 7		
verses 8, 9		
verse 14		
verse 16		

My New Bumper Sticker!

Today's story teaches lessons about deep faith and commitment to God. Are you able to express your faith as eloquently as Ruth? Make a concise statement of faith or commitment to the Lord by creating a bumper sticker. You may use up to two lines. However, remember that bumper stickers are concise. Here are a few starter lines that may stimulate your thinking: "When life is tough . . ." "Rough days mean . . ." "I may be moving, but . . ."

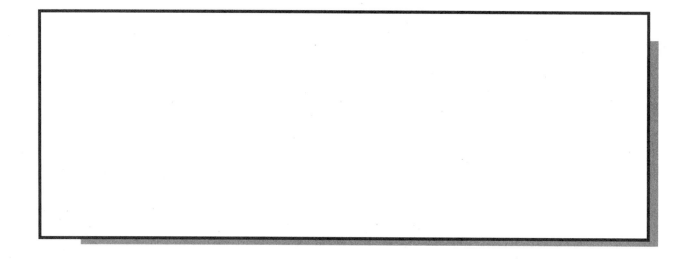

Who Said It?

The beautiful story of Ruth and Boaz is filled with dialogue that reflects attractive character traits and values. Identify who said the following statements by marking them with an R (Ruth) or B (Boaz). Following the quotation, jot a word or note that identifies a character trait or value you will emulate.

1. ___ "Please let me glean and gather among the sheaves." (Ruth 2:7)
The character trait or value I will emulate here is . . .

2. ___ "My daughter, . . . stay here with my servant girls." (Ruth 2:8)
The character trait or value I will emulate here is . . .

3. ___ "I have told the men not to touch you." (Ruth 2:9)
The character trait or value I will emulate here is . . .

4. ___ "I've been told all about what you have done for your mother-in-law . . . and [how you] came to live with a people you did not know before." (Ruth 2:11)
The character trait or value I will emulate here is . . .

5. ___ "I am your servant . . . you are a kinsman-redeemer." (Ruth 3:9)
The character trait or value I will emulate here is . . .

6. ___ "You are a woman of _____ _____." (Ruth 3:11)
The character trait or value I will emulate here is . . .

WWBD

We are acquainted with the acronym *WWJD* ("What Would Jesus Do?"). In the notebook to the right, you will have the opportunity to write a devotion titled *WWBD* ("What Would Boaz Do?"). Imagine you are leading a devotional for a group of high-school students on the theme of practicing compassion and kindness as illustrated by Boaz. Use the following questions to jot a few notes about what you would use in the devotion.

1. Why is kindness an important trait for Christians?
2. What illustration of Christian compassion will you use?
3. What challenge will you give to these teens?

Sorrow to Joy

The following story is a modern example of how God turn our sorrows into joy.

Many years after his father's death in the jungle of Ecuador, Steve Saint traveled as part of a relief team to West Africa during the middle of a famine. The seat he thought he would occupy on his return flight was inadvertently given to a UNICEF doctor. This left Steve alone in a Muslim country where he feared for his life.

Through a series of events, Steve was befriended by a man named Noah. Noah did not speak English, so he began to look for a translator. Through the translator Steve listened to Noah's story. As a teenager, Noah had become a Christian in Timbuktu, but when his mother found out she threw him out of the house and then tried to poison him. Even though he was alone in the world, Noah determined to live for Christ in the Muslim city of Timbuktu. Steve Saint was moved by this testimony and asked Noah where he had found the strength to live this life of persecution. Noah replied that the hope he had was based on what God had done for him and not what he could do for God. Then he went on to explain he had received a book in French about "five Christians who had risked their lives to take their faith to another group of violent people in a fearful part of the world covered in dense jungles. He said, 'When I read of five young men from North America who were willing to die for their faith in the Amazon jungles so far from home, I decided I could live for my faith at home'" (www.pastors.com/article).

Imagine Noah's surprise and joy when Steve told him, "I know that story. My dad was one of those five young men." Imagine Steve's joy years later when he was able to introduce one of those Waodani warriors who had killed his father to Noah—three brothers in Christ united by the same sorrowful event. Later, Steve would write, "Who could imagine that the painful chapter that shredded my young heart would be used by God to bring peace to another boy in Timbuktu."

Now think about a sorrow you have experienced and write how God has turned that sorrow (or could turn that sorrow) into joy:

Living in the Light of God's Love

Unscramble the anagram phrases below to identify actions John says are characteristic of those who "walk in the light."

hits her slob over

for the new thank

tom hero violence eve

dwelt good ole fish

answers: loves his brother; known the Father; overcome the evil one; does the will of God

Lighting the Living of God's Love

As we live lives of love, we are to do so in such a way that we become "the light the world." See if you can unscramble part of Matthew 5:14, 16 in the "fallen phrase" puzzle below. Each of the letters at the bottom can be used in only one of the empty boxes in the column directly above it. There are three boxes with periods and one with a comma, so don't put letters in those. The answer, of course, is in Matthew 5:14, 16, but try not to look!

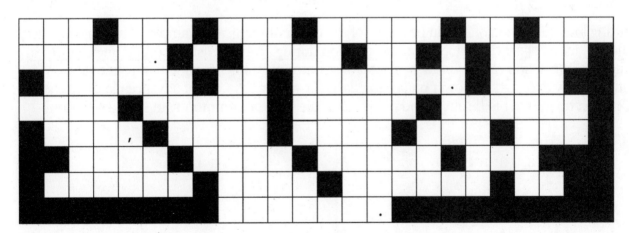

```
                        E
        R               A  O        Y  E  A
    C  Y  L             Y  C     T  H  I  N  N              O  T
    P  A  R  U  O  E    B  T  E  H  H  N  D  H  M     R  L  S  E
    M  E  N  D  R  I  G  T  H  U  S  I  E  Y  E  S  A  A  F  I  T  H
    Y  O  R  A  I  S  T  H  O  O  A  V  E  D  G  E  H  A  Y  N  E  N  L
    Y  O  U  N  A  R  T  A  H  E  I  R  L  F  O  D  N  B  O  F  I  R  E
    W  O  U  O  N  L  E  G  H  T  D  T  D  I  E  T  T  E  E  H  D  L  E  E
```

The Law and the Prophets

Our Scripture text for today reminds us that all the law and the prophets hang on the two commandments to *love the Lord your God with all your heart, soul, and mind* and *love your neighbor as yourself*. Confirm the validity of that statement by matching the imperatives to the right with commandments to the left. Expected answers are in the box below, although there may be room for debate on some.

_____ 1. Have no other gods before me

_____ 2. Do not murder

_____ 3. Repay justly for an injury

_____ 4. Do not make and worship idols

_____ 5. Do not commit adultery

_____ 6. Deal justly with the poor

_____ 7. Do not hold back your offering to God

_____ 8. Do not steal

_____ 9. Do not misuse the Lord's name

_____ 10. Be reverent in your worship

_____ 11. Be generous to those in need

_____ 12. Honor your father and your mother

_____ 13. Do not lie

A. Love the Lord your God with all your heart, soul, and mind.

B. Love your neighbor as yourself

Expected answers:
"A" for 1, 4, 7, 9, and 10
"B" for 2, 3, 5, 6, 8, 11, 12, and 13

Planning to Put Love into Action

Putting love into action often can be a spur of the moment thing. An example is meeting the needs of others in terms of providing food or transportation during a family crisis. At other times, however, putting love into action can require a great deal of advance planning. Imagine that your region of the country is hit with a massive power outage that lasts for several days. What advance planning should your church do in order to be an "island of love and care" for the community in such a situation?

THINGS MY CHURCH NEEDS TO STOCKPILE

PLANS/PROCEDURES MY CHURCH NEEDS TO CREATE

Come to the Feast

Jesus contrasts the kingdom of God with the world by telling about two feasts in Luke 14. Listed below are the characteristics of the world mentioned in these parables. Beside each worldly characteristic, write how the kingdom of God is different.

1. The world honors itself. In the kingdom of God, . . .

2. The world serves those who are "acceptable." In the kingdom of God, . . .

3. The world offers excuses for not "attending the feast." In the kingdom of God, . . .

4. The world limits its invitations for the feast to friends and family. In the kingdom of God, . . .

Potential answers and discussion starters:
1. . . . God honors the humble.
2. . . . the lame, poor, blind, and crippled are served.
3. . . . those in the "streets and alleys" will come to the feast.
4. . . . there is room for all who will accept the invitation.

Excuses, Excuses!

Evaluate your response to God's invitations by completing the following sentences.

One of God's invitations that I have not yet accepted is . . .

Some of the excuses I've given for not accepting it are . . .

I think God might respond to my excuses by saying . . .

A Growing Church

A growing church increases not just in the number of active Christians but also in the spiritual maturity of those Christians. On the church building images here, identify some elements and practices that cause and indicate both kinds of church growth.

How is your congregation doing? What do you and your class need to do to enhance both kinds of congregational growth?

Living as a Saint: How Am I Doing?

Paul commends the Christians in the first century church at Colosse for a variety of characteristics and behaviors. A twenty-first century Christian needs to consider how he or she compares. Mark each of the following elements as a personal evaluation. Use the scale of *1* for "need a new commitment to maturing in Christ" to 5 for "doing very well."

Faithfulness to the saint's calling 1	2	3	4	5
Faith in the lordship of Jesus 1	2	3	4	5
Love expressed to all the saints 1	2	3	4	5
A driving hope for a heavenly future. 1	2	3	4	5
Showing the fruit of a Spirit-led life 1	2	3	4	5
Filled with the knowledge of God's will. 1	2	3	4	5
Increasing in my knowledge of God. 1	2	3	4	5
Sensing the power of God's might 1	2	3	4	5
Feeling like an heir to God's riches. 1	2	3	4	5
Leaving behind the power of darkness. 1	2	3	4	5
Assured of redemption and forgiveness 1	2	3	4	5

Perhaps you will want to state a commitment to going higher and deeper in one or more of these elements of maturity in Christ. Tell him here what you will do:

Three Ways to Go Wrong

From Colossians 2:8, we may conclude three related sources of teaching that can contradict or distort the truth of the gospel. The first is from faulty thinking. The second is from not thinking. The third is thinking that comes from the devil and his agents. One sample is given under each heading below. Write in other errors based on their source. (There may be some overlap since the categories are not exclusive or "air tight.")

Philosophy (possible "faulty thinking")	Traditions (possibly "not thinking")	Worldly Principles (possibly "thinking like Satan")
Man is the measure of all things.	*Might makes right.*	*Right and wrong are relative to circumstance.*
WRONG WAY	WRONG WAY	WRONG WAY

In Control of My Sailboat

By the Spirit, Paul writes that we must resist being "tossed back and forth by the waves, and blown here and there by every wind" of false teaching and deception by evil teachers (Ephesians 4:14). Complete the following confession and personal statement:

At the helm of my own spiritual sailboat, moving only at the impulse of his power and Spirit, I am occasionally threatened by the storm-tossed waves of doubt that tend to capsize my faith, including doubts about . . .

1.

2.

3.

Today, I make this commitment to the lordship of Jesus Christ:

I will . . .

"Well, Shut My Mouth!"

Today's text begins with Paul's admonition for the Colossian Christians (and us) to eliminate sins of the mouth (Colossians 3:8, 9). Put a check mark by each you have you heard in the past week. Put a sad face by any that you have heard from your own mouth during that same time. Put a line through any you have uttered and to which you are willing to say, "No more!"

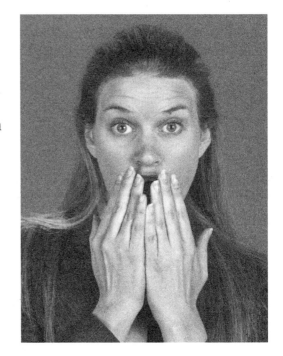

_____ Anger   _____ Slander

_____ Rage   _____ Filthy Language

_____ Malice   _____ Lying

Time to Sing

Paul admonishes us to "sing psalms, hymns and spiritual songs with gratitude in [our] hearts to God" (Colossians 3:16). The following verse can be sung to the Philip P. Bliss tune "Gladness," to which many congregations sing the song titled "Jesus Loves Even Me." Notice the relationship of the words to today's text. If you don't sing it as a class, you can still sing it to yourself or with someone in need of Christ's encouragement during the week ahead.

Singing with grace in my heart to the Lord;

Risen with Christ, seeking him in his Word;

Looking to Heaven, where Jesus is King;

Those are the reasons in grace I can sing!

Christianity and Slavery

Some consider Christianity to have been "soft" on slavery in the Roman world and at other times in the church's history. Paul's words in Ephesians 6:5-9 and in the context of the book of Philemon are sometimes cited in the attack. Consider each of the following reasons for the apostles' and the church's stance. Number these ideas as to their validity: 1 for most valid to 8 for least valid.

____ "God does not expect good behavior from bad people; neither can the church."

____ "Socioeconomic status is irrelevant in redemption and in church relationships."

____ "Christianity does condemn slavery and open the way to its abolition in its emphasis on personal will and personal worth."

____ "A direct attack on slavery is only an indirect attack on evil; conversion is better than legislation."

____ "The rise of Christianity and its rapid growth relied on the political stability and freedom of travel the Roman government provided; thus, an attack on the institutions of Roman law was counterproductive."

____ "Christianity is committed to institutional change only as it convicts individuals of the lordship of Jesus."

____ "The church's concern with slavery is slavery to sin and the redeemer's slavery to the lordship of Jesus."

____ "Christianity is a matter of the will and heart, not a matter of forced behavior, not a matter of armed might, so it does not/cannot impose a godly morality."

What is the way you can best explain the church's stance in the first century? How do you explain the twenty-first century's church attitude toward peoples other than "their own kind"?

A Noted Prayer List

Paul often writes of his prayers for those to whom he writes. List names of Christians for whom you are praying. When you write a note (or e-mail) informing and encouraging each one, jot down at the right the day and time you prayed.

1. _____   _____
2. _____   _____
3. _____   _____
4. _____   _____

Jude the Describer

Match the adjectives on the left with their nouns on the right. The verse numbers where the correct answers are found in Jude are given in the box to the right.

A. celestial ____ beings
B. entrusted ____ chains
C. eternal [first use] ____ clothing
D. eternal [second use] ____ Day
E. everlasting ____ faith [first use]
F. glorious ____ faith [second use]
G. godless ____ fire
H. great [first use] ____ God
I. great [second use] ____ immorality
J. holy ____ instincts
K. natural ____ joy
L. only ____ life
M. sexual ____ men
N. shared ____ presence
O. stained ____ salvation

Here's where to find the answers in Jude:
A, verse 8; B, verse 3; C, verse 7; D, verse 21; E, verse 6; F, verse 24; G, verse 4; H, verse 6; I, verse24; J, verse 20; K, verse 19; L, verse 25; M, verse 7; N, verse 3; O, verse 23.

Benediction

In the pattern of Jude's final word to the Christians he addresses in verses 24 and 25, write a benediction you can use in your communication to other Christians.

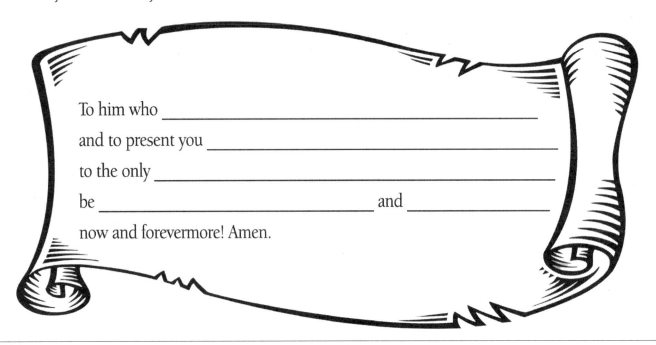

To him who _____

and to present you _____

to the only _____

be _____ and _____

now and forevermore! Amen.

Summer Quarter 2010

Christian Commitment in Today's World

(1 and 2 Thessalonians, Philippians)

Special Features

Lessons

Unit 1: The Nature of Christian Commitment

Unit 2: The Foundation of Christian Commitment

Unit 3: The Marks of Christian Commitment

About These Lessons

Are you "committed"? Almost everyone is committed to something, if only to personal comfort. The question is, "To what or whom are you committed?" This quarter's lessons will help you focus your commitment on Christ.

Jun 6

Jun 13

Jun 20

Jun 27

Jul 4

Jul 11

Jul 18

Jul 25

Aug 1

Aug 8

Aug 15

Aug 22

Aug 29

Quarter Review

Use this page to form questions for the class to answer and discuss. Then provide the information as a handout to summarize the lessons of the past quarter.

LESSON 1: VISIBLE FOR GOD

How can people see the invisible God? Paul taught that he is seen in the lives of his people. He commended the Thessalonians for their exemplary faith, love, and hope. Can people see God in your life?

LESSON 2: PLEASING TO GOD

Paul's own example is in focus in this lesson. He had come to Thessalonica with a mission, and his intention was to please God first and foremost. The result honored God and was beneficial to people. Are you pleasing to God?

LESSON 3: SUSTAINED THROUGH ENCOURAGEMENT

Paul had left Thessalonica too abruptly. He missed the believers there and they missed him. So he sent Timothy to encourage them, and Timothy's report back to Paul was encouraging to him. Whom can you encourage today?

LESSON 4: DEMONSTRATED IN ACTION

Is faith a private matter or public? For Paul the answer was obvious. He commended the Thessalonians for living in such a way that they had become an example for others. Is your faith on display as a good example to others?

LESSON 5: GOD'S COSMIC PLAN

Sometimes life is hard. Standing up for one's faith is challenging. It's tempting to quit, to go with the flow. The Thessalonians were almost to that point, but Paul reminded them that God is faithful. Are you needing such a reminder?

LESSON 6: GLORY TO CHRIST

"Oh that will be glory for me!" So says the old hymn, and it's right. But the glory is to Christ first. When he comes in glory, only then will we have glory. In the meantime, we give all the glory to him. Can you do that?

LESSON 7: CHOSEN AND CALLED

The deceiver is at work. He would like nothing more than for us to abandon hope, to forget that God himself has chosen and called us. He will protect his own until the day comes when the deceiver is destroyed. Can you wait for that?

LESSON 8: GOD'S OWN FAITHFULNESS

God is faithful; of that we can be sure. Because of that, we must be faithful too—in the big things as well as the little things. Like pulling our own weight; like continuing to do good even when we are tired. Are you doing that?

LESSON 9: SHARING GOD'S GRACE

Some people do the right thing for the wrong reason. It's hard to appreciate the right of their actions in the middle of the wrong of their attitude. Paul said give it to the Lord, and praise him when good is done. Will you do that?

LESSON 10: GIVING OF ONESELF

"Your attitude should be the same as that of Christ Jesus." It's a familiar verse, but it's a tough assignment. We want to be stroked, admired, even pampered. We at least want what's due us. Are we really ready to act with the selfless attitude of Christ?

LESSON 11: LIVING INTO THE FUTURE

As much as some people want to "live in the past," we are all living into the future. We can hold on to neither the past nor the present, but must keep moving into the future. Will you go reluctantly, or will you press on with zeal?

LESSON 12: GROWING IN JOY AND PEACE

Sometimes even good people quarrel. It happened in Philippi, and it happens in your town. What a contrast with Paul, who had learned to be content in all things. Can you be content even when you don't get you way?

LESSON 13: UPHELD BY GOD

The book of Acts ends with Paul in Roman custody over a period of some five years (in Caesarea, en route to Rome, and then in Rome). He could have despaired, but instead he continued his ministry. What would you have done?

Our Commitment

by John C. Nugent

Genuine, long-term commitment seems to be a rare thing today. This trend to shorter-term arrangements is closely tied to the expectations of a consumer-driven economy. I wish I could say that Christians are immune to such a trend in the spiritual arena, but I cannot. Church-hopping has replaced long-term membership for some Christians as they "shop around" for an experience to meet the moment's felt needs. Some Christians have taken to experimenting with non-Christian forms of spiritual fulfillment. Those tempted by this kind of thinking will especially benefit from this quarter's lessons.

UNIT 1: THE NATURE OF CHRISTIAN COMMITMENT

Lesson 1 reveals Paul's gratitude that the Thessalonians were committed to enduring in the faith, receiving the gospel message, turning from idols, and awaiting Christ's return. Their example remains an example for us.

Lesson 2 teaches that Christian commitment can be emulated. Paul was able to encourage the Thessalonians to live lives worthy of their calling because he lived that kind of life while among them. The integrity of the church's witness today depends on leaders who model such commitment.

Christian commitment will be tested, as **Lesson 3** reveals. Paul knew it was difficult to endure trials, and he was encouraged to learn that testing had made the Thessalonians stronger. Christians today endure trials and tests of many kinds. May we be encouraged by the example of Paul and the Thessalonians.

Our commitment to Christ involves not just our spiritual dedication, but also the physical side of our being. In **Lesson 4,** Paul instructed the Thessalonians that Christians must be faithful in everyday behavior, including abstaining from sexual immorality, loving fellow disciples, and having a good work ethic.

UNIT 2: THE FOUNDATION OF CHRISTIAN COMMITMENT

Unit 1 emphasized that Christian commitment must be expressed in actions. But such commitment is not founded on human effort. Rather, it is by divine initiative. **Lesson 5** teaches about the fact and significance of Christ's promise to return and finish his saving work. Paul taught the Thessalonians that they did not need to know precisely when Christ would return. What they needed to know—as do we—is that God is faithful to fulfill his promise, and he has called us to be prepared.

In **Lesson 6** we learn that a key part of Christian commitment is the faithfulness of the persecuted. The same God who worked through the persecuted Thessalonians will complete that work and glorify himself through us.

Christian commitment is founded on God's sovereignty or control of world history, as **Lesson 7** firmly establishes. God knows that lawless forces are at work in the world, and he allows their operation for a time. God's people must stand firm in full assurance that God will, indeed, accomplish his purposes both to condemn the lawless and to save his people.

God's faithfulness is to be a model for our commitment. **Lesson 8** points out certain ungodly attitudes and behaviors within the church that work against our commitment to Christ. Paul shows us how to recognize attitudes

JUNE

JULY

and behaviors that distract and mislead. These are not problems to be ignored! Believers must spend their time wisely and productively in the service of God. Part of that service involves admonishing those who do not.

UNIT 3: THE MARKS OF CHRISTIAN COMMITMENT

We discern various marks of Christian commitment in Paul's letter to the church in Philippi. **Lesson 9** teaches us that Christian commitment must be unwavering. Paul conducted his ministry under opposition. He was able to endure by placing Christ first. His letter encouraged the Philippians to follow his example in that regard. So must we.

Christian commitment must be humble and selfless, as **Lesson 10** establishes. For the church to flourish under suffering, its members must follow the example of Christ, who humbled himself and put the needs of others first.

Lesson 11 brings us the challenge of distinguishing between past and future orientations. Paul is clear in this regard: Christian commitment must be oriented to the future, to be oriented toward a heavenly goal. We must resolve to know Christ alone as we press forward in him. In so doing, we experience both the fellowship of his sufferings and the power of his resurrection in the present.

Lesson 12 teaches us that Christian commitment involves a zeal for peaceful, joyous fellowship within the church. Churches that are fractured by strife will not endure. No one wants to be part of a joyless church.

Believers are to be at peace not only with fellow believers but also with whatever uncertainties the future may hold. Rather than dwell on what we cannot control, we are to focus on the good that we know and have in Christ. Like Paul, we must exhibit unflinching confidence that God will meet all our needs.

Lesson 13 shows us how Paul embodied Christian commitment during his last recorded days under house arrest in Rome. Here we see unwavering commitment under persecution. Here we see a steadfast commitment to proclaiming the reality of the present and future kingdom of God that has been made possible by Christ. Paul lived what he taught until his dying days. So must we.

CONCLUSION: GETTING COMMITTED

In our day, sometimes it seems that the only cause worth obligating oneself to is personal freedom, and the only time frame worth committing to is one that may be abandoned when deemed inconvenient. Indeed, to the modern mind it seems entirely irrational to commit to just about anything on a long-term basis. To do so would be to limit one's options and to surrender one's flexibility.

That was not the mind-set of Paul. That apostle's unwavering commitment to Christ is a refreshing break from the "commitment to noncommitment" of our culture. A primary long-term commitment we should make is to adopt his outlook as our own. In so doing, we immerse ourselves in a commitment worth living and dying for: a commitment to Jesus Christ.

Television commercials, blockbuster Hollywood films, and "the latest buzz" on the Internet capture our imagination and cloud our vision in the process. The Christians of Thessalonica and Philippi may not have had mass media outlets to compete with, but they had to practice unflinching Christian commitment when reputations, occupations, and the security of future generations were on the line. Though times have changed in many ways, the need for commitment to Christ has not.

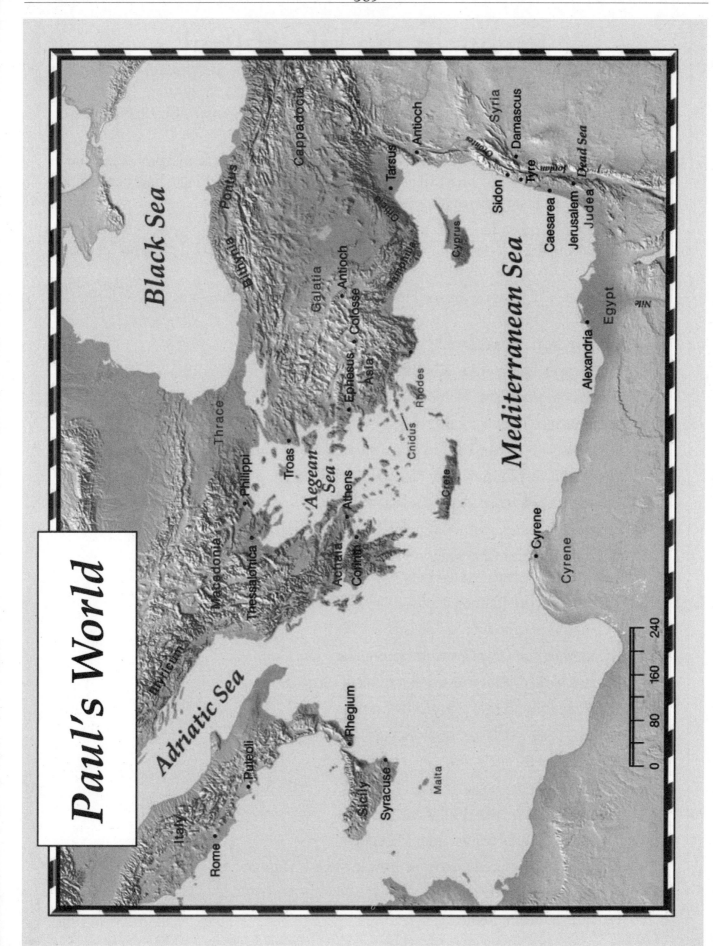

Paul's World

Black Sea

Adriatic Sea

Mediterranean Sea

Aegean Sea

Italy

Rome

Puteoli

Rhegium

Sicily

Syracuse

Malta

Illyricum

Macedonia

Thessalonica

Philippi

Troas

Athens

Achaia

Corinth

Thrace

Bithynia

Pontus

Cappadocia

Galatia

Antioch

Colosse

Ephesus

Asia

Pamphilia

Cnidus

Rhodes

Crete

Cyrene

Cyrene

Tarsus

Cilicia

Antioch

Syria

Damascus

Sidon

Tyre

Jordan

Dead Sea

Orontes

Caesarea

Jerusalem

Judea

Egypt

Alexandria

Nile

Cyprus

240

160

80

0

Events in the Life of Paul

DATE	EVENT
2	Birth in Tarsus; named Saul. That Saul was a "young man" (Acts 7:58) at the stoning of Stephen suggests he was about 30 at that time.
30	Pentecost (Acts 2). Saul was probably not in Jerusalem during the ministry of Jesus or at this great feast that occurred 10 days after his ascension. His writings show no evidence of first-hand knowledge of Jesus' ministry.
32	Stoning of Stephen in Jerusalem (Acts 7:54–8:1). Saul was probably one of those from Cilicia who the first to dispute with Stephen (Acts 6:9, 10), one of those who "could not stand up against his wisdom or the Spirit by whom he spoke."
34	Appearance of Jesus on the road to Damascus; baptism in Damascus (Acts 9:1-19; 22:6-16; 26:12-23)
34-37	Three years in Arabia, learning of Jesus (Galatians 1:17, 18)
37	Saul escapes Damascus in a basket (Acts 9:23-25; 2 Corinthians 11:32, 33)
37	First visit to Jerusalem; escape to Tarsus (Acts 9:26-30)
45	Barnabas recruits Saul for the work in Antioch (Acts 11:25, 26).
46	Paul assists in carrying relief to Jerusalem; returns to Antioch (Acts 11:27-30; 12:25)
47-49	First Missionary Journey, with Barnabas (Acts13–14))
51	Jerusalem Conference (Acts 15; Galatians 2)
52-54	Second Missionary Journey, with Silas (Acts 15:36–18:22))
52	Churches established in Philippi, Thessalonica, and Corinth (Acts 16–18); 1 & 2 Thessalonians written from Corinth
54-58	Third Missionary Journey, ending in Jerusalem (Acts 18:23–21:16)
56	1 Corinthians written from Ephesus
57	2 Corinthians & Galatians written from Macedonia
58	Romans written; Paul arrested in Jerusalem (Acts 21)
58-60	Transferred to and held prisoner in Caesarea (Acts 23:31-35; 24:27)
60	Paul appeals his case to Caesar (Acts 25:11)
60-61	Trip to Rome (Acts 27–28)
61-63	Paul is held under house arrest in Rome (Acts 28:16, 30)
63	Prison Epistles written; Paul is released
65	1 Timothy & Titus written from Macedonia
67	Paul arrested in Macedonia, or perhaps in Troas (2 Timothy 4:13)
67	2 Timothy written
67/68	Paul is executed in Rome

Applying the Bible to Life

THE OTHER HALF OF THE LESSON
by James Riley Estep, Jr.

"Students should just make the lesson application themselves. That's not really the teacher's responsibility." Is that your viewpoint as a teacher? Many Sunday school teachers resist the idea of making application, perceiving their role to be a teacher of Bible content and little more.

WHY TEACHERS HESITATE

There are various reasons why teachers hesitate when it comes to application. Some teachers avoid making application to life out of fear of appearing authoritarian or intrusive into students' personal lives. Other teachers resist making application because they don't want to be seen as "offensive." They don't want to "step on people's toes." The result in these cases may be Bible lessons that are taught in a vague, general way in order to avoid controversy.

But if a student is offended by a suggested application to life, could that not mean that the student is living his or her life in a way that is contrary to the Scriptures? We recall this warning: "Do not merely listen to the word, and so deceive yourselves. Do what it says." (James 1:22). This means that teaching the Bible text is incomplete without application. Application to life is more likely to happen when the teacher recognizes his or her responsibility in this regard.

THE TEACHER'S TASK

The simple diagram below depicts the teaching process in its most complete form. The first step, naturally, is to read the biblical text. From there we move on to explaining its meaning. This step involves coming to grips with what the Bible author intended the original readers to understand (the fancy word for this is *exegesis*).

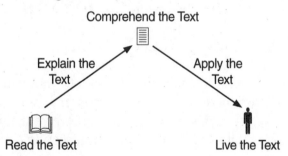

Comprehend the Text

Explain the Text

Apply the Text

Read the Text

Live the Text

The third step, comprehension, involves helping the student begin to see how his or her understanding of the text can form a general principle of life. This step is your vital bridge between explanation of the text and application to life. When the learner studies a passage and comprehends it (not just memorizes it), then the teacher is ready to move to application of the passage. Until comprehension is achieved, application is virtually impossible because the text is still too "distant" from the life of the learner. Our study of the passage must take us successfully through this point.

WHY TEACHERS HESITATE

Fear of appearing authoritarian or intrusive.

Don't want to be seen as "offensive."

Don't want to "step on people's toes."

THE TEACHER'S TASK

Read the biblical text.
Explain its meaning.
Help the student begin to understand.
Apply the passage.
Live the text.

We can help our learners form these general principles of life by considering *life parallels*. How does the situation of the biblical author's message parallel our situation today? In those parallels, how does the biblical message address the culture, congregation, and general life situation of the student? It is here the learner should begin to see similarities between the lives of biblical characters and their own regarding circumstances, challenges, and decisions.

Help learners form general life principles.

Consider, for example, Paul's discussion in Galatians about the relationship between Jews and Gentiles in the church. That situation in and of itself is probably rather "distant" to your learners. Chances are they have never experienced a conflict between Jew and Gentile in the churches they have attended. Thus the issue by itself doesn't carry the immediacy today that it did in the first century.

However, the nature of relations between people of different races or cultural backgrounds is a very real issue in the twenty-first century. In this light, Paul's discussion about the relationship between Jews and Gentiles informs what our response should be to twenty-first century parallels. Now the text is definitely getting closer to our life, society, and world.

Help students develop a specific plan for Biblical life change.

After establishing a general arena of application (in this case, race and/or cross-cultural relationships), we ask ourselves, "What specific *life applications* can be made? What are students expected actually to do about it?" As teachers, we prepare for a lesson by thinking through these questions, but ultimately we have to ask how we can help students develop a specific plan for biblical life-change. It is never enough merely to draw parallels for students or have them brainstorm about possible applications before you move on to the next verse. Students must be asked, "So, what are you going to do about it? What changes do you need to make to reflect the biblical text in your life?" After all, this is ultimately how Scripture is to affect students.

CLASSROOM TIPS

MOVE FROM GENERAL TO SPECIFIC

The next question is "But how do we set this process in motion in the classroom? What's the best way to move from *general life-principle* to *specific application*?" The Lesson Aims of each study in this commentary form a good starting point for you in this regard. The first and second aims deal with knowing and comprehending the lesson text. The third aim always addresses application.

The Lesson Aims of each study in this commentary form a good starting point.

There is more than one way to achieve those Lesson Aims, depending on your teaching style. If you like to use a learning-activity approach, the Learning by Doing section in each lesson can help you achieve all three aims. After an attention-getter ("Into the Lesson"), you move to Bible study proper ("Into the Word"); this is where you achieve your first and second Lesson Aims. That is followed by an application section ("Into Life") to achieve the third aim.

There is more than one way to achieve the Lesson Aims:

Learning-activity approach

Discussion approach

You can also use a discussion approach to achieve your application aim. After helping your learners comprehend the biblical message, you can lead them in a discussion of possible applications of the biblical principle. Students actively participate by suggesting parallels between the situation of the people in the Scriptures with those in our own world today. Your task is to help the students push their comprehension to application.

For example, after studying Paul's praise of the Thessalonian church, you can ask, "How does our congregation measure up to what Paul expected in a church?" After a time of class or small-group discussion, the next question can be, "How can you, individually, help our church become what God expects it to be?" This brings the biblical text into "real life" application for the student.

For an Old Testament example, consider Moses' educational mandate in Deuteronomy 6. After addressing what this text meant "back then," you can ask students to suggest general applications of the biblical text for modern parenting. Classes can brainstorm possible applications, and the more the better! After the brainstorming winds down, you can ask your learners to select one possible application to put into practice in the week ahead. (You may have to distinguish between applications for parents and non-parents among your students.) Thus the application can result in biblically informed life-changes.

The advantage of this kind of approach is that your learners will have a greater sense of "ownership" of the action plan because of their participation in helping create it. If you, the teacher, want to retain a bit more control during a discussion (to keep the class from going off on tangents), you can provide the life parallels yourself. You can do this by bringing newspaper or magazine articles that address the issue at hand. If your classroom is equipped to do so, you can show video clips from a movie, documentary, or Internet sites such as *YouTube* or *GodTube*.

Keep in mind that after a season of general discussion, the lesson focus must shift to the life of the individual student. At the beginning of a discussion the teacher may ask, "What are *we* going to do about this?" but the question eventually must move to "What are *you* going to do about it?" Asking students to identify a biblical life-change they can make in the week ahead is somewhat easy given the fact that they have spent time discussing possible general applications. Moving from the general application to the specific application simply becomes a matter of determining what God wants each one of them to do about it.

Move from the general application to the specific application.

The creation of a specific application also provides a point of assessment for the lesson itself: the following week the teacher simply asks students if they followed through with the application of the previous week's lesson. This builds a sense of spiritual accountability among your class members. When application is done in this way, it becomes a natural extension of biblical study, which is exactly what it should be.

Even if your preferred teaching style is primarily lecture, you can move your class from comprehension to application by selective and occasional use of discussion questions. The discussion questions included with each lesson can serve you well in this regard.

COMPLETE INTERPRETATION

As one student has pointed out, "The interpretation of Scripture is not complete until its application is found for the reader in his or her present situation." This means that an explanation of the Bible text must be followed by coming to grips with how that text is to be lived out.

The teacher's job is to assist the students in making their own applications.

Keep in mind that leading your students to make application of the biblical text in their own lives does not require you, the teacher, to directly make the application *for* them. Your job is to assist your students in making their own applications. That's complete interpretation!

How to Say It

Use this list to help you pronounce the names and hard-to-pronounce words in the lessons of the summer quarter.

A

Achaia. Uh-KAY-uh.
Agnes Bojaxhiu. AG-ness Boh-yah-JOO.
Agrippa. Uh-GRIP-puh.
Albanian. Al-BAY-nee-un.
Amish. AW-mish.
antichrist. AN-tee-christ.
Antioch. AN-tee-ock.
Apollos. Uh-PAHL-us.
Arminian. Ar-MIH-nee-un.
Augsburg. Ogz-burg.

B

Barack Obama. Buh-ROCK O-BAH-muh.
Barnabas. BAR-nuh-bus.
Berea. Buh-REE-uh.

C

Caesar Augustus. SEE-zer Aw-GUS-tus.
Caesar. SEE-zer.
Caesarea Maritime. Sess-uh-REE-uh MARE-uh-time.
Calcutta. Cal-CUT-uh.
centurion. sen-TURE-ee-un.
Cilicia. Sih-LISH-i-uh.
Clairvaux. Clare-VOE.
Clement. KLEH-munt.
Clodovaeus. Kluh-DOE-vee-us.
Corinth. KOR-inth.

D

Damascus. Duh-MASS-kus.
Diet. DEE-ut

E

Epaphroditus. Ee-PAF-ro-DYE-tus.
Ephesus. EF-uh-sus.
Euodia. You-O-dee-uh.

G

Gamaliel. Guh-MAY-lih-ul or Guh-MAY-lee-al.
Gentile. JEN-tile.

H

heretical. heh-REH-tih-cul.

I

Ignatius. Ig-NAY-shus.
Irenaeus. I-ree-NEE-us.

J

Jerusalem. Juh-ROO-suh-lem.
Judaism. JOO-duh-izz-um or JOO-day-izz-um.
Julius Caesar. JOO-lee-us SEE-zer.

L

Ludovicus. Luh-DOE-vih-kus.
Lydia. LID-ee-uh.
Lystra. LISS-truh.

M

Macedon. MASS-uh-don.
Macedonia. Mass-eh-DOE-nee-uh.
Malta. MAL-tuh.
Meidung. MY-dohn(g).
Mennonites. MEH-nuh-nights.
Messiah. Meh-SIGH-uh.
millennial. muh-LEN-ee-uhl.

N

Naboth. NAY-bawth.
narcissism. NAR-sih-SIZ-um.

P

papacy. PAY-puh-see.
Pas-de-Calais. Pah`d-cuh-LAY.
Pax Romana. PAX Roe-MAH-nuh.
Pentecost. PENT-ih-kost.
Pharisaic. FAIR-ih-SAY-ick.
Pharisees. FAIR-ih-seez.
Philippi. Fih-LIP-pie or FIL-ih-pie.
Polycarp. PAW-lee-carp.
proconsul. pro-CAHN-suhl.

R

rabbi. RAB-eye.

S

Sadducees. SAD-you-seez.
sanctification. sank-tih-fuh-KAY-shun.
Smyrna. SMUR-nuh.
Socrates. SOCK-ruh-teez.
synagogue. SIN-uh-gog.
Syntyche. SIN-tih-key.

T

Talmudic. Tal-MOOD-ick.
Tarsus. TAR-sus.
Thessalonica. THESS-uh-lo-NYE-kuh (TH as in THIN).

W

Wartburg. VORT-berg.
Worms. Vormz.

VISIBLE FOR GOD

LESSON 1

INTRODUCTION

A. WHAT YOU SEE IS WHAT YOU GET

Do you remember using a personal computer in the 1980s? If you do, you probably remember being amazed at all the things it could do. Personal computers made it easy to do what was tedious on a typewriter. They fit the text to the length of the line, started a new page at just the right point, and even helped check the spelling.

But with their dark monitors with green or amber dots forming the letters, those early computers did not show exactly how a document would look when it was printed. It was a later generation of computers that offered WYSIWYG (pronounced WIH-see-wig), or "what you see is what you get," a feature that today's computer users take for granted.

Today's text is about what-you-see-is-what-you-get faith. It describes a group of young-in-the-faith Christians whose lives were changed by the gospel. There was no questioning whether their inward and outward lives were in tune with each other. Since they had come to believe in Jesus Christ, they were visibly, obviously becoming a new kind of people.

If we are content with the idea that faith in Jesus is an inward, private matter that does not affect our public life, this text will challenge us!

B. LESSON BACKGROUND

Thessalonica was a prosperous port and center of trade in the region of Macedonia, the northern part of the Greek peninsula. Like most cities of its kind, it was filled with all kinds of people and all kinds of beliefs. Economically there was a wide gap between the rich merchants and poor laborers. Socially there was powerful pressure to conform to established standards. Religiously there were many followers of pagan cults, some encouraging grossly immoral practices, but also a notable number of faithful Jewish worshipers of the God of Israel.

When Paul first visited the city, on what we call his second missionary journey (Acts 17:1-10), his preaching there led many to believe in Jesus. But it also provoked persecution, and Paul was forced to leave after only a short time. The new believers were left alone to face the pressures of their environment. Would they persist in their new faith or go back to their old lives?

When he was able, Paul sent his assistant Timothy to visit the Thessalonian Christians and report back (1 Thessalonians 3:1-5). Timothy's visit confirmed that the new believers were faithful and growing. Though not without problems, the church was demonstrating its faith through action (vv. 6-8).

Paul wrote 1 Thessalonians probably just a few months after leaving the city and soon after receiving Timothy's report. He begins with a thankful celebration of the Thessalonians' transforming faith. Far from succumbing to

DEVOTIONAL READING:
TITUS 2:11-15

BACKGROUND SCRIPTURE:
1 THESSALONIANS 1

PRINTED TEXT:
1 THESSALONIANS 1

LESSON AIMS

After this lesson each student will be able to:

1. Tell what Paul gave thanks for concerning the Thessalonians.

2. Contrast the old life of the Thessalonian believers with their new life in Christ.

3. Describe one way that his or her church can and should imitate the example of the church at Thessalonica.

KEY VERSE:

You welcomed the message with the joy given by the Holy Spirit. —1 Thessalonians 1:6

LESSON 1 NOTES

DAILY BIBLE READINGS

Monday, May 31—God Sees All (Ezekiel 14:1-8)

Tuesday, June 1—A Purified People (Titus 2:11-15)

Wednesday, June 2—Faith and Convictions (Romans 14: 22, 23)

Thursday, June 3— Imitators of Christ (1 Corinthians 10:23–11:1)

Friday, June 4—The Outcomes of Faith (Hebrews 13:1-7)

Saturday, June 5— Following Christ's Example (John 13:3-15)

Sunday, June 6—An Exemplary Faith (1 Thessalonians 1)

the pressures of their culture, they have become examples to believers in their region and beyond. Through the centuries, their example continues to speak to us today.

I. TRANSFORMED RELATIONSHIP (1 THESSALONIANS 1:1, 2)

1. Paul, Silas and Timothy,

To the church of the Thessalonians in God the Father and the Lord Jesus Christ: Grace and peace to you.

In the world of ancient Greece and Rome, it is customary to begin a letter with a salutation that names the writer and the addressees and that offers a brief greeting. *Paul* uses this format, but he deliberately alters it to express the profound relationship he has with his fellow Christians. After naming himself and his assistants, *Silas and Timothy,* Paul addresses his readers as *the church . . . in God the Father and the Lord Jesus Christ.* Though the word *church* sounds conventional to us, it has a rich meaning for Paul's readers. For those who had been Greek pagans before their conversion, the word reminds them of the assemblies of citizens common in Greek government. Now they are part of an assembly that belongs to the one true God, whom they know as Father and who has entered the world to save it in the person of Jesus Christ. The term reminds Jewish believers of the assembly of Israel as God's people. Now, however, they realize that they are God's people because of God's saving work in Christ, not because of their ethnic identity. Both Gentiles and Jews are now together in a great assembly of people, the very people of God.

Typical Greek letters in New Testament times offer a conventional word of "Greetings." (See James 1:1.) Among Jews another word is often used, a Hebrew word meaning *peace.* Paul adapts both of these conventions in his letters. In place of the Greek "greetings," he uses a word that sounds very much like it but means *grace.* And he combines that with the Greek translation of the Hebrew "peace." Those two words epitomize the blessings of the gospel that Paul has shared with the Thessalonians: God's grace, his favor and blessing granted freely to those who do not deserve it, and his peace, the well-being and assurance that he grants in all circumstances. Grace and peace now describe the relationship that believers enjoy with God and with each other.

2. We always thank God for all of you, mentioning you in our prayers.

Following the greeting in a Greek letter comes a word of thanksgiving, which Paul begins here. But Paul's thanksgiving is no mere formality. He goes to great lengths to describe exactly why he thanks God constantly for the Thessalonian Christians.

These believers are not just people whom Paul happens to know from the short time he was in their city. They are of the utmost importance to him as fellow members of God's family. That reality is reflected in his constant prayer on their behalf.

II. TRANSFORMED LIFESTYLE (1 THESSALONIANS 1:3-6)

A. BEHAVIORAL CHANGE (v. 3)

3. We continually remember before our God and Father your work produced by faith, your labor prompted by love, and your endurance inspired by hope in our Lord Jesus Christ.

WHAT DO YOU THINK?

How much are you experiencing God's grace and peace today? If you feel this is a deficiency in your life, why do you think that is? If it is abundant, what can you share with the rest of us to help us experience that?

As soon as Paul begins to recall what he knows about the Thessalonian Christians, he focuses on the way their lives are visibly different. Each term that he uses emphasizes that they are active and vibrant in living out what they believe.

Paul notes first their *work produced by faith*. Paul is well known for emphasizing that faith, not works, is the basis on which God gives salvation (Ephesians 2:8, 9). But he also stresses that true faith always leads to action (Ephesians 2:10). A person who believes that Jesus is Lord will always seek to do what honors and pleases him.

The next phrase is *labor prompted by love*. Faith prompts action, and the love of God reinforces that prompting. The biblical God is the God of love, who showed his love by giving his Son to die for unworthy sinners. His love is poured into the hearts of those who believe in him, and they in turn share that love with others. Biblical love is not just sentiment or feeling; it is a powerful impulse to act for the benefit of others, even when such action is costly.

The third phrase is *endurance inspired by hope*. We use the word *hope* for things about which we are uncertain ("I hope it stops raining soon," or "I hope my team wins its game tonight"). In the New Testament, however, hope always expresses confidence based on the character and power of God. Believers in Christ can have assurance about the future, knowing that God loves them and is faithful and powerful to deliver what he has promised. In the end, God has promised that Christ will return for all of his people (1 Thessalonians 1:10; 3:13; 4:13–5:11; 5:23). Believers can be confident that the powerful God who loves them will be faithful to finish his saving work in the end.

That confident hope is the basis for their present patience. This word suggests not just passively waiting but actively enduring hardship and suffering. Christians are able to bear up under the burdens of life and even persecution for their faith because they are confident of the future that God will give to them.

The combination of the terms *faith, love,* and *hope* is found many times in the New Testament (Romans 5:1-5; 1 Corinthians 13:13; Galatians 5:5, 6; Ephesians 4:2-5; Colossians 1:4, 5; 1 Thessalonians 5:8; Hebrews 6:10-12; 1 Peter 1:3-8, 21, 22). These terms summarize the nature of the Christian life.

TRANSFORMED!

A generation ago a new type of toy captured the fancy of children: the Transformer. It took various forms—as you might expect of a toy with that name! Typically, it would be a machine such as a car that, through bending and twisting of its pieces, could be turned into a sort of science-fiction humanoid figure. Then came the animated television series and movie (in 1986). The latter depicted an epic battle in the future (2005!) on a far-off planet. It was the classic story of good-against-evil. Heroic Autobots fought the evil Decepticons to save their planet. The story line was reprised in a 2007 movie.

Paul's letter to the Thessalonians approaches the subject of transformation from an entirely different perspective. Paul does not deny the evil forces in the world that work to destroy the good. Far from it! However, Paul focuses on the transformation that had occurred in the lives of the Thessalonians. Because of the gospel, their lives had become characterized by faithful good works, the diligence with which their love for God was shown to others, and an unwavering hope based on the Lord Jesus Christ. No twisting and bending necessary!   —C. R. B.

VISUALS FOR THESE LESSONS

The visual pictured in each lesson (example: page 399) is a small reproduction of a large, full-color poster included in the Adult Resources *packet for the Summer Quarter. That packet also contains the very useful* Presentation Helps *on a CD for teacher use. The packet is available from your supplier. Order No. 492.*

WHAT DO YOU THINK?

We have often heard lessons on faith and love, but what about hope? What are some specific ways hope is manifested in the lives of believers? How do you think we can grow in the area of hope?

B. BASED ON GOD'S WORK (vv. 4, 5)

4. For we know, brothers loved by God, that he has chosen you,

The Thessalonians' transformed behavior is nothing less than the result of their new standing with *God* in Christ Jesus. Here Paul refers to God's choice of them as his people. The Thessalonian believers now belong to God as his *chosen* people just as Israel belonged to him in the time of the Old Testament. Some teach that such terms as this require us to believe that God determines beforehand who will believe and who will not. In the New Testament, however, God's choice is based on the believers' faith. God chooses those who put their trust in Christ. He makes believers in Jesus His chosen people.

This reminds us that salvation is entirely God's initiative. God planned from the beginning to save sinners by sending his Son. He declares that people belong to him on the basis of their faith in what he has done. The steadfast work of God's people is their response to what God has done. It is never their effort to earn God's favor or pay God back!

5. . . . because our gospel came to you not simply with words, but also with power, with the Holy Spirit and with deep conviction. You know how we lived among you for your sake.

Just as today, the world of the New Testament was filled with competing religious and philosophical ideas. Why should anyone believe that the Christian *gospel* is different or better than the others? Paul here reminds the Thessalonians that they witnessed the gospel's *power* when Paul first brought the message to them. It was not a "word-only" message; it was accompanied by evidence of its truth and authority.

The Holy Spirit is at the heart of the gospel's power. The gospel promises God's Spirit to all who receive Christ. And the power of God's Spirit is evident in those who bring the message. By referring to power and to the Holy Spirit, Paul may be reminding the readers that they had witnessed miracles performed through the Spirit's power when Paul and his associates were in their city. But Paul's view of the Spirit's power is not limited to what we strictly label as miraculous. It also embraces the powerful life change that the Spirit brings to those who believe.

Part of that change is confidence in the truth of the gospel message. Thessalonica had probably seen its share of traveling religious teachers who cared more about the money they made than about the truth of their message. Paul reminds his readers that he and his associates were different. Their deep commitment to their message was demonstrated by the lives that they lived. They worked to support themselves, spoke boldly despite persecution, and demonstrated with personal sacrifice their sincere love. They were examples to the Thessalonians of the transformation that the gospel brings to those who trust its saving message.

C. BEING LIKE CHRIST (v. 6)

6. You became imitators of us and of the Lord; in spite of severe suffering, you welcomed the message with the joy given by the Holy Spirit.

The Christ whom Paul preaches is also the Christ whom Paul follows. His Christ-centered message comes both through what he says and how he lives. He reminds the Thessalonian believers that they saw something powerfully attractive in the lives of the Christian missionaries, something that matched the message that they heard. So they committed to the same kind of life. In following Paul, they follow *the Lord* whom Paul follows.

WHAT DO YOU THINK?

The lesson writer says that the work of God's people is never an effort to earn God's favor or to pay God back for what he has done. If you don't have to earn your salvation, what motivates your best efforts for God's kingdom?

HOW TO SAY IT

Achaia. Uh-KAY-uh.

Berea. Buh-REE-uh.

Macedonia. Mass-eh-DOE-nee-uh.

Philippi. Fih-LIP-pie or FIL-ih-pie.

Silas. SIGH-luss.

Thessalonica. THESS-uh-lo-NYE-kuh (TH as in THIN).

As a result, these new believers have now suffered for their faith. We can easily understand why. The new Christians are severing old loyalties and changing old relationships. Family and community often react with hostility to such transformation. But even more important is the connection between their persecution and the experience of other believers and of Christ himself. They can see that their faith is genuine like Paul's as they face persecution for their faith as he does. And they can see how their experience is like that of the Lord himself, who suffered and died on their behalf.

That understanding enables the new believers to receive persecution with *joy*. Suffering is never fun, but knowing that we stand together with other believers and with Christ himself reminds us that our *suffering* is not meaningless or random. The *Holy Spirit* enables believers to endure persecution with joy. There is no greater demonstration of the transforming power of the gospel than for believers to reflect the Spirit's joy in suffering.

III. TRANSFORMED REPUTATION (1 THESSALONIANS 1:7-9)

7. And so you became a model to all the believers in Macedonia and Achaia.

The Thessalonian Christians may think of themselves as a small, insignificant group of people. But they are a vital part of God's plan to reclaim the world. Their faith is now known well beyond their own city. Just as they imitated the faith of Paul, now others are imitating their faith.

Macedonia is the region of northern Greece of which Thessalonica is the capital. We know from Acts 16 and 17 that Paul has also made converts in Philippi and Berea, other cities of Macedonia. We can also assume that the gospel has spread through some of those early believers to smaller towns in the surrounding region. *Achaia* is the region of Greece to the south of Macedonia. Paul has also preached in the Achaian cities of Athens and Corinth (Acts 17, 18) and now writes this letter from Corinth. The two regions together represent a span of hundreds of miles, a great distance for the new believers' reputation to have spread.

8. The Lord's message rang out from you not only in Macedonia and Achaia — your faith in God has become known everywhere. Therefore we do not need to say anything about it,

In fact, their reputation has spread beyond those regions. Everywhere the gospel is preached, people are learning about the Thessalonian believers.

The Lord's message is more literally *the word of the Lord,* an expression we usually expect to be used for the gospel message itself, not for stories of how people have come to believe in it. But Paul does not hesitate to call the story of the Thessalonian believers the "word of the Lord." This should not surprise us. We regard the book of Acts as authoritative Scripture, part of God's written Word. That book contains a brief account of the gospel's reception in Thessalonica, along with similar reports from other cities visited by Paul and other early Christian preachers. Those accounts provide us with definitive examples of what it means to become a Christian and to live by faith in Christ.

Certainly something similar continues to happen today. Faith in Jesus is as much "caught" as it is "taught." We observe how others live out their faith, and we imitate their example. Our own lives in turn become the examples that still others will follow. We should never underestimate the impact of a life transformed by the gospel.

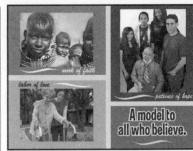

Visual for Lesson 1. *Display this visual as you discuss verse 7. Note the way faith crosses boundaries of race, age, and physical abilities.*

PRAYER

Almighty God, we confess that sometimes we are content to keep you in a corner of our lives. Today we offer ourselves to you to be remade. We invite you into every part of us, so that we can be clearly yours in every way. In Jesus' name, amen!

9. . . . for they themselves report what kind of reception you gave us. They tell how you turned to God from idols to serve the living and true God,

Paul says that the story of the Thessalonian believers is so widely known that he hears about it before he can tell it. Specifically, the Thessalonians' story is about their forsaking the idolatrous practices that are a pervasive feature of their culture.

The pagan people of this time worship *idols* not out of love, gratitude, or awe, but to placate the whims of the gods so their own lives will go well. Pagan worship is like ritualized bribery, offering the gods a payoff in return for favors.

Paul says that the Thessalonians serve *the living and true God.* God is often called "the living God" in contrast with idols, which have no life at all (compare, Daniel 6:26). The trouble and difficulty that the new believers have experienced is more than compensated by the realization that they now stand with the one true God who both made them and saved them.

EXAMPLES BAD AND GOOD

Recent years have seen the rise of what can be called the "professional athlete/lawbreaker." Their offenses range from the drug—to enhance athletic performance or for "recreational" purposes—to violent criminal behavior. When confronted with the effects of such behavior on young people who look to them as heroes, a common excuse has been "I'm not trying to be anybody's role model." However, denying it does not change the fact that young people look up to adults, regardless of the type of behavior they exhibit.

Fortunately, there are refreshing examples on the other side of the ledger. Around the country, various mentor/protégé programs have been developed. For example, in Washington, D.C. for more than 20 years, Mentors, Inc. has been helping at-risk young people to become mature, responsible adults. The mentors are not celebrities. They are just common people who care about what is happening to young people.

Like it or not, our lives affect the behavior of others. Adults who spurn good behavior will find young people scorning the values that promote a decent, law-abiding, and moral society. As the Thessalonians lived out their commitment to Christ, their example influenced others both near and far. Whose life is affected by *your* behavior?

—C. R. B.

IV. TRANSFORMED FUTURE (1 THESSALONIANS 1:10)

10. . . . and to wait for his Son from heaven, whom he raised from the dead — Jesus, who rescues us from the coming wrath.

The new believers now have a different expectation of the future, a "hope" that impels them to be steadfast in trials. The object of their hope is the very *Son* of the one true, living God. He has already died and risen again on their behalf. He has promised to return to gather his people to himself. The rest of the world, still in rebellion against the true God, will be subject to God's wrath, his holy judgment against those who have rebelled against him. But the believers expectantly await their Lord's arrival to deliver them from that *wrath* and bless them as his people.

The bleak hopelessness of paganism has been replaced. Gone is the expectation that life ends in cold, unforgiving death. The promises of Christ give us the confidence to expect much more.

WHAT DO YOU THINK?

The Thessalonian Christians faced persecution when they turned from idols to the living and true God. What problems do we face today when we turn away from the idols of our culture?

WHAT DO YOU THINK?

When you read that Jesus "rescues us [present tense] from the coming wrath" (a future event), what is your response? What encouragement does this provide for you?

CONCLUSION

Paul describes Christian faith as more than mere ritual. It embraces every aspect of life, bringing purpose, direction, and confidence. It transforms ordinary people into world-changers. It gives meaning to the most mundane of daily affairs. It provides assurance that the future contains boundless blessing.

Knowing Jesus Christ makes us the people God intended us to be, living as God intended us to live. The change is public, visible, and unmistakable. And it continues for a lifetime.

THOUGHT TO REMEMBER

"You are the light of the world. A city on a hill cannot be hidden" (Matthew 5:14).

Discovery Learning

The following is an alternative lesson plan emphasizing learning activities. Classes desiring such student involvement will find these suggestions helpful. At the back of this book are reproducible student pages to further enhance activity learning.

INTO THE LESSON

Before the lesson, collect childhood pictures of class members. Have these on display on the wall or on a bulletin board. As students arrive, hand each person three index cards and have them guess the names of three people pictured (writing one name per card) and attach the name below the picture. When everyone has finished (there may be more than one name per picture), have the class members move their own names to the correct picture. (If you are not able to get childhood pictures of your students, search the Internet for childhood pictures of celebrities and use those.)

Then as a class, identify ways each person has changed since the pictures were taken. Write these changes on the board and then discuss why the changes occurred. Transition to the next part of the lesson by saying, "As Christians, we should be able to see how we have changed since our conversion. In today's lesson we will identify ways the Thessalonian Christians changed as a result of their conversions."

INTO THE WORD

As a class, read aloud 1 Thessalonians 1 (one or two members can read, or students may take turns reading the text). As students read the verses, have the class members who are not reading aloud identify the behaviors that are characteristic of the Thessalonians now that they are Christians. Write these on the board as students call them out. Your list may look something like this: work produced by faith (v. 3), labor prompted by love (v. 3), en-durance inspired by hope (v. 3), imitators of Paul and God (v. 6), welcomed the Word with joy (v. 6), model to all believers (v. 7), God's message rang out from them (v. 8), their faith is known everywhere (v. 8), turned to God from idols (v. 9), waiting for Jesus to return (v. 10). As the class discusses each verse, use the lesson commentary to give more explanation or insight where it is needed or to comment on what Paul gives thanks for (vv. 1, 2).

Once you have completed the verse study, divide students into groups of two or three. Distribute the reproducible activity "Transforming Behaviors" from page 500. Have students identify possible behaviors the Thessalonians might have exhibited before they were Christians that are contrary to the behaviors you have on the board. (An example is given on the reproducible). When the groups have had sufficient time to identify two or three contrary behaviors, bring the class back together and have each group share their thoughts. Write these behaviors on the board opposite the "changed" behavior. Write these behaviors on the board opposite the "changed" behavior.

Next, have the class identify some behaviors that people who are not Christians may exhibit today that are not representative of the phrases you identified in the Scripture text (for example, rather than exhibit a "labor prompted by love," someone today may ignore a homeless man asking for money). Write these on the board and then write a specific behavior that represents what this person would do if he became a Christian (such as, giving the man the help he needs or taking him to a homeless shelter or asking the benevolence committee to assist the man).

INTO LIFE

Make the transition to application by asking the students, "How well do you think our church does at living the 'changed' life of the Thessalonians? Let's rate ourselves to find out." Give each student a set of three index cards you have prepared before class. One card will say "Great," one will say "OK," the third one will say "Not so good." As you go down the list of present-day behaviors you constructed on the board, have students show which card they believe best represents the church's performance in that area. When students show a consensus of "not so good" for a behavior, stop and talk about ways the church could change that rating. (Place a star beside each of these behaviors on the board.) When you have completed the list, return to those behaviors that you put stars beside. Choose one the class will commit to improving within the church at large. For example, perhaps the class has decided that the church's performance on the message "rang out" is "not so good." After some discussion, the class may decide to ask the church leadership about beginning a radio ministry. Determine how the class will encourage the church in this endeavor and ask God's guidance.

For a more personal application, use the reproducible activity "Am I Transformed?" from page 500.

PLEASING TO GOD

LESSON 2

INTRODUCTION

A. More Than a Sales Pitch

Very few people can say they have never given in to a sales pitch. When we do give in, too often we get less than we have bargained for; the reality of the product does not match the sales pitch. And usually there is nothing we can do about it.

The apostle Paul wanted to be sure that his readers knew that the gospel is more than just an effective sales pitch. It transforms the lives of those who believe it. Christian believers become people whose chief desire is to please God. They want to live in a way that is consistent with what God has done for them, to please God all the time, even in those things that God alone can see.

B. Lesson Background

In the Roman Empire in Paul's time, traveling religious teachers were very common. They were also notorious for operating unscrupulously. Many would slip into a city, work their way into the confidence of the wealthy, live sumptuously at the expense of their students, and then quietly slip out of town when people began to question the value of their teaching and the integrity of their lives.

When Paul wrote to the Thessalonian Christians, he realized that his own actions might appear to fit that stereotype. He had come to Thessalonica as a traveling religious teacher. He had spent a short period of time in the city before leaving suddenly when trouble arose (Acts 17:1-10). Since then, he had not returned. Certainly the Thessalonian Christians had to wonder whether they had been persuaded to adopt their new faith by a man who cared more about "making the sale" than telling the truth.

To set their minds at ease, Paul reminded the Thessalonian Christians how he lived when he was among them. Every aspect of his behavior expressed deep integrity. Paul was committed to pleasing the God who had saved him, so he lived in a way that reflected the character of God as revealed in the gospel of Jesus Christ. His life was very different from those of the stereotypical religious teacher. It was probably very different from the life of anyone the Thessalonians had known before! Now they themselves were becoming like Paul, committed to pleasing God with lives that reflect the good news.

I. PLEASING GOD IN PERSECUTION (1 THESSALONIANS 2:1, 2)

1. You know, brothers, that our visit to you was not a failure.

Paul begins to recount his experiences in Thessalonica, reminding his readers that his behavior among them had been very different from what they had expected. While the stereotype is of a deceptive, selfish con artist, Paul is different. His *visit . . . was not a failure,* or without meaning, as is the teaching of those who take advantage of the gullible for selfish ends.

DEVOTIONAL READING:
GALATIANS 1:1-10

BACKGROUND SCRIPTURE:
1 THESSALONIANS 2

PRINTED TEXT:
1 THESSALONIANS 2:1-13

LESSON AIMS

After this lesson each student will be able to:

1. Identify ways that Paul's behavior among the Thessalonians demonstrated his commitment to pleasing God.

2. Explain why pure motives are important to behavior that pleases God.

3. Identify a personal motive or behavior that needs to be changed for him or her to be more pleasing to God and tell how he or she will change it.

KEY VERSE:

We speak as men approved by God to be entrusted with the gospel. We are not trying to please men but God, who tests our hearts.
—1 Thessalonians 2:4

LESSON 2 NOTES

2. We had previously suffered and been insulted in Philippi, as you know, but with the help of our God we dared to tell you his gospel in spite of strong opposition.

People who are "in it for themselves" are not willing to undergo hardship. But the Thessalonian Christians know that Paul is different. Before coming to their city, he had preached in nearby Philippi. There he had been insulted (Acts 16:20), beaten and imprisoned (Acts 16:22, 23), and treated dishonorably and illegally (Acts 16:37), all because of his fearless proclamation of the *gospel*. Such experiences would have meant the end of the road for a person who preached for selfish gain. But Paul had continued to preach in Thessalonica even though he met with similar *opposition* there (Acts 17:5-7).

For those who know Jesus Christ, faithfulness in difficulty springs from something other than personal determination. It is based on the gospel itself. Jesus endured the cross for unworthy sinners, and he told his followers to expect similar treatment. Paul's faithfulness in persecution is an expression of his commitment to please the God who sent his Son to die. To please God is to follow the Christ of the cross.

WHAT DO YOU THINK?

What does being persecuted say about the genuineness of one's faith or message?

SUFFERING FOR CHRIST

American Christians sometimes complain about being "persecuted" because of an occasional insult or issues such as prayer in school. But Christians actually suffer for their faith today, especially in nations where Islam is the dominant religion. For example, in 2007 Dimiana Hanna's parents reported to the police in her village in Egypt that she was missing. They were later informed that she had been found and was married to a Muslim, but they were not allowed to see her. In June 2008 Dimiana took her 10-month-old baby and ran away to escape her husband's abusiveness. As news of the escape spread, Muslim citizens in her husband's village of Nazla rioted against Coptic Christians, beating them and destroying businesses, homes, and churches.

When Paul wrote about the beating and imprisonment he had experienced in Philippi, it was not for the purpose of complaining about the mistreatment. It was as a reminder of the power of the gospel to accomplish God's purpose in spite of opposition. Whatever difficulties we face in living for Christ, Paul would have us focus on the positive results of our witness for the Lord. —C. R. B.

II. PLEASING GOD WITH HUMILITY (1 THESSALONIANS 2:3-6)
A. PURE SPEECH (v. 3)

3. For the appeal we make does not spring from error or impure motives, nor are we trying to trick you.

The Thessalonians have seen for themselves that Paul is unconcerned about what will happen to himself, about money, social status, or approval from others. He is consistently ready to take the lowly position for the sake of others, just as Jesus took the lowliest of positions for the sake of sinners.

So Paul reminds the Thessalonian Christians that his actions had no hint of deception in the attempt to benefit himself. He had done nothing out of an attempt to mislead people or out of *impure motives* (this term has a sexual connotation).

B. SACRED TRUST (v. 4)

4. On the contrary, we speak as men approved by God to be entrusted with the gospel. We are not trying to please men but God, who tests our hearts.

WHAT DO YOU THINK?

What are some ways we may be tempted to use deceptive means to make Christian teaching more attractive to people?

Paul now comes to the heart of the matter. Paul has become captive to the grace of God. The Lord who asked him, "Why do you persecute me?" (Acts 9:4) had forgiven him and had called him to be an apostle, a witness of the Lord's resurrection. For Paul God's grace can never be less than amazing.

So Paul here speaks of the good news as a sacred trust. God's amazing grace compels Paul to be concerned ultimately about nothing except pleasing the one who has been so generous to him. Whatever Paul may receive from other people through his preaching is nothing compared to what he has already received from the gracious hand of God.

That concern to *please* God and not other people gives Paul even greater integrity. Other people see only our outward behavior. We can fool them, at least much of the time. But God looks at the heart; he is not fooled by an outward show. The heart that belongs to God seeks to become conformed to the image of Christ, who surrendered all his privileges as the divine Son of God to give his life for others. That cross-shaped life is what Paul had lived before the Thessalonians, just as he constantly lives it before God.

C. SELFLESS APPEAL (vv. 5, 6)

5. *You know we never used flattery, nor did we put on a mask to cover up greed —God is our witness.*

Once again, Paul's appeal is not just to the memories of the Thessalonian Christians. He invokes *God* as his *witness,* affirming that even in those parts of his life that God alone can see, he lives with complete integrity.

In Paul's time flattering the audience is a standard strategy for public speakers. It is common practice among other, less scrupulous religious teachers whom the Thessalonian Christians have encountered. But Paul is notable for his lack of *flattery.* He feels no need to soften up his audience with false compliments. The focus of Paul's message is neither himself nor his audience but Jesus Christ.

Nor does Paul deceive people for monetary gain. In fact, Paul has been notable for refusing gifts while preaching, supporting himself through his trade of tentmaking. Nothing in Paul's life can reasonably be attributed to selfishness or deception.

6. *We were not looking for praise from men, not from you or anyone else.*

   As apostles of Christ we could have been a burden to you,

Typical human behavior is driven by selfish desires like greed (v. 5). Parallel to that is the desire for prominence and status. But seeking *praise* from other humans makes no sense for the person who follows the Christ, who was "despised and rejected by men" (Isaiah 53:3). The only glory that Paul seeks as a follower of Christ is the glory of the cross (Galatians 6:14), the glory of a life given to serve others.

The term *apostle* carries great authority among early Christians, for it is used for those who are witnesses of Jesus' resurrection and have been explicitly designated by Jesus as his authoritative spokesmen. For Paul this term is even more special, for he witnessed the risen Jesus and was called as an apostle in a unique event on the road to Damascus. But Paul is not willing to take advantage of his apostolic office. Unlike those who parade their religious credentials for personal privilege, Paul takes a position as servant when he wears the title apostle.

HOW TO SAY IT

Cilicia. Sih-LISH-i-uh.

Damascus. Duh-MASS-kus.

Philippi. Fih-LIP-pie or FIL-ih-pie.

Thessalonica. THESS-uh-lo-NYE-kuh (TH as in THIN).

WHAT DO YOU THINK?

What is the difference between the flattery that Paul renounces and being complimentary to a person? When do compliments become sinful?

What Do You Think?

Some people today think preachers and missionaries should work in secular jobs to support themselves so they will have more credibility in the world. Tell why you agree or disagree. What are the advantages and disadvantages of this approach?

Paul's description of his behavior is the description of a life shaped by the cross. The normal human tendency is to act selfishly, seeking wealth, power, and prominence. Paul's life by contrast is characterized by unselfish lowliness, the willingness to serve others at any cost. Such is the life of one who is captivated by the gospel of Jesus Christ.

III. PLEASING GOD WITH LOVE (1 THESSALONIANS 2:7-9)
A. Gentle as a Nursing Mother (v. 7)

7. *. . . . but we were gentle among you, like a mother caring for her little children.*

Unlike the proud, selfish, demanding behavior of the typical traveling teacher, Paul's life with the Thessalonians has been characterized by gentleness. This is not mere passivity, sitting back so that others can have first place, but positive concern and care for the new believers. The term *mother* provides a keen image of love that forms a deep bond and gives of oneself for the good of the other. As Paul had worked through the day and stayed up nights to support himself and nurture the Thessalonians in their faith, he had been very much like a nursing mother with her children.

B. Generous with the Gospel (vv. 8, 9)

8. *We loved you so much that we were delighted to share with you not only the gospel of God but our lives as well, because you had become so dear to us.*

Preaching the *gospel* of God's love makes little sense if the preacher does not live the message of God's love. The expression that is translated *loved you so much* is an unusual one, used only here in the New Testament and seldom outside it. Some think it is part of the dialect of Paul's home region of Cilicia. If so, perhaps he uses it here because it expresses in his "heart language" the deep attachment that he has for his fellow believers.

Love shaped by the gospel is never just a matter of feeling. It always translates into action. Paul demonstrates that here, expressing his desire to give his soul or his very life for the Thessalonian Christians. Again we see that Paul is different from that of other teachers of his day, who want to enhance their own lives at the expense of others. Paul has been transformed by Christ's giving his life for him, and so Paul follows Christ by giving his life for others. This is not something that Paul does grudgingly. The Thessalonian Christians are beloved to him, as *dear* and precious as the closest family member.

9. *Surely you remember, brothers, our toil and hardship; we worked night and day in order not to be a burden to anyone while we preached the gospel of God to you.*

Paul now cites an obvious demonstration of his love for the Thessalonians: he supported himself by working as a tentmaker rather than accepting money for preaching to them. Paul will later explain in 1 Corinthians 9:1-18 his practice of self-support. There he asserts that he has the right to expect to be paid for his preaching, no less because he is an apostle of Christ. However, he willingly surrenders that right so that his support will not be a *burden* for those to whom he preaches or an impediment to their listening to *the gospel*. It is a practice that imitates Christ's own loving self-sacrifice.

We learn from Acts 18:3 that Paul's trade is tentmaking, which in his time includes all kinds of leatherworking. We can expect that Paul rented a small space in the marketplace of Thessalonica, where he could work at his trade, accept jobs and make sales, but also speak about the gospel with those who passed through or worked nearby.

When the market closed, Paul was then free to preach and teach in the synagogues and homes of Thessalonica. So he does not exaggerate when he says that he *worked night and day* on behalf of the Thessalonian Christians. If you have ever felt that you are working "24/7" between your job and your volunteer commitments, you have a companion in the apostle Paul!

But Paul's talk about his hard work is not to garner sympathy or to impress readers with his importance. He mentions his hard work as a reminder of his profound love for his fellow believers, a love grounded in Christ's love.

LIVING THE GIFT OF LOVE

Numerous stories of sacrifice have come out of the war in Iraq, just as they have from other wars. Somehow, in the brutality of armed conflict, sparkling examples of the best in the human spirit come to the fore. On November 15, 2005, Marine Lance Cpl. Adam Morrison and several other Americans entered a house in Fallujah. Insurgents hidden inside began firing at them, wounding Sgt. Rafael Peralta. A grenade landed inches from Peralta's face and blocked the exit from the building. Morrison reported later that Peralta reached out his hand, grabbed the grenade, and pulled it under his chest. That selfless act resulted in his own violent death, but saved the lives of his comrades.

Throughout the New Testament, love is characterized by sacrifice. So it is in Paul's description of his love for his readers. The image is that of a nursing mother, readily giving of the substance of her own body and spirit so that her child might live. We may never be called on to give our lives for another, but we can tenderly "live the gift of love" for them. Can you think of examples? —C. R. B.

IV. PLEASING GOD BY EXAMPLE (1 THESSALONIANS 2:10-13)
A. GODLY BEHAVIOR (vv. 10-12a)
10. You are witnesses, and so is God, of how holy, righteous and blameless we were among you who believed.

Paul's behavior was not just an expression of his life before *God.* It also provided the example that shaped the lives of the Thessalonians. It is often said that the gospel is better "caught" than taught. Paul demonstrates that truth in this section.

Paul describes his example as *holy,* demonstrating proper reverence for almighty God. It was *righteous,* reflecting adherence to God's standards of right and wrong. And it was *blameless,* consistent in a way that left him above criticism.

Again Paul appeals to the witness of God, his final witness of his character and integrity. But he also reminds the readers that they are his witnesses as well. Paul deliberately had lived such a life before them so that they could both hear and see what the gospel is all about.

11, 12a. For you know that we dealt with each of you as a father deals with his own children, encouraging, comforting and urging you

Having previously compared himself with a mother (v. 7), Paul now compares himself with a *father* providing instruction to his *children.* He says he encouraged them, a term that stresses urging on toward a goal, in this case a

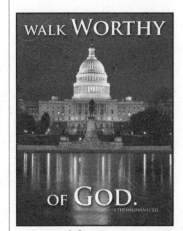

Visual for Lesson 2. *Display this visual as you discuss verse 12. Ask, "What does it mean to 'live . . . worthy of God'?"*

PRAYER

Gracious God, we want our lives to be fitting reflections of your love. We submit ourselves to your transforming power, that by your grace we can please you with our lives. In Jesus' name, amen!

WHAT DO YOU THINK?

Someone might say that one who believes himself to be "worthy of God" is hypocritical. In fact, a common criticism of the church is that it is "full of hypocrites." How would you respond to an unbeliever who made this statement?

righteous life. He had comforted them, implying fatherly consolation in difficult times. With the word *urging* Paul expresses that his teaching had been urgent and insistent.

Stressing that he had acted this way toward *each of you*, Paul reminds the Thessalonian Christians of his individual attention and concern for them. Just as a good father treats his children as unique individuals, so Paul deals with new Christians as unique individuals.

B. WORTHY GOAL (vv. 11, 12)

12b. . . . to live lives worthy of God, who calls you into his kingdom and glory.

Just as Paul's life has been forever changed by the good news, so now have the Thessalonian Christians' *lives* been changed in the same way. Paul's teaching and witness are aimed at transforming the way that they live in the world moment by moment.

The standard of their new life is to be *worthy of God.* In a very obvious sense, this is impossible, of course. No sinful human can ever be worthy of the holy God. But Paul here and elsewhere calls on Christians to live or walk in a manner worthy of God and the gospel (Ephesians 4:1; Colossians 1:10). His point is to urge Christians to conform their lives to the character of God as revealed in the gospel of Jesus Christ. When we know God as the God who entered the world as a human being to die for unworthy, rebellious sinners, we are compelled to submit to his authority and become conformed to his image. We want to grow in Christlikeness in response to the wonderful gift we have received.

That is Paul's point as he reminds his readers that they have been called into God's kingdom and glory. The kingdom of God in the New Testament is God's reign or rule. Jesus taught his followers that God's kingdom was already breaking into the world because he was present (Matthew 12:28) but would not be fully realized until his return (Matthew 25:34). In the meantime, followers of Jesus experience already the blessings of God's kingdom even while they suffer the hardships and indignities of this present, evil age. Paul reminds the readers of this key teaching in this verse. The God to whom they belong has made them subjects of his glorious kingdom, in which they already experience the peace, unity, and contentment of living under God's rule.

C. WORD OF GOD (v. 13)

13. And we also thank God continually because, when you received the word of God, which you heard from us, you accepted it not as the word of men, but as it actually is, the word of God, which is at work in you who believe.

Paul now describes the way that his example has taken root in the lives of the Thessalonians. They have seen his evident integrity. They understand his commitment. So they have accepted his teaching as not just his but God's. That *word* is not an abstract message but something that is now actively *at work* in them, empowering and changing their lives as they put their confidence in the gospel message.

CONCLUSION

In recent years Christianity has been plagued with scandals. The media have repeatedly drawn attention to prominent Christians whose lives have not matched their words. Beyond those notable cases, many of us have been personally disappointed by Christians who have professed one thing and lived another. Worst of all, sometimes the Christians who disappoint us are ourselves.

This passage reminds us that such failure is not inevitable. It is not even normal. When the gospel takes hold in a life, as it did in Paul's life, the person is forever changed. Our focus is taken off of ourselves and placed on the God who saved us with his amazing grace. We center our lives on reflecting his sacrifice in Christ in the way that we live with humility and love for others. Lives like that show us that the gospel is more than a good sales pitch. It is "the power of God for . . . salvation" (Romans 1:16), a salvation that we can see in transformed lives.

THOUGHT TO REMEMBER

"Live a life worthy of the calling you have received. Be completely humble and gentle; be patient, bearing with one another in love" (Ephesians 4:1, 2).

Discovery Learning

The following is an alternative lesson plan emphasizing learning activities. Classes desiring such student involvement will find these suggestions helpful. At the back of this book are reproducible student pages to further enhance activity learning.

INTO THE LESSON

Before class, collect various newspaper or Internet articles that depict people with integrity and others without integrity. Have these articles spread out on the table next to a stack of large index cards as students arrive. On the board have the words *Integrity* and *Immorality* written at opposite ends. Ask each student to choose an article and take a card, read the article, and then write on the card a brief summary of the action that exhibited either integrity or immorality. As students complete the assignment, have them place their cards under the appropriate headings on the board. When everyone is finished, discuss what it means to have integrity. (According to The *American Heritage Dictionary,* integrity is "moral soundness, especially as it is revealed in dealings that test steadfastness to truth, purpose, responsibility, or trust.") Say, "As we'll learn today, the best way to have integrity is to live in a way that pleases God."

INTO THE WORD

Use the background commentary to set the context for today's Scripture text, 1 Thessalonians 2:1-13. Then divide the class into groups of three. Distribute copies of the reproducible activity "Having Integrity Before God" from page 501. Have each group read the entire text and record on the activity page phrases describing actions that demonstrate Paul's integrity. Your results may resemble the following:

- preached boldly in spite of strong opposition (v. 2);
- never had impure motives or used deceit (v. 3);
- approved by God (v. 4);
- actions pleased God (v. 4);
- never used flattery (v. 5);
- did not put on a mask (v. 5);
- received no praise from men (v. 6);
- gentle among believers (v. 7);
- shared their lives with believers (v. 8);
- worked hard to pay their own way (v. 9);
- conduct was holy, righteous, and blameless (v. 10);
- treated them as a father treats his children (v. 11);
- urged others to live worthy of God (v. 12).

When the groups have completed the assignment, have them report their findings. Record their phrases on the board. Compare these behaviors with those you recorded at the beginning of class from the articles and discuss why it is important for a Christian to possess integrity (because it reveals a life that is focused on pleasing God). Use the lesson commentary to add any insights relevant to the discussion.

INTO LIFE

Make the transition to application by saying, "Now that we understand why it is important to possess integrity, let's determine whether we as individuals reveal integrity in our actions." Form groups of three or four and distribute the following list of situations. Ask the groups to discuss these questions: "Has any of the following happened to you? Were you able to act with integrity? If not, what made it difficult?"

- You are given too much change at a grocery checkout.
- You find a purse or wallet containing a large sum of money with the person's name and address inside.
- Your boss thinks someone else made a costly mistake that was actually your fault.
- You pick up an unscratched lottery ticket that you saw someone drop, and it has the potential of winning $10,000,000.

- You spot the teenage daughter of a friend shoplifting in a store.
- You back into another car in an isolated spot and make a small dent in it; your insurance premiums have recently gone up and you're pretty sure no one is watching.

Give each student a copy of the reproducible activity "Defining Integrity" from page 501 and have him or her write down an action he or she has exhibited that may not reveal integrity. (Assure the students that what they write will not be shared publicly; this is between them and God.) Have students also identify what they need to do to redeem this action before God.

Read Titus 2:7 aloud to the class. Ask students to look at what they've written on the "Defining Integrity" activity and determine whether what they intend to do is part of a pattern of good works and sincerity. Have the class rewrite Titus 2:7 into a prayer and read it in unison to close the session.

SUSTAINED THROUGH ENCOURAGEMENT

LESSON 3

Jun 20

INTRODUCTION

A. CAST AWAY OR IT'S A WONDERFUL LIFE

The movie *Cast Away* was a big hit a few years ago. It vividly depicted the struggles of a man left alone on a deserted island after an airplane crash. He struggled to survive, to find food, water, and shelter. But more than that, he struggled against his loneliness. Desperate for a friend, he began to speak to a volleyball as if it were a human being.

Contrast that with the famous old movie *It's a Wonderful Life*. In that film the main character is also desperate. But he comes to appreciate how much his life is worth when he realizes the value of his relationships. "No man is a failure who has friends" is a famous line from the close of that movie.

These movies ring true for audiences because they reflect a truth about how God made us. Human beings were made for relationships. When life is challenging, Christians can find encouragement from their sisters and brothers in the faith. Real Christian fellowship gives us comfort, example, support, and even correction. It restores our strength and keeps our minds and hearts set on the gospel that brought us together. That is the central idea of today's text.

B. LESSON BACKGROUND

Paul wrote his first letter to the Thessalonians after a forced absence. Persecution had forced Paul to leave the city (Acts 17:1-10), and as his absence stretched on, it was clear that the church faced difficulties and uncertainties. Paul wrote the letter to address those issues.

But Paul also wanted the young church to know that he, no less than they, was pained by his absence from them. Paul carried a deep burden for the welfare of these new converts. Wanting to know about their situation, Paul sent Timothy, his assistant in ministry, to visit the church and report back. So in 1 Thessalonians 3 Paul expresses his concern for the Thessalonians, his desire to be reunited with them, and his motivation for sending Timothy. But he also expresses the joy he experienced when Timothy returned with a good report.

This passage raises some questions about the details in Acts. Some have even alleged that Luke is in error! In Acts 17:14, 15, Paul leaves Berea for Athens while Timothy and Silas stay behind with instructions to "join him as soon as possible." But no mention is made of their arrival in Athens. Instead, Luke says they rejoin Paul in Corinth (Acts 18:5). The passage before

DEVOTIONAL READING:
ACTS 4:32-37
BACKGROUND SCRIPTURE:
1 THESSALONIANS 3
PRINTED TEXT:
1 THESSALONIANS 3

LESSON AIMS

After this lesson each student will be able to:

1. Identify expressions of Paul's encouragement to the Thessalonian Christians.

2. Tell how sharing in other believers' experiences gives encouragement in difficult circumstances.

3. Write a note of Christian encouragement to a fellow believer.

KEY VERSE:

Therefore, brothers, in all our distress and persecution we were encouraged about you because of your faith.
—1 Thessalonians 3:7

LESSON 3 NOTES

WHAT DO YOU THINK?

Timothy left Paul in order to minister in Thessalonica. Have you ever had a friend or family member leave you for ministry purposes? How did you—or how would you— deal with that loss?

DAILY BIBLE READINGS

Monday, June 14—"Son of Encouragement" (Acts 4: 32-37)

Tuesday, June 15— Encouraging New Leaders (Deuteronomy 3:23-29)

Wednesday, June 16— Encouraging the Fearful (Isaiah 35:1-4)

Thursday, June 17—Encouraged by the Script ures (Romans 15:1-6)

Friday, June 18— Supported by God's People (Acts 18:1-11)

Saturday, June 19—A Ministry of Encouragement (Acts 18:18-23)

Sunday, June 20— Encouraged in Distress (1 Thessalonians 3)

us says Paul decided to be "left by ourselves in Athens" in order to send Timothy to Thessalonica. This makes us think Paul sent Timothy to Thessalonica from Athens.

This is entirely possible. The fact that Acts has no record of that is not really a problem. Timothy is not mentioned at all from the time he joins Paul's team in Acts 16:3 until the mention in Berea. He must have been with Paul in Philippi, where Luke tells of Paul and Silas's imprisonment, but Timothy is not mentioned (Acts 16:19-40). So he and Silas could have rejoined Paul in Athens and then returned to Thessalonica, Silas perhaps being sent to another Macedonian city such as Philippi. The two then rejoined Paul in Corinth, coming "from Macedonia" (Acts 18:5). Or the decision to be "left by ourselves in Athens" could have been made in Berea. Perhaps Paul sent Timothy to Thessalonica and Silas to Philippi (or elsewhere in Macedonia) at the time he left for Athens. Paul's ministry in Athens was brief, so by the time the two coworkers got there, Paul had already gone to Corinth. Silas and Timothy then followed and joined him there. Either way, the integrity of Luke's account in Acts need not be questioned.

I. TIMOTHY'S VISIT (1 THESSALONIANS 3:1-5)
A. PAUL'S ANXIETY (v. 1)
1. So when we could stand it no longer, we thought it best to be left by ourselves in Athens.

Paul was deeply stressed at being away from his Christian friends in Thessalonica. The only solution was for him to give up the assistance of Timothy and send him to visit the Thessalonians and report back.

Such a decision meant that Paul would be alone in *Athens,* with all the emotional toll of loneliness. Acts 17:32 tells us that the progress of the gospel was difficult there. So Paul would have had little by way of Christian fellowship in Timothy's absence. But Timothy's departure also meant that Paul would be without assistance in his missionary work or day-to-day affairs. The burden of Timothy's departure was considerable, but for Paul, the opportunity to reconnect with the Christians of Thessalonica made it imperative that he bear that burden.

WHEN THE STRESS BECOMES TOO GREAT
In February 2007 a female astronaut was arrested in Florida on charges of trying to kidnap and kill a woman whom she perceived as a rival for the romantic attention of another astronaut. As a result, NASA reexamined its preparations for dealing with a possible emotional breakdown of an astronaut on board the space shuttle or International Space Station. Severe depression or a psychotic breakdown could produce an incident on board that would threaten the lives of everyone on the crew.

Paul was concerned for the Thessalonians' spiritual well-being. So he sent Timothy to Thessalonica to reassure and encourage the Christians there. In so doing Paul sacrificed the fellowship that Timothy provided for him in Athens. Christians are together in their mission, not vying for the attention of one another. We must encourage each other, even if it costs us something personally.   —C. R. B.

B. TIMOTHY'S MISSION (vv. 2, 3)
2. We sent Timothy, who is our brother and God's fellow worker in spreading the gospel of Christ, to strengthen and encourage you in your faith,

Paul describes Timothy in a way that indicates how significant his visit was to the Thessalonians and how valuable he is to Paul. *Timothy* is called *our brother*. Though it is common in the New Testament for Christians to call each other "brother" or "sister," we should not minimize the significance. Paul's relationship to Timothy is like a close family relationship. Paul sent his dear brother Timothy to the Thessalonians because Timothy is also their dear brother.

Paul is fond of expressions that start with *fellow* in his letters. They stress the shared blessings and responsibilities of the gospel that bind Christians together in encouraging fellowship. Thus Timothy is called a *fellow worker*. His visit, in addition to relieving Paul of his distress about the Thessalonians' welfare, would provide them with renewed fellowship. The outcome of Timothy's visit was to *strengthen* their *faith* and to *encourage* them to continue in their Christian walk.

3. . . . so that no one would be unsettled by these trials. You know quite well that we were destined for them.

The Thessalonian Christians are continuing to experience the pressure and opposition that had arisen while Paul was present. Such *trials* might induce them to give up their faith and return to their old lives. Probably these afflictions are mostly the social pressures they receive from neighbors and family who object to their new faith. To stand against such pressure, they need a strong social network of faith, a fellowship of believers who support each other in hard times. Timothy would help strengthen their new fellowship so that they can stand firm and not be moved.

C. PAUL'S REMINDER (v. 4)

4. In fact, when we were with you, we kept telling you that we would be persecuted. And it turned out that way, as you well know.

Paul wants the readers to remember that persecution and suffering should not surprise them. He reminds them of a point that has been a common part of his teaching, something that he had taught them in his brief time among them: that suffering is an expected part of the lives of God's people who live in a world of evil. God has intended all along that his people will experience trials in the world, testing and proving their faith as they resist the evil that surrounds them. When believers suffer, it does not mean that God has lost control. Just as Christ suffered, so those who follow him suffer as well.

D. PAUL'S CONCERN (v. 5)

5. For this reason, when I could stand it no longer, I sent to find out about your faith. I was afraid that in some way the tempter might have tempted you and our efforts might have been useless.

This verse repeats a part of what Paul said in verse 1, that he *sent* Timothy when he could wait *no longer* to learn about the Thessalonians' welfare. Paul's primary concern was for the faith of these new Christians. The threat to their faith was no less than the devil himself. The repetitive-sounding phrase *the tempter . . . tempted* puts strong emphasis on the possibility that a Satanic attack might have shaken the young believers' trust in Christ.

The outcome of such an attack, if successful, would mean that Paul's labor had been meaningless. Paul's missionary work is entirely focused on bringing people to faith in Jesus and the salvation that their faith receives. His work will be for nothing if they do not persist.

HOW TO SAY IT

Berea. Buh-REE-uh.

Corinth. KOR-inth.

Macedonia. Mass-eh-DOE-nee-uh.

Philippi. Fih-LIP-pie or FIL-ih-pie.

Silas. SIGH-luss.

Thessalonica. THESS-uh-lo-NYE-kuh (TH as in THIN).

WHAT DO YOU THINK?

How much should Christians fear a satanic attack? What are the extent and limitations of the tempter's power in the lives of believers?

II. TIMOTHY'S REPORT (1 THESSALONIANS 3:6)

6. But Timothy has just now come to us from you and has brought good news about your faith and love. He has told us that you always have pleasant memories of us and that you long to see us, just as we also long to see you.

We can appreciate the power of Timothy's report to Paul only when we listen carefully to what Paul wrote in the preceding verses. Having made clear how anxious he was to learn whether the Thessalonian Christians remained faithful, Paul now speaks of what he learned when *Timothy* returned to him.

The report was *good news*. Normally Paul uses this expression for the gospel, the good news of Jesus. Here he uses it for Timothy's report of the effects of the gospel. This is probably no accident. For Paul, the Thessalonians' faithfulness is an outgrowth of the saving message of Jesus, a direct consequence of the gospel's good news. It is worth remembering that the saving work of God, centered on Jesus' death and resurrection, continues wherever people come to faith in that message.

Paul mentions *faith* as the first element of that good-news report. It is the foundation of everything else. *Love* is mentioned next: the practical and necessary result of faith in the Christ who with his death fulfilled God's love for sinners. Thus, the Thessalonian Christians continue to hold Paul in high regard, longing to see him as much as he longs to see them. Faith and love always create this kind of bond between believers. But to have good remembrance of the person who taught one the Christian faith is more than just a strong personal attachment. It means that the person is following the teaching diligently. Paul's encouragement comes from knowing that the Thessalonians are actively faithful to the gospel of Jesus.

The way that Paul expresses this idea suggests that he writes this letter immediately after receiving Timothy's report. The Greek word translated *now* suggests immediacy. Paul's passion for the welfare of his brothers and sisters is demonstrated by how quickly he responds with this letter.

A "VIRTUAL" MEETING

LifeChurch.tv is a virtual "church" created by Craig Groeschel in Oklahoma City. His audience sees him in what computer gamers call a "metaverse," an apparently three-dimensional world in which the gamer—in this case, the worshiper—manipulates an on-screen pixilated character representing himself. The on-screen character is called an avatar, and the worshiper can make the avatar stand, kneel, or do whatever he wishes. This virtual approach to life goes by the name of Second Life. Advocates for Second Life churches claim that communication there is more intimate and honest than can be found in "real" churches.

One can't help but think something is missing. It was lack of actual contact with his brethren in Thessalonica that caused Paul to send Timothy to them. When Timothy returned with good news of their faith and witness, it provided Paul with what he could not have experienced in any other way. What do you think: will human beings *ever* derive meaningful intimacy—let alone communal worship—from a "virtual" world?   —C. R. B.

III. PAUL'S RESPONSE (1 THESSALONIANS 3:7-13)
A. PAUL'S COMFORT (vv. 7, 8)

7. Therefore, brothers, in all our distress and persecution we were encouraged about you because of your faith.

WHAT DO YOU THINK?

Paul responded immediately to Timothy's report about the Thessalonians. When is it important to respond quickly to a situation, and when is it better to be more slow and deliberate?

Visual for Lesson 3. *As one climber helps another, so Timothy encouraged the apostle Paul (vv. 6, 7). Discuss how we can do that for one another today.*

In verse 2 Paul had said that he wants to "encourage" the Thessalonian Christians. Now he says that the report of their faith has *encouraged* him. We might think that a mature Christian leader such as Paul does not need encouragement, but here he expresses how important it is for him to know about the faith of these young Christians.

That news overcomes the difficulties that Paul has faced. To be alone in a pagan environment, without brothers and sisters nearby, and worried about the lives of those far away, had been *distress and persecution,* words that suggest extreme hardship and pressure. The antidote to that anguish is the renewing of his relationship with the Thessalonian Christians through Timothy's good report.

8. For now we really live, since you are standing firm in the Lord.

Paul expresses his relief in terms of life and death. That may sound exaggerated, but we can appreciate it when we realize that Paul teaches that death is more than what lies at the end of natural life. It is the sentence of sin (Romans 6:23), and so "death" is what a person experiences in a sinful world. But the life of Christ constantly overcomes that death (2 Corinthians 1:9; 4:10-12), bringing the comfort, peace, and joy of the Lord into the very worst of circumstances. So it is here: in the midst of difficulty, trials, and pressure, Paul has experienced the new life given by Christ through Timothy's assurance that the Thessalonian Christians' faithfulness is intact. That experience of life is a glimpse in the present of the life that believers will experience when Christ returns (2 Corinthians 4:17).

B. PAUL'S JOY (v. 9)

9. How can we thank God enough for you in return for all the joy we have in the presence of our God because of you?

Paul credits the good news of the Thessalonians' faith to God's blessing. So now he exclaims that he cannot possibly pay God back for the blessing of knowing that his Christian friends remain firm. Whatever thanks Paul offers, whatever good he can do, whatever sacrifices he makes, they can never repay God for what God has given to Paul.

Paul uses a strong expression for *joy* here, for his joy is more than ordinary happiness. It is the joy that the people of God experience when they recognize that God is at work. It comes to its climax when Jesus returns and all his people stand together, as Paul says in 1 Thessalonians 2:19: "For what is our hope, our joy, or the crown in which we will glory in the presence of our Lord Jesus when he comes? Is it not you?" Real joy is to be found only in Christ, and it is experienced best when we share our lives with other Christians with whom we will spend eternity in Christ's *presence.*

C. PAUL'S PRAYER (vv. 10-13)

10. Night and day we pray most earnestly that we may see you again and supply what is lacking in your faith.

Paul's joy is coupled with an ongoing desire not just to hear a good report but also to be reunited in person with the Thessalonian Christians. So just as Paul had worked night and day for the good of the Thessalonians while he was with them (1 Thessalonians 2:9), now he prays for them *night and day.*

Paul's prayer is first of all to be reunited with the Thessalonian Christians in encouraging fellowship. That fellowship means not just casual

WHAT DO YOU THINK?

Paul was confident the Thessalonian believers would stand firm in the Lord. How confident are you that you will do so? What can you do to increase your confidence in this area?

WHAT DO YOU THINK?

Paul's exclamations of joy ring hollow for some believers. Why do you think this might be?

PRAYER

O God our Father, we thank you that you did not leave us alone. You gave us each other. Please help us love, support, and cherish each other so that we can receive the encouragement that you send us through each other. In Jesus' name, amen!

WHAT DO YOU THINK?

Think about the fact that you will spend eternity with many of the people in your church. How does this affect the way you relate to them today?

friendship but active, purposeful ministry. Their *faith* is strong, but Paul knows that it is not complete. So Paul says he prays to return to Thessalonica. For Paul, staying connected to other Christians and serving their needs in the gospel so that they can be made stronger in their faith is the only right response to the wonderful gift God has given in Jesus Christ. If Paul has been encouraged by Timothy's report, it is encouragement to continue to spend his life leading people to come to faith and to move on to greater faith.

11. Now may our God and Father himself and our Lord Jesus clear the way for us to come to you.

Now Paul expresses directly the content of his prayer to *God* for the Thessalonians. As is common in the New Testament, Paul refers to God as *Father*, emphasizing God's loving care and provision for his people. The God who treats his people as a good father treats his children can always be counted on to give them exactly what they need.

Paul also addresses *Jesus* Christ, calling him *Lord*. That emphasizes Christ's authority, the authority of God himself. Praying at once both to the Father and to Christ demonstrates the conviction that Christ is fully God. Paul's assurance of the future is based on his confidence that the God who saved his people by sending his Son to die will also do everything necessary to see his people through to the end.

The first petition of Paul's prayer is that God will put Paul back on the road to the Thessalonians. Their connection of faith, an eternal connection, needs to be renewed, so Paul asks God to bring that about.

12. May the Lord make your love increase and overflow for each other and for everyone else, just as ours does for you.

Paul knows the Thessalonians have been living out the gospel's mandate of *love* (1 Thessalonians 1:3). But he knows their love needs to be sustained and to *increase*. If the gospel is about God's love, then people who believe it should be known as those who abound in that love—not just for each other, but also love for the unlovely. So Paul prays that the readers will love all people just as Paul had demonstrated his love to them.

13. May he strengthen your hearts so that you will be blameless and holy in the presence of our God and Father when our Lord Jesus comes with all his holy ones.

Paul's prayer continues with the request for strong, faithful *hearts*, purely and thoroughly devoted to God. Closing with anticipation of Christ's return, Paul emphasizes a key theme of the passage. What motivates his deep desire for fellowship with the Thessalonian Christians is the profound truth that they will stand together with Christ when he returns. What motivates Paul to work for their faithfulness and growth is knowing that they will all stand before Christ with a desire to be pleasing to the one who gave his own life to save them.

The encouragement that believers receive from each other comes from this place. Our Christian brothers and sisters are the people with whom we will spend eternity. Together we are the greatest objects of God's love, the sinners for whom Christ died. Knowing that implants in us a deep desire to be together and a deep desire to serve Christ in a way that honors him. So we take encouragement in our service as we share our lives with other Christians.

CONCLUSION

Think about what have been some of the best experiences of your Christian life. Chances are good that they were experiences when you were actively working and sharing with other Christians. We naturally take encouragement and derive joy from our fellowship with other followers of Jesus.

Paul and the Thessalonian Christians had the same experience. For them, separation was agony, but a report of steadfast faith was tremendous joy.

In hard times, when we are discouraged or when we just feel empty, it is time for us to reconnect with the family of faith. When we keep those faith relationships strong, we will always know where to go for encouragement, where to find the joy of the Lord afresh.

THOUGHT TO REMEMBER

"No man is an island, entire of itself; every man is a piece of the continent, a part of the main" (John Donne, 1624).

Discovery Learning

The following is an alternative lesson plan emphasizing learning activities. Classes desiring such student involvement will find these suggestions helpful. At the back of this book are reproducible student pages to further enhance activity learning.

INTO THE LESSON

The week before class secure some large colored index cards, butcher paper, spray adhesive, colored markers, several thesauruses, strips of paper with Scripture references on them (as described below), a list of the missions your church supports and/or a list of people for whom the church members are praying, including those who are sick or are shut-ins (with addresses), and small note cards. Put the bulletin board or butcher paper on a wall near the front of the classroom. Spray it with the adhesive before class, following the directions on the can.

As students arrive, instruct them to take two index cards each. On one they are to write a synonym for the word *encouragement*. (Let them use a thesaurus if they need help.) Ask students to write on the second card an encouraging word or phrase they like others to say to them. As cards are completed, have the students put the cards on the adhesive paper.

Option: Distribute copies of the reproducible activity "Words of Encouragement" from page 502. Give students time to discover the encouraging words in the puzzle; then have them call these out as you write them on the board.

Discuss how these words (whether on the index cards or in the puzzle) make the students feel. Then say, "It is good that we are sharing these good feelings because the body of Christ is supposed to encourage one another. Today we'll see how encouragement can help us stand firm in our faith."

INTO THE WORD

Ask students to share circumstances that cause discouragement in their lives or the lives of others. If no one suggests persecution as a circumstance of discouragement, offer it into the discussion. Use the information in the background commentary to set the context for today's Scripture, 1 Thessalonians 3.

Ask students to work in pairs and read the passage and to complete the reproducible activity "Prescription for Encouragement" from page 502.

Here are the answers they should discover:

Occasion: *the afflictions or trials the Thessalonians are suffering (v. 3)*; acts: *strengthen and encourage (vv. 2, 7), concern for others (v. 5), faith and love (v. 6); desire to see and be with each other (vv. 6, 11); prayer for others (v. 10); love for one another and for others (v. 12); results of the encouragement: renewed life (v. 8), thanks to God (v. 9); motivation: to strengthen their faith as they anticipate the Lord's return (v. 13).*

When students finish the assignment, discuss the passage, focusing on these key elements. Use the lesson commentary to add to the discussion so students understand that the encouragement offered in this passage was a "two-way road" and is given to strengthen the believers' faith.

Have students write the "acts of encouragement" from today's lesson on index cards (one act per card) and put them on the adhesive paper with the cards from earlier in the lesson. Note that there are other types of encouragement identified in the Scripture.

Then distribute strips of paper with one of the following Scripture references on each strip. Have the groups look up each reference and write the form of encouragement on an index card (Acts 9:31, *Holy Spirit;* Romans 15:4, *Scripture;* 2 Corinthians 7:13, *refreshing each other's spirit;* Philippians 2:1, *union with Christ;* 1 Thessalonians 4:17, 18, *promise of eternity with Christ;* 2 Thessalonians 2:16, *God's grace;* Titus 1:9, *sound doctrine;* Hebrews 10:25, *fellowship*). Put these cards on the paper as well. Discuss how each additional items bring encouragement.

INTO LIFE

Say, "I want to give you the opportunity today to exercise your role as encouragers in the body." Distribute copies of the list of missions and prayer requests to the students, along with the addresses and the small note cards. Ask each student to choose one or more names from the list and write a note of encouragement to that person this week. Tell students to be intentional about using some of the words/phrases from the adhesive board at the front of the class in their notes (for example, mention they are praying for the person, quote Scripture in the note, remind the person of God's grace, etc.).

Before you dismiss the class, lead a prayer that specifically asks God to bless those who receive these notes and to grant them his peace and encouragement.

DEMONSTRATED IN ACTION

LESSON 4

INTRODUCTION

A. SACRED OR SECULAR?

People commonly distinguish between the sacred and the secular—between things that have to do with God and things that are ordinary. Musicians distinguish between sacred and secular music. In times past some communities would force businesses to close on days that were deemed sacred. In certain sacred places special clothing may be expected.

However, there is a problem with this distinction if we think we can exclude God from anything that is "secular." When we think we can divide our lives so that God's part is set off from the rest, we may well keep God confined to that part alone. Faith is then just for special days, holy places, and religious observances.

The Bible's perspective is different. God made all of life, not just a few parts of it. God rules over every aspect of life, not just those we want to allow to him. In Jesus Christ, God entered the world as a human being, living every part of life just as you and I, showing us that the whole of life belongs to him.

When we realize that truth about God, we cannot divide our lives into sacred and secular portions. The whole of life becomes sacred, and pleasing God by fulfilling his purpose in all parts of our lives becomes our focus.

B. LESSON BACKGROUND

The readers of Paul's first letter to the Thessalonians lived in an environment in which religion was seldom seen as altering a person's way of life. In Greek religions the worshiper seldom was expected to obey the god in any way. The Greek gods simply were not interested in that kind of thing.

While many pagan religions of the day simply called on worshipers to observe certain rituals, others offered something more. Some invited worshipers to engage in promiscuous sexual activity as part of the cults' observance. Such practices were almost taken for granted by many citizens.

In addition to its difficult religious environment, Thessalonica presented a challenging economic setting. The city was the site of a major harbor. Work in the harbor was plentiful, but there were often more workers than work to do. Furthermore, a small number of extremely rich people controlled enormous wealth, far beyond what they could use for themselves. As a result of these tensions, a system arose in which workers who did not have work received small sums of money from rich patrons, for whom the workers were then obligated to do favors. Such a practice encouraged some to avoid work altogether and simply live from patronage.

DEVOTIONAL READING:
HEBREWS 11:1-6

BACKGROUND SCRIPTURE:
1 THESSALONIANS 4:1-12

PRINTED TEXT:
1 THESSALONIANS 4:1-12

Jun
27

LESSON AIMS

After this lesson each student will be able to:

1. Describe the kind of life Paul said the Thessalonian Christians ought to live.

2. Compare and contrast this lifestyle with the secular lifestyle common today.

3. Pair up with another student or join a small group for mutual accountability and covenant with one another to help one another grow in living holy and pure lives.

KEY VERSE:

Finally, brothers, we instructed you how to live in order to please God, as in fact you are living. Now we ask you and urge you in the Lord Jesus to do this more and more. —1 Thessalonians 4:1

Lesson 4 Notes

The God whom Paul preached was more than a pagan deity who accepted gifts and doled out favors. The Thessalonian Christians needed to be conscious of this difference, remembering that God had made them and saved them for a purpose. That purpose extended to every part of their lives.

I. CALL TO PLEASE GOD (1 THESSALONIANS 4:1, 2)

A. Earnest Entreaty (v. 1)

1. Finally, brothers, we instructed you how to live in order to please God, as in fact you are living. Now we ask you and urge you in the Lord Jesus to do this more and more.

Paul's readers have come out of their old lives and into faith in Jesus (1 Thessalonians 1:9; 2:13). That change of faith means a change of life, something that they already have been taught and already have begun to demonstrate. The essence of that new way of life is *to please God*. And this is no ordinary God. He is unlike the pagan gods who are aloof and indifferent. He is the God who has saved his people through the *Lord Jesus* Christ. So as Paul says that he urges the readers by the Lord Jesus, he reminds them of this important difference. The readers have a reason to want to please this God. In Jesus he has given himself for their sakes.

Pleasing God is more than just doing the right religious things. Paul says that it has to do with how God's people ought *to live*. The readers have made an excellent start in this God-pleasing life. But by its nature, this new kind of life always offers the prospect of growth.

B. Imperative Instructions (v. 2)

2. For you know what instructions we gave you by the authority of the Lord Jesus.

What Paul says here is nothing new. From the beginning he has taught the new converts about the nature of their new life. This is not just good advice but *instructions* that are imperative. Nor are they just on Paul's *authority* but that of Jesus himself, what Jesus taught his followers. Transformed behavior with actions that reflect God's will is absolutely necessary to demonstrate transformed lives.

PLEASING GOD

Rick Nelson was a star in the early days of rock-and-roll. His music career peaked in 1961 with "Hello, Mary Lou." In October of 1971 he was part of a reunion show at Madison Square Garden with other early rock-and-roll stars. Nelson had shifted to country rock by then and mixed his new music with the old. The crowd started booing, and Nelson walked off the stage. (It was later reported that police were trying to break up a problem at the back of the hall while Nelson was singing, and some believe that the booing was actually directed at the police.) Out of that experience came a song that spoke autobiographically of the "Garden Party." A key theme of the song was that "you can't please everyone, so you got to please yourself."

Paul reminds us that the Christian life is all about pleasing God, not ourselves. However, the great thing about pleasing God is that pleasing him is exactly what we need to do in order to be pleasing to our deepest selves. In other words, pleasing God makes us fully human, just as God intended us to be in the beginning! Isn't that amazing?   —C. R. B.

What Do You Think?

The Christian life "always offers the prospect of growth." If you were put in charge of growth development at your church, what would you do to promote spiritual growth among the members?

II. PLEASING GOD WITH SEXUAL PURITY
(1 THESSALONIANS 4:3-8)
A. PURITY PRESCRIBED (vv. 3, 4)
3. It is God's will that you should be sanctified: that you should avoid sexual immorality;

Paul summarizes *God's will* for the Christian's life in a single word: *sanctified.* Sanctification is the state of being set apart from common usage for something distinctly sacred, belonging entirely to God. Paul stresses this point at the beginning of his discussion of *sexual* behavior to make a very clear point: the way a person behaves sexually is not a "private" matter but affects the person's relationship to God. In the ancient world as much as the modern world, people insisted that their sex lives were no one's business but their own. Paul asserts that our sex lives are very much the business of God.

Specifically Paul says that sanctification means abstaining from *immorality.* In this context the term refers to all sexual activity outside the context of marriage. God created human sexuality to be expressed in the context of faithful marriage between one man and one woman (Genesis 2:23, 24). Sex was part of what God pronounced "very good" on the sixth day of creation (Genesis 1:28, 31), but it remains such only when it is exercised in the context for which God created it. Those who belong to God in Christ, who understand God's purpose in creation and want to honor God and his purpose, will understand why the Bible forbids sexual activity outside marriage.

4. . . . that each of you should learn to control his own body in a way that is holy and honorable,

This verse continues to set forth sexual purity as an expression of a right relationship with God. Again Paul says that one's sexual behavior should express sanctification, and he adds honor to the proper understanding of sexuality. To act with honor means to treat sexual behavior as something extremely valuable, demanding the utmost discipline and sensitivity.

This verse contains a difficult figure of speech, hidden in this translation by the word *body.* The Greek here is actually the same word Peter uses for a man's wife in 1 Peter 3:7, but its more usual meaning is that of a container of some kind, as in 2 Corinthians 4:7. Like Peter, Paul may use the word to refer to a man's wife. (See the *NIV* footnote.) Or it may be an indirect, polite expression for the sexual organs. In either case, Paul's point is that one's sexuality is not to be used however one wishes. It is not something for which we can exploit other people. It is a valuable, sacred trust given us by God, to be used in a way that honors him and expresses our belonging to him.

B. BAD BEHAVIOR BANNED (vv. 5-7)
5. . . . not in passionate lust like the heathen, who do not know God;

Here Paul draws a sharp contrast with the understanding of sexuality that many of the Thessalonian Christians would have had before they came to faith. *Passionate lust* is a dramatic phrase. Paul suggests that, apart from our relationship with God, we have nothing other than our desires to act on, and so we will be controlled by them. If we know God, we can submit our sexuality to his will. This statement implies that the person

WHAT DO YOU THINK?
Paul was writing to the church, not the city council, in Thessalonica. To what extent is it right to expect the secular culture to observe Christian sexual standards?

Visual for Lesson 4. Display this poster as you discuss verse 7. Ask, "What does holiness *look like in today's world?"*

who refuses to discipline his or her sexual behavior to the will of God is acting like someone who does not know God, a pagan (*heathen*). The desire for sex is perhaps the strongest urge that a human being experiences, but for those who know God, it is something that can be brought into submission to him.

6. . . . and that in this matter no one should wrong his brother or take advantage of him. The Lord will punish men for all such sins, as we have already told you and warned you.

Paul insists that our sexual behavior is of vital importance for our relationship to God. But here he also asserts that it is important for our relationship with other people. If my sex life is no one's business but my own, then the same is true for other people as well. In that case, a person reasons that he or she can use another for sexual gratification without any sense of harming another person. But if sexuality was created for expression in a faithful marriage between one man and one woman, any sex outside marriage amounts to cheating another person.

The person who has sex outside marriage cheats his or her present or future spouse out of what should be an exclusive relationship. Likewise, the person with whom the immoral act is committed is deprived of the same exclusive relationship, as is that person's present or future spouse. Then there are the further implications for the families of all those involved. While people imagine that sex has no consequences, sexual immorality hurts other people at least as much as any other offense we can commit against them.

Unlike the pagan gods, the God of the Bible is not indifferent to such matters. He cares too much for his people to let them damage one another with sexual immorality. His will in this matter is expressly stated, and Paul reminds the Thessalonian Christians that they have heard from him on this subject before. God will not allow sexual immorality to go unanswered. It is far from a "victimless crime," and it is subject to God's judgment just as all sinful behavior.

7. For God did not call us to be impure, but to live a holy life.

To live in sexual immorality, cheating others for the sake of one's own gratification and ignoring God's purpose for our lives, is unthinkable for the follower of Christ. Through the gospel *God* has called us to belong to him in every aspect of our lives. There can be no "secular" territory when we know what God has done to make us his. We are to be his in holiness, belonging to him as consecrated people who exclude no corner of our lives from submission to his will.

It is worth remembering that our purity before God is based on God's grace and forgiveness. Sexual sin has enormous consequences, but it is not unforgivable. Many in the Thessalonian church probably joined in immoral practices prior to their conversions. Perhaps some have not overcome their old habits. Paul tells them that God calls them to purity that begins now. The blood of Christ can take an *impure* life and make it clean again, no less with sexual immorality than with any other sin.

C. Weighty Warning (v. 8)

8. Therefore, he who rejects this instruction does not reject man but God, who gives you his Holy Spirit.

Today there are many people who like to blame the apostle Paul for what they see as a narrow, negative, and ignorant view of sexuality. They equate Paul's teaching with mere human *instruction*. This verse shows us that in Paul's time people argued against him in the same way. So he closes his discussion of sexual behavior by insisting that his teaching is not merely his. Paul's teaching on sexual behavior is identical with that of Jesus and the Old Testament. From the beginning with the creation of one man and one woman, God's will for human sexuality has been utterly clear. So the person who treats that teaching with contempt, who openly *rejects* it or secretly acts against it, rejects not just a human teaching but the very will of *God*, announced from the beginning of time.

But the God who is rejected is not just the Creator God but also the Redeemer God. He has given his *Holy Spirit* to those who follow Jesus Christ. The Holy Spirit provides guidance and power to the believer to follow the will of God as expressed in his Word. It is the Holy Spirit who empowers God's people to live as his holy people. Consequently, to receive this gift and persist in unholy behavior is a severe affront to God. How can a person who has even modest respect for God act against both his teaching and his Spirit?

III. PLEASING GOD WITH BROTHERLY LOVE
(1 THESSALONIANS 4:9, 10)

9. Now about brotherly love we do not need to write to you, for you yourselves have been taught by God to love each other.

From the subject of sexual behavior, Paul moves on to a wider subject that takes in all aspects of our behavior: *love* for others. Paul has already commended the Thessalonians for their "labor prompted by love" (1 Thessalonians 1:3), their active work in living out the love that they have for *each other*. So here he asserts again that the readers know well what they must do in this regard. But love is so central and imperative to the Christian life that Paul is compelled to mention it again.

The love that the Christians have for each other is brotherly love. Prior to the New Testament, this term was used almost always for the love one naturally has for family members. But Paul applies the term broadly: all Christians should love each other as brothers and sisters because in Christ we have become members of the same family.

The basis for this wide, deep love is the wide, deep love of God. Christians, Paul says, *have been taught by God to love each other*. In other words, the gospel story itself, God's sending his Son to die for sinners, is the supreme demonstration of love. If we believe that message, we are compelled by it to change our outlook and bring as many into the circle of our love as God brought into his circle through Jesus.

10. And in fact, you do love all the brothers throughout Macedonia. Yet we urge you, brothers, to do so more and more.

Again, there is no doubt that these Christians have *love* for each other. Their circle of love now embraces not just the Christians they know well in their own city but those throughout the region of *Macedonia*. But how can a person have love for people far away, people whom he or she barely knows? God's love shown through Jesus Christ makes that possible. Just as God loved the unlovely, so those who know God through Jesus learn to love the unlovely.

HOW TO SAY IT

Macedonia. Mass-eh-DOE-nee-uh.

sanctification. sank-tih-fuh-KAY-shun.

Thessalonica. THESS-uh-lo-NYE-kuh (TH as in THIN).

WHAT DO YOU THINK?

Paul said the Thessalonian church's love for others was known throughout Macedonia. How can a church today become known for its love?

PRAYER

Father in Heaven, we surrender our lives to you again. Forgive us for holding back parts of ourselves as if they belonged to us. Make every part of us your sacred, holy territory. In Jesus' name, amen!

WHAT DO YOU THINK?

Paul tells the Thessalonian Christians they are to work. What exceptions, if any, do you think are applicable to that principle today?

WHAT DO YOU THINK?

What does it mean to be "model citizens" in a democratic society? To what extent does leading a quiet life and minding one's own business permit or prohibit political activism?

IV. PLEASING GOD IN THE COMMUNITY (1 THESSALONIANS 4:11, 12)

A. WORKING RESPONSIBLY (v. 11)

11. Make it your ambition to lead a quiet life, to mind your own business and to work with your hands, just as we told you,

The command to love is not just a matter of warm feelings. It is a practical matter of day-to-day life, touching every way that a person lives. The aspect that Paul stresses here is the way a person lives as part of the community.

Loving community life begins with orderly citizenship. In this context *to lead a quiet life* expresses the ideal of responsible, law-abiding citizenship. Paul stresses that the gospel does not change this essential feature of human society. In fact, it strengthens it. Certainly a Christian who knows the love of God cannot ignore others' rights or take advantage of others in any way.

Loving community life also means honest labor. God created human beings *to work* and placed them in a world that responds to their work (Genesis 2:15). By using our capacity to be creative and to use the resources God provides on the earth, we create goods and services that provide benefit to others, and so we support ourselves. This is true for Paul's readers, whether they are dockworkers, shipowners, farmers, craftsmen, or merchants. It is true in our time as well, regardless of our occupations.

But in the environment of Thessalonica, it is easy for some to shirk their responsibility. The culture of patronage prevails, allowing some to avoid work and receive the support of wealthy patrons in exchange for favors and acclaim. Some may have carried these habits into the church, taking advantage of the loving generosity of brothers and sisters in the faith.

Paul reminds these people to renew their commitment to work and so to take care of their own needs. Love compels Christians to be generous with each other, but it also compels that they never take advantage of such generosity when they have the means and opportunity to support themselves.

B. ACTING HONESTLY (v. 12)

12. . . . so that your daily life may win the respect of outsiders and so that you will not be dependent on anybody.

Honest work is also vital to the reputation of the church among unbelievers. Because their beliefs challenge accepted ideas and practices, early Christians are often regarded as subversive. Paul wants to be sure that the Thessalonian Christians do not supply any valid reason for such suspicions. If the Christians become well known for their honest labor and generosity toward the genuinely needy, their reputation will change from subversives to model citizens.

"NEO-ATHEISTS" VS. "REAL CHRISTIANS"

Many critics of religion are now calling themselves "neo-atheists." What makes them "neo" is their equation of Islamic suicide bombers and other such radicals with Christianity. "Neos" have trouble fitting into their scheme anyone who believes in God and the principles of the Christian faith and yet is still able to talk about faith in reasonable terms in a moderate tone of voice. They are attacking a caricature of Christianity, not the real thing.

Paul reminds us of the effects of real Christianity: it empowers people to be upstanding citizens and to do good to others. It motivates people to be hard-working and law-abiding members of society and thus not burden the welfare and justice systems of their nation. Real Christianity motivates people to be gracious and kind to their enemies—even those who unfairly criticize the Christian faith and arrogantly seek to limit its positive effects on society!   —C. R. B.

CONCLUSION

As Paul reminds the Thessalonians about Christian behavior, we see that no part of their lives has been excluded. Whether it is the very private matter of sexuality or the very public matter of community life and work, new life in Christ transforms it. Whether it is those closest to us or those farthest away, the love of Christ compels love for all. God has made his will and purpose clear in all these matters. Those who are captivated by God's grace and love will want to do nothing so much as to please him by fulfilling his will and purpose in all areas of their lives.

When we become Christians, what part of our lives is left just to us? None! And that is a good thing for us. By pleasing God, fulfilling his purpose in every area, we discover the purpose for which we were made: to be his entirely.

THOUGHT TO REMEMBER

"It was character that got us out of bed, commitment that moved us into action, and discipline that enabled us to follow through"

—Zig Ziglar.

Discovery Learning

The following is an alternative lesson plan emphasizing learning activities. Classes desiring such student involvement will find these suggestions helpful. At the back of this book are reproducible student pages to further enhance activity learning.

INTO THE LESSON

Before class, make a copy of reproducible page 503 for each student. Have the papers, some colored pencils, and several markers on a table as students arrive. Ask students to draw lines to divide the gingerbread men so they accurately represent the various parts of each student's life, and then to color the various parts and label them (You may want to color and label one ahead of time to serve as an example; for instance, 1/3 of the gingerbread man may be colored green and labeled "work," 1/4 may be colored purple and labeled "sleep," another 1/4 may be colored red and labeled "family," 1/12 may be colored blue and labeled "recreation," and 1/12 may be colored orange and labeled "church," or any such combination). When students finish the assignment, have them display their "works of art" and compare them with that of other class members.

After a few moments, ask whether anyone sees a problem with the pictures. If no one mentions it, ask students where the part is that represents God. (Many will probably say that's the "church" part.) Say to students, "Don't we as Christians belong

100% to God?" Lead into a discussion about this, referring to the lesson commentary introduction and saying, "We cannot divide our lives into sacred and secular portions. The whole of life becomes sacred, and pleasing God by fulfilling his purpose in all parts of our lives becomes our focus. Driving that point home is what the apostle Paul was doing in today's text."

INTO THE WORD

Use the information from the background commentary to set the context for today's Scripture study, 1 Thessalonians 4:1-12. Emphasize the sexual immorality that was prevalent within the pagan society of Thessalonica. Then divide the class into an equal number of groups. Half of the groups will read verses 1-8 of the lesson text and the other half of the groups will read verses 9-12. Ask both groups to answer the following two questions: (1) What behaviors or attitudes does Paul instruct the Thessalonians to adopt in order to observe the "will of God"? (2) If the Thessalonians do not follow Paul's instruction and find themselves outside the will of God, what will happen? (Group A: 1: *Be sanctified or holy, v. 3; avoid sexual immorality , v. 3; control one's own body, v. 4. 2: God will punish them, v. 6; they will be unclean rather than holy, v. 7. Group B: 1: Practice brotherly love even more, vv. 9, 10; lead a quiet life, take care of their own business, and work with their hands, v. 11. 2: They will set a bad example for the pagans, v. 12.)*

After the groups finish their assignments, have them report their findings. Discuss each behavior or attitude they identify and each outcome, using the lesson commentary to bring out relevant information to expand on their understanding.

Then ask students to compare the Thessalonian society with our society today, noting where the two societies are similar and where they are different. (Examples: sexual sin is still rampant; self-control is important for the Christian life; some Christians do not behave much differently from their pagan counterparts; working with one's hands is not so common today.) Then ask students, "What do you think we as Christians need to do to be sure we are in God's will and our behavior is a testimony to the world?" Allow for some discussion on this and then make this transition to application: "I think the one thing we need to do is to realize we are accountable to God for our actions; the next step may be to begin to hold each other accountable."

INTO LIFE

Say to students, "Let's look at your gingerbread men from the beginning of the lesson. What did we determine was wrong with those pictures?" (*God should represent all of our lives, not just part of them.*) "How can we 'fix' our pictures so they represent this truth?" (*Students could choose yellow or some other transparent color and color over the entire picture, representing the fact that God is, in fact, in all aspects of their lives.*) When students have completed their revisions, ask them to consider the various aspects of their lives and determine whether there are any areas where they may not be in the will of God. Have students pair off and share with each other as much as they are comfortable concerning this question. Then ask students to spend the rest of the class time in prayer with one another, asking God to hold them accountable this week.

GOD'S COSMIC PLAN

LESSON 5

INTRODUCTION

A. TOYING WITH TIME

My girls despise cleaning the basement. That's where they keep their toys, and like many children they tend to pick up one, play with it awhile, and leave it on the floor before picking up another. So after a long day of playing hard, they dread clean-up time. They know that books, puzzle pieces, and doll paraphernalia are strewn about the room and that it will take a while to pick it all up. Unfortunately, if we fail to provide a time limit and negative reinforcement, like loss of snack, it is almost certain that they will be distracted and never clean up. It is usually not enough, however, simply to give them an ending time. They typically require reminders like "10 minutes left" and "you've got only 60 seconds!" As you may suspect, my girls cover nearly as much ground in the last minute as in the preceding 10 combined.

So one day I thought I would break them of their procrastination. I told them that I had set a reasonable time limit for them to finish cleaning but that they would have no reminders and no knowledge of the deadline. I hoped that the lack of a verbal security blanket would unleash their potential for more efficient use of time. The results were terrible. The girls were nearly paralyzed by the uncertainty and spent more time whining and begging for clues than cleaning. The mystery was simply more than they could bear.

As Christians we sometimes feel as if we are in a similar situation. We do not know when Jesus will return to fulfill his mission and bring God's kingdom in its fullness. This accounts for the widespread appeal of books claiming to provide concrete information about Christ's return. Hal Lindsey's *The Late Great Planet Earth,* for instance, went through 16 printings within two years of being released. Such curiosity is not new, and it caused considerable anxiety for believers in Thessalonica.

B. LESSON BACKGROUND

The believers in Thessalonica were suffering a variety of temptations to abandon their faith. The Jewish community as a whole had rejected Paul's message of Christ (Acts 17:1-9). So the Jews who became believers faced continuing opposition from that community. Thessalonica was predominantly Greek, however, and not Jewish. The people worshiped the supposed gods on nearby Mt. Olympus. In addition, Thessalonica was a key Roman colony, devoted to the imperial cult of Rome. These Greek and Roman pagans exerted considerable pressure on the Christians there, pressing them to join in their worship of the gods and devotion to Caesar.

It also appears that people of influence, whether inside or outside the body, were causing the believers to doubt the prophecies of God's coming judgment. As a result some questioned whether Christ was returning to judge, so they began to flirt with loose living. Some worried that those who

DEVOTIONAL READING:
JOEL 3:11-16
BACKGROUND SCRIPTURE:
1 THESSALONIANS 4:13–5:28
PRINTED TEXT:
1 THESSALONIANS 5:1-11, 23, 24

Jul
4

LESSON AIMS

After this lesson each student will be able to:

1. Summarize Paul's instructions for being prepared for Christ's return.

2. Explain the connection between (a) the need for self-control and mutual encouragement and (b) the expected return of Jesus.

3. Confess one area of self-control weakness and make a commitment to an accountability partner to strengthen that area.

KEY VERSE:

God did not appoint us to suffer wrath but to receive salvation through our Lord Jesus Christ.

—1 Thessalonians 5:9

died before Christ returned would miss out on his kingdom. Some feared that those still living would be trapped on the earth and caught in the crossfire as God vanquished his enemies. Others were so convinced that Christ would soon return that they no longer took any thought of the future and even quit working. Still others believed that Christ had already come and that they had missed out on it.

Paul wrote to empathize with the believers' suffering, clear up their confusion, and urge them to remain firm in their faith. He reaffirmed the prophecies of future judgment, taught that Christ would return at an unknown time, and assured them that no one would be able to miss it. He then clarified that the faithful who had died and those who were still living would escape Christ's judgment on the wicked; both would gain entrance into his eternal kingdom.

On that basis, Paul exhorted the Thessalonians to live modest yet active lives consistent with their salvation in Christ. Our text today picks up near the end of 1 Thessalonians as Paul finished clarifying the doctrine of the last days and commended the Thessalonians to live appropriately.

I. CHRIST WILL RETURN (1 THESSALONIANS 5:1-3)
A. NO NEED TO KNOW WHEN (v. 1)
1. Now, brothers, about times and dates we do not need to write to you,

In some of his letters, Paul addresses disputes about special *times and dates*. (See Galatians 4:9, 10; Colossians 2:16.) In such letters the believers wonder whether key events of the Jewish calendar are mandatory for Gentile Christians. That is not the issue here. The pair of terms concerning time in this verse combine to point to the ultimate time in history for which God's people have been waiting: the day of the Lord. It is a continuation of the theme of Christ's return already introduced in 4:15. We see a similar pair of words in Acts 1:7, where Jesus tells the curious apostles that it had not been given to them to know when Christ would return.

It is only natural to wonder and to ask when the day of God's ultimate salvation will be. Daniel wondered "How long?" (Daniel 12:6), as did Jesus' closest followers (Mark 13:1-4). When one has the luxury of consulting an angel or the Messiah himself, one cannot help but ask the question everyone has been asking, in hopes that this exceptional figure might have inside information. Apparently the Thessalonians hoped that someone like Paul, who had personally encountered the exalted Christ, might know. But they are quickly reminded that "when?" is still the wrong question to ask. The Thessalonians need to be reminded of the implications of the more fundamental truth that they already know.

B. LIKE A THIEF (v. 2)
2. . . . for you know very well that the day of the Lord will come like a thief in the night.

The day of the Lord is a phrase that points to God's final judgment—a phrase with a rich biblical history (see Isaiah 2:12-22; Jeremiah 46:10; Ezekiel 30:2, 3; Amos 5:18-20; Zephaniah 1:14-18). In most cases, it concerns God's wrath on his enemies. This focus on divine judgment suggests that the Thessalonians are not simply curious about when they will be saved, but anxious about being in the world when God's anger is poured out on his enemies.

WHAT DO YOU THINK?

Why do you think the question of "when" is so important to us in regards to the return of Christ? How can we stay focused on the right questions?

WHAT DO YOU THINK?

Paul uses the word pictures of the thief in the night and a woman in the pains of childbirth in speaking of the coming of Christ. What is your reaction to these word pictures?

Even so, the answer they receive is no different from what Christ taught his followers (Matthew 24:43, 44; Luke 12:39, 40) and what his followers, in turn, taught others (2 Peter 3:10; Revelation 3:3; 16:15). That day *will come like a thief in the night.* It will come suddenly, when it is least expected. It will come at a time when the people of this world are least vigilant and most ignorant as to what God is doing around them.

C. WITH DESTRUCTION (v. 3)

3. *While people are saying, "Peace and safety," destruction will come on them suddenly, as labor pains on a pregnant woman, and they will not escape.*

The bad news continues. God's judgment comes when the *people* of this world think they have secured *peace* and tranquility for themselves. In Thessalonica, a Roman province packed with Roman patriots, this warning likely resounds quite profoundly. They think Caesar is securing the world's peace: the Pax Romana. They are like the wicked of ancient Israel who cried peace when there was no true peace (Jeremiah 6:14; Ezekiel 13:10, 16; Micah 3:5).

The wicked have no clue when the hour of their *destruction will come,* but it will come. A *pregnant woman* knows that her time will eventually come. There will be no crying baby without the pain of childbirth, as it has been since the Fall. It is inevitable. Jesus himself used this metaphor to describe God's judgment (Matthew 24:8; Mark 13:8).

Paul provides no particular details here about the nature of the final judgment. His concern is that the readers know it will be unexpected, unstoppable, and inescapable. This is bad news for God's enemies.

II. BELIEVERS BE READY (1 THESSALONIANS 5:4-8)

A. BE CHILDREN OF LIGHT (vv. 4, 5)

4, 5. *But you, brothers, are not in darkness so that this day should surprise you like a thief. You are all sons of the light and sons of the day. We do not belong to the night or to the darkness.*

At least part of the reason Paul provides no details about the coming judgment is that such details need not worry these believers. It simply does not pertain to them. They are dwelling on possibilities that should be of no concern to them. Paul uses a common metaphor for distinguishing those who do and do not have reason to fear the *day* of the Lord—that of *light* and *darkness.* (See Luke 16:8; John 12:35, 36; Ephesians 5:8-14.)

Children *of the day* live in *the light,* who is Jesus, and thus need not fear. Only those who live the *night* life, the life of *darkness,* are vulnerable to the intrusion of the *thief.* In Jesus' teaching, walking during day or night was a powerful image for conveying rival ways of living (John 11:9, 10). This image is particularly vivid for those who live before the widespread use of electricity. Without proper illumination one is susceptible to stumbling and injuring oneself on rocks in the path, getting lost without the benefit of visible landmarks, or suffering the attacks of crooks who spring from the shadows to prey on unsuspecting travelers.

Paul does not explain in great detail how to live in the light. These believers already know that. He simply reminds them who they are in Christ. They are already children of light. It is pointless for those who travel only during the day to anticipate what it means to safely navigate the nighttime world. Dwelling on such matters reflects spiritual amnesia and should not be encouraged.

HOW TO SAY IT

Caesar. SEE-zer.

Gentile. JEN-tile.

Messiah. Meh-SIGH-uh.

Macedonia. Mass-eh-DOE-nee-uh.

Olympus. Oh-LIM-pus.

Pax Romana. PAX Roe-MAH-nuh.

Thessalonica. THESS-uh-lo-NYE-kuh (TH as in THIN).

DAILY BIBLE READINGS

Monday, June 28—*The Day of the Lord (Joel 3:11-16)*

Tuesday, June 29—*Hearing the Word of the Lord (Acts 19:1-10)*

Wednesday, June 30—*Watch for the Lord's Coming (Matthew 24:36-44)*

Thursday, July 1—*Prepared for the Lord's Coming (Matthew 25:1-13)*

Friday, July 2—*The Coming of the Lord (1 Thessalonians 4:13-18)*

Saturday, July 3—*Blameless at Christ's Coming (1 Thessalonians 5:12-24)*

Sunday, July 4—*Obtaining Salvation in Christ (1 Thessalonians 5:1-11)*

ACCUSTOMED TO DARKNESS

Nighttime satellite images of Earth show that South Korea is bathed in light, with its cities gleaming in the blackness, while North Korea is dark. But it's more than just the lack of visible light. Intellectual and moral darkness also covers the nation of North Korea. The government is one of the most repressive on earth. Radio and television sets are hardwired to receive only government propaganda. In 2004, the government banned cell phones. North Koreans still have no access to the Internet—a source of information readily available in other impoverished countries around the world.

There is another significant contrast: the North is officially atheist—the last remaining "Stalinist" communist society. The South has known Christian influence for more than a century. The technological difference between the two nations illustrates the difference between spiritual darkness and light.

Scripture uses the darkness/light contrast frequently to illuminate the difference between Christian behavior and that which characterizes people in the world. Just as the citizens of North Korea are accustomed to darkness because they have never known modern lighting, many people the world over have lived in spiritual darkness all their lives and do not comprehend how the darkness affects them. Do we Christians show them the benefits of living in the light? —C. R. B.

B. BE FULLY AWAKE (vv. 6, 7)

6, 7. So then, let us not be like others, who are asleep, but let us be alert and self-controlled. For those who sleep, sleep at night, and those who get drunk, get drunk at night.

Here the metaphor of *sleep* is introduced to distinguish different ways of living. Those who love the nightlife and the darkness sometimes appear to experience life more fully. Christians in places like Thessalonica have to watch their words and be careful not to offend the locals. By contrast, those who worship pagan deities or hail Caesar as savior attend all the lively parties, spend money liberally, and rest peacefully under the blankets of influential friendships.

Paul, however, knows that looks can be deceiving. So he asks the Thessalonians to adjust their perspective. Upon closer examination, children of the light can see that their carefree pagan neighbors are still sleeping, still stumbling about in a drunken stupor. Why imitate them? Why long for their slumbering ways? Those who continually walk in their sleep will eventually tumble down the stairs, walk into traffic, or fall into a pit. Believers, on the other hand, are blessed with true wakefulness. They walk with purpose.

Paul sees an important connection between one's thinking about end-times and his or her morality. What one believes about the future that God is bringing has everything to do with how one lives in the present. This has important implications for Christians today. When we see fellow believers stumbling in darkness, we need to engage them in candid conversations about the future. Sometimes we wrongly assume that our brothers and sisters in Christ think clearly about God's future. More often than one might suspect, their minds are clouded with confusion and doubt.

C. BE PROPERLY CLOTHED (v. 8)

8. But since we belong to the day, let us be self-controlled, putting on faith and love as a breastplate, and the hope of salvation as a helmet.

Visual for Lesson 5. *Display this visual throughout the lesson time. At some point ask, "What truth from today's study most inspires you to hope? Why?"*

Paul again reminds the Thessalonians of who they are in Christ. The English is not as clear as it could be expressing what this verse is saying. The believers, or day-dwellers, are encouraged to remain alert, but not by *putting on faith, hope,* and *love;* they already have been clothed in these since the day they accepted Christ. Paul is reminding them of that and stressing that those who bear the spiritual armor of Christ (see Isaiah 59:17; Ephesians 6:14-17) are engaged in a battle that demands their full attention.

Paul frequently discusses this metaphor of being newly clothed in Christ (Romans 13:12-14; Galatians 3:27; Colossians 3:9-14). Doubt and insecurity about one's standing in the final judgment is as unbecoming as wearing the old garments of immorality. Christ has equipped his followers with faith, hope, and love (see 1 Corinthians 13:13; 1 Thessalonians 1:3) so they may make a positive difference in this world. Though *helmets* and *breastplates* primarily served to protect the head and heart, this protection is not simply for defense. It emboldens warriors to move forward confidently into battle.

III. GOD WILL FINISH WHAT HE STARTED
(1 THESSALONIANS 5:9-11, 23, 24)
A. GOD SAVES THROUGH CHRIST (vv. 9, 10)
9, 10. For God did not appoint us to suffer wrath but to receive salvation through our Lord Jesus Christ. He died for us so that, whether we are awake or asleep, we may live together with him.

The Thessalonians desire information about the day of the *Lord,* so Paul shares the most relevant information they could hear about God's *wrath.* It pertains not to *when* but to *whom.* Those who have been clothed in *Christ* look forward to *salvation,* not wrath; to life *with* Christ, not fear of him. In dying *for us* (Isaiah 53:12; Romans 5:6, 8; 1 Corinthians 15:3; 2 Corinthians 5:14; Galatians 1:3, 4; 2:20), Christ exempted us from the wrath to come.

The fact that believers will live with Christ, *whether . . . awake or asleep,* can be confusing. In verses 6 and 7, wakefulness and sleepfulness represent godly and ungodly living. This leads some to surmise that Christ will save us regardless of how we live, as if the only relevant factor is whether God has appointed us or not. Such a position undercuts the force of everything else we have read so far.

To get the context for this statement, one must go back to 4:13-15 and note that one of the questions that vex the Thessalonians is whether or not those who die before Christ comes would share in Christ's salvation. In those earlier verses, *sleep* functions as a metaphor for death. Thus the authors may be suggesting that Christ died for us so that, whether we are still living or whether we die prior to his coming, we will participate in the fullness of salvation he has in store for children of light.

This solution makes good sense in the context of the entire letter. There is a problem with this view, however. The Greek word for *sleep* in verse 10 is not the same as in 4:13-15. Instead, it is the same one Paul used in 5:6, 7, where it refers to immorality. This leads some to suggest that verse 10 is also talking about moral living and not life and death. Paul's point in this case would not be that moral living is optional. Rather, he emphasizes that Christ is in control of our salvation and that those clothed in him have no need to fear.

WHAT DO YOU THINK?

How can your holy armor—your breastplate of faith and love, and your helmet of hope—be evident in your life day by day?

WHAT DO YOU THINK?

Why do some Christians often live in fear instead of hope concerning the return of Christ?

PRAYER

Patient God, we are a curious people. We're curious to know what you, in your wisdom, keep hidden. Teach us the grace of humble ignorance. Teach us to accept the limits of our knowledge and to respect the depths of yours. In Jesus' name we pray. Amen.

WHAT DO YOU THINK?

What are some of the works that you believe God desires to complete in you?

B. BELIEVERS ENCOURAGE ONE ANOTHER (v. 11)

11. Therefore encourage one another and build each other up, just as in fact you are doing.

Paul knows that the Thessalonians must not remain dependent on the repeated affirmation of a traveling evangelist. They are part of a body of believers, all of whom are responsible for encouraging and edifying one another in the faith (see Romans 14:19; 1 Corinthians 14:5, 12, 26). Had they reminded one another of the teaching they originally had received, they may not have needed this pep talk. They must be confident in their standing in Christ and boldly *build each other up* in that faith.

C. GOD FINISHES HIS WORK (vv. 23, 24)

23, 24. May God himself, the God of peace, sanctify you through and through. May your whole spirit, soul and body be kept blameless at the coming of our Lord Jesus Christ. The one who calls you is faithful and he will do it.

Paul first encouraged the believers by reminding them who they are in Christ. Second he challenged them to encourage each other in their shared identity in Christ. As he concludes the letter, he reminds them that their confidence does not rest in the work of diligent humans alone. The entire work of faith is God's work. It is God who has called them to faith, God who has made them new in Christ, God who encourages them through one another, and God who will complete their sanctification—and ours—upon Christ's return. The certainty of Christian identity is not our ability to keep ourselves blameless, but God's faithfulness to continue and complete what he has begun in us.

PRESERVATION

The Springfield, Illinois, area is a center for preserving the memory of Abraham Lincoln. The only home he ever owned is there, as is the old state capitol building where the future president argued cases before the state Supreme Court. Also in Springfield one can find the Lincoln Presidential Library and Museum, which opened in 2005 and where the history of Lincoln's presidential years is brought vividly to life. A high-tech timeline helps the visitor to visualize the ebb-and-flow of the Civil War. An audio-visual exhibit presents the vociferous voices that argued over Lincoln's worth as a president (and even as an individual). Remnants of an earlier, formative stage of his life have been preserved at the New Salem State Historical Site. The village has been restored to a semblance of its appearance during the 1830s. It was there that he became a merchant, surveyor, postmaster, and captain of the local militia.

The point of these memorials is to preserve for coming generations the memory of the man who may have been America's greatest president. God is involved in an even more important act of preservation. Our spirit, soul, and body—our whole being—will be preserved without condemnation as we await God's consummation of the salvation process when Christ returns.   —C. R. B.

CONCLUSION

"When?" is such a tantalizing question. But it is clearly the wrong one. I suspect that my girls are not unique. In fact, my experience with college students is nearly identical. We humans simply prefer to know our limits. We want to know exactly how long we have to do what we want to do before we have to buckle down and do what others require of us.

Yet God would not have us play such games with him. It is dangerous, indeed, to know when Christ will return. We might be tempted to pace ourselves when it comes to discipleship, to wait until the last minute before we "go all out" for Christ. Before then, we might cling to the toys of this world and lose ourselves in our own amusement.

So Scripture discourages questions about timing and replaces them with the challenge of Christian identity. Will we walk in the light of day? Will we encourage our brothers and sisters in the faith? Will we place our confidence in God's faithfulness to finish the work he began in us?

THOUGHT TO REMEMBER

All we need to know is our true identity in Christ.

Discovery Learning

The following is an alternative lesson plan emphasizing learning activities. Classes desiring such student involvement will find these suggestions helpful. At the back of this book are reproducible student pages to further enhance activity learning.

INTO THE LESSON

Blow up two balloons and give each balloon to a student. Tell the group that you're going to play a recording (either music or someone speaking) and that they are to keep passing the balloons to one another until you turn the recording off. (Make sure no one can see you stop the recording.) When the recording stops, the two students who have balloons must squeeze their balloons until one of them pops. Whoever pops his or her balloon first is the "winner."

Repeat the game three or four times, each time with the "winner" of the previous game controlling when the recording is turned off. Ask him or her to observe how people anticipate the balloons' "pop!"

Tell your students that today's lesson is about staying alert and maintaining a sense of expectation for Christ's return, and that the intention of the game was to remind them what it's like to be on the edge of your seat, anticipating the inevitable. Probably very few of your students felt complacent as the balloons were passed around, as each student wondered whether he or she would be one of the people holding a balloon when the music stopped. In a similar way, we must not become complacent as we do the work God has given us to do while we await the Lord's return.

Option: For a quieter opening activity, distribute copies of the reproducible activity "Great Expectations" from page 504 and follow the directions there.

INTO THE WORD

Read 1 Thessalonians 5:1-11, 23, 24 aloud, and ask the students to raise a hand whenever they hear a command. Their sense of attention should be heightened as they wait for the commands. Read slowly to build up a sense of expectation.

Here are the commands: "let us not be . . . asleep" (v. 6a); "let us be alert and self-controlled" (v. 6b); "let us be self-controlled, putting on faith and love . . . and the hope of salvation" (v. 8); "encourage one another" (v. 11); "build each other up" (v. 11).

Split the class into five groups and assign one command per group. Ask each group to describe some practical ways Paul might expect us to live out each of these commands. For example, "let us not be . . . asleep" means we need to be careful not to take the apparent delay of the Lord's return for granted and act as if he's not coming back for a very long time. For "let us be alert and self-controlled," we can foster a sense of expectation in our prayers, asking the Lord what we can do to hasten his return. Again, ask each group to be very specific about what Paul meant when he offered each of these commands.

Read the description of the armor of God in Ephesians 6:10-18, and compare what Paul says there with his "armor admonitions" in verse 8. Ask your students to explain why they think Paul also admonished the Ephesians to be alert and watching (Ephesians 6:18) after describing the armor of God.

End this section by pointing out the contrast of dark and light represented by the false sense of peace and security that the people of the world hold on to (described in vv. 1-5) and the peace of God (described in vv. 23, 24). The world's sense of security is based on God's apparent delay and the ignorance that results from living in the dark. The believer's sense of security is based on God himself, the God of peace. God is faithful, and he will accomplish our deliverance.

INTO LIFE

Paul tells his readers to encourage one another and build each other up. He notes that they are, in fact, doing that. Wrap up today's lesson by having the students do the same thing for one another. Hand students index cards and ask them to put their names at the top of the cards. Then have each of the students pass the card to the person on his or her left.

When everyone has a card in hand, have the students write one encouraging thing about the named person that they have observed. What are some of the biblical commands that they see this person consistently living out on a day-to-day basis? Encourage your students to call attention to the person's spiritual gifts, especially the ways they exercise those spiritual gifts in the congregation. Pass the cards to the left again and have students write more encouragement. Continue passing and writing until the cards get back to the original owners. Most of your students will probably treasure these cards for many years to come.

Distribute copies of "Keep It Up!" from page 504. Have students complete these as time allows.

GLORY TO CHRIST

LESSON 6

INTRODUCTION

A. FINDING INSPIRATION

Our culture loves violent movies. This should not surprise us. These are violent days. Homes, schools, and public venues have suffered a great deal from the devastating effects of violence. What I find more surprising is that many Christians also love violent movies. Though we follow the Prince of Peace, many of us are still captivated by violence's deadly allure. Sure, we long for the day when swords are beaten into plowshares, but until then we are content to entertain ourselves with reenactments of the world's most tragic and gruesome events and portrayals of unspeakable acts of violence dreamed up by Hollywood's most "creative" filmmakers.

I recently asked a good friend for his opinion about why this is so. His response was thought provoking. He suggested that we watch violent movies because tragedy often brings the best out of people. We find inspiration in a heroine's bravery. We admire those who give their all to protect a worthy cause. We may not identify with their particular cause, but we wish to associate with their fierce loyalty. My friend further suggested that violence-filled movies are really the only place in his life where these particular emotions are evoked. They touch a nerve deep within him that Bible lessons, song services, and sermon illustrations simply do not reach.

My point is neither to condemn the church for not engaging every aspect of every person's being nor to promote the watching of violent films. I tend to find them more disturbing than inspiring. My friend made me wonder, however, whether there were actually resources within the Christian faith that might inspire courage and loyalty among God's people. Of course, we do not have to look far because our Scriptures are filled with them. A few examples that come to mind include Daniel and his friends, Jeremiah, Stephen, and our Lord Jesus Christ. But our faith legacy does not end with the narratives of Scripture. Christian tradition is filled with stories of brave believers who gave their all to advance God's kingdom. Their stories are told in collections like Foxe's *Book of Martyrs* and van Braght's *Martyrs Mirror*. Yet persecuted Christians were not perfect. They were sometimes doctrinally confused and needed sensitive pastoral guidance. Such was the case in Thessalonica.

B. LESSON BACKGROUND

Thessalonica was the capital of Macedonia and thus a Roman province of considerable political clout. A Roman proconsul resided there, and strict measures were taken to assure cordial relations with Rome. Loyalty to the emperor was thus of utmost importance, as evident in this city's construction of a temple dedicated to Caesar and coins minted with the images of Caesar Augustus and Julius Caesar, both of whom were considered divine. In such a climate, Thessalonian Christians constantly walked on eggshells. They taught

DEVOTIONAL READING:
1 PETER 5:6-11

BACKGROUND SCRIPTURE:
2 THESSALONIANS 1

PRINTED TEXT:
2 THESSALONIANS 1:3-12

Jul
11

LESSON AIMS

After participating in this lesson, each student will be able to:

1. Tell why Paul thanked God for the Thessalonians and what he prayed for on their behalf.

2. Compare and contrast the Thessalonians' reality of suffering with their future reality of glory.

3. Write a prayer of thanksgiving for his or her church's perseverance.

KEY VERSE

We constantly pray for you, that our God may count you worthy of his calling, and that by his power he may fulfill every good purpose of yours and every act prompted by your faith.
—2 Thessalonians 1:11

DAILY BIBLE READINGS

Monday, July 5—Remain Steadfast in the Faith (1 Peter 5:6-11)

Tuesday, July 6—A Night-long Farewell (Acts 20:7-12)

Wednesday, July 7—Worthy Is the Lamb (Revelation 5:9-14)

Thursday, July 8—The Saved Praise God (Revelation 7:9-17)

Friday, July 9—The Eternal Gospel Is for All (Revelation 14:6-13)

Saturday, July 10—Give God the Glory (Revelation 19:1-8)

Sunday, July 11—Worthy of Christ's Call (2 Thessalonians 1:3-12)

WHAT DO YOU THINK?

If someone were to write a letter to your church thanking God for you, what things might be included in that letter?

about another king and his kingdom, another Lord whom they also deemed divine. It is not surprising, then, that when the Jewish opponents of Paul's preaching had wanted to discredit him before the authorities, they used loyalty to Caesar as the benchmark: "'They are all defying Caesar's decrees, saying that there is another king, one called Jesus.' When they heard this, the crowd and the city officials were thrown into turmoil" (Acts 17:7, 8).

In his previous letter to the Thessalonians, Paul was looking to encourage these believers in their trials and to correct doctrinal confusion, especially pertaining to the coming judgment. Apparently, things had since become worse. In this second letter, Paul addressed these persecutions in a more prominent place, right at the beginning. Likewise, confusion remained concerning the day of the Lord. Apparently an apostle's work is never done, and we continue to find inspiration in this follow-up letter to a persecuted church.

Our target passage, 2 Thessalonians 1:3-12, is a thanksgiving prayer. This is the way Paul often began his letters (see Philippians 1:3-11; Colossians 1:3-14; 1 Thessalonians 1:2-4), yet it was more than a mere formality. In these prayers, Paul often communicated his deep love and respect for the letter's recipients. They also serve to establish the particular aims of the entire letter. So we must not skip past these thanksgivings in an effort to rush to the letter's main concerns. To do so risks missing the crucial context that sets the stage for the teachings within. Divorced from their context, specific verses are often misinterpreted, which contributes to bad doctrine and practice.

In the Greek, verse 3 begins a sentence that does not actually end until verse 10. Keeping this in mind should help us realize that all these thoughts hang together. What begins in thanks for human faith ends in glory to Christ. Here we see that God's glory is not in competition with human effort, though human initiative that is not directed to God's glory can often end in idolatry.

I. FAITH OF THE PERSECUTED (2 THESSALONIANS 1:3, 4)
A. WORTHY OF THANKS (v. 3)
3. We ought always to thank God for you, brothers, and rightly so, because your faith is growing more and more, and the love every one of you has for each other is increasing.

Paul feels obligated to continually *thank God* for the Thessalonian believers. This is not because God commands him to or because someone is somehow checking up on him. He is obligated because God is clearly at work in these *brothers* and sisters. Their *faith* never ceases to grow, and their mutual *love* abounds.

We are thus reminded that God is not simply concerned with our relationship with him. Paul knows that faith in Christ cannot be separated from love for his body, the church. Regular tokens of kindness and love to one another speak volumes of our devotion to God. Distance from God's people, on the other hand, conveys confusion about God's will for our lives.

Conspicuously absent from this thanksgiving, however, is the middle component of the common Pauline triad of "faith, hope, and love." This cluster of core Christian attributes, most associated with 1 Corinthians 13:13, was present both at the beginning and near the end of the first letter (1 Thessalonians 1:3; 5:8; see a list of nine New Testament references to *faith, hope,* and *love* on page 397). Its absence here may be an early indicator that these believers are still somewhat confused about the future God has in store. Their hope is uncertain not because of any deficiency in Christ's work but because they are listening to the wrong people and are thus receiving mixed signals about Christ's coming judgment.

B. WORTHY OF PRIDE (v. 4)

4. Therefore, among God's churches we boast about your perseverance and faith in all the persecutions and trials you are enduring.

Paul is not silent in his thanksgiving for what God is doing among the Thessalonians. He cannot help but tell the story of the Thessalonians' *faith* wherever he goes. First-century *churches* are not formally connected by a denominational structure or creedal statement. They are bound in an indissoluble kinship of shared commitment to Christ. Those who travel from church to church spread the news of the gospel's advance from city to city, and churches thus encourage one another. Paul is especially fond of spreading the news of the Thessalonians' *perseverance* through their *persecutions*. Their faithfulness under fire provides strong evidence that these new believers have truly embraced Jesus as Messiah.

PRAYING FOR THE PERSECUTED

Have you prayed for other Christians lately? No, not just your Christian friends or family, but for Christians who live where it is dangerous to be a Christian? The annual International Day of Prayer for the Persecuted Church is dedicated to encouraging Christians around the world to pray for our brothers and sisters who live where lives and livelihoods are threatened.

In many countries in the world, the government places limits on Christian gatherings. Some countries have laws in place that make it illegal to convert to Christianity. As of 2008, at least seven states in the Hindu nation of India had enacted falsely named "Freedom of Religion" legislation specifically designed to prevent conversion to Christianity. Christians are fallaciously accused of bribing, "alluring," or coercing converts to the faith. Missionaries are accused of conspiring to turn India into an American satellite nation. The government often turns a blind eye to the persecution.

Paul set an example for us in his prayers for the Thessalonian Christians. Just as he did, we should thank God for the faith shown by our persecuted brothers and sisters and for the faithfulness of their testimony. We should also pray for their power to resist the evil forces aligned against them.   —C. R. B.

II. VINDICATION OF THE PERSECUTED (2 THESSALONIANS 1:5-10)

A. RELIEF FOR THE PERSECUTED (vv. 5-7)

5. All this is evidence that God's judgment is right, and as a result you will be counted worthy of the kingdom of God, for which you are suffering.

Paul views persecution quite differently from the way many Christians do today. Those who seldom suffer for their faith typically count it a great privilege to live on friendly turf. The apostle, however, counts it a great honor to suffer for God's *kingdom* and share in Christ's sufferings (see Philippians 3:10, 11). What a privilege that the righteous God of this world would include us in his pain and grant us a share in his reign.

It is important to note, however, that not all *suffering* is honorable. The apostle Peter reminds us that Christians who suffer for wrongdoing are far

WHAT DO YOU THINK?

Have you, or has your church, ever faced persecution? If so, in what ways? If not, why not?

WHAT DO YOU THINK?

What positive results of persecution can you think of?

HOW TO SAY IT

Caesar Augustus. SEE-zer
  Aw-GUS-tus.
Irenaeus. I-ree-NEE-us.
Julius Caesar. JOO-lee-us
  SEE-zer.
Macedonia. Mass-eh-DOE-
  nee-uh.
Messiah. Meh-SIGH-uh.
Polycarp. PAW-lee-carp.
proconsul. pro-CAHN-suhl.
Smyrna. SMUR-nuh.
Thessalonica. THESS-uh-
  lo-NYE-kuh (TH as in
  THIN).

PRAYER

*Our Father in Heaven,
we hesitate to pray out loud
about persecution. To lift
up those who suffer for faith
is to identify with them. It
means confessing that we are
like them and that if only we
were in a similar situation,
then we would do what they
are doing. So we fear, Lord,
that by extolling their faithful
endurance that we may be
inviting you to make us like
them. Forgive us, Lord, for
not truly wanting that and
for wanting, instead, to keep
them at a safe distance. Make
us a people who so desire to
make you known that we welcome the opportunity to suffer
publicly so that your gospel
may be made visible. In Jesus'
name we pray, amen.*

from commendable (1 Peter 4:12-19). Only those who suffer for Christ will share in his blessings. Paul expresses full confidence that this is precisely the kind of suffering being endured in Thessalonica. They are suffering for *the kingdom of God.*

6. God is just: He will pay back trouble to those who trouble you

God is righteous not only to include his suffering faithful ones in his king-dom, but to punish their persecutors. God's people have always affirmed God's just retribution (Deuteronomy 32:35, 36, 43). He keeps tabs on op-pressors and brings judgment on the unrepentant. What we Christians must never do, however, is take such judgment into our own hands. Since God will avenge us, we are free to love our persecutors and overcome their evil with the love of Christ (Romans 12:17-21). Our hope is to turn them from their self-defeating ways, but we are not responsible to ensure their repentance or judge their stubborn resolve. God alone knows their hearts, and we can be sure that he will judge them appropriately at the right time.

7. . . . and give relief to you who are troubled, and to us as well. This will happen when the Lord Jesus is revealed from heaven in blazing fire with his powerful angels.

God's justice is not one-sided. God will not only bring low all oppressors; he will also end all suffering. Paul can sympathize with this need for *relief.* As God's traveling missionary, he encounters new trials and tribulations wher-ever he goes. Having found a way to coexist peacefully in one region, he is beset by a new adversary in the next. In his previous letter to the Thessalo-nians this partnership in suffering received greater attention (2:1, 2; 3:4, 7). It is important for the Thessalonians to know that they are not alone. Many of Christ's followers long to enter God's rest, many are tempted to relax their convictions, and many are waiting patiently for God to finish what he has started in them.

God's relief is not promised, however, in this lifetime. It will not arrive fully until Christ returns to earth with his heavenly host. These *angels* are not merely a heavenly escort for God's Son. In Mark 13:24-27 they assist in the gathering of God's people from the ends of the earth, and in Matthew 13:41, 42 they are agents of God's judgment. Until Christ returns in power, we can-not fully know his peace, and we may also find ourselves called to join those counted worthy to suffer for him.

B. PUNISHMENT FOR THE PERSECUTORS (vv. 8, 9)

8. He will punish those who do not know God and do not obey the gospel of our Lord Jesus.

God's fiery judgment was predicted long ago by the prophets (Isaiah 66:15, 16) and figures prominently in New Testament teaching as well (1 Corinthians 3:13; Hebrews 10:26, 27; Revelation 20:11-15). This verse specifies that it is reserved for two groups of people: *those who do not know God* and those who *do not obey the gospel.* This puts responsibility not only on the persecutors but also the persecuted. Although the persecuted can do little about those who reject the gospel, it is well within their ability to make that gospel known. God has called us to be his witnesses precisely so no one will have to suffer out of ignorance (Romans 10:14, 15).

Paul thanks God for these believers because their suffering is making God known to those who would otherwise burn in ignorance. The Thessalonians have every reason to keep their faith private. Yet their faith in God and love for one another stand as a public testimony to Christ (Matthew 5:14-16). Though perceived as heresy to Jews, as atheism to pagan Greeks, and as threatening to faithful patriots of the Roman regime, it is the only way they can know God and escape his vengeance.

9. They will be punished with everlasting destruction and shut out from the presence of the Lord and from the majesty of his power

In 1 Thessalonians 4:17, Paul assured the believers that Christ's coming means that they will be with him forever. In this second letter he notes the reverse consequence for those who disbelieve. Their destruction is not a temporary setback but an *everlasting* lot (see Mark 9:42-48). Worse than that, they will be permanently separated from the only true *Lord*, Jesus Christ, whose very presence is salvation. They will be barred from his glorious *power*, which far exceeds whatever limited power they may attain in this world.

C. GLORY FOR THE LORD (v. 10)

10. . . . on the day he comes to be glorified in his holy people and to be marveled at among all those who have believed. This includes you, because you believed our testimony to you.

The Lord is not slow to share his glory with those who embrace the gospel. Paul acknowledges these believers as *holy people*. This title does not indicate that God's people are somehow blameless or perfect. Rather, they are set apart by God for salvation, set apart from their old way of life, and set apart from the worldly ways around them. Amidst persecution it is tempting for them to believe that they are set apart only for shame and ridicule. But when Christ returns, they will "appear with him in glory" (Colossians 3:4).

III. PRAYER FOR THE PERSECUTED
(2 THESSALONIANS 1:11, 12)

A. THAT GOD FULFILLS HIS WORK IN US (v. 11)

11. With this in mind, we constantly pray for you, that our God may count you worthy of his calling, and that by his power he may fulfill every good purpose of yours and every act prompted by your faith.

Though Paul has reason to hope in the future glory of the Thessalonian believers, he is nonetheless aware that the race is not finished. He continues to pray for these believers and the powerful work *God* is doing in and through them. Though God has counted them *worthy* to receive his call and to suffer for his call, this does not mean they will automatically remain faithful to that call. Since God is not finished with them, Paul must continue to pray for them.

This also means that God has much more in store for his church. He is pleased for us to surpass previous accomplishments and move faithfully into his future work of faith. He also provides us the *power* we need to accomplish this work. Now is not the time for rest. It is the time to remain alert and stay active so God may finish what he started with us (see 1 Thessalonians 5:6, 7).

B. THAT CHRIST IS GLORIFIED IN US (v. 12)

12. We pray this so that the name of our Lord Jesus may be glorified in you, and you in him, according to the grace of our God and the Lord Jesus Christ.

Though the Thessalonians may not know the specific plans God has for them, all such plans entail *Christ* being *glorified* in them. Christ's glory is

WHAT DO YOU THINK?

Suppose a fellow Christian said, "I love these verses. It's just like I tell my pagan neighbor—'God is going to get you for this!'" How would you respond?

Visual for Lesson 6.
Make a list of missions your class or church supports and develop a plan to pray regularly for the people served by those missions.

the rudder that guides all Christian actions (1 Corinthians 10:31). It is the constant criterion for faithfulness. This is not a task, however, that we may accomplish by our own strength. We are only capable by *the grace of our God*. God calls us to this task and empowers us for it, and he is faithful to see it to completion.

We should not mistake God's overarching involvement in his saving mission for human passivity. Paul prays this prayer precisely in order to encourage the Thessalonians to remain active. Persecution must weigh heavily on these believers. It is one thing to absorb an insult or two or even to suffer unfair prices in the marketplace, but these believers likely have had to watch their loved ones suffer as well. Parents watched their children suffer exclusion. Spouses watched their mates endure public shame and disrespect. Paul therefore knows that he needs to pray for these believers and to remind them of their faithfulness up until this point. Without the power of prayer and memory of God's previous provision, they might easily succumb to temptation, and so might we.

WHAT DO YOU THINK?

What are some of the ways that God is being glorified in our lives and in our church?

MARTYRDOM—A WORTHY CALLING

Polycarp is the author of some of the earliest postapostolic Christian writings. He apparently was acquainted with the apostle John and was thus a bridge between the end of the apostolic age of the church and that which followed. Irenaeus, Polycarp's most famous pupil, wrote that he heard his teacher speak of his discussions with John and others who had seen Jesus and that Polycarp had been converted to Christ through the testimony of the apostles. His life came to an end during one of the extensive persecutions of Christianity by the Roman government in the middle of the second century. The Roman proconsul told Polycarp he could save his life merely by renouncing Jesus. Polycarp's famous words were, "For 86 years I have served him and He has never wronged me. How can I renounce the King who has saved me?" He was burned at the stake in Smyrna, where he had led the church for years.

The early church—from Stephen onward—bravely faced death for its faith. It is a theme that runs through the New Testament and was acted out in the lives of countless Christians who were crucified, beheaded, or burned for their faith in Christ. Our self-centered age thinks of such willingness to suffer as a quaint relic of the past, but Paul calls it a worthy calling. What will be the verdict of history on our generation of Christians?

—C. R. B.

CONCLUSION

The believers in Thessalonica had a particular calling: to glorify Christ by suffering for him. Paul gives thanks to God because these believers have previously risen to this task. Yet past performance is no guarantee of future success. So he encourages these Christians by affirming their flagging hope and lifting them before God in prayer.

Our calling will look different in some ways, but in others it will be the same. We, too, have been called to glorify Christ to the point of suffering, over against the arrogant taunting of today's power brokers and idol worshipers. We too must remember that the momentum of our past faithfulness is not enough to carry us into the uncertain future. Each day we must choose anew to glorify Christ with our life, since each day we are tempted to glorify ourselves or seek to secure our identity by our own strength. We need to encourage one another by telling the stories of Christians who have remained and continue to remain faithful in the midst of tribulation. We need to lift one another up in prayer and beseech our God to finish the work he has begun in us.

Christians need not consult Hollywood to be inspired by radical devotion and fierce loyalty. We need to stay attuned to the testimony of God's faithful witnesses.

THOUGHT TO REMEMBER
Thank God for his persecuted followers.

Discovery Learning

The following is an alternative lesson plan emphasizing learning activities.
Classes desiring such student involvement will find these suggestions helpful. At the
back of this book are reproducible student pages to further enhance activity learning.

INTO THE LESSON

Provide everyone with a piece of graph paper and a pencil. Ask your students to create a "life graph," an up-and-down line that marks the mountain peaks and valleys of their lives so far. Have them go as far back as they can remember, and mark the milestones in their lives. Have the students recall what God taught them during each peak and valley. (They might discover that they learned more from the valleys than during the good times.) Encourage your students also to identify key people who provided support and those who stirred up difficulty for them.

In today's passage Paul comments on how his readers have increased in their faith and in their love for one another. Use this graph as an opportunity for your students to mark their spiritual growth.

Option: Use the reproducible activity "Growing in the Dark" from page 505 to introduce today's lesson.

INTO THE WORD

Read 2 Thessalonians 1:3-12 out loud, and ask your students to make another graph as you read. When Paul mentions something growth-oriented, like growing faith or increasing love, have the students mark their graphs upward. When Paul mentions something like persecutions or trials, have them draw their graphs downward. When Paul promises vindication by God, have the lines go upward; when he speaks of being troubled, have the lines go down.

Use the questions below to discuss how the promise of vindication, given over and over in this passage, was supposed to help the Thessalonians persevere. They were still struggling with some doctrinal confusion, especially about the return of Christ, but the persecutions seem to have increased.

1. Why did Paul expect the Thessalonians' faith to increase while they were being persecuted? Wouldn't one expect doubts to increase instead? Explain.

2. Why do you think Paul kept promising the Thessalonians that someday God would vindicate them and punish their persecutors? How would knowing this help them to persevere during times of hardship?

3. Why is it easier to forgive someone when you know that God will have the final word in regard to any injustice that a believer experiences?

4. What specific things does Paul pray about concerning the Thessalonians? (*Answers include that God would count them worthy of this calling, that by God's power he would fulfill every good purpose for them, that by God's power he would fulfill every act prompted by faith, that God would be glorified through their lives.*)

5. What does it mean for God to be glorified through the life of a believer?

INTO LIFE

Say, "Since Paul is praying for the Thessalonians in this passage, let's imitate his actions and make our own prayer lists, using Paul's criteria." First, ask each student to think of a person who is going through a difficult time and write that person's name on the top of a sheet of paper. Then ask your students the following questions, and have them write their answers (privately) on their papers. These questions follow those offered by Paul in today's passage:

1. What are three things, in regard to this person, that motivates you to thank God for him or her?

2. How have you observed this person's faith grow and love increase, even during this time of difficulty?

3. How has this person experienced suffering, especially in regard to his or her faith?

4. Who is causing trouble in this person's life?

5. How would knowing that God will vindicate him or her help this person to persevere?

6. How is God bringing relief to this person?

7. What are some ways that the coming of Christ will bring this person joy?

8. What will this person marvel at when he or she finally sees Christ?

9. What kinds of acts are consistently prompted by this person's faith?

10. How do you see God being glorified in this person's life, even during times of tribulation?

Option: For a different application activity, distribute copies of the reproducible activity "A Greater Purpose" from page 505. If students cannot identify people and issues relevant to any of the seven statements, encourage them to pray that they can participate in these ways in the future.

Close the class in prayer, giving each student enough time to pray through these issues.

CHOSEN AND CALLED

LESSON 7

INTRODUCTION

A. FALSE ALARM

In August of 2008 alarms sounded in 20 government offices in Japan. Red lights flashed, and the central government's Fire and Disaster Management Agency broadcast a dire message: "This is information about a ballistic missile attack." The Japanese people had not forgotten that North Korea had fired test missiles over their island nation in 1998 and then again in 2006. They remained concerned about the Communist nation's intentions.

It turned out to be only a test, but a switch had been left on so the "emergency" message was mistakenly broadcast to the government offices. There was no ballistic missile attack; it was a false alarm.

As it turned out in Japan, the Fire and Disaster Management Agency was able to send a second message immediately so that no action was taken in response to the false alarm. But we've all heard of police and firefighters dispatched to emergencies that did not exist, rescuers searching for children who weren't lost, and families upset and worried over reports that turned out to be untrue. A false alarm can create panic and confusion; it must be exposed as false as quickly as possible.

B. LESSON BACKGROUND

An alarm was sounded in Thessalonica. A letter or some other communication had been received, supposedly from the apostle Paul. It said the day of the Lord had already arrived (2 Thessalonians 2:2). The believers there were panicked. Had they missed it? Would they be caught in the destruction of the wicked? Was the persecution they were facing a part of God's judgment? Had God left them to suffer for their sin instead of redeeming them?

Paul wrote to address this issue and to quell the panic. The Lord had not returned. In a nutshell, Paul said the fact that they faced persecution by the wicked was proof of that, for when Christ returns he will "overthrow" and "destroy" the evil one (v. 8). If the Lord had returned, evil would have been vanquished by now!

Most interpreters take this passage to refer to a rebellion in the far-off future (at least from Paul's perspective). Some impressive figure will arise and lead a rebellion against God. Things will get worse and worse until Christ returns and leads in a great cosmic battle against this "antichrist," resulting in the Lord's eventual victory. Depending on one's millennial view, this will either usher in the 1000-year reign of the Lord or bring it to a close.

Many of the Reformers thought this figure was the pope (or the papacy in general). Since then, others have been identified with this great evil one, including Adolf Hitler, Ronald Reagan, and Barack Obama!

DEVOTIONAL READING:
PSALM 33:4-12
BACKGROUND SCRIPTURE:
2 THESSALONIANS 2
PRINTED TEXT:
2 THESSALONIANS 2:7-17

LESSON AIMS

After participating in this lesson, each student will be able to:

1. List three things that Paul expected the Thessalonians to know about the end times.

2. Compare and contrast the confusion of the Thessalonians regarding the end times with modern-day confusion on the subject.

3. Write a note of encouragement to a fellow believer that uses one or more of Paul's observations.

Jul 18

KEY VERSE

So then, brothers, stand firm and hold to the teachings we passed on to you, whether by word of mouth or by letter.
—2 Thessalonians 2:15

Lesson 7 Notes

While Paul assured the Thessalonians that the day of the Lord had not come, he did not suggest it could not come for many more years. Paul taught that "the Lord is near" (Philippians 4:5). Paul's teaching allows for an imminent return of Christ, so nothing he says here can be expected to mean Christ cannot return until the rise of some religious or political figure as much as 20 centuries later.

When Paul writes of a "rebellion" (v. 3), he uses a term that Jewish writers before him have used of the Jewish people's turning from the truth. Paul's experience in Thessalonica, when Jewish leaders rejected his message and forced him out of town (Acts 17:5-9), might be on his mind. It would surely come to the mind of his readers. Paul elsewhere expresses great concern for the failure of Israel to accept her Messiah (cf. Romans 9–11). So it does not have to be a future event that he has in mind in this passage. The rebellion is in progress, but the evil one behind it has yet to be revealed, or exposed. He is at work, but his identity remains a secret to most.

I. END OF THE WICKED (2 THESSALONIANS 2:7-12)

A. Dark Mystery Exposed (vv. 7-9)

7. For the secret power of lawlessness is already at work; but the one who now holds it back will continue to do so till he is taken out of the way.

Usually Paul uses the word *mystery* (here translated *secret power*) to refer to God's purpose as revealed in the gospel (Romans 16:25; Ephesians 1:9; 3:3-9; 5:32; 6:19; Colossians 1:26, 27; 2:2; 4:3; 1 Timothy 3:16). The world did not recognize that until God revealed it by apostolic preaching. And the world does not recognize the work of the lawless one until God reveals or exposes that. Even so, it is *already at work*.

A question arises about the identity of *the one who now holds it back*. It seems that some person or force is restraining this lawless one, but for some reason will cease to do so at some future time. This sounds confusing, and even more so if we understand that the Greek word used here almost never means "restrain" or "hold back" unless it is used with an object. Since there is no object used here, we want to know what is the more ordinary meaning of this term in such cases. Without an object, this word more usually means to "prevail." That sounds less confusing. This lawless one is at work behind the scenes, unknown to most. And he will continue to prevail until he is exposed and *taken out* of the picture. The persecuted Thessalonians know this lawless one is prevailing. They look forward to the time when he is exposed!

The verb for "holds back" is the same one used in verse 6. In each case it is used as an intransitive verb (that is, it has no object), so we expect the meaning in each case to be that of "prevail." What is different in these two verses is that the subject is neuter in verse 6 ("what") and masculine ("he") in verse 7. This subtle change indicates that Paul can speak of this prevailing evil either as an impersonal force (v. 6 and carried over into v. 7 as "secret power") or as a person (v. 7 and later in the passage; compare also v. 3, "man of *lawlessness*"). The evil that prevails is the work of the evil one who prevails. But neither will prevail forever.

8. And then the lawless one will be revealed, whom the Lord Jesus will overthrow with the breath of his mouth and destroy by the splendor of his coming.

How to Say It

antichrist. AN-tee-christ.
Barack Obama. Buh-ROCK O-BAH-muh.
Clodovaeus. Kluh-DOE-vee-us.
Ludovicus. Luh-DOE-vih-kus.
Messiah. Meh-SIGH-uh.
millennial. muh-LEN-ee-uhl.
papacy. PAY-puh-see.
Pas-de-Calais. Pah'd-cuh-LAY.
Pharisees. FAIR-ih-seez.
Thessalonica. THESS-uh-lo-NYE-kuh (TH as in THIN).

There will come a time when *the lawless one* will be exposed. It will be climactic and sudden. At the Lord's return this pretentious imposter will be destroyed. There will be no siege, no long battle. As Jesus calmed the storm with a rebuke of his mouth, so the evil one will be conquered in an instant. If the power of evil is still at work in the world, then the Lord's *coming* has not happened yet!

9. *The coming of the lawless one will be in accordance with the work of Satan displayed in all kinds of counterfeit miracles, signs and wonders,*

Paul uses a play on words here. The word for *coming* in this verse is the same as the one in the previous verse. This term's focus is not only on the act of coming but also its result, the presence of the one who comes. The coming (presence) of Christ will completely destroy the coming (presence) of the evil one.

The presence or influence of this evil one is *in accordance with the work of Satan*. That is, it is Satan's influence at work. In fact, Paul probably intends us to understand that this *lawless one* is in fact Satan. Paul has used terms such as "man of lawlessness" (v. 3), "secret power of lawlessness" (v. 7), and "lawless one" (v. 8) to show that there is a secret power at work. When he exposes that power in verse 9, we see it is none other than Satan himself behind it all. Attempts at identifying some human "man of lawlessness" are unnecessary. Satan is our adversary. He is a great deceiver, so most people do not recognize his work in the world. But in the end he will be exposed and disposed of.

IDENTIFYING THE LAWLESS ONE

Christians have long speculated about the identity of the "man of lawlessness" or "lawless one" that Paul mentions. Many believe he is one of the beasts mentioned in Revelation 13, the one whose "number is 666" (Revelation 13:18).

Among the more imaginative approaches used many times in Christian history has been that which substitutes numerical equivalents for the letters in the names of various world leaders. One such attempt named Clodovaeus, supposed to be the first French king to submit to papal power, as the wicked one. The theory is that he was also known as Ludovicus (which is better for "proving" this theory). Using Roman numeral equivalents—where they exist—for the letters in Ludovicus's name, see what develops: L=50, U[V]=5, D=500, O=0, V=5, I=1, C=100, U[V]=5, S=0. The total when added is 666.

Other theories do the same thing with the title of the Roman Catholic popes and secular world leaders at various times in history. A Bible college student had a bit of fun with the idea and used the same process to "prove" that the children's cartoon character Barney the Purple Dinosaur is the lawless one!

The point is that the apostle Paul's purpose is not to offer an end-times theory or identify a character who will oppose God in those days. Rather, he assures us that the Lord will see his plan for saving and securing his chosen ones come to completion, regardless of who may oppose him.   —C. R. B.

B. CONSEQUENCES OF UNBELIEF (vv. 10-12)

10. . . . *and in every sort of evil that deceives those who are perishing. They perish because they refused to love the truth and so be saved.*

Paul continues to describe the activities of the wicked one. Deceit is his major weapon. Those who believe his lies instead of *the truth* are described

---

WHAT DO YOU THINK?
How does the promise in verse 8 encourage you?

DAILY BIBLE READINGS

Monday, July 12—Chosen as God's Heritage (Psalm 33:4-12)

Tuesday, July 13—The Confidence of Hope (Hebrews 3:1-6)

Wednesday, July 14—Called to Liberty (Galatians 5:7-14)

Thursday, July 15—Called to God's Purpose (2 Timothy 2:8-13)

Friday, July 16—Finishing the Course (Acts 20:17-24)

Saturday, July 17—The Danger of Deception (2 Thessalonians 2:1-12)

Sunday, July 18—Stand Firm, Hold Fast (2 Thessalonians 2:13-17)

WHAT DO YOU THINK?

What can a Christian do to be assured that he or she will not be deceived?

as those who *perish*. It is a present tense rather than future. They are already under God's judgment for rejecting the truth. Had they accepted it, they would have been *saved*, but they deliberately follow the deceiver. Satan's activity and deceit do not cancel human responsibility.

DECEIVING THE ENEMY

Operation Fortitude was one of the most important events in World War II. As Allied forces were preparing to retake the European mainland, it was obvious that a straightforward assault would fail. In a classic example of what we now call *disinformation,* a scheme using false radio "chatter" made it seem as if a huge invasionary force was preparing for the landing at Pas-de-Calais (at the shortest distance across the English Channel). A large book eight inches thick scripted the radio activity in detail with cues for time and date. Visual authentication came in the form of inflatable rubber tanks and "practice beach landings" across the Channel from Pas-de-Calais. The dummy tanks were moved to new locations at night and a single tank made tracks to complete the subterfuge. False information about troop movements was printed in British newspapers. Hitler swallowed the trickery "hook, line, and sinker." He moved his troops away from Normandy Beach, where the successful landing on June 6, 1944, became a turning point in the war.

A battle of far greater significance is yet to come. God will use the human inclination to forsake the truth and trust in lies as a means of accomplishing his victory over the forces of Satan. We who have made a practice of trusting in the truth of the gospel will have nothing to fear in that day.   —C. R. B.

11, 12. *For this reason God sends them a powerful delusion so that they will believe the lie and so that all will be condemned who have not believed the truth but have delighted in wickedness.*

These verses trouble some Bible students. The idea that God causes these people to *believe* a *lie* seems to be a contradiction of the nature of God as a God of truth. But there are at least two ways to view this that do not make God the author of a lie.

First, we may take it as hyperbole. Luke 14:26 says, "If anyone comes to me and does not hate his father and mother, his wife and children, . . . he cannot be my disciple." We do not expect disciples literally to hate their families in order to follow Christ. Instead, we understand this to be hyperbole. The text here is hyperbole as well. Its message is that God is still sovereign in spite of Satan's activity. Satan is not deceiving people without God's knowledge; God has not become distracted while Satan steals his sheep. Nothing happens in the world without God's knowledge and, to some degree, his permission. So God allows—*sends,* if you please—a *delusion* so that the unbelievers are deceived. In the book of Job, we know that Satan afflicts Job, but only with God's permission. In Job 1:12, God grants Satan permission to test Job. But after that test, in Job 2:3, God says Satan incited him (that is, God) against Job, "to ruin him without any reason." God speaks of what he allowed in such a way that we would think he was the cause if we had no other context. That may well be the case here as well.

Another way to understand this is that it declares God's judgment. In verse 10 we see this happens because these perishing ones "refused to love the truth." They have already made up their minds, and they have rejected *the truth*. They have, in fact, chosen to be deceived. So when Paul says God

PRAYER

Heavenly Father, thank you for the promise of our Lord's imminent return. We sometimes grow anxious for his return. But we trust you and know that you are in control. When we suffer, may we bring you glory with perseverance. When we have rest, may we thank you for your gifts. And when he returns, may we find the realization of your promises even more wonderful than we have imagined them to be. In Jesus' name we pray, amen.

sends them a delusion, he is using the same kind of language as he uses in Romans 1. There he says of the ones who deliberately rejected the truth God "gave them over" (vv. 24, 26, 28). They have made their choice, and God passes judgment.

WHAT DO YOU THINK?

How might Christians be deluded so that they believe a lie?

II. COMFORT TO THE CHOSEN (2 THESSALONIANS 2:13-17)

A. SALVATION THROUGH SANCTIFICATION (vv. 13, 14)

13. But we ought always to thank God for you, brothers loved by the Lord, because from the beginning God chose you to be saved through the sanctifying work of the Spirit and through belief in the truth.

Here Paul makes a dramatic shift from the work of Satan and those who are deceived by him to the believers. Paul is confident that his friends in Thessalonica are not among the deceived. By their response to the gospel they are among the chosen. This verse has been used to support the idea that God chooses certain ones for salvation without regard to their response—that, in fact, he has chosen them from before time. But the context of the passage as a whole does not square with that understanding. Indeed, if their election is guaranteed by God's choice alone and not their response, what is the point of telling them to "stand firm" in verse 15?

Instead, we understand God's calling to be conditional. God's plan *from the beginning* was to send Christ to defeat Satan and his deceptive work. As early as Genesis 3:15 God announces this plan. Revelation 13:8 speaks of the "Lamb that was slain from the creation of the world." God chose from that time that all who believe *the truth* and turn to Jesus will be *saved* and sanctified by his Holy *Spirit*.

14. He called you to this through our gospel, that you might share in the glory of our Lord Jesus Christ.

The instrument to call people to faith is the preaching of the *gospel*. As Paul writes in Romans 10:13, 14, "'Everyone who calls on the name of the Lord will be saved.' How, then, can they call on the one they have not believed in? And how can they believe in the one of whom they have not heard? And how can they hear without someone preaching to them?"

WHAT DO YOU THINK?

Paul mentions some important facts about our salvation in this text. Which ones stand out to you or give you the most comfort? Why?

The purpose of this call is, in this context, *the glory* to be shared by the faithful when they are gathered to the *Lord Jesus Christ* at his return. If the Thessalonians are worried that they have missed out on this, Paul assures them that the promise is still theirs. They need to stand firm and to resist the temptation to quit. The persecution they face is nothing compared with the glory they will share (Romans 8:18).

B. ENDURANCE THROUGH SOUND TEACHING (v. 15)

15. So then, brothers, stand firm and hold to the teachings we passed on to you, whether by word of mouth or by letter.

What was implied in the previous verse is now stated explicitly. The disciples in Thessalonica need to *stand firm*. They need to persevere. They can do this, in part, by being careful to observe what they have been taught. The word *teachings* here refers to something *passed on* from one to another, particularly *by word of mouth*. Printed Bibles are not available in Paul's day (and most of the New Testament has not even been written yet), so they cannot look things up as we do. They have to be careful to recall what Paul and other faithful teachers told them when they were present (compare v. 5). They also

Visual for Lessons 7 & 9. *Display this visual as you discuss verse 15. Ask, "What traditions and teachings most help you to hold fast to your faith?"*

WHAT DO YOU THINK?

Many Christian leaders lament the high level of "biblical illiteracy" in the church today. Why do you think Bible knowledge is as low as it is? How can it be increased?

have Paul's first *letter* to which they can refer. It deals with some of the same matters they are concerned about now. Of course, by the time they read this, they have the second letter as well!

The admonition to hold fast to the teachings they have received addresses the problem of listening to the wrong people. The language imitates that of verse 2, where Paul says he wants them not to be alarmed by "report or *letter*" about the second coming. Now he tells them to hold fast to what they have been taught, by word, or our epistle. The different translation, "report" in verse 2 and "word of mouth" here, mutes Paul's similarity of expression somewhat; in the Greek the words are the same. Any word or letter that contradicts the word and letter they have from Paul is false! The same is true today. Any teacher who has a message that contradicts what we have in the Bible must be rejected as a false teacher.

C. HOPE THROUGH GRACE (vv. 16, 17)

16, 17. May our Lord Jesus Christ himself and God our Father, who loved us and by his grace gave us eternal encouragement and good hope, encourage your hearts and strengthen you in every good deed and word.

Paul closes this section with a prayer, which he will follow with a request that the Thessalonians pray for him (3:1). They are in this together; they need mutual support, both in fellowship and in prayers. His prayer is rooted in the love of *God*. Paul can pray this with confidence because he knows it is the Father's will to respond. In fact, God has already given much of what the prayer asks for. Paul prays for encouragement; God has already given *encouragement*.

God has also given them *hope*, something that has not been apparent in the Thessalonians' experience. They have allowed false reports to cloud and blur their hope. But if they understand God's *grace*, they will realize they have great hope of the kind that does not disappoint (Romans 5:5).

Finally Paul prays that they will bear fruit. God's grace in their lives should find expression, both in what they say and in what they do. There is no conflict between grace and work (deeds) in Paul's teaching. The former leads naturally to the latter. If the believers in Thessalonica and in our churches today understand the role of God's grace in their lives, then *good* deeds and words will follow naturally.

WHAT DO YOU THINK?

How has the Lord given you encouragement and hope?

CONCLUSION

On November 3, 1948, people in Chicago picked up their morning edition of the *Chicago Daily Tribune* and read in the headline the results of the previous day's Presidential election: "Dewey Defeats Truman." It was a reliable source; it was the expected outcome of the election; but it was false.

Apparently some in Thessalonica had read a letter or had other information supposedly from a reliable source (2 Thessalonians 2:2). But that information was also wrong. It alleged that the return of Christ had already occurred. But that was wrong.

Today many will claim to have insight into the Lord's return. They will set dates. They will identify world leaders or political candidates with the antichrist. They will write books and fill columns on their blogs. But don't believe everything you read!

There is one source of reliable information. Return to the Scripture and see what God has to say through his inspired writers. Then hold firmly to what you've been taught. By the grace of God, and until the Lord does return, be diligent in every good deed and word.

THOUGHT TO REMEMBER

Until the Lord returns, be diligent in every good deed and word.

Discovery Learning

The following is an alternative lesson plan emphasizing learning activities. Classes desiring such student involvement will find these suggestions helpful. At the back of this book are reproducible student pages to further enhance activity learning.

INTO THE LESSON

Ask for volunteers to come to the front of the class and offer three apparently little known facts or stories about themselves. However, one of the three facts or stories needs to be false but not unbelievable.

After each person has given his or her "set of three," give the class a few minutes to think about which one was false. Have them write their decisions down, and then ask for volunteers to offer their opinions on which fact or story was false. Ask them to go into detail as to why they think the person was fibbing . . . because he shifted his eyes or she became fidgety, etc.

Say, "In today's passage, Paul talks about how Satan uses what is counterfeit to distract people from the truth. So we need to be careful to separate the false from the true when we hear others discussing the Word of God. Even though a teaching may contain a nugget of truth, we need to be on our guard against those who try to slip something false by us."

INTO THE WORD

The Thessalonians had been misled by teachers whose corrupting doctrines contained nuggets of truth but did not present the entire Word of God. Paul's readers had been confused by these teachers, so Paul wanted to set these believers straight about the true motivations of these false teachers.

Distribute copies of the reproducible activity "Stark Contrast" from page 506 and ask your students to follow the directions given. Here are some possible answers for the left-hand columns: v. 7: lawless (*immoral, boundary violators, unethical*); v. 10: "those who are perishing" (*self-destructive, falling further and further away from God*);

v. 11: under a "delusion" (*fooled, blind, duped, gullible*); v. 12: "condemned" (*guilty, tainted, unrepentant*); v. 12: "have not believed the truth" (*faithless, skeptical, sarcastic, filled with contempt*); v. 12: "delighted in wickedness" (*warped, taking pleasure in perversion*).

Here are some possible answers for the right-hand columns: v. 13: "loved by the Lord" (*treasured by God*); v. 13: chosen by God (*objects of grace*); v. 13: "saved" (*delivered from wickedness, sealed by the Holy Spirit*); v. 13: believers "in the truth" (*full of faith, ready to obey*); v. 14: "called" (*lives full of significance and purpose*); v. 14: sharing in Christ's "glory" (*looking forward to the reward, praise for their perseverance*); v. 15: "stand firm" (*unwavering in the faith, able to hold one's position*); v. 16: given "eternal encouragement" (*motivated, refusing to be held back*); v. 17: "strengthen you" (*having the power to complete the tasks God has given them*).

INTO LIFE

Bring in enough newspapers for each student to have at least 10 pages of news. Tell them they are going on a "nuggets of truth" hunt. They'll be looking for news stories or gossip about celebrities that contain something that is true, but presents a nonbiblical worldview in a very persuasive way.

Examples: (1) A story of a famous couple who keeps adopting children, even though they are not married. Why don't they marry? They want to keep their options open, while remaining "role models" for adopting parents. (2) An ad for condoms encourages men not to be "pigs" by refusing to use one during sex, but seems to imply that promiscuous sex is OK as long as one uses "protection." (3) A young female celebrity, in and out of rehab, seems to have stabilized after finding a "girlfriend," implying that "love," even between homosexuals, is all that really matters in the world.

When you've completed this exercise, switch gears and focus on some positive role models in your students' circle of influence. Describe the following "four acts of internalization," and ask your students to identify one person they know who exemplifies the particular trait.

1. This person takes responsibility for his or her sin and refuses to blame others.

2. This person takes responsibility for nonsinful mistakes and learns something from each of them.

3. This person recognizes his or her gifts and is confident in the talents and abilities given to him or her by God.

4. This person is careful and diligent to use his or her gifts to advance the kingdom of God.

Distribute copies of "I Thank God for You" from page 506. Give students a few minutes to complete the activity. Then close the class in prayer, asking God for discernment to tell truth from falsehood.

GOD'S OWN FAITHFULNESS

LESSON 8

INTRODUCTION

A. TO EACH HIS OWN

In many passages, Jesus warns his followers not to judge other people. The most famous of such passages is his somewhat humorous rebuke of the critic who seeks to remove a speck of dust from someone's eye while the critic himself has a log in his own eye. That is enough to convince many Christians not to meddle in others' affairs—after all, no one is perfect. If one combines this with Jesus' warning that each believer will be judged with the same judgment by which he or she has judged others (Matthew 7:2), then an entirely hands-off approach to others' sin seems justified.

This logic seems right, but it's wrong because it leaves others in their sin (Jude 23). It is wrong because it ignores Jesus' teaching about confronting those who sin (Matthew 18:15-20). It is wrong because sins are contagious and can spread to infect the whole church (1 Corinthians 5:6, 7). It is wrong because it allows people to dishonor Christ's name before nonbelievers. It is wrong, finally, because it takes a few verses out of context in order to avoid what is arguably one of the most awkward tasks that Scripture commands us to carry out—that of lovingly confronting a sinning brother or sister.

In Matthew 18:15-20 Jesus sets forth a process for dealing with sin in a fellow believer's life. After studying this passage, it is helpful to see examples of the process in action. A common place to turn for this is 1 Corinthians 5:9-13. Less commonly cited, but nonetheless instructive, is 1 Thessalonians 3.

B. LESSON BACKGROUND

In the first two chapters, Paul affirmed the Thessalonians' endurance under persecution and corrected their confusion about the Day of the Lord. In this last chapter, he addresses a specific problem that likely resulted from this confusion. Some insiders had convinced many believers in Thessalonica that the persecutions they suffered were signs that the Day of the Lord had begun. This announcement could have influenced people in many ways. It could have produced panic among those who feared being firsthand participants in the intense suffering they expected to accompany the last days. It could have paralyzed others, who would not have known what to expect or how to handle whatever may come their way. It could have excited still others, who would leave behind the responsibilities and routines of everyday life to fully engage the challenges ahead.

DEVOTIONAL READING:
PSALM 89:1-8

BACKGROUND SCRIPTURE:
2 THESSALONIANS 3

PRINTED TEXT:
2 THESSALONIANS 3:1-15

LESSON AIMS

After this lesson each student will be able to:

1. Summarize Paul's warnings on idleness.

2. Predict some results of unchecked idleness, as Paul uses that concept, in his or her church.

3. Plan an event that encourages 100 percent participation in ministry so that idleness is not found among the church members.

Jul
25

KEY VERSE

The Lord is faithful, and he will strengthen and protect you from the evil one.
—2 Thessalonians 3:3

It is difficult to know how exactly the Thessalonians responded and exactly what problems elicited the practical advice that Paul gave in 2 Thessalonians 3. There we see him engage this community in prayer, lifestyle mentoring, and basic advice for admonishing believers whose confusion had become a burden to the church and a detriment to their witness. He therefore furnished helpful guidelines for churches of all eras that struggle with internal and external strife.

I. EVIL OUTSIDE (2 THESSALONIANS 3:1-5)

A. PRAYER FOR THE EVANGELISTS (VV. 1, 2)

1, 2. Finally, brothers, pray for us that the message of the Lord may spread rapidly and be honored, just as it was with you. And pray that we may be delivered from wicked and evil men, for not everyone has faith.

Paul does not think he is superior to the Thessalonian believers. He and his companions (Silas and Timothy; see 1:1) are coworkers with these churches, who depend daily on their prayers and aren't too proud to ask. It is tempting for leaders to think more highly of themselves than they ought. It is tempting to think that since they are the ones who pray for others, then asking for prayer would express weakness. Paul likely would agree that it expresses weakness, but he does not believe human weakness should be hidden. It is precisely through human weakness, he says, that God's greatness is made known (2 Corinthians 12:9, 10).

We learn much from how this prayer request begins. Paul first asks that the believers *pray* for the gospel's advance. Though he has personal needs that he later shares, he begins by focusing on the cause of Christ. This order echoes Jesus' example in the Lord's Model Prayer. He instructs us to pray first that God's kingdom come and his will be done before asking that God provide for our daily needs and protect us from *evil* (Matthew 6:9-13).

Note also the source of human wickedness: it is not simply a matter of upbringing and poor life choices. It flows from lack of *faith*. Believers must accept the reality that not all men possess faith and so not all will accept Christ. It is this resistance to the Spirit's work that makes them so dangerous. To properly identify this cause is to look in the right direction for a solution. Paul is dedicated to proclaiming the Lord's Word so that people may come to faith and leave their *wicked* ways behind.

B. PRAYER FOR THE EVANGELIZED (VV. 3-5)

3. But the Lord is faithful, and he will strengthen and protect you from the evil one.

In stark contrast to "wicked and evil men" (v. 2, above), *the Lord is faithful*. Though Paul acknowledges his vulnerability to wicked schemes, he refuses to linger there. He refuses to sulk about specific harms suffered or specific men who cause him pain. Instead, he directs our focus to the Lord's faithfulness. Human wickedness must never be the last or even loudest word. We must not give it more exposure than it deserves. Though faithless people would rob us of stamina and standing, our faithful Lord strengthens and protects us.

Paul offers similar words of encouragement in 1 Corinthians 10:13: "No temptation has seized you except what is common to man. And God is faithful; he will not let you be tempted beyond what you can bear. But when you are tempted, he will also provide a way out so that you can stand up under

WHAT DO YOU THINK?

What are some specific areas for prayer for your church leaders?

WHAT DO YOU THINK?

How has the Lord demonstrated his faithfulness to you? How does this affect your life?

it." Paul has no desire to ignore the reality of evil and the schemes of *the evil one* (2 Thessalonians 2:9), but believers must remain confident that God's faithfulness is of such superior power that our victory is guaranteed as long as we remain in him (see 1 Thessalonians 5:24).

4. We have confidence in the Lord that you are doing and will continue to do the things we command.

In this verse, Paul begins switching gears. He expresses *confidence* in God's work in the Thessalonian church, but he draws on this confidence to issue a *command*. It is uncommon, but not unheard of, for the apostle Paul to issue commands to churches. He prefers gentle exhortation. The fact that he is preparing them for a command indicates that something critical is at stake.

5. May the Lord direct your hearts into God's love and Christ's perseverance.

Before issuing this command, Paul pauses to lift these believers before *the Lord* in prayer. He asks God to *direct* their *hearts* in a twofold manner patterned after God himself. This text has been translated in two ways. The *King James Version* places the emphasis on the believers' action and encourages them to love God and patiently wait for Christ: "direct your hearts into the love of God, and into the patient waiting for Christ." But the grammatical structure here can also emphasize God's example and represent a command to direct their hearts to *God's love* and *Christ's perseverance,* as in our text here. We need not choose between these two meanings. God's love is always the pattern for human love, and Christ's patience the pattern for human patience. Either way, Paul prays that God will engender a proper heart condition as he lays before these believers a sensitive command.

II. DISORDER INSIDE (2 THESSALONIANS 3:6-15)

A. HEEDING THE TRADITION (vv. 6-10)

6. In the name of the Lord Jesus Christ, we command you, brothers, to keep away from every brother who is idle and does not live according to the teaching you received from us.

Finally, Paul issues his *command:* that the church distance itself from certain members who do not follow Paul's *teaching* and example.

The exact nature of their transgression is not clear. Our text here describes it as idleness, but the original word means something like "not in proper order." The issue of idleness is clearly in view, for Paul spends much time persuading his readers to work responsibly. He even specifies laziness in verse 11. Probably the problem involves many forms of disorder, one of which (and probably the root of which) is idleness. The failure to work apparently has led to the tendency to meddle excessively in others affairs, as these same persons obviously are doing (v. 11).

The point Paul begins to make here is that such disorderly believers are compromising the church's integrity in such a way as to require some form of separation. Before describing what this separation should and should not look like, which he does in verses 13-15, he first reminds them that such living is not in keeping with the faith tradition they *received* and explains why it has become such a problem.

SHUNNING

The practice of shunning is widely practiced among a number of religious groups, both Christian and non-Christian. Many Muslim, Hindu, and Orthodox

HOW TO SAY IT

Amish. AW-mish.
Corinth. KOR-inth.
Meidung. MY-dohn(g).
Mennonites. MEH-nuh-nights.
Messiah. Meh-SIGH-uh.
Silas. SIGH-luss.
Thessalonica. THESS-uh-lo-NYE-kuh (TH as in THIN).

WHAT DO YOU THINK?

Paul urges what has been called "excommunication" in verse 6. Under what circumstances do you think he expects us to apply such an extreme measure?

Jewish converts to Christianity are cut off from their families and treated as if they were dead. Jehovah's Witnesses and Mormons follow similar practices in regard to those who leave their faith.

Probably the most famous context of shunning is the Amish, where the practice is referred to as Meidung, the German word for "avoidance." In the 1690s, Jacob Ammann felt the Mennonites were not being sufficiently faithful to the practice of Meidung, so he split off from the parent group. Others coalesced around his leadership, becoming known as the Amish.

Numerous novels have been written about the practice, usually painting it in a negative, narrow-minded light. But used sensitively, the practice can be helpful as a disciplinary tool to maintain uniformity in belief and practice. The threat of Meidung can be a strong deterrent to those who are tempted to push the boundaries.

Both in 2 Thessalonians and 1 Corinthians, Paul endorses withdrawal as a means of discipline to rectify sinful behavior. Both for the purity of the body and for the salvation of the sinner, it is a practice that the church needs to take seriously today. —J. B. N.

7. For you yourselves know how you ought to follow our example. We were not idle when we were with you,

Paul believes that the churches he has influenced ought not only obey his teaching but to *follow* his *example*. Like Jesus, he not only speaks about the gospel, he also attempts to live it out in every aspect of his life.

This is not simply an effective teaching strategy; it is an essential part of the gospel message. The gospel means more than that Christ has died for our sins so that we may be united with God someday. It also means that in Christ's life, death, resurrection, and ascension, God has changed the course of world history. He has made possible new and abundant life even now for those who accept him.

WHAT DO YOU THINK?

In what areas are you setting an example for others to follow? What are some areas for improvement or correction?

So all Christians have the responsibility both to speak of what Christ has accomplished and to show its fruits by how they live. Christians have both a message to communicate and a witness to maintain. We are to be salt and light (Matthew 5:13-16). God wills the world to see our witness and to be drawn to him through it. When it comes to evangelism, the medium is also the message. When the two are separated, our mission is compromised. Paul is diligent to live out his convictions wherever he goes. This empowers him to highlight his own example.

8. . . . nor did we eat anyone's food without paying for it. On the contrary, we worked night and day, laboring and toiling so that we would not be a burden to any of you.

Not only did Paul, Silas, and Timothy live orderly lives in Thessalonica, but they *worked night and day* to provide for their own physical needs. We should probably not interpret this to mean that they never accepted others' hospitality and always felt obligated to repay anyone who gave them the gift of a meal. Rather, they made sure not to lay any unnecessary *burden* on their hosts by requiring these churches to supply their room and board.

9. We did this, not because we do not have the right to such help, but in order to make ourselves a model for you to follow.

The apostle clarifies at this point, however, that he is in fact entitled to call on the believers to provide for his needs. Jesus gives him that *right* (see Matthew 10:5-16; Luke 9:2-5; 10:1-12), Paul argues for that right persuasively from the Old Testament Scriptures (Deuteronomy 25:4) in his letter to the believers in Corinth (1 Corinthians 9:3-14), and later extends that right to those functioning as elders (1 Timothy 5:17, 18). The bottom line is that those who labor for the gospel possess the right to earn their keep from those whom they serve.

Nonetheless, Paul chooses not to exercise that right. He chooses, instead, to work because he does not want people to confuse his motives. He is not proclaiming Christ in order to get out of working a real job. Nor is he proclaiming a Messiah who calls everyone to leave behind their former occupations. He proclaims a Christ who transforms people's occupations and calls them to faithful witness as a part of their occupation. In this way, he sets an example for all believers to follow, especially those who remain in their hometowns rather than join the traveling missionaries.

10. For even when we were with you, we gave you this rule: "If a man will not work, he shall not eat."

Paul's example in Thessalonica has been reinforced with clear teaching. Why have some chosen to ignore it? One reason could be that they are imitating the wrong teachers. There are at this time traveling Cynic philosophers who shun work, embrace philosophy, and encourage others to do the same. Maybe the Thessalonians have been influenced by these Cynics.

Another reason could be that the poorer converts have noticed that rich believers feel obligated to give to them, so they have begun taking advantage of them. Another possibility is that the believers who have accepted the false teaching that the day of the Lord has already begun (2 Thessalonians 2:2) are so distressed or excited that they have quit their jobs, only to become a burden to other believers who continue to supply their needs. A final possible reason is that some may think that the second coming of Christ means the abolition of the everyday structures of living, perhaps drawing on Jesus' teaching in Matthew 6:26-34 to justify their position.

Because of the emphasis on end-time confusion in chapter 2, one or both of these final two options seems most likely. Now that Paul exposes the error of such thinking, it is necessary that the people's behavior adjust accordingly.

WORK TO EAT

We live in a day where the challenges of welfare are enormous. It is a highly controversial subject—politically, economically, and socially. There are many who believe that we have created a society with a permanent welfare class. According to this view, welfare recipients simply live on governmental handouts and are never concerned about getting a job. I knew an unmarried woman who had three children from three different men because she loved children, and the welfare checks made it possible for her to get along without working.

I also knew a man who made a good living as a bulldozer operator. But he lived in a northern area of the country where his heavy equipment operating skills were not needed during the winter. He collected unemployment checks during these months. He told me he could get other work, but unemployment paid more than the jobs he could get, so why should he work?

In Paul's day there were no unemployment checks or welfare payments for unmarried mothers. But almost everyone had a bit of land and/or a trade passed down from earlier generations. Paul's comments were addressed to that situation, but even today the principles he enunciates are valid. Able-bodied people should work for their liv-

DAILY BIBLE READINGS

Monday, July 19—God's Steadfast Love (Psalm 89:1-8)

Tuesday, July 20—Ready to Die for the Lord (Acts 21:1-14)

Wednesday, July 21—God Is Faithful (1 Corinthians 1:4-9)

Thursday, July 22—A Sure and Steadfast Anchor (Hebrews 6:13-20)

Friday, July 23—Faithful Promises (Hebrews 10:19-25)

Saturday, July 24—Faithful to Forgive (1 John 1:5-10)

Sunday, July 25—God Will Strengthen and Guard (2 Thessalonians 3:1-15)

WHAT DO YOU THINK?

What impact does idleness have on the work of Christ?

WHAT DO YOU THINK?

What causes a Christian to become tired of doing what is right? (Display the visual for Lesson 8 as you discuss this question.)

Be not weary in well doing.

PRAYER

Forgiving Father, we thank you for teaching us that forgiveness is not simply a state of mind, but a holistic practice that requires painful choices. Increase our faith so we can see the needs of our brothers and sisters. Increase our resolve that we may do the right thing. Faithful God, you have been faithful to us; may we be faithful to you and to one another through Jesus Christ our Lord. Amen.

ing and not expect the church (or the government!) to supply their needs when they refuse to do the job themselves. No work, no eat!   —J. B. N.

B. HELPING THE TROUBLESOME (vv. 11-15)

11. We hear that some among you are idle. They are not busy; they are busybodies.

Such laziness not only flows from faulty doctrine and ignores Paul's positive example, it also results in people meddling excessively and disrupting others' lives. With too much time on their hands, some believers are apparently forcing both their personal needs and their twisted views on other members in the community who do not share in their disorderly practice.

It is not uncommon for people who do not occupy their time with constructive endeavors to engage in destructive habits. There is truth in the classic adage that "an *idle* mind is the devil's workshop." So Paul invites these believers to judge this disorderly tree by its meddlesome fruit.

12, 13. Such people we command and urge in the Lord Jesus Christ to settle down and earn the bread they eat. And as for you, brothers, never tire of doing what is right.

These busybodies must get back to work and stop causing trouble. They must *earn* their keep and stop draining the church's funds without cause. There will be others in the church who truly need help (1 Timothy 5:3-16).

14, 15. If anyone does not obey our instruction in this letter, take special note of him. Do not associate with him, in order that he may feel ashamed. Yet do not regard him as an enemy, but warn him as a brother.

Paul now turns to address the faithful in the church and to answer the question that has likely been weighing most on their minds: "What do we do with those who ignore this teaching?" This is likely weighing on their minds because it is not the first time that these busybodies have been instructed to get their act together. They have been instructed firsthand by Paul (v. 10) and reminded again by way of a letter (1 Thessalonians 5:14), yet still they persist in their misconduct.

So Paul instructs these faithful believers to continue doing the right thing and to part company with those who refuse to do the same. This may mean excluding them from the regular meals at which they have been freeloading or excluding them from the Lord's Supper, which itself is tied to larger communal meals. It may also mean ceasing to initiate contact with such persons and using uninitiated contacts as opportunities to admonish their behavior so that full fellowship may be restored.

The reason for such avoidance is not punishment, scorn, or vengeance. The reason is shame. Some people cannot recognize their shameful behavior until those they respect make it crystal clear to them. Apparently several rounds of instruction have not made an impact. Yet the intended result is reconciliation. One shames a good friend only when he or she has failed to heed reason. One's hope is that the person will finally come to his senses. This is the reason Paul makes explicit that the faithful must not regard errant members as enemies, but as estranged family. Such exclusion is an act of love. Sometimes the first step to getting closer is to create some distance. In reality that distance is already there, but the offender is blind to the distance that his sin has caused. He needs his family to open his eyes. Only after he sees the truth and repents of his ways can the gulf truly be bridged.

CONCLUSION

When we truly love a brother or sister, we will not let that person go down without a fight. To fight for a loved one begins with prayer, but it doesn't always end there. It requires ending her illusion that all is well between her and God and his people. A church that believes each member is vitally important will intervene decisively to bring order to disordered lives.

In 2 Thessalonians 3:1-15 we see such intervention unfold. It begins with correct teaching and positive examples; it continues with verbal warning and admonition. It may lead even to spatial separation until the problem is resolved. Though it is painful to withdraw from someone we love, it is far more agonizing to watch that person destroy his or her life and that of others. Since each member of Christ's body is one with it, it is the business of all to call the wanderer back.

THOUGHT TO REMEMBER
Care enough to admonish the disorderly ones in your life.

Discovery Learning

The following is an alternative lesson plan emphasizing learning activities. Classes desiring such student involvement will find these suggestions helpful. At the back of this book are reproducible student pages to further enhance activity learning.

INTO THE LESSON

Ask for two people to role-play a job interview in which the candidate really does not want the job—any job. He lives with his widowed mother, who willingly provides shelter, food, and free laundry service. He is going through this interview only as a favor to his minister, who has been trying to get him out from under his mother's wing and into the workforce. The interviewer will try to help the candidate look good by asking "set up" questions. But the candidate will keep giving slacker-type responses.

After the interview, say, "Today's passage is about the importance of working and making a contribution to the church as long as you are able to do so."

If your class is less dramatic, use the reproducible activity "The Laborer Is Worth His Wages" from page 507 as an opening activity.

INTO THE WORD

Then say, "Some of the Thessalonians had been so focused on the return of Christ that they quit making a living and simply kept their eyes on the skies, looking for the Lord's return. Of course, after a while they started to get hungry. Since they had no means, some of them were looking to the church for sustenance. At this point, Paul had to draw the line and say, 'If a man will not work, he shall not eat' (2 Thessalonians 3:10). In fact, the apostle said that these slackers should be excluded from the congregation!"

• Read 2 Thessalonians 3:1-15, and then split the class in two. The first half is to describe the actions (or nonactions) of those who were idle. The second half is to point out the positive examples of Paul and those Thessalonians who continued to work.

Here are some possible answers:

1. Those who were idle: they were lazy and refused to work; they would not accept the teachings of the apostles; they were not busy; instead, they were getting into other people's business, probably criticizing those who were working; they were tired of doing the right thing; they would not obey Paul's teachings.

2. Those who worked (including Paul): they were spreading the message of Christ; they were being delivered from wicked men; they were strengthened and protected from the evil one; they continually put Paul's teachings into action; they were not idle; they set an example; they ate no one's food without paying; they worked night and day not to be a burden; they never tired of doing the right thing; they disassociated themselves from the idle; they treated the idle person not as an enemy but as a brother.

INTO LIFE

The purpose of this activity is to draw a distinction between those who refuse to work and those who are legitimately poor due to circumstances beyond their control. Using the same two groups as were used in the previous activity, give these tasks: Group 1: Define the characteristics of the slacker, a person who's only looking for a handout and wants someone else to support him or her on an ongoing basis. Group 2: Define the characteristics of a poor person who simply wants help to get back on his or her feet.

Here are some possible answers:

1. *The Slacker:* has a sense of entitlement; feels like he's paid his dues, and now it's time for a free ride; seems indignant that others are rich while he has very little, and so the rich should distribute their wealth, particularly to him; he is controlled by his circumstances; he always has an excuse why he cannot work, why the establishment is against him, why no one will hire him; he feels that the church and self-sustaining Christians exist in order to sustain him; it is their duty to give and his privilege to receive.

2. *The Poor:* they are doing the best they can; they want to work, and they diligently look for work; they may have physical or mental challenges that prevent them from working, but they want to make whatever contribution they can; if they are able to work but facing legitimate obstacles, they seek out temporary help to overcome the obstacles so that they can eventually make it on their own; once they are on their own, they seek ways to help people who are currently in the difficult situations they used to be in.

Use the reproducible activity "Legitimately Poor" from page 507 to explore how students can help those who are poor. Then close the class in prayer, praying for the poor, asking God to encourage and support them, and ask specifically how he would like you to do the same.

SHARING GOD'S GRACE

LESSON 9

INTRODUCTION

A. THE NEW GOLDEN AGE OF PREACHING

Preaching, the public proclamation of God's Word, has been God's chosen means of spreading the gospel since the time of the apostles. Paul asked, "How can they hear without someone preaching to them?" (Romans 10:14). Paul saw his vocation as a "preacher" just as important as his status as an apostle (see 1 Timothy 2:7). Revelation 14:6 pictures the preaching of an "eternal gospel" with the implication that this mode of delivery is also eternally ordained.

For the last several generations, there have been those who have forecast the end of preaching. Public proclamation is pronounced an archaic method of communication. People look back on the preachers of the past and see a "golden age" of preaching. It seems that no current preacher can stand with such preachers as Charles Spurgeon and D. L. Moody. In a local church, it is often said by old-timers that the current preacher cannot hold a candle to the former minister or the preacher of their youth. Others say that in our fast-paced and visually driven world, oral communication is a lost and unappreciated art, and traditional preaching is in its death throes.

This is a distorted view of the past and the present. There have always been excellent preaching and mediocre preaching. There have always been learned preaching and simple preaching. Styles and methods have changed. Consider that the most celebrated preacher of the Middle Ages, Bernard of Clairvaux, preached an unfinished series of sermons on the Song of Solomon. Bernard preached 86 sermons from this little book and had only progressed to chapter 3 (out of 8)! That most preachers today would never spend nearly two years' worth of sermons on the most obscure book in the Bible cannot be considered a bad development in the history of preaching!

Technological advances have made an impact on preaching in the last 50 years. Many preachers use projected visuals, including pictures and video clips. Some large venues project a live image of the preacher, making him 20 feet tall so all can see. The traditional wooden pulpit has been replaced with a clear plastic lectern or done away with entirely.

Sermon preparation has also changed. The proliferation of sermon resources on the Internet has made excellent material very accessible. (An unscrupulous preacher may thus preach a downloaded sermon without attribution, as if it were his own.) Some believe that new media has decreased the patience and attention span of congregations, forcing quick, shallow exposition of Scripture. Overall, though, there are many excellent sermons delivered every week in churches all over the world. Preaching's doomsayers must wait; their prophecies will not be fulfilled in the near future.

DEVOTIONAL READING:
ACTS 9:10-16
BACKGROUND SCRIPTURE:
PHILIPPIANS 1
PRINTED TEXT:
PHILIPPIANS 1:15-29

LESSON AIMS

After participating in this lesson, each student should:

1. List the sources of joy Paul mentions in today's passage.

2. Compare and contrast Paul's attitude about slanderers and imprisonment with his or her own attitudes about adversity.

3. Make a plan to conduct himself or herself in a manner worthy of the gospel in the face of some specific opposition.

Aug 1

KEY VERSE

Whatever happens, conduct yourselves in a manner worthy of the gospel of Christ. Then, whether I come and see you or only hear about you in my absence, I will know that you stand firm in one spirit, contending as one man for the faith of the gospel.
— Philippians 1:27

Fifty years from now some will probably decry the preaching of their time and yearn for the early days of the twenty-first century as a "golden age of preaching."

The apostle Paul was aware that there were many preachers in his day. We do not know much about them. We are told of the eloquent Apollos, but we have no samples of his preaching (Acts 18:24). Paul did speak of false and heretical preaching (see Galatians 1:8, 9) and warned his people to be on guard for such. In today's lesson, Paul speaks not so much of the doctrinal purity of other preachers, but of the spirit in which they deliver their messages. Paul's insights in this area are surprisingly fresh and have application for us today.

B. Lesson Background

In Paul's day, Philippi was a leading city of Macedonia. It derived its name from Philip II of Macedon, the father of Alexander the Great. Philip prized the site because of its strategic location and nearby gold mines, so he founded the city and named it after himself. It later served as a base of operations for Alexander's conquests.

In the Roman civil wars following the murder of Julius Caesar, a major battle was fought near Philippi. When Caesar Augustus emerged as the undisputed ruler of Rome, he resettled the city with veterans from his legions, making it a Roman colony. It became an outpost for Roman culture in the Greek world, although it never became a large city. When Paul visited Philippi, the city probably had fewer than 20,000 inhabitants, but it enjoyed close and important connections with the imperial city itself.

Acts 16 records Paul's visit to Philippi, often celebrated as his first ministry in Europe. In Philippi, Paul converted the rich and generous businesswoman Lydia (Acts 16:14, 15) and the Roman soldier who had been his jailer (Acts 16:25-33). Paul called his experience with the Roman authorities of the city an insult (see 1 Thessalonians 2:2), for he and Silas were beaten and jailed illegally and then encouraged to leave the city (Acts 16:38, 39).

Paul's letter to the Philippian church is counted among the "Prison Epistles," written by Paul while under house arrest in Rome about AD 63. The other three Prison Epistles—Ephesians, Colossians, and Philemon—are directed to a connected pair of churches (or to an individual in one of those churches) in Asia Minor. Philippians is from the same period, but it addresses a completely separate audience with different issues.

The Philippian church had continued to support Paul financially, sending a monetary gift to Rome via one of its members, Epaphroditus (Philippians 4:18). Epaphroditus had dutifully delivered the gift, but while in Rome he had become deathly ill (Philippians 2:25-30). After his recovery, Paul sent Epaphroditus back to Philippi with his thanks and with encouragement and advice for several issues the church was experiencing. This encouragement and advice are what make up the book of Philippians, one of the most beloved books of the New Testament and the source of our lessons for the next four weeks.

I. TWO KINDS OF PREACHING (PHILIPPIANS 1:15-18)
A. Selfish Proclamation (v. 15)
15. It is true that some preach Christ out of envy and rivalry, but others out of goodwill.

How to Say It

Antioch. AN-tee-ock.

Apollos. Uh-PAHL-us.

Arminian. Ar-MIH-nee-un.

Caesar Augustus. SEE-zer Aw-GUS-tus.

Clairvaux. Clare-VOE.

Epaphroditus. Ee-PAF-ro-DYE-tus.

Ignatius. Ig-NAY-shus.

Jerusalem. Juh-ROO-suh-lem.

Julius Caesar. JOO-lee-us SEE-zer.

Lydia. LID-ee-uh.

Macedon. MASS-uh-don.

Macedonia. Mass-eh-DOE-nee-uh.

Philippi. Fih-LIP-pie or FIL-ih-pie.

It is easy for us to understand how *Christ* could be preached from *goodwill*. The essence of the gospel is good news, that all men and women can be saved through faith in Christ. We should want to deliver this message to every person on this earth.

But how can Christ be proclaimed from a spirit *of envy and rivalry?* How can the gospel be preached of "selfish ambition" (v. 17)? A deeper look at the word *ambition* will help us understand. It is used in the sense of one who is ambitiously striving or competing for position. The position of a preacher can be very powerful and lucrative if he is able to persuade many people to be loyal to him. He is able to carve out a personal empire of influence and wealth within the Christian community. If the preacher is enticed by such goals, his preaching will be motivated by his own self-interests. He might seek to discredit any rivals, stirring up strife and being motivated by selfish envy.

Although Paul gives no names, apparently there are such men who are disparaging him in his absence and feathering their own nests. With this debasing of the preacher's role, along with personal attacks on Paul, these self-exalting preachers are trying to hurt the apostle, thinking to add to his affliction while he remains helpless in Rome.

B. Loving Proclamation (vv. 16-18)

16, 17. *The latter do so in love, knowing that I am put here for the defense of the gospel. The former preach Christ out of selfish ambition, not sincerely, supposing that they can stir up trouble for me while I am in chains.*

Paul does not understand this commercialized type of preaching. He is not motivated to preach for financial gain, but simply out of *love.* He is an ambassador of goodwill, even while imprisoned (see Ephesians 6:20). His concern is to *preach* the gospel faithfully, to preach simply (see 1 Corinthians 2:2), and to defend *the gospel* against those who would distort or demean it.

18. *But what does it matter? The important thing is that in every way, whether from false motives or true, Christ is preached. And because of this I rejoice. Yes, and I will continue to rejoice,*

Despite Paul's lack of appreciation for those who would preach for personal gain, he says that in the end it matters only that *Christ is preached.* No preacher has entirely pure motives. All are tainted with a measure of selfishness and ignorance. Paul is convinced, however, that the message of the gospel is more powerful than the shortcomings of the preacher. The treasure of the message of salvation is contained in earthly, human vessels (2 Corinthians 4:7). The power of persuasion in the message is not through lofty rhetoric (1 Corinthians 2:1), but in the convicting power of the Holy Spirit (John 16:7, 8). Paul's joy in this type of preaching is not forced, but sincere. He echoes the example of Jesus, who did not allow his disciples to forbid outsiders from casting out demons in his name (Mark 9:38-40).

CHRIST IS PREACHED

John Wesley and George Whitefield were significant evangelists during the Evangelical Revival in England during the eighteenth century. It was Whitefield who introduced Wesley to the practice of field preaching, which involved delivering sermons outside the confines of a church building. The two were good friends

WHAT DO YOU THINK?

Paul said that some people would preach Christ out of envy and rivalry, but others out of goodwill. What are some bad reasons to get involved in ministry today? What good can come out of poorly-motivated ministry?

DAILY BIBLE READINGS

Monday, July 26—Paul's Call to Service (Acts 9:10-16)

Tuesday, July 27—Paul's Arrest (Acts 21:27-36)

Wednesday, July 28—Paul's Trial Before the Council (Acts 22:30–23:11)

Thursday, July 29—Paul's Appeal to Caesar (Acts 25:1-12)

Friday, July 30—Paul's Prayer for the Philippians (Philippians 1:3-11)

Saturday, July 31—Paul's Imprisonment Spreads the Gospel (Philippians 1:12-18a)

Sunday, Aug. 1—Paul's Struggle with His Future (Philippians 1:18b-29)

and supportive of each other's work, but they also had differences. Wesley believed in the Arminian doctrine of free will; Whitefield accepted the Calvinist doctrine of predestination. Because of this doctrinal difference, they were unable to work together and ultimately formed different groups of churches.

Wesley was still living when Whitefield died in 1770. A person who knew of their doctrinal disagreement once jokingly asked him, "Mr. Wesley, do you think you will see Mr. Whitefield in Heaven?"

Wesley simply replied, "No."

The other man was shocked. "You think Whitefield won't go to Heaven?"

"Oh, that wasn't what you asked," replied Wesley. "You asked, 'Will I see him in Heaven?' and my answer was 'No.' When I get to Heaven," Wesley continued, "Whitefield will be so close to the throne of God and I will be so far away that I won't be able to see him!"

Wesley and Whitefield had their differences, but Wesley acknowledged Whitefield as a great man of God. Wesley never compromised his doctrinal beliefs because of Whitefield, but he also knew that Whitefield was preaching Christ and the salvation found in him alone. For that Wesley gave thanks. Are we able to give thanks to God for brothers and sisters in Christ with whom we have significant disagreements?   —J. B. N.

II. TWO KINDS OF FUTURE (PHILIPPIANS 1:19-26)
A. DYING WITHOUT SHAME (vv. 19-21)

19. . . . for I know that through your prayers and the help given by the Spirit of Jesus Christ, what has happened to me will turn out for my deliverance.

Paul is confined and, though he is able to receive guests (Acts 28:30), he surely experiences times of loneliness. He faces an uncertain future, and his day-to-day existence is probably spartan and bleak. Yet he never ceases to hope and to pray. He is sustained by the *Spirit of Jesus Christ* and in the knowledge that the Philippians still care about him. They have sent him financial help and the companionship of the trusty Epaphroditus, and they continue to pray for their beloved apostle.

20. I eagerly expect and hope that I will in no way be ashamed, but will have sufficient courage so that now as always Christ will be exalted in my body, whether by life or by death.

Paul's ministry may be limited by circumstance and physical frailty, but never by embarrassment or fear. He is never *ashamed* of the gospel (Romans 1:16) or of his calling to preach it (1 Corinthians 9:16). A characteristic description of Paul's preaching is *courage* (see Acts 13:46; 19:8; 28:31; Ephesians 6:19). This history of faithful and consistent preaching allows Paul to face the future with confidence. If he lives, he still has work to do. If he dies, he has no regrets, for his entire life has been dedicated to being a witness of *Christ*.

Paul seems to believe that his *life* is in danger. He may suspect the ruthlessness and capriciousness of the emperor. He may be aware of plots against his life by Jewish opponents in Rome as they had conspired in Jerusalem (Acts 23:12). Paul is not expressing a misguided desire for martyrdom, a sentiment that appears a few decades later in the church. He is convinced that even his *death* can bring glory to Christ. Here he may be remembering the tragic yet noble death of Stephen, to which he had been a witness (Acts 7:58; 8:1).

21. For to me, to live is Christ and to die is gain.

WHAT DO YOU THINK?

Paul was confident that everything that had happened to him would in some way result in his deliverance. In what ways can God use everything in our lives, both difficult and joyful?

WHAT DO YOU THINK?

For Paul, to live was Christ, but to die was gain. What are some of the benefits of staying right where God has us, and what are some benefits of leaving our earthly homes to be with Christ?

This brings Paul to one of the grandest statements in all of Scripture: *to live is Christ and to die is gain.* This is not rhetorical flourish. Paul believes it to the core of his soul. In Paul's mind every day is another opportunity to exercise his God-appointed ministry for his Lord Jesus Christ. To serve is his privilege and honor. Yet there is nothing to fear about death, because Paul is confident of the reward and rest that await him (2 Timothy 4:6-8).

To Die Is Gain

Ignatius was bishop of Antioch in the late first and early second centuries. He was arrested for his Christianity, marched all the way across Asia Minor, Greece, and Italy, and then was executed in Rome about the year 110. While traveling through Asia Minor, he wrote seven letters (mostly to churches), urging the recipients to maintain unity in their fellowship while resisting the incursions of false teaching. One of his letters was to the church in Rome, and in it he talks about his desire for martyrdom.

He begs the Roman Christians not to interfere with his death. If they extend his life, he becomes a meaningless noise; if he dies, people will see God's Word in him. He desires no more than to be a sacrifice for God. He hopes to become fodder for the wild beasts and that they will make short work of him. He claims he is God's wheat that will be ground by the teeth of wild beasts to become a pure loaf for Christ. Whatever execution comes—beasts, cross, burning, wrenched bones, mangled limbs, crushed body—he wants only to get to Jesus Christ.

The words of Ignatius may seem macabre and masochistic to us, but they reflect a man who has realized that to die for Christ is pure gain. Is that confidence evident in our lives?

—J. B. N.

B. Living to Labor (vv. 22-26)

22, 23. *If I am to go on living in the body, this will mean fruitful labor for me. Yet what shall I choose? I do not know! I am torn between the two: I desire to depart and be with Christ, which is better by far;*

Paul is unsure whether his death is imminent or will be delayed. Tradition tells us that Paul was released from this imprisonment and traveled another four or five years before returning to Rome to meet his death in AD 66 or 67. But in AD 63, the prospect of death does not discourage the apostle. He echoes the sentiment of the famous Queen Esther, "If I perish, I perish" (Esther 4:16).

24. . . . *but it is more necessary for you that I remain in the body.*

There is one thing that causes Paul to desire continued life: he is needed. As long as he survives, he can minister to the Philippians and other believers. He does not worry about leaving a wife or dependent children behind, for he has none. His concern is for his sons and daughters in the faith, his beloved sisters and brothers in Christ.

25, 26. *Convinced of this, I know that I will remain, and I will continue with all of you for your progress and joy in the faith, so that through my being with you again your joy in Christ Jesus will overflow on account of me.*

Now Paul looks to the future with expectancy and *joy.* He looks forward to a reunion with the Philippian church and anticipates it as a great time of rejoicing. This change of attitude does not come because Paul receives news of his release while writing the letter. He is simply making plans for ministry and taking joy in the prospects of seeing his friends *again.* It is this type of hope that sustains Paul during his dark days of imprisonment.

Visual for Lessons 7 & 9. *Display this visual as you discuss verse 27. Ask, "How does standing together help us to stand fast?"*

What Do You Think?

Paul understood that it was important for him to stay for the sake of other believers. In what ways do our priorities affect the decisions we make every day?

WHAT DO YOU THINK?

Paul's presence would provoke joy in the lives of these believers. What person provokes joy in your life, just by showing up? What sets this person apart from the rest?

PRAYER

O God our Father, the one who is always faithful and true, may we be given clear times to serve you. May we embrace these opportunities and may we too be found faithful. We pray this in the name of the one who gives meaning to living and who promises life beyond death, Jesus Christ our Lord. Amen.

WHAT DO YOU THINK?

Paul told us not to be intimidated by those who oppose us. Why are we better off if we expect resistance, to consider it as something normal, when we are preaching the gospel and leading others to a deeper maturity in Christ?

III. STRIVING TOGETHER (PHILIPPIANS 1:27-29)

A. STANDING IN ONE SPIRIT (v. 27)

27. *Whatever happens, conduct yourselves in a manner worthy of the gospel of Christ. Then, whether I come and see you or only hear about you in my absence, I will know that you stand firm in one spirit, contending as one man for the faith of the gospel*

Having raised the prospect of a future return to Philippi, Paul now tells some of his expectations. In short, he wants the good reports that he has received from Epaphroditus to continue. He does not want to be ashamed by what he finds when he revisits. He expects the church to guard its *conduct.* This must be *worthy of the gospel of Christ,* absent of hypocrisy or malice.

Furthermore, Paul expects to find the congregation standing united, *in one spirit* and in one mind. Paul knows of some minor issues of division within the church and will address these later in the letter. He reminds the Philippians of one of the great keys of church unity: a common purpose. Congregations may be very inclusive and diverse if all members are unreservedly committed to *the gospel.* Unity based on personality or tradition will falter and crumble. We are one body because we have one Lord and one *faith* (Ephesians 4:4, 5).

B. SUFFERING FOR CHRIST (vv. 28, 29)

28. *. . . . without being frightened in any way by those who oppose you. This is a sign to them that they will be destroyed, but that you will be saved—and that by God.*

The adversaries of the Philippians may be within the church, but more likely they are outsiders. These may be Jews, who have been known to harass the churches in Macedonia (Acts 17:13). They may be pagans in the city who belittle the message of the gospel (Acts 16:20, 21). It is also possible that Paul has in mind the spiritual forces of evil, which seek to undermine the church at all times (Ephesians 6:12). The bold, strong, unified faith of the Philippians stands as a testimony to their salvation and to the perdition, that is, the eventual destruction, of their adversaries. Those holding fast to the gospel are on the side of God, and their enemies know this in their heart of hearts.

29. *For it has been granted to you on behalf of Christ not only to believe on him, but also to suffer for him.*

Paul concludes this section with a sober reminder. Being a believer is not always joy and happiness. If we are committed to serving the Lord, we must be ready to *suffer for him.* This suffering can take many forms. It can be ostracism, including painful separation from friends and family. It can be slander, the loss of one's good name through gossip and lies. It can be illness or deprivation in the course of ministry. Epaphroditus had risked his life and health to minister to Paul in Rome. It can even be physical pain, imprisonment, and/or torture by the authorities. Paul and Silas spent a night shackled in a dark cell in a Philippian jail after receiving a beating (Acts 16:22-24). All Christians will undergo various forms of suffering for Christ. This seems to be promised by Paul and by Jesus himself (see Matthew 5:11). When these times come, we must remember, "For me, to live is Christ and to die is gain."

CONCLUSION

The Bible often pictures the lives of Christians in terms of a military struggle. We are soldiers in the cosmic battle being waged by servants of the Lord against the forces of evil. The ironic thing about this is that there is no gigantic battle-field for this warfare. It is a battle in the life of each individual believer.

In Ephesians, Paul develops a wonderful allegorical presentation along these lines, exhorting his readers to don the spiritual protection offered by the "full armor of God." Paul says that the purpose of wearing this battle gear is so that when the battle is over, the soldier will be able "to stand" (Ephesians 6:13). The word picture he presents means that Paul is praying that his readers will not end up as casualties from the spiritual battles of life. At the end, they will still be standing, not among the fallen. They will have neither fled the battle nor succumbed to enemy attacks. They will die while yet spiritually alive and kicking. They will be found faithful.

THOUGHT TO REMEMBER
Even in the worst of times, God is faithful and desires that we continue to serve him.

Discovery Learning

The following is an alternative lesson plan emphasizing learning activities. Classes desiring such student involvement will find these suggestions helpful. At the back of this book are reproducible student pages to further enhance activity learning.

INTO THE LESSON

Bring a trophy to class or display a large picture of one at the front of the class. Tell the students you'd like them to be thinking of who should receive the award for "World's Greatest Preacher." Write their suggestions on the board.

When you have a list of six or eight suggestions, ask the class why they chose these "candidates." If your current preacher is there, ask why he should receive the award. (If he's not, ask why not!) What distinguishes these preachers? Is it a great voice? Good story-telling ability? A keen way of tying in current news to the messages?

Say, "Today we'll see that Paul thinks the most important thing for a preacher is to preach Christ."

INTO THE WORD

When you are ready to give attention to today's text, Philippians 1:15-29, have one of your good oral readers read verses 12-14 to establish the context. Then say, "Philippians 1 reveals Paul's attitudes about and motives for preaching and ministry. The text reveals there were other preachers with different motives." Recruit two learners to stand before the group and read the following alternately. Give your readers labels indicating *Preacher X* and *Preacher Paul (P)*.

X: "I think some preachers get too much attention."

P: "I want people to give their attention to the gospel, not to me."

X: "If I preach eloquently, I know it could make other preachers appear second-rate—but I gotta' be me!"

P: "The gospel wants good for all; that's what I want too."

X: "Naturally, I believe what I preach; but I don't want to belittle or exclude the beliefs of others."

P: "I consider my preaching to be truth; I'll defend it wholeheartedly against false teaching."

X: "You know, there are some preachers of the gospel I wish would just be quiet!"

P: "Whatever their motives, truth is truth, and I want it heard."

X: "With hard work, persistence, and skill, I have made myself into a really good preacher!"

P: "My success is due to the prayers of those saved by the gospel and the blessing of the Holy Spirit."

X: "Some preachers do such a poor job they should be ashamed to call themselves preachers!"

P: "I have godly pride in my evangelism and teaching words. God has honored me by letting me do this."

X: "I like to preach, but it would be foolish to risk imprisonment or death for the gospel."

P: "Whether I live or die—that's not the issue. Being faithful to my call is the issue."

X: "I preach for myself. I'm just driven to do it and do it well enough to be appreciated."

P: "I preach to meet the needs of the unsaved and for the joy and depth of faith it produces in those who hear and obey the gospel. That's the goal."

X: "There are some limits to what I will do and say. Some of the gospel's enemies are capable of hurting Christians. Paul should know that!"

P: "I strive in every way to fear God only. Men can take away only one thing: physical life. But God—God gives eternal life."

These statements reflect issues raised in today's text. Ask the learners to look at the text and match the ideas with specific verses as you discuss them.

INTO LIFE

Remind your learners that Paul's epistle to the Philippians is all about joy, even though he had been arrested, illegally beaten, and jailed in the city to which he is writing. Have someone read Acts 16:22-25, and then say, "Joy is unrelated to circumstances. Joy is related to faith in Christ."

Distribute copies of the reproducible activity "I've Got the Joy" from page 508. Have students identify the verses that reveal Paul's joy. Discuss how much joy we today find in those same things.

Ask your class to identify circumstances that try—and sometimes succeed at—robbing them of their joy. Solicit an admission that such surrender to the devil is a sin; solicit a resolve to find joy in hard circumstances by dwelling on the good things happening among God's people, as Paul did. Distribute copies of "To Be or Not to Be" from reproducible page 508. Encourage your students to write their commitment in the space provided.

If your class knows the old children's chorus, "I've Got the Joy, Joy, Joy, Joy Down in My Heart," have them sing it as class ends.

GIVING OF ONESELF
LESSON 10

INTRODUCTION

A. WILLINGLY HUMBLED

"Reality" programs continue to be popular with the worldwide TV audience. Many of these follow the old talent-show formula, where amateurs perform for a panel of judges who then evaluate them. If a performer adequately impresses the judges, he or she may progress to a higher level of competition or even gain a monetary prize. There seems to be an endless supply of willing contestants.

Viewers of these talent competition programs are often amazed at the humiliation suffered by some of the amateur performers. Some judges, previous unknowns themselves, have achieved a degree of celebrity for their biting criticism of inept performances. We, the viewing public, shake our heads and ask, "Why would anyone be willing to suffer such public humiliation?" The answer is complex, having to do with our increasingly narcissistic culture and the tremendous lure of wealth and fame.

One of the central themes of the New Testament is the story of one who was willing to be humbled. This person had no trace of narcissism, and he did nothing to deserve his dishonor. He was not motivated by money or fame, but by love—love for all humankind. This person, of course, was Jesus. The second chapter of Philippians is a powerful expression of his willing self-humbling, which is central to understanding Jesus and his work on the cross. This is the focus of our lesson today.

B. LESSON BACKGROUND

The book of Philippians has the most joyous and celebratory tone of any of Paul's letters. It was written to a church where Paul was deeply appreciated. He did not write the letter to scold or to correct serious error, but to thank the Philippians for their faithfulness and support.

Furthermore, Philippians is loaded with useful, encouraging content for us today. One of the central features of the book is a passage sometimes called the "Philippian Hymn" (Philippians 2:6-11). Because of its rhythm and use of words not typical of Paul's writing, many students believe that Paul did not write this section but quotes a hymn already in use in the churches.

This passage has been the inspiration for many hymns of the church (such as "He is Lord" and "All Hail the Power of Jesus' Name") and innumerable sermons. While there are several passages in the New Testament with a parallel theme of Jesus' self-humbling (particularly the first part of John 13), there are some unique expressions here that help us understand the mystery of God becoming human. Without this passage, our understanding of the Son of God would be immeasurably poorer.

Paul's purpose in this section of the letter is to remind the Philippians that living for Christ means living life as Christ lived his. There is no place for

DEVOTIONAL READING:
MATTHEW 20:20-28

BACKGROUND SCRIPTURE:
PHILIPPIANS 2:1–3:1A

PRINTED TEXT:
PHILIPPIANS 2:1-18

LESSON AIMS

After participating in this lesson, each student will be able to:

1. List the imperatives in today's passage.

2. Tell how the nature of Christ, as described in today's text, demands certain behaviors of believers today as it did in Paul's time.

3. Describe at least one way he or she plans to behave in a manner that is consistent with the nature of Christ.

Aug
8

KEY VERSE

Your attitude should be the same as that of Christ Jesus.
—Philippians 2:5

ruthless ambition and selfish promotion. The church is to be known for its true concern for the well-being of others. The essence of this is the idea that church members serve one another rather than seeking to control others for their own benefit. Satisfaction comes from serving, not from being served. This is the example of Christ.

I. GIVING THROUGH RESPECT (PHILIPPIANS 2:1-4)
A. STANDING WITH OTHERS (vv. 1, 2)
1, 2. If you have any encouragement from being united with Christ, if any comfort from his love, if any fellowship with the Spirit, if any tenderness and compassion, then make my joy complete by being like-minded, having the same love, being one in spirit and purpose.

This is deeply personal and sincere. Paul uses four parallel expressions to express the depth of his relationship with the Philippian Christians.

First is the mutual *encouragement* they share in *Christ*. Second, there is the *comfort* of *love*, the loving desire to ease the pain of others. Third, there is the *fellowship* that is enjoyed by the shared Holy *Spirit* of God. This is closely tied to the first two, encouragement and comfort, for the word *Counselor* in John 14:16, used of the Spirit, comes from the same root as *encouragement* here. The presence of the Holy Spirit should bring peace and encouragement to the individual believer and to the church as a whole. Fourth, Paul appeals to the *tenderness and compassion* of the Philippians. These powerful words express a compassion and kindness that are much like God's (2 Corinthians 1:3).

Paul calls upon these qualities so that his beloved Philippians might fulfill his *joy*. He dearly wants them to be united with him and with each other. This is summed up in Paul's final expression, *being one in spirit and purpose.* Paul's joy will come from the common determination and loving purpose of the Philippians, as shared with him.

B. WATCHING OUT FOR OTHERS (vv. 3, 4)
3, 4. Do nothing out of selfish ambition or vain conceit, but in humility consider others better than yourselves. Each of you should look not only to your own interests, but also to the interests of others.

Selfish ambition is characteristic of the selfish preachers in Philippians 1:17. It describes the ambitious person who promotes division within the church for his or her own advantage. *Vain conceit* implies an obsession for honor or glory based on pride. For Paul, this is nothing but empty.

At the other end of the scale from this ambitious pride is lowliness of mind. Paul is not describing the person who has been humbled or numbed by the cruel circumstances of life, but persons who willingly put themselves in a position where they esteem *others better than* themselves. They have taken the focus off themselves and think first of the well-being and *interests of others.*

II. GIVING THROUGH SUBMISSION (PHILIPPIANS 2:5-11)
A. RELINQUISHING REPUTATION (vv. 5-7)
5, 6. Your attitude should be the same as that of Christ Jesus: Who, being in very nature God, did not consider equality with God something to be grasped,

How can a community survive where members are willing to put others first? Is not such a congregation ripe for exploitation by selfish people, intent

WHAT DO YOU THINK?
How can people in the congregation be like-minded and be one in spirit and purpose, and still respectfully disagree on things? How do we know where to draw the line?

WHAT DO YOU THINK?
Paul wanted the Philippians to look out not only for their own interests, but also for the interests of others. Why is it important to put others' interests ahead of our own? When, if ever, should we not do this?

on satisfying their own interests and needs? This is precisely Paul's point. The church must be single-minded, unanimous in its desire to care for each other. One selfish person can upset and even destroy this ideal model. This is not a matter of direction from church leadership. Such an ideal can be approached only through the commitment each believer has to *Christ* and a willingness to follow his example.

Paul explains the example of Jesus by first affirming the full deity of the Christ, and here we are in deep waters. No matter how much we study the relationship between the persons in the Godhead, we will never understand it fully. Paul gives a hint by saying Christ was *in very nature God.* This relationship is also described as being equal with God. Christianity does not teach that there are two or three equal gods, only one. God is revealed to us in three persons, and all are equal in the sense of equal and complete divinity.

Paul's purpose here is not to explain the mystery of the Trinity, but to use it to illustrate the great sacrifice that Christ made in becoming a human being. Christ did this willingly, not holding on to his high position in glory. Paul says, however, that Christ had every right to hang on to this *equality with God.*

7. . . . but made himself nothing, taking the very nature of a servant, being made in human likeness.

Despite this inconceivably lofty position, Christ took it upon himself to redeem humankind. Paul says he *made himself nothing.* This is gladly to take on a position of serving others. Jesus often taught that he had been sent to serve, not to be served. His greatest act of service was to ransom men and women from the power of sin. To do this he had to become flesh and blood so that he could die for us (see Mark 10:42-45).

B. HUMBLING HIMSELF (v. 8)

8. And being found in appearance as a man, he humbled himself and became obedient to death — even death on a cross!

To obey sincerely is to recognize a higher purpose and authority than oneself. This is the essence of humility. When we believe there is an all-powerful God and that our power and authority are insignificant when compared to God's, then we are on the path to wise humility.

That should seem obvious to us, but we find it hard to do. So Jesus becomes the perfect model for us. As a man, he had put aside his earthly entitlements. *He humbled himself,* and thus obedience was the natural result. If we find it hard to obey, we need to look again at Jesus. His obedience was extreme, taking him to the *death* of the *cross.*

C. GAINING GLORY (vv. 9-11)

9. Therefore God exalted him to the highest place and gave him the name that is above every name,

The self-humiliation of Christ is not the end of the story. *God* took the heroic sacrifice of Jesus and rewarded him by lifting him high *above* all creation.

Paul describes this honor in three ways. First, his *name.* Paul is not implying that Jesus received a new, different name when God honored him. He is saying that Jesus' name, which stands for his person, is in a position of absolute, unchallenged supremacy. He is the King of kings (Revelation 17:14).

WHAT DO YOU THINK?

Paul admonishes us to imitate Christ, both in his attitude and obedience. What are things we grasp onto that might prevent us from taking on a servant role? What does it mean to be Christlike in our attitudes as well as our actions? How does our attitude affect our actions?

DAILY BIBLE READINGS

Monday, Aug. 2—The Greatness of a Servant (Matthew 20:20-28)

Tuesday, Aug. 3—Revealing a Conspiracy (Acts 23:12-24)

Wednesday, Aug. 4—Sacrifices Pleasing to God (Hebrews 13:12-18)

Thursday, Aug. 5—A Living Sacrifice (Romans 12:1, 2)

Friday, Aug. 6—Poured Out in Sacrifice (Philippians 2:14-18)

Saturday, Aug. 7—Concerned for Others' Welfare (Philippians 2:19-30)

Sunday, Aug. 8—Looking to Others' Interests (Philippians 2:1-13)

WHAT DO YOU THINK?

Paul is not talking about earning salvation by works, but the "working out" or exercising of our spiritual gifts. What are you doing to "work out your salvation"? What kinds of things do you do that you would not do if you weren't saved?

There is none above him in honor or authority. He has not fought his way to this pinnacle, but has been placed there by God himself, for this position is given to him. Since this is a description that fits God alone, we conclude that Jesus returned to his position of equality with God.

10. . . . *that at the name of Jesus every knee should bow, in heaven and on earth and under the earth,*

Second, Jesus is honored through worship. To *bow* the *knee* is more than an act of deference. It is an act of worship. All creation is obliged to worship the Christ, for he is worthy (Revelation 5:12). This is what separates Christianity from other monotheistic religions. Christians believe that Jesus was God incarnate, and as God he is to be worshiped.

11. . . . *and every tongue confess that Jesus Christ is Lord, to the glory of God the Father.*

Third, Jesus is honored through confession. Confession is acknowledgement, and here it serves as an oath of allegiance. Christians *confess that Jesus Christ is Lord* (compare Acts 2:36; Romans 10:9). Paul indicates that there is nothing deviant or heretical about claiming Jesus to be Lord, for it is done in accordance with God's will, *to the glory of God the Father.*

EVERY KNEE WILL BOW

Several years ago I was teaching one of my college classes and was talking about the development of theological liberalism. Liberalism tends to take the Bible as literary symbolism instead of taking it literally. Biblical miracles are reinterpreted to remove the supernatural, and everything is explained as human causation in one form or another. Biblical teaching on morality is often dismissed as an older, restricted way of looking at things, while modern society is not bound by such limitations. While the Bible presents Jesus as the only way to salvation, modern liberalism says that all religions will lead to God. These same liberal views emphasize gender equality and dismiss the apparent gender roles reflected in Scripture.

To illustrate these views to my class, I quoted from a woman who had spoken at a religious conference. She denied both gender limitations and the exclusivity of the Christian faith. She concluded by stating, "I have never and will never bow my knee to Jesus Christ or any other man!" When I finished that quotation, a student right down front said, "She will!"

Indeed, Paul emphasizes that ultimately every knee will bow and every tongue confess that Jesus Christ is Lord. Paul's assertion remains a firm anchor of the Christian faith!

—J. B. N.

III. GIVING THROUGH SHINING (PHILIPPIANS 2:12-18)
A. NO NEED FOR SUPERVISION (v. 12)

12. *Therefore, my dear friends, as you have always obeyed—not only in my presence, but now much more in my absence—continue to work out your salvation with fear and trembling,*

Paul's desire to see his readers serve each other and live in humility is a call for action. He wants them to *work out* their *salvation,* even in his *absence.* Paul is not teaching salvation through works. He is saying: "As people saved by Jesus, live out the redeemed life by your selfless service to others. In this you are following the example of Jesus and truly confirming that he is the Lord of your life." We do not serve to be saved. We are saved to serve.

B. NO NEED FOR COMPLAINING (vv. 13, 14)

13. . . . for it is God who works in you to will and to act according to his good purpose.

For the Christian, living the life of a servant comes naturally if we yield to God's power in our lives. Our service to others is not contrary to God's will, but allows God to work in and through us. We do not serve to heap honor on ourselves, but obediently to fulfill the *purpose* of God. God is pleased when we love others through our actions.

14. Do everything without complaining or arguing,

This obedient service must be sincere, however. It cannot be done from guilt or compulsion (see 2 Corinthians 9:7). It should not be accompanied by complaints (compare James 5:9) or diminished by arguments. Service is always more pleasurable, even fun, if one feels part of a group with a common purpose and goal. This is another way of manifesting the congregational "one mind" that Paul values so highly (Philippians 2:2).

C. ENLIGHTENING THE WORLD (vv. 15, 16)

15. . . . so that you may become blameless and pure, children of God without fault in a crooked and depraved generation, in which you shine like stars in the universe

This dedication to service is more than an internal matter for the church. There is a public side too. When the church is seen as a harmonious, unselfish group of people who esteem each person in the group, outsiders will notice. To get joy from serving others is not the norm of the world.

An example from the Roman world can help us understand this. The verbal idea of "serving" in this context is taken from the world of slavery. Literally, Paul says that Jesus took on the form of a slave (Philippians 2:7). In wealthy Roman society, status was sometimes measured by how many slaves a person owned. It was not unknown for some powerful landowners to possess tens of thousands of slaves. The most esteemed people were those who were served by the largest number.

This, for Paul, is *crooked* and perverse. It is a disregard for God and his will to strive for personal enrichment, pleasure, and satisfaction. Things have not changed much, and Paul's disapproval of this type of life still rings true today.

Paul's readers are called to be radically different. To serve others without regard to self will seem like the contrast between night and day to the people of the world. They will stick out, *shine like stars*. In so doing, they will light the way for people to come to Christ.

A PERVERSE NATION

"What's the world coming to?" We have heard that rhetorical question numerous times. It is sometimes comforting to refer to the "good old days," but we have to acknowledge that even the good old days had their problems. Things just seem to be so much worse today!

Indeed, there is much to be concerned about. The divorce rate is frightful, even among Christians. Suicide is the leading cause of death among teenagers. Use of illegal drugs has become common, even among athletes. Abortion claims more than a million babies annually. Unmarried cohabitation was bad enough, but now homosexuality is popularly accepted, and the courts are legalizing homosexual

Visual for Lesson 10. *Display this visual as you look at verse 14. Discuss, "What lesson about serving is this boy learning?"*

"marriages." Politics and business are rocked by one scandal after another. Homicides are increasing in many cities. "What's the world coming to?"

If it is any consolation, the same question could have been raised two millennia ago. Infanticide was common in the time of Paul. Prostitution was widely practiced, even as religious worship. Professional gladiators killed each other in the name of sport, to the delight of audiences of thousands. The inner cities were notoriously dangerous. Fathers could sell their children into slavery. Slaves were approximately one-third of the population of the Roman Empire. Married women could not own property, and the testimony of a woman could not be used in court. "What's the world coming to?"

Yet Christianity was birthed in this culture and ultimately transformed it. If Christians are blameless and harmless in today's culture, they can transform modern society as well.

—J. B. N.

16. . . . as you hold out the word of life—in order that I may boast on the day of Christ that I did not run or labor for nothing.

Acts 16 tells us that Paul had suffered physically for the opportunity to preach the gospel, *the word of life,* in Philippi. His goal had been to plant a congregation of Jesus' followers in the city, to bring them the message of salvation. To have *run* or labored *for nothing* would mean that the effects of his work are only temporary. Paul's cause to rejoice is the faithfulness and unity of the Philippian church. When Paul meets *Christ* face to face, whether at death or at his return, he wants to be able to report the steadfastness of this congregation.

D. BASKING IN JOY (vv. 17, 18)

17, 18. But even if I am being poured out like a drink offering on the sacrifice and service coming from your faith, I am glad and rejoice with all of you. So you too should be glad and rejoice with me.

Paul does not suffer from any delusions that his plight in Rome is not serious. He may be offered as a *sacrifice* for his service to Christ. His life may be forfeit. But for Paul, this is not a cause for despair. It is a time for joy, an occasion to rejoice. He hopes that the Philippians will share his joy, but this will be done only if they remain faithful in commitment and service to Christ and to one another.

CONCLUSION

Sometimes, even secular observers of culture get it right. One of the most respected and honored persons of the 20th century was an Albanian nun, Agnes Bojaxhiu. She was sent to India in 1929 to teach schoolchildren and enjoyed it. However, she was troubled by the grinding poverty she encountered on a daily basis, so she turned her attention to helping the poor.

She founded the Missionaries of Charity, an organization dedicated to serving the "shunned of society," those whom no one else was helping. This became an international relief organization. She was known to the public as Mother Teresa of Calcutta, and in 1979 was awarded the Nobel Peace Prize for her ministry. Despite her international celebrity, Mother Teresa never used her public reputation for her own sake. All the money she received for books, speaking, and prizes like the Nobel was poured back into her ministry to the poor. She never tired of this work, even until the day of her death in 1997.

PRAYER

Holy God, we understand only partially the sacrifice made by Christ to take on human form. We grasp imperfectly why he loved us enough to assume the position of a slave. We appreciate better why he is exalted above all others. May we exalt him through our own obedient service to others. We pray this in his holy name, amen.

HOW TO SAY IT

Agnes Bojaxhiu. AG-ness Boh-yah-JOO.
Albanian. Al-BAY-nee-un.
Calcutta. Cal-CUT-uh.
heretical. heh-REH-tih-cul.
narcissism. NAR-sih-SIZ-um.

What motivates a person like Mother Teresa? Why would she give her life to helping people others had forgotten? How do we explain her fierce love for the unlovely? Only Mother Teresa knew this for sure, but we can attribute a lot of it to her love for God and her consequent desire to be of service to him.

It is more difficult to understand the sacrifice made by the Son of God for our salvation. Emily Elliott, taking her cue from Paul's Philippian Hymn, wrote, "Thou didst leave Thy throne and Thy kingly crown, When Thou camest to earth for me." If we are to be like Christ, we too should be of this mind. We cannot be found holding too tightly to earthly position or riches. May there be no need for God to humble us in preparing us for Heaven because we have already humbled ourselves in obedience to him.

THOUGHT TO REMEMBER
There is great joy to be found in serving God by serving others.

Discovery Learning

The following is an alternative lesson plan emphasizing learning activities. Classes desiring such student involvement will find these suggestions helpful. At the back of this book are reproducible student pages to further enhance activity learning.

INTO THE LESSON

Prepare two pieces of opaque paper of about 9 by 12 inches in this fashion: on one put a four-inch I on one side and an eight-inch I on the other. On the second, put a similar small U on one side, a larger U on the reverse. As class begins, show each paper to your class, first one side and then the other. Ask, "What do you think is the best way for me to display these letters? Why?" After some discussion, or if the group seems confused and unable to come up with ideas, display the smaller I and the larger U. Have someone read Philippians 2:3, noting the idea, "As a Christian, I must consider *you* to be more valuable than *I* at times."

INTO THE WORD

Prepare the following completion statements as strips that can be distributed to learners. Include the numbers, which are text verse numbers. Send the strips around in a container from which learners can draw one (or more). Give this introduction: "We live in an *IF-THEN* world. If certain things are true, then certain attitudes and behaviors are both logical and appropriate. This is true both in the physical world and in the spiritual world. Look at the IF half of the statement(s) on the strip(s) you have drawn. Write the THEN half of each statement in a way that you think is

logical and appropriate. I'm not looking for the 'right' answer, only your answer."

Here are the IF's:

¹If there is any encouragement in being in Christ . . .

¹If there is any loving desire to ease the pain of others . . .

¹If there is a comforting presence of the Holy Spirit . . .

¹If there is a godly sense of kindness and compassion . . .

²If Christian joy results from seeing true unity of purpose in all Christians . . .

³If we can eliminate self-importance and social strife over differences . . .

³If we were to consider others more important than ourselves . . .

⁵If we had the mind and attitude of Christ . . .

⁷If Jesus took on the form and behavior of a servant . . .

⁹If God has exalted Jesus to the highest place . . .

⁹If Jesus has a name that is above every name . . .

¹¹If Jesus Christ is Lord . . .

¹²If we must work out our salvation in fear and trembling . . .

¹⁴If we could eliminate complaining and arguing . . .

¹⁵If we are the children of God in the midst of an evil, depraved generation . . .

[16]If we truly hold out the word of life . . .

[17]If leaders can see the sacrifice and service issuing from our faith . . .

Allow three or four minutes for learners to think and respond. Then say, "Paul introduces today's text in an *IF-THEN* context. He affirms that spiritual realities can be expected to issue forth in spiritual life choices and practices. Let's see what we say and what he says." Allow learners the freedom of their responses, but tie their thoughts as you can to the text. Note the appropriate verse in Philippians 2 as you consider each statement. Some have specific consequences identified in the text; some are actually given as consequences of preliminary truths.

As you come to verses 17, 18, return to the letters with which you began the class (Into the Lesson). Note that as far as the consequences of our godly behavior is concerned, we can "turn both letters to the larger ones, for you and I share equally in the joys of Christ and fellowship."

Option: Use the reproducible activity "At the Center" from page 509 to explore today's text and begin to make application.

INTO LIFE

Buy a package of small, self-sticking stars. Give each learner five or six of those stars after you have the class complete the reproducible activity "How Bright Is Your Star?" (page 509). Give these directions, "Take these stars home and affix them in places you spend a good deal of time each week—car, desk, kitchen, office—to remind yourself of Philippians 2:15, 16." Have a learner reread those verses. Continue, "Let each star remind you of your role 'in the universe' as a witness to 'a crooked and depraved generation.' Let each star help your mind and attitude to reflect that of our Lord, reminding you of our need to be others-oriented rather than self-centered and conceited."

LIVING INTO THE FUTURE

LESSON 11

INTRODUCTION

A. FAILURE VS. SUCCESS

An old lesson in business asks the question, "How many attempts does it take to be successful?" Answer: "Only one, but it may take many failures." City histories are littered with restaurants that closed quickly, shops that folded within a few months, and even megastores that shut down. In the city where I live, one of the most famous bookstores in the nation recently announced it would close because of changing consumer habits. One estimate is that, sadly, half of small business start-ups fail within the first four years.

Older adults can look back on their careers and see failures and successes. Most people follow several career paths in a lifetime, and often a change makes a huge difference. Maybe a person did poorly in school but flourished in business. Perhaps one languished as a salaried employee but excelled in running her own business. Some who flounder in the for-profit world thrive with a nonprofit organization.

The story is reversed for many, however. People who achieve early success may fail repeatedly later in life. The music industry speaks of "one-hit wonders," artists who have a highly ranked song that propels them to prominence but are never able to repeat that success. Literary critics can point to authors who produce a profound, important novel but never write a comparable book again.

If we evaluate the career of the apostle Paul objectively, we would say that he had both successes and failures. In Ephesus, his preaching was so popular that he moved to a better location and stayed there for two more years (Acts 19:9, 10). In Athens, though, Paul's debut before the philosophers received a mixed reception, and he seems to have left the city without having founded a church (Acts 17:32–18:1).

Paul was not driven by the goal of personal success. He never changed the essence of his preaching or his basic methods in order to get better results. He preached whether it was popular or unpopular (see 2 Timothy 4:2). Paul says that his ministry was based on "forgetting what is behind" (Philippians 3:13). His goal was simple: serving Jesus by spreading the gospel. His measure of success was equally basic: to remain faithful to his calling (Philippians 3:14).

B. LESSON BACKGROUND

We wish we knew more about Paul's background. As recorded in Acts 9, Paul had a dramatic, personal encounter with the risen Christ. We think that Paul was in his early or mid-twenties when this happened. He came out of this experience with both faith in Christ and a divine appointment to preach the gospel to the Gentiles (Acts 26:16-18). But what were the dynamics of his life that had brought him to this point? We have only bits and pieces of this information scattered throughout several New Testament books.

DEVOTIONAL READING:
1 JOHN 4:7-12
BACKGROUND SCRIPTURE:
PHILIPPIANS 3:1–4:1
PRINTED TEXT:
PHILIPPIANS 3:4B-16

LESSON AIMS

After this lesson each student will be able to:

1. Tell what Paul gave up in order to serve Christ and some of what he gained in that pursuit.

2. List some things people today give up in order to serve Christ.

3. Identify one area in his or her life that results in a loss of focus on Christ and describe the corrective action to be taken.

KEY VERSE

One thing I do: Forgetting what is behind and straining toward what is ahead, I press on toward the goal to win the prize for which God has called me heavenward in Christ Jesus.
—*Philippians 3:13, 14*

Aug
15

When Paul addressed the crowd of Jerusalem on a stairway near the temple, he asserted that he had been born in Tarsus (Acts 22:3). Tarsus was an important city roughly 400 miles north of Jerusalem and 125 miles west of Antioch. Tarsus was known in the ancient world as a center of learning and philosophy, but not for having a large Jewish presence. We assume that Paul's family was engaged in the business of tent manufacture and distribution, for this was the trade he knew (Acts 18:3). This could be lucrative, although the sewing of large tents from leather was arduous work. Paul seems to have been something of a child prodigy, and his desire for learning soon outstripped the resources available to a Jewish boy in Tarsus. Therefore, he was sent to Jerusalem to study under the famous rabbi Gamaliel (Acts 22:3). This was because Gamaliel was a leading teacher of the day among a group of the Jews called Pharisees (Acts 5:34).

Paul's father had been a Pharisee (Acts 23:6). Mentioned frequently in the New Testament, the Pharisees were a super sect among the Jews of Paul's time. They had an outsized influence in proportion to their relatively small numbers. Scholars today estimate that there were no more than 10,000–20,000 Pharisees during this period.

The Pharisees were scrupulous in keeping the Jewish law and the traditions that had built up around it. This emphasis meant they were not as tied to the temple as were their rivals, the Sadducees. Because of this, when the temple was demolished by the Romans in AD 70, the Pharisaic type of Judaism survived, eventually to become Talmudic Judaism (which persists to this day).

By today's standards, Pharisees were highly educated laypersons. To study successfully under a great teacher such as Gamaliel was the equivalent of doing doctoral work at a famous university. We surmise that Paul was one of the most educated people in all of Judaism, even in the entire Roman world (see Acts 26:24).

When Paul was called by Christ on the road to Damascus, he was already on the high road to grand success in the Jewish world. Doors were open to him for unrivaled fame and much wealth. When he submitted to the will of God to serve Christ, he turned his back on all of this potential but brought along his great intellect and education.

I. SELF-CONFIDENCE: FALSE CONFIDENCE (PHILIPPIANS 3:4b-6)

A. PAUL'S CAUSE FOR CONFIDENCE (v. 4b)

4b. If anyone else thinks he has reasons to put confidence in the flesh, I have more:

When he sensed the need, Paul did not hesitate to produce his Jewish credentials (see Acts 26:4, 5; 2 Corinthians 11:22; Galatians 1:13, 14). Why does he do so here? Although we have only hints about the threat that Paul perceived for the Philippians, part of it seems to have been encroaching legalism from false teachers. We know that the early church had converts from the ranks of the Pharisees (Acts 15:5). The churches planted by Paul had a mix of Jews and Gentiles. Some of these churches were beset by teachers who came after Paul and taught the people that adherence to the Jewish law was necessary for Christians, both Jews and Gentiles.

Paul fought this false teaching whenever he became aware of it. The clearest example of this is the book of Galatians, where Paul is particularly refuting

Antioch. AN-tee-ock.

Athens. ATH-unz.

Damascus. Duh-MASS-kus.

Gamaliel. Guh-MAY-lih-ul or Guh-MAY-lee-al.

Gentiles. JEN-tiles.

Jerusalem. Juh-ROO-suh-lem.

Judaism. JOO-duh-izz-um or JOO-day-izz-um.

Pharisaic. FAIR-ih-SAY-ick.

Pharisees. FAIR-ih-seez.

rabbi. RAB-eye.

Sadducees. SAD-you-seez.

Talmudic. Tal-MOOD-ick.

Tarsus. TAR-sus.

the idea that Gentile men needed to undergo Jewish circumcision in order to be saved. He condemns these teachers with unusually harsh language (Galatians 5:12). This may be the situation in Philippi too, for Paul speaks of "those mutilators of the flesh" (Philippians 3:2).

B. PAUL'S ANCESTRY OF HONOR (v. 5)

5. . . . circumcised on the eighth day, of the people of Israel, of the tribe of Benjamin, a Hebrew of Hebrews; in regard to the law, a Pharisee;

Paul presents himself as the ideal Jew. As was proper, he had been ritually *circumcised* a week and a day after his birth (Leviticus 12:3). This is a tip of the cap to his observant parents. He claims to be *of the people of Israel*, probably indicating that his ancestry is not tainted by Gentile wives for many generations. He is *of the tribe of Benjamin*, the tribe of the first monarch of Israel, King Saul (1 Samuel 9:21). Benjamin was the final and very dear son of Jacob, for his beloved wife Rachel died at his birth (Genesis 35:18).

Paul also describes himself as *a Hebrew of the Hebrews*. This means that his family had not adopted Greek ways (become "Hellenized") as had many of the Jews of the day. He has been numbered among the Hebrew/Jewish elite. This is reaffirmed in his final heritage claim: he is *a Pharisee*. He had been an insider, a member of a very exclusive club in the Jewish world.

C. PAUL'S RÉSUMÉ OF RUTHLESSNESS (v. 6)

6. . . . as for zeal, persecuting the church; as for legalistic righteousness, faultless.

Paul continues listing his Jewish credentials, now turning to his accomplishments. He has been blameless as regards any violation of the law (see Mark 10:20). This does not mean he is sinless, for he understands his pre-Christian life as full of sin (see 1 Timothy 1:15). His religious fervor had been misdirected into a persecution of *the church,* to the point of murdering Jews who were disciples of Christ (Acts 9:1). Paul is not revealing this side of his life as a positive thing, but to show any challengers that he cannot be bested by anyone who questions his commitment to Judaism. It is as if he were the previous champ who has retired undefeated.

II. LOSING: WINNING (PHILIPPIANS 3:7-16)

A. GAINING THE KNOWLEDGE (vv. 7, 8)

7, 8. But whatever was to my profit I now consider loss for the sake of Christ. What is more, I consider everything a loss compared to the surpassing greatness of knowing Christ Jesus my Lord, for whose sake I have lost all things. I consider them rubbish, that I may gain Christ

Commonplace advice after a devastating loss or tragedy is something like, "Cheer up kid, you'll get over it." How often, though, do we hear the flip side? After a great victory or a great honor, does anyone say, "Tone down kid, you'll get over it"?

Paul does not cruise through life based on his great education and heritage. Instead, all his accomplishments and privileges he has counted *loss* for *Christ.* This does not mean he is trivializing or dismissing these things; after all, he just listed them! It means that even the greatest honors of human life are of small value in comparison to his driving passion: the knowledge of *Christ Jesus my Lord.* Paul is not talking about *knowing* about Jesus—the

WHAT DO YOU THINK?

Paul had many reasons to put his confidence in his religious résumé. What types of accomplishments are Christians tempted to place their confidence in (instead of Christ)?

DAILY BIBLE READINGS

Monday, Aug. 9—God's Love Perfected in Us (1 John 4:7-12)

Tuesday, Aug. 10—Trust in the Lord (Jeremiah 17: 7-13)

Wednesday, Aug. 11—A Place Prepared for You (John 14:1-4)

Thursday, Aug. 12—Trust with All Your Heart (Proverbs 3:3-8)

Friday, Aug. 13—Breaking with the Past (Philippians 3:1b-6)

Saturday, Aug. 14—Our Citizenship in Heaven (Philippians 3:17-21)

Sunday, Aug. 15—The Heavenly Call of God (Philippians 3:7-16)

knowledge that might come if one were to read every book written about Christ. Paul is concerned with knowing Jesus, being in an intimate relationship with him.

For Paul, this means serving Christ as his Lord and gladly offering up any abilities or advantages he might have in this service. Paul uses unusually strong language here, saying that his previous life is of no value (politely translated here as *rubbish*). This is hyperbole, but drives home his point. He is no more concerned with his past life than he is with yesterday's garbage. His focus is on the present, his ministry for Christ. He has willingly released hold on his previous life's accomplishments. Paul does not broodingly resent the hardships he endures for Christ. He rejoices over these things as a privilege (Colossians 1:24).

B. GAINING THE POWER (vv. 9, 10)

9, 10. . . . and be found in him, not having a righteousness of my own that comes from the law, but that which is through faith in Christ — the righteousness that comes from God and is by faith. I want to know Christ and the power of his resurrection and the fellowship of sharing in his sufferings, becoming like him in his death,

Paul had been raised to understand *righteousness* as a legitimate outcome of good works according to the Jewish *law*. He was "a Pharisee, the son a of Pharisee" (Acts 23:6). Paul knows that no one can accumulate enough good works to be truly righteous (Romans 3:10). Righteousness is reckoned according to one's *faith*, one's commitment and trust in God (Romans 4:24, 25).

The central feature of this faith is the *resurrection*. This is the source of *power* for Paul's ministry. He is utterly convinced that Christ was risen from the dead and that the price for sin has been paid. Jesus' crucifixion was done in weakness and vulnerability. Jesus' resurrection was a mighty deed of power (2 Corinthians 13:4). The followers of Christ share in both weakness through *sufferings* and, therefore, *his death*, and in his power through his resurrection. Personal power is not found in accomplishment or pedigree, but in absolute surrender to Christ.

PEDIGREES

Pedigrees are interesting things. Some people take great pride in their genealogical ancestry. Many are in awe of such great American families as the Roosevelts, the Vanderbilts, the Rockefellers, or the Kennedys. Some people claim descent from those who first arrived on the Mayflower. In Virginia, the FFVs (First Families of Virginia—descendants of those who arrived in the 1600s) comprise a prestigious group of bluebloods. Other groups, such as the Sons of the American Revolution or Sons of Union Veterans (Civil War), perpetuate the honor of involvement in great American causes.

I am proud to be a flag-waving American, and I have the pedigree to support it. My dad served in World War II, my great-grandfather in the Civil War, and two great-great-great-grandfathers in the American Revolution. (Thus my daughters could also join the prestigious Daughters of the American Revolution.) According to an old family history, one line of my ancestors came from Scottish nobility, arriving in western Pennsylvania in 1765. Other branches of the family came to Virginia in the 1700s. According to an old family Bible, I am a distant cousin of a previous Prime Minister of Great Britain.

WHAT DO YOU THINK?

Everything Paul had accomplished prior to knowing Christ he considered loss. Why is it so difficult to give up our sense of security in those things with which we were once comfortable?

WHAT DO YOU THINK?

We know that righteousness that comes from the law and that which comes by faith are different. One is an earned righteousness, from doing good things; the other is an imputed righteousness, having it credited by God's grace. But what, if any, is the difference in action?

Visual for Lesson 11. Display this visual as you discuss verse 14. Ask, "What role models inspire you to 'press on' in your faith?"

Yet, what does all this amount to? It does not make me a better person. It doesn't give me a larger vote. It doesn't lower (or raise!) my taxes. I am simply an ordinary American whose ancestors arrived on earlier boats. My pedigree does not change the quality of who I am.

—J. B. N.

C. GAINING THE RESURRECTION (vv. 11-13a)

11-13a. . . . and so, somehow, to attain to the resurrection from the dead. Not that I have already obtained all this, or have already been made perfect, but I press on to take hold of that for which Christ Jesus took hold of me. Brothers, I do not consider myself yet to have taken hold of it.

Paul now picks up his earlier imagery of being a runner for *Christ* (Philippians 2:16). He humbly looks forward to the greatest prize of all: *resurrection from the dead.* If this life is all there is, if there is no resurrection, then our selfless service to Christ and his church is pathetic and ridiculous. We might as well live selfishly, seeking only our own pleasures (see 1 Corinthians 15:32). We need not run any races. Let's stop this foolishness now! Let's just go to the tavern on the side of the race road and have a jolly old time!

But Paul will have none of that. He is committed never to swerve from the course or abandon the race. This is ensured by his desire to follow after Christ, to pursue the path Christ has already traversed.

Paul makes his point here with a play on words. He says *Christ Jesus* has taken *hold of* him. The phrase *take hold of* has the sense of "make something one's possession." Paul has been taken hold of by Christ. He is Christ's own, Christ's possession. But part of this process is Paul's taking hold of or capture of himself. Here, he knows that his efforts are not complete. He has not fully captured himself. His job is *not* done, and his life is not *perfect.* He still has some race to run.

D. GAINING THE PRIZE (vv. 13b, 14)

13b, 14. But one thing I do: Forgetting what is behind and straining toward what is ahead, I press on toward the goal to win the prize for which God has called me heavenward in Christ Jesus.

Paul continues to make his point by using the analogy of a footrace. The great runners do not look back to see where they have been. Their focus is dead *ahead,* on *the goal* and *the prize* that await the winner. As Christ said, "No one who puts his hand to the plow and looks back is fit for service in the kingdom of God" (Luke 9:62).

The thing to remember is that this is not a quick sprint but a marathon, a life race. It is not a competitive race, a matter of beating other runners. It only matters that you finish the race. Paul makes his race imagery more vivid by picturing *Christ* at the finish line, calling us home. This is a high calling, a calling from above, a call to our heavenly home. We finish this race at the end of our lives. We have crossed the finish line and remain eligible for the prize if we remain faithful to this call.

WHAT DO YOU THINK?

Paul made it clear that he had not yet completed his journey in Christ. Why is it important not to convey an attitude that "we've arrived" when it comes to full spiritual maturity in Christ?

WHAT DO YOU THINK?

Paul pressed on to win the prize in Christ Jesus. To what extent should our spiritual growth be motivated by reward? Explain.

I PRESS FORWARD

I have a good friend who is a marathoner. I used to be a morning jogger, but I never contemplated doing a marathon. The winning times for a marathon are often just over two hours. Many people take four hours. The idea of running nonstop for four hours makes me tired and sore just thinking about it! But for many people, running marathons is a fun-filled hobby.

It takes a lot of training to do a marathon. These runners spend months getting ready. Ten-mile runs are considered warm-ups. Just before a marathon they may do a 20-mile run just to prove they can do it. Weather is not a deterrent. They run in sun or shower, heat or cold.

In the marathon everything is focused on crossing the finish line. Often they get painful blisters. I have seen my friend hobble for days after a marathon before his muscles began to loosen up. During one race, the weather turned nasty, with dropping temperatures and a cold rain setting in. But my friend kept pushing himself. He was tired, sore, and uncomfortable, but he wanted to cross the line and collect his medallion.

I admire his zeal and perseverance. Paul says that's what the Christian life is like. We press forward to collect the prize.   —J. B. N.

E. GAINING THE MATURITY (vv. 15, 16)

15, 16. All of us who are mature should take such a view of things. And if on some point you think differently, that too God will make clear to you. Only let us live up to what we have already attained.

This race is the most important thing in all of life. It is for the *mature*. We become mature in this task as we refine our focus and continue the race along with our fellow believers. With maturity comes agreement. We figure things out. We yield to the power of God to reveal his will to us. This makes for a church in which members walk by the same rule and mind the same thing. They are united in their commitment to Christ and encouraged by the promise of his resurrection.

CONCLUSION

Today's Olympic athletes compete for gold, silver, and bronze medals. Outside the games, however, many of these athletes receive rich monetary rewards. Some receive cash payments from their government for winning. Others reap the benefits of celebrity through product endorsements and personal appearance fees.

In the ancient version of these games (the type that was familiar to Paul), the athletes competed for honor and a laurel wreath worn as a crown. To win was to receive one's "laurels." If handled carefully, these organic crowns probably lasted for a long time, but they had no cash value. Yet the potential of being honored as a victor in an Olympic event caused many to undergo strict training and preparation leading up to the games. To win was their goal, and to be honored was their prize.

Most people have many goals in their lives. Some are short term. In times of great hardship, the goal might be to make it through another week or another day. The prize is that life usually improves; things do get better. A longer personal goal might be to lose 10 pounds or to pay off a credit card. The prize comes from better physical and fiscal health. Still longer term might be the goal of early retirement. At one time, I had hoped to retire by age 50. Since that age is now seen only in my rearview mirror, it is a goal I will not attain (nor do I want it anymore). I still have the goal of being able to retire with adequate financial resources in place. The prize will be reasonable comfort and security in my old age. Personal goals change over the years, and the attraction of various prizes shifts as we mature.

WHAT DO YOU THINK?

Which do you think comes first, maturity or like-mindedness? Explain.

PRAYER

Dear Lord, serving you comes at a cost. We must give up things that the world thinks are important. May you give the strength to run your race, through your gate, down your straight and narrow road, for all of our lives. May we run and not grow weary. May we finally attain the prize of the high calling that is found only in serving Christ. In his name we pray, amen.

My primary goals in life have not changed for many years, though. Each year, I want to know Christ more fully (Philippians 3:10). I have chased this goal for many decades, and while I have made progress, there is still more track to run. I want to live in service to Christ in such a way that people will look at me and say, "That was a life well lived." And when I die, I want to hear the words, "Well done, faithful servant. Come and share my happiness!" (see Matthew 25:23). That is my goal. May my prize be to be with the Lord forever (1 Thessalonians 4:17).

THOUGHT TO REMEMBER
Our past failures and successes become less important as we know Christ more fully.

Discovery Learning

The following is an alternative lesson plan emphasizing learning activities. Classes desiring such student involvement will find these suggestions helpful. At the back of this book are reproducible student pages to further enhance activity learning.

INTO THE LESSON

Consider coming to class in running clothes and running shoes. Put a race number on your back. A checkered flag on display or winner's tape across the room will set a context for today's study and the imagery Paul uses. As the class assembles, say, "Are you ready to run?" Note that Paul concludes today's text with a footrace analogy.

Ask volunteers to stand and read the following "testimony" statements after you ask, "What do some people consider to be evidence of their right relationship to God?" (1) *"When it comes to being spiritual, I am more so than most."* (2) *"I spend more time at our church building than 95 percent of the congregation."* (3) *"My family has been part of this church for generations."* (4) *"No one has a stricter view of the binding nature of the Scriptures than I do."* (5) *"I'll match my prayer life against anyone's."* (6) *"I've been opposing those who distort God's Word every chance I get."* (7) *"I consider myself a serious and diligent student of the Bible. My knowledge of the Word rivals most members."* (8) *"I can't remember the last time I missed Sunday morning worship."*

Reflect on the eight remarks: "Well, you know, some of the things we think really matter are insignificant in relation to knowing Christ intimately. That's Paul's conclusion in today's study in Philippians 3."

INTO THE WORD

Prepare sheets with the following headings and 14 phrases on the sheet in equal blocks lined off (blocks about 4¼" by 1¼"). Headings: *WHAT*

MATTERS and *WHAT DOESN'T MATTER*. Phrases: *Family Heritage, A Faith in Christ That Comes of God, Ethnic Heritage, The Unity of True Believers, Zeal for a Religious Point of View, Having Confidence in Jesus' Resurrection and Sharing in It, High Personal Morality and Character, Careful Adherence to Dos and Don'ts, Being Able to Forget Past Sins and Weaknesses, Resistance to Cultural Influences, Being Found in Right Relationship to Christ, Participation in Religious Rites, A Sense of Needing Spiritual Completion, Personal Knowledge of Christ Jesus as Lord.*

Give a sheet to each learner with the directive to cut (or fold and tear) the sections and then establish two stacks under the two headings.

After a few minutes, ask one or two to read their stacks. Learners may disagree on the placement of some items, such as "resistance to cultural influences." For that example, Paul's claim of staying Jewish when many had been Hellenized may be considered to matter if one sees it as "keeping oneself unblemished from the world," but Paul says that his being "a Hebrew of the Hebrews" really doesn't matter.

Then say, "Now let's look at today's text; here Paul identifies what really matters and what is but rubbish." Have the text read aloud slowly and prompt learners to interrupt with relevant phrases from the sorting activity. Some will be more obvious than others, but all are related to the text.

Ask the class to look at verses 10, 11, where Paul says, "I want to know. . . ." Then ask, "What would be a good question to ask that would have these verses as the answer?" Allow a variety of responses. If no one says, "What is the goal of the Christian's life?" then offer that as "your" question. Note that the daily value of this vow can work wonders in the Christian's life. Suggest that your learners read this daily through the next week as their personal statement of their life's goal and see what a difference it can make each day.

Option: Use the reproducible activity "Anything [Jewish] You Can Do I Can Do Better" from page 510 to explore the lesson text.

INTO LIFE

Note that many are living life out of focus, with no real sense of what matters. Ask, "What are most people focused on?" Accept responses and then remark, "What really matters is what I'm focused on and what you're focused on: a relationship with Christ that carries the hope of resurrection." Lead the class in a time of directed prayer (in which you suggest subject matters as class members pray silently). Include such elements as "confidence in and hope for resurrection," "an increasingly intimate knowledge of Jesus," "unity of mind in our congregation on what really matters," "God's help in forgetting the past," "a desire to reach completion, maturity in Christ." Add other elements from today's study, as you choose.

Option: The reproducible activity "Credentials" on page 510 is an alternative application activity.

GROWING IN JOY AND PEACE

LESSON 12

INTRODUCTION

A. JOY VS. HAPPINESS

Is it possible to be too happy? This may seem like a silly question, but it speaks to the heart of what drives much of our society today. We are forever engaged in Thomas Jefferson's elusive "pursuit of happiness." The problem is in determining what makes us happy and at what cost. If more and better possessions make us happy, is it worth it to work three jobs in order to afford them? If deep personal relationships make us happy, what will we do when they end? If winning in competition makes us happy, how can we survive losing?

Some writers today, both religious and secular, question this all-consuming focus on happiness. It is argued that a well-rounded person is one who experiences pain as well as happiness. These writers claim that there is value in melancholy, strength in sadness. Jesus himself pronounced a blessing on those who mourn (Matthew 5:4).

In today's text Paul exhorts the readers to rejoice continually. This presents us with a conundrum if we equate joy with happiness. How can I be happy when I am unhappy? Am I just supposed to fake being happy all the time? Should I paint a smile on my face or wear a mask? This misses the important point that happiness and joy are not the same thing. Joy is not a fleeting and easily manipulated emotion. Joy is hopeful, deep-seated confidence in our existence as children of God. Joy is a positive look at the present because we know our future is secure through faith in Christ. Joy is based on never having to doubt the acceptance of a loving and caring heavenly Father. We may not always be happy. In fact, it is unreasonable and unhealthy to expect to be happy all the time. But we may always rejoice, even in the darkest experiences of our lives.

B. LESSON BACKGROUND

Throughout the Christian era, churches have been known to raise funds for purposes outside their own congregations. One of Paul's great projects was raising relief money "for the poor among the saints in Jerusalem" (Romans 15:26). This was a widespread effort brought on by a famine of several years' duration in the temple city.

Today's churches give large amounts of money to various ministries and parachurch organizations. Some churches do this through coordinated denominational efforts. Independent churches support such works on an individual basis according to the policies and decisions of each congregation. All churches, however, like to support people and ministries with which they

DEVOTIONAL READING:
PSALM 85:4-13

BACKGROUND SCRIPTURE:
PHILIPPIANS 4

PRINTED TEXT:
PHILIPPIANS 4:1-14

LESSON AIMS

After participating in this lesson, each student will be able to:

1. Identify some of the attitudes and priorities that Paul says will lead to a life of spiritual joy and peace.

2. Explain why joy and contentment are not dependent on possessions or circumstances.

3. Choose one attitude or priority for special focus in the coming week in order to pursue peace and joy in his or her life.

KEY VERSE

Whatever you have learned or received or heard from me, or seen in me—put it into practice. And the God of peace will be with you.
—*Philippians 4:9*

Aug
22

feel a personal connection. Modern opportunities for travel allow churches to send representatives to foreign fields to assist and to evaluate the ministries they support. Reports from these travelers energize the congregations and spur even greater giving.

We do not know exactly how Paul funded his travels. His first missionary journey included three passages onboard ship, which would have been costly. These may have been funded by Barnabas, who was a person of some means (see Acts 4:36, 37). Paul's later journeys (without Barnabas) seem to have been more on the order of shoestring operations. He spoke of times of hunger and hard work (2 Corinthians 6:5). He seems to have taken temporary employment as a tentmaker to support himself when necessary (Acts 18:3; compare 1 Thessalonians 2:9; 2 Thessalonians 3:7-10).

Paul's relationship with the Philippian church was unique. This church supported him long after he left its city (see Philippians 4:15, 16; compare 2 Corinthians 11:8, 9). They received no direct benefit from his ministry, yet they understood Paul's burning desire to take the gospel to people all over the Roman world (see Romans 1:14, 15). They even sent Epaphroditus to help Paul while he was imprisoned in Rome (Philippians 2:25, 30). They shared with him monetarily because they believed they shared his ministry.

The Philippian church was the result of Paul's ministry, but Paul's ongoing work was an extension of the Philippians' ministry. This made them willing to share generously and selflessly. Is it any wonder, then, that Paul is so full of joy when he writes to them? And wouldn't the Philippians have been energized and encouraged when they received a letter from the missionary they were supporting, along with a firsthand report from their messenger? The financial matters of this affiliation cannot be separated from the deep personal relationship between Paul and his beloved Philippians.

I. GENERATING JOY (PHILIPPIANS 4:1-7)

A. CONFLICT RESOLUTION (vv. 1-3)

1. Therefore, my brothers, you whom I love and long for, my joy and crown, that is how you should stand firm in the Lord, dear friends!

Paul's affection for the Philippians can be seen by the ways he addresses them in this, the final section of the letter. First, they are his *brothers*. This is an inclusive term, not confined to the male believers. Paul often uses the metaphors of family to describe the church (see Galatians 6:10). These descriptions are founded on the spiritual kinship all believers have with their common Father through the Son (see John 1:12).

Second, the Philippians are ones whom Paul loves, an expression of deep tenderness. The depth of Paul's *love* for the Philippians is made especially clear by the repetition of this expression at the end of the verse, where it is translated *dear friends*. Third, the Philippians are those Paul has longed for. Ministry and circumstance have separated them, but Paul treasures the memories of his times of fellowship with the Philippian church. He has not forgotten any of the bad parts of his Philippian sojourn, but he sincerely loves these people.

Finally, Paul addresses the readers as his *joy and crown*. This may seem like a curious combination of words, but Paul has chosen them carefully. The Philippians are his joy because their faithfulness brings a smile and sense of hope to Paul whenever he remembers them. The Philippians are the church

HOW TO SAY IT

Augsburg. Ogz-burg.
Barnabas. BAR-nuh-bus.
Clement. KLEH-munt.
Diet. DEE-ut
Epaphroditus. Ee-PAF-ro-
    DYE-tus.
Euodia. You-O-dee-uh.
Philippi. Fih-LIP-pie or FIL-
    ih-pie.
Syntyche. SIN-tih-key.
Wartburg. VORT-berg.
Worms. Vormz.

that Paul has hoped all his churches would be. They have listened to his message and are now living out their faith in Christ through their actions. *Crown* has the sense here of "reward," not royalty. The shining example of the Philippians and their faith is a precious payoff for Paul. He does not expect to become wealthy in ministry. He wants to become rich in relationships and in the fathering of many spiritual children for the Lord.

2. I plead with Euodia and I plead with Syntyche to agree with each other in the Lord.

Not everything is perfect in Philippi, though. Somehow Paul has learned that two prominent women in the church, *Euodia* and *Syntyche,* are feuding about something. Epaphroditus may have reported this to Paul. Or there might have been additional communication from Philippi—the same source by which Epaphroditus knows the folks back home have learned of his illness (Philippians 2:26)—and in that communication was the report of the feud between Euodia and Syntyche.

This feud is ironic given the meanings of the women's names. Euodia means "pleasant journey" and has the connotation of "success." Syntyche means "good fortune" and also has the connotation of "success." In this case, two successes apparently have collided! These women have positive, optimistic names that mean nearly the same thing, yet they are being dragged down by an unspecified dispute. Significantly, Paul does not try to resolve the disagreement, but exhorts them to work it out themselves. This can be done only if they remember that they are Christian sisters and find agreement *in the Lord.*

3. Yes, and I ask you, loyal yokefellow, help these women who have contended at my side in the cause of the gospel, along with Clement and the rest of my fellow workers, whose names are in the book of life.

Paul enlists the help of an unnamed Philippian church leader, described only as a *loyal yokefellow.* This is a metaphor drawn from the world of working animals in which two oxen or horses might be joined by a common yoke, a harness contraption that allows them to pull a cart or wagon. This has to be done in unison, equally. If one ox pulls harder or gets ahead, the wagon goes off kilter. Paul sees this leader as in complete harmony with himself. No doubt he also wants this analogy to be extended to the disputing women, so that they might begin to work together.

Paul is not taking sides here, for he loves all of these people. The *women,* along with a man named *Clement,* have been *fellow* laborers, coworkers with Paul in the gospel, evangelizing their community. These are not false believers or outsiders who have infiltrated the church. They are Paul's brothers and sisters in Christ, Christians with their eternal destiny secured by faith, believers with their *names* in *the book of life* (see Revelation 20:12).

B. Consistent Rejoicing (vv. 4-7)

4. Rejoice in the Lord always. I will say it again: Rejoice!

Having dealt with this matter between the two women, Paul returns to general advice for the congregation. His first appeal is that the Philippians be in a state of ongoing rejoicing. How can this be? Do they not have the right to sulk a bit occasionally? Is it realistic to command people to *rejoice*? This is not a command that says, "Don't worry, be happy," in mindless, oblivious fashion. It is a call to remember all the things that give them reason to rejoice.

WHAT DO YOU THINK?

Paul addressed an ongoing dispute between two women in this congregation. What does God-honoring resolution in such arguments usually look like?

WHAT DO YOU THINK?

Paul was able to rejoice in all of his circumstances. What can we legitimately rejoice about during difficult times? How does it help to know that God is going to use everything that happens to us for his glory?

DAILY BIBLE READINGS

Monday, Aug. 16—God Speaks Peace (Psalm 85: 4-13)

Tuesday, Aug. 17— Facing Danger with Peace (Acts 27:33-44)

Wednesday, Aug. 18—Reap in Shouts of Joy (Psalm 126)

Thursday, Aug. 19— Finding Joy and Peace (Isaiah 55:6-13)

Friday, Aug. 20—Peace Be with You (John 20:19-23)

Saturday, Aug. 21— Focusing on the Spirit (Romans 8:1-8)

Sunday, Aug. 22— Experiencing God's Peace (Philippians 4:1-14)

WHAT DO YOU THINK?

Paul wanted his readers to focus their thoughts on particular kinds of things. What in your life can be categorized under each of the descriptors in Philippians 4:8?

They have been blessed by the gospel (Philippians 1:5). Their future destiny is secure because of the resurrection of Christ (3:10, 11). They have a dear fellowship founded in the sharing of the Holy Spirit (2:1). When they stop to consider these blessings, how can they help but rejoice?

5. *Let your gentleness be evident to all. The Lord is near.*

Paul never claims to know the exact date or time when Christ will return, but he always has believed that this day *is near.* He believes that the Lord's return might occur during his lifetime, and that all believers should be in a constant state of readiness (see 1 Thessalonians 5:23). In regard to the Philippians, it is important for Paul that they live in a manner that is courteous and gentle. They are to be seen as solid, dependable people in the eyes of outsiders, not as fanatics or extreme zealots, for these characteristics are repellent to nonbelievers.

6, 7. *Do not be anxious about anything, but in everything, by prayer and petition, with thanksgiving, present your requests to God. And the peace of God, which transcends all understanding, will guard your hearts and your minds in Christ Jesus.*

We lose our focus when we begin to *be anxious,* worrying and piling concerns on ourselves. We must release our cares to the Lord (1 Peter 5:7). When we understand that *God* is in control and is watching over us, it does not mean that all of those things that concern us suddenly disappear. We still face challenges and hardships, but we begin to live in *the peace of God.* This process is not fully explainable. How can God bring peace to a troubled life without taking away all the problems? While not completely rational, it is true. It is a peace that exceeds all understanding. It is the comforting presence of the Holy Spirit (see Acts 9:31).

II. FINDING PEACE (PHILIPPIANS 4:8, 9)

A. THOUGHT TARGETS (v. 8)

8. *Finally, brothers, whatever is true, whatever is noble, whatever is right, whatever is pure, whatever is lovely, whatever is admirable—if anything is excellent or praiseworthy—think about such things.*

Today's news is full of the sordid, the tragic, and the violent. It was no different for the Philippians. Paul says, though, that we have control over our thought lives. We should concentrate on virtuous things, examples of honesty, justice, beauty, and good reputation.

These things are happening all around us all the time, but they rarely make the evening news or headlines. Society can become ugly and mean because we are fascinated by ugliness and meanness. We should seek to add virtue to our faith (2 Peter 1:5). We should celebrate great deeds of nobleness, inspiring and uplifting music, and beautiful works of art wherever they might be found.

THINKING

The novel *Silas Marner* by George Eliot, first published in 1861, tells the story of a disillusioned recluse. Marner, an active member of an evangelical church and engaged to be married, was falsely accused of theft. His church excommunicated him, his fiancée abandoned him (actually marrying the real thief), and he relocated to a small town. For 15 years he shut himself off from everything else except his work as a weaver, meanwhile hoarding his growing supply of gold. Abandoned by everything he thought stable and foundational, he now found his only comfort in amassing money. It was his driving thought, and his life became consumed by its accumulation, and he became a bitter miser. As he thought in his heart, so he had become.

Then his money was stolen and a little orphan girl came into his life. Now concerned for her welfare, Marner changed his life's priorities. As the girl blossomed into a winsome young woman, Marner earned the respect of the town. Now consumed with the girl's best interests, Marner's heart changed, and his life was enriched by her love. His money was restored as well.

Paul encourages us to think about good and lofty things. If we think about these virtues, they will become our lifestyle as well.   —J. B. N.

B. BEHAVIOR BAROMETERS (v. 9)

9. Whatever you have learned or received or heard from me, or seen in me— put it into practice. And the God of peace will be with you.

The best standard for behavior is not a list of rules but an example. The musician does not gain her skill by reading a book, but from a teacher and *practice*. Paul never portrays himself as having reached perfection (Philippians 3:12), but he is confident enough in his track record to encourage the readers to live as he lives. He has devoted his life to ministry and service to others. He has been content with very little. He has cherished and guarded his relationships with fellow believers. This lifestyle has not deprived him of anything he counts as significant. Instead, he has been granted *peace* from God's presence in his life, and this benefit is available to those who imitate him (1 Corinthians 11:1; Philippians 3:17).

III. GRASPING CONTENTMENT (PHILIPPIANS 4:10-14)

A. FRIENDS WHO COMFORT (v. 10)

10. I rejoice greatly in the Lord that at last you have renewed your concern for me. Indeed, you have been concerned, but you had no opportunity to show it.

Although they may have been out of contact for a time, Paul never doubted the *concern* of the Philippians. Communication and travel are difficult in the ancient world. Letters can go undelivered. Months, even years, might pass with no word. The Philippians did not forget Paul, though. When they learned of his situation in Rome, they had sent Epaphroditus with money, allowing the relationship to be *renewed* (see v. 18). Even at a distance, their love for each other has flourished again.

B. CHRIST WHO STRENGTHENS (vv. 11-14)

11, 12. I am not saying this because I am in need, for I have learned to be content whatever the circumstances. I know what it is to be in need, and I know what it is to have plenty. I have learned the secret of being content in any and every situation, whether well fed or hungry, whether living in plenty or in want.

Paul is no masochist, one who enjoys suffering. He does not find pleasure in pain. But life has sent him more than his share of hardship, mainly because of his commitment to spreading the gospel. No matter what harsh realities and cruelties he encounters, Paul has learned *to be content*. He does not complain, crying out to the Lord that he deserves better. There is no hardship that can separate him from the love of Christ (Romans 8:35). His goal is not a life of ease, but the salvation of souls (2 Timothy 2:9, 10).

THE GOD OF PEACE SHALL BE WITH YOU

Visual for Lesson 12. *Display this visual as you discuss verse 9. Ask, "Who can claim this promise? Why?"*

Paul's pain is caused by the unbelief of his fellow Jews (Romans 9:1-3), by the betrayal of the gospel (Galatians 1:9), and other matters.

CONTENTMENT

Martin Luther experienced both plenty and scarcity. In his early days as a monk, he lived on a spartan diet. Later, as a highly successful reformer and a respected religious leader, he ate well. At one time he was an unknown; later he hobnobbed with some of the greatest of the German princes. Yet when the princes were debating Lutheranism's future at the Diet in Augsburg in 1530, Luther quoted Psalm 118:9: "It is better to take refuge in the Lord than to trust in princes."

Luther could be content in his small monk's cell or under house arrest at the Wartburg; he could also be content in his home surrounded by his wife and six children. He was willing to risk his life defending his religious views at the Diet of Worms; later he could yield to his prince who refused to allow him to go to Augsburg because it was too risky. He received rich gifts, but he would often give a gold or silver platter to a beggar or send booklets off to the printer without even thinking about royalties. He had learned the principle of contentment that Paul discusses.

—J. B. N.

WHAT DO YOU THINK?

How would you respond to a fellow believer who tells you he is going to stop taking his diabetes medicine, claiming the promise that "I can do everything through him who gives me strength"?

13. I can do everything through him who gives me strength.

This is one of the most quoted yet misapplied verses in the Bible. Some have taken it to mean that nothing should be impossible for the faithful Christian. Thus, when things seem impossible, they say it must be that we lack faith. But there were many things that Paul was unable to do. He was unable to persuade God to remove a physical infirmity from which he suffered, his "thorn in [his] flesh" (2 Corinthians 12:7-9). He was unable to keep Demas from deserting him (2 Timothy 4:10). Paul was no ancient superman.

In context, Paul is speaking about enduring hardship. He admits to times of plenty and times of want. He understands being loved and accepted, as well as being rejected and persecuted. In all these times, he continues to do, to function, because of the strengthening grace he receives from his faith in Christ. Because of this ministry of the Lord, Paul is able to claim *strength* in his weakest moments (see 2 Corinthians 12:10). He may live a penniless, physically battered, unappreciated life, but he is still strong in Christ.

14. Yet it was good of you to share in my troubles.

Paul compliments the Philippians for remembering him and trying to ease his suffering. They know of his hardships in Rome and have sent Epaphroditus with a monetary gift to help him (Philippians 2:25; 4:18). Paul is saying in effect, "I would have survived without you because of the strengthening power of Christ. I have done it before. But I sure do appreciate your help."

CONCLUSION

An old saying claims, "Money cannot buy happiness." We often joke about this, saying that we would at least like to give it a try. We look at our lives and wonder whether more money would make things better. Would it relieve stress? Would it allow us to bless other people? Would it get me the new car or house I have always wanted?

The truth is that the happiness that money can purchase is fleeting. It is not satisfying in the long run and does not give us real contentment. The

PRAYER

Gracious Father, help us to find contentment in our lives. Give us the peace that passes human understanding. May we be satisfied with your provision. In the name of Jesus we pray. Amen.

desire for money will cause evil in one's life (1 Timothy 6:10). It causes a soul-poisoning restlessness, the uncontented life always wanting more.

Some of the most joyful, contented, purposeful people I have known were people of very modest means. Some of the most miserable were very wealthy. Paul's emphasis here is that we can be content in poverty or wealth if we trust in God. Personal peace does not come from controlling our situation through abundant wealth, but in yielding that control to God and trusting him to provide. Jesus taught that concern over wealth and security was driven by a lack of faith (Luke 12:27, 28). May we seek peace through our relationship to God and our service to him.

THOUGHT TO REMEMBER

May we experience lives of ongoing joy and peace as we find contentment in our relationship with God.

Discovery Learning

The following is an alternative lesson plan emphasizing learning activities. Classes desiring such student involvement will find these suggestions helpful. At the back of this book are reproducible student pages to further enhance activity learning.

INTO THE LESSON

Cut three 3" by 27" strips from poster board. Draw nine boxes of 3" squares on each and also on the back of two strips. On one side of each of the double-sided strips, put the word *REJOICING* vertically, one letter per square. On the other side put an H and an A in the top two boxes and an S in the bottom box of each. On the third strip write the word *TEMPORARY* and cut the boxes apart.

As class begins, display the two strips side-by-side, with the *H*, *A*, and *S* showing along with the six blank squares. Say, "There are some letters missing from these 'Ha Ha' strips. As you correctly suggest the missing letters, I'll fill them in." The two words you want are *HARDTIMES* and *HAPPINESS*.

When you have both words completed, divide the class in half and direct each group to make an acrostic with one of these words. One will identify components and descriptions of hard times. The other will do the same for happiness. If they need a sample to get started, suggest *homelessness* for the "hard times" group, *health* for the "happiness" group. If examples are needed, consider these: "hard times": *homelessness, anxiety, recession, death/ depression, threats, inflation, misery, estrangement, scarcity;* "happiness": *health, accomplishment, prosperity, pleasure, independence, nurture, employment, satisfaction, security.*

Start putting up the letters *T-E-M-P-O-R-A-R-Y* a letter at a time, between your *HARDTIMES* and *HAPPINESS* strips. As a class member notices

and identifies the word you are adding, complete putting all the letters up and then say, "Both hard times and happiness are temporary. But [turn the strips over to reveal the word *REJOICING*] rejoicing is eternal!"

INTO THE WORD

Read today's Scripture text, Philippians 4:1-14. Give a copy of the following word search puzzle (which you will have prepared in advance) to each learner. Say, "In Philippians 4 Paul makes a continuing plea for each Christian to fill his or her life with joy. But he also calls for other emotions and lifestyle choices for the believer. Find a variety of characteristics or descriptions in this word search." Some words are quoted from the text; others are synonyms.

REJOICING PLUS

```
J  G  E  N  T  L  E  N  E  S  S  P  O  Y
S  J  G  N  I  C  I  O  J  E  R  I  A  F
U  T  O  Y  J  O  Y  J  O  A  I  Y  J  E
O  O  E  Y  J  S  O  Y  Y  J  M  O  U  X
R  D  L  A  T  Y  J  E  O  Y  I  R  J  C
E  L  B  R  D  O  R  Y  J  O  T  Y  T  E
N  T  O  L  J  F  O  Y  J  O  A  Y  S  L
E  N  N  J  U  O  A  Y  P  R  T  U  E  L
G  E  J  L  N  F  O  S  I  U  O  Y  N  E
J  T  O  Y  I  J  E  G  T  U  R  O  O  N
Y  N  J  O  T  Y  H  C  T  N  S  E  H  T
J  O  O  S  Y  T  Y  R  A  J  E  O  L  Y
J  C  U  O  E  Y  I  J  O  E  Y  S  O  O
Y  J  Y  L  E  V  O  L  J  O  P  Y  S  J
```

Words in the puzzle are *content, excellent, fair, generous, gentleness, honest, imitators, just, lovely, noble, peaceful, prayerful, pure, rejoicing, right, steadfastness, strong, true, unity, virtuous.*

As the words are identified, make a public list and stop to note how and where the concepts are included in today's text. Use the lesson commentary to note the significance of the terms, both for the Philippians in Paul's day and for believers today. Follow up with the reproducible activity "Joy Is . . ." from page 511.

INTO LIFE

Paul's challenge in Philippians 4:8, 9 is one we should carry with ourselves daily. Distribute copies of "Thought Life" from page 511. After students compete that activity, have the class read verse 9 in unison. Give each learner a sheet with the following stimulus statements and ask them to give attention to it during the coming week:

• Here are some of the important things I have learned about Christian behavior.

• Here are some of the spiritual things I have received from Christian family and friends.

• Here are some of the most important things I have heard from Christian teachers and preachers.

• Here are some of the delightful behaviors I have seen in the people of Christ.

At the bottom of the list, put this imperative from Paul's challenge: THOSE THINGS . . . DO!

UPHELD BY GOD

LESSON 13

INTRODUCTION

A. WHY DID THE JEWS REJECT JESUS?

After the Roman governor, Pontius Pilate, condemned Jesus to be executed, he commissioned that a sign be placed on Jesus' cross. The sign—written in Hebrew, Greek, and Latin—identified Jesus as the "King of the Jews." All four Gospels tell of the sign, but John's Gospel includes this unique detail: the Jewish leaders were offended and objected to Pilate. They wanted no part of any sort of legitimate recognition of Jesus (John 19:19-22).

This little story is consistent with the general pattern portrayed in the New Testament. For the most part, the Jewish people of Paul's day were unreceptive to Paul's claims that Jesus was the prophesied Messiah, the heir of David. The Jews who accepted the claims of the early Christian evangelists such as Paul—like many who accepted Jesus from his own teaching—were often driven from the synagogue and cut off from the Jewish community. (See John 9:22.) Why?

There is no clear answer to this. We can say that faith is an individual decision and that each Jewish person in the ancient world made a personal choice concerning Jesus. This is true, but it does not fully explain the widespread and violent opposition to the Christian message, particularly by Jewish leaders in various locations. After Paul's final, fateful confrontation with the temple leaders in Jerusalem, they characterized him as a "troublemaker" who was causing trouble among Jews all over the world (Acts 24:5). This animosity erupted with such force on one occasion that the governing Romans had to use military force to rescue Paul from his imminent death at the hands of a Jewish mob (Acts 21:31-36).

This never caused Paul to reject his people. He was a Jew until the day he died. He longed for the salvation of his Jewish brothers and sisters (Romans 9:2, 3). He took no pleasure in Jewish unbelief. He spoke with great anguish when he told King Agrippa that he was accused of betrayal by the Jews, when he was simply proclaiming the fulfillment of Jewish hopes and prophecy (Acts 26:7). Elsewhere, Paul looked at the unbelief of the Jewish nation as an opportunity for Gentiles to become grafted into the people of God (Romans 11:17). Even in this, Paul held out the hope that the Jews would be grafted back in at a later date (Romans 11:23).

In many ways, the book of Acts is the chronicle of this unfortunate rejection of Jesus by the Jews. Paul often began his work in a new city by going to the synagogue. There, using scriptural arguments, he would attempt to prove that Jesus was indeed the promised Messiah (see Acts 17:1-3). This strategy generally produced a few disciples, but often resulted in Paul's being driven from the synagogue and the city. In Lystra, the unbelieving Jews even attempted to kill Paul by stoning him (Acts 14:19).

Acts ends with Paul in Rome, the great imperial city. He used this opportunity to preach Christ to the Jews there, but he received a mixed reception

DEVOTIONAL READING:
ACTS 9:23-30
BACKGROUND SCRIPTURE:
ACTS 28; PHILIPPIANS 4:
15-23
PRINTED TEXT:
ACTS 28:16-25a, 28-31

LESSON AIMS

After participating in this lesson, each student will be able to:

1. Describe the situation Paul endured in Rome while writing Philippians.

2. Give an example of a time when the gospel advanced in seemingly unfavorable circumstances.

3. Write a prayer that asks God for strength to proclaim the gospel boldly in all circumstances.

KEY VERSE

For two whole years Paul stayed there in his own rented house and welcomed all who came to see him. Boldly and without hindrance he preached the kingdom of God and taught about the Lord Jesus Christ.
—Acts 28:30, 31

LESSON 13 NOTES

and many did not believe him. At this point, Paul saw that the Old Testament prophets not only spoke of the Messiah, but they also foresaw the unbelief of Israel. Paul quoted Isaiah 6:9, 10 to the crowd, a horrifying prediction of the rejection of God's message. Why did they rebuff Paul's preaching? Acts does not give us a specific reason. Whatever the cause, Luke (the author of Acts) is more interested in the result: Paul turns to the Gentiles with the offer of salvation through faith in Christ (Acts 13:46; 28:28).

B. LESSON BACKGROUND

Both the book of Acts and Paul's writings testify to the apostle's strong desire to preach the gospel in the great city of Rome. This was based on Paul's conviction that God had destined him to do this (Acts 23:11) and a personal yearning to do so (Romans 1:15). Paul had grown up in Tarsus and had significant ministries in Antioch, Corinth, and Ephesus. These were major, important cities in the Roman Empire, but they did not compare with Rome itself. The old saying that "all roads lead to Rome" was true in many ways. Rome was the center of power, of wealth, and of culture for the entire empire. It had no peer.

Some have compared Paul's desire to go to Rome with that of the aspiring actor who goes to Hollywood or the talented songwriter who goes to Nashville. This is a false portrayal! Paul did not want to go to Rome to further his career. His motivation was a strategic move for the success of the gospel. If Rome could have a strong Christian presence, it would have an oversized impact on the rest of the empire. Just as all roads led to Rome, those roads carried people and ideas from Rome to the farthest corners of the world.

Christian tradition credits Peter and Paul with founding the church in Rome, but this is almost certainly not accurate. There was already a church in Rome when Paul arrived, about AD 60. We know there were residents of Rome in the crowd in Jerusalem some 30 years earlier on the Day of Pentecost to hear Peter preach the first gospel message (Acts 2:10). It is likely that the church was present in Rome for many years before Paul's arrival. This does not deny, however, that the two great apostles had a huge positive impact on the Roman church and helped to increase its size and influence.

Paul got the first hint of his eventual ministry in Rome during his Damascus road experience. At that time, it was revealed that he would preach to "Gentiles and their kings" (Acts 9:15). The ultimate Gentile king was the Roman emperor, and Paul's appeal to Caesar (see Acts 27:24) gave him the potential opportunity to share the gospel with this very person. This did not happen quickly. Paul endured two years imprisonment in Caesarea Maritime before making his appeal (Acts 24:27). His trip to Rome was not a pleasant journey. He was under armed guard and had to live through a terrifying storm and a shipwreck on Malta (Acts 27:14–28:1). The book of Acts ends with Paul having finally reached Rome and awaiting his audience with the emperor. This is the backdrop for today's lesson.

Visual for Lesson 13.
This map will be useful throughout the quarter to give your students a geographical perspective.

HOW TO SAY IT

Agrippa. Uh-GRIP-puh.
Antioch. AN-tee-ock.
Caesar. SEE-zer.
Caesarea Maritime. Sess-uh-
    REE-uh MARE-uh-time.
centurion. sen-TURE-ee-un.
Corinth. KOR-inth.
Damascus. Duh-MASS-kus.
Ephesus. EF-uh-sus.
Judaism. JOO-duh-izz-um or
    JOO-day-izz-um.
Lystra. LISS-truh.
Malta. MAL-tuh.
Messiah. Meh-SIGH-uh.
Naboth. NAY-bawth.
Pentecost. PENT-ih-kost.
Socrates. SOCK-ruh-teez.
synagogue. SIN-uh-gog.
Tarsus. TAR-sus.

I. ROME AT LAST! (ACTS 28:16-22)

A. HOME DETENTION (vv. 16, 17a)

16, 17a. When we got to Rome, Paul was allowed to live by himself, with a soldier to guard him. Three days later he called together the leaders of the Jews.

Paul's sea voyage to *Rome* had been overseen by Roman soldiers, but this had not ensured his safety. The shipwreck on the island of Malta had stretched what should have been a few weeks' sailing into a voyage of several months. We can imagine the relief of the responsible centurion who had traveled with Paul when finally he was able to turn Paul and the other prisoners over to the authorities in Rome. We should note that the author of the book, Luke, is with Paul during this odyssey, as indicated by the *we* in his narrative.

As in today's world, Roman legal appeals can move at a snail's pace, so arrangements are made for Paul's detention while awaiting his hearing before the emperor. He is *allowed to live* in a house, under the *guard* of a Roman *soldier*. This is probably at Paul's expense, including the cost of the soldier, but Paul seems to have access to funds that make this possible. His freedom to move about is restricted by the use of a chain (Acts 28:20), probably an ankle fetter.

The house is more than a small hovel, for it is able to accommodate the many people who will come to hear Paul's message at a future date (Acts 28:23). Paul takes little time to be settled, for after only *three days* he invites the local Jewish *leaders* to meet with him. This is not an example of Paul's authority to order these men around, but a reflection of the circumstance of his detention.

B. DISTINGUISHED VISITORS (vv. 17b-20)

17b, 18. When they had assembled, Paul said to them: "My brothers, although I have done nothing against our people or against the customs of our ancestors, I was arrested in Jerusalem and handed over to the Romans. They examined me and wanted to release me, because I was not guilty of any crime deserving death.

Paul's initial message is not about the gospel, but an explanation of the events that have caused him to be in Rome. In this, he claims categorical innocence, that he has committed *nothing* that could be considered a legitimate offense according to Jewish laws and traditions. Even so, he has been accused, and this has placed him in Roman custody. Paul contends that *the Romans* have found no reason to detain him, and certainly nothing that deserves execution. In this, his situation mirrors that of Jesus in his trial before Pilate (Luke 23:13-16; compare Acts 26:30-32).

INNOCENT OF CHARGES

In Frank Capra's classic 1936 film, *Mr. Deeds Goes to Town*, a simple honest man from Vermont inherits a fortune and heads to New York City. There, many people try to take advantage of him to get some of his money. When he puts it to use helping disadvantaged folks get back on their feet, distant relatives try to get Deeds declared mentally incompetent so they can take over the money. In the end, Deeds proves his sanity, gets the girl, and is set free.

It is all too common in history for people to be accused of crimes of which they are innocent. Jesus experienced this, as did Socrates, Naboth (1 Kings 21:13), and Paul. If you've ever been falsely accused, you are in good company! People who have an evil agenda will make false accusations against an innocent person to accomplish their own agenda.

Paul was accused and put in prison. Even so, he continued to preach and teach, and he wrote letters to churches and individuals. When you are falsely accused, will you handle it as well as he?

—J. B. N.

DAILY BIBLE READINGS

Monday, Aug. 23—An Encouraging Advocate (Acts 9:23-30)

Tuesday, Aug. 24—Our Refuge and Strength (Psalm 46)

Wednesday, Aug. 25—The Lord Is Your Keeper (Psalm 121)

Thursday, Aug. 26—God's Promise and Protection (Psalm 119:114-117)

Friday, Aug. 27—Protected on the Journey (Acts 28:1-15)

Saturday, Aug. 28—God Will Satisfy Every Need (Philippians 4:15-20)

Sunday, Aug. 29—The Unhindered Gospel (Acts 28:16-25a, 28-31)

WHAT DO YOU THINK?

Paul proclaimed his innocence to the Jewish leaders. When is it wise to make a public response to false accusations, and when should we just let them go?

19, 20. But when the Jews objected, I was compelled to appeal to Caesar—not that I had any charge to bring against my own people. For this reason I have asked to see you and talk with you. It is because of the hope of Israel that I am bound with this chain."

Paul's account of his *appeal to Caesar* includes an interesting note of explanation. He has no desire to accuse his nation, meaning he has not done this to embarrass or bring shame on the nation of Israel. He has not come to Rome with a determined hostility toward the Jewish *people*. They are still his "brothers" (v. 17) and sisters, and *for this reason* he has arranged to meet with the Jews of Rome.

Paul gives a bottom line for all of his problems: his preaching of *the hope of Israel*. This is an inclusive phrase to describe Paul's preaching of Jesus as the Messiah, but it is focused especially on the hope of the resurrection (see Acts 24:14, 15). Paul has previously encountered unbelief on this very point (see Acts 17:32; 24:21).

C. TO BE CONTINUED (vv. 21, 22)

21, 22. They replied, "We have not received any letters from Judea concerning you, and none of the brothers who have come from there has reported or said anything bad about you. But we want to hear what your views are, for we know that people everywhere are talking against this sect."

The initial reaction of these Roman Jews is guarded. They seem to have no specific knowledge of Paul, and no one has *come from* Jerusalem to accuse him. However, they have heard of the Christians, whom they consider to be a divisive *sect*, a perversion of Judaism that is notorious and spoken against. Nevertheless, they appear to be fair-minded and curious. They have been impressed by Paul enough to *want to hear* him more fully. This delay is probably so that they can bring others, perhaps respected elders of the Roman synagogues that are not present for this initial meeting.

II. ROMAN AUDIENCE (ACTS 28:23-25a)

A. PLEADING OF PAUL (v. 23)

23. They arranged to meet Paul on a certain day, and came in even larger numbers to the place where he was staying. From morning till evening he explained and declared to them the kingdom of God and tried to convince them about Jesus from the Law of Moses and from the Prophets.

When the *day* comes, many come to hear what Paul has to say. His credentials as a well-educated rabbi and his notoriety produce a strong turnout. The theme of Paul's message is *the kingdom of God*. This is a characteristic expression of *Jesus* (see Luke 4:43) and describes Jewish belief in the providential activity of God on behalf of their nation (Luke 23:51). Paul's message in a synagogue context often had taken this tack (see Acts 19:8).

Paul gives an exhaustive address, lasting 10 hours or more. This probably includes some give-and-take dialogue with the hearers. Paul's method, however, is to examine passages in the writings *of Moses* (Genesis through Deuteronomy) and in *the Prophets* (Isaiah through Malachi; perhaps some others).

We know from Paul's letters, most of which have been written by this time, that he uses a wide range of Scripture to understand the significance of the gospel message. For Paul, his message of "Christ crucified" (1 Corinthians 1:23) is not at odds with the Jewish Scriptures, but a fulfillment of them. It is

WHAT DO YOU THINK?

The Jewish leaders in Rome were curious and wanted to hear Paul's explanation about Christianity. Why is evangelism so much more effective when a non-Christian asks us to explain what we believe? How can we create more situations like these?

WHAT DO YOU THINK?

Paul appealed to the Old Testament prophecies to affirm that Jesus was the Messiah that the prophets predicted. Why is fulfilled prophecy a powerful tool for evangelism?

possible that the Jews who have come have brought scrolls of these books to be consulted rather than trusting their memories. The unrolling of the various scrolls may help explain the extended nature of this dialogue.

B. MIXED REACTION (vv. 24, 25a)

24, 25a. Some were convinced by what he said, but others would not believe. They disagreed among themselves and began to leave after Paul had made this final statement:

At best, we can say Paul is partially successful. Some believe, but others (maybe most) do not. Their own discussions apart from Paul do not result in any sort of consensus, and the meeting breaks up. Before they go, though, Paul gets in one last word of a long day. He begins by quoting Isaiah 6:9, 10 (Acts 28:26, 27). Then he makes a stunning pronouncement.

III. TURNING POINT AT ROME (ACTS 28:28-31)

A. HISTORIC PRONOUNCEMENT (vv. 28, 29)

28. "Therefore I want you to know that God's salvation has been sent to the Gentiles, and they will listen!"

Paul's final pronouncement is not uttered in bitterness or frustration. He has done his duty by presenting the claims of the gospel in great detail to the Jewish community in Rome, and with some success. He knows from experience that the Gentile community is receptive to his preaching. He is announcing that within the constraints of his detention, he intends now to seek converts among these non-Jews. We should not understand this as meaning that he has given up on the Jews. He wants to be clear that this message is not just for the people of Israel. It is for everyone.

THEY WILL HEAR

William Lloyd Garrison was one of the leading figures in the American fight against slavery in the early 19th century. In 1831 he became the editor of the *Liberator,* probably the leading anti-slavery magazine of the century. He was also involved in several anti-slavery societies. Under his influence the Massachusetts Anti-Slavery Society in 1843 resolved that the U.S. Constitution, because it sanctioned slavery, was "a covenant with death and an agreement with hell." In 1854 he publicly burned a copy of the Constitution declaring, "So perish all compromises with tyranny."

But it was his editorials in the *Liberator* that achieved the most fame—or infamy, depending on one's viewpoint. In violation of federal law, southern postmasters confiscated and destroyed copies of his magazine that came under their jurisdiction, refusing to send these inflammatory materials on to subscribers. In his first editorial in 1831, Garrison vehemently assailed those who urged moderation in this cause, writing, "I will not equivocate—I will not excuse—I will not retreat a single inch—AND I WILL BE HEARD."

It was with a similar conviction and fervency that Paul stated to the Jewish leaders in Rome that the message of salvation was sent to the Gentiles, and they would hear it.

—J. B. N.

29 (footnote). After he said this, the Jews left, arguing vigorously among themselves.

This verse appears only in a footnote in the *New International Version* because it is not in some of what are considered the better manuscripts of Acts.

WHAT DO YOU THINK?

Paul was able to convince some, but not others. How, if at all, is that encouraging to you as you try to share your faith with others?

It mostly repeats the information we have in verse 25, that *the Jews* "disagreed among themselves and began to leave after Paul had made [his] final statement." We can easily see how the disagreement noted in that verse erupted into vigorous arguing as the Jews *left.* Paul has certainly succeeded in spurring them to think carefully about what he has said about Jesus.

B. Accelerating Expansion (vv. 30, 31)

30, 31. For two whole years Paul stayed there in his own rented house and welcomed all who came to see him. Boldly and without hindrance he preached the kingdom of God and taught about the Lord Jesus Christ.

Acts does not tell us what eventually happens to Paul, but finishes with him still under *house* arrest awaiting his appeal. *Two whole years* are spent this way. Paul does not have freedom to move about the city, but he has no restrictions on visitors. In this way, he is able to use this imprisonment in a productive fashion, preaching *boldly* to any audience he can get. We are given the impression that many people visit Paul to hear his message and that the church in Rome gains many converts.

Although the author of Acts does not mention it, during this time Paul also has a ministry of writing. He sends out four letters that we still have: Ephesians, Philippians, Colossians, and Philemon, or the "Prison Epistles." Tradition claims that Paul was released from his detention after the two years. One theory is that his accusers in Jerusalem never came to Rome, so there was no basis for the charges against him.

We do not know whether he ever appeared before the emperor, who at this time was Nero Caesar. If not, this may have been a blessing, for Nero was growing increasingly erratic and paranoid during this period. To have a hearing before him was no guarantee of justice. We know, though, that Paul longed for such an audience, and there are hints in Acts that he may have had it (Acts 27:24). Tradition has it that Paul did appear before Caesar after a second arrest and imprisonment. That hearing resulted in Paul's execution.

CONCLUSION

A popular theory in the church today is that God makes "divine appointments" for believers to share the gospel with nonbelievers. Whether this is true or not, we should not deny that opportunities are presented to us in unexpected ways. Perhaps a coworker turns to us for comfort or advice. Maybe a relative asks us about our church or our faith. There might be a friend or neighbor who opens the door for sharing one's faith in a casual conversation.

Paul's evangelistic efforts in Rome were not the culmination of a well-executed strategic plan. He found himself in the imperial city after a lengthy, unjust imprisonment in Caesarea and with a legal cloud hanging over him. His initial outreach to the Jews of Rome did not receive the response for which he had hoped. It may have seemed that the timing was wrong, that he should have hunkered down to wait for a better time to preach the gospel to the Romans.

But Paul was not wired that way. There was no wrong time for him to tell people about Jesus. He did not wait for a divine appointment. When he was unable to preach in a certain region, he went elsewhere. When he encountered stubborn unbelief, he moved on to find those who were more receptive.

Whenever the gospel is preached, some believe and some do not. Some believe only after many encounters with Christians and the Word. Some hear

---

What Do You Think?

Through at least two years of confinement in Rome, Paul continued to preach and teach the gospel with bold confidence. What do you think was the source of his boldness? How can you increase your boldness in sharing your faith?

Prayer

Holy Father, we, like Paul, are not in complete control over where we live and whom we meet. May we always be ready to share the hope of salvation that you have given us through the gospel of Jesus Christ. May we be godly men and women for all times and opportunities. May you give us courage and strength, no matter what the circumstance might be. We pray this in the name of our Savior, Jesus Christ, amen.

many times but never do submit to the lordship of Jesus. But we, in our limited knowledge and perception, never know which person is in what category at any particular time. May we follow Paul's example and always be ready to present and defend Jesus (1 Peter 3:15). If it is a divine appointment, we have no right to cancel it.

THOUGHT TO REMEMBER

When a door of opportunity for sharing the gospel closes, God will open a different one.

Discovery Learning

The following is an alternative lesson plan emphasizing learning activities. Classes desiring such student involvement will find these suggestions helpful. At the back of this book are reproducible student pages to further enhance activity learning.

INTO THE LESSON

Under the heading *The Perils of Paul*, display the following list of locations: (A) Athens, (B) Damascus, (C) Ephesus, (D) Jerusalem, (E) Lystra, (F) Malta, (G) Perga, (H) Philippi. Distribute copies of the reproducible activity "The Perils of Paul" from page 512, and ask the students to write down at which location each event occurred. Encourage the learners to make random choices if they do not know; assure them the point of the activity goes beyond the details.

When they have had time to finish, read the statements with the correct answers inserted. (The correct answers are as follows: 1. Lystra; 2. Jerusalem; 3. Malta; 4. Philippi; 5. Ephesus; 6. Perga; 7. Damascus; 8. Athens.)

After the reading, ask, "Which of these hard events caused Paul to stop teaching and preaching the good news?" Of course, the answer is *none*. Once that has been stated—whether by you or a student—say, "Today's text presents one more occasion when circumstances—as bad as they were—did not keep Paul from wanting others to know the gospel. Let's look at Acts 28."

INTO THE WORD

Give learners a sheet on which you have the heading *RE: Paul in Rome* and this list of words: *rejection, restriction, review, redeemed, released, responsive, reactive, received, reflected, resigned, refusal, resolution*. Provide each a copy of today's text, Acts 28:16-25a, 28-31. (The *NIV® Bible Student* student book includes the printed text.) Give these directions: "Write each of these words by a verse or verses of today's text, at a place you consider appropriate."

Allow time to complete the assignment, which can be done in groups or pairs. Though several words could be assigned to more than one verse, with varying explanations, here is one possible list of answers: rejection, verse 24 (some would not believe); restriction, verse 16 (Paul has a Roman guard); review, verses 17-19 (Paul's explanation of his predicament); redeemed, verse 20 (the "hope of Israel" is redemption); released, verse 18 (Roman authorities in Judea wanted to release Paul); responsive, verse 24 (some were persuaded by Paul's arguments); reactive, verse 25 (Paul's ultimate response at the many leaving unconvinced); received, verses 23, 30 (Paul received many into his house); reflected, verse 22 (Jews wanted to ponder Paul's teaching); resigned, verse 28 (Paul's resignation to take the gospel to the Gentiles); refusal, verse 19 (Paul refuses to accuse Israel and those who accused him); resolution, verse 31 (Paul resolves to teach and preach no matter what the circumstances). Allow learners to identify their choices and their reasoning.

INTO LIFE

Distribute copies of the reproducible activity "Circumstances and the Gospel" from page 512. Encourage students to fill in the blanks and to keep this where they will see it often in the coming week.

Have a time of directed prayer in which you verbalize certain hard circumstances. Those who are following your directions in prayer are to respond with their commitment to proclaiming the gospel and their request for appropriate blessings of the Spirit for dealing with the circumstances. These responses can be done aloud by individuals or silently by the group.

Give an example to help the learners express their responses: "If I suggest a time when a member of your family is ill and in the care of medical professionals, say something like, 'Lord, give me the boldness to express a confidence in your goodness to the nurses and doctors.'" Here are other prayer stimuli possibilities: (1) "A time when a major appliance has quit working and a service person has arrived"; (2) "You are being taken advantage of and overlooked at work, or your child is at school"; (3) "The business whose employment supports you and your family has just announced major layoffs, with you a likely victim"; (4) "A major weather disaster has struck your community, and you and your friends have suffered significant losses"; (5) "A family member or a friend's family member has been killed in an auto accident caused by a drunken driver."

Add other circumstances, but avoid those that are immediately relevant to a class member. Suggest that learners ponder devotionally during the coming week a prayer opportunity in this format: "When _____ happens to me, my prayer will be _____."

Reproducible Activity Pages

Each of the following pages is designed to be used with one of the lessons of the current quarter. You'll find the activities have a variety of helpful applications. Here are a few suggestions on how to use an activity:

- Use it to supplement the discovery learning plan.

- Use it to introduce the lesson concept.

- Use it to make application near the close of your class time.

- Create an overhead transparency with the page, and use it to have the class do the activity together.

Sometimes there are two or more activities on a sheet. Sometimes there is just one. Use each activity as it best suits your own teaching style and the personality of your class.

Transforming Behaviors

The phrases below on the right represent behaviors the Thessalonians exhibited "after" they became Christians. In the space on the right, record a behavior they may have exhibited "before" they were Christians. (The first one has been done for you.)

BEFORE CONVERSION	AFTER CONVERSION
Trusted in their own power to succeed	work produced by faith (v. 3)
	labor prompted by love (v. 3)
	endurance inspired by hope (v. 3)
	imitators of Paul and God (v. 6)
	welcomed the Word with joy (v. 6)
	model to all believers (v. 7)
	God's message rang out from them (v. 8)
	their faith is known everywhere (v. 8)
	turned to God from idols (v. 9)
	waiting for Jesus to return (v. 10)

Am I Transformed?

Are you exhibiting the same changed behaviors the Thessalonians exhibited? Complete the phrases below to identify how you have grown in your Christian walk.

Before I was a Christian, I . . .

After I became a Christian, I . . .

Having Integrity Before God

Use the verse references below from 1 Thessalonians 2 to identify characteristics of integrity Paul exhibited.

v. 2 _____

v. 3 _____

v. 4 _____

v. 4 _____

v. 5 _____

v. 5 _____

v. 6 _____

v. 7 _____

v. 8 _____

v. 9 _____

v. 10 _____

v. 11 _____

v. 12 _____

Defining Integrity

In the space below, write down an action you have exhibited that may not reveal integrity. Also identify what you need to do to redeem this action before God.

_____

_____

_____

_____

Read Titus 2:7 and then write it as a prayer to God on the lines below.

_____

_____

_____

_____

Prescription for Encouragement

First Thessalonians 3:1-13 gives a prescription for encouragement that we would do well to follow. For the verses assigned to you, fill in the table below by reading the Scripture references and identifying the occasion that prompts Paul's concern, the acts of encouragement that Paul and the Thessalonians render to each other, the results of that encouragement, the goal of Paul's encouragement to the Thessalonians—in each verse indicated.

VERSE	OCCASION	ACTS	RESULTS	MOTIVATION
2				
3				
5				
6				
7				
8				
9				
10				
11				
12				
13				

Words of Encouragement

Within the puzzle find the phrases of encouragement listed below and circle them. Make an effort this week to speak these words, if appropriate, to each person God puts in your path.

```
G I D I I L O V E Y O U B L E Y O Y O U L
N O L E G C P W B L R E G O O O D O O T E
R K D J L G O O D W O R K Y O U O U F M T
Y O U B L G E S S N P X M E P D I A R E M
E S T H L E S N B O J W K A W I T R E S E
S K C N L E S S B P R H M S A D I E R E G
Y O U T H I S I S F U N G Y Y I M A T R I
I M F K B S P S R J L S N E T T H W E R V
Y A M R K B M E Y O L P R Y O V M E R E E
E Y E N L R S P B O H B L E G R E S T O Y
L I M R H T H O U O U Y E M O O D O O D O
T H A T L O O K S G R E A T H A T M A K U
H E Y M R T H A P R T H R M W I H E L R A
E L P B I A M P R A Y I N G F O R Y O U H
L P R A H V M E R S T H P I O R A Y T H A
M Y O U C A N D O I T H A Y P L E S S G N
R O U N M R E S T K E E P T R Y I N G I D
M U Y O U G O G I R L B R I G E N T H A R
```

FIND THESE EXPRESSIONS:

You go girl
I love you
May I help you
I am praying for you
This is fun
Good work
Keep trying
God bless you
Way to go
You did it
That looks great
You are awesome
You can do it
Yes
Let me give you a hand

Where Does God Fit into Your Life?

The picture below represents your life. To determine what part of your life belongs to God, begin by dividing the figure into various sections. Each section should represent the amount of time various aspects of your life take up. Color each part of the figure a different color. (For example, 1/3 of the gingerbread man may be colored green and labeled "work," 1/4 may be colored purple and labeled "sleep," another 1/4 may be colored red and labeled "family," 1/12 may be colored blue and labeled "recreation," and 1/12 may be colored orange and labeled "church," or any such combination). Now decide whether God is part of all of your life or just select portions. If you need to make some changes to assure God is in all parts of your life, find someone who will help hold you accountable as you make those changes.

Great Expectations

Today's lesson is about being alert and ready for the return of Christ. On a scale of one to five, with five representing the highest of expectations, rank the following possible events in your life according to your expectation level.

1 2 3 4 5   It's going to rain sometime in the next three days

1 2 3 4 5   Your net worth will be greater a year from now than it is today.

1 2 3 4 5   You will be presented with an opportunity to share the gospel this week.

1 2 3 4 5   Someone is going to tell you that things are better than they actually are.

1 2 3 4 5   You will be tempted, in some way, today.

1 2 3 4 5   Someone is going to significantly encourage you by next Sunday.

1 2 3 4 5   You are going to be more like Christ tomorrow than you are today.

1 2 3 4 5   You're going to discover a new way to use your spiritual gifts very soon.

1 2 3 4 5   God is going to provide everything you need this year.

1 2 3 4 5   You're going to face an opportunity to help the poor this month.

1 2 3 4 5   You will live long enough to see the return of Christ.

1 2 3 4 5   Christ is going to return very soon.

Keep It Up!

The apostle Paul told the Thessalonians to encourage one another and build each other up, just as they were doing.

Make a list of the top 10 things you do well. Next to each thing, describe how you're using that talent or skill to advance the kingdom. An example is given to stimulate your thinking.

MY GIFT: *I'm good at making my home a warm and inviting place.*	HOW I'M USING IT: *We host Bible studies in our home.*
1.	
2.	
3.	
4.	
5.	
6.	
7.	
8.	
9.	
10.	

Growing in the Dark

God can cause our faith to grow, even during times of persecution and hardship. In the space to the left below, write a one- or two-word description of a difficult experience you went through. On the right, draw some sort of picture that symbolizes how God used that difficult event in your life.

Difficult Experience	*How God Used It*

A Greater Purpose

Paul prayed that God would fulfill every good purpose he intended for them. In the house below, complete the following purpose statements. (If you haven't done any of these things recently, describe how you might fulfill them in the coming week.)

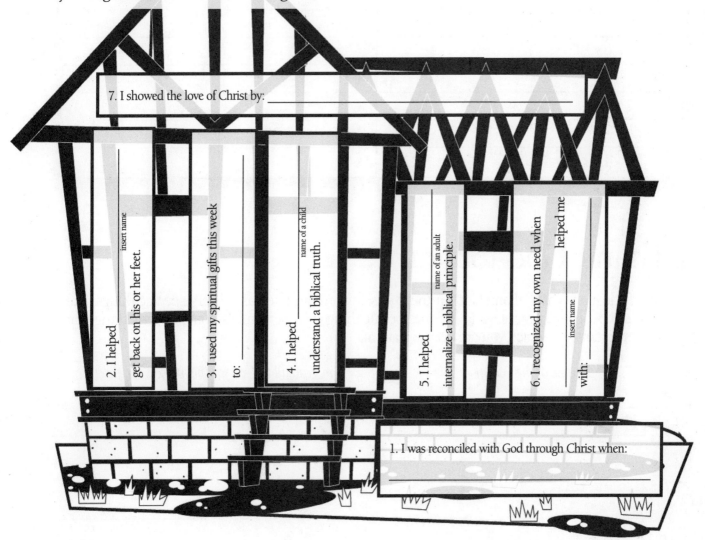

7. I showed the love of Christ by: _____

2. I helped _____ *insert name* get back on his or her feet.

3. I used my spiritual gifts this week to: _____

4. I helped _____ *name of a child* understand a biblical truth.

5. I helped _____ *name of an adult* internalize a biblical principle.

6. I recognized my own need when _____ *insert name* helped me with: _____

1. I was reconciled with God through Christ when: _____

Stark Contrast

The Thessalonians had been misled by teachers whose corrupting doctrines contained nuggets of truth but did not present the entire Word of God. Paul's readers had been confused by these teachers, so Paul wanted to set the believers straight about the true motivations of these false teachers. Study 2 Thessalonians 2:7-12 and find words and phrases in the passage that identify these corrupting people. Then come up with synonyms or short phrases that define or describe these characteristics. Write them in the left-hand columns.

Paul sets up a contrast with the believers in Thessalonica, who had not given themselves over to these false teachers. Read verses 2 Thessalonians 2.13-17 and find the descriptive phrases of these believers and expand the definitions. Write these in the right-hand columns.

| FALSE TEACHERS | | FAITHFUL THESSALONIANS | |
Identification	Description	Identification	Description
v. 7		v. 13	
v. 10		v. 13	
v. 11		v. 13	
v. 12		v. 13	
v. 12		v. 14	
v. 12		v. 14	
		v. 15	
		v. 16	
		v. 17	

I Thank God for You

Paul made it a point to thank God for the Thessalonians, and he named very specific things. Name half a dozen people in your life, and list one specific thing each person has done, or something that person represents, for which you are deeply grateful.

Name of the Person	*I'm grateful to God for this person because:*
1. _____	_____
2. _____	_____
3. _____	_____
4. _____	_____
5. _____	_____
6. _____	_____

The Laborer Is Worth His Wages

Paul warned the idle people in the church that if they refused to work, they should not eat. But most people, especially believers, want not only to work, but also to enjoy the fruit of their labor.

In the "vocational scale" below, the left side, describe the type of work you do, whether outside or inside the home. On the right side of the scale, describe the rewards of your labor in each of the blocks.

Legitimately Poor

Paul told the believers at Thessalonica not to support the idle; however, we are still obligated to help the poor get back on their feet, or at least to become self-sustaining, if at all possible. Once you have identified a person who is legitimately poor, describe below specific ways that you can help him or her.

This year, I can help a poor individual (whom I know) by assisting that person in the following areas:

1. Adequate shelter:

2. Adequate clothing:

3. Enough to eat:

4. Sufficient medical and dental care:

5. Help in securing employment:

6. Show person how to be a steward over personal resources:

7. Helping person to see his or her worth in God's eyes regardless of economic status:

I've Got the Joy

Paul could sing with us the simple chorus, "I've got the joy, joy, joy, joy down in my heart." Which of the following sources of joy in Paul do you find in today's text in Philippians 1:15-29? For those you find, indicate the verse or verses. Then note to the right any occasions when you have found joy in the same thing. Add any other source of joy you find in the text.

Verse	Source of Joy for Paul	Source of Joy for Me
	Meeting the spiritual needs of others	
	Good behaviors with bad motives	
	Death whenever it comes	
	Reunion with Christian friends	
	Being restricted in doing what you want	
	Faith growing in others	
	Hearing of a church's unity and growth	
	Conflicts between the temporal and the eternal	
	Confidence in dealing with threats	
	Other:	

To Be or Not To Be

In Shakespeare's play, Hamlet contemplated suicide with the expression, "To be or not to be, that is the question." That was not Paul's question in Philippians 1:20-27. Though he was eager to be with the Lord, he was committed to serving Christ on the earth. Make your own expression of resolution to "continue with all of you for your progress and joy in the faith."

Lord, though I am sometimes discouraged and always eager for your return, while I remain in this life I am committed to . . .

At the Center

At the center of today's text, verses 6 through 11 are a magnificent poem describing the nature of Christ. His attributes there form the basis for Paul's admonitions for godly behavior. Over the image at the right, write in the grand truths you read. At the end, complete the "If-Then" statement.

"If I accept all these truths regarding Jesus and he becomes the center of my life, then I must . . .

How Bright Is Your Star?

In Philippians 2:15 Paul characterizes those who wear the name of Christ among "a crooked and depraved generation" to be those who "shine like stars in the universe." Using Paul's admonitions in today's text in Philippians 2:1-18, decide how bright your star is for Christ. Shade in a star that represents the "size of your brightness."

Sharing a unity of spirit and purpose
  with your congregation ☆ ☆ ☆ ☆ ☆ ☆ ☆

Considering others better than yourself ☆ ☆ ☆ ☆ ☆ ☆ ☆

Obeying the gospel whether other
  Christians are present or not ☆ ☆ ☆ ☆ ☆ ☆ ☆

Avoiding complaining and grumbling ☆ ☆ ☆ ☆ ☆ ☆ ☆

Filling your life with joy and gladness ☆ ☆ ☆ ☆ ☆ ☆ ☆

Unashamedly confessing that Jesus
  Christ is Lord ☆ ☆ ☆ ☆ ☆ ☆ ☆

Eliminating selfish ambition and vain
  conceit ☆ ☆ ☆ ☆ ☆ ☆ ☆

Allowing God to work in me to will and
  act according to his good purpose ☆ ☆ ☆ ☆ ☆ ☆ ☆

Anything [Jewish] You Can Do, I Can Do Better

In Philippians 3 Paul responds to the personal attacks of his enemies, defending his Jewish heritage and faith. He claims he was the most Jewish of Jews. In some of his other letters, Paul was forced to make similar claims. Match each of the following attributes of Paul's Jewishness to a relevant text.

___ 1. Descendant of Abraham

___ 2. Circumcised on the eighth day, per the law

___ 3. Of the people of Israel

___ 4. Of the tribe of Benjamin

___ 5. A Pharisee and the son of a Pharisee

___ 6. Persecuting the church on the authority of the chief priests

___ 7. A diligent student of noted Rabbi Gamaliel

___ 8. Advanced in Judaism beyond his peers

A. Acts 22:3

B. Acts 23:6

C. Acts 26:9-11

D. Romans 9:3, 4

E. Romans 11:1

F. 2 Corinthians 11:22; Romans 11:1

G. Galatians 1:14

H. Philippians 3:5a (cf. Leviticus 12:3)

SOLUTION:
1. F; 2. H; 3. D; 4. E; 5. B; 6. C; 7. A; 8. G.

Credentials

Challenged by false teachers, probably Judaizers, Paul produced his "spiritual credentials" in Philippians 3. The Scripture cited for the first part of each statement below reveals the "credentials" you had before Christ's death atoned for your sins. The second Scripture has some of the "credentials" you can claim in Christ. Examine each Scripture and indicate an "I was" or an "I am" for each.

1. *I was* _____ (1 Corinthians 6:9, 10),

   but now I am _____ (Colossians 1:12).

2. *I was* _____ (Ephesians 2:12),

   but now I am _____ (Ephesians 2:19).

3. *I was* _____ (Romans 3:23),

   but now I am _____ (Ephesians 2:19).

4. *I was* _____ (1 Corinthians 6:9-11a),

   but now I am _____ (1 Corinthians 6:11b).

5. *I was* _____ (Romans 5:10),

   but now I am _____ (1 John 3:2).

SOLUTION:
1. I was not an heir, but now I am qualified to share in his inheritance. 2. I was separate, excluded, a foreigner, but now I am a citizen and member of God's household. 3. I was falling short, but now I am justified by faith. 4. I was wicked, but now I am washed, justified, and sanctified. 5. I was God's enemy, but now I am a child of God.

Joy Is . . .

Ponder each of the following affirmations regarding what joy is and what it accomplishes in the life of the believer. Based on each statement, make a related personal observation or commitment.

"Joy is not a fleeting and easily manipulated emotion."

Therefore, I will . . .

"Joy is hopeful, deep-seated confidence in our existence in God."

Therefore, I will . . .

"To find joy in unhappy and sad situations is the great blessing and privilege of the believer."

Therefore, I will . . .

"Joy is a positive look at the present because we know our future is secure through faith in Christ."

Therefore, I will . . .

"Joy is based on never having to doubt the acceptance of a loving and caring heavenly Father."

Therefore, I will . . .

Thought Life

Belief is foundational. Behavior is paramount. It is the thought life of the believer that connects the two. Paul emphasizes the thought life of the believer in Philippians 4:8, 9 which he ends with the challenge: "Put it into practice." Look at Paul's attributes of what he considers thoughtworthy. Beside each concept write yourself a challenge for this week's thought life. Include some of the behaviors you hope to incorporate.

TRUE

NOBLE

RIGHT

PURE

LOVELY

ADMIRABLE

EXCELLENT

PRAISEWORTHY

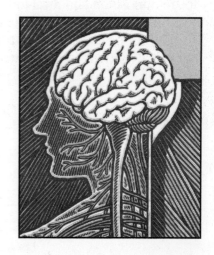

The Perils of Paul

Look at the list of "perils" that Paul faced in his ministry and write down the location at which each event occurred.

1. In _____ Paul was stoned and left for dead outside the city gates. (Acts 14:8-19)

2. In _____ Paul was shunned because some were suspicious of his conversion. (Acts 9:26)

3. Paul was shipwrecked on _____. (Acts 27:40 44; 28:1)

4. In _____ Paul was beaten and put into stocks in prison. (Acts 16:12, 22-24)

5. Paul was forced to leave the city of _____ after a riot over an idol's value. (Acts 19:23–20:1)

6. In _____ Paul was abandoned by one of his young associates. (Acts 13:13)

7. Paul had to leave the city of _____ by stealth at night because his life had been threatened. (Acts 9:22-25)

8. Paul was alone in the deeply pagan and idolatrous city of _____. (Acts 17:16)

Which of these hard events caused Paul to stop teaching and preaching the good news?

Circumstances and the Gospel

Paul's house arrest and shackles did not deter him from teaching and preaching the gospel. Violent opposition and royal indifference to his case mattered little to him. He was "sold out for the gospel." Fill in the blanks for this grand challenge to present the gospel, as it was written to Timothy, but personalize it, putting your own name in the blank added to the text. Let this be your watchword for your own witness, no matter the circumstances. Consider memorizing this text—with your name inserted appropriately.

"In the presence of _____ and of _____ _____, who will _____ the _____ and the _____, and in view of his _____ and his _____, I give you this charge, _____: Preach the _____; be prepared in _____ and out of _____; _____, _____ and _____ —with great _____ and careful _____" (2 Timothy 4:1, 2).